SEX AND PERSONALITY

SEX AND PERSONALITY

Studies in
Masculinity and Femininity

BY

LEWIS M. TERMAN AND CATHARINE COX MILES

Assisted by

JACK W. DUNLAP	E. ALICE MCANULTY
HAROLD K. EDGERTON	QUINN MCNEMAR
E. LOWELL KELLY	MAUD A. MERRILL
ALBERT D. KURTZ	FLOYD L. RUCH
HORACE G. WYATT	

NEW YORK / RUSSELL & RUSSELL

FIRST PUBLISHED IN 1936

REISSUED, 1968, BY RUSSELL & RUSSELL

A DIVISION OF ATHENEUM HOUSE, INC.

L.C. CATALOG CARD NO: 66-27163

PRINTED IN THE UNITED STATES OF AMERICA

PREFACE

Sex differences in personality and temperament are matters of universal human interest. Among all classes of people, from the most ignorant to the most cultivated, they provide an inexhaustible theme for light conversation and humorous comment. They have always been and perhaps always will be one of the chief concerns of novelists, dramatists, and poets. They are rapidly coming to be recognized as one of the central problems in anthropology, sociology, and psychology.

It is well that they should be so recognized; for sex differences are more than a perennial stimulus to idle speculation, wit, and literary art. Mass theories in regard to them are one of the most potent of all the forces that operate in the shaping of human societies, from the most primitive to the most modern. In every culture they help to determine the accepted patterns of family life, of education, of industry, and of political organization. Anthropologists have shown that the standard patterns of male and female behavior present every shade and degree of variety, even to the well-nigh complete reversal of the roles commonly prevalent in Occidental society. Sometimes the male and female patterns are virtually nonoverlapping and arbitrarily enforced; sometimes they are less differentiated and less rigidly maintained. Nearly always, however, there is a recognized dichotomy which seems to be based on the tacit assumption that men and women, by the mere fact of their sex, differ more than they resemble, and that the members of either sex considered alone make up a population which, biologically and psychologically, is relatively homogeneous.

Many students of human nature, especially the anthropologist, the psychiatrist, and the psychologist, have questioned this assumption. The anthropologist encounters so many varieties of dichotomy with respect to masculine and feminine behavior that it seems impossible to explain them wholly in terms of biological factors. The psychiatrist in his clinical practice finds a large proportion of his patients among men and women who, because of either their exceptional nature or their exceptional nurture, have had major difficulties in adjusting to the sexual patterns society has assigned to them. The psychologist of individual differences has so often found his results in opposition to popular views with respect to the existence of human types; has so often discovered wide variation within and consequent overlapping of alleged types; has become so familiar with the possibilities of psychological conditioning to gradations of behavior, that he, too, views with suspicion the categorical explanation of any aspect of human nature in terms of well-defined dichotomies\

Unfortunately, investigations of masculinity and femininity have been retarded by lack of definiteness with respect to what these terms should connote. Gross departures from even a vaguely defined norm have of course long been recognized, but in the absence of quantitative methods the less extreme deviations are overlooked or misunderstood. The present situation resembles that which obtained a few decades ago with respect to mental deficiency or insanity, when, in default of quantitative concepts, the psychiatrist classified his subjects as "normal" or "feeble-minded," "normal" or "insane," etc. Thanks largely to Binet and his successors on the one hand, and to modern psychiatry on the other, no competent investigator in abnormal psychology now regards such classifications as adequate or even possible. No more adequate, we believe, is the classification of subjects as "normal" or "invert" with respect to masculinity or femininity.

The purpose of the investigations here reported has been the accomplishment in the field of masculinity-femininity of something similar to Binet's early achievement in the field of intelligence—a quantification of procedures and of concepts. No one can better realize than the authors how imperfectly they have succeeded in their pioneer attempt. The problem of temperament is no less complex than the problem of abilities. The concepts of masculinity and femininity are even more vague than the nineteenth century concepts of intelligence. Clarity and exactness are seldom attained by a single effort. Indeed, the investigations to be reported have been shaped by the conviction that only the simplest and roughest kind of quantification is at present possible, and that any attempt at exact measurement of the traits in question would, in the present state of psychometric development, be fatuous and unprofitable. The experiment will have justified itself if in some degree it opens the way to more precise measurements and methods.

During the eleven years since the experiment was undertaken, the authors have accumulated a great load of indebtedness to those who have helped to bring the study to its present stage of development. Most of all, they are under obligation to the Committee for Research on Problems of Sex, of the National Research Council, for a series of grants which made the investigation possible, and to Mr. George Frick for additional financial support. The names of the research assistants who have contributed most heavily appear on the title page, but the authors wish to record here their appreciation of the skilled and devoted services rendered by these younger colleagues. Drs. Jack W. Dunlap, Harold K. Edgerton, Albert D. Kurtz, Floyd L. Ruch, and Miss E. Alice McAnulty assisted in the technical and statistical detail of the test standardization. Dr. Quinn McNemar collaborated in this part of the work, in the standardization of Exercise III as an intelligence test, and in a preliminary study of the M-F scores of married couples. Special recognition is due to Dr. E. Lowell Kelly for providing the data presented in the three chapters on homosexuality in males, to Professor Maud A. Merrill for providing the case information on which Chapter XIV is based, and to Mr. Horace G. Wyatt for bringing together the detailed material for the chapter on "Sex Temperaments as Revealed by the M-F Test."

The authors gratefully record other valued assistance. Mary A. Bell contributed in the development of the ink-blot association technique and administered other tests to various populations. Dr. Psyche Cattell helped assemble the test items in a first trial series, particularly those for the interest test. Madeline Frick carried out the study of trait ratings of college students described in Chapter V. The teachers' ratings of masculinity and femininity mentioned in the same chapter were provided by Lela Gillen.

Helen McCreery assisted in bringing together some of the data for the case notes of Chapter XV. Much of the computational work was done by Kirk Miles. For assistance in proofreading the authors are indebted to Gladys Buttenwieser, Helen McCreery, and Frances S. Shaffer. Tests were administered to the students at the University of California by Professor George M. Stratton, at the University of Oregon by Professor Howard Taylor, and at the University of Utah by Professor Dorothy Nyswander. Mention should also be made of those who aided the research by securing data from other school and college groups. These include especially Professors Charles A. Breck, Jack W. Dunlap, Ll. Wynn-Jones, Ellen B. Sullivan, J. St. Clair Price, Drs. Esther A. Gaw and Hazel M. Stanton, Miss Rosalind Cassidy, Mr. Walter R. Chivers, and Miss Helen Marshall. Finally, the authors acknowledge with appreciation their indebtedness to the thousands of subjects who have provided the fundamental data and to the teachers and school officials who made possible the administration of the test to school populations.

The senior author is responsible for the original plan of the investigation, for bringing the testing techniques to essentially their present form, and for the plan and preparation of the present volume. The junior author assisted in the final standardization of the two forms of the test, arranged for administration of the tests to all the main populations with the exception of the male homosexuals, directed jointly with the senior author the work of most of the assistants for four years, and provided the original draft of Chapters V to X, and the material in Appendix VII. The authors have collaborated in the final revision of the manuscript.

Lewis M. Terman.
Catharine Cox Miles.

August, 1936.

CONTENTS

LIST OF ILLUSTRATIONS

Acknowledgment

THIS VOLUME OF STUDIES
WAS MADE POSSIBLE BY A SERIES OF GRANTS FROM
THE COMMITTEE FOR RESEARCH ON PROBLEMS OF SEX
OF THE NATIONAL RESEARCH COUNCIL

SEX AND PERSONALITY

CHAPTER I

RATIONALE OF THE MASCULINITY-FEMININITY TEST

The belief is all but universal that men and women as contrasting groups display characteristic sex differences in their behavior, and that these differences are so deep seated and pervasive as to lend distinctive character to the entire personality. That masculine and feminine types are a reality in all our highly developed cultures can hardly be questioned, although there is much difference of opinion as to the differentiae which mark them off and as to the extent to which overlapping of types occurs. It is true that many social trends, of which the recent development of psychological science is one, have operated to reduce in the minds of most people the differences that had long been supposed to separate the sexes in personality and temperament. Intelligence tests, for example, have demonstrated for all time the falsity of the once widely prevalent belief that women as a class are appreciably or at all inferior to men in the major aspects of intellect. The essential equality of the sexes has further been shown by psychometric methods to obtain also in various special fields, such as musical ability, artistic ability, mathematical ability, and even mechanical ability. The enfranchisement of women and their invasion of political, commercial, and other fields of action formerly reserved to men have afforded increasingly convincing evidence that sex differences in practical abilities are also either nonexistent or far less in magnitude than they have commonly been thought to be.

But if there is a growing tendency to concede equality or near equality with respect to general intelligence and the majority of

1

special talents, the belief remains that the sexes differ fundamentally in their instinctive and emotional equipment and in the
sentiments, interests, attitudes, and modes of behavior which
are the derivatives of such equipment. It will be recognized
that these are important factors in shaping what is known as
personality, hence the general acceptance of the dichotomy
between the masculine and feminine personality types. The
belief in the actuality of M-F types remains unshaken by the fact,
abundantly attested, that observers do not agree in regard to the
multitudinous attributes which are supposed to differentiate
them. Although practically every attribute alleged to be characteristic of a given sex has been questioned, yet the composite
pictures yielded by majority opinion stand out with considerable
clearness.

In modern Occidental cultures, at least, the typical woman is
believed to differ from the typical man in the greater richness and
variety of her emotional life and in the extent to which her everyday behavior is emotionally determined. In particular, she is
believed to experience in greater degree than the average man the
tender emotions, including sympathy, pity, and parental love; to
be more given to cherishing and protective behavior of all
kinds. Compared with man she is more timid and more readily
overcome by fear. She is more religious and at the same time
more prone to jealousy, suspicion, and injured feelings. Sexually
she is by nature less promiscuous than man, is coy rather than
aggressive, and her sexual feelings are less specifically localized in
her body. Submissiveness, docility, inferior steadfastness of
purpose, and a general lack of aggressiveness reflect her weaker
conative tendencies. Her moral life is shaped less by principles
than by personal relationships, but thanks to her lack of adven-
turousness she is much less subject than man to most types of
criminal behavior. Her sentiments are more complex than man's
and dispose her personality to refinement, gentility, and preoccupation with the artistic and cultural.

But along with the acceptance of M-F types of the sort we have
sketchily delineated, there is an explicit recognition of the existence of individual variants from type: the effeminate man and the

masculine woman. Grades of deviates are recognized ranging from the slightly variant to the genuine invert who is capable of romantic attachment only to members of his or her own sex, although, as we shall see later, judges rating their acquaintances on degree of masculinity and femininity of personality seldom show very close agreement. Lack of agreement in such ratings probably arises from two sources: (1) varying opinion as to what factors truly differentiate the M-F types, and (2) varying interpretations of specific kinds of observed behavior. Some raters base their estimates largely upon external factors, such as body build, features, voice, dress, and mannerisms; others, more penetrating, give larger weight to the subtle aspects of personality which manifest themselves in interests, attitudes, and thought trends.

For many reasons, both practical and theoretical, it is highly desirable that our concepts of the M-F types existing in our present culture be made more definite and be given a more factual basis. Alleged differences between the sexes must give place to experimentally established differences. A measure is needed which can be applied to the individual and scored so as to locate the subject, with a fair degree of approximation, in terms of deviation from the mean of either sex. Range and overlap of the sexes must be more accurately determined than is possible by observational and clinical methods.

It is to this end that the researches set forth in the present volume have been directed. As the result of empirical investigations, over a period of several years, a test of mental masculinity and femininity has been devised which is based upon actual differences between male and female groups ranging in age from early adolescence to life's extreme. The reliability of the instrument, in the sense of consistency of its verdicts, qualifies it for the comparative study both of groups and of individuals. The test has been applied to samplings of populations of each sex differing in age, education, occupation, cultural interests, and familial background. Two groups of male and a few female homosexuals have been studied. Scores on the M-F test have been correlated with physical measurements and with rated estimates of several personality variables. The possibility of subjects faking their scores has been investigated. The mean, the range, and the overlapping of sex groups have been determined for numerous populations. The degree to which M-F traits enter into marital selection has been measured, and (by the use of a modified M-F test) spouse resemblance in M-F score has been correlated with marital happiness. The test items carrying masculine weights have been compared with those carrying feminine weights in an effort to arrive at a more exact and meaningful description of characteristic sex differences as they exist in the culture of our time and country.

The M-F test is made up in two equivalent forms, A and B. It is entirely a pencil-and-paper test, of the questionnaire variety, composed of 910 items (Form A, 456; Form B, 454). In the interests of anonymity, as well as to insure speed in administration and scoring, all the items are responded to by checking one of four, three, or two multiple responses. The test is administered without a time limit, a single form requiring forty to fifty minutes for the majority of subjects, rarely an hour. It is hardly applicable to subjects of less than seventh-grade education and ability. The scoring is done by the use of stencils and is therefore entirely objective. Scoring by the Hollerith machine is possible but is not economical except for fairly large populations. Each response carries a weight of one and is scored either $+$ or $-$, that is, masculine or feminine. Weighted scores were originally used but were discarded in favor of unit weights for reasons which will be given in Chapter IV.

The purpose of the test has been disguised by the title, "Attitude-Interest Analysis." This was made necessary by the fact that subjects who know what the test is intended to measure are able to influence their scores so greatly as to invalidate them entirely.[1]

Both forms of the test are reproduced in Appendix I, with $+$ and $-$ signs inserted to show how each item is scored. It will be noted that in subtests 2, 3, 5, and 6 omissions as well as actual responses are scored. There are seven subtests (or "exercises") as follows:

[1] For data on this point see pp. 77 *ff.*

	Form A	Form B
Exercise 1. Word Association......................	60 items	60 items
Exercise 2. Ink-blot Association...................	18 items	18 items
Exercise 3. Information.........................	70 items	70 items
Exercise 4. Emotional and Ethical Response........	105 items	105 items
Exercise 5. Interests...........................	119 items	118 items
Exercise 6. Personalities and Opinions..............	42 items	41 items
Exercise 7. Introvertive Response.................	42 items	42 items
Total..	456 items	454 items

Examination of the seven exercises will show that with the exception of No. 6 each is composed of items of a fairly homogeneous type. Exercise 6 contains two parts, the first of which logically belongs with Exercise 5. The make-up of this exercise was influenced by space requirements in printing the blanks, and the same fact accounts for the addition to Exercise 4 of a small group of items which logically belong with Exercise 6. This does not greatly matter, as it was not the intention that each of the seven exercises should necessarily measure a unitary trait. All of them together present a wide sampling of sex differences and it is the total score with which we are chiefly concerned. The range of scores in the general population of adults is roughly as follows: for males, from $+200$ to -100, with a mean of $+52$ and S.D. of 50; for females, from $+100$ to -200, with a mean of -70 and S.D. of 47. The score, as we shall see, is influenced by age, intelligence, education, interests, and social background, and to such an extent that groups differing in these respects often show markedly contrasting score distributions.

The M-F test does not represent any radical departure in principle from methods previously employed in the study of sex differences. A majority of the earlier studies also resulted in comparisons stated in quantitative terms. For example, the sexes were found to differ numerically in the number liking or playing particular games; the number liking or disliking particular colors, books, or school subjects; the number preferring this or that occupation, literary style, historical character, or ideal; or they were found to differ in the degree of introversion, dominance, inferiority feeling, conservatism, emotional stability, sense of humor, religious attitudes, or other alleged traits. The present study differs from its predecessors primarily in the fact that it represents a more systematic attempt to sample sex differences in a large variety of fields in which such differences are empirically demonstrable. The literature of the subject, both theoretical and experimental, was canvassed for clues as to the types of test responses most likely to reveal sex differences. Of the thousands of items which have been tried out only those have been retained which satisfied in some degree this criterion of discriminative capacity. The test is based, not upon some theory as to how the sexes may differ, but upon experimental findings as to how they do differ, at least in the present historical period of the Occidental culture of our own country.

The purpose of the M-F test is to enable the clinician or other investigator to obtain a more exact and meaningful, as well as a more objective, rating of those aspects of personality in which the sexes tend to differ. More specifically, the purpose is to make possible a quantitative estimation of the amount and direction of a subject's deviation from the mean of his or her sex, and to permit quantitative comparisons of groups differing in age, intelligence, education, interests, occupation, and cultural milieu. By comparing the responses made by groups of subjects on the several parts of the test we secure a basis for qualitative as well as quantitative studies of sex differences.

The M-F test rests upon no assumption with reference to the causes operative in determining an individual's score. These may be either physiological and biochemical, or psychological and cultural; or they may be the combined result of both types of influence. The aim has been merely to devise a test which would measure existing differences in mental masculinity and feminity, however caused. It is only when a test of this kind has been made available that it becomes possible to investigate with any degree of precision the influence of the numerous physical, social, and psychological factors that may affect a subject's rating.

At present extreme differences of opinion are to be found with reference to this question. Many if not the majority of students of homosexuality accept the theory that sexual inversion is not a product of psychological conditioning but is inborn. This seems to be also the almost universal belief of homosexuals themselves, though one would of course hesitate to give much weight to their unsupported opinion. So far as animals below man are concerned, the facts available point unmistakably to the conclusion that maleness and femaleness of behavior are biochemically determined. Transplantation of male gonadal tissue into the ovariectomized domestic fowl induces not only male secondary sexual characters but also typical male behavior. A corresponding effect in the reverse direction is produced by ovarian transplants in the castrated male fowl. Spontaneous sex reversals in pigeons and domestic fowls, ordinarily initiated by pathological conditions in the gonads, have been described in detail by Riddle, Crew, and others. In one case, reported by Crew, a hen which had been the mother of two broods of chicks lost her ovaries from a tubercular infection, developed male sexual organs, and later became the father of another brood of offspring.[1] The injection of the female hormone into the blood of virgin female white rats is followed by maternal behavior patterns otherwise observed only in late pregnancy and the postdelivery period, particularly nest building and retrieving of young. The impressive contrast between the "personality" of stallion and gelding, or of bull and steer, is familiar to every farm boy. In a majority of mammals and birds in which castrated subjects have been experimentally studied, the effect of this operation on the male is to produce a temperament (personality) more or less approximating that of the normal female. Castration of the female, on the other hand, has little effect except upon the specific patterns concerned with mating and with maternal behavior.

Strong as the temptation is to draw inferences from lower mammals and fowls to man, it must be resisted in view of man's enormously greater modifiability by psychological conditioning. Although early castration of the human male is well known to be followed by the development of a temperament lacking a number

[1] CREW, F. A. E., Abnormal sexuality in animals. III. Sex reversal, *Quart. Rev. Biol.*, 1927, **2**, 427–441.

of the usual attributes of masculinity, we are not able to disentangle the biochemical from the psychological factors which may have combined to produce the total result.

Our investigations offer considerable evidence of the influence of nurture on the masculinity and femininity of human personality, although we regard our results as far from conclusive. Perhaps cross-parent fixation followed by homosexuality is one of the most convincing illustrations of environmental influence, but even here biochemical abnormalities have not been ruled out as possible contributing causes of the mother-son or father-daughter attraction. In view of the scanty and conflicting data of strictly scientific nature it would seem that the only just course is to keep an open mind and to investigate every possible influence that is subject to even approximate measurement. One awaits with special interest the results of biochemical studies of homosexual subjects, particularly those which will establish the behavioral effects induced by synthetic preparations of male and female hormones. In these and other experiments it is hoped that the M-F test will prove a helpful research tool.

In view of the myriad known physiological and biochemical differences between men and women, any degree of overlap of the sexes on a masculinity-femininity test of the type used in the investigations to be described must be regarded as psychologically and sociologically very significant. If it can be shown that despite the biological dichotomy between males and females of the genus Homo a few members of each sex rate as masculine or as feminine as the average member of the opposite sex, a heavy burden of proof devolves upon anyone who doubts the weighty influence of environment in shaping the patterns of male and female behavior. Certainly any such finding must constitute a challenge of the first order to the search for possible physiological and biochemical correlates of extreme deviation from the respective sex norms in M-F score. It is only by the discovery of such correlates that it will become possible to establish any definite limits to the effect of environmental influences. In the meantime, studies of sex differences by the use of subjective methods will remain of indeterminate value.

At this point it may be well to give a few words of warning in regard to possible misuses of the M-F test.

In the first place, one must bear in mind that since the test does not sample every conceivable kind of sex difference and does not sample with perfect reliability even those fields which it attempts to cover, the score it yields cannot be regarded as an adequate index of the totality of a subject's mental masculinity and femininity. It would doubtless be possible to find enough additional valid items to make up several other tests as lengthy as the one we have devised. This would especially be the case if the test were not exclusively of the pencil-and-paper variety.

Secondly, a more serious limitation to the present usefulness of the test lies in the fact that as yet too little is known about the behavior correlated with high and low scores. Painstaking clinical studies of large numbers of high-scoring and low-scoring subjects will be necessary to remedy this defect. Most emphatic warning is necessary against the assumption that an extremely feminine score for males or an extremely masculine score for females can serve as an adequate basis for the diagnosis of homosexuality, either overt or latent. It is true, as we shall show, that male homosexuals of the passive type as a rule earn markedly feminine scores, and that the small number of female homosexuals of the active type whom we have tested earned high masculine scores. That the converse of these rules is in accord with the facts, we have no assurance whatever; indeed, our findings indicate that probably a majority of subjects who test as variates in the direction of the opposite sex are capable of making a perfectly normal heterosexual adjustment. Mental masculinity or femininity is at most only one of a number of factors predisposing to homosexuality; one must even bear in mind the possibility that it may be a secondary rather than a primary condition, an effect rather than a cause.

Used with suitable precaution we believe that the M-F test will be found valuable both as a clinical and as an investigational tool. The application of a single form is adequate for comparison of population groups and also for securing approximate ratings of individual subjects. When it is important that a subject's rating be as accurate as possible, both forms of the test should be administered and the average taken of the two scores. Types of investigation in which the test should be helpful include, among others, the relationship of masculinity and femininity of temperament to body build, metabolic and other physiological factors, excess or deficiency of gonadal and other hormone stimulation, and homosexual behavior, and to such environmental influences as parent-child attachments, number and sex of siblings, sex of teachers, type of education, marital compatibility, and choice of friends or of occupations. It will be especially interesting to compare M-F differences in different cultures, and in the same culture at intervals of one or more generations. In short, the measurement of M-F differences will make it possible greatly to expand our knowledge of the causes which produce them.

Our primary task has been to throw light on the meaning of the M-F score. For this reason we have presented only a relatively brief summary of the extensive experimental work which was necessary to bring the test to its present form, and have devoted the bulk of our volume to the relationships found to obtain between M-F score and other variables, including physique, personality traits as rated and measured, achievement, age, education, intelligence, occupational classification, interests, domestic milieu, delinquency, and homosexuality. It is hoped that the reader will thus be sufficiently impressed by the multiplicity of factors which go to determine an individual's score and by the complexity of interaction among them. In the interest of concreteness and in order to illustrate some of the major questions that arise in score interpretation, three chapters have been devoted to case studies. We believe that many of these will be of surpassing interest to the general reader as well as to the professional student of personality and temperament.

CHAPTER II

ORIGIN OF THE M-F TEST

The idea of developing a test of masculinity and femininity first occurred to the senior author in 1922 in connection with an investigation of intellectually superior children. One division of that investigation had for its purpose comparison of gifted and unselected children with respect to their interest in, practice of, and knowledge about plays, games, and amusements. Each of 90 such activities was rated three times by each subject; first for acquaintance with it, secondly for interest in it, and thirdly for frequency with which it was practiced. There followed a list of 45 questions about experience or accomplishment in a wide variety of activities hardly to be classed as plays or games, such as "Have you ever cooked a meal?" "Have you ever taken part in a play?" etc. Finally, there were 123 information questions designed to test the subject's actual knowledge about the plays, games, and other activities. (Examples: "A singing game is follow-the-leader, London Bridge, poison"; "A game in which you must not smile is fruit-basket, old-witch, tin-tin.")

The test was given to 303 boys and 251 girls of IQ 140 or above, ages 6 to 14, and to a control group of 225 unselected boys and 249 unselected girls, ages 8 to 17.[1]

Sex differences between unselected boys and girls were computed for the composite of the two ratings given by the subjects for interest in and practice of the 90 plays, games, and activities. Next a masculinity index was computed for each of the activities,

[1] Subjects in the control group could not read well enough to take the test below the age of 8 years. As the test was given only through the eighth grade, in which gifted children above the age of 14 are rarely found, the age range for the gifted group does not run as high as for the control group. The unselected children accordingly have a considerable advantage in the comparison of the entire gifted and control group; only for ages 8 to 14 inclusive are the two groups strictly comparable.

based upon the sex differences found in the control group. These indices ranged from 2 to 24, those above 13 indicating greater preference by boys, those below 13 greater preference by girls. They are shown in Table 1.

TABLE 1.—MASCULINITY AND FEMININITY INDICES OF NINETY ACTIVITIES

13	Anty over	18	Fish	12	Post office
12	Authors	13	Follow the leader	11	Puss in corner
14	Backgammon	20	Football	15	Racing or jumping
19	Baseball	13	Fox and geese	13	Red rover
16	Basketball	12	Fox and hounds	9	Ring around rosy
20	Bicycle	16	Garden work	13	Roly-poly
14	Billiards	13	Geography cards	15	Row a boat
12	Blackman	9	Guessing games	6	School, play
10	Blindfold	14	Handball	8	Sewing
17	Bow and arrow	11	Hide-and-seek	15	Shinny
14	Bowling	14	Hike	21	Shoot
20	Boxing	13	History cards	11	Simon says thumbs up
13	Cards	15	Hoops	10	Skate
9	Cat and mouse	4	Hopscotch	17	Ski
9	Charades	14	Horseback riding	13	Snap
14	Checkers	5	House, play	15	Snap the whip
14	Chess	15	Hunt	17	Soccer
11	Church, play	9	In and out window	11	Solve puzzles
14	Coast or toboggan	10	Jackstones	16	Stilts
5	Cook a meal	12	Jackstraws	8	Store, play
13	Crokinole	9	Jump rope	15	Swim
13	Croquet	20	Kites	11	Tag
8	Dance	7	Knit or crochet	12	Tennis
11	Dare base	14	Leapfrog	13	Tiddly-winks
2	Dolls, play	9	London Bridge	24	Tools, use
13	Dominoes	19	Machinery, work with	19	Tops
3	"Dress up," play	20	Marbles	17	Tug of war
10	Drop handkerchief	13	Parchesi	13	Volleyball
14	Duck on rock	13	Pom-pom pull-away	13	Word building
9	Farmer in the dell	16	Pool	20	Wrestling

By use of the above data it was possible to derive a masculinity rating of each subject based upon the score weights given to "masculine" and "feminine" activities. The distributions of these masculinity ratings are given in Table 2 separately by sex, for the gifted and control groups.

A certain amount of historic interest attaches to the data presented in Table 2. Here, for the first time, we have distributions

TABLE 2.—MASCULINITY RATINGS OF GIFTED AND UNSELECTED CHILDREN*

	Control group		Gifted group	
	Boys	Girls	Boys	Girls
20	1		1	
19	1		3	
18	4		6	
17	14	1	33	1
16	34	. .	76	1
15	40	1	92	6
14	34	7	62	16
13	31	17	8	23
12	1	56	6	54
11	. .	39	2	69
10	1	36	. .	34
9		15	. .	20
8		5	. .	4
7			. .	4
6			. .	
5			1	
N	161	177	290	232
Mean	14.90	11.23	15.22	11.35
S.D.	1.49	1.45	1.45	1.65

* Compiled from Tables 153a and 153b, *Genetic studies of genius*, vol. I., pp. 411–412, by Lewis M. Terman, *et al.*, Stanford Univ. Press, 1925.

by sex of masculinity ratings based upon an extensive sampling of behavior responses. We see that the range for each sex is very wide and that there is a considerable amount of overlap between the sexes; that there are indeed a few members of each sex who test beyond the mean of the opposite sex. Incidentally, though the fact is not of prime interest for our present purpose, little difference in masculinity was found for the gifted and control groups at any age.

It is possible that the masculinity test would have been allowed to rest at this point but for facts which came to light in a comparison of scores and case-history data for a number of subjects deviating greatly from their sex norm. Some of these comparisons indicated that the scores tended to be correlated with general masculinity and femininity of behavior and to reveal an important line of cleavage in personality and temperament. One of the deviating cases in particular furnished considerable motivation to further experimentation in the field of M-F testing.   This was the gifted boy who can be identified in Table 2 as receiving a masculinity rating not only below all the other boys, of either the gifted or the control groups, but also below that of any girl.   The following account of the case offers spectacular evidence of the significance that may attach to M-F ratings of the kind in question.

An assistant who was tabulating the masculinity scores of gifted boys noted what seemed to be an error, a score that was more feminine than any for the girls.   The score was accordingly checked for error, as was also the sex classification of the subject, but no error was found.   Reference to the field assistant's case history revealed the fact that the boy in question (age nine) had become a problem to his mother because of his persistent and overpowering desire to play the role of a girl.   Besides showing a distinct preference for feminine plays and games, X frequently dressed himself in girl's clothes and "dolled" his face with rouge, lipstick, and other cosmetics.   When he found that his feminine behavior was beginning to attract the attention and disapproval of his parents and playmates he cleverly found a way to continue it without criticism by writing little plays for neighborhood performance, each carefully provided with a feminine role for himself.   A follow-up study six years later showed that the feminine inclinations of X had become more rather than less marked.   For now, at the age of fifteen, one of his favorite amusements was to dress himself as a stylish young woman, apply cosmetics liberally, and walk down the street to see how many men he could lure into flirtation.   It is practically certain that at this time X had no knowledge whatever about the existence of such a thing as homosexuality.

So striking a case of inverted behavior in childhood naturally provoked speculation in regard to the course of development that would ensue.   To secure the facts, however, was not easy.   Letters of inquiry were addressed to the mother from time to time, but as these were couched in general terms to avoid the risk of causing offense or shock their import was not understood and they elicited little information. Finally, one of these letters which was somewhat more pointed than usual was shown to X by his mother. X understood immediately the purpose of the inquiry and informed his mother that there was something he had kept from her, namely, that his love interests were unlike those of other men in that only boys had the slightest attraction for him. He denied, however, that he had engaged in any kind of overt homosexual behavior. As a result of this confession X was asked to fill out the "Attitude-Interest Analysis Test" (M-F test). The score of -71 which he now earned places him near the 50th percentile for women, or more feminine than 999 men out of 1,000.

A few weeks before this chapter was written the mother of X requested information about the possibility of normalizing her son's emotional life by the use of testoserone, a recently developed synthetic preparation of male hormone.[1]

The case we have just described raises in dramatic form the question as to the age when an individual's M-F status becomes relatively fixed. To what extent is the adult M-F status of a subject foreshadowed in the years of middle childhood and preadolescence? Does the very feminine boy usually become a very feminine man, or is X an exception to the rule? Similarly, does the tomboy usually develop into the masculine type of woman, or is tomboyishness more commonly but a passing phase?

The question is a very interesting one, but at present no answer can be given. It cannot be answered until a more satisfactory M-F test has been devised for use with young children. The Plays, Games, and Amusements test is both too crude and too

---

[1] This youth, now in his twenties, is well started on what promises to be a brilliant career in one of the arts. There were several factors which may have contributed to the development of his homosexual tendencies. The mother married in the late thirties a man some twenty years her senior. When X was born he was definitely marked to remain an only child, and the stage was thus set for an excessive attachment to his overcherishing mother. Masculine contacts were largely lacking, as he did not spend much time with other boys and had little in common with his elderly father. His artistic temperament and refined sensibilities may also have played a part. X is an example of the highest type of mental sexual inversion; he has high principles, is passionately devoted to his work, and seems to have rejected all overt expression of his homosexual inclinations.

limited in scope to afford a measure comparable in reliability and validity to the M-F test we have devised for adults. Even so, the reader will want to know to what extent this test, given in the preadolescent years, agrees with scores made by the same subjects on the M-F test several years later.

Six years after the P. G. and A. test was administered to the gifted subjects, the M-F test described in this volume was given to 94 boys and 99 girls of the same group. The ages at the time of the earlier test averaged about 10½ years and ranged from 6 to 13, giving a mean age of about 16½ at the time of the M-F test.

In the case of the boys the correlation between the two sets of scores was .30 ± .08, which is large enough to be statistically significant but too small to serve as a basis of prediction in the case of individual subjects. For the girls the correlation was .24. In the case of both boys and girls, however, there were striking differences in the M-F scores of subjects who scored at opposite extremes on the P. G. and A. test. For example, the 11 most masculine boys on the P. G. and A. test had a mean M-F score of +78 six years later, as compared with a mean of +37 for the 6 most feminine. The two M-F scores, +78 and +37, are separated by approximately one S.D. of the distribution of a typical male group. (See norms, Appendix I.) The 12 most masculine girls on the P. G. and A. test had a mean M-F score of −50 six years later, as compared with −106 for the 12 who had been rated most feminine by the P. G. and A. test. This difference is about 1.5 S.D. of a typical female distribution.

On the whole, these results suggest that there is a certain amount of "constancy" with regard to a subject's M-F status from middle childhood to the adult period. We are inclined to think that improved tests for the earlier years will reveal a considerable degree of constancy. The case history data presented in Chapters XIII to XV lend considerable support to this view. Because of the far-reaching effects which extreme M-F deviation may have upon an individual's social and sexual adjustment, the problem should be thoroughly investigated. In this connection one would like to know whether the child's progress toward the adult M-F status is related to early or late puberty, or influenced by forced association with older or younger children as in the case of pupils who are markedly accelerated or retarded in school.

The facts that have been presented, representing, as they do, the only examples of subjects being given an objective M-F test and later followed on to the adult period, are surely challenging enough to justify all the labor that has been expended in improving the test, in securing norms for a large number of population groups, and in correlating the scores with other variables.

CHAPTER III

EXTENSION OF THE M-F TEST TO NEW TECHNIQUES

Each exercise of the M-F test in its present form required a large amount of preliminary investigation, including the examination of experimental literature in the search for clues, selection of tentative lists of items, trial for rejection of non-discriminating items, application of retained items to numerous groups of subjects, computations of reliability and of overlap of sex groups, trial of different response methods, and comparison of the merits of various scoring and weighting techniques. The reader would hardly be interested in a minute account of this exploratory work and we shall therefore summarize in a single chapter the thousand or more pages of material representing this stage of the investigation.

It was not until the summer of 1925 that opportunity arose to provide a broader basis for the M-F test than sex differences in the field of plays, games, and amusements. Examination of the literature suggested many possible lines of extension, but consideration was given only to methods which would permit group testing, pencil-and-paper responses, and objective scoring. Within a few months experiments were begun with five techniques: word association, ink-blot association, information, interests (likes and dislikes), and tests of introvertive tendencies. Two other methods were added to the experiment in 1926, a test of emotional and ethical response and a test of common beliefs.

Apart from a few minor experiments which were quickly found to be unpromising, the investigations at this stage were confined to the above seven techniques. All of these turned out favorably with the exception of the test of opinions, which netted only a small proportion of items showing reliable sex differences. Although the investigation proceeded upon several lines simultaneously, often with application of the various tests to identical groups, the account which follows will deal with the seven techniques successively.

THE WORD ASSOCIATION TEST

The so-called free association method employing words as stimuli has been used by numberless investigators since the work by Aschaffenburg was first published in 1889. Among these, Jastrow, Calkins, Washburn, and others had made note of sex differences revealed by the method.[1] The sex differences that had been found were usually the by-products of studies primarily designed either to establish the general laws of associative response or to bring out the influence of individual differences other than sex, including personality type, psychotic tendency, mental complexes, consciousness of guilt, etc. It was reasonable to suppose that if a list of stimulus words was chosen specifically on the basis of significant response differences yielded by male and female subjects, it would prove a valuable addition to the test of masculinity and femininity.

Dr. J. B. Wyman, in connection with the Stanford study of gifted children,[2] had already demonstrated that a word association test can be constructed which is effective in discriminating between groups of subjects differing in interests, attitudes, and thought trends. Her investigation was not primarily concerned with sex comparisons, but with groups representing the extremes of intellectual interests, social interests, and activity interests. The same principle, however, was involved. If the free association technique is capable of differentiating between subjects having much or little of one of three types of interest, it should be capable of discriminating between subjects differing in mental masculinity and femininity. Dr. Wyman's adaptation of the method to group testing, making feasible its application to large populations, was also an important consideration. Her pro-

---

[1] For a summary of the literature on this point see Catharine Cox Miles and Lewis M. Terman, Sex differences in the association of ideas, *Am. J. Psychol.*, 1929, **41**, 165–206.

[2] TERMAN, LEWIS M., *et al.*, *Genetic studies of genius*, vol. I, pp. 455–484, Stanford Univ. Press, 1925.

cedure was to expose the stimulus word visually, printed in giant type on a card 3 by 12 in., and have the subjects write in a numbered space the one word it made them think of. The responses were scored by the use of weights assigned to them on the basis of the frequency difference between subjects rated high

FORM A

TABLE	NAKED	EVIL
BLUE	CASTLE	ARTIST
RAIN	CHEAT	RADIO
TURNIP	ATHLETE	SAFETY
BOOK	FEELING	BATTLE
PURE	FELLOW	MAIDEN
KITCHEN	WAR	EMBRACE
FLESH	BABY	WASH
ADMIRE	PAIN	ANKLE
SICK	MONEY	WISH
HAIR	SQUEEZE	BULL
FLIRT	ACTOR	WEEP
MOON	PROTEST	WASTE (WAIST)
MODEST	KNEE	HERO
HUNT	DEVIL	PHYSICAL
FRESH	ENJOY	SERVE
FASHION	JEALOUS	ROSE
DANGER	SHOP	MAGIC
DECENT	DIMPLE	SKIRT
WEDDING	AFRAID	MANNERS
NECKLACE	LIPS	PROPOSE
COLOR	CLOTHES	RING
RELIGION	ANGER	BUILD
HANDSOME	BREAST	MOUSE
VIRTUE	PROMISE	LOVE
WANT	GENTLE	FOOT
SHOULDER	FAME	HANDKERCHIEF
CLOSET	BOSS	BOLD
DUTY	TOMBOY	DARLING
FEMALE	GIVE	SCREAM
PICNIC	FAITHFUL	
DELICATE	AUTOMOBILE	
FAIR	BLUSH	
GARDEN	FORM	
POWER	CHILD	
HOME	BALL	
HAND	SNAKE	
THIRTEEN	STOUT	
FILTHY	POWDER	
SOCIETY	SWEETHEART	

or low in a given type of interest. A majority of the stimulus words in the final form of her test yielded responses which could be weighted for two or all three of the types of interest the author was attempting to measure. Reliability coefficients found for the list of 120 stimulus words ranged from .83 to .87 for intellec-

FORM B

CHAIR	BARE	DARKNESS
GREEN	KNIGHT	ART
WIND	SNEAK	ELECTRICITY (ELECTRIC.
CARROT	STRONG	SAVE
LETTER	MEMORY	KILL
TRUE	MATE	YOUTH
CELLAR	FIGHT	KISS
BODY	BIRTH	SOAP
DESPISE	HUNT	SLENDER
ILL	EARN	DESIRE
FACE	HUG	ROOSTER
SPOON	STAGE	CRY
TWILIGHT	POLICEMAN	SKIN
BASHFUL	LEG	LEADER
GUN	ANGEL	IDEAL
CHEEK	FUN	SUBMIT
TASTE	VAIN	LILY
ESCAPE	BARGAIN	CHARM
PROPER	CURL	CLOTHING
MARRIAGE	FEAR	RUDE
DIAMOND	MOUTH	ENGAGEMENT
PINK	DRESS	BELL
WORSHIP	CURSE	MAKE
LOVELY	HIPS	WORM
HONOR	SUCCESS	PASSION
LONGING	TENDER	ARM
THROAT	AMBITION	GARTER
SECRET	MISTRESS	DARE
SACRIFICE	SISSY	BELOVED
MALE	GIFT	THRILL
PARTY	IMMORTAL	
COARSE	MACHINE	
BRAVE	SHAME	
FLOWERS (FLOWER)	FIGURE	
RULE	MOTHER	
FAMILY	PLAY	
LIMB	TOAD	
SIXTEEN	THIN	
NASTY	PAINT	
SOCIAL	LOVER	

tual interests, from .82 to .87 for social interests, and from .48 to .87 for activity interests.   After correction for attenuation the correlations of the scores with teacher ratings of the subjects for the three types of interests averaged, for six groups of subjects, .65 for intellectual interests, .50 for social interests, and .31 for activity interests.

In devising the M-F association test the procedure followed was in all essential respects that used by Dr. Wyman.   First a short English dictionary was scanned in the search for words which looked as though they might bring sex differences in responses if used as stimulus words in an association test.   A tentative list of about 500 such words was selected by the senior author, with the assistance of Edith M. Sprague.   The selection was based in part on investigational data in the field of sex differences, but to a greater extent on subjective "hunches."   Each word in this list was next rated by three judges for probable merit in bringing out sex differences, with the result that the list was reduced from 500 to 220 (110 in each of two forms).   The 220 stimulus words were printed in large type on cards like those used by Dr. Wyman and were administered to 400 high-school and university subjects equally divided between the sexes.   The words were divided into two forms, A and B, as shown on pages 20 and 21.

A few examples of responses found to be predominantly masculine or feminine which will give an idea of the possibilities of a test of this kind in the study of sex differences are shown on the following page.

Reliabilities were secured by application of the test to 128 boys and 134 girls in the junior high school and 87 boys and 92 girls in the senior high school.   Even-numbered items were correlated with the odd-numbered and the coefficients were corrected by the Spearman-Brown formula.   This was done for scores obtained by two methods: (a) by weighting responses from +6 to −6 according to the amount of sex difference shown, and (b) by weighting each response as either +1 or −1 (masculine or feminine).   The two sets of scores will hereafter be designated by the terms "weighted scores"[1] and "unit scores."   For single-sex groups

[1] See pp. 52ff. for method of deriving score weights.

Stimulus word	Responses given more often	
	By males	By females
BLUE	spectrum	dress
FLESH	meat	pink
CLOSET	door	clothes
GARDEN	weeds	flower
HOME	house	happy
POWDER	bullet	rouge
CHARM	snake	beauty
ARM	leg	limb
FAIR	weather	blonde
RELIGION	God	church
WAR	soldiers	hate
STOUT	strong	fat
GENTLE	horse	mother
HUNT	shoot	find

the reliabilities (based on 220 words) ranged from .45 to .64 for weighted scores, and slightly lower for unit scores. Weighted score reliabilities for the sexes combined ranged from .60 to .81.

An association test of the kind just described has three serious disadvantages. (1) A majority of the responses have such low frequency that very large numbers of subjects must be tested in order to secure reliable sex differences for a reasonable proportion of the responses occurring. This means that of the entire number of responses given by a subject, many will be responses which cannot be scored. This, of course, seriously reduces the reliability of the test. (2) Scoring is laborious and time consuming, as each of the responses must be looked up in a tabulated list to find the weight it carries. (3) Occasionally a subject with defective vision fails to perceive correctly the stimulus word, while others, failing to find a response to a given stimulus word in the time allowed (10 seconds), lose their place in the column of spaces and misplace succeeding responses. Such misplacement is likely to cause errors in scoring.

Because of these defects the type of association test first used was finally abandoned in favor of one which required the subject to check that one of four given responses which seemed "to go best with" the stimulus word. The stimulus words were no longer presented on cards, but were printed in capital letters in a test booklet. Each stimulus word was followed by the four response words printed in lower case and smaller type. Response words were selected which had shown differences in frequency between male and female subjects, and of the four following each stimulus word two were "masculine" and two "feminine." The masculine and feminine responses were arranged in chance order to allow for the tendency of some subjects to check more often the response standing in a particular serial order.

An experiment was made to find out whether it is possible to make up valid items of this kind without first giving them to subjects in the form of a free association test in order to find response words that have different frequencies for males and females. A list of 51 untried stimulus words was made up, each followed by two response words selected as likely to be masculine and two as likely to be feminine. Of the 51 items devised in this way 28 proved to be usable and in no way inferior to those for which response words were selected on the basis of empirically ascertained sex differences in frequency. This method saves much time and could probably be used advantageously in adapting the multiple-response association test to purposes other than the study of sex differences.

The multiple-response form of the association test is better adapted to group testing, requires less time for its administration, and can be scored with far greater rapidity. However, the reader will naturally raise the question whether the test thus altered does not lose its essential character as an association technique. Certainly the association is less "free," since response is limited to choice among the four alternatives presented. Even if these have been selected from among responses showing high frequency by the earlier method it will nevertheless often happen that in the case of a particular subject no one of the four would have been given by the method of free association. However, the relative merits of the two methods can only be judged by their results. Our data show that by every criterion the multiple-response method is as good for the present purpose as the older method. It is fully as reliable, gives as wide separation of sex groups, and in fact correlates with scores obtained by the standard method almost as highly as the latter correlate with themselves.

The experimental form of the multiple-response association test was composed of 171 items, 120 from the 220 of the original list and 51 items artificially constructed. It was given to 600 subjects: 100 of each sex in the seventh grade, the junior year of high school, and the university. Both weighted and unit scores, based upon the sex differences found by item tabulation, were used in computing reliabilities and sex overlap. The weighted scores showed only a slight superiority when judged by these two criteria and were discarded in favor of the simpler unit scores.[1]

All of the types of association tests we have used as measures of M-F differences have low reliability. It will be recalled that the free association list of 220 stimulus words used in the first experiment had a reliability of only .45 to .64 for single-sex groups, and of only .60 to .81 for the sexes combined. The reliabilities of the multiple-response association test, with 171 stimulus words, averaged .59 for single-sex groups and .78 for the sexes combined. The amount of sex overlap was close to 10 per cent for each of the three groups tested.[2]

For the final M-F test 120 words were selected from the 171 used in the experiment just described. These have been equally divided between Form A and Form B and are reproduced in Appendix IV. The words retained include only those from the original list which showed sex differences in the same direction for at least three out of the four multiple responses in all the groups tested. The reliabilities were then computed for the retained lists of 60 words, both by the split-half method and by the correlation of Form A against Form B. Average reliabilities did not differ significantly for the two methods, averaging about .40 for single-sex groups and .55 for the sexes combined. By application of the Spearman-Brown formula the reliability of the

---

[1] See pp. 53 *ff.* for discussion of considerations leading to this choice.

[2] Throughout the M-F study the percentage of overlap has been computed by the method described on pp. 66 *ff.*

120 words of Form A and Form B combined is estimated to be about .57 for single-sex groups and .71 for the sexes combined. These figures would have been somewhat higher if less homogeneous groups had been used, that is, if subjects from junior high school, senior high school, college, and a wide variety of adult populations had been thrown together. Even so, the reliability of a test of this type tends to be low. The score on Exercise 1 should not be used by itself for the comparison of individuals unless both forms (120 words) have been given, and then only with due caution. It is estimated that a test of nearly 300 words would be required to give a reliability of .75 for a single-sex group and of .85 for the sexes combined.

The amount of sex overlap based upon 60 words was 22 per cent in the seventh grade, 14 per cent in the high school, and 12 per cent for the college subjects. Overlap has not been computed on the basis of 120 words, but it would of course be appreciably less.

Score norms for Exercise 1 are given in Appendix II. We are here concerned only with the outstanding facts brought out in the adaptation of the word-association technique in the study of M-F differences. We feel warranted in concluding that the test has demonstrated its value for this purpose when used as one of a battery of tests, though in the interest of reliability the number of items should be considerably increased if it is to be used independently in profile studies of individual subjects.

INK-BLOT ASSOCIATION

This form of the association test has an extensive history extending from the time it was suggested by Binet in 1895 to recent and current work with the Rorschach test. Dearborn, Sharp, and Bartlett have used the method in qualitative studies of the imagination; Kirkpatrick and Pyle in investigations of the associations of school children; Brown as a test of suggestibility; Rorschach and his followers as a test of personality type.[1] Extravagant claims have been made with respect to its value in

[1] See WHIPPLE, G. M., *Manual of mental and physical tests; Part II, Complex processes*, pp. 254 *ff.*, Warwick and York, 1915.

the classification of abnormal types, but as a test of a somewhat "freer" kind of association than is called forth by word stimuli it would seem to have a distinct place in the investigation of personality differences.   A disadvantage is that so many associations are possible with the usual kind of ink blot that it is very difficult to devise a scoring technique which gives high enough reliability to make the test worth using.

The ink-blot test in the study of M-F differences began in 1925 when the senior author and Mary A. Bell produced a series of 40 blots according to the directions of Dearborn.[1]   In this case blots were so made as to suggest responses which it was thought might show sex differences.   For example, one blot was made to look something like a hill and also something like a colonial hat, on the theory that the latter association would be more often given by women than by men if, as is commonly believed, women are more interested than men in wearing apparel and less in the kind of outdoor life that would suggest the response "hill." Another was devised to resemble both a pistol and a cradle, with the idea of tapping man's pugnacious and woman's maternal attitudes; and so with the entire series.   The trial series also included the 20 blots used by Whipple.

Tryout of these 60 ink blots with men and women college students brought to light various imperfections, the most serious of which was the wide range of responses with consequent low frequency for the greater number and low reliability of sex differences.   It was found that stimuli with simple outlines were better suited to the purpose at hand than those that were more complex and irregular.   The first series was therefore discarded and a new series of 100 drawn in printer's heavy ink with a paint brush wielded in rather sweeping strokes.   By this method it was easier to devise stimuli offering a more strictly dichotomous ambiguity.   For example, one blot might very well be taken either as a pipe or as a mailbox, one as a snake or a tulip, one as a snowshoe or a spoon, one as the moon or a ship, etc.

[1] DEARBORN, G., A study of imagination, *Am. J. Psychol.*, 1898, **9**, 183–190. Also WELLS, F. L., Rorschach and the free association test, *J. Gen. Psychol.*, 1935, **13**, 413–433.

After trial of the new series with 100 male and 100 female students in high school and college, 30 of the 100 were discarded. Photographic plates were made of those retained and the blots were printed in a 3 by 5 in. booklet of 70 leaves, one blot to a leaf. On the outside cover were the following directions: "On each leaf of this booklet is a kind of ink blot or drawing. They are not pictures of anything in particular but might suggest almost anything to you, just as shapes in the clouds sometimes do. Below each drawing write the *first* thing it makes you think of." At intervals of ten seconds the subjects were instructed to turn the leaf to the next drawing.

The test in this form was given to 460 subjects in the following groups, each evenly divided between males and females: 120 seventh-grade pupils, 180 high-school freshmen, 80 students in the State Teachers College of San Jose, and 80 nonacademic adults. The last group included 40 members of a professional and business women's club and 40 members of a men's church club. The responses given by these subjects were tabulated and the frequencies were computed separately by sex. Only those responses were retained for scoring which were given by as many as four subjects in at least three of the four groups tested and which showed a sex difference in the same direction for at least three of the four groups. Each retained response was then assigned a weight in proportion to the standard error of the difference between the percentage of males and females giving it. The weights ranged from 0 to 15. The total score of a subject taking the test was computed by taking the average weight of his scorable responses. The average of the weights, instead of their sum, was used because the number of scorable responses varied from subject to subject. The score distributions of 230 male and 230 female subjects, together with their accumulative per cents, are given in Table 3.

The reliability of the 70-blot test, computed by the split-half method, for the 180 high-school freshmen was found to be .64 for the sexes combined but only .48 and .31, respectively, for males and females taken separately. The validity of the test is indicated by the smallness of sex overlap shown in Table 3.

TABLE 3.—DISTRIBUTION OF INK-BLOT SCORES OF MALES AND FEMALES

Score	Male	Female	Cumulative per cent males	Cumulative per cent females
7.	1		100.	
..				
..				
..				
6.2	1		99.6	
6.1			99.1	
6.0	2		99.1	
5.9	2		98.3	
5.8	6		97.4	
5.7	4		94.8	
5.6	10		93.0	
5.5	14	1	88.7	100.
5.4	7		82.6	99.6
5.3	20		79.6	99.6
5.2	25		70.9	99.6
5.1	14	1	60.0	99.6
5.0	25		53.9	99.1
4.9	17	2	43.0	99.1
4.8	15	4	35.7	98.3
4.7	14	7	29.1	96.5
4.6	15	14	23.0	93.5
4.5	11	10	16.5	87.4
4.4	8	17	11.7	83.0
4.3	7	13	8.3	75.7
4.2	5	25	5.2	70.0
4.1	4	22	3.0	59.1
4.0		21	1.3	49.6
3.9		24	1.3	40.4
3.8	2	29	1.3	30.0
3.7		17	.4	17.4
3.6		6	.4	10.0
3.5		7	.4	7.4
3.4	1	3	.4	4.3
3.3		2		3.0
3.2		1		2.2
3.1		2		1.7
3.0				.8
2.9		2		.8
Total	230	230		

In a later edition of the test the number of blots was reduced to 50 by elimination of those which had been found least satisfactory. As in the case of the word-association test, the original procedure was discarded in favor of the multiple-response technique. All the considerations which favored this change in the test of word association apply with equal force to the ink-blot test. For each item four responses were selected from those secured by the free association method, two which had been given more often by males and two more often by females in at least three of the four groups of subjects, all with as high frequencies as could be found satisfying this criterion.

The 50 blots were printed in a booklet with six to eight on a page. Beside each blot were the four responses arranged in chance order in a column. The first page contained the instructions and two blots used as a fore-exercise.

The test was given in this form to 600 subjects, 200 in the eighth grade, 200 in the junior year of high school, and 200 in college. Each group contained 100 males and 100 females. Reliabilities and sex overlap were computed separately for weighted and unit scores. The superiority of weighted scores was so slight by both criteria that they were abandoned in favor of the more readily computed unit scores. By both methods of scoring the reliability for 50 items is low and the overlap of sexes large. An average reliability of .43 was found for the sexes combined; the reliabilities for single-sex groups ranged from .00 to .35.

In the final edition of the M-F test the number of blots was further reduced to 36, equally divided between Form A and Form B. Reliabilities found for eight new groups, each numbering 50 subjects of one sex, ranged from almost zero to .56 for the 36 items. The 18 items in a single form have an average reliability of .28 for groups homogeneous as to sex and school grade, with consequent heavy overlap between the score distributions for male and female subjects. The test could therefore have been eliminated from the battery without appreciable loss, but has been retained partly because of its appeal to subjects and partly in the hope that its retention would stimulate further experimentation. It seems in fact to have all the merits possessed by the word-association method and possibly others. Certainly it would seem to evoke associations less stereotyped by habit than those evoked by words. In order to make the test produce a reasonably reliable score it would of course be necessary to increase the number of stimuli to something like 200. As this test stands its score should not be used by itself for the comparison either of individuals or of moderate-sized groups.

THE INFORMATION TEST

Tests of general information of the type commonly used in group tests of intelligence usually show relatively small sex differences in total score. This seems to be explained by the conscious intent, on the part of those who devise such tests, to make them equally "fair" to male and female subjects, or, when this is not deemed feasible, to select items equally divided between those which favor males and those which favor females. The Army Alpha information test is an exception; its items were selected for testing only male subjects, with the result that when otherwise comparable sex groups are given this test the mean information score is usually found to be lower for females. There is abundant evidence in the literature of sex differences that particular items of information are more often answered correctly by males and others by females, and it was this fact which gave rise to Exercise 3 of the M-F test.

Early in 1926 the literature on sex differences in information was canvassed by the senior author and the first M-F information test of 200 items was made up. The selections were based in part upon the direct evidence offered by tabulations of successes and failures by males and females on various information tests, and in part on indirect evidence from sex differences in interests, reading preferences, etc. The 200 items may be roughly classified as follows: 28 historical; 26 from the physical sciences; 23 from the biological sciences; 35 literary (relating to books, authors, and literary characters); 17 items of general information, mostly of a practical kind; 38 related to household arts; 16 from religion and mythology; and 17 miscellaneous.

The items were set up in the multiple-response form, the subject's task being that of underlining the correct response out of four given. The test was administered to 800 subjects, 100 of each sex in each of four populations: seventh-grade pupils, high-school students, college students, and nonacademic adults. The successes and failures on each item were tabulated separately by sex in each of the four populations, and only those items were retained which showed a probably significant sex difference in the same direction for at least three of the four populations. Of the 200 items, 91 satisfied this criterion. These were assigned M-F weights in proportion to the amount of sex difference.

The reliabilities computed for the eight single-sex groups ($N = 100$ each) of the original populations tested averaged .50 for single-sex groups and .71 for the sexes combined. Unit scores and weighted scores gave about the same reliability.

The 91 items were then administered to new groups, as follows: 127 eighth-grade boys, 134 eighth-grade girls, 88 high-school boys, 122 high-school girls, 212 college men, 170 college women. Reliabilities for these groups, based on weights derived from the four populations previously tested, averaged .41 for single-sex groups and .69 for the sexes combined. These reliabilities are much lower than those found when the same items are used simply as a measure of information. The latter was found to be .89 for high-school girls and .79 for high-school boys, as compared with about .40 when scored for masculinity or femininity of response.

In an effort to improve the reliability, a search was begun for new information items which would yield sex differences. Data were tabulated from an information test of 491 items which had been administered to a total of 200 subjects of each sex in grades 8, 11, and 12. The experiment yielded 95 additional items which seemed to merit further trial. This new set was given to 121 boys and 112 girls in the eighth grade, and to 102 boys and 118 girls in the high school. In the further interest of reliability a new method of scoring was tried out. Previously a subject's total score was the number of masculine items correctly answered minus the number of feminine items correctly answered. It was found, however, that in the case of nearly all the items there was a significant sex difference in the number of subjects underlining one or more of the three wrong responses, and also in the number failing to answer at all. It was accordingly found advantageous to score wrong responses and omissions, instead of mere success and failure. By this "all-possible-response" method of scoring the average reliability for eight single-sex groups of 50 subjects each was raised to .70, and for sexes combined to .82. These figures are for the populations from which the unit weights were derived and so are somewhat spuriously high, but the superiority of the "all-possible-response" method is unmistakable.

The final M-F information test was made up of the best 140 items selected from the two series above described containing, respectively, 91 and 95 items. These 140 are equally divided between Form A and Form B of the test, the items of each series being arranged in order of frequency of correct response. Unit scores are used, based upon the "all-possible-response" method. The reliability of 70 items varies according to the heterogeneity of the groups tested, but is in the neighborhood of .45 for a single sex and .65 for the sexes combined. It is only by using both forms, totaling 140 items, that the reliability of Exercise 3 taken by itself reaches a figure which justifies more than a very tentative rating of the individual subject.

The validity of the 70-item test is indicated by sex overlap ranging from 12 to 23 per cent in the various groups tested, the average being about 16 per cent.

Our final appraisal of the information test as an approach to the study of M-F differences is that it has demonstrated its value when used in conjunction with other tests. Its rather low reliability can be raised to any figure within reasonable limits by increasing the number of items. However, like all the other tests in the battery, it is capable of measuring only one aspect of sex difference, whereas measures of several aspects are necessary in order to secure a more balanced picture of an individual's M-F status. The amount of one's information depends upon schooling and intelligence; its content depends largely upon interests.

That sex differences in information are perhaps almost wholly due to environmental causes (granting sex equality in general intelligence) does not seem to us a valid criticism of the test as we have used it.   It remains true that, generally speaking, male and female subjects acquire funds of information which differ considerably in content, and it must be held significant when the information of a given man or woman includes a disproportionately large amount of those kinds that are more frequently encountered among members of the opposite sex, whatever causes may be responsible for the departure from norm.   It will be granted that these are probably in the main environmental; certainly there are many kinds of information exposure to which is unequal for the two sexes.   We have sought to minimize the influence of this constant environmental factor in two ways.   In the first place we purposely excluded from our trial series items to which both sexes have not had reasonable exposure in school, home, or other environment.   It was hoped that by this means whatever differences were found would be more indicative of interests or temperament than would otherwise be the case. Secondly, the method of unit scores avoids giving undue weight to the very large sex differences which might reasonably be held to reflect largely differences in environment.   By the unit method an item showing the largest sex difference contributes no more toward the total score than one showing a barely significant difference.   The amount of sex overlap by this method is increased, but we believe that the psychological significance of the score has been enhanced.

A special advantage of including a test like Exercise 3 in the M-F battery lies in the fact that it offers a rough measure of intelligence when it is also scored as a straight information test.   The intelligence score thus derived has a reliability (Form A against Form B) of .77 and yields a correlation of .67 with mental age on the Terman Group Test for eighth-grade subjects. It predicts M.A. on the T.G.T. with a probable error of 12 months. Although only a very rough measure of the intelligence level of a single individual, it is sufficiently reliable and valid to be very useful in the comparison of groups.

Test of Emotional and Ethical Attitudes

Perhaps no other differences between the sexes have been so much stressed as those in the field of emotions. Psychologists, psychiatrists, sociologists, novelists, dramatists, and poets are in fairly general agreement that the affective life of women tends in a number of ways to be unlike that of men. In the first place, women are characterized as having a higher degree of affectibility than men in the sense that they respond emotionally to a greater variety of stimuli and experience more intense feeling. Secondly, it is commonly believed that there are important sex differences in the relative contribution of the specific emotions to the total affective life; man, for example, is supposed to be more given to anger and woman to the sympathetic emotions. Thirdly, sex differences are alleged with respect to the stimuli that are effective in calling forth a given emotion; men and women do not fear the same things, are not angered by the same things, do not pity the same people or withdraw in disgust from the same objects. Finally, there are thought to be qualitative as well as quantitative differences in the emotional experiences of the sexes. It may well be that a man's fear or anger or love does in fact have a different existential quality from the corresponding emotion of a woman, but whether this is true is a question that can never be answered in terms of objective data; introspective testimony is at best only able to suggest clues as to the nature of qualitative differences that may exist.

The first three types of sex difference mentioned above are amenable to scientific investigation, and there exists already a respectable body of experimental literature dealing with them. A survey of this literature suggested that a contribution could best be made to the study of M-F differences by asking subjects to rate the effectiveness of specific stimuli in provoking them to a particular emotional response. Anger, fear, disgust, and pity were the emotions chosen for investigation.

The experimental edition of the test was composed of 218 items: 35 relating to anger, 45 to fear, 41 to disgust, 33 to pity, and 64 to ethical attitudes. The items on ethical attitudes were included on the theory that responses of the kind in question are fundamentally emotional rather than intellectual. In form the test was in all essential respects identical with Exercise 4 of the present M-F battery. The subject checked *VM*, *M*, *L*, or *N* (very much, much, little, none) to indicate the extent to which a given situation tended to provoke in him the emotion in question. The ethical attitude items were responded to by checking 3, 2, 1, or 0 to indicate the degree of moral seriousness of a given type of behavior.

Here, as in the case of the other trial series of M-F tests, the selection of items had to be based chiefly on subjective opinion as to ways in which the sexes are likely to differ. First, several persons working independently, including both professors and graduate students of psychology, made up lists of stimuli which in their opinion tend to rouse more anger (or fear, etc.) in one sex than in the other. Next, conferences were held for discussion of individual items proposed, in order to eliminate those not favored by at least a strong minority of opinion. In that part of the test dealing with ethical attitudes it was possible to base the selection of items largely on the data of earlier investigations by others.

The trial series of 218 items thus selected was administered to 854 subjects: 148 boys and 172 girls enrolled in the eighth grade, 116 boys and 128 girls in high school, and 144 men and 146 women attending college. Responses were tabulated separately by sex for each of the three populations tested and scoring keys were made for computing both weighted and unit scores. Items which did not yield a significant sex difference on at least two of the four multiple responses (*VM*, *M*, *L*, *N* or 3, 2, 1, 0) were disregarded in scoring. In this experiment a total score was computed for each of the four parts of the test; that is, for anger, fear, disgust, pity, and ethical attitudes.

The emotional-attitude test proved successful beyond all expectations. In the first place, approximately 90 per cent of the items in the trial series were sufficiently discriminative to justify their retention, whereas in the case of several of the other tests discards from the trial series ran as high as 60 to 75 per cent. In the second place, the reliabilities were surprisingly high even when computed separately for the four parts of the test. These (based on unit weights) averaged as follows for six single-sex groups: anger, 34 items, .74; fear, 40 items, .81; disgust, 36 items, .83; pity, 29 items, .86; ethical attitudes, 56 items, .88. The reliabilities based on weighted scores were of about the same magnitude as those found for unit scores. Sex overlap was approximately 30 per cent for anger, fear, and disgust, and 35 per cent for pity and ethical attitudes.

The 195 items retained were divided between Form A and Form B of the final M-F test. In making the division care was taken to balance the A and B lists as accurately as possible both for content and for comparability of means and score ranges. As the number of items available for one form of the test (A or B) is only 15 to 28 for each section of the test, the four sections are combined into a single total score. Both forms of the test as thus made up were given to new groups of subjects in the eighth grade and high school and reliabilities of total score on Form A or Form B were computed for eight single-sex groups of 50 subjects each. The average was .88. Reliability of total score for mixed-sex groups is .90 or better by the same method (split-half). These reliabilities are remarkably high for a test composed of less than a hundred items. Sex overlap on total score ranges from 21 per cent to 34 per cent, with little difference between Form A and Form B.

We have been somewhat puzzled to account for the high reliability of this test as compared with the association and information tests. It appears that 20 items in any division of the test yield as consistent results as several times that number of association or information items, and that the total score based upon less than 100 items is as reliable as the best tests of intelligence requiring an hour for their administration. One explanation may be the greater homogeneity of the test items. The items of the association and information tests constitute an extremely heterogeneous and small sampling of a vast multitude of possible sex differences. The number of situations to which we are likely to respond with anger, fear, etc., is much more limited than our

associations with a given list of word stimuli, or than the countless
bits of factual information which one may be more or less likely
to possess than the average person of his sex.   That heterogeneity
of content does ordinarily tend to lower reliability of a test is a
well known fact.   One sees its effect in the total score of the
emotional-attitude test, for the reliability of this total is lower
than would be predicted by the Spearman-Brown prophecy
formula from the reliability of any one of the four sections taken
singly.

Another factor contributing to reliability is probably the
graded type of response.   A subject's response indicates not
whether a given situation arouses in him a given emotion, but to
what extent it does so.   Moreover, any tendency a subject may
have to high or low emotivity would operate throughout the test
as a constant factor making for increased consistency.   The same
effect would be produced, regardless of emotivity differences, by
a subject's strictness or looseness of standard in the use of the
response words.   One who is given to careless use of superlatives
may be expected to check *VM* (very much) with unusual frequency in all parts of the test.   The reliability of the test in
question is perhaps fully accounted for by homogeneity of content,
graded responses, and a constant factor of high or low emotivity
(or an equivalent constant factor in language usage).

At this point attention may be called to a persistent sex difference in the frequency with which male and female subjects check
VM or *N* in the first four parts of the test and 3 or 0 in the section
dealing with ethical attitude.   For example, *VM* and 3 together
receive a masculine score in the case of only 9 of the 195 items
in the two forms of the test, as compared with 152 which receive a
feminine weight and 34 no weight at all.   On the other hand, *N*
and 0 together have a masculine weight in 133 items as compared
with 12 which are feminine and 40 which receive no weight.
The question whether women are in fact so much more emotional than men cannot be answered by the data at hand; their
appearance of being so may be entirely an artifact of a sex
difference in language usage.   That the latter explanation can
alone be responsible for the results hardly seems to us probable,

especially as the ethical-attitude items show about the same sex difference as those dealing more strictly with the emotions. Since there is abundant outside evidence that in our culture women do in fact tend to be more severe than men in their judgment of offenses, the sex difference in this section of the test cannot be entirely one of language usage. One might infer that if language is not the sole factor here it probably is not in the other four sections of the test.

TEST OF INTERESTS

We have already seen how the conception of a masculinity-femininity test had its origin in the treatment of data relating to interest in and practice of plays, games, and amusements in a study of gifted and control groups of school children. When an extension of the M-F test was undertaken one of the first things done was to make a collection of items sampling a wider variety of interests than the original test. As a result of rather thorough-going search of the literature of sex differences in interests, 456 items were assembled. About three-fourths of these were new items; the remainder were selected from the 1924 edition of the Strong-Cowdery[1] test of occupational interests after giving the test to 50 adults of each sex and tabulating the responses for the individual items.

The 456 items were made up in two equivalent forms of 228 items each. In the case of each item, the subject's task was to check L, D, or N to indicate "like," "dislike," or "neither." The items were listed in the following groups, each form containing half the items of a given group: occupations, 78; people, 72; games and amusements, 78; movies, magazines, and school studies, 56; books and literary characters, 68; travel and sight-seeing preferences, 52; special interests, 52. This edition of the test was given to the 245 subjects listed on the following page.

Item responses were tabulated by sex and only those were retained for scoring which showed sex differences that were

[1] COWDERY, KARL M., Measurement of professional attitudes, *J. Person. Res.*, 1926, **5**, 131–141.

	Form A		Form B	
	Male	Female	Male	Female
Seventh grade.............................	79	79	46	46
High school...........................	100	100	94	94
College.............................	26	26	54	54
Nonacademic.........................	40	40	38	38
Total..............................	245	245	232	232

large enough for two of the three responses (*L, D,* or *N*) to be probably significant and that were in the same direction in all four groups tested. The reliability of one form of the test (A or B) averaged .55 for single-sex groups and .84 for sexes combined. The sex overlap was slightly less than 10 per cent. These figures are for unit scores and agree very closely with those based upon weighted scores.

A selection was made of the best 170 items from the 456 of the original set. They included the following: occupations, 30; people, 18; movies, magazines, and school studies, 26; games and amusements, 27; books and literary characters, 36; special interests, 33. These were administered to 127 males and 134 females in the seventh grade, to 88 males and 122 females in the first year of high school, and to 177 males and 156 females in college. For single-sex groups the average reliability (unit score) was .70, and for the sexes combined .86. The superiority of this selected list of items over the trial series is seen in the higher reliability and in the decreased overlap of sex groups (6 per cent as compared with 10 per cent).

Shortly after the above experiment was completed a trial was made of 60 newly assembled items relating to historical characters. Four populations were tested, each containing 50 males and 50 females. The reliability of these 60 items averaged .83 for the eight single-sex groups—higher than had been found for much longer lists made up of items from a number of widely different fields. This is another illustration of the effect of homogeneity of content upon a test's reliability. Fifty-five of the historical items discriminated sufficiently between male and female subjects to justify their retention, 28 being assigned to Form A and 27 to Form B of the present M-F test. Though logically belonging in Exercise 5, which contains the other items on likes and dislikes, these items were located in Exercise 6 with a group of others relating to opinions.

Another group of 40 interest items tried out at this time should be mentioned here. In these the subject was asked to give his preference between two kinds of activities or situations such as: (a) camping, (b) living in good hotels; (a) a well cooked meal with soiled linen, (b) a poorly cooked meal with linen spotless. The 15 items of this list which gave significant differences between 239 male and 280 female subjects were printed in the present M-F test with Exercise 4, although, like the historical items, they logically belong in Exercise 5.

Exercise 5 as it now stands in the test contains 187 items, 93 in Form A and 94 in Form B. They include 50 relating to occupations, 24 to people, 27 to movies, magazine reading, and studies, 40 to games and activities, and 26 to books. The reliability of one form, based on eight single-sex groups each numbering 50 subjects, ranged from .54 to .79 with an average of .66. For mixed-sex groups the reliability of Form A against Form B is .86 to .88. The overlap of sex groups ranges from 6 to 12 per cent.

The test of interests and attitudes has proved to be one of the most valuable in the entire M-F battery, as there are several types of populations which it especially helps to differentiate from the generality of a given sex. Among these are male (and probably also female) homosexuals. It would have been strengthened, however, by the inclusion of the items in the first part of Exercise 6 dealing with historical characters, and the small group of items at the end of Exercise 4 on preference between two activities. For profile studies it would be desirable to regroup the items in this way, also to give both forms of the test in order to enhance reliability. The scores so obtained could be counted upon to yield reliability coefficients around .85 for single-sex groups and close to .95 for the sexes combined.

In view of the fact that more than a third of the total number of "interest" items in the M-F test are identical with or similar to items in Strong's test of vocational interests, it occurred to the senior author that it would be desirable to derive a masculinity-femininity scoring key for the Strong test to supplement the keys giving measures of occupational interest. Arrangements were made in 1932 for this to be done by Dr. Harold Carter. With the assistance of Dr. Strong, 114 blanks of males who had taken the vocational interest test were matched with those of 114 females and item tabulations were made. Of the 420 items, 156 were found which could be classified as masculine or feminine and these were weighted in proportion to the sex differences found. The total score so derived had a reliability of .86 for males, .78 for females, and .94 for the combined groups of male and female subjects used in deriving the weights. The figures would of course be lower for new groups. It was found to correlate with the present M-F test to the extent of .43 for a group of 41 males and .62 for a group of 62 females. These items do not constitute a satisfactory substitute for our M-F test, but they make possible interesting comparisons between groups which have been given the vocational interest test and not the M-F test. Data are presented elsewhere (pp. 117 *ff.*) on the relation of the occupational M-F score to marital compatibility.

Dr. Strong has carried further the work initiated by the senior author and Dr. Carter by utilizing the data on sex differences for 603 adults of each sex who had taken his vocational interest test. The M-F test which he has derived from these data includes 202 of the 420 items in his vocational interest test. This form of the Strong M-F test will be found very useful in investigations dealing with sex differences in the restricted field of interests, but like its predecessor it has too little in common with our M-F test to serve as an adequate substitute for it, the coefficient of alienation between the two being somewhere in the neighborhood of .80, if we base the calculation on the intercorrelations for female subjects, and about .90, if based on the intercorrelations for male subjects. In other words, the two tests are not measuring the same thing to the extent of more than 10 or 20 per cent. Basing the calculations on intercorrelations corrected for attenuation would increase the 10 or 20 per cent to something like 20 or 40 per cent. It is obvious, therefore, that even if both tests had a reliability of 1.00 they would still be measuring traits that have too little in common to warrant the use of either measure as an equivalent of the other.[1]

A TEST OF OPINIONS

Women are frequently depicted in literature and in the popular press as holding opinions different from those of men on innumerable matters. The belief that such is the case seems to be fairly general, for no doubt as to its truth was expressed by a single man or woman of many who were interviewed on the question. "Men believe so many things which we women know are not true" was a formulation encountered a number of times; "Women have such silly opinions about a lot of things" was the way men sometimes expressed it. The M-F information test had shown that the factual repertories of men and women are not the same, and one would naturally infer that this would inevitably result in sex differences with respect to opinions held. Studies of superstitious beliefs had presented considerable evidence of sex differences in that particular realm of belief. Moreover, if belief is in part an emotional response, as some have held,[2] one would expect this to produce sex differences in the opinions which are accepted as true or rejected as false.

The task of devising a test of opinions was undertaken hopefully and 201 items were assembled, of which 25 were taken from Garrett and Fisher's study of 140 women and 219 men in Columbia University,[3] and 25 from Jones's study of the opinions of college students.[4] The remaining 150 items were new. From

---

[1] STRONG, EDWARD K., JR., Interests of men and women, *J. Soc. Psychol.*, 1936, **9**, 49–67.

[2] See, for example, MCDOUGALL, WILLIAM, Belief as a derived emotion, *Psychol. Rev.*, 1921, **28**, 315–328.

[3] GARRETT, H. E., and T. R. FISHER, The prevalence of certain popular misconceptions, *J. Appl. Psychol.*, 1926, **10**, 411–420.

[4] JONES, VERNON, Disagreement among teachers as to right and wrong, *Teach. Coll. Rec.*, **21**, 34–36.

the entire number, 96 were selected by the composite ratings of several judges as most likely to prove valid for the purpose at hand.

The test was given to somewhat more than 100 of each sex in the seventh grade, to the same number in the high school, and to 50 of each sex attending college. The task as set forth in the instructions was to read each statement and "consider whether it is mostly true or mostly false," and to encircle T or F accordingly.

The results of the response tabulations were disappointing, for only 28 of the 96 items yielded sufficiently large and consistent sex differences in the three populations to warrant their inclusion in the M-F battery. These have been divided equally between the two forms and appear as part of Exercise 6. Reliability of the 28 items separately computed for nine single-sex groups of approximately 50 subjects each averaged only .40. For all the subjects below college level, sexes combined, the reliability was .68. These figures are based upon unit scores, though weighted scores were tried out and discarded as in the case of all the other M-F studies. Overlap of sex groups ranged from 22 to 28 per cent.

The outcome of the experiment was so meager that it is obvious the test of opinions could have been eliminated from the battery without serious loss. It was finally retained in the interest of making the total score of the M-F battery a wide sampling of sex differences. Even when both forms of the opinions test have been given their combined score is still entirely too unreliable to justify its separate use except in the comparison of exceedingly large populations.

What conclusions can be drawn with respect to the importance of beliefs or opinions as differentiating the personalities of the sexes? Unless the items used in this experiment represent an unfortunate selection it would appear that sex differences of the kind in question have probably been much exaggerated; that they are perhaps almost negligible. It is of course conceivable that a much better selection of trial items could have been made by a more penetrating observer of people. The result cannot, however, be attributed to lack of industry in assembling items for consideration or to lack of attempt to apply critical judgment in selecting from the larger number those most worthy of trial. Each item was selected either on the basis of its relationship to known data or on the basis of a definite hypothesis. The trial list is reproduced at the end of this section in order that the reader may judge for himself whether the relative failure of the experiment can be justly blamed upon the selection of items. The few which discriminated appreciably between sex groups are indicated by an asterisk.

A few illustrations may be given of the kind of reasoning that went into the construction of the test. Statements like 2, 18, 29, 36, 53, 57, 63, 78, 84, and 95 were selected on the theory that women tend to be more religious than men and to be somewhat more orthodox in their religious beliefs. Statements 12, 23, 33, 39, 54, 59, 60, 68, 73, and 85 were expected to be more acceptable to men because of the element of aggression or will to power which they involve. Item 8 was chosen because women are supposed to be more conservative about divorce than men; items 14, 16, and 30 because investigations have shown them to be more superstitious; items 4, 5, 13, 28, 34, 35, and several others because women are thought to be more tender and sympathetic; item 43 because they are often said to be more given to "white lies"; item 34 because Lincoln symbolizes feminine sympathy and Washington masculine strength. And similarly throughout the test. The frequency with which seemingly good hunches were belied by the response statistics inclines us to believe that men and women do not differ from each other very greatly in the opinions they hold about commonly discussed issues.

*1. The face shows how intelligent a person is.
2. Laws should be passed to compel people to observe the Sabbath.
*3. Blondes are less trustworthy than brunettes.
*4. The weak deserve more love than the strong.
*5. The hanging of murderers is justifiable.

6. A square jaw indicates will power.
7. It is better to be poor in the city than rich in the country.
8. Nine-tenths of the divorces granted are unjustified.
9. Character is indicated by the shape of the head.

*10. The world was created in six days of twenty-four hours each.

*11. Married women ought not to be permitted to teach school.
 12. Will power is supreme.
 13. It is justifiable to whip a baulky horse.
*14. One usually knows when stared at from behind.
 15. Silent men are good thinkers.

*16. Lines in the hand foretell the future.
 17. The "insanity plea" as a defense in murder trials should be abolished.
*18. Preachers have better characters than most persons.
 19. The world is rapidly getting better.
*20. Men are created equal in mental capacity.

 21. Conscience is an infallible guide.
 22. It is silly to let others see your emotions.
 23. Individual liberty is more to be desired than wealth.
 24. A wicked person cannot be happy.
 25. The pen is mightier than the sword.

*26. Love "at first sight" is usually the truest love.
*27. Inventors deserve more honor than artists.
 28. Criminals are really sick and should be treated like sick persons.
 29. God is a real personality who thinks and feels and wills.
 30. The stars have an influence on character.

*31. Girls are naturally more innocent than boys.
*32. An ugly face usually goes with a kind heart.
 33. A person is justified in taking another's life to save his own.
*34. Lincoln was greater than Washington.
*35. Hunting and fishing are wrong because cruel.

 36. In Bible times miracles actually occurred.
 37. Human beings are descended from the lower animals.
 38. Brains and beauty do not go together.
*39. The United States should adopt a more aggressive foreign policy.
*40. There is plenty of proof that life continues after death.

*41. The largest fortunes should be seized by the government and divided among the poor.
 42. All human lives are equally sacred.
 43. "White lies" are sometimes justifiable.
*44. Opportunity knocks but once for any man.

45. What we call conscience is mainly the fear of being caught.

*46. Children should be taught never to fight.
47. Immorality is as wicked in men as in women.
48. Paupers are usually themselves to blame for their condition.
49. A shifty eye indicates dishonesty.
50. Children should sometimes be punished by whipping.

51. Rich men give to charity mainly to advertise themselves.
*52. It is more important to be just than to believe in God.
53. The clergyman's profession is nobler than the physician's.
54. God is more a being of power than of tenderness.
*55. It is better to tell your troubles to your friends than to keep them to yourself.

56. Only those of average or superior intelligence should be allowed to vote.
57. The wicked will suffer eternal punishment in the life to come.
58. Students these days are not required to study hard enough.
59. We are sometimes justified in returning evil for evil.
*60. Wealth, power, and honor usually go to those who deserve them.

61. Suicide is never justifiable.
62. A receding chin means a weak character.
63. Faith can heal a broken bone.
*64. There should be perfect equality between men and women in all things.
65. To be well liked while living is better than eternal fame after death.

66. The artist is more to be admired than the statesman.
67. The humblest laborer should be paid as much as the good mechanic because his family needs as much.
68. The soldier is more to be admired than the musician.
69. Riches should be totally disregarded in choosing a husband or wife.
70. We should never send a man to prison for his first offense.

*71. Green-eyed people are not to be trusted.
*72. Women are purer than men by nature.
73. We are sometimes justified in refusing to forgive our enemies.
74. "Our nation, right or wrong," is a good slogan.
75. Success depends more on luck than on ability.

76. It can be proved that the soul is immortal.
77. If a man becomes a criminal it is usually the fault of society.
78. The religious missionary is a meddler and nuisance.
79. Handsome men are less dependable than homely men.
80. No one is entirely unselfish.

81. Exactly the same standard of morality should apply to men as to women.
82. It is better to live a coward than to die a hero.
83. Unclean bodies are as bad as unclean thoughts.
84. When science and the Bible disagree we should always believe the Bible.
85. The United States should take possession of Mexico and civilize that country.

86. It is possible even today to live exactly as Christ would have us.
87. No one ever truly loves but once.
88. There is no real justice in the United States.
89. Killing animals for meat is morally objectionable.
*90. We should never give to beggars.

91. An illegitimate child should have the rights of inheritance.
92. War is certain to be abolished sometime.
93. The morals of the young are growing worse.
94. If a man is moral it doesn't matter whether he is religious.
95. The laws of nature are sometimes suspended in answer to prayer.

96. The unmarried mother deserves the scorn she gets.

TEST OF INTROVERTIVE RESPONSE

An experiment was initiated in 1926 for the purpose of exploring sex differences in introvertive tendency. Cady's modification of the original Woodworth personal data sheet[1] served as a point of departure. As the Cady test had been administered a few years previously to the Stanford group of gifted children (IQ 140 and above) and to a control group of unselected children, this offered an opportunity to discover whether any considerable number of its 85 items were promising for inclusion in the M-F test. Item counts were therefore made for 100 boys and 100

[1] CADY, V. M., The estimation of juvenile incorrigibility, *J. Delinq. Monog.*, 2, Whittier (Calif.) State School, 1923, pp. 140.

girls, between the ages of 12 and 15. Half belonged to the gifted and half to the control group. Of the 85 items, 51 yielded sex differences large enough to warrant further trial. Only those were retained which gave critical ratios of 2 or higher for either the yes or the no response. The wording of many of the items was changed before printing for tryout. These 51 items will be referred to as Introversion, Series 1.

Introversion, Series 2, was prepared concurrently with Series 1. It consisted of 47 items, about half of which were borrowed either from Laird's C1 and C2 or from the Heidbreder[1] list, the latter in advance of publication. The remainder of the items were new.

Series 1 was given to 261 subjects in the seventh grade and to 210 who were in the first year of high school. Series 2 was given to 231 subjects in the seventh grade and to 231 in high school. All the groups were composed of boys and girls in approximately equal numbers. On the basis of item counts for both series, scoring keys were made for both weighted and unit scores. As in all the other experiments, weighted scores showed so little superiority over the unit scores that they were discarded.

The average reliability of Series 1 for four single-sex groups of 100 subjects each was .44, and for a combined-sex group of 200 subjects, .59. The sex overlap for seventh-grade and high-school subjects combined was 28 per cent. The average reliability of Series 2 for eight single-sex groups of 50 subjects each was .24, and for all subjects, sexes combined, .43.

The 84 items composing Exercise 7 of the present M-F test (42 in each form) were selected as the best from Series 1 and Series 2. The 14 discarded were items which did not show a significant sex difference in both the yes and the no response. The retained items of both Series 1 and Series 2 were equally divided between Form A and Form B of Exercise 7.

As was to be expected from previous data, the reliability of Exercise 7 is very low, averaging only .24 for eight single-sex

[1] HEIDBREDER, EDNA F., Introversion and extroversion in men and women, *J. Abn. and Soc. Psychol.*, 1927, **22**, 243–258. The authors are indebted to Dr. Heidbreder for supplying a manuscript copy of her test.

groups. A sex overlap of 25 per cent was found for seventh-grade subjects, of 33 per cent for high-school subjects, and of 34 per cent for college subjects. Reliability of the total score of Form A and Form B combined is only in the vicinity of .40 for a single sex, so that there is no warrant for the use of Exercise 7 in the comparison of individual subjects. Its use, with due caution, is permissible only in the comparison of rather large populations.

As in the case of the test of opinions, the question arises whether the results of this experiment should have been discarded altogether. The answer would have to be in the affirmative if the purpose of the M-F battery had been to provide a basis for profile ratings of individual subjects in a number of aspects of human personality. Several measures of sufficient reliability to be used in this way are unquestionably a desirable objective for future work, but the goal of the present series of experiments has been primarily the more modest one of sampling a wide field of sex differences the significance of which would be reflected in a single total score for the battery. Exercise 7 has, therefore, been retained for whatever it may add to the general picture.

In the period that has elapsed since the M-F test was devised many studies have been made of the aspect of personality commonly designated by the term introversion-extroversion, and several scales for its measurement have been devised. The concept is one which varies greatly from author to author, with the result that some of the tests designed to measure the trait in question yield very low correlations with some of the others. However, three of the best known (Laird's, Thurstone's, and Bernreuter's) yield intercorrelations which approximate unity when corrected for attenuation, though whether the aspect of personality measured by these three tests has been suitably named is a question with which we need not here concern ourselves. Exercise 7 closely resembles in content the three tests just mentioned. Its low reliability, especially as compared with the Thurstone and Bernreuter tests, is in part attributable to the smaller number of items, but chiefly to the fact that it is here scored as a sex difference test instead of as a direct measure of introversion-extroversion.   Its use in this way is justified not only by the data presented in this section but also by the sex differences which several later investigations have brought to light.   These are unanimous in showing females somewhat more introverted than male subjects of comparable populations.   The fact that the sex difference is not large probably has some connection with the low reliability of the test when used as a measure of masculinity-femininity.[1]

[1] The reader who is interested in the field of psychological sex differences drawn upon in the construction of the seven exercises constituting the M-F Test is referred to a summary of the recent literature with a bibliography of older summaries by Catharine C. Miles, *Sex in Social Psychology*, Chapter 16, pp. 683–797, in A Handbook of Social Psychology (Ed. C. Murchison) Worcester, Mass.: Clark Univ. Press, 1936.   Pp. 1195.

CHAPTER IV

THE M-F TEST AS A WHOLE

The preceding chapter has given a brief and rather general account of the experiments which resulted in the various "exercises" or parts of the M-F test. It remains to present certain data and to discuss a number of issues which concern the test as a whole, including the weighting of items, method of deriving a total score, intercorrelation of the subtests, reliability, validity, establishment of norms, equivalence of Form A and Form B, correlations with other measures, sample score distributions, and desirable lines of extension and revision.

THE WEIGHTING OF ITEMS

The question of chief concern in this connection is whether the plan adopted whereby each item is given a unit score (M or F) is as satisfactory as giving the item a score weight in proportion to its efficiency in discriminating between comparable sex groups. If it is not, then no ordinary degree of economy of time in scoring the test and in dealing with the measures it yields would justify our choice of the simpler method. By what criteria shall the relative merits of the two methods be judged? We are aware of only three: (1) reliability, (2) validity as indicated by per cent of overlap of score distributions for comparable male and female groups, and (3) validity as indicated by correlations with independent measures or ratings of masculinity and femininity.

The third criterion should theoretically be the one most nearly crucial, especially if it includes correlations with clinical case histories as well as correlations with more strictly quantitative data. Unfortunately, it is a method we have not been able to use. There is available no other psychometric technique for measuring M-F differences against which the present test can be validated, and clinical data in sufficient quantity have not yet been accumulated. There remains the outside criterion of M-F ratings of subjects by presumably competent judges, the difficulty here being that we have not been able to find two observers whose ratings of the same subjects agree to more than a trifling extent. The choice between unit scores and weighted scores has accordingly been determined primarily by the effect upon reliability and sex overlap and secondarily by considerations of convenience and economy.

When the experiments in M-F testing were undertaken it was assumed that weighted scores would probably be found both more reliable and more discriminative. Their desirability was questioned only on certain theoretical grounds; whether, for example, the decrease in sex overlap which weighted scores were expected to bring about is necessarily a desirable result from the psychological point of view. No one knows what amount of overlap would be found if the totality of M-F traits were adequately and reliably measured. It is conceivable that the use of weighted scores might result in a spuriously small amount of overlap and thus exaggerate the sex differences which actually exist. It can be plausibly argued that heavy weights for individual items place a premium on sex differences that are accidental rather than fundamental—accidental in the sense that they reflect almost entirely sex differences in experience. There are doubtless a few items of information which practically every woman but only a few men could answer correctly which would have a high discriminative index but which would have no psychological significance in the present study, and similarly, items of specifically male knowledge could be propounded. Items of this kind tell us nothing beyond the fact that the subject is male or female, which we already know. The principle involved here does, as a matter of fact, apply in greater or less degree to every item in the M-F test. One may reasonably argue that the only way to avoid making the test too much a measure of accidental differences in experience is to take account only of the *number* of M-F differences without regard to their size.

It was this point of view which led us in the first place to compare weighted and unit scores for reliability and validity, though it was hardly hoped that the data in these criteria would warrant the adoption of the method which we regarded as otherwise theoretically preferable. As it turned out, more than a hundred reliability coefficients computed by the two methods showed an average difference of less than .05 in favor of weighted scores. Even more unexpectedly, the average difference in sex overlap was less than 2 per cent. Although the average difference both for reliability and for overlap favored the weighted scores, it was so small as hardly to justify the retention of a method which was both clumsy and psychologically questionable. Unit scores are therefore used throughout the test. Each response of the subject is scored $+$ or $-$, that is, masculine or feminine. The total score of a given exercise is the algebraic sum of the $+$ and $-$ scores. It will be noted that in Exercises 2, 3, 6, and one section of 5 omissions as well as positive responses are scored.

The weighted item scores used for a time and then discarded in favor of unit scores were derived by the formula:[1]

$$W = 10\beta = \frac{10\phi}{(1 - \phi^2)\sigma_x}$$

where

$$\phi = \frac{ad - bc}{\sqrt{(a + c)(b + d)(a + b)(c + d)}}$$

This formula takes account of the fact that the reliability of the sex differences with respect to relative frequency of a given response is lower when the frequencies are small than when they are large.

WEIGHTING OF EXERCISES FOR TOTAL SCORE

The weighting of subtests in a battery of intelligence or special ability tests has become a fairly standardized procedure. Everything else equal, those subtests are assigned the most weight which have highest reliability, which correlate best with independent measures of the ability, and which duplicate least the

[1] COWDERY, K. M., *op. cit.*

other subtests of the battery. While agreement is general that these are the important factors to be taken into account, the precise weight to be given to each is a matter on which experts sometimes differ. Over and above these three factors is the problem of equating the several subtests for variability. This, however, is a question of *un*weighting rather than weighting, for it is clear that a given subtest A yielding score distributions with twice as large standard deviations as those of subtest B carries automatically twice the weight of the latter. In order to give the two subtests a truly equal weight, the score on B must be multiplied by 2.

The weighting of subtests in a battery of the type with which we are here concerned should take account of reliability, sex overlap (validity), intercorrelations, and dispersion of scores. The following data are pertinent:

The subtests	1	2	3	4	5	6	7
Approximate average reliability, ten single-sex groups	.40	.25	.50	.89	.60	.54	.24
Approximate average reliability, sexes combined	.62	.34	.68	.90	.80	.64	.32
Average per cent of overlap	17	30	17	26	10	31	31
Average correlation with the other subtests, single-sex groups	.01	.07	.19	.15	.10	.09	.13
Average correlation with the other subtests, sexes combined	.40	.30	.47	.39	.49	.27	.38
Approximate average of S.D.'s of 16 groups	7	1	8	20	30	7	2

The intercorrelations of the exercises may be ignored, as they are all relatively low. As for reliabilities, those of Exercises 4 and 5 are highest, those of 2 and 7 very low, and the others medium. Overlap is least for 5, greatest for 2, 4, 6, and 7, and moderate for 1 and 3. The standard deviations of scores are large for 4 and 5, very small for 2 and 7, and intermediate for 1, 3, and 6. The weights we have assigned are as follows, the figures given being the multipliers to apply to the raw scores of the several exercises before adding for total score:

Exercise	1	2	3	4	5	6	7
Multiplier	1	⅓	1	1	2	1	⅓

Perhaps no two psychologists on the basis of the available data would have arrived at exactly the same weights; certainly it would not be easy to defend those assigned as the best possible. As a matter of fact, within reasonable limits the weights assigned to the separate exercises have little effect on the correlations which the total score will have with other variables. The low weights given Exercises 2 and 7 would seem to be justified by the low reliability and large overlap of these tests. It is possible that the weight assigned to Exercise 5 is higher than it should be as compared with that of 4 and especially as compared with those of 1, 3, and 6. However, the sex overlap for Exercise 5 is the lowest found for any of the tests.

EQUIVALENCE OF FORMS A AND B

In apportioning the items between Form A and Form B considerable effort was made to insure that the two forms would be as nearly as possible equivalent both in respect to content and in respect to the mean scores which they would yield. Items were first laid out in pairs in such a way that the two items of a given pair would be psychologically as similar as possible. Account was next taken of the degree of the masculinity or femininity of each member of a pair, and pairings were juggled so as to arrive at a reasonable compromise between psychological and statistical equivalence of the forms. As more weight was given to psychological similarity of content, it turns out that scores on the two forms are not exact equivalents, those of Form B averaging a few points more masculine than Form A scores. The difference in mean total score on the two forms was 6.7 points for high-school boys, 10.2 points for high-school girls, 4.2 points for eighth-grade boys, and 3.4 for eighth-grade girls, all these differences being in the same direction.[1] Separate norms have accordingly been provided for the two forms.

---

[1] Groups to whom both forms of the test were administered took them half in the AB order and half in the BA order, although as it turned out the order of taking the forms did not seem to affect the score.

INTERCORRELATIONS OF THE EXERCISES

Table 4 gives the intercorrelations of the seven exercises of Form A for two populations of 50 each, the upper triangle for eighth-grade girls and the lower for high-school junior girls. The reliabilities, which are underlined, are in each case the average computed from several populations. Table 5 gives the algebraic averages of the correlations for the two groups.

TABLE 4.—INTERCORRELATION OF EXERCISES, FORM A
(Upper right, eighth-grade girls; lower left, high-school girls)

Ex.	1	2	3	4	5	6	7
1	+.40	−.02	+.26	−.21	.00	+.11	−.06
2	+.12	+.28	+.04	+.24	+.05	+.04	−.08
3	+.02	+.07	+.45	+.35	+.18	+.46	+.17
4	−.08	+.20	+.11	+.89	+.03	−.03	+.20
5	+.14	+.06	.00	+.26	+.60	−.01	−.01
6	−.15	−.17	+.47	+.21	+.05	+.54	+.07
7	−.01	+.20	+.17	+.52	+.40	+.02	+.24

TABLE 5.—AVERAGE OF CORRELATIONS FOR THE TWO GROUPS OF TABLE 4

Ex.	2	3	4	5	6	7
1	+.05	+.14	−.15	+.07	−.02	−.04
2		+.06	+.22	+.06	−.07	+.06
3			+.23	+.09	+.47	+.17
4				+.15	+.09	+.36
5					+.02	+.20
6						+.05

It is evident that the several parts of the M-F test have little in common. In the preceding table of average intercorrelations only two values are found which can be regarded as clearly significant: (1) the correlation of .47 between Exercise 3 (information) and Exercise 6 (historical characters and opinions); (2) the correlation of .36 between Exercise 4 (emotional attitude) and Exercise 7 (introvertive response). The intercorrelations would still be very low even if they were corrected for attenuation.

The two exercises which have highest reliability (4 and 5) yield an average intercorrelation of only +.15 and +.10, respectively, for the two populations.

The intercorrelations would be slightly higher with populations less homogeneous than those of Tables 4 and 5. The intercorrelations of the exercises are higher when computed for the sexes combined, but intercorrelations thus derived have doubtful significance.

The only conclusion possible from the data at hand is that M-F differences are so largely specific for the various types of items composing the separate exercises that search for a general factor or group factors by the application of factor-analysis techniques would be futile. It is doubtful in any case what, if any, psychological meaning attaches to the alleged factors disclosed by such techniques. Instead of adding to the controversial literature on this question we have employed (in Chapter XVI) a method of analysis which we regard as psychologically more meaningful.

The total M-F score, as the test is now constituted, is a composite of samplings from several areas not highly correlated with each other. Warrant for its use rests on the hypothesis that a high *average* of masculinity or femininity in the fields covered by the test probably affects the total personality picture and has significant correlates in everyday behavior. The correctness of this hypothesis has not been conclusively demonstrated but is supported by a certain amount of clinical and other data. It is desirable at present to keep an open mind, for it is conceivable that behavioral correlates of appreciable amount will turn out to be for the most part specific to particular M-F fields, such as information, emotional attitudes, interests, etc. The specificity may carry even further; for example, to anger, fear, pity, etc., in the field of emotional attitudes, and to occupations, people, books, etc., in the field of interests.

Perhaps the next step in M-F research should be to devise highly reliable subtests in as many fields of sex differences as possible so as to make profile studies of individual subjects feasible. The requisite reliabilities could doubtless be obtained for at least one form of each of the following subtests: word association, information, anger response, fear response, pity response, disgust response, ethical response, and interests. The sacrifice of duplicate forms would not be a serious loss, as these are not required for the types of research and clinical practice which are at present most needed. Pending such revision, provisional profile studies should be carried out with three or four of the present subtests by combining the scores of Forms A and B to improve reliability.

RELIABILITY

The reliability of total score of the M-F test has been computed both by the split-half method and by correlating Form A with Form B. The average of six reliabilities by the split-half method, for single-sex populations ranging from 50 to 170, was .78, and for three combined-sex groups, .92. The corresponding correlations of Form A against Form B were .72 and .90. The reliability of the composite score of Form A and Form B is .88 by the split-half method for single-sex groups, and .96 for mixed-sex groups. The probable error of an individual's score in M-F points is for one form of the test approximately 15 score points, roughly a third of the standard deviation of the score distribution of a typical single-sex group. If both forms of the test are administered the average score of the two has a probable error slightly in excess of 10 points, or about 22 per cent of the standard deviation of a typical distribution. It is of course extremely important not to lose sight of the measure's probable error in comparing the scores of individual subjects.

Split-half reliabilities of the seven exercises have been computed for seven to ten different narrow-range populations with N's ranging from 50 to 100 each (eighth-grade, high-school, and college students). The averages of these reliabilities for the several exercises are given in Table 6.

The total score of one form of the test is reliable enough (.92 for sexes combined) to determine a subject's status fairly accurately in the total M-F range. The combined score of the two forms of the test accomplishes this with exceptional accuracy

TABLE 6.—RELIABILITIES OF THE SEPARATE EXERCISES

Exercise	Single-sex groups		Sexes combined	
	No. of groups	Av. rel.	No. of groups	Av. rel.
1	5	.40	3	.62
2	7	.25	2	.34
3	10	.50	2	.68
4	7	.89	2	.90
5	8	.60	2	.80
6	7	.54	2	.64
7	8	.24	2	.32

(reliability .96). The reliabilities of the seven parts of the test taken separately vary greatly—from .24 to .89 for single-sex groups and from .32 to .90 for sexes combined. Only Exercise 4, emotional attitudes, is reliable enough to locate an individual subject with reasonable accuracy if only one form of the test has been given. If both forms have been given, all the other exercises except two are reliable enough to be useful in comparisons of moderately small populations, but not reliable enough for comparing individual subjects. The two exceptions are Exercise 2, blots, and Exercise 7, introvertive response, both of which are so unreliable that they can be used separately only in comparing extremely large populations. Accordingly, if profiles are made of individual subjects these by rights should be based upon the combined score of Form A and Form B, and Exercises 2 and 7 should even then be omitted from the profile.

As we see it now, it would perhaps have been preferable to have included in the M-F test only such subtests as could have been made highly reliable, even if only a single form could have been provided. Exercise 4, emotional attitudes, already satisfies this standard. Exercises 2 and 7 (blots and introvertive response) could not be made to do so without lengthening them to an extent hardly practicable. Exercises 1 (word association), 3 (information), and 5 (interests) would satisfy the standard well if provided with 50 per cent to 100 per cent more items than are included in both forms as they stand at present.

Typical Correlations with Other Variables

We have brought together in Table 7 some of the more interesting correlation coefficients found for M-F scores and other measures. Most of the relationships which enter into this table have been treated at length in other chapters, especially those with age, education, intelligence, interests, occupation, family background, and physical measurements. At this point we should call the reader's attention to the following outstanding results of the correlational work:

1. Nearly all the correlations are low.

2. Correlations of total M-F score with age, within the relatively narrow range represented by the populations in question, are so low as to be merely suggestive of a slight positive relationship (though we shall see later that over wide age ranges the correlation is significantly negative for males).

3. Correlations of total score with intelligence approximate zero for males and tend to be slightly positive for females.

4. Total score shows a significant positive correlation with Stenquist mechanical-ability test for males but not for females, and a lower but possibly significant correlation with McQuarrie mechanical-ability scores.

5. M-F total correlates negatively with both the Laird and the Conklin tests of introversion, but not with the Neyman-Kohlstedt test.

6. Correlations with Conklin introversion, Allport ascendance-submission, Pressey X-O, and Watson fair-mindedness differ as between college men of high scholarship and low scholarship, Conklin introversion being more negative and Allport ascendance more positive with the high-scholarship group, and the Pressey X-O more negative with the low group.

7. College women who engage in many extracurricular activities do not tend to test especially masculine.

8. M-F score shows no appreciable correlation with the total score (or with any of the seven parts) of the Raubenheimer-Cady battery of character tests.

TABLE 7.—CORRELATIONS OF M-F SCORES WITH OTHER VARIABLES

Variables correlated	Population	Sex	N	r	P.E. of r
Total M-F and age..............	Eighth grade	M	95	.03	.07
	Eighth grade	F	84	.28	.07
	H.S. juniors	M	79	−.03	.08
	H.S. juniors	F	86	−.08	.07
	Eighth grade and juniors	M	174	.14	.06
	Eighth grade and juniors	F	170	.16	.05
	Stanford students	F	91	−.03	.08
	Gifted	M	79	.08	.08
	Gifted	F	81	.20	.07
Total M-F and Thorndike intel.....	Stanford students	M	97	.00	.07
	Stanford students	F	92	.16	.07
Total M-F and Terman group M.A..	Eighth grade	M	95	.13	.07
	Eighth grade	F	79	−.01	.08
	H.S. juniors	M	78	.03	.08
	H.S. juniors	F	85	.27	.07
	Student nurses	F	74	.20	.07
Total M-F and Scholarship av......	Stanford students	F	89	−.12	.07
Total M-F and Binet IQ...........	Gifted	M	79	.06	.08
	Gifted	F	81	.05	.08
Total M-F and Extra-curric. act....	Stanford students	F	90	−.09	.07
Total M-F and Stenquist.........	H.S. juniors	M	64	.24	.08
	H.S. juniors	F	64	.06	.08
Total M-F and Laird C2..........	Stanford students	F	90	−.29	.09
Total M-F and total of 7 Raubenheimer character tests...........	Older delinquents	M	329	.06	.04
Total M-F and Neyman-Kohlstedt introversion...................	Older delinquents	M	329	.02	.04
Total M-F and Stenquist.........	Older delinquents	M	329	.30	.04
Total M-F and McQuarrie mechanical ability.....................	Older delinquents	M	329	.13	.04
Total M-F and Conklin..........	High-scholarship college	M	46	−.52	.07
	Low-scholarship college	M	46	−.24	.09
Total M-F and Allport A & S......	High-scholarship college	M	46	.36	.09
	Low-scholarship college	M	46	.08	.10
Total M-F and Pressey X-O.......	High-scholarship college	M	46	.03	.10
	Low-scholarship college	M	46	−.44	.08
Total M-F and Watson fair-mindedness.........................	High-scholarship college	M	46	.18	.10
	Low-scholarship college	M	46	−.17	.10
Total M-F and $\dfrac{\text{girth of 9th rib (expanded)} \times 100}{\text{stature}}$.	Stanford students	F	82	.26	.07
	Stanford students	F	70	.04	.08
Total M-F and height.............	Stanford students	M	32	.33	.11
Total M-F and $\dfrac{\text{sitting height} \times 100}{\text{stature}}$.	Stanford students	M	35	−.30	.10
Exercise 4 and Terman group M.A..	Student nurses	F	74	.38	.07
	H.S. juniors	F	85	.31	.07
Exercise 4 and Terman group IQ...	H.S. juniors	F	85	.28	.07
Exercise 4 and Thorndike intel.....	Stanford students	M	97	.16	.07
	Stanford students	F	92	.36	.06
Exercise 4 and Laird C2..........	Stanford students	F	55	−.20	.09
Exercise 5 and Thorndike intel.....	Stanford students	M	97	−.09	.07
Exercise 5 and Terman group M.A.	Student nurses	F	74	−.08	.08
Exercise 5 and Stenquist..........	H.S. juniors	M	64	.20	.08

9. There is suggested a small but significant correlation between M-F score and certain physical measures.

10. Exercise 4 (emotional attitudes) correlates positively and to a significant degree with intelligence.

It is interesting to examine the data of Table 7 for such bearing as they may have upon the question of validity of the M-F test. Among the correlations which may be interpreted as supporting its validity are those between M-F total and mechanical-ability scores, introversion, Allport ascendance, Pressey X-O, general intelligence of female subjects, and physical measurements (relationship here more doubtful). At least these findings are in line with beliefs that seem to prevail with regard to differences between the masculine and feminine extremes within either male or female groups. Certainly the opinion is commonly held that short men tend to be more effeminate and athletic women less ladylike than the average of their sex, that highly intellectual women are likely to be somewhat masculine, and that emotionality and introvertive or inferior attitudes are more characteristic of femininity than of masculinity. Data reviewed in later chapters tend on the whole to support our interpretation of the above evidence as indicative of validity.

Overlap of Comparable Sex Groups

One of the customary procedures used in validating a test of ability or of personality is to select two criterion groups of subjects on the basis of some outside measure and find out how well the two groups are differentiated by the test in question. In the case of ability tests this method of validation is readily applied because of the reliability with which such contrasting groups can be selected; the experimenter usually has little difficulty in making up groups which contrast greatly in general intelligence, artistic ability, musical ability, or mechanical ability. In the case of personality traits the task is much more difficult. Independently validated outside measures of such traits are not ordinarily available, and the nature of the traits is such that they cannot be reliably rated for a subject by his intimate acquaintances. For one thing, it is harder to define what the experimenter means by introversion, fair-mindedness, inferiority attitudes, social intelligence, etc., than it is to define what is meant by intelligence or musical ability.   In the second place, the manifestations of personality differences are less clear-cut, less easily observable, than differences in ability.   The result is that authors of nearly all kinds of personality tests have had difficulty in setting up criterion groups that could be known to represent extremes with reference to the personality trait in question.

The same difficulty would have been experienced in devising the M-F test had it been necessary to select criterion groups on the basis of M-F ratings of subjects by their teachers or other intimate acquaintances.   In fact M-F ratings, as we have shown by several experiments, seem to be less reliable than ratings of almost any other personality trait.   Fortunately, however, we do not have to select our criterion groups in this way in order to validate the M-F test; the criterion groups are everywhere at hand—boys and girls, men and women—and the maleness or femaleness of either group is known with practically 100 per cent certainty.   It is only necessary to administer the test to comparable sex groups and note the amount of overlap in the distributions for the two sexes.   This has been done for several pairs of sex groups, the amount of overlap for each pair having been computed both for the total score and for the separate exercises.

Before presenting the statistics on overlap of sex groups it may be well to point out that the figures given are valid only for the total score of the particular items which compose the test as a whole or the subtest in question.   The very method of selecting these individual items insures that the overlap will be relatively small.   Certainly if all possible items of the general type found in a given exercise had been included, the overlap would have been much greater than has been found.   The smallness of overlap is simply an index of the extent to which the items included bring sex differences in response.   It is not to be supposed that the sexes really differ from one another in their interests, attitudes, and thought trends as much as the small overlap on the M-F test and its exercises might at first suggest; the fact that the test is composed entirely of items selected on the basis of their M-F discrimination necessarily exaggerates the true differences. The excuse for using a method which has this effect is that the primary purpose of the test is to bring sex differences into relief by measuring the extent to which a subject's responses diverge from the mean of his sex on *just those test items to which the sexes do tend to respond differently.*

The reader will observe that the seven parts of the M-F test present considerable diversity with regard to amount of sex overlap in scores. This is partly a function of the length and reliability of the exercises, but it seems to be in part a function of their content. The relatively large overlap for Exercise 2 (blots) and Exercise 7 (introvertive response) is largely accounted for by low reliability. On the other hand, Exercise 4 (emotional attitudes) has also a very large overlap notwithstanding the fact that it is highly reliable. The explanation may be connected with the fact that this exercise calls for a graded response instead of the all-or-none type. For this reason, and possibly for others, it would be a mistake to interpret the per cents of overlap as accurate indices of the relative validity of the exercises. Such would be the case only if all other factors were equal. Exercise 5 (interests) stands out from all the others in the smallness of its overlap; it contains more items than any of the other exercises, holds second place for reliability, and contains a large proportion of items with a strong tendency to sex dichotomy of responses.

The cautions that must be observed in interpreting overlap of the different exercises apply equally to the overlap figures for total score. These figures are valid only for a test composed of items identical with or very similar to those of the present M-F test. If, for example, we say that a given male subject tests as feminine as the average female, that a given female rates at the 30th percentile for males, etc., it will be understood that the comparison is based strictly on the test as it stands. If all possible likenesses and differences between the sexes were taken into account the relative status of the subjects compared might be considerably altered.

The expression "per cent of overlap" has been used with various meanings by various writers. Overlap as we have used the term is computed as follows:

Cumulate (upwards) in terms of percentages the distribution having the higher mean. Cumulate downwards the distribution having the lower mean. Then the percentage found at the point in the two distributions where the cumulated percentages are equal is the index of overlapping. Interpolation is of course often necessary if one wishes to locate the points exactly. The percentages do not need to be cumulated much beyond the point where their values for the groups compared become equal. The following example will make the procedure clear.

Score intervals	Frequency		Cumulative percentages	
	Males	Females	Males	Females
20	1			
19	0			
18	3			
17	7			
16	12			
15	16			
14	23			
13	31		62.2	
12	28	1	43.3	.7
11	17	1	26.2	1.4
10	13	3	15.9	3.5
9	6	7	7.9	8.5
8	3	14	4.3	18.4
7	2	23	2.4	34.8
6	1	28	1.2	54.6
5	1	26	.6	73.0
4		15		83.7
3		9		
2		7		
1		4		
0		3		
N	164	141		

In the above illustration it is obvious that the percentages at the point of equality are approximately 8.2, hence the index of overlap can be expressed as 8 per cent. By this method the overlap shown in Fig. 1 is the area *AON* (or *AOM*), and not (as it is sometimes expressed) the area *AMN*.

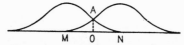

Fig. 1.—Illustration of the measure of overlapping.

TABLE 8.—PER CENT OF OVERLAP OF SEX DISTRIBUTIONS FOR TWO POPULATIONS

($N = 100$ in each)

	Eighth grade	Eleventh grade	Average
Exercise 1			
Form A...................................	23.33	14.67	
Form B...................................	21.14	15.11	18.56
Exercise 2			
Form A...................................	30.80	36.63	
Form B...................................	29.80	25.23	30.61
Exercise 3			
Form A...................................	12.00	14.63	
Form B...................................	17.64	23.60	16.97
Exercise 4			
Form A...................................	34.25	21.43	
Form B...................................	27.14	30.43	28.31
Exercise 5			
Form A...................................	6.00	10.21	
Form B...................................	12.29	6.89	8.84
Exercise 6			
Form A...................................	29.43	29.59	
Form B...................................	38.00	26.55	30.89
Exercise 7			
Form A...................................	32.57	29.59	
Form B...................................	24.56	33.49	30.07
Total score			
Form A...................................	8.71	8.36	
Form B...................................	7.66	7.21	8.02

Correlation of M-F Scores with Teachers' Estimates

One of the usual methods of "validating" a mental test is to correlate its scores with ratings of the tested subjects by teachers or others. It is notorious, however, that the reliability of such ratings is usually low even for abilities (general intelligence, etc.) and that they are still lower in the case of personality traits. For general or special abilities the ratings of two supposedly competent judges do not ordinarily correlate more than .4 to .6 and for personality traits from .2 to .4. Perhaps some would expect masculinity-femininity to be an exception to the rule in view of the confidence with which most of us judge our acquaintances on this personality trait. However, far from being an exception, M-F ratings yield particularly low reliabilities. The reasons for this have not been experimentally investigated, but probably lie in the varying concepts which people have in regard to what constitutes masculinity or femininity. Whatever the explanation, the limitations of ratings as a method of validating M-F scores are obvious.

In one of our experiments 200 subjects of each sex enrolled in the eighth and tenth school grades were rated for masculinity-femininity by from one to six teachers who had had them in their classes for several months. The ratings were secured with the help of one of our former graduate students of psychology, Miss Lela Gillan, who taught in the school system where the experiment was made and who took over the entire task of instructing the raters and getting their fullest cooperation. The ratings were made, we believe, with more than ordinary care. Each teacher was given two lists of names of the subjects enrolled in her classes (one list for each sex) and was asked to take them home and at her leisure consider each pupil with respect to masculinity and femininity of behavior. Her task was to check in each list those she would rate among the one-fourth who were most masculine, and those she would rate among the one-fourth who were least masculine, leaving unmarked the middle 50 per cent.

The subjects were given one of the preliminary series of M-F tests including 91 information items, 170 interest items, 51 introversion-extroversion items, and 60 word-association items. The correlation between composite teacher ratings and the M-F scores on these tests were +.10 for information, +.15 for interest, +.02 for introvertive response, and +.03 for word association. However, the reliability of the ratings was so low as to preclude any very considerable correlation with the test scores. The reliabilities were .142 for ratings of boys and .216 for ratings of girls by a single judge. These figures become .332 for ratings of boys and .453 for ratings of girls by three judges, and .498 for boys and .623 for girls when there are six judges.

When the M-F test had reached its present stage one form of it (A) was given to 82 male Stanford students who, immediately after taking the test, were asked to rate themselves on degree of masculinity with respect to (a) childhood interests, (b) occupational interests, (c) present method of spending leisure time, (d) emotionality, and (e) general personality make-up. The ratings were made by the cross-on-a-line method and were preceded by a brief discussion designed to promote frankness of ratings. The subjects did not know the purpose of the test and it is believed that most of them were successfully misled to believe that the ratings had no connection with the test they had just taken. The five ratings correlated as follows with total M-F score: childhood interests, .08; vocational interests, .06; use of leisure, .22; emotionality, .21; general make-up, .13; average of the five self-ratings, .19 ± .07.

A more careful experiment was carried out later to determine whether the correlations of ratings with M-F scores would be higher if judges were asked to rate, not masculinity or femininity in general, but more specifically defined traits which are presumably related thereto. For each trait a composite rating was computed based upon the independent ratings of the two (or three) judges, and the correlation was found between this composite and the total score of the M-F test. Most of the correlations were in the expected direction, but only three of them were as large as three times their probable error. These were: with "tomboyishness," .33 ± .08; with leadership,. 24 ± .07; with having manual interests typical of women, −.25 ± .07.

The fact that the M-F test is composed of items empirically selected as showing sex differences in responses makes it, *ipso facto*, a measure of mental masculinity and femininity in the scope embraced by its contents. One may therefore say that the test is inherently and of necessity valid. However, this kind of validity becomes a rather empty merit unless the scores yielded by the test can be shown to have demonstrable correlates in behavior. We believe that some of the data presented in later chapters strongly suggest the reality of such correlates, especially in the case of subjects who deviate from their sex norm to an extreme degree in either the masculine or the feminine direction. For validation of the test in this sense we shall have to look to clinical studies of such deviates rather than to personality ratings of the kind that are based upon relatively superficial and unreliable observations. The data on score distributions and score means in the following section constitute interesting evidence of validity.

SCORE DISTRIBUTIONS FOR SELECTED GROUPS

In Tables 9, 10, and 11 score distributions are given for a number of selected groups of both sexes. The data which they contain are fragments of material dealt with more fully in later chapters, but the reader may wish to examine a few distributions at this point both because of their general interest and because of their bearing upon the question of validity. In comparing the scores of the different groups the reader should consider whether the distributions and means are in line with what could be expected on the basis of common observation regarding the degree of masculinity or femininity of population classes of the kind in question. Is the small overlap of distributions for analogous sex groups a general phenomenon or will it perhaps fail to appear with English youths, Americanized Japanese, negro college students, or delinquent boys and girls? Do athletes and professionally trained engineers, believed by many to be characterized by masculine behavior, actually test more masculine than male groups commonly characterized as somewhat effeminate, such as artists, musicians, ministers, and theological students?

Do passive male homosexuals score as feminine as they are reputed to be? Is the highly intellectual woman holding the M.D. or Ph.D. degree shown by the test to be more masculine-minded than the typical housewife or female domestic employee?

Before examining the tables the following facts should be noted regarding the composition of some of the groups. The "general population" of Table 9 is fairly representative of the younger educated adults in California. The negroes were students in prominent negro colleges. The Japanese were school children in Hawaii and were almost all of the second generation of immigrants. "Office workers," both male and female, included office managers, secretaries, clerks, accountants, etc. The delinquents were inmates of two California state institutions, the Whittier school for boys and the Ventura school for girls; they are believed to be fairly representative of male and female delinquents of the late teens who have received court commitments.

The male athletes (Table 10) were mostly football players; the female athletes (Table 11) were somewhat less specialized. The engineers were university trained and were practicing their profession. The males classed as "teachers" were in many cases supervisors or principals, but the women so classed were nearly all actual teachers. The "gifted" represented a random selection of the older of the 1,000 gifted children studied by the senior author; when given the M-F test they were nearly all between the ages of fifteen and twenty. The music groups were students in one of the best known schools of music in the country. The theological group was made up of three subgroups whose score distributions were very similar: students preparing to become Catholic priests, Protestant theological students, and Protestant ministers. The "artist" group was composed chiefly of professional painters in California. The homosexuals were nearly all male prostitutes, which means that the majority of them would probably classify as of the passive homosexual type.

Table 9 illustrates a fact to which we have found no exception, namely, that markedly contrasting distributions are always found when comparable male and female groups are tested. We have no doubt that this will hold for all modern Occidental cultures.

TABLE 9.—COMPARISON OF HOMOLOGOUS MALE AND FEMALE GROUPS

Score	General population A & B M	General population A & B F	College A M	College A F	High school A M	High school A F	Eighth grade A M	Eighth grade A F	Office workers B M	Office workers A & B F
+201–220										
+181–200	6		1		1					1
+161–180	4		2		4		1			
+141–160	14		3		6		3			
+121–140	36		8		9		5		2	
+101–120	42		10		9		6		3	
+81–100	72		36		13		9		9	
+61–80	95		18		10		16		10	
+41–60	101	5	18		19		17		5	1
+21–40	78	18	15	2	11		12	1	14	1
+1–20	60	30	7	8	9	3	7	2	5	1
−0–19	51	50	5	14	4	5	12	3	5	12
−20–39	32	76	4	15	1	4	7	8	2	36
−40–59	6	104	2	20	1	14	3	3	2	39
−60–79	6	103	1	24		17	2	16		54
−80–99	1	117		27		8		10	1	60
−100–119		85		15	1	14		26		47
−120–139		58		5		14		13		28
−140–159		32				9		9		15
−160–179		12				2		2		5
−180–199		5						2		2
−200–219		1						1		1
N	604	696	130	130	98	90	100	98	58	303
M	+52.58	−70.65	+67.42	−60.81	+72.68	−85.50	+46.10	−96.04	+43.43	−80.85
S.D.-dist.	49.93	47.51	47.65	39.15	51.99	46.01	53.93	46.20	47.22	41.75
S.D.-M	2.03	1.80	4.18	3.43	5.25	4.77	5.39	4.67	6.20	2.40

TABLE 9.—COMPARISON OF HOMOLOGOUS MALE AND FEMALE GROUPS.—(Continued)

Group	Delinquents		English students		Negro college students		Honolulu Japanese	
Form	A	A	B	B	A	A	B	B
Sex Score	M	F	M	F	M	F	M	F
+201–220								
+181–200								
+161–180								
+141–160	4							
+121–140	5		5					
+101–120	7		2		2		1	
+ 81–100	9		17		4		5	
+ 61– 80	17	1	12		5		4	
+ 41– 60	27		14	1	3		6	
+ 21– 40	20		4	1	8		4	
+ 1– 20	15		2	3	7		5	
– 1– 19	14	1	2	4	7		3	2
– 20– 39	8	4		8	9	4	1	9
– 40– 59	2	6	1	19	2	1	1	5
– 60– 79	1	9		16	3	3		8
– 80– 99		14		5	1	7		7
–100–119		5		1		3		2
–120–139		7		2		3		3
–140–159		5				2		
–160–179		2				2		
–180–199								
–200–219								
N	129	54	59	60	51	25	32	41
M	+43.66	–88.02	+28.46	–70.50	+14.50	–94.30	+25.50	–74.88
S.D.dist.	46.62	42.08	35.45	33.55	51.45	41.29	43.01	39.27
S.D.M	4.10	5.73	4.62	4.33	6.15	8.26	7.60	6.13

TABLE 10.—COMPARISON OF TEN MALE GROUPS

Group / Score	College athletes	Engineers	Gifted	Teachers	Who's who	Fathers of gifted	Music students	Theological group	Artists	Homo-sexuals
Form	A & B	A & B	A	B	A	A	A	A & B	A & B	A
+201–220	1	1	1							
+181–200			1	1						
+161–180	2	3	1	2						
+141–160	6	4	7	1	1	1				
+121–140	11	8	3	9	2	1				
+101–120	8	6	13	12	2	4	2	2	1	
+ 81–100	11	6	18	16	1	5	6	4	1	2
+ 61– 80	6	4	13	23	5	7	8	7	5	1
+ 41– 60		7	7	31	6	13	12	20	5	2
+ 21– 40		2	4	24	6	10	7	33	9	4
+ 1– 20	1	2	5	9	5	2	5	33	7	14
− 0– 19		1	1	2	3	2	4	27	7	11
− 20– 39				1		8	3	26	2	17
− 40– 59			1			2		5	4	14
− 60– 79						1	2	4		7
− 80– 99				1			1	1		4
−100–119										3
−120–139										1
−140–159										
−160–179										
−180–199										
−200–219										
N	46	44	75	132	31	56	50	162	41	80
M	+92.54	+77.32	+66.22	+44.58	+31.15	+19.44	+15.70	+10.62	+0.26	−19.75
S.D.-dist.	33.35	48.61	45.44	40.80	42.04	49.13	48.63	37.02	39.04	43.50
S.D.-M	4.92	7.33	5.28	3.55	7.55	6.57	6.88	2.91	6.10	4.86

TABLE 11.—COMPARISON OF TEN FEMALE GROUPS

Group / Score	College athletes (A)	M.D. or Ph.D. (A & B)	Who's who (A)	Gifted (A)	Student nurses (A)	Music students (A)	Teachers (B)	Chinese students (B)	Mothers of gifted (A)	Domestic employees (A & B)
+201–220										
+181–200										
+161–180										
+141–160										
+121–140										
+101–120										
+ 81–100										
+ 61– 80	4				1			1		
+ 41– 60	4	2	1	1						
+ 21– 40	7	2	1	2			1			
+ 1– 20	9	3	2	4			1			
– 1– 19	6	1	3	6	3	2	1	1	2	2
– 20– 39	2	1	3	10	4	4	4	6	2	4
– 40– 59	3	7	3	17	12	3	5	3	3	12
– 60– 79	1	2	8	7	11	13	17	6	8	7
– 80– 99	1	2	1	16	16	6	31	11	9	10
–100–119		1	3	3	15	7	23	5	20	15
–120–139				3	8	11	25	10	17	4
–140–159	1			3	2	3	23	3	10	2
–160–179					4		13	3	6	
–180–199					1	1	2	2	1	
–200–219					1		2			1
N	38	20	25	72	78	50	149	51	78	57
M	−13.71	−34.50	−45.50	−57.80	−68.99	−71.10	−72.06	−75.00	−91.64	−103.89
$S.D._{dist.}$	22.26	48.53	42.33	43.28	44.26	39.57	42.81	49.95	37.65	37.79
$S.D._{M}$	3.61	10.85	8.47	5.10	5.01	5.60	3.51	6.99	4.26	5.01

The difference between the means of comparable male and female groups is an expression of the test's validity. The smallest difference we have found—that of 48 score points between female prostitutes and male homosexual prostitutes— is 3.4 times its standard error, and the majority of differences are from three to four times as great. The following score differences between the sex means are typical:

Group	Score difference between means	No. of males	No. of females
Eighth-grade children........................	143	200	196
High-school juniors..........................	155	196	180
Gifted children (age 16–18)..................	123	75	72
Delinquents.................................	132	129	54
English private-school children..............	99	59	60
Japanese adolescents........................	100	32	41
College sophomores..........................	128	130	130
College athletes.............................	114	29	53
College-of-music students....................	87	50	50
Negro college students......................	109	51	25
Prostitutes.................................	48	52	12
Adult population, age 20 to 29...............	131	138	285
Adult population, age 50 to 59...............	115	82	162
Adult population, age 70 to 85...............	89	28	94

The above differences between means are nearly all between twice and three times the S.D. of the usual score distribution. Sexual inverts seem to be the only exception to the rule that males score far more masculine than females, and this exception is of course the best of evidence of the test's validity. Male inverts (passive male homosexuals) commonly score between +25 and −60, with a mean around −20. The small number of female inverts (active female homosexuals) we have tested have nearly all scored between +75 and −30. This reversal of the direction of sex difference in the case of inverts presents, in our opinion, one of the most challenging problems in the psychology of personality.

DANGER OF SCORE-FAKING

In any pencil-and-paper test of the questionnaire type that requires the subject to answer questions about how he thinks or feels, what he is interested in, or how he is accustomed to react in given situations, it is assumed that the subject will cooperate by responding as truthfully as he can. Failure thus to cooperate would probably invalidate the subject's score on almost any of the current personality tests. One would not need to be a psychologist to be able to score as fair-minded on the Watson test, extroverted on the Laird C2, or self-sufficient on the Bernreuter inventory, provided one knew what the test was intended to measure. Unfortunately the authors of personality tests have ordinarily not taken the trouble to investigate the extent of this danger, although precautions are sometimes taken to keep the subject in the dark with respect to the purpose of the test.

With the assistance of Dr. Lowell Kelly the M-F test was given three times to a group of 52 college sophomores (33 women and 19 men) under the following conditions. (1) At the time of the first test the subjects were merely informed that the investigator was making a study of the interests and attitudes of college students; the real purpose of the test, we learned by later inquiry, was not suspected by a single one of them. (2) One week later they were again tested, but were first told what the test measures and were asked to show us how much they could influence their scores at will. More specifically, half of the men were requested to make their scores as masculine as possible, the other half to make them as feminine as possible. Similarly for the women. (3) A week later those who had been asked to make their scores masculine in the second test were now asked to make them as feminine as possible, and vice versa.[1]

The subjects were promised that they would be informed of their scores, and they entered into the experiment with great zest, as

[1] KELLY, E. LOWELL, CATHARINE COX MILES, and LEWIS M. TERMAN, Ability to influence one's score on a pencil-and-paper test of personality, *Char. and Personality*, 1936, **4**, 206–215.

though it were a kind of game.   The results gave a very emphatic answer to the question as to whether M-F scores can be faked.
Following are the means and S.D.'s of the naïve scores, the
masculinized scores, and the feminized scores:

	Males		Females	
	M	S.D.	*M*	S.D.
Naïve scores......................	+ 66.8	39.2	− 56.2	48.1
Masculinized scores.................	+208.8	68.9	+189.1	93.9
Feminized scores....................	−140.5	51.8	−147.6	62.6

In other words, a typical group of males at the most masculine
age are able to earn a mean score more feminine by far than the
mean of any female group we have tested; a typical female
group can make itself appear far more masculine than any male
group we have tested!   The distance between the masculinized
and feminized means is 349.3 score points for the males and 336.7
score points for the females.   The shift amounts to seven or eight
times the standard deviation of the usual naïve score distribution.   Male subjects are able to shift their scores more in the
feminine than in the masculine direction, females more in the
masculine direction: the explanation doubtless lies in the fact
that the test gives more room for reverse shifts.   The ability to
influence score was found to be uncorrelated with age, intelligence, or scholastic achievement within the ranges provided by
this group.   The ability should be further investigated as a
possible index of "social intelligence" or "psychological insight."
    Since the faking of scores is so easy, it is fortunate that subjects
almost never suspect the purpose of the test.   Of the hundreds
who have been asked, immediately after taking the test, what
they thought we were trying to measure, so far not one has
guessed correctly.   As the test comes into more general use the
possibility of score-faking will of course increase, but we do not
believe that its validity for most purposes is ever likely to be
jeopardized from this cause.   The danger is present only when

the subject has a definite motive in appearing other than he is. One of us gave the test to 31 college students (17 men and 14 women) after explaining to them carefully what the test is intended to measure, yet the resulting mean for neither sex differed significantly from the college norms. The mean for the men was 3.6 points more masculine than the norm, that for the women 5.1 more masculine.

CHAPTER V

CORRELATIONS OF M-F SCORE WITH PHYSICAL MEASUREMENTS AND TRAIT RATINGS

If masculinity and femininity are thought of in relation to health, robust would be popularly regarded as the masculine and frail as the feminine adjective. Furthermore, a correlation between M-F score and physical build should be expected if masculinity-femininity is an expression of personality type grounded in innate constitution. Popular belief rates the large woman as masculine, the small man as feminine; a man with large hips or a woman with broad shoulders is likely to be suspected of an anomalous constitutional trend. Fortunately we have been able to check these popular beliefs against physical data for sizable groups for whom M-F scores were available.

M-F SCORE AND HEALTH RATINGS

The M-F blank used in our later work calls for a self-rating of each subject with regard to health. The categories provided, one of which the subject is asked to check, are *robust, above average, average, below average, frail.* Table 12 gives the mean M-F scores of males and females of our adult population with high-school education in each of the five categories; also the means for the two highest categories combined and the three lowest combined.

In view of the highly masculine scores of athletes, both male and female, and in view of the popular belief that frailty is associated with femininity, it is interesting to find that in this group of adult men those who rate themselves as robust or above average have a mean score which is 7 points, or .15 of a standard score,[1] lower than the mean of those in the three lower categories.

---

[1] See p. 477 ff. for table of standard scores.

TABLE 12.—HEALTH AND M-F SCORE. HEALTH IS MEASURED IN TERMS OF
SELF-RATINGS ON A FIVE-POINT SCALE
Subjects: Adults of high-school education, ages twenty to sixty-five years

	No. of cases	Mean M-F score	Combined mean	$S.D._M$	$\dfrac{\text{Diff.}}{S.D._{\text{diff.}}}$
Males:					
Robust.............	29	+ 47.1 ⎱	+45.3	5.68 ⎞	
Above average.......	67	+ 44.5 ⎰		⎟	
Average............	87	+ 51.4 ⎱		⎬	.96
Below average.......	3	+ 57.2 ⎰	+52.7	5.22 ⎠	
Frail...............	2	+105.5			
Omissions..........	24	+ 58.8		10.73	
Total.............	212	+ 50.0			
Females:					
Robust.............	63	− 85.1 ⎱	−79.5	3.04 ⎞	
Above average.......	121	− 76.6 ⎰		⎟	
Average............	288	− 89.0 ⎱		⎬	2.44
Below average.......	26	− 89.5 ⎰	−88.9	2.38 ⎠	
Frail...............	3	− 76.2			
Omissions..........	32	− 78.6		7.28	
Total.............	533	− 85.5			

The difference, however, is not significant, as it is just less than
its standard error. We cannot, of course, assert on the basis
of our findings that men of average or inferior health are more
masculine than those who have superior health, but we can
perhaps safely say that the converse is not true. The subjects
who gave these self-ratings ranged in age from twenty to sixty-five
years, and since frailty and femininity of M-F score both increase
with age one might have expected the age factor itself to insure
a positive correlation between good health and masculinity.
The 24 men who did not rate their health averaged 13.5 M-F
points more masculine than the men with superior health and
6 M-F points more masculine than the group with average or
inferior health, another bit of evidence, possibly, of the relation
of indifference or noncooperation to masculinity.

The results for women are just the reverse of those for men;
women who rate themselves as *average, below average,* or *frail*

in health have a more feminine score than those who rate themselves as *above average* or *robust*. The difference is 2.44 times its standard error and therefore probably significant. Women who omit the rating, like men who do so, average more masculine than either of the other groups, but the difference is not reliable.

Incidentally it is interesting to note that relatively twice as many women as men rate themselves as below average or frail: 5 per cent as against 2½ per cent. We are unable to say whether this represents a true sex difference in physique or whether it merely reflects the greater respectability of ill-health among women. It is unfortunate that the health ratings could not have been made by physicians on the basis of a thorough medical examination. It is possible that an investigation of this kind would disclose significant relationships between M-F score and special conditions of health, apart from any correlation that might be found between score and a generalized health rating.

M-F Score and Physical Measurements

It has been thought that a man being "a man to his finger tips" and a woman being "a woman even to her little toes," correlations should be demonstrable between physical measures and M-F scores. To test this view we have correlated M-F scores with (1) measures of physical size and (2) such measures of physical proportion as are recognized expressions of sex contrast or difference.

Series of measurements of 152 women and 138 men were available for correlation.[1] Height, weight, and pulse were correlated directly with M-F score. Other measurements were transformed into ratios to stature so that the specific factor rather

[1] The women's measurements were available through the courtesy of Professor Helen Bunting of the Department of Physical Education for women, Stanford University. The measurements of the men were obtained with the kind permission of Dr. Thomas A. Storey of the Department of Physical Education for men. All besides the height and weight measurements for the men were made under the direction of Professor W. R. Miles of the Psychology Department in connection with another psychophysical research.

than the general size element might be isolated for comparison with M-F score.

TABLE 13.—CORRELATIONS BETWEEN M-F SCORE AND PHYSICAL MEASUREMENTS IN TWO GROUPS OF SUPERIOR COLLEGE WOMEN

Physical measures	Correlation with M-F score Group I (82 cases) Group II* (70 cases)	Physical measures	Correlation with M-F score Group I (82 cases) Group II* (70 cases)
Pulse (before exercise).	+.152 ± .07	*Ratio to stature* × 100 *of:*	
Weight...............	+.07 ± .07	100 *of:*	
Height (standing).....	−.025 ± .07	Girth of chest (ex-	
Ratio to stature × 100 *of:*		panded)........	+.080 ± .07
Height (sitting).....	−.046 ± .07	Girth of chest (con-	
Girth of waist.......	+.120 ± .07	tracted)........	+.075 ± .07
		Girth of 9th rib	+.261 ± .07
Depth of abdomen...	+.174 ± .07	(expanded).	*+.037 ± .08
	*−.084 ± .08	Girth of 9th rib	+.212 ± .07
Depth of chest (con-		(contracted).	*+.033 ± .08
tracted).........	+.082 ± .07	Lung capacity.....	+.185 ± .07
			*−.055 ± .08
Breadth of shoulders	+.027 ± .07	Expansion (breadth	
Breadth of chest (ex-		of chest)........	−.065 ± .07
panded)..........	+.072 ± .07	Expansion (girth of	
Breadth of chest	+.138 ± .07	chest)...........	−.086 ± .07
(contracted).	*+.002 ± .08	Expansion (depth	
		of chest)........	−.191 ± .07

* The starred coefficients refer to Group II.

For a group of 82 women coefficients were derived for the correlation between score and (1) measurements of pulse, weight, and height, and (2) fifteen ratios to height as follows: sitting height, girth of waist, depth of abdomen, depth of chest (contracted), breadth of shoulders, breadth of chest (contracted), same (expanded), girth of chest (contracted), same (expanded), girth at ninth rib (expanded), same (contracted), lung capacity, expansion (breadth of chest). Of the 18 coefficients 2 were three times the P.E., 5 others were twice the P.E., and the remaining 11 were less than 2 P.E. The two of possible statistical significance were between score and (1) the contracted and (2) the expanded girth at the ninth rib (indirectly vital capacity). In order to check the results for these two and certain of the other coefficients that deviated farthest from zero, correlations were derived for 70 other Stanford women for whom M-F scores were available. None of the coefficients in the second series was larger than its probable error, and the relationships that appeared largest in the first series were small in the second. One factor of difference between the two groups that has been suggested by later findings should, however, be mentioned. The first group included a considerable number of the best women athletes in college, as well as a general selection of college women. The second group included few women who were very superior in athletics. This difference in the composition of the groups might account for the regular and persistent discrepancy between the two series of coefficients and if so would leave us with some evidence of a tendency for M-F score to correlate with athletic physique. We have seen (Tables 10 and 11) that groups of college athletes, both male and female, do make outstandingly masculine scores on the M-F test. The matter deserves further investigation, but from the data at hand one cannot infer that there is any dependable relationship between M-F score and physical measurements in the case of women. The relationship vaguely hinted at in a single group is, if other than a chance occurrence, associated with the presence of an interest or behavior type already shown to correlate to some extent with M-F score.

A group of 32 men of small stature (height range 160 to 179 cm.) was examined as to the relation of physical traits and M-F score. Their average M-F score of +61.7 (s.s. of +.45) is lower than that of all but one of our groups of college men in their own or any similar institution. The one group that rates as low is a group of 46 men of exceptionally high scholarship (upper quartile). The men in the small stature group do not owe their placement to a like cause, as their average scholarship rating is just below the general average for the institution. Not only do these men as a group score low on the M-F scale, but the 12 smallest of their number average even lower (+48) and the correlation between height and M-F score for the group is

$+.33 \pm .11$, indicating a probably significant relationship. Correlations for this group have also been worked out between M-F score and (1) weight, (2) ratio of weight to height, (3) ratio of height to weight, (4) ratio of shoulder to hip, and (5) ratio of hips to weight. Correlations were also made between score and shoulder width, and score and hip width. Of these correlations that with weight is two and a half times its P.E. The others are all nearer one than two times the P.E. Evidently an indication of a correlation between an M-F index of build and the mental M-F score is not found in this group except as stature alone is such an index.

Correlations between M-F scores and four ratios of body build have been derived from the data for a group of 106 college men in an elementary psychology class. These give the following values:

$$r$$

$$\text{M-F score with ratio } \frac{\text{hip width} \times 100}{\text{stature}} \cdots\cdots -.20 \pm .11$$

$$\text{M-F score with ratio } \frac{\text{shoulder width} \times 100}{\text{stature}} \cdots -.08 \pm .11$$

$$\text{M-F score with ratio } \frac{\text{weight} \times 100}{\text{stature}} \cdots\cdots +.04 \pm .07$$

$$\text{M-F score with ratio } \frac{\text{sitting height} \times 100}{\text{stature}} \cdots -.30 \pm .10$$

It may or may not be significant that one of these correlations (M-F score with ratio of sitting height to standing height) is three times, and another (that with ratio of hip width to stature) is twice, its probable error. Both of these correlations are in the direction to be expected if masculinity of build is associated with masculinity of score. It is well known that greater length of trunk in proportion to total height is one of the most characteristically feminine traits disclosed by physical measurements, and the correlation of $-.30$ means that *for this particular sample of the male population* this factor is definitely associated with less masculine score. We can by no means be sure, however, that a larger and therefore more reliable sampling would yield the same result.

At this point the reader may want to examine the data on physical measurements of 24 male homosexuals in Chapter XI. These subjects belonged to our most feminine-testing male group, but apart from stature, in which they were significantly below both unselected army recruits and college students, their physical measurements showed no significant departure from the male norms. No ·anomalies of the sexual organs were found.

Summarizing, it is obvious that no definite conclusion can be ventured with regard to the existence or nonexistence of a relationship between M-F score and physical measurements; the available data are based on small populations and contain contradictions. One can only say that if there is any correlation between score and any of the physical measures we have used it is probably not very large. The data available suggest that there may be for males a positive correlation between masculinity and height, and also between femininity and length of trunk in relation to height. In the case of females the only significant relationship suggested at present is the apparently positive correlation between score and ratio of girth at ninth rib (either expanded or contracted) to stature. The latter correlations for one group, partly composed of outstanding athletes, are for contracted girth three times the P.E., and for expanded girth nearly four times the P.E. A more searching investigation is urgently called for. Large populations should be measured and tested and if more than one measure yields an apparently reliable correlation the technique of multiple correlation could be applied. It is conceivable that the combination of a number of small but reliable correlations would yield a sizable multiple correlation with M-F score. Measures should also be made of amount and distribution of hair growth, of metabolism, and, when reliable techniques are available, of amount of gonadal hormones in the blood.

M-F Score and Age of Puberty

The question was raised in an earlier chapter whether the course of M-F development is affected by early or late puberty. Such an influence might occur either as a direct effect of endocrine factors or as the effect of differential social treatment based upon recognized physical maturity or immaturity.

It happens that records of approximate age of puberty are available for 80 boys and 96 girls who took the M-F test at the average age of 16½, the range of ages falling between 13 and 19. The subjects were members of the California group of "gifted children" who had been under observation for several years. The record was the mother's statement as to the age when her daughter first menstruated or when her son's voice changed. Although records of this kind are known to involve appreciable error, especially in the case of voice change, they are probably accurate enough to reveal any close association that might exist between M-F score and age of sexual maturation.

According to these records the ages at which puberty was attained were distributed as follows:

Age	10*	11	12	13	14	15	16	17	18	19
Boys...................	..	..	2	11	21	33	11	..	2	..
Girls...................	4	15	28	25	10	11	2	..	..	1

* Age 10 means 10 but not yet 11, etc.

Each sex group has been divided into two categories by age, and biserial r's have been computed. Boys were classed as less than 15, or 15 or over; girls as less than 13, or 13 or over. The resulting correlations with M-F score were +.30 for boys and +.10 for girls.

Only the first of these correlations suggests a genuine relationship. However, in the case of both boys and girls a significant difference in M-F score is found where we limit the comparison to the extremes of the age distributions. For example, the 13 boys whose voice changed before 14 had a mean M-F score of +65; the 13 whose voice changed at 16 or later, a mean of +44. The difference is about .5 S.D. of a typical male distribution. The mean M-F score of the 19 girls who menstruated before 12 was −64; of the 24 who first menstruated at 14 or later, −33. The difference is approximately .75 S.D. of a typical female distribution. The data therefore rather strongly suggest that decidedly early, as compared with decidedly late, puberty is associated with greater masculinity in boys and greater femininity in girls.

If this apparent influence of early and late puberty should be confirmed it would remain to discover whether the effect persists through adult life or disappears as maturity is reached; also to determine, if possible, whether the influence is primarily bio-chemical or mainly the result of social pressures.

We have tried to estimate the possible effect of one type of social influence in the case of these subjects, by correlating M-F score with age-grade status in school. One might assume that marked acceleration of a subject, bringing him or her into close association with older and sexually more mature children, would be found associated with increased masculinity in boys and increased femininity in girls. Data on this point were available for 80 boys and 130 girls of the gifted group. The age-grade status of each sex ranged from one year retarded to 5 years accelerated, but the biserial correlation with M-F score for each sex was less than its probable error. Comparison of extremes with respect to degree of acceleration showed no significant difference in the case of girls. On the other hand, the 22 boys who were accelerated three years or more scored markedly *less* masculine than the 11 who were not at all accelerated; the scores were, respectively, +44 and +95. It would seem that in the case of boys the influence, if real, is in the opposite direction from the tentative assumption. Possibly the assumption was wrong; it may be that the boy who is excessively promoted becomes so isolated socially from inability to share the activities of his school fellows on equal terms that his mental masculiniza-tion is actually retarded.

M-F SCORE AND TRAIT RATINGS

In Chapter IV summary data were presented which resulted from attempts to validate M-F scores in terms of ratings of subjects by their teachers or acquaintances (or by themselves) on masculinity-femininity of personality. It was shown that the extremely low correlations found could be accounted for in large part by the unreliability of the ratings, but that the coefficients would still be low even if the M-F scores were correlated with the composite of the ratings of several judges. If the validation of the M-F test hinged upon our ability to establish fairly high correlations with such ratings one could claim for its scores only the slightest validity. However, the method of deriving the test (by the retention only of such test items as actually yield sex differences in responses) automatically validates the test as a measure of masculinity and femininity in the particular area (a fairly broad one) embraced by the test items retained. Why a measure derived from such a test should agree so little with subjective ratings has been a puzzling question.

In the M-F scale we have a technique that measures masculinity-femininity in both sexes, differentiates sex groups unmistakably, and rates single individuals at various points over a wide range. Individual scores have been found that deviate from the general mean as much as three or four times the S.D. of the distribution for the sex in question. Individual men have been found who rate more feminine than the average woman, and women who exceed the average man in mental masculinity. We have found that occupation, interest, age, education, intelligence, and homosexuality (at least in males) account for large deviations in group averages, and that home environment and marital experience are not without influence. It is perhaps not unreasonable to suppose that these influences operative in groups are discernible for individuals also, and furthermore that other elements in nature and nurture might be isolated which would account for some or part of the deviations of individuals within groups. One would expect that definite and probably rather easily distinguishable traits of character or personality could be described and measured which would show a considerable degree of correlation with the M-F scores if a sufficiently wide range of the latter were included.

The low correlations found in the comparisons of scores with ratings on all-round masculinity-femininity suggested that the latter trait is perhaps too complex and vague to permit of reliable or valid ratings based on observation, and that higher correlations might be obtained between scores and ratings on specific aspects of masculinity and femininity. The terms masculine and feminine had perhaps been variously conceived by different raters; perhaps also the significance of particular behavior manifestations in the individuals rated had not been similarly interpreted. In an effort to test this hypothesis an elaborate correlation study was carried out which involved the rating of three groups of subjects on 19 different aspects of personality which were thought to be probably associated with the kind of mental masculinity and femininity measured by the test. The 19 traits were selected partly on the basis of the clearness with which they could be defined, in the hope that this would make for agreement among judges as to the degree of their presence or absence. The ratings were made on a four-page blank 8½ by 11 in., carrying directions for rating and succinct definition of the traits in question (see Appendix V).

The rating blank was first used with a small group of orphan children to see how it would work. The main study was directed to the data from sizable populations of both sexes at the eighth-grade and eleventh-grade levels, and of one sex at the college level. The eighth-grade subjects numbered approximately 75 of each sex, the eleventh-grade subjects approximately 50 of each sex. The college group was composed of 92 women, members of sororities at Stanford University. Each subject was rated on each of the 19 traits by either two or three judges, the school boys and girls by their teachers, the college women by fellow members of the sororities to which they belonged. For all three groups raters were selected who were considered to be specially qualified as discerners of character traits. Some, but not all of them, had had previous experience in rating personality traits.

The ratings for the three groups were not, however, uniformly competent. Some of the teachers who rated the school boys and girls stated that they did not know the pupils well enough to feel satisfied with their ratings, even though they had had them in one or more classes daily for several months. This lack of acquaintance was indicated by the small range in the ratings given; the expected discrimination being evident only in the case of the more conspicuous traits of a given subject. The ratings of the college women were made with considerable care. A graduate student in psychology, Madeline Frick, assisted in obtaining the ratings and served as one of the raters. Miss Frick had given special attention to problems of personality and was exceptionally well equipped, both professionally and personally, for the task of rating the subjects herself and securing the intelligent cooperation of other raters. All who assisted

TABLE 14.—CORRELATION BETWEEN PERSONALITY TRAIT RATINGS AND M-F SCORE AT THREE AGE LEVELS

No.	Trait	Women and girls			Boys	
		92 college women's ratings, standard scores from averages of ratings by 3 judges	52 high-school-junior girls' ratings, averages of 2 or 3 judges	76 8th-grade girls, averages of 2 or 3 judges	48 high-school-junior boys, averages of 2 or 3 judges	78 8th-grade boys, averages of 2 or 3 judges
1	Leadership	+.01 ± .07	+.193 ± .09	−.111 ± .074	*	+.24 ± .07
2	Personality	+.19 ± .07	+.220 ± .09	−.079 ± .075	*	+.17 ± .07
3	Attractiveness to persons of the opposite sex	+.07 ± .07	*	*	*	*
4	Attractiveness to persons of the same sex	−.05 ± .07	*	*	*	*
5	Seeks the society of the other sex	+.10 ± .07	*	*	*	*
6	Seeks the society of the same sex	−.08 ± .07	*	*	*	*
7	Typical intellectual interests of own sex	+.03 ± .07	*	*	+.06 ± .10	*
8	Typical intellectual interests of opposite sex	+.15 ± .07	*	*	*	*
9	Typical social interests of the same sex	−.08 ± .07	*	*	*	*
10	Typical social interests of the opposite sex	−.04 ± .07	*	*	+.05 ± .10	*
11	Typical manual interests of the same sex	−.25 ± .07	−.182 ± .09	*	*	*
12	Typical manual interests of the opposite sex	+.04 ± .07	+.098 ± .095	*	*	*
13	Tomboyishness (in girls); sissiness (in boys)	+.11 ± .07	+.327 ± .085	*	+.03 ± .10	+.18 ± .075
14	Has crushes on persons of same sex	−.08 ± .07	*	*	+.06 ± .10	*
15	Aggressiveness	+.08 ± .07	*	*	*	*
16	Objective-mindedness	−.03 ± .07	*	*	*	*
17	Subjective-mindedness	−.05 ± .07	*	*	*	*
18	Effectiveness	−.13 ± .07	*	*	*	*
19	Originality	+.10 ± .07	*	*	*	*

* Correlation estimated from scatter diagrams as being within the range +.10 to −.10.

were fully instructed as to rating methods, essential objectivity of attitude, and the necessity of avoiding "halo" effects. Three independent ratings were secured for the 92 women who were members of five sorority groups, the ratings for each group being made by the three of its members selected for the task on the basis of fitness and cooperativeness.

The three ratings for each subject on each trait were averaged to secure a composite rating score. When the distributions of the composite scores for the different living groups were examined it was found that the absolute standard had evidently varied from house to house; accordingly the trait scores were transformed into standard scores for the several house groups. The resulting scores are as well equated as we could make them where different groups of raters provided different segments of the data. The correlations of M-F scores with the composite ratings thus treated are presented in Table 14 for the college women and also for the public-school boys and girls.

A multiple correlation for 92 college women between M-F score and four variables (intelligence score and ratings on traits 8, 11, and 18) is $+.347 \pm .061$. Multiple correlations have also been computed for 78 of the 92 on M-F score with these same 4 variables ($r = +.327 \pm .067$); with these four combined with six others (pulse rate, and five ratios to stature, namely, depth of abdomen, breadth of chest, girth of ninth rib, lung capacity, girth of waist), $r = +.443 \pm .061$; and between M-F score and the last named six variables, $r = +.358 \pm .061$.

The correlations of ratings with M-F scores are again disappointingly low. In the case of the college women only one of the correlations in Table 14 is more than three times its probable error: that of $-.25 \pm .07$ between M-F score and "having typical manual interests of the same sex." Two others are more than twice the probable error: that with "personality" ($+.19 \pm .07$), and that with "intellectual interests of the opposite sex" ($+.15 \pm .07$). One other, that with "effectiveness," is just below this magnitude ($-.13 \pm .07$), in this case the direction of the correlation being the reverse of what most observers would probably have expected. For the high-school girls one correlation is nearly four times its probable error, that of +.327 ± .085 for "tomboyishness." Three others for this group are more than twice their probable errors: "leadership" (+.19 ± .09), "force of personality" (+.22 ± .09), and "typical manual interests of the same sex" (−.182 ± .09). In the case of the eighth-grade girls and the high-school boys there is not a single correlation that even suggests statistical significance. For the eighth-grade boys, one is more than three times its probable error ("leadership," +.24 ± .07) and two are more than twice their probable errors ("force of personality," +.17 ± .07, and "sissiness," +.18 ± .075). That with "sissiness" is in the unexpected direction in eighth-grade boys perhaps because the early adolescent interest in girls of the older and hence more masculine-scoring boys in the group is mistakenly interpreted as an evidence of "sissiness."

It will be noted that masculinity of score shows a possibly significant positive correlation with "leadership" in two of the five groups (high-school girls and eighth-grade boys) and "force of personality" in three of the five groups (college women, high-school girls, and eighth-grade boys). "Typical manual interests of the same sex" correlates negatively with masculinity, and "tomboyishness" positively, in two of the three female groups. All these trends are in the expected direction and, although each coefficient considered alone is of doubtful significance, the correlations fit together in a way to indicate the existence of small but fairly definite relationships. The small negative correlation between M-F score and "effectiveness," in the case of the college women, may not be a result of chance factors; it is quite possible that the kind of effectiveness the raters had in mind was effectiveness in activities essentially feminine in character. The reason for the positive correlation between masculinity score and "sissiness" in the case of eighth-grade boys is obscure, assuming it is not a chance result. There are two or three circumstances, however, that taken together may account for it. (1) The more masculine-scoring boys are probably on the average somewhat older, as it has been shown that at this age there is an appreciable correlation between age and score in the case of boys. (2) The older boys at this school level may be growing out of the boisterous period and therefore tend on the average to present the picture of a quieter and less obstreperous (less masculine) personality, an effect which could easily be interpreted by the teacher as bordering upon "sissiness."

The evidence with reference to the attractiveness or unattractiveness of the more or less masculine girl or young woman is one of the most interesting and perhaps one of the more surprising contributions of this experiment. At the grammar-school and high-school levels the correlation between M-F score and the groups of traits indicating attractiveness to and interest in their own and the opposite sex are all zero. At the college level attractiveness to and interest in the opposite sex tend if anything to be associated with the more masculine M-F scores, while attractiveness to and interest in their own sex tend to be associated with the more feminine scores. In view of the fact that intelligence also correlates positively with the M-F score, these findings, even if they are accepted only to the extent that they do not support the opposite trends, are biologically encouraging. Similarly, it is interesting to know that in these groups there was no correlation, either positive or negative, between M-F score and proneness to form emotional attachments to members of the same sex, though it is unlikely that there were genuine cases of homosexuality in these groups.[1]

[1] Of the 92 women for whom trait ratings were made at college in 1928 the marital status eight years later is as follows: 66 married, 23 unmarried, 2 married and divorced, 1 (unmarried) deceased. Comparing the 66 married with the 23 unmarried with respect to total M-F score, intelligence score, and each of the 19 trait ratings we find the results shown in the table on page 95. (A plus difference means that the women of the group who are married have the higher rating in the trait in question.)

Definitely significant is the leadership difference only, possibly also that for objective-mindedness. A glance at the other differences shows that the married group tend to exceed in reasonableness, attractiveness to their own sex (including the raters), strength of personality, effectiveness, and having the typical intellectual and manual interests of the opposite sex and of their own. A combined personality rating for leadership, balance, attractiveness to the raters, and breadth of interests would give a significantly higher score to the married group. The three traits in which the differences have negative signs are, having the typical social interests of their own sex, having crushes,

How shall we interpret the scantiness of positive results from this experiment in trait rating? Would the conclusion be warranted that M-F scores are almost totally uncorrelated with any of the various aspects of behavior which go to make up what is known as personality? In our opinion such a conclusion would be premature. We have shown in other chapters that the scores of this test are definitely related to occupational interest, mechanical interest (in the case of men), religious interest, culture, intelligence, age, education, aggressive independence, and homosexuality. We have also found that composite subjective rankings of both male and female groups for masculinity-femininity agree fairly closely with the rank orders of the same groups based upon mean M-F scores.

One can only conclude either (1) that the type of masculinity and femininity tested by the test has few conspicuous correlates in everyday behavior, or (2) that these correlates cannot be accurately identified by teachers or close acquaintances. That the latter explanation is generally speaking correct is, we believe,

---

and emotionality and excitability, but none of these differences is statistically significant. The differences in M-F score and in intelligence are positive but not statistically significant. Of the seven women who were rated above 1 in standard

Trait†	Diff.*	$\frac{\text{Diff.}}{\text{S.D.}_{\text{diff.}}}$	Trait	Diff.*	$\frac{\text{Diff.}}{\text{S.D.}_{\text{diff.}}}$
1	+.77	+3.35	12	+ .29	+1.28
2	+.38	+1.67	13	+ .05	+ .21
3	+.25	+ .97	14	− .03	− .13
4	+.40	+1.76	15	+ .20	+ .90
5	+.05	+ .18	16	+ .47	+2.25
6	+.07	+ .29	17	− .32	−1.53
7	+.30	+1.10	18	+ .30	+1.39
8	+.42	+1.71	19	+ .12	+ .45
9	−.04	− .16	M-F score....	+2.3	+ .25
10	+ 25	+ .88	Intelligence		
11	+.34	+1.39	Thorndike score.......	+1.7	+ .77

† See Appendix V for rating sheet with names of traits.
* The differences are in terms of ratings expressed as standard scores.

score on "having crushes" five are married, one has been married and is divorced, one is single. Of the two women in the total group of 92 who rated above 2 in standard score on "having crushes" one is married, the other single.

supported by our data on occupations, interests, culture, age, and homosexuality. The small amount of agreement between two or more raters who judge the masculinity-femininity of the same subjects is corroborative of this interpretation. In Chapter IV it was shown that a composite of several ratings of masculinity-femininity by teachers would be necessary to afford even a very modest reliability. The ratings of the more specific aspects of masculinity-femininity just described have on the average higher reliabilities. These are shown in Table 15 for eight of the traits. It will be noted that the reliabilities for these more specific traits run much higher than for ratings of all-round masculinity. Even so, we have seen that there is little evidence of correlation between composite ratings and M-F score.

TABLE 15.—RELIABILITY OF CERTAIN TRAIT RATINGS OF COLLEGE WOMEN

	Reliabilities
1. Leadership..............................	.74 (av. of 3)
2. Force of personality......................	.43 (av. of 15)
8. Having typical intellectual interests of opposite sex................................	.45 (av. of 15)
9. Having typical social interests of same sex...	.45 (av. of 3)
11. Having typical manual interests of same sex..	.39 (av. of 15)
13a. "Tomboyishness".......................	.44 (av. of 3)
14. Having crushes on persons of same sex......	.41 (av. of 3)
18. Effectiveness	.59 (av. of 15)
Effectiveness	.72 (av. of 3)

SUMMARY

1. No reliable correlations have been found between M-F scores and self-ratings on health in the case of our adult population.

2. Most of the correlations between M-F score and physical measurements are within one or one and a half probable errors of zero. The data suggest that there may be for males a positive correlation between masculinity and height and also between femininity and length of trunk in relation to height. In the case of females the only significant relationship suggested is the positive correlation between masculinity of score and ratio of

girth at ninth rib to stature. No other relationships between M-F score and physical secondary sexual characteristics were suggested.

3. It is conceivable that the apparent correlation with height is not the result of an intrinsically more masculine element expressed in relatively greater size, but rather the result of a correlation between masculinity of score and the kind of ascendancy and domination which is associated with superior strength and athletic ability; in other words, whatever relationship exists may be due to psychosociological rather than psychobiological factors.

4. Exceptionally early puberty appears to be associated, in the case of boys, with excess masculinity of score in the late teens; in the case of girls, with excess femininity of score at this age.

5. Ratings on 19 personality traits commonly believed to be associated with mental masculinity-femininity have yielded only negligible or very low correlations with M-F scores. Indications of small relationships are found in the case of the following rated traits: "Having the typical manual interests of their own sex," "force of personality," and "tomboyishness."

6. Since intelligence correlates positively with M-F score in women it is perhaps fortunate that "attractiveness to persons of the opposite sex" shows no evidence of negative correlation with test standing.

7. The reliabilities of the ratings on the fairly specific personality variables entering into this investigation are considerably higher than we have found for ratings of all-round masculinity, but except in the case of leadership are still unsatisfactorily low.

8. Further investigation is urgently needed to throw light on the behavioral correlates of the kind of masculinity and femininity measured by this test.

CHAPTER VI

CORRELATION OF M-F SCORE WITH PERSONALITY AND ACHIEVEMENT MEASURES

EXTROVERSION-INTROVERSION AND THE M-F SCORE

Two measures of the habit systems which type psychology attempts to differentiate in an extrovert-introvert dichotomy have been applied and correlated with ratings on the M-F scale. Scores on the Laird C2 Personal Inventory[1] (higher the score, the more introvert) have been correlated with M-F scores (higher, the more masculine) for 90 men in an elementary psychology class $(r = -.25 \pm .07)$, for 46 men of high (upper quartile) scholarship $(r = -.29 \pm .09)$, for 46 men of low (lower quartile) scholarship $(r = +.20 \pm .10)$, and for 55 college women in a mixed group $(r = -.19 \pm .09)$. The M-F scores of 329 older delinquent boys were correlated with the Neyman-Kohlstedt scores by Casselberry[2] $(r = -.02 \pm .04)$.

In three of the four groups for which correlations were obtained the coefficients indicated a low negative correlation. Two of the correlations for men are high enough to be fairly reliable. The women's correlation suggests that the same trend is present for them also. The third correlation for the men, although not definitely significant, is curiously divergent from the general trend indicated in the other groups, but it may be noted that both the M-F scores and the Laird C2 scores cover much narrower ranges for this group than for the others. Altogether it seems probable that for unselected groups of college men there is a small negative correlation between Laird introversion and

---

[1] The items included in the Laird C2 are essentially those enumerated by Max Freyd (Introverts and extroverts, *Psychol. Rev.*, 1924, **31**, 74–87) in so far as they were found valid by Edna Heidbreder (Introversion and extroversion in men and women, *J. Abn. and Soc. Psychol.*, 1927, **22**, 52).

[2] CASSELBERRY, W. S., Analysis and prediction of delinquency, *J. Juv. Res.*, 1932, **16**, 1–31.

masculinity as measured by our test, and that the same general trend may be present to a somewhat less extent in the women also. The trend is not unexpected in view of the M-F culture relationship: the more masculine college men are the more extroverted, the more feminine are the more introverted, and the same may be true for the women.

A study by Oliver[1] gives corroboration to the proposition just stated and adds further interesting sidelights on the relation between extroversion-introversion and M-F score. Oliver selected for comparison small groups of extreme extroverts and introverts, the 10 per cent tail from each end of a normal distribution of college students. The 12 extrovert and 11 introvert men so selected were given a number of personality tests in an effort to determine some of the traits associated with extreme extroversion and extreme introversion. On the M-F scale the 12 extroverts rated at +108.3, the 11 introverts at +66.8. The difference between these two means is 5.5 times its standard error. The characteristics which Oliver discovered for his extrovert group we may therefore fairly accept as (indirectly) the more masculine traits, the introvert traits as (also indirectly) the more feminine. An added justification for this interpretation is found in the relationship between M-F score and extroversion-introversion in high- and low-scholarship men studied by Tinsley (see pp. 101 ff.). For them also the Laird scores and M-F scores were negatively correlated. The high-scholarship group with average Laird C2 score of 18 rated at +61.1 on the M-F scale; the low-scholarship group with average Laird C2 score of 14 rated at +92.3 M-F. Here again extroversion is associated with masculinity, introversion with femininity. The difference between the M-F means is 3.8 times its standard error; that between the Laird C2 means 3.1 its standard error.

The other tests used by Oliver to define the traits of extroverts and introverts were Strong's vocational-interest test, the Kent-Rosanoff free association test given as a group test, the Pressey X-O test, Allport's A-S reaction test, the Watson test of fair-

---

[1] OLIVER, R. A. C., The traits of extroverts and introverts, *J. Soc. Psychol.*, 1930, **1**, 343–665.

mindedness, and the George Washington test of social intelligence. Comparison of Oliver's (masculine) extroverts with his (less masculine) introverts on these various tests suggests at least what may be expected from a direct comparison between the measures used and the masculinity-femininity score. The 15[1] extrovert men showed less vocational aptitude, as measured by Strong's test, than the 13[1] introvert men for the occupations of their choice. These were mechanical engineering, personnel psychology, law, advertising, and architecture. The introverts chose journalism, law, authorship, medicine, advertising, executive administration, and insurance. It is of interest to note that the extrovert who chose to be a mechanical engineer was the only one in the extrovert group who received a rating of A in the Strong test for the occupation of his choice. None of the group rated B+. Among the introverts the choices of journalism, law, and authorship received Strong ratings of A; medicine, authorship, and law, B+. Furthermore, the extroverts were not only less well suited to the professions they had chosen, but it was also found that fewer of them than of the introverts had made a decision in the matter. This agrees with our findings reported in Chapter VIII, that the more masculine men have less intense positive interests than the less masculine. The contrast between mechanical interest and culture is further brought out by the ratings of all the members of both groups on the two occupations "author" and "engineer." The former occupation proves by this comparison to be, as we might expect, quite definitely introvert and less masculine, the latter extrovert and more masculine.

In the Kent-Rosanoff free association test both of Oliver's groups gave a larger percentage of unique responses than the norm, as was to be expected in view of their more than average education. But the introverts (less masculine) gave significantly more of the unique responses than the extroverts, whatever that may mean. The introverts showed on the Pressey X-O tests

[1] Three subjects (extreme extroverts) were added by Oliver to his original group of 12 extroverts, and two extreme introverts to his original group of 11 introverts.

higher affectivity, greater idiosyncrasy, and greater self-con-
sciousness; the last two differences are statistically significant.
These results agree with expectation regarding introverts and
extroverts, and also with the culture interpretation of femininity
in men and its contrast in the indifferent, hard-boiled, over-
masculine type.   Allport's A-S reaction test showed the extroverts to be more ascendant, the introverts more submissive than
the norm.   The difference is not entirely reliable, but the direction in the contrast is worthy of note.   Since the extroverts
are more masculine, it is not surprising that they should also
be more ascendant.   The Watson test of fair-mindedness
showed no difference between the two groups in general level of
prejudice, and none in any particular aspect of religious opinion.
There appeared, however, to be a definite tendency for introverts
to hold more liberal views on economic issues and to favor
stricter moral standards.   On the social-intelligence test there
was no difference found between the two groups.

Additional data with reference to the relation of M-F score to
Conklin scores on introversion-extroversion come from Tinsley's[1]
study of the traits of high- and low-scholarship men.   Her high-
scholarship men with low M-F mean (+61.1) rated introvert;
her low-scholarship men with high M-F mean (+92.3) rated
extrovert.   The difference between the two groups on Laird C2
score was 3.1 times its standard error.   The correlation between
Conklin introversion score and M-F rating was $-.52 \pm .07$ for
the high-scholarship men and $-.24 \pm .09$ for the low-scholarship
men, which agrees in direction with the Laird C2 results, but
brings out also a difference that should be further investigated;
namely, the higher correlation of M-F with Conklin than with
Laird.

Scores on the tests secured by Tinsley have been correlated by
us with the other measures in her battery (Table 16) and we
quote in addition her own correlations and averages (Table 17).
These results, especially the contrasting traits of the high-

[1] TINSLEY, RUTH, Personality traits of high and low scholarship men with
equal aptitude ratings, M.A. thesis directed by P. R. Farnsworth, Stanford
University, 1930, unpublished.

scholarship (more feminine) group, when compared with the low-scholarship (more masculine) group, corroborate Oliver's results from another angle. The more feminine, high-scholarship group differs from the more masculine, low-scholarship group in being (1) more submissive in terms of Allport's test (critical ratio 2.7), (2) less prejudiced in terms of Watson's test (critical ratio 2.1), (3) more self-conscious, having higher affectivity scores in terms of the Pressey X-O test (critical ratio 1.8), (4) more unstable emotionally as measured by the Laird B2 personal inventory (critical ratio 1.3), and (5) as we have already seen,

TABLE 16.—CORRELATIONS BETWEEN PERSONALITY SCORES AND M-F SCORES IN HIGH- AND LOW-SCHOLARSHIP GROUPS

	46 college men of high scholarship	46 college men of low scholarship
Laird B2	$-.31 \pm .09$	$.00 \pm .10$
Laird C2	$-.29 \pm .09$	$+.20 \pm .10$
Conklin	$-.52 \pm .07$	$-.24 \pm .09$
Pressey X-O	$+.03 \pm .10$	$-.44 \pm .08$
Allport A-S	$+.36 \pm .09$	$+.08 \pm .10$
Watson fair-mindedness	$+.18 \pm .10$	$-.17 \pm .10$

TABLE 17.—CORRELATIONS BETWEEN PERSONALITY SCORES AND SCHOLARSHIP SCORES (GRADE-POINT AVERAGE)

Laird B2	$+.11 \pm .06$	Good scholarship (indirectly femininity) and instability associated to this extent.
Laird C2	$+.27 \pm .06$	Good scholarship (indirectly femininity) and introversion associated to this extent.
Conklin	$+.23 \pm .06$	Good scholarship (indirectly femininity) and introversion associated to this extent.
Pressey X-O	$+.13 \pm .06$	Good scholarship (indirectly femininity) associated with affectivity and self-consciousness to this extent.
Allport A-S	$-.25 \pm .06$	Good scholarship (indirectly femininity) and ascendancy associated to this extent, *i.e.*, negatively.
Watson fair-mindedness	$-.18 \pm .06$	Good scholarship (indirectly femininity) and prejudice associated to this extent, *i.e.*, negatively.

more introverted (critical ratio Laird, 3.1; Conklin, 2.7). Tinsley's correlations between scholarship and the various measures are a further indirect evidence of the correlation between these measures and the M-F score. The correlations between M-F score and each of the other measures suggest the desirability of further investigation using unselected groups with wide score ranges.

In summary it may be said that there is considerable evidence that more masculine college men tend to be extroverted, more feminine college men to be introverted. This is true with respect to the elements of extroversion-introversion measured in the Laird C2 test and even more clearly the case with respect to the more restricted type of extroversion-introversion measured by the Conklin test.[1] Furthermore, the (masculine) extrovert men are found to be less sure of the vocations they should follow than the (feminine) introvert men. They are less well fitted for those they choose, unless these be in the field of engineering. The (introvert) feminine group is more affective and self-conscious in response on the Pressey test and shows greater idiosyncrasy. Its members are more submissive, hold more liberal economic views, and favor stricter moral standards. The two groups do not differ in fair-mindedness nor in social intelligence. That the traits in question tend to persist as characteristic of the more masculine and the more feminine groups respectively is shown by a contrast between high-(feminine) and low-(masculine) scholarship groups. This comparison adds to the traits already mentioned a difference in prejudice: the data indicating that prejudice is more characteristic of men rating high than of men rating low in masculinity.

College women seem to show a slight tendency for introversion to be associated with femininity, extroversion with masculinity, but further evidence is needed to confirm or disprove the slight trend suggested. In teen-age delinquent boys there is no relation between M-F score and introversion-extroversion as measured by the Neyman-Kohlstedt test.

[1] The Bernreuter test of introversion has not been correlated with M-F scores but it is known to correlate very highly with Laird C2.

Correlation of M-F Score with Character Measures

Information concerning the relation between character traits and masculinity-femininity has been contributed by Casselberry, who compared M-F scores of 329 older delinquent boys with their standing in the series of character tests developed by Cady and Raubenheimer and used in the Stanford study of gifted children. The battery included two overstatement tests, tests of questionable reading preferences and character preferences, a trustworthiness test (the tracing of circles and squares with opportunity for cheating), and Cady's adaptation of the Woodworth emotional-stability test.[1] The weighted character index developed from these tests by Terman and Goodenough was also derived for the delinquent boys. Scores on the separate parts of the battery and the final indices were correlated with the M-F scores.

The first overstatement test, which consists in marking book titles, some of them fictitious, gave a correlation of $+.19 \pm .04$ between M-F score and amount of overstatement regarding books claimed to have been read. Overstatement B, the second test in the series, gives an opportunity for overstatement with reference to general information. The correlation coefficient for this test and the M-F is $+.10 \pm .04$, showing a less clear relation than was found for overstatement A. Questionable reading preferences and questionable character preferences, both of which rank very low in their contribution to the general character index, show no correlation with M-F score; the coefficients are $+.00 \pm .04$ and $-.01 \pm .04$. The activity interest test, also based upon questionable preferences, shows the small but reliable correlation with masculinity of $+.18 \pm .04$. This test is heavily weighted in the character index. The trustworthiness test adapted by Cady and used in accordance with the technique developed for the gifted-children study shows a correlation of $+.06 \pm .04$ with M-F scores for the delinquent group. The Woodworth-Cady emotional-stability test gives a

[1] The tests and testing procedure are described in Terman, *et al.*, *Genetic studies of genius*, vol. I, Chapter XVII, 1925.

correlation of $+.04 \pm .04$ with M-F. The weighted character index which combines scores from all seven tests in the battery correlates $+.06 \pm .04$ with the M-F test, showing no appreciable relationship between masculinity-femininity and the character index as a whole. Such correlation as is indicated appears to be limited to (1) overstatement with reference to reading matter, and (2) choice of questionable or undesirable activities, both of which are natural opposites to the more introvert and cultural pursuits of the boys who tend toward femininity on the M-F scale.

MECHANICAL ABILITY AND MASCULINITY

There was no more striking result in the occupational and interest comparisons (Chapters VIII and IX) than the influence of mechanical pursuits on the M-F score at every educational level. It is no wonder then that a positive correlation is found between M-F ratings and scores on a test of mechanical ability. It is perhaps also to be anticipated that this positive relationship will appear for males only, as nothing equivalent to the high means of the engineers and architects and the mechanical occupations appeared for the women. The first correlation between mechanical ability (Stenquist I) and M-F test scores was noted in the small group of 15 orphan boys ($rho = +.55 \pm .13$). For 15 orphan girls the correlation coefficient was $+.03 \pm .20$. The Stenquist test was then given to 64 boys and 64 girls in the junior year of high school, the resulting correlations with M-F scores being as follows: for the boys, $+.237 \pm .079$; for the girls, $+.055 \pm .083$. Correlations between Stenquist scores and the scores on the separate parts of the M-F test, Exercises 3, 4, and 5, showed that Exercise 5 (interests; $r = +.20 \pm .08$) was contributing the major part of the correlation with the M-F score. The coefficients for the boys between scores on the other exercises and the Stenquist scores were all less than their probable errors, as were also those for the girls on each of Exercises 3, 4, and 5.

A further group consisting of 329 delinquent boys in the teen age was given the Stenquist test by Casselberry, its scores correlating +.306 ± .038 with M-F scores. The McQuarrie mechanical-ability test given by Casselberry to the same group yielded a correlation of +.125 ± .038 with M-F score.

From these findings it may be stated that mechanical ability measured by test is a masculine trait for boys and young men as it is for older men when measured by occupation. It has no correlation whatever with mental masculinity-femininity in girls, and this agrees with the apparent absence of any such relationship in the occupational findings for adult women (Chapter VIII).

Scholarship and M-F Score

We have investigated the relation of scholarship to masculinity-femininity only in the case of college students. The factors that contribute to college marks are so numerous that one could hardly expect a very high correlation between scholarship and M-F score. Intelligence, which is more closely related to scholarship than any other single factor, is positively correlated with mental masculinity in the case of college women but not to any appreciable extent in the case of men. However, several investigations have shown that college men who rate as introverts on the Laird or Bernreuter tests display a small but reliable superiority in scholarship over men who rate as extroverts, and

Table 18.—Scholarship and M-F Scores

A. Average M-F scores of college men above and below (1) the college scholarship mean, (2) the college intelligence mean.

	Mean M-F score
1. 69 men, intelligence below average, scholarship below average.	+77.0
2. 40 men, intelligence above average, scholarship below average.	+74.2
3. 44 men, intelligence above average, scholarship above average.	+71.7
4. 39 men, intelligence below average, scholarship above average.	+77.5

Combinations of the above:

a. Scholarship comparison
83 men above average in scholarship...................... +74.4
109 men below average in scholarship.................... +75.8

b. Intelligence comparison
84 men above average in intelligence..................... +72.8
108 men below average in intelligence.................... +77.1

TABLE 18.—Scholarship and M-F Scores.—(*Continued*)

B. Average M-F scores of college men (1) in the upper and lower scholarship quartiles and (2) above and below the college intelligence mean.

	Mean M-F score	S.D.	S.D.$_M$
1. 43 men, high intelligence, low scholarship......	+89.9	43.2	6.6
2. 53 men, low intelligence, low scholarship.......	+88.1	42.0	5.8
3. 62 men, high intelligence, high scholarship.....	+74.4	41.8	5.3
4. 27 men, low intelligence, high scholarship......	+52.9	43.8	8.4

Combinations of the above:

a. Scholarship comparison

	Mean M-F score
89 men in the upper scholarship quartile......	+67.8
96 men in the lower scholarship quartile......	+88.6

b. Intelligence comparison

	Mean M-F score
105 men above average in intelligence........	+80.6
80 men below average in intelligence........	+76.1

C. Average M-F scores of college men who have been in college 6 or more terms (2 college years or more) and who are (1) in the upper and lower scholarship quartiles and (2) above and below the college intelligence mean.

	Mean M-F score	S.D.	S.D.$_M$
1. 28 men, intelligence above college average, scholarship in lowest quartile..............	+100.5	43.8	8.3
2. 18 men, intelligence below college average, scholarship in lowest quartile..............	+ 81.1	36.6	8.6
3. 27 men, intelligence above college average, scholarship in upper quartile..............	+ 69.2	42.4	8.2
4. 19 men, intelligence below college average, scholarship in upper quartile..............	+ 52.9	49.2	11.3

Combinations of the above:

a. Scholarship comparison

	Mean M-F score	S.D.	S.D.$_M$
46 men in the upper scholarship quartile.....	+ 61.1	46.0	6.8
46 men in the lower scholarship quartile......	+ 92.3	41.9	6.2

b. Intelligence comparison

	Mean M-F score
55 men above average in intelligence........	+ 87.4
37 men below average in intelligence........	+ 66.6

since introversion, as we have seen, is for men negatively correlated with mental masculinity, it would not be surprising to find a small negative correlation between scholarship and masculinity. The culture factor which in men seems to be associated with low M-F score would support the same expectation. In the case of women the expectation is reversed, since with them both superior intelligence and superior culture are associated with mental masculinity. Table 18 gives mean M-F scores of college men in their relation to both scholarship (as measured by grade-point ratio) and intelligence (as measured by Thorndike's college aptitude test).

It will be noted that Table 18 contains three sections, *A, B,* and *C*. Section *A* compares the M-F mean of all who are above average in scholarship with the mean of all who are below, separately for groups of high and low intelligence. Section *B* makes the same comparisons between highest and lowest quartiles with respect to scholarship. Section *C* is like *B* except that in this case the data are confined to the men whose scholarship quartile classification could be based upon at least two full years of college work, whereas in *A* and *B* the scholarship record was for varying periods from a third of a year to three and two-thirds years.

Section *A* of the table shows practically identical M-F means for men above and men below average scholarship (74.4 and 75.8) where intelligence is disregarded. When the same subjects are divided into two groups according to intelligence, the lower intelligence group rates slightly more masculine; 77.1 as compared to 72.8. The difference is not reliable but is in the expected direction. When the comparison is between upper and lower scholarship quartiles (Section *B* of the table) a relationship of considerable magnitude is found between scholarship and M-F score, and this relationship obtains in both intelligence groups. When the scholarship quartile classification is based upon grade-point average for two years or more (Section *C* of table) the relationship is still further enhanced. We find here a mean M-F score of 92.3 for the lower scholarship quartile as compared with 61.1 for the upper scholarship quartile. The corresponding means for those of more than average intelligence are 100.5 and 69.2; for those below average intelligence, 81.1 and 52.9. It appears, therefore, that whatever the level of intelligence there is a considerable negative correlation between scholarship and mental masculinity in the case of men. The matter deserves to be investigated with larger groups, for if the trends here shown should be confirmed the M-F test might prove a useful aid in the prediction of college success.

The interests expressed by Tinsley's high- and low-scholarship groups (Table 19) throw light on the grade-getting success of the one and the lack of it in the other.   The averages for both groups having each of the 12 interests, positive and negative, follow the usual trends.   In general the devotees of any given interest have a mean M-F score above or below the mean of the group as a whole according as the interest in question is masculine or feminine (see Chapter IX).   For example, the men who

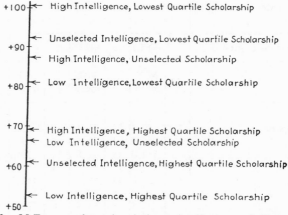

FIG. 2.—M-F scores of men in relation to intelligence and scholarship.

care much for mechanics in the high-scholarship group are as masculine as the mechanically interested in the low-scholarship group.   The single individual in the low-scholarship group who is interested in religion has a very feminine score indeed.   Comparison of the percentages of each group that shows positive interests in the various pursuits gives some indication of the characteristic contrast between the individuals of high and low scholarship.   The high-scholarship group is more interested than the low-scholarship group in (1) politics, (2) travel, (3) religion, (4) literature.   The differences are not large, but taken together they quite clearly indicate a cultural trend in the high-scholarship men.   The negative interests of these men are social life, mechanics, music, pets, and in these a larger percentage of them than of the low-scholarship men have little or no interest.

It may seem surprising that music is included here, but we are inclined to think that musical interest among these western college students may not be really cultural. It is perhaps connected rather with sports and social life than with cultural life.

TABLE 19.—MEAN M-F SCORES OF HIGH- AND LOW-SCHOLARSHIP MEN HAVING (1) MUCH, OR (2) LITTLE OR NO INTEREST IN CERTAIN PURSUITS

	Much interest				Little interest			
Interest	High-scholarship group		Low-scholarship group		High-scholarship group		Low-scholarship group	
M-F means of groups	+61.1		+92.3		+61.1		+92.3	
	N	M-F mean	N	M-F mean	N	M-F mean	N	M-F mean
Travel.....................	34	59.9	31	93.5	..	..	..	..
Outdoor sports.............	22	69.5	21	95.4	1	65.5	2	89.5
Religion...................	3	55.5	1	24.5	18	69.9	29	98.2
Mechanics.................	6	118.8	15	99.8	12	39.6	2	72.0
Social life.................	8	70.5	12	96.1	4	63.0	..	..
Literature.................	15	54.8	14	80.2	3	142.1	4	114.5
Music.....................	15	40.8	18	88.9	4	110.5	2	84.5
Art.......................	2	5.5	5	84.5	10	96.5	11	123.5
Science...................	15	84.8	18	97.8	1	55.5	5	86.5
Politics...................	12	73.8	7	73.0	10	72.5	14	83.7
Domestic art..............	..	..	..	..	23	67.6	22	95.4
Pets......................	7	64.0	9	76.7	11	57.3	9	103.3

The low-scholarship group (Table 20) has a slightly stronger inclination to both positive and negative interests. The difference is small, 2 per cent for each interest in both groups of interests. The positive interests of the low-scholarship group show a strong predilection for mechanics, social life, art, music, science, and pets, in that order. Their negative interests show a striking dissimilarity as compared with those of the high-scholarship group with respect to attitude toward religion. The other pursuits for which they have expressed less interest than the high-scholarship group are science and politics. Again it may be seen that the intellectual pursuits as a whole, excepting art and music, are more attractive to the high- than to the low-scholarship group. The outstanding characteristic of the high-scholarship group is its significantly smaller number of individuals who have very great interest in mechanics. The

TABLE 20.—POSITIVE AND NEGATIVE INTERESTS OF HIGH AND LOW SCHOLARSHIP GROUPS OF COLLEGE MEN

	High-scholarship group, per cent with positive interests	Low-scholarship group, per cent with positive interests	Diff.	High-scholarship group, per cent with negative interests	Low-scholarship group, per cent with negative interests	Diff.
Sports.............	48	46	2	2	4	− 2
Social life..........	17	26	− 9	9	0	9
Mechanics..........	13	33	−20	26	17	9
Science............	33	39	− 6	2	11	− 9
Literature..........	33	30	3	7	9	− 2
Travel.............	74	67	7	0	0	0
Pets...............	15	20	− 5	24	20	4
Politics............	26	15	11	22	30	− 8
Art................	4	11	− 7	22	24	− 2
Music.............	33	39	− 6	9	4	5
Religion...........	7	2	5	39	63	−24
Domestic arts.......	..	..	..	50	48	2
Average per cent.....	25.2	27.3		17.7	19.1	

striking characteristic of the low-scholarship group is the significantly larger percentage of individuals who have little or no interest in religion. On the basis of these expressions of interest alone it could have been predicted that the high-scholarship group would register less masculine on the M-F scale than the low-scholarship group.

Among college women there is evidence of about the same degree of correlation between scholarship and the M-F score as among the men. At each of two intelligence levels scholarship above average is associated with a more feminine score as follows:

Mean M-F
score

1. 22 women, intelligence above average, scholarship below average........................ −13.5
2. 93 women, intelligence above average, scholarship above average........................ −26.9
3. 24 women, intelligence below average, scholarship below average........................ −41.3
4. 36 women, intelligence below average, scholarship above average........................ −49.6

Combinations of these scores show, however, that the scholarship element is small in comparison with the contribution of
intelligence:

Mean M-F
score

a. Scholarship comparison
 129 women, above average in scholarship..... −33.1
 46 women, below average in scholarship...... −27.9

Difference.... + 5.2

b. Intelligence comparison
 115 women, above average in intelligence..... −24.3
 60 women, below average in intelligence...... −46.2

Difference.... −21.9

Low scholarship for the women, as for the men, is associated
with more masculine M-F scores, and this persists in the more
intelligent (more masculine) and in the less intelligent (more
feminine) college women's groups. This seems especially
interesting and important in view of the fact that intelligence
operates in the opposite direction for the women (*i.e.*, makes for
masculinity), while for men intelligence shows no consistent
relationship to M-F score.

RELATION OF M-F SCORES TO ATHLETIC ABILITY

The scores of a group of 43 male college athletes average
+92.5, which is reliably more masculine than the mean (+67.4)
for college men in general. They are more masculine than
groups of either high or low scholarship unselected as to athletic

ability. They are also more masculine than either high- or low-intelligence groups unselected as to athletic ability. The one-third of them who have intelligence scores above average score +95.0; the two-thirds whose intelligence scores are below average score +98.5. The half whose scholarship is above average rates +91.0, or .25 s.s.[1] higher than the low-scholarship

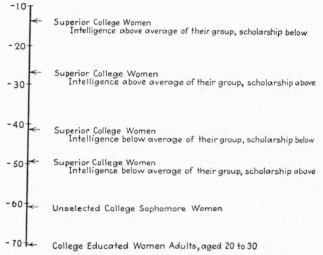

FIG. 3.—M-F scores of women in relation to intelligence and scholarship.

half, which rates at +104.0. This is in line with expected cultural and personality differences found to be correlated with the M-F score.

Two sets of data on women athletes are available:

1. A group of 53 college athletes from two higher institutions in the West, women of exceptional skill in games and sports, yields a mean M-F score of −21.7. This is almost one standard deviation above the generality of college women.[2]

[1] See Appendix II for table of standard scores for adult population.

[2] Scores were also secured for 25 physical education majors in a middle-western university. These show an M-F average at just the same level as the 130 college sophomores upon whom the college norm is based. But it may be noted that these physical education majors, many of them, are interested in the artistic rather than the athletic side of the profession. Hence, we incline to ascribe the difference between these scores and the athletic women's scores, not

2. At Stanford University, with the assistance of Miss Helen M. Bunting, Associate Professor of Physical Education, and three women athletes of recognized standing and wide acquaintance, ratings of athletic ability were made on 100 women students. The individuals rated included about 70 women who had played on teams and about 30 women chosen at random from the list of others for whom M-F scores were available. Ratings were made on a seven-point scale the items of which are as follows:

1. (a) Exceptional all-around athlete, very unusual skill and ability, outstanding in several sports. (b) Eminent athlete distinguished as an exceptional record holder or champion in one sport.
2. Very skillful athlete but not most eminent. Member of first team or teams, consistent point winner.
3. Fair athlete above average of college women. Dependable member of second team. Somewhat less able than average member of first team. May be substitute on first team.
4. Average athletic ability among college women. Exercises whether requirements demand it or not. Likes out-of-door activity and regularly indulges in it.
5. Plays games in gymnasium but does not go out voluntarily for sports. Chooses the less active physical education requirements.
6. Not athletic, utmost exercise is walking. Avoids games.
7. Avoids physical exertion entirely.
x Means you do not know the person.

The resulting distribution was naturally much skewed in the direction of the superior athletes. The small group of non-athletic individuals served as a satisfactory check in the rating, and the ranks obtained by these women indicated by comparison that the athletic ability of the others was probably not overrated. On the basis of the combined ratings of the four judges 55 women were found who rated 2.0 or better in athletic ability. The average of the M-F scores of these exceptional athletes was −25.8, which has a standard score index of +1.40 and is +.85 s.s. above the college sophomore norm for women.

In order to isolate the factor of athletic achievement or interest from other masculine trends in women the athletes in each of four

to a geographical difference, but rather to the probability that a good many of the physical education majors included here are not athletes, but dancing experts.

groups were compared with the group as a whole as follows: (1) those above the college average in intelligence and in college grades, (2) those above the college average in intelligence and below it in college grades, (3) those below the college average in intelligence and above it in college grades, (4) those below the college average both in intelligence and in college grades. "Above average intelligence" means a score of 80 or above on the Thorndike college aptitude test, "below average intelligence" means rating at 79 or below. "Above average in college grades" means having a grade point rating of 1.5 or better; "below average in college grades," 1.49 or lower.

TABLE 21.—M-F SCORES OF ATHLETIC AND NONATHLETIC COLLEGE WOMEN

	N	Mean M-F score	S.D.$_M$
1. AI college athletes, total group................	44	−21.1	7.9
a. with aptitude score of 80 or higher.........	30	−11.5	8.6
b. with aptitude score below 80..............	14	−38.1	16.4
2. Nonathletic college women, total group.........	122	−37.1	3.6
a. with aptitude score of 80 or higher.........	77	−31.0	4.2
b. with aptitude score below 80..............	45	−47.6	6.5

In each of the four subgroups the superior athletes of that group score more masculine than the group as a whole except in the case of the women of low intelligence and high scholarship. Here the 14 superior athletes included score .2 of a standard score more feminine than the group as a whole. Although the groups compared are not large, it seems possible that this difference is not due to chance. We suggest that these women of lower intelligence who have made good in both scholarship and athletics in such an exceptional way possess a trait of *effective conformity* which is probably mentally feminine. We have found in another experiment that the mean M-F score of college women who rated below average in "effectiveness" was −29.3, as compared with −38.8 for those above average in "effectiveness." The difference between the two averages is just more than its standard error.

It seems not improbable that effectiveness in women represents the opposite of independence, that it involves an element of conformity and cooperation which is feminine in its influence. If this is so it is also not purely a matter of chance that the athletes below the college average in intelligence and above it in scholarship represent the most feminine extreme, while the

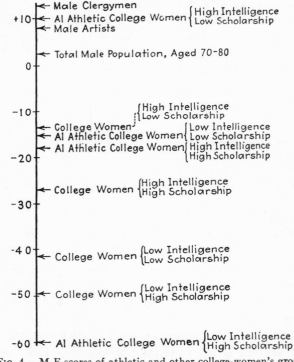

Fig. 4.—M-F scores of athletic and other college-women's groups.

athletes above the college average in intelligence and below it in scholarship represent the most masculine extreme. We believe that the same indifference and independence of this last-named gifted galaxy makes them poor scholars and at the same time the most masculine group we have discovered among more than 2,000 women tested. These women doubtless lack the feminine "effectiveness" which is associated with "having the manual interests of their own sex," and which is associated with making good college marks. They are able, and they are independent. In a sense, this small group of seven unusual individuals epitomizes the characteristics of the mentally masculine college woman: (1) superior intelligence, (2) marked indifference to traditional female college aims, (3) athletic prowess. This is the only female group whose mean M-F score overlaps the normal male range of means. These women, who are 2.25 s.s. removed from the mean of their own sex, are only .45 s.s. below the male mean. It would probably be a surprise to all in the following groups to know that these unusual women rate at about the same point on the M-F scale as male clergymen, and the generality of males aged 60 to 70, or that they rate more masculine than male artists or the generality of males above age 70.

RELATION OF MASCULINITY-FEMININITY TO MARITAL COMPATIBILITY

It would not be unreasonable to suppose that a relationship might exist between marital happiness and the mental masculinity or femininity of spouses. Inquiry discloses that various opinions are prevalent in regard to the types of M-F matings that would probably be most favorable to happiness. A majority of those to whom the question has been put are inclined to believe that the best combination is superior masculinity of husband and superior femininity of wife, though a few have argued strongly for the mating of "likes," some even in favor of the feminine-husband, masculine-wife combination.

It has not been possible to investigate this question with the present M-F test, but an investigation was carried out by Terman and Buttenwieser[1] with the use of a substitute M-F test. The reader will recall that certain items in the M-F test were taken from the Strong test of occupational interests, particularly items in Exercise 5 relating to interests. It happened that Terman and Buttenwieser had administered the Strong test to 341 married couples and to 100 divorced couples,

---

[1] TERMAN, LEWIS M., and PAUL BUTTENWIESER, Personality factors in marital compatibility, *J. Soc. Psychol.*, 1935, **6**, 143–171, 267–289.

and that for each of the married couples a marital-happiness score was available based upon confidential information furnished by both spouses. It seemed desirable, therefore, to derive a masculinity-femininity score from the Strong test for use with these groups.

At our suggestion an M-F scoring key was worked out for the Strong test by Dr. Harold Carter. The key was based on the responses of 114 males and 114 females to the Strong test, a majority of the subjects being of high-school age. Of the 420 items in the test, 156 yielded sex differences of probably significant magnitude, and weights were assigned to these items in proportion to the amount and reliability of difference found. The score derived by the use of this key will be designated the occupational M-F score.[1] It is not identical with the Terman-Miles M-F score but correlated with it to the extent of .43 for 41 males and .62 for 62 females. Any relationship that may be found to hold between the occupational M-F score and marital happiness will at least suggest the direction of relationship that would be found for the Terman-Miles M-F score.

First the husband-wife correlation in occupational M-F score was found for 126 of the married couples having high happiness ratings, and also for 215 married couples with low happiness ratings. These were as follows: for the more happy group, .029 $\pm$ .060; for the less happy group, .085 $\pm$ .046. In other words, happy spouses were no more and no less alike in masculinity-femininity than unhappy spouses; marital selection based upon this personality trait had not occurred to any appreciable degree in either group.

Next, the husband's happiness score was correlated with his score on the occupational M-F test (.085 $\pm$ .031), and the wife's happiness score with hers (.047 $\pm$ .031). Again no significant relationship with marital happiness appears. The result is the same when the combined happiness score of husband and wife is correlated with the husband-wife difference in Strong M-F score (r = .108 $\pm$ .03).

[1] For a later version of the Strong M-F test see Edward K. Strong, Jr., Interests of men and women, *J. Soc. Psychol.*, 1936, **7**, 49–67.

Finally, a comparison was made of the mean occupational M-F scores, separately by sex, for the following groups: 100 most happily married couples, 100 most unhappily married couples, and 100 divorced couples. The results, in terms of mean standard scores on the occupational M-F test, were as follows:

	Husbands			Wives		
	Happy	Unhappy	Divorced	Happy	Unhappy	Divorced
Mean occupational M-F standard score.	4.67	5.14	4.29	4.71	4.56	5.45
σ_M.	.20	.19	.18	.24	.21	.20

The critical ratios of the differences between M-F scores of happy, unhappy, and divorced are as follows, a plus sign indicating a higher mean standard score for the first member of the pair concerned, a minus sign a lower score.

Husbands			Wives		
Happy-unhappy	Happy-divorced	Unhappy-divorced	Happy-unhappy	Happy-divorced	Unhappy-divorced
−1.67	+1.41	+3.24	+0.47	−2.39	−3.08

Here the outstanding difference among men is the markedly masculine rating of the unhappy group as compared with the divorced group, the happy group being about halfway between the two. For the women the outstanding fact is the marked masculinity of the divorced group as compared with either the happy or the unhappy wives.

It would be interesting to know why divorced women and unhappily married men tend to rate more masculine than the other groups with which they are compared. Analysis of the responses made by the three groups to the 420 items of the Strong occupational-interest test and to the 125 items of the Bernreuter personality inventory brings out a number of facts which are in line with the test results for the two groups in question.[1] For example, the item responses of unhappily married men strongly suggest that this group is characterized by less tolerance, less sympathy, less amiability, less interest in uplift activities, and definitely less interest in such cultural things as symphony concerts, modern languages, philosophy, literature, and art. Nearly all of these characteristics would stamp them as masculine rather than feminine. The differentiating traits of the divorced women stand out even more clearly. The item responses of this group indicate that the typical divorced woman differs from both the happily and the unhappily married in being more self-assertive, more ambitious, less docile, more of an individualist, more intellectual, less moved by sympathy, and less interested in social welfare schemes; in short, her personality lacks the element of sweet femininity but may command respect for its masculine qualities of rugged strength and self-sufficiency. It is impossible to say to what extent these characteristics of divorced women are to be attributed to the selective effect of divorce itself, or to what extent they are the result of the broader contacts and outside employment which in the case of women are so likely to follow divorce. Perhaps both factors are involved.

Summary

1. Masculinity and femininity as measured by the M-F test is definitely (though not closely) correlated with introversion-extroversion as measured both by the Laird and by the Conklin tests, masculinity being an extrovert trait, femininity an introvert trait. The relationship holds for both sexes at the college level, but is more marked for men than for women. In the case of delinquent boys no correlation was found between M-F scores and introversion-extroversion as measured by the Neyman-Kohlstedt test.

[1] JOHNSON, WINIFRED BENT, and LEWIS M. TERMAN, Personality characteristics of happily married, unhappily married, and divorced persons, *Char. and Personal.*, 1935, **3**, 290–311.

2. No reliable correlation was found between the M-F scores of delinquent boys and scores on the Cady and Raubenheimer battery of character tests.

3. M-F scores are positively correlated in the case of males with scores on both the Stenquist and the McQuarrie tests of mechanical ability; this correlation does not hold for young women or girls. This is in agreement with the data on interests in Chapter IX.

4. High-scholarship college men are more feminine, low-scholarship men more masculine. This is in contrast to the finding for college students in general that intelligence has a small positive correlation with masculinity (Table 34). The interests of high-scholarship men are more cultural, those of low-scholarship men more mechanical and athletic. Scholarship correlates negatively with M-F score for college women as well as for college men, but this trend is slight as compared with the large (opposite) influence of intelligence. Both trends are persistent and the results are in agreement with data presented in preceding chapters.

5. The M-F scores of athletes tend to be strongly masculine. This is true of both sexes but is especially marked in the case of women. The mean M-F score of 55 outstanding women athletes was by far the most masculine found for any female group of this size.

6. No reliable correlation was found between husband-wife resemblance or difference in M-F score (on a substitute test) and an index of their marital happiness. It appears, however, that men who are unhappily married tend to test reliably more masculine than divorced men, and that divorced women as a group test definitely more masculine than either happy or unhappy wives.

CHAPTER VII

RELATION OF M-F SCORE TO AGE, EDUCATION, AND INTELLIGENCE

The M-F test consistently differentiates the sexes. Any pair of comparable sex groups which if combined form a single homogeneous social unit always yield average scores that are widely divergent for the two sexes. Groups of men test on the average within well-defined limits on the masculine half of the M-F range and groups of women within a narrower range on the feminine half of the scale. However, there are often wide and significant differences between the means of groups within the same sex. In the present chapter we shall discuss some of the factors which influence these placements in the case of the large representative groups which make up the bulk of our test population, particularly the factors of age, education, and intelligence.

THE INFLUENCE OF AGE

Age and M-F score are found to be correlated in youth and in maturity, but the relationship, far from a close one at any period, is reversed in the later as compared with the earlier period of life. Intercomparison of the means of large and homogeneous groups from the early and middle adolescent years shows a fairly well-defined tendency in both sexes for masculinity to be correlated with increase in chronological age (see Figs. 5 and 6). In late adolescence or early maturity a change takes place in the direction of the trend so that as age increases the M-F score becomes less and less masculine until the close of life.

There is a sex difference as to the age at which the reversal of the relationship occurs and also with respect to the amount of age influence. The mean score of males reaches its masculine peak somewhere during the high-school years and from this time onward through early and late maturity it declines steadily toward the feminine end of the scale, though no male group equals in femininity the corresponding female group (see Fig. 5). The mean of females continues to become more and more masculine from early adolescence to early maturity, the peak of masculinity being reached in the college years. From then on

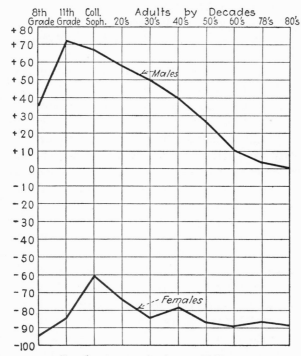

FIG. 5.—Age trends of mean M-F score.

mental masculinity declines slightly and irregularly but unmistakably until old age.

In Fig. 5 it will be noted that the distance between the most masculine and the most feminine mean score is just twice as great for males as for females. In the case of males the difference is about 70 points, the distance between the means of high-school juniors and of eighty-year-old men. The most feminine mean for females, that for the eighth grade, is 35 points below the mean of college women, the most masculine female group. The mean score of men in old age is far below the mean position of the eighth-grade boys, but the final point reached by women in their later decades is not the lowest score norm. The eighth-grade girls are in terms of this test more feminine than the elderly women. From fifty years onward the women score lower on the scale than girls in the junior year of high school, but not so low as eighth-grade girls. Throughout this period their average score is some 25 points more feminine than the average college sophomore woman.

The age trends indicated above may be described as we follow the curves from the point of view of the course of development of the average individual, boy or girl, man or woman. We may think of the endogenous predispositions and the exogenous influences that affect mental masculinity-femininity as operative continuously from birth onward. We have as yet no measures of the trait in early childhood. But as the average child enters adolescence he already registers upon the M-F scale within the range characteristic of his sex. From his last years in the grammar school onward until he reaches approximately his third year of high school the combined effect of nature and nurture makes the boy mentally more and more masculine. The increase in his masculinity from the fourteenth to the sixteenth or seventeenth year is considerable. During the later high-school years, however, the boy's score ceases to gain in masculinity and by the college sophomore year it registers in the feminine direction. The difference is not large, less than once its standard deviation, but decade by decade the modification continues. In the thirties the eighth-grade score point is passed. Each decade up to the sixties brings a larger drop than the decade preceding. In his seventies and eighties the average man in our test population has traversed about half of the distance that in the adolescent period divides the sexes in respect of mental masculinity and femininity.

The course of the M-F trait in the average woman's life is rather different from this. In early adolescence she, like her brother, is becoming mentally more masculine. The difference between her scores at fourteen years and at sixteen or seventeen years is, however, considerably less than in the case of the boy. This is not mathematically a significant difference in our data. But after the third high-school year and if the girl goes on to college her score becomes increasingly masculine and the difference between her M-F score in grammar or high school and in the college years is statistically significant. The average college girl registers 35 points more masculine on the M-F scale than the average eighth-grade girl, the difference being six times its standard deviation. In the same period the boy has gained 27 points but has lost 5 of them. By the time he is a college sophomore he is 22 points above the average eighth-grade boy. The latter difference is three times its standard deviation. The woman declines from her peak of mental masculinity reached during college days until in her sixties she is only 6 points more masculine than the average eighth-grade girl and is 29 points below her masculine high point. At or near this position she tends to remain to the end of her life.

The conspicuous contrasts between the sexes with respect to the influence of age upon M-F score are (1) in the extent of the initial rise from eighth grade to the third high-school year; (2) in the direction of the trend from the third high-school year to the second college year; (3) in the extent of change in score at that period; (4) in the age at which the turning point in development of the M-F trait occurs; (5) in the extent of decrease in masculinity from twenty years of age onward. It is noteworthy that at all ages and whatever the trends, in any comparable pair of groups the sexes retain their characteristic positions relative to each other. The scores for the sexes diverge more at the high-school than at the grammar-school age because, although both sexes have become mentally more masculine than before, the boys have gained more than the girls. The sex difference is less in the college period than in the high-school period because the men have become more feminine, the women more masculine.[1] From this age onward the sexes differ less and less

[1] The possibility of college acting as a selective factor should not be overlooked; perhaps the more feminine type of girl is more likely than the masculine type to abandon her education at this point with a view to early marriage.

because of the feminizing of the men's scores. Both sexes are becoming continually less masculine, but the change is more marked in men than in women. At eighty years of age they are closer together than at any other period. The distance here is 89 points as compared with 157 points at the high-school age.

Statistical evidence of the relationship of M-F score to age is in the form of (1) comparisons of the means of age groups in terms of the ratio between their difference and the standard deviation

TABLE 22.—COMPARISON OF MEAN M-F SCORES OF HOMOGENEOUS GROUPS AT DIFFERENT AGE LEVELS (MALES)

Groups	No. of cases	Age	M-F score		
			Mean score	S.D.M	Diff. / S.D.diff.
Eighth grade (unselected)......	95	14+	+45.6	5.42⎫	−3.59⎫
High-school juniors (unselected)	79	16+	+72.7	5.25⎬	⎬−3.19
College sophomores (unselected).	130	20+	+67.4	4.18⎭	+.78⎭
Eighth grade (unselected)......	95	14+	+45.6	5.42⎫	
Adults: Grade-school education				⎬	+3.73
(unselected)...............	208	20 to 90	+21.8	3.40⎭	
High-school juniors (unselected).	79	16+	+72.7	5.25⎫	
Adults: High-school education				⎬	+4.54
(unselected)...............	344	20 to 90	+45.4	2.92⎭	
College sophomores (unselected).	130	20+	+67.4	4.18⎫	
Adults: College education (unse-				⎬	+3.65
lected).....................	531	20 to 90	+50.4	2.05⎭	
Gifted boys..................	79	16+	+66.2	5.28⎫	−1.99⎫
Superior college students.......	45	18 to 25	+79.5	4.12⎬	⎬+3.81
Who's Who men	30	30 to 50	+31.1	7.55⎭	+5.63⎭
Younger delinquents...........	124	15	+43.7	4.10⎫	−1.89⎫
Older delinquents..............	131	17+	+55.7	4.89⎬	⎬−2.78
Adult army prisoners..........	44	26+	+66.2	6.97⎭	−1.23⎭
Catholic student priests........	46	21	+19.4	5.14⎫	+.99⎫
Protestant theological students..	53	26	+ 9.0	9.12⎬	⎬+.99
Clergymen and ministers (prot-				⎬	−.35⎭
estant)	63	20 to 90	+12.6	4.52⎭	

of the difference (Tables 22, 23, and 24) and (2) correlations between age and M-F score (Table 26). Both kinds of evidence are available for all parts of the curve. In connection with the correlation material an attempt has been made to isolate from the age factor certain other influences, such as those of mental age and marital experience.

We shall present first the data for each sex derived from the comparison of means. The differences have been found between successive means from the youngest to the oldest groups and the ratios of these to their respective standard deviations have been computed. In general we may regard a difference as definitely significant and indicative of a clear trend when it is

TABLE 23.—COMPARISON OF THE MEAN M-F SCORES OF HOMOGENEOUS GROUPS
AT DIFFERENT AGE LEVELS (FEMALES)

Groups	No. of cases	Age	M-F score		
			Mean score	S.D.$_M$	$\dfrac{\text{Diff.}}{\text{S.D.}_{\text{diff.}}}$
Eighth grade................	84	14+	−95.3	4.62 ⎱	− .57 ⎱
High-school juniors...........	86	16+	−84.8	4.77 ⎰	⎱ −5.99
College sophomores...........	130	20+	−60.8	3.43 ⎰	−4.08 ⎰
Eighth grade................	84	14+	−95.3	4.62 ⎱	−1.72
Adults: Grade-school education.	287	20 to 90	−86.2	2.53 ⎰	
High-school juniors...........	86	16+	−84.8	4.77 ⎱	− .02
Adults: high-school education...	820	20 to 90	−84.7	1.47 ⎰	
College sophomores...........	130	20+	−60.8	3.43 ⎱	+3.68
Adults: College education......	760	20 to 90	−74.7	1.60 ⎰	
Gifted girls.................	81	16+	−57.3	5.10 ⎱	−3.13 ⎱
Superior college students.......	92	20+	−36.3	4.38 ⎰	⎱ −1.19
Who's Who women...........	25	30 to 50	−45.5	8.47 ⎰	+2.12 ⎰
Student nurses...............	78	21+	−63.3	4.47 ⎱	+ .15
Adult nurses.................	64	20 to 90	−64.4	5.27 ⎰	
Music students..............	50	18 to 25	−71.3	5.60 ⎱	+1.89
Musicians and music teachers...	41	20 to 90	−85.8	5.27 ⎰	

as great as three times its standard deviation. When the difference continues to be even twice its standard deviation in successive groupings a trend is fairly definitely indicated. We

TABLE 24.—AGE DIFFERENCES IN M-F SCORES OF ADULTS

Single decades	Male				Female			
	No. of cases	Mean	S.D.$_M$	Diff./S.D.$_{diff}$	No. of cases	Mean	S.D.$_M$	Diff./S.D.$_{diff}$
20's	342	+57.9	2.76		604	− 74.2	1.82	
				}+2.04				}+3.90
30's	330	+49.5	3.05	}+2.97	488	− 84.5	1.93	}+1.36
				}+2.05				}−1.91
40's	178	+39.7	3.64	}+4.24	328	− 78.4	2.54	}+ .64
				}+2.28				}+2.28
50's	108	+26.6	4.46	}+4.68	234	− 86.5	2.50	}+2.71
				}+2.37				}+ .66
60's	75	+10.8	4.99	}+2.81	153	− 89.1	3.02	}− .15
				}+ .75				}− .55
70's	38	+ 3.7	8.03	}+ .87	100	− 86.5	3.70	}− .43
				}± .26				}+ .21
80's	6	+ .5	9.13		18	− 88.4	8.24	
90's					1	−121.0		
Combined decades								
20's & 30's	672	+53.8	2.06		1092	− 78.8	1.34	
				}+2.45				}+1.60
30's & 40's	508	+46.0	2.37	}+5.39	816	− 82.0	1.54	}+1.32
				}+2.04				}− .11
40's & 50's	286	+34.8	2.85		562	− 81.8	1.82	
				}+3.31				}+2.17
50's & 60's	183	+20.1	3.39	}+5.75	387	− 87.5	1.93	}+2.13
				}+2.37				}+ .18
60's & 70's	113	+ 8.4	3.60		253	− 88.1	2.34	
				}+ .66				}− .23
70's & 80's	44	+ 3.2	7.04		119	− 87.2	3.37	

have made combinations in our groupings where the trend was suggested in this way, continuing the combining process until the evidence was convincing either for or against the apparent tendency.

Our analysis proceeds from the youngest groups to the oldest. The first step shows an increase of 27.1 points in score between eighth-grade and high-school junior boys, or 3.59 S.D.$_{\text{diff.}}$ (Table 22). The next step, a drop of 5.3 points from the high-school norm to the college sophomores is less than its S.D. and therefore only meaningful in connection with other results. It is worthy of note that the pronounced change in score before age twenty-five occurs between the eighth grade and the junior year of high school and that the former group is significantly less masculine as compared with the latter and also as compared with the college norm. High-school juniors and college sophomores, however, are not significantly divergent.

From the turning point, the mean score of the high-school junior boys, the line of direction is toward the feminine end of the scale. Pursuing the course of the total population group (Table 24) we find each successive decade position less masculine than the preceding one. The difference between the means for the high-school junior boys and the twenty-year-old men is almost twice (1.9) its S.D. The means for succeeding decades up to the sixties differ by something over 2.0 S.D.$_{\text{diff.}}$. From the sixties to the seventies the curve still falls in the feminine direction, and similarly from the seventies to the eighties, but in these cases with their small populations the differences are less than their respective S.D.'s. Enlarging populations by combining groups anywhere along the line gives statistically reliable differences between stages. It is to be noted that we are following here the total population group only. The separate groups of adults representing three educational levels will be considered later.

Turning now to the norms for the girls and women we find a similar but statistically less significant tendency. The first step, from the eighth grade to the high-school-junior level (Table 23) is not statistically reliable. The second step, from the high-school-junior to the college sophomore level, 24.0 points, is more than 4 S.D.$_{\text{diff.}}$, whereas the corresponding step for the boys is not significant statistically and is in the opposite direction. The step from college sophomores to twenty-year-old women

combining all degrees of education is 13.4 M-F points or 3.45
S.D.$_{\text{diff.}}$. In the general population group (Table 24) that from

TABLE 25.—COMPARISON OF MEAN SCORES OF MALE AND FEMALE GROUPS AT
SUCCESSIVE AGE PERIODS

	Mean	S.D.$_M$	Diff.	$\dfrac{\text{Diff.}}{\text{S.D.}_{\text{diff.}}}$
School and college groups:				
14⅓ years (Eighth-grade pupils)				
Male	+45.6	5.42⎫	+140.9	+19.8
Female	−95.3	4.62⎭		
16½ years (High-school junior pupils)				
Male	+72.7	5.25⎫	+157.5	+22.2
Female	−84.8	4.77⎭		
20½ years (College sophomore students)				
Male	+67.4	4.18⎫	+128.2	+23.7
Female	−60.8	3.43⎭		
Decade groups of adults:				
20's				
Male	+57.9	2.76⎫	+132.0	+39.9
Female	−74.2	1.82⎭		
30's				
Male	+49.5	3.05⎫	+134.0	+37.1
Female	−84.5	1.93⎭		
40's				
Male	+39.7	3.64⎫	+118.1	+26.6
Female	−78.4	2.54⎭		
50's				
Male	+26.6	4.46⎫	+113.1	+22.1
Female	−86.5	2.50⎭		
60's				
Male	+10.8	4.99⎫	+99.9	+17.1
Female	−89.1	3.02⎭		
70's				
Male	+ 3.7	8.03⎫	+90.2	+10.2
Female	−86.5	3.70⎭		
80's				
Male	+ 0.5	9.13⎫	+89.0	+ 7.2
Female	−88.4	8.24⎭		

the twenties to the thirties is 3.9 S.D.$_{\text{diff.}}$. The step from the
thirties to the forties is in the reverse direction and is almost

2 S.D.$_{\text{diff}}$.. From the forties to the fifties, the trend is again feminine and the distance is 2.3 S.D.$_{\text{diff}}$.. From the fifties to the sixties the feminine tendency continues but the difference is less than its standard error. The remaining steps, one upward from the sixties to the seventies and one downward from the seventies to the eighties, are small and unreliable. Irregularity is obviously a feature of the course of the women's decade norms. Combination into successively larger groups, however, shows differences between younger, middle, and older adult groups that are at least twice their respective S.D.'s; and comparison of persons under fifty with those over sixty years 4.7 its S.D.

The two most important differences between the curves for the sexes are again emphasized by the statistical treatment: (1) the difference in the age level at which the curves turn from their early masculine to a feminine direction, and (2) the range from the most masculine to the most feminine score in the life of each sex. The latter sex difference is emphasized statistically by the fact that the successive steps in the male curve are so much greater, so much more consistently in the same direction, and so much more reliable.

The differences between corresponding sex groups are indicated in Table 25. These show the three younger sex groups differing by 128 to 157 M-F points; 20 or more times the standard errors. The adults compared by decades show the largest sex differences in the twenties and thirties (over 130 M-F points with critical ratios of 37 and 40), but all the sex differences are significant even among the older, smaller populations. Those at the forties and fifties are more than 110 M-F points; the sixties, the seventies, and the eighties have differences of 89 to 100 M-F points. In spite of the modifying influence of age the M-F scale continues to differentiate the central tendencies of the two sexes from youth to old age.

We may turn now to the correlational evidence bearing on the relationship between age and M-F score (Table 26). Correlations are available for six groups of boys and for seven groups of girls, together with a correlation for each sex from two of the respective groups combined into a single population. The correlations in this age range are all quite small. The coefficients for the boys include only one significant value and it is for a very small and probably not unselected population, the orphans. Eighth-grade boys, high-school juniors, gifted boys, younger and

TABLE 26.—CORRELATIONS BETWEEN M-F SCORES AND CHRONOLOGICAL AGE IN YOUNGER POPULATIONS

Male groups	No. of cases	Mean C.A. Yr. mo.	Age range	Correlation between C.A. and M-F scores	Correlation between C.A. and M-F score with M.A. constant	Correlation between M-F score and M.A. with C.A. constant
Orphans	15	14-2	11-11 to 16-7	+.60 ± .12	+.55 ± .13	−.20 ± .16
Eighth grade	95	14-4	12 to 17	+.03 ± .07	..	..
High-school juniors	79	16-8½	14 to 21	−.03 ± .08	..	..
Combined grade and high school	173	15-4	12 to 21	+.14 ± .06	+.08 ± .05	+.15 ± .05

					Correlation between C.A. and M-F score with educational placement constant	Correlation between educational placement and M-F score with C.A. constant
Gifted boys	79	16-9	11 to 20	+.08 ± .08	+.12 ± .08	.00 ± .08
Young delinquents	124	15	12 to 17	+.02 ± .06	.00 ± .06	+.05 ± .06
Older delinquents	131	17-6	10 to 20	+.05 ± .06	+.04 ± .06	+.13 ± .06
Superior college men	97	21	18 to 25	.00 ± .07	..	..
Superior college men with high scholarship	46	21	19 to 25	−.15 ± .10	..	..
Superior college men with low scholarship	46	21	19 to 25	−.13 ± .10	..	..

Female groups					Correlation between C.A. and M-F score with M.A. constant	Correlation between M-F score and M.A. with C.A. constant
Orphans	13	14-9	12-1 to 17-2	+.39 ± .16	..	..
Eighth grade	84	14-2	12 to 19	+.28 ± .07	+.29 ± .07	+.10 ± .07
High-school juniors	86	16-5	14 to 21	−.08 ± .07	..	..
Combined grade and high school	170	15-3	12 to 21	+.16 ± .05	+.07 ± .05	+.14 ± .05

					Correlation between C.A. and M-F score with educational placement constant	Correlation between educational placement and M-F score with C.A. constant
Private school	28	15-11	13 to 19	+.31 ± .11	+.02 ± .13	+.35 ± .11
Gifted girls	81	16-2	13 to 19	+.20 ± .07	+.10 ± .07	+.05 ± .07
Superior college women	91	20-2	18 to 24	−.03 ± .08	..	..
Student nurses	78	21-1½	18 to 25	−.15 ± .08	..	..

older delinquents, and even the combined grade and high-school groups show correlations that are with one exception no larger than their probable errors.

For the girls also the coefficients are low, though not generally so low as for the boys. Two of them are three times the P.E. and two others almost reach this criterion of reliability. The correlations between M-F score and age seem from these figures to be significant in the eighth grade, and in the combined eighth-grade and high-school group. They appear to be nearly so for the orphans, the private-school girls, and the gifted girls. Apparently a slight but fairly persistent relationship is indicated in the case of the girls, whereas for the boys there is barely a suggestion of relationship.

The single significant coefficient in the case of the boys is that for the small group of orphans. The mean M-F score of this group is so unusual for this age in its intense masculinity as to suggest that many of the individuals in the group may have been responding to a special social influence at the time the test was taken. Several of them, especially the older ones, were antagonistic to the management of their Home at the time the test was given and behaved in an aggressively hostile manner during the test. This might account not only for the unusually masculine mean score but also for the correlation with chronological age. For this reason and also because of the small size of the group the mean and the correlation can be given little weight. The only other correlation of any consequence among the boys' groups is that for the combined eighth-grade and high-school groups. The coefficient, .14 ± .06, although small is of interest because the population in question represents the most considerable age range analyzed in this connection by the correlation method. We have probed its possible significance by deriving the correlation between age and M-F score with mental age constant and find it to be negligible, +.08 ± .05. The relation, however, between M-F score and mental age, with age constant, is +.15 ± .05, indicating a small but probably true correlation. The negligible correlation for the high-school-junior group is to be expected, as the trend of development of the M-F score is altered at about this age.   Among college men the relationship between age and M-F score is also negligible.

More detailed analysis of the coefficients for the girls' groups gives evidence of an age correlation, but does not make clear whether this is due to age alone or to some related factor.   In the eighth-grade group the relation between age and M-F score appears to be a genuine one, not attributable to the mental-age factor.   In the combined eighth-grade and high-school group, however, mental age appears to contribute the larger influence. Thus it seems that the relationship has shifted between the eighth grade and the third high-school year.   Among private-school girls and gifted girls there is a suggestion of correlation between age and M-F score.   This is found for the first named to be chiefly associated with grade placement, perhaps a measure of mental age; for the latter also mental age is probably account-able.   Among the older school groups of girls no correlation between age and M F score appears.   This is, of course, to be expected in view of the fact that the direction of the trend in M-F score is turning among the girls at about the age represented by the groups in question.

Summarizing the correlational data for the younger groups, we find that the relationship between age and M-F score is positive but very slight in the regular school groups of adolescent boys living under normal home conditions, and that this relationship is probably largely a matter of mental age.   Among older adolescent boys the relationship is negligible, and in the college years also it is not demonstrable.   The M-F scores of girls in the teens apparently correlate slightly with age.   It is not clear that this is attributable to the influence of mental age, though there is some indication that mental age is involved. With college girls there does not seem to be any clear relationship between M-F score and age.

In addition to the correlations between age and M-F score for the younger groups, coefficients between age and M-F score have also been derived for both sexes in the populations of adults who had been married and who reported having had all or part of a high-school education.   The group in question is called the high-school adult group. As was to be expected from the comparison of age means, significant correlations were found for both sexes, though the coefficient for the women's group was exceedingly small. They are: for the men, $r = -.26 \pm .04$; for the women, $r = -.09 \pm .02$. The scores of the unmarried members of the same educational group were also correlated with age. The coefficients for these were as follows: for the men, $r = -.12 \pm .09$; for the women, $r = -.11 \pm .06$. It should be mentioned that in the case of the single men the age range was much narrowed. There was only one unmarried man over thirty-one years of age, but the ages of the single women extended from twenty to eighty years of age as did those of both married groups.

In order to test whether married life itself was the chief factor in the feminine trend with increasing age, the correlations between M-F score and the number of years married were calculated. They were found to be as follows: for the men, $r = -.28 \pm .05$; for the women, $r = -.07 \pm .03$. Partial coefficients were then derived between age and M-F score with the number of years of married life constant. These resulted as follows: for the men, $r = -.02 \pm .05$; for the women, $r = -.06 \pm .03$. The converse coefficients (M-F score correlated with the number of years of married life, age being constant) were as follows: for the men, $r = -.11 \pm .05$; for the women, $r = +.01 \pm .04$.

Reviewing the correlations between age and M-F score among married and unmarried adults of high-school education and the correlations between number of years married and M-F score in the married part of the group, it appears that, among the married at least, age and M-F score are somewhat correlated negatively in both sexes, but that in the case of the women the relationship is very slight. As far as married life is concerned, while for the men the number of years thus spent is slightly but significantly correlated negatively with mental masculinity there is no significant correlation either positive or negative in the case of the women. When the element of age is made constant the correlation with number of years married disappears for the men.

Summarizing all of the data with respect to age and M-F score, we find that there is a demonstrable relationship between these two in both sexes from the earliest to the latest age for which scores are available. We have discovered further that the direction of the influence changes, during adolescence for the men, in early maturity for the women, and that whereas before the change age correlated positively with M-F scores, after the change the correlation is a negative one. Possibly mental age is involved in the positive correlation in childhood and also in the negative correlation in later maturity. It is suggested by the data that the correlation with age is greater for the younger girls than for the younger boys. The correlation in later years is greater for the men than for the women.

In childhood and youth both boys and girls become mentally more and more masculine as they proceed through the later grammar grades and high school. Thereafter the boys become mentally more feminine, while the girls wax increasingly masculine until some time during the college years. Then they too begin gradually to lose their masculinity, although unlike the men they never again become quite so feminine mentally as they were before they left the grammar school. In contrast to this the men are on the average never again after their thirties as masculine in this test as they were in the eighth grade, in high school, or in college.

The most striking contrast between the sexes is in the greater modification of the men from decade to decade, as compared to the slight alteration in the women during the same periods. The limits between which the mean scores of females register are set by the beginning and the end of adolescence. Those for males are set by middle adolescence and late senescence. Apparently man draws nearer and nearer to woman's norm, whereas woman deviates little from her fundamental position.

Finally it seems important in view of the changes that do take place to reiterate that in no case does the mean of either sex pass over the mid-line between the sexes. At no age do corresponding groups from the two sexes ever approach each other in mean

M-F score, although *individuals* of either sex may score far within the range of the other.

TABLE 27.—SCORE DISTRIBUTIONS OF ADULT POPULATION BY AGE DECADES

Score	20–29 M	20–29 F	30–39 M	30–39 F	40–49 M	40–49 F	50–59 M	50–59 F	60–69 M	60–69 F	70–89 M	70–89 F	Total M	Total F
221– 240														
201– 220														
181– 200	3		2										5	
161– 180	2												2	
141– 160	10		7		3								20	
121– 140	19		11		6		3						39	
101– 120	37		28		13	1	3		2				83	1
81– 100	41	2	44		14		5		3		1		108	2
61– 80	64	3	42		22	3	14		3		3		148	6
41– 60	43	3	46	1	29		15	1	9		5		147	5
21– 40	49	8	45	1	28	2	23	1	16		2		163	12
1– 20	30	11	40	10	25	6	15	1	12	3	4		126	31
0–– 19	21	39	20	16	18	18	14	6	10	4	10	2	93	85
− 20–– 39	14	56	15	44	13	34	7	19	8	4	4	9	61	166
− 40–– 59	3	97	7	70	4	43	6	27	5	20	2	11	27	268
− 60–– 79	1	100	3	74	2	55	2	44	3	27	2	17	13	317
− 80–– 99	4	106	3	91		58		44	1	35		24	8	358
−100––119	1	90		79	1	52		51		28		15	2	315
−120––139		53		60		32	1	19		15		22	1	201
−140––159		25		26		13		18		11	1	5	1	98
−160––179		6		8		9		3		4		2		32
−180––199		4		7		1								12
−200––219		1				1								2
−220––239				1										1
Mean M	58.16		48.75		39.71		26.61		12.44		1.68		44.27	
Mean F		−74.17		−84.50		−77.98		−85.91		−88.57		−91.00		−81.02
S.D. M	51.15		51.27		48.53		46.31		43.23		48.31		51.68	
S.D. F		45.19		42.61		45.91		38.31		37.82		36.35		43.22
N M	342		313		178		108		72		34		1047	
N F		604		488		328		234		151		107		1912

Decade comparisons in Chapter VII and references in other chapters to the means for the total population show slightly different values from those in this table. The discrepancy, in no case significant, is due to the exclusion or inclusion of small special groups.

In Table 27 are distributions of scores for unselected adults of each sex by decades from the twenties through the eighties.

The Influence of Education

The course of mean M-F scores of typical groups has been followed from youth to old age. We have seen it in both sexes rise in the early years toward a masculine peak and then fall gradually, as age advances, toward a feminine limit. In viewing the changes from grammar school to high school and from high school to college the question naturally arises whether in the mature groups the M-F score might be found correlated with education as well as with age. Only a few correlations are available on this point. The chief evidence is contained in a comparison of the means at given ages for groups of varying amounts of education. The means for the younger school groups range themselves according to the level of education reached. We have subdivided the adult population of each sex into three groups: (1) persons whose education went no further than the eighth grade, (2) those who had all or part of a high-school education or its equivalent, and (3) those with all or part of a college course. Examination of the curves for each of these three educational levels shows that they tend severally to follow the course of the group as a whole. Comparing the means for these groups we have computed the differences between them at successive ages and the reliability of the differences.

In Fig. 6 we observe certain striking and persistent features in the mean M-F scores at the three educational levels. For the men the differences between the adult populations of high-school and of college education are generally insignificant; the scores of the grammar-school group show a decided tendency to be persistently and, for combined groups, significantly more feminine than the scores of high-school or college men. In the case of the women, the adults of high-school and of grammar-school education do not differ significantly except at the seventh decade, but the women of college education diverge from both the other educational groups regularly and significantly. An attempt to interpret this sex difference may make it more meaningful.

It appears that the greatest masculinizing influence in boys (1) is present and becomes operative at this time in those individuals who pursue their education beyond the eighth grade to the high-school-junior level or (2) is developed in them through exogenous pressures at this period. Whether inherent

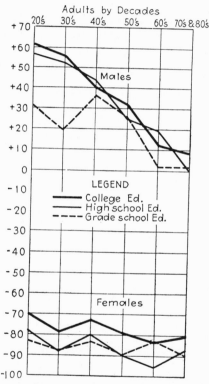

Fig. 6.—Age trends of mean M-F score in relation to schooling.

or induced, the mental masculinizing that occurs at this period persists in its expression in terms of the M-F score throughout life. Somewhat similarly in the case of the girls, the effect appears chiefly in those who pursue part or all of a college course. It appears most pronouncedly at the period between the third high-school year and the second college year and its effect as expressed in the M-F score persists thereafter throughout life.

Girls who leave school at or before the close of the grammar grades and even those who continue through part or all of the high-school years do not at any age average as masculine as college women.

Statistical evidence for the educational differences consists chiefly in comparisons between the averages. A few correlations between M-F scores and educational status are available (Table 28) but these are usually of slight interest in the present connection because they are for atypical groups and for short ranges. So far as they go the correlations offer no contradiction to the

TABLE 28.—CORRELATIONS BETWEEN M-F SCORE AND SCHOOL GRADE REACHED

Groups	No. of cases	Correlation between M-F score and school grade	Correlation between M-F score and school grade with C.A. constant
Boys' groups:			
Young delinquents............	124	+.05 ± .06	+.05 ± .06
Older delinquents............	131	+.14 ± .06	+.13 ± .06
Gifted boys.................	74	+.01 ± .08	.00 ± .08
Men 25 to 29 years old........	126	+.10 ± .06	
Girls' groups:			
Private-school girls...........	28	+.45 ± .11	+.35 ± .11
Gifted girls.................	80	+.18 ± .07	−.05 ± .07
Women 25 to 29 years old.....	175	+.27 ± .05	

data already given. The coefficients for both the delinquent groups and for the two gifted populations are positive but small. They and possibly the coefficients for the private-school group may be disregarded since they are based on nonrepresentative groups and offer no contradiction to the manifest trends. The correlations for the two young adult populations are probably worthy of consideration since they represent the scores of persons who are just entering maturity, who have generally reached the end of their educational training, and who are drawn from all three educational levels. For the men the correlation is +.10 ± .06, which is not significant. For the women, however, $r = +.27 \pm .05$, suggesting a small but probably actual relationship.

We may consider next the mean scores of certain school groups ranging from the preadolescent to the early adult years (Tables 22 and 23). The eighth-grade boys, as we have seen, are definitely more feminine than high-school-junior boys or college sophomores. Both differences are more than 3 S.D.$_{\text{diff}}$.. Unfortunately for purposes of calculation the comparison shows age as well as education as a variable. Young delinquents whose age is intermediate between the eighth-grade boys and the high-school

TABLE 29.—COMPARISON OF M-F SCORES OF ADULT POPULATION AT THREE EDUCATIONAL LEVELS (DECADE PERIODS)

Group	Male					Female				
	No. of cases	Mean	S.D.$_M$	Diff. / S.D.$_{\text{diff}}$		No. of cases	Mean	S.D.$_M$	Diff. / S.D.$_{\text{diff}}$	
20's:										
Grade.....	21	+31.4	10.56 }			28	−83.1	8.63 }		
High school	117	+56.6	5.07 }	−2.15 }	−2.69	257	−78.1	2.76 }	−.54 }	−1.43
College....	204	+61.3	3.36 }	−.76 }		319	−70.2	2.55 }	−2.12 }	
30's:										
Grade.....	46	+19.2	7.08 }			54	−88.0	6.28 }		
High school	113	+52.1	5.06 }	−3.78 }	−4.63	208	−88.2	2.96 }	−.02 }	−1.30
College....	164	+55.9	3.55 }	−.61 }		204	−79.0	2.88 }	−2.21 }	
40's:										
Grade.....	44	+36.0	7.70 }			70	−83.2	5.76 }		
High school	44	+43.2	7.39 }	−.68 }	−.43	118	−80.0	4.00 }	−.59 }	−1.37
College....	83	+39.9	5.16 }	+.37 }		109	−73.0	4.71 }	−1.14 }	
50's:										
Grade.....	55	+25.8	5.93 }			52	−89.5	5.22 }		
High school	27	+24.6	7.97 }	+.12 }	−.59	110	−89.9	3.41 }	+.06 }	−1.44
College....	46	+31.4	7.38 }	−.63 }		72	−79.2	4.84 }	−1.80 }	
60's:										
Grade.....	28	+ 1.9	9.55 }			48	−82.8	5.31 }		
High school	29	+18.8	6.86 }	−1.43 }	−.73	74	−95.4	4.17 }	+1.87 }	−.10
College....	18	+11.6	9.23 }	+.62 }		31	−83.7	6.90 }	−1.46 }	
70's and 80's:										
Grade.....	14	+ 1.9	9.19 }			37	−90.0	6.19 }		
High school	14	− .9	17.46 }	+.14 }	−.48	57	−87.0	4.91 }	−.38 }	+1.08
College....	16	+ 8.0	8.64 }	−.46 }		25	−80.7	5.99 }	−.82 }	

juniors but whose average school grade is much nearer the former than the latter, perhaps even below the former in terms of accomplishment, rate in M-F score not more masculine, but a shade more feminine than the eighth-grade boys. The older delinquents, whose chronological age is beyond that of the high-school juniors but whose educational status is near the eighth-grade level, are 17 M-F points below the high-school norm; a difference that is 2.4 S.D._{diff.}. When the two delinquent groups are combined their average age approximates that of the high-school-junior group, although their educational standing, cer-

TABLE 30.—COMPARISON OF M-F SCORES OF ADULT POPULATION AT THREE EDUCATIONAL LEVELS (TWO-DECADE PERIODS)

Group	Male				Female			
	No. of cases	Mean	S.D.$_M$	$\dfrac{\text{Diff.}}{\text{S.D.}_{diff.}}$	No. of cases	Mean	S.D.$_M$	$\dfrac{\text{Diff.}}{\text{S.D.}_{diff.}}$
20's and 30's:								
Grade.....	67	+23.0	5.92	−4.57	82	−86.3	5.09	− .68
High school	230	+54.4	3.49	} −5.59	465	−82.6	2.03	} −2.33
College....	368	+58.9	2.45	−1.05	523	−73.6	1.93	−3.21
30's and 40's:								
Grade.....	90	+27.4	5.29	−3.29	124	−85.3	4.26	− .03
High school	157	+49.6	4.20	} −3.81	326	−85.5	2.36	} −1.70
College....	247	+50.5	2.96	− .17	313	−76.9	2.50	−2.49
40's and 50's:								
Grade.....	99	+30.3	4.78	− .79	122	−85.9	4.00	− .23
High school	71	+36.1	5.59	} −1.03	228	−84.8	2.67	} −1.98
College....	129	+36.9	4.25	− .10	181	−75.5	3.43	−2.49
50's and 60's:								
Grade.....	83	+17.7	5.23	− .56	100	−86.3	3.74	+1.27
High school	56	+21.6	4.49	} −1.01	184	−92.1	2.65	} − .87
College....	64	+25.8	6.01	− .57	103	−80.6	3.98	−1.90
60's and 70's:								
Grade.....	39	+ 2.3	6.57	−1.14	79	−86.0	4.22	+1.17
High school	42	+11.9	5.27	} − .94	121	−92.3	3.40	} − .69
College....	32	+11.1	6.70	+ .09	53	−81.6	4.78	−1.83
70's and 80's:								
Grade.....	14	+ 1.9	9.19	+ .14	37	−90.0	6.19	− .38
High school	14	− .9	17.46	} − .48	57	−87.0	4.91	} −1.08
College....	16	+ 8.0	8.64	− .46	25	−80.7	5.99	− .82

tainly in terms of achievement, is not above the eighth-grade level. The difference between the two groups of equal age but of divergent educational status is 23 scale points and considerably more than 3 S.D.$_{diff}$. Similarly the gifted boys, younger than the older delinquents, but averaging four years beyond them in educational advancement, score several points above them. That they do not score so far or so significantly above them as the high-school juniors is probably, at least in part, to be attributed to the fact that in the gifted boys the turning point associated with greater maturity has already been

TABLE 31.—COMPARISON OF M-F SCORES OF ADULT POPULATION AT THREE EDUCATIONAL LEVELS (THREE-DECADE PERIODS)

Group	Male				Female			
	No. of cases	Mean	S.D.$_M$	$\dfrac{\text{Diff.}}{\text{S.D.}_{diff}}$	No. of cases	Mean	S.D.$_M$	$\dfrac{\text{Diff.}}{\text{S.D.}_{diff}}$
20's, 30's, 40's:								
Grade......	111	+28.2	4.74	-4.26 } -5.19	152	-84.9	3.82	$-.66$ } -2.69
High school.	274	+52.6	3.74	$-.70$ }	583	-82.1	1.81	-3.36 }
College.....	451	+55.4	2.24		632	-73.5	1.79	
40's, 50's, 60's:								
Grade......	127	+24.0	4.40	-1.12 } -1.64	170	-85.0	3.24	$+.59$ } -1.86
High school.	100	+31.1	4.51	$-.45$ }	302	-87.4	2.27	-2.78 }
College.....	147	+33.8	3.96		212	-76.7	3.11	
60's, 70's, 80's:								
Grade......	42	+ 1.9	6.42	-1.06 } $-.88$	85	-86.0	4.05	$+1.13$ } $-.58$
High school.	43	+12.4	7.47	$+.25$ }	131	-91.8	3.20	-1.67 }
College.....	34	+ 9.9	6.36		56	-82.4	4.67	

passed and in terms of mental maturity they should perhaps be compared in M-F standing with college sophomores rather than with high-school students of equal age. That there are other trends operative will be brought out in succeeding chapters.

From the twenties onward the decade norms for the three educational levels in the above tables show persistent and fairly regular divergence. In the twenties and thirties the norms of adults of grade-school education appear to diverge significantly from the high-school and college norms. Norms for combined decades show the differences to be reliable in the earlier decades and the trends to be persistent thereafter. Finally three combined groups including respectively the adult populations at the three educational levels show differences with large critical ratios.

TABLE 32.—COMPARISON OF M-F SCORES OF ADULT POPULATION AT THREE EDUCATIONAL LEVELS (ALL AGES COMBINED)

Group	Male			Female		
	Mean	S.D.$_M$	$\dfrac{\text{Diff.}}{\text{S.D.}_{\text{diff.}}}$	Mean	S.D.$_M$	$\dfrac{\text{Diff.}}{\text{S.D.}_{\text{diff.}}}$
Grade..................	+21.8	3.40 } −5.27 }		−86.2	2.53 } −.48 }	
High school.............	+45.4	2.92 } −7.00		−84.7	1.47 } −3.82	
College.................	+50.4	2.05 } −1.40 }		−74.7	1.60 } −4.62 }	
General population........	+36.5	2.28 } +3.60		−85.1	1.27 } + .37	
Grade..................	+21.8	3.40 }		−86.2	2.53 }	
General population........	+36.5	2.28 } −2.41		−85.1	1.27 } − .19	
High school.............	+45.4	2.92 }		−84.7	1.47 }	
General population........	+36.5	2.28 } −4.53		−85.1	1.27 } −5.10	
College.................	+50.4	2.05 }		−74.7	1.60 }	

It may have been noted that a number of selected adult male groups of unquestionably superior education score in scale positions unwarranted by the educational trends just noted. In the last section of this chapter (the relation of intelligence to M-F score) and in later chapters some of the other influences to which these divergences must be attributed will be discussed. For the present the comparison is between typical, representative, unselected populations of adults at the three educational levels in question. These comparisons show that for the men there are fairly definite trends of score divergence in relation to education.

For the women the differences between the educational groups are not as a rule as large as for the men, but they are as persistent and tend generally in the same direction. With both sexes a higher educational level is associated with greater masculinity in the younger years and throughout life. As we have seen, the larger differences for the men are between the grade-school groups on the one hand and the high-school and college groups on the other; for the women they are between the grade- and high-school groups on the one hand and the college groups on the other. This sex difference is statistically valid.

The mean of eighth-grade girls is 10.5 M-F points more feminine than that of high-school-junior girls, but the difference is less than half its standard error. The difference between the high-school juniors and the college sophomores is 24 M-F points, or 4.1 S.D.$_{diff}$. The difference between the eighth-grade group and college sophomores is 28.1 M-F points, or 6.0 S.D.$_{diff}$. As in the case of the boys the comparisons are not entirely satisfactory because the groups differ in age as well as in education. Certain control comparisons may be made between selected groups and the unselected general populations (Table 23). For example, 72 gifted girls in the fourth year of high school whose average age is 16 years and 2 months, 3 months younger than the high-school-junior girls, score far more masculine than the high school juniors. The difference of 27.6 M-F points is four times its S.D. On the other hand, 54 delinquent girls whose average age is 17 years, 4 months are in the ninth school grade and score in accordance with this placement between the eighth-grade and high-school-junior norms rather than between high-school juniors and college sophomores as their age might lead one to expect. In contrast to these group placements, which harmonize with the expectations based on educational considerations, is the mean for a group of 20 part-time schoolgirls whose average age is 16 years, 5 months and whose educational placement is equivalent to the sixth or seventh grade but whose mean M-F score places them at a point just above the high-school juniors. The mean mental age of this group is 11 years, 9½ months yet they score as high as a group of average high-school juniors whose mental age is not less than 16 years.

A group of 28 private-school girls makes an average score of −65.9 on the M-F scale, approaching the college sophomores and differing from the high-school junior rating by 1.5 S.D.$_{diff}$.

These girls are only 15 years and 11 months old on the average, yet they score far nearer to the gifted girls and the college-sophomore norm than to schoolgirls of their own age. Their school placement averages at the same point as the high-school juniors. In the case of both part-time schoolgirls and the private-school girls, neither age nor educational status accounts for the M-F score position. The explanation will have to be sought in some other factor or factors as yet unrevealed.

The steps in M-F development at the three educational levels show for the decades from the twenties to the eighties the trend revealed in the curve for the total population. There is considerable crossing and recrossing of the lines for the women of grade-school and those of high-school training. The grade-school women even pass the college norm in the sixties, but in general the college norm is for this sex distinct from the other two and maintains a distance from each of them in successive decades that amounts to 8 or 10 M-F points and ranges up to 1.3 S.D.$_{diff}$. Combined decade norms emphasize rather than lessen these differences and the total divergence of college women from high-school women in the populations studied is 10 M-F points in the masculine direction, which is 4.6 S.D.$_{diff}$. The divergence of college women from the population of women with a grade-school education is 11.5 M-F points or 3.8 S.D.$_{diff}$. A general-population group so made up as to match as nearly as possible the adult female population of the country as given in the United States census differs from this grade-school group by only 1 M-F point and from women of high-school education by less than half a point, but from the college women's group by 10.4 M-F points or 5.1 S.D.$_{diff}$.

Summarizing, we may say that mental M-F scores are correlated with education to an appreciable extent. In the male population the order from greatest to least masculinity shows first the college group, then the high-school group, and last the grade-school group. The differences between these three are statistically demonstrable for sufficiently large populations. A representative general-population group is more masculine than the men of grade-school education, but less masculine than the

men of high-school or college education. In the female populations education makes noteworthy differences at all ages for
which norms have been derived, especially between the more
feminine groups of grade-school and high-school women on the
one hand and the more masculine college women on the other.

TABLE 33.—COMPARISON OF MEAN SCORES OF MALES AND FEMALES (*a*) OF
GENERAL POPULATIONS AT THREE EDUCATIONAL LEVELS, AND (*b*) OF A
COMPOSITE REPRESENTATIVE GENERAL POPULATION

Populations compared	Mean	S.D.$_M$	Diff.	$\dfrac{\text{Diff.}}{\text{S.D.}_{\text{diff.}}}$
General population:				
Adults of grade-school education				
Male...........................	+21.8	3.40	+107.9	+42.4
Female.........................	−86.2	2.53		
Adults of high-school education				
Male...........................	+45.4	2.92	+130.1	+39.8
Female.........................	−84.7	1.47		
Adults of college education				
Male...........................	+50.4	2.05	+125.1	+48.1
Female.........................	−74.7	1.60		
A composite representative general-popula-tion group (conforming in age and educa-tional constitution to the U.S. census populations):				
Male...........................	+36.5	2.28	+121.6	+46.6
Female.........................	−85.1	1.27		

A representative general population of women scores virtually
at the same point as do women of grade-school or of high-school
education, but is significantly more masculine than the women
of college training.

Regardless of education, the differences between the mean
scores of the sexes are very great. The largest difference is
between the means of the men and women of high-school education, 130 M-F points. The next largest is between the two
college means, 125 points. The smallest difference, but still a

tremendous one, is that between the means for the men and women of grade-school education: 108 points. The two typical composite sex groups representing as nearly as our data permit the general population of the United States differ from one another by 122 M-F points.

THE INFLUENCE OF INTELLIGENCE

Evidence as to the influence of intelligence upon M-F scores will be shown in correlations between M-F scores and scores on various intelligence tests, and in comparisons between groups otherwise as similar as possible but divergent with respect to intelligence. The correlations most useful in this connection are those from groups of at least fair size and those having a fairly wide range in educational status and mental age. Two such correlations have been made, one for each sex for the combined eighth-grade and high-school-junior groups. These are between M-F scores and mental ages derived from the Stanford Binet, the Terman Group Test, and the National Intelligence Test. For the boys the correlation is .19 ± .05; for the girls it is .20 ± .05. The correlations between M-F score and IQ when mental age is made constant become, respectively, +.08 ± .05 for boys and +.07 ± .05 for girls, indicating no significant relationships. When chronological age is rendered constant, we have, respectively, +.15 ± .05 and +.14 ± .05, correlations which are probably indicative of a small but genuine relationship.

Correlations for boys and men within small grade or other limited groupings give practically no evidence of either positive or negative relationship between M-F score and mental age. For the girls, however, there is repeated evidence that such a relationship is present after the eighth-grade level is passed. The coefficient for the high-school juniors is higher than that for the combined eighth-grade and high-school-junior groups. Student nurses and superior college women show a fairly definite tendency for mental level to be correlated positively with M-F score.

A sex difference is probably present in youth in the extent to which mental maturity as measured by intelligence tests is

TABLE 34.—CORRELATIONS BETWEEN M-F SCORES AND INTELLIGENCE SCORES

Population	No. of cases	C.A. range in years	M.A. range in years	Correlation between M-F score and mental age
Males:				
Large group representing a wide range				
Eighth grade and high-school juniors	173	12 to 22	11 to 21	+.19 ± .05
Small and select groups, or groups representing narrower ranges				
Orphans.....................	15	11 to 16	11 to 18	+.33 ± .16
Eighth grade..................	95	12 to 18	11 to 18	+.13 ± .07
High-school juniors..............	79	14 to 22	12 to 21	+.03 ± .07
			Ranges of Thorndike test scores	
University men (psychology class)	97	18 to 32	52 to 111	+.00 ± .07
University men: upper quartile scholarship..................	46	19 to 24	59 to 106	+.20 ± .10
University men: lower quartile scholarship..................	46	19 to 24	59 to 106	+.24 ± .10
			M.A. range in years	
Females:				
Large group representing a wide range				
Eighth grade and high-school juniors	164	12 to 19	11 to 21	+.20 ± .05
Small and select groups, or groups representing narrower ranges				
Orphans.....................	13	12 to 17	12 to 18	+.27 ± .18
Eighth grade..................	79	12 to 19	11 to 17	−.01 ± .08
High-school juniors..............	85	14 to 19	13 to 22	+.27 ± .07
			Terman group score	
Student nurses..................	74	18 to 25	90 to 199	+.20 ± .07 (+.24 ± .08 corrected)
Superior university women.......	175	18 to 24		+.16 ± .05

associated with M-F score. Coefficients from separate and combined groups suggest that for younger boys there would probably be found a small but significant correlation between M-F score and mental age in a representative population drawn from more than one grade. At the high-school-junior level and thereafter it is probable that no such correlation exists. In the case of the girls the youngest ages show no significant correlation between M-F score and mental age but from the high-school-junior level onward and including the college and student-nurse populations a positive correlation is found.

There is nothing in these results to contradict the findings respecting the relation of M-F score to chronological age. They help to interpret certain puzzling differences between the M-F curves of the two sexes. The gain in masculinity by the boys from the eighth-grade to the high-school-junior level is not duplicated by the girls; it is at this period that mental age is a factor in relation to M-F score of boys but not of girls. On the other hand, the upward trend of the girls from the third high-school year to the second college year is not duplicated by the boys; it is at this period that intelligence enters as an important factor in the case of girls. Why the intellectual factor should exert its influence at different ages in the two sexes is not clear.

We may next compare the means of groups of corresponding ages but of varying intelligence (Tables 22 and 23). The average age of the gifted group falls for each sex between sixteen and seventeen years, as does also that of the high-school juniors. Of the two groups, however, the former is much superior in intelligence. The mean M-F score of the gifted boys is +66.2, or 5.5 points below the mean of the high-school-junior boys. The difference is not statistically significant. However, the mean M-F score of the gifted girls is 27.6 points higher than that of the high-school-junior girls; the means are, respectively, −57.3 and −84.8. The difference is four times its S.D. For the college students we may compare the M-F scores of those who have rated above the average for their institution on the Thorndike Intelligence Test for High School Graduates with the scores of those who have rated below this average in intelligence. In the case of men the difference is not significant, the high-intelligence group yielding a mean M-F score of +79.5, the low-intelligence group a mean of +74.[1] The corresponding means for girls are −24.3 for the high-intelligence group and

[1] These averages are for the groups A,B,C of Table 18 combined.

—46.2 for the low-intelligence group. The difference is 2.6 times its S.D.

In the case of our adult groups, since no intelligence test scores are available for them, the best we can do is to compare the M-F means of the three large populations belonging to three educational levels. Owing to the influence of selective elimination in the schools, it is well known that men or women who have

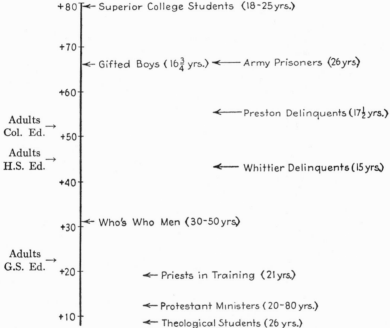

FIG. 7.—Age influence upon mean M-F scores of certain male groups.

graduated from high school excel in average mental ability those who have completed only the eighth grade, and that college graduates are on the average superior to the general run of high-school graduates. The M-F standing of the three adult groups is shown in Figs. 7 and 8 in comparison with several other groups. We have seen that certain special groups do not follow closely the course described by the general population. Comparison of the means of these special groups of known characteristics with the means for the unselected population in part corroborates our findings regarding the influence of age, education, and intelligence and suggests other factors operative in the M-F ratings of the groups in question. Three unusually interesting groupings have been selected for each sex.

The first of these permits of intercomparison of markedly superior individuals at three age levels: gifted boys in their teens

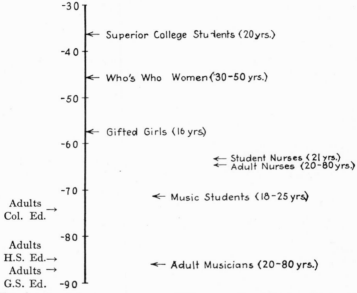

FIG. 8.—Age influence upon mean M-F scores of certain female groups.

whose IQ ratings seven years earlier averaged 150; superior college men in their early twenties whose college aptitude score was above the mean for their institution, *Who's Who* men, an unselected group of forty- and fifty-year-old married men listed in the well-known volume. The age curve described by the means of these three groups is similar to that of the general population, but somewhat exaggerated in its main features. The gifted boys are less masculine than average schoolboys of their age. The superior college students rate highest. The *Who's Who* men are more feminine than the other adult groups which have had college or high-school education and approach more nearly than these to the adults of grade-school education. Special factors must be operative to make gifted boys and distinguished men more feminine, and superior college men more masculine, than corresponding age groups of the general population.

A second example is found in three delinquent populations. The younger delinquent boys score more feminine than the eighth-grade boys who are on the average younger. Older delinquents show the expected gain in masculinity from the younger position, but they score decidedly more feminine than either high-school juniors who are younger or college sophomores who are older. Army offenders, in their twenties, are more masculine than either of the adolescent groups, but they do not reach the masculinity of college sophomores or high-school juniors.

Three interesting male religious groups are available: a group of Catholic priests in training, a group of Protestant theological students, and an adult group of Protestant clergy and ministers. The Catholic student priests score at a point far less masculine than any other male group of their age; in their early twenties they are more feminine than the general male population at middle life. The Protestant theological students in their middle twenties are, however, more feminine than they and exceed in femininity the sixty-year-old men of equal education. The adult ministerial group is barely more masculine than the Protestant theological students and less so than the student priests. They exceed in femininity the college men of the seventh decade. It is obvious that the age element is practically erased here by other influences. Some dominant factors must be present in all three groups to make them, without regard to age, conspicuously and almost equally lacking in mental masculinity.

Three groups from the female populations may be briefly examined: gifted adolescent girls of average IQ 149; superior college women whose intelligence ratings are above the mean for their university; and a group of married women in their forties and fifties listed in *Who's Who*. These three groups, like the three comparable groups of men, diverge from the general population norms of corresponding age. The gifted girls are far more masculine than the high-school juniors of almost equal age, and slightly exceed in masculinity the college women's norm. The superior college women exceed the college women's norm in their masculinity. They are much nearer in score to the male theological students than to the high-school junior girls. The most comparable adult group, the *Who's Who* women, score more feminine than they. The *Who's Who* women are mentally more masculine than any of the three main groups of the general female population at any age. They are only one-fifth as far below the special group of superior college women as *Who's Who* men are below superior college men. Although the gifted boys are less masculine than the most comparable group of average schoolboys, the gifted girls are more masculine than any group of schoolgirls and even exceed average college girls. The superior college women exceed the gifted girls in masculinity by more than the difference between the superior college men and the gifted boys. This comparison indicates again that the factors operative in mental masculinity-femininity are not identical for the sexes. Intellectual superiority or some factor associated with it seems to incline far more to mental masculinity in women than in men. In fact, in the *Who's Who* men intellectual superiority strongly favors femininity.

A second age comparison among the women is between the student nurses in the early twenties and the adult group of professional female nurses. The student nurses are less masculine than any of the college groups of equal age. They are less feminine than the (younger) high-school juniors and rate the same as older, practicing nurses. The latter score more masculine than any of the general population groups of adult women of any educational level. Here age is apparently without influence; some other factor or factors, perhaps occupational interests and habits, are evidently dominant.

A third age comparison among women may be made between music students in their early twenties and a group of adult musicians and music teachers. The music students are more feminine than the student nurses or any of the groups of college women. They are more masculine than the (younger) high-school-junior girls or than any of the decade norms for the general population. The musicians and music teachers are as feminine as the general female population in middle life. In mental masculinity they rate as far below the professional nurses as these do below the *Who's Who* women. In these musical groups we find the same age tendency as was noted in the general population, namely an increase of femininity with increase of age.

Consideration of the above special groups of both sexes shows that whereas the age factor is important, other influences are at times dominant. Some of the other influences will be treated in later chapters. It is sufficient here to point out that numerous factors enter to affect the M-F score and that these frequently operate dissimilarly for the sexes.

Summary

1. The course of mental M-F scores is generally similar for the sexes: an initial rise in youth to a more masculine level is followed in both sexes by a decline throughout maturity toward femininity.

2. At no time do the means for comparable groups of opposite sex approach one another closely. Sex difference measured by the M-F score is preserved in all general unselected groups from childhood to old age.

3. The range between the means of the most masculine and the least masculine male groups is about twice that between the means of the least feminine and the most feminine female groups.

4. The peak of masculinity in average males is reached in the high-school period; the most feminine scores are found in old age.

5. The greatest extreme of femininity found among females is in the eighth grade, the greatest extreme of masculinity in the college period.

6. The feminizing of men in maturity is associated with the effect of influences represented in part by a composite of increasing age and length of married life. For women the relation of this composite to the M-F score is less demonstrable.

7. In general the same trends are followed and the same sex differences shown by populations at three important educational levels.

8. For the men, college and high-school education seem to exert a more masculinizing influence than grade-school education. For the women, college training apparently has a significantly more masculinizing influence than high-school or grade-school education. We do not know whether or to what extent selection may be responsible for these results.

9. A general population of males made up in such a way as to conform to the United States census proportions for the adult population of the country differs by 121.6 M-F points from a similarly constituted population of females. This difference is approximately twice the range from the most to the least masculine mean for the general male populations and more than three and a half times the range from the most to the least feminine mean for the general female populations.

10. Intelligence is probably positively correlated with mental M-F score for both sexes at certain ages. The relationship appears to be more pronounced for the youngest boys than for the youngest girls, but thereafter more pronounced for the female than for the male populations.

11. Age, education, and intelligence explain only the differences between the large general-population groups. Special groups selected with respect to occupation or other characteristics do not always conform to the expectations based on the findings for the general populations. Interesting examples are the extremely feminine male religious groups, the *Who's Who* men, so much less masculine than others of equal education, and among women the relatively masculine professional female nurses and the extremely masculine intellectual groups.

CHAPTER VIII

RELATION OF M-F SCORE TO OCCUPATION

In the preceding chapter we found that age was slightly but definitely correlated with M-F score from the youngest to the oldest groups. Education and intelligence were also discovered to be related factors determining to a measurable extent M-F scores of most of the groups studied. The scores of all groups were not explainable in the terms of these correlations. It appeared that other factors were at work that sometimes entirely upset our expectations. For example, two groups of younger men, and another averaging at middle age, all well educated, scored at approximately the same point as men of the general population at sixty years of age; two groups of women, one in the early twenties, the other averaging at middle maturity, scored at the same point, which was above all the decade averages for all adult women without respect to the level of their education. In both these illustrations age was not a common factor. Education was probably about equal for the combinations in question, as was also intelligence. But as these groups did not score near others of the same educational and intelligence level it was manifest that some other factor was strongly active. The most natural suggestion was that interests and occupations were playing a part in influencing the score. One of the nonconforming groups was made up of Catholic student priests in their early twenties, Protestant theological students in their middle twenties, and ministers and clergymen representing all ages from twenty to ninety. In spite of the differing ages, sects, and experience of these three groups all scored near the same point on the scale, and at a position nowhere near the scores for other groups comparable to them in schooling or in intelligence. A similar situation was found for two groups of women. Student nurses and women engaged in the profession of nursing, although diverse in age, scored at the same point and quite apart from any others of comparable intelligence and schooling. In both these comparisons, occupational interest seems a very potent influence. The present chapter is devoted to an analysis and discussion of M-F scores in the light of the occupations and interests of both sexes.

Total populations for the sexes separately, including all persons tested between twenty-five and sixty-five years of age, were classified into occupational groups. Several hundred occupations were found represented. Many of the groupings were very small and wherever possible these were combined into larger homogeneous populations. Where there were four or more individuals from a given occupation a distribution of the M-F scores was made and the mean calculated. The dispersion in such groups was much less than is expected in small random populations. On the basis of (1) means of the small groups, (2) dispersion, and (3) intrinsic homogeneity of activity, subjectively rated, the small groups were combined and recombined into about 45 groups for the men and 74 for the women. These were in turn reduced by further amalgamation to 9 principal men's groups and 4 most important women's groups. The situation regarding occupations for the sexes is quite dissimilar. There are many activities for the men any one of which may be pursued throughout life with profound interest and devotion. For the women there is one chief occupation, that of housewife, and there is no other that compares with it in number. Hence, it is not possible to discuss occupations for the two sexes in a single analysis. We shall present first the relation of men's occupations to their standing on the M-F scale and then take up women's occupations.

Score Trends of Male Occupational Groups

Each M-F test calls for an entry under the caption, "Profession or Occupation." More than 150 different male activities have been listed from the information received in answer to this item. These occupations have been combined into nine groups by the method indicated above. Listed in order from most to least

TABLE 35.—MEAN M-F SCORES OF MALE OCCUPATIONAL GROUPS AND SUBGROUPS

Profession or occupation	No. of cases	Mean score	S.D. dist.	S.D.M	Standard score
A. Professions					
I. Engineers, architects	41	+81.2	51.9	8.10	+ .80
1. College engineers (no other occupation)	21	+94.3	45.2	9.87	+1.05
2. College engineers (other occupation)	15	+70.5	45.0	11.62	+ .60
3. Architects	5	+58.5	..	..	+ .40
II. Professional business	162	+57.3	47.5	3.73	+ .35
1. Bankers	17	+68.1	34.3	8.31	+ .55
2. Lawyers	17	+62.3	37.0	8.97	+ .45
3. Realtors	16	+61.8	46.8	11.71	+ .45
4. Executive managers, superintendents	26	+58.9	37.7	7.39	+ .40
5. Salesmen	60	+58.2	50.5	6.52	+ .40
a. Salesmen, special lines	12	+63.8	..	..	+ .50
b. Salesmen	45	+58.5	..	..	+ .40
c. Traveling salesmen	3	+30.5	..	..	− .10
6. Insurance	26	+40.5	58.0	11.37	+ .05
7. Manufacturers	5	+70.5	..	..	+ .60
8. Bankers, realtors, insurance, executive managers, superintendents	85	+55.7	47.1	5.11	+ .35
III. Physical-social welfare	166	+45.1	41.6	3.23	+ .15
1. Dentists	14	+49.1	50.9	13.61	+ .20
2. Physicians, surgeons	20	+45.5	39.4	8.82	+ .15
3. Teachers	132	+44.5	40.8	3.55	+ .10
a. Teachers (college)	27	+45.3	47.9	9.22	+ .15
b. Teachers (general)	75	+44.6	39.4	4.55	+ .15
c. Teachers (educational administration)	30	+43.8	36.6	6.69	+ .10
d. Teachers (physical education coaches)	5	+82.5	..	..	+ .85
4. Scientific workers	9	+54.9	..	..	+ .30
B. Occupations					
IV. Mechanical occupations	87	+44.8	50.1	5.37	+ .15
1. Draftsmen	7	+64.8	..	..	+ .50
2. Electricians	14	+57.6	..	..	+ .35
3. Engineers (noncollege)	9	+41.6	..	..	+ .05
4. Machinists, mechanicians	43	+40.7	..	..	+ .05
5. Chauffeurs, truck drivers	14	+33.4	..	..	− .05
V. Clerical, mercantile	95	+43.2	51.3	5.26	+ .10
1. Clerks, bookkeepers, office managers, secretaries, accountants	58	+43.4	47.2	6.2	+ .10
a. Accountants	14	+50.5	..	..	+ .25
b. Clerks	34	+49.3	..	..	+ .20
c. Bookkeepers	4	+30.5	..	..	− .10
d. Office managers, secretaries	6	+ 3.8	..	..	− .60
2. Postmasters	4	+45.5	..	..	+ .15
3. Printers	9	+43.8	..	..	+ .10
4. Merchants, druggists, pharmacists	37	+42.9	57.0	9.37	+ .10
a. Druggists, pharmacists	14	+46.1	..	..	+ .15
b. Merchants	23	+37.6	73.1	19.6	0
5. Confectioners	4	+10.5	..	..	− .45
6. Grocers	8	+ 8.0	..	..	− .50
VI. Building trades, contractors, painters, builders	45	+36.3	42.1	6.27	0
1. Contractors, builders	14	+51.9	..	..	+ .25
2. Building trades	23	+32.2	..	..	− .05
3. Painters	8	+20.5	..	..	− .25
VII. Farmers	58	+32.9	43.9	5.8	− .05
VIII. Policemen, firemen	23	+27.9	43.0	8.97	− .15
1. Firemen	10	+28.5	54.7	17.3	− .10
2. Policemen	13	+27.4	31.2	8.66	− .15
C. Vocations					
IX. Vocational groups	113	+13.0	38.2	3.59	− .40
1. Editors, journalists	12	+27.2	52.2	15.1	− .15
2. Clergymen	63	+12.7	35.8	4.52	− .40
3. Artists	38	+ 8.4	34.9	5.7	− .50

masculine, these are as follows: (I) professional engineers and architects; (II) professional businessmen: lawyers, salesmen, bankers, and executives; (III) professional physical-social welfare group: teachers, physicians, surgeons, dentists; (IV) mechanical occupations; (V) clerical and mercantile occupations;

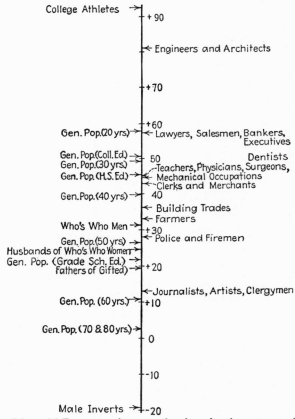

Fig. 9.—Mean M-F scores of occupational and other groups (males).

(VI) building occupations; (VII) farming occupations; (VIII) public-safety occupations: policemen and firemen; (IX) vocational group: editors, journalists, clergymen, ministers, and artists. Reference to Fig. 9 will show the position of these groups on the scale with respect to each other and in relation to norms. There is a tendency for the groups to bunch on the scale. For example, farmers and builders are in close proximity, and the three large groups (III) teachers, physicians, surgeons, dentists, (IV) mechanical occupations, (V) clerks and merchants are within 2.5 M-F points of one another. However, we could see no justification on the basis of inherent interest for combining any of the nine groups further among themselves. We could make a professional, an occupational, and, as we already have it, a vocational group, but to do this to any greater extent we should have to overlook the occupational differences actually indicated.

Comparing the professions, the occupations, and the vocations with one another, we find the three large classes rating in the order indicated. The professional rate most masculine and somewhat higher than the mean for adults with college training; higher also than the mean for age twenty-five of the general population. Their position is approximately the same as that of the college graduates in their twenties. The occupations rate in an intermediate position and at about the same point as the general-population group. This places them midway between the adults of high-school education and those of grade-school training and somewhat below the mean for all adults in their forties. They are at the scale position for combined high-school and grade-school adults between their forties and fifties. The vocations rate lowest. Their position on the scale is far below all the general-population averages including that for adults of grade-school education. The combined group of editors, journalists, clergymen, and artists rates just above the norm for sixty-year-old adults. Its mean indicates less masculinity than any other general-population group except the sixty-, seventy-, and eighty-year-olds.

Consideration of the positions of the three main activity groupings of men shows certain new and important trends. (1) Mechanical occupation is strongly masculine in its influence, but it does not entirely obliterate the effect of educational level. (2) Social or humane pursuits, those concerned with people rather than with things, have a feminine influence, but they do not eliminate the effect of education on the score. (3) Culture and philanthropy, concerns of the spirit as contrasted with material objectives, have a profoundly feminizing influence. Apparently this is as strong as the influence of age, and in groups of any size it tends to override and obliterate almost completely the effect of the educational level. Each of the three trends must be considered in greater detail.

The influence of mechanical occupations is seen in two conspicuous instances in the nine activities. Engineers and architects are far more masculine than any other group. The difference between them and the professional business group is 23.9 points or 2.68 S.D.$_{diff.}$. The difference between them and the teachers, physicians, surgeons, and dentists is 4.14 S.D.$_{diff.}$. They are 31 points more masculine than the general average of men of college education, a difference that is more than 3.5 times its S.D. Men in the mechanical occupations are significantly less masculine than the engineers and architects; the difference is 36.4 points, or 3.74 S.D.$_{diff.}$. But just as the engineers and architects score significantly more masculine (1) than either of the other professional groupings, (2) than the mean for the appropriate decade group, and (3) than the mean for all college-trained men, so, too, the mechanical occupations score (a) at the masculine limit of the occupational groups, and (b) significantly more masculine than the grade-school mean. The respective differences among the four occupational groups are neither as large nor as significant as those among the (larger) professional groups, but the trend from the least masculine groups, firemen and policemen, to the most masculine, mechanical occupations, seems to support the hypothesis of a mechanical element in mental masculinity. The professional and the occupational groups meet where the mechanical workers register a high point for the occupational groups and where the professional group concerned with human welfare (teachers, physicians, surgeons, dentists) register the most feminine mean for the professions.

The second trend noted was for occupations dealing with people and social interests to tend in the feminine direction, and for those concerned with finance, manufacture, industry, and mercantile pursuits to tend in the masculine direction. This is seen in the placements in the occupational and professional groups respectively and in the relation to them of the vocational group, especially the clergymen. In both the first-named groupings the interest order is (1) mechanical, (2) business and financial, and (3) social and human welfare. The last-named is exemplified in the professional groups by the teachers, physicians, surgeons, and dentists, and in the occupational groups by the policemen and firemen. The most conspicuous example of the human or social interest is of course in the clergymen and these rate more feminine than any other occupational group except the artists'.

A third important general trend is the cultural. This is indicated, first, by the position of the editors, journalists, clergymen, and artists, and second, by the position of three special groups not included in the occupational populations: fathers of gifted children, *Who's Who* men, and husbands of *Who's Who* women. Probably the individuals who make up the three last-named groups average in ability and achievement considerably above any of the occupational groups and probably above the other professional groups. The common factor which makes *Who's Who* men, fathers of gifted children, editors, journalists, artists, and clergymen score significantly less masculine than any other group of superior ability cannot be attributed to age, education, or intelligence. Subjective considerations suggest that it is probably closely related to cultural interests and activity. This will also be indicated later by comparison, in terms of general populations, of the dominating interest of such persons with their M-F scale positions. In the meantime it is apparent that the culture factor has for the *Who's Who* groups, the editors, journalists, clergymen, and artists overridden the trends for age, education, and intelligence. The principal evidence for and against the trends summarized is found in the more detailed analysis of each of the nine groups. Table 36 gives the statistical intercomparisons of the male occupational groups.

I. **Professional Engineers and Architects.**—The group of 41 engineers and architects is made up of (*a*) 21 engineers, college trained and having had no other occupation besides engineering,

TABLE 36.—INTERCOMPARISON OF THE MEAN M-F SCORES OF 15 OCCUPATIONAL, PROFESSIONAL, AND VOCATIONAL GROUPS

Professions, occupations, vocations	No. of cases	Mean M-F score	S.D._M	Engineers, architects (41) +81.2 ± 8.10		Lawyers (17) +62.3 ± 8.97		Salesmen (60) +58.2 ± 6.52		Bankers, Bus. Admin. (85) +55.7 ± 5.11		Physicians, surgeons, dentists (34) +47.0 ± 7.64	
				Diff.	$\frac{\text{Diff.}}{\text{S.D.diff.}}$	Diff.	$\frac{\text{Diff.}}{\text{S.D.diff.}}$	Diff.	$\frac{\text{Diff.}}{\text{S.D.diff.}}$	Diff.	$\frac{\text{Diff.}}{\text{S.D.diff.}}$	Diff.	$\frac{\text{Diff.}}{\text{S.D.diff.}}$
Engineers, architects	41	+81.2	8.10	..	..	+19.0	1.57	+23.1	2.22	+25.6	2.67	+34.3	3.08
Lawyers	17	+62.3	8.97	−19.0	1.57	..	..	+ 4.1	<1	+ 6.6	<1	+15.3	1.30
Salesmen	60	+58.2	6.52	−23.1	2.22	− 4.1	<1	..	..	+ 2.5	<1	+11.2	1.11
Bankers, business administrators..	85	+55.7	5.11	−25.6	2.67	− 6.6	<1	− 2.5	<1	..	..	+ 8.7	<1
Physicians, surgeons, dentists....	34	+47.0	7.64	−34.3	3.08	−15.3	1.30	−11.2	1.11	− 8.7	<1	..	..
Mechanical occupations	87	+44.8	5.37	−36.5	3.75	−17.5	1.67	−13.4	1.64	−10.9	1.54	− 2.2	<1
Teachers	132	+44.6	3.55	−36.7	4.14	−17.7	1.83	−13.6	1.78	−11.1	1.18	− 2.4	<1
Clerical workers	58	+43.4	6.20	−37.8	3.71	−18.8	1.73	−14.7	1.62	−12.3	1.50	− 3.6	<1
Merchants, druggists, pharmacists	37	+42.9	9.37	−38.3	3.09	−19.3	1.49	−15.2	1.33	−12.7	1.19	− 4.0	<1
Building trades	45	+36.3	6.27	−45.0	4.39	−26.0	2.37	−21.9	2.42	−19.4	2.40	−10.7	1.08
Farmers	58	+32.9	5.77	−48.3	4.86	−29.3	2.75	−25.2	2.90	−22.8	2.95	−14.1	1.47
Policemen, firemen	23	+27.9	8.97	−53.3	4.41	−34.4	2.71	−30.3	2.73	−27.8	2.69	−19.1	1.62
Editors, journalists	12	+27.2	15.08	−54.1	3.16	−35.1	2.00	−31.0	1.89	−28.5	1.79	−19.8	1.17
Clergymen, ministers	63	+12.7	4.52	−68.5	7.43	−49.5	4.93	−45.4	5.73	−43.0	6.30	−34.3	3.86
Artists	38	+ 8.4	5.66	−72.8	7.37	−53.9	5.08	−49.8	5.77	−47.3	6.20	−38.6	4.06

TABLE 36.—INTERCOMPARISON OF THE MEAN M-F SCORES OF 15 OCCUPATIONAL, PROFESSIONAL, AND VOCATIONAL GROUPS.—*(Continued)*

Professions, occupations, vocations	No. of cases	Mean M-F score	$S.D._M$	Mechanical occupations (87) +44.8 ± 5.37		Teachers (132) +44.6 ± 3.55		Clerical workers (58) +43.4 ± 6.20		Merchants, druggists, pharmacists (37) +42.9 ± 9.37		Building trades (45) +36.3 ± 6.27	
				Diff.	$\frac{Diff.}{S.D._{diff.}}$	Diff.	$\frac{Diff.}{S.D._{diff.}}$	Diff.	$\frac{Diff.}{S.D._{diff.}}$	Diff.	$\frac{Diff.}{S.D._{diff.}}$	Diff.	$\frac{Diff.}{S.D._{diff.}}$
Engineers, architects	41	+81.2	8.10	+36.5	3.75	+36.7	4.14	+37.8	3.71	+38.3	3.09	+45.0	4.39
Lawyers	17	+62.3	8.97	+17.5	1.67	+17.7	1.83	+18.8	1.73	+19.3	1.49	+26.0	2.37
Salesmen	60	+58.2	6.52	+13.4	1.64	+13.6	1.83	+14.7	1.62	+15.2	1.33	+21.9	2.42
Bankers, business administrators	85	+55.7	5.11	+10.9	1.54	+11.1	1.78	+12.3	1.50	+12.7	1.19	+19.4	2.40
Physicians, surgeons, dentists	34	+47.0	7.64	+ 2.2	<1	+ 2.4	<1	+ 3.6	<1	+ 4.0	<1	+10.7	1.08
Mechanical occupations	87	+44.8	5.37	..	..	+ .2	<1	+ 1.3	<1	+ 1.8	<1	+ 8.5	<1
Teachers	132	+44.6	3.55	— .2	<1	..	..	+ 1.2	<1	+ 1.6	<1	+ 8.3	1.15
Clerical workers	58	+43.4	6.20	— 1.3	<1	— 1.2	<1	..	..	+ 1.6	<1	+ 7.2	<1
Merchants, druggists, pharmacists	37	+42.9	9.37	— 1.8	<1	— 1.6	<1	— .5	<1	..	..	+ 6.7	<1
Building trades	45	+36.3	6.27	— 8.5	<1	— 8.3	1.15	— 7.2	<1	— 6.7	<1	..	..
Farmers	58	+32.9	5.77	—11.8	1.44	—11.7	1.72	—10.5	1.26	—10.0	<1	— 3.4	<1
Policemen, firemen	23	+27.9	8.97	—16.9	1.57	—16.7	1.73	—15.5	1.44	—15.0	1.16	— 8.4	<1
Editors, journalists	12	+27.2	15.08	—17.6	1.10	—17.4	1.12	—16.3	<1	—15.8	<1	— 9.1	<1
Clergymen, ministers	63	+12.7	4.52	—32.0	4.56	—31.9	5.54	—30.7	4.00	—30.2	2.91	—23.6	3.05
Artists	38	+ 8.4	5.66	—36.4	4.66	—36.2	5.42	—35.0	4.18	—34.5	3.15	—27.9	3.30

TABLE 36.—INTERCOMPARISON OF THE MEAN M-F SCORES OF 15 OCCUPATIONAL, PROFESSIONAL, AND VOCATIONAL GROUPS.—(Continued)

Professions, occupations, vocations	No. of cases	Mean M-F score	S.D._M	Farmers (58) +32.9 ± 5.77		Policemen, firemen (23) +27.9 ± 8.97		Editors, journalists (12) +27.2 ± 15.08		Clergymen, ministers (63) +12.7 ± 4.52		Artists (38) +8.4 ± 5.66	
				Diff.	$\frac{Diff.}{S.D._{diff.}}$	Diff.	$\frac{Diff.}{S.D._{diff.}}$	Diff.	$\frac{Diff.}{S.D._{diff.}}$	Diff.	$\frac{Diff.}{S.D._{diff.}}$	Diff.	$\frac{Diff.}{S.D._{diff.}}$
Engineers, architects	41	+81.2	8.10	+48.3	4.86	+53.3	4.41	+54.1	3.16	+68.5	7.43	+72.8	7.37
Lawyers	17	+62.3	8.97	+29.3	2.75	+34.4	2.71	+35.1	2.00	+49.5	4.93	+53.9	5.08
Salesmen	60	+58.2	6.52	+25.2	2.90	+30.3	2.73	+31.0	1.89	+45.4	5.73	+49.8	5.77
Bankers, business administrators	85	+55.7	5.11	+22.8	2.95	+27.8	2.69	+28.5	1.79	+43.0	6.30	+47.3	6.20
Physicians, surgeons, dentists	34	+47.0	7.64	+14.1	1.47	+19.1	1.62	+19.8	1.17	+34.3	3.86	+38.6	4.06
Mechanical occupations	87	+44.8	5.37	+11.8	1.44	+16.9	1.57	+17.6	1.10	+32.0	4.56	+36.4	4.66
Teachers	132	+44.6	3.55	+11.7	1.72	+16.7	1.73	+17.4	1.12	+31.9	5.54	+36.2	5.42
Clerical workers	58	+43.4	6.20	+10.5	1.26	+15.5	1.44	+16.3	<1	+30.7	4.00	+35.0	4.18
Merchants, druggists, pharmacists	37	+42.9	9.37	+10.0	<1	+15.0	1.16	+15.8	<1	+30.2	2.91	+34.5	3.15
Building trades	45	+36.3	6.27	+ 3.4	<1	+ 8.4	<1	+ 9.1	<1	+23.6	3.05	+27.9	3.30
Farmers	58	+32.9	5.77	..	..	+ 5.0	<1	+ 5.8	<1	+20.2	2.76	+24.5	3.03
Policemen, firemen	23	+27.9	8.97	− 5.0	<1	..	..	+ .7		+15.2	1.51	+19.5	1.34
Editors, journalists	12	+27.2	15.08	− 5.8	<1	− .7	<1	..	..	+14.4	<1	+18.8	1.17
Clergymen, ministers	63	+12.7	4.52	−20.2	2.76	−15.2	1.51	−14.4		..	..	+ 4.3	<1
Artists	38	+ 8.4	5.66	−24.5	3.03	−19.5	1.84	−18.8	1.17	− 4.32	<1	..	..

(*b*) 15 engineers college trained and having had other occupations, and (*c*) 5 architects. The subgroups score in the order named. The first constituent, the 21 engineers, holds the position of highest M-F score among adults. The difference between them and the engineers who have had other occupations and between both of these and the architects seems to give evidence of the strength of the mechanical influence. Architects, being akin to artists, should be expected to score less masculine than other engineers of equal training, as they actually do. The 5 manufacturers, who were assigned to the business group, perhaps in fact belong to the engineers' group, as their score seems to indicate. The proximity should also be noted of men of clear mechanical bent who have been assigned to the mechanical occupations because they were less well trained than the graduate engineers. These include 7 draftsmen and 14 electricians; the first are considerably above, the second almost equal to the architects in average score. The position of 9 scientific workers, at a point a little below the architects, may perhaps also be attributed to the mechanical factor.

The engineers and architects rank well above the professional business group; the difference in average score is 23.9 points (2.68 S.D.$_{diff.}$). As compared to the seven other professional and occupational groups and to the vocational groups, and to the principal subgroups, the engineers and architects are significantly more masculine, the differences all exceeding the criterion of 3 S.D.$_{diff.}$. The difference between this group and the principal others is as follows: teachers, physicians, surgeons, and dentists, 36 points; building trades, 45 points; farmers, 48.3 points; policemen and firemen, 53.3 points; and vocational group, 68 points. The engineers and architects are undoubtedly high-grade individuals with superior training, both general and special, but these qualifications do not account for their position with respect to the other groups and subgroups. The hypothesis of positive correlation between M-F score and mechanical ability and interest, a correlation which we shall find persisting at every educational level, does, we believe, account for the exceptionally masculine score.

II. Professional Businessmen.—This group is made up of 17 bankers, 17 lawyers, 16 realtors, 26 executive managers and superintendents, 60 salesmen, including traveling salesmen, salesmen in special lines, salesmen in general, and 26 insurance salesmen and brokers. The six subgroups score on the M-F scale from the most to the least masculine in the order named. The range is from the bankers at +68.1 to the insurance salesmen and brokers at +40.5. It is quite probable that individuals are included in some of these groups who have had less than full college training. The average is, however, that of college-trained individuals and should, we believe, rank the class as a professional group. It is somewhat difficult here to identify the factors which make for higher and lower scoring. The individuals dealing with financial and administrative business on a large scale apparently are those who rate more masculine, while the businessmen who are concerned with individual contacts score more feminine, notably the insurance salesmen. Two factors seem to make for greater masculinity: (1) executive and administrative work, (2) financial work that is largely free from the social aspects. Both of these either demand individuals of greater masculinity or else create greater masculinity. Both trends are probably included in the element which we have called the financial versus the social interest in business and in occupations in general. All but one of the subgroups included in Class II score well above Class III, the physical-social welfare group. In fact, they average at a point approximately halfway between the two other professional groups.

The professional business group is significantly more feminine in average (23.9 M-F points) than the engineers and architects. The mean difference is 2.68 S.D.$_{diff.}$. All the other large occupational groups are more feminine and diverge from Class II as follows: mechanical occupations, 12.5 points (1.0 S.D.$_{diff.}$); building trades, 21 points (2.88 S.D.$_{diff.}$); farmers, 24.4 points (3.55 S.D.$_{diff.}$); policemen and firemen, 29.4 points (3.03 S.D.$_{diff.}$); and the vocational group, 44.3 points (8.55 S.D.$_{diff.}$). As far as M-F ratings are concerned the superior business group presents a marked contrast to the engineers and architects on the one hand, and to the farmers, policemen and firemen, editors, journalists, clergymen, ministers, and artists on the other. It is more closely related to the group of physicians, surgeons, dentists, and teachers, to the mechanical occupations, to the clerical and mercantile group and to the representatives of the building trades. The first of the contrasts, that which divides the professional businessmen from the engineers and architects, seems to involve both a lesser degree of mechanical interest and a greater degree of the general social element. The second difference, exemplified in the divergence from farmers, policemen, and firemen, may well be largely due to the educational factors; the professional businessmen are in general more highly trained. As contrasted with the farmers the difference seems to be attributable to financial versus social-welfare interests. The large divergence between the professional businessmen and the vocational groups indicates the contrast between financial and cultural interests. The superior businessmen rate more masculine than the general population, college educated. Their mean is above all the educational means and general-population means, and they exceed in their masculinity all the general decade norms except that for the twenty-year-olds, which they closely approximate. We may in summary attribute the position on the M-F scale of our professional Class II to superior educational status and to financial and administrative versus social or cultural interests.

III. Professional Physical-social Welfare Class.—The group of 166 teachers, physicians, surgeons, and dentists is made up of three subgroups which rank from most to least masculine as follows: 14 dentists, 20 physicians and surgeons, and 132 teachers. In view of our previous discussions this arrangement of the subgroups is to be expected. The dentists have doubtless more concern with mechanical aspects in their profession than the average physician, surgeon, or teacher. The teachers on the other hand would probably, in general, have the least interest of this kind. The educational difference, if present, would place the physicians and surgeons at the highest point, with the average for dentists and teachers approximately equal. The college professors rate at exactly the same point as the medical men, a combined group of approximately equal college and advanced training. We are not inclined to see in the respective divergences of the subdivisions of Class III any new contribution to our financial-social hypotheses. The pressure of other influences than the mechanical adequately accounts for the fact that Class III shows no overlap with Class I. The dentists who mark the most masculine limit of Class III score at 49.1, and the most feminine subgroup of I, the architects, at 58.5, a difference of 9.4 score points.

Class III rates probably significantly less masculine than Class I; the difference in score is 23.9 points (2.68 S.D.$_{diff.}$). The difference between III and II may also be significant, amounting as it does to 12.2 points (2.47 S.D.$_{diff.}$). Educational or cultural factors appear to account for the greater femininity of Classes IV to IX as compared with the physicians, surgeons, dentists, and teachers who make up Class III. From the smallest to the largest the differences between III and later groups are as follows: IV, mechanical occupations, .3 points (difference less than its S.D.); V, clerical and mercantile occupations, 1.8 points (difference less than its S.D.); VI, building occupations, 8.8 points (1.25 S.D.$_{diff.}$); VII, farming occupations, 12.2 points (1.85 S.D.$_{diff.}$); VIII, public-safety occupations, 17.2 points (1.80 S.D.$_{diff.}$); and IX, vocational group, 32.1 points (6.65 S.D.$_{diff.}$). Class IX, comprising the editors, journalists, clergymen, ministers, and artists is the only one of the six that is reliably more feminine in score than Class III. A complexity of interacting factors doubtless accounts for the similarity in score averages of the six classes in the central scale positions. As we have seen, Class III scores at the extreme feminine position for the professions. Class IV, the mechanical occupations, is the most masculine within the distinctly occupational groups, and, we believe, owes its position primarily to the specific mechanical-interest element. The social-welfare interest apparently tends about as strongly in the feminine direction as the mechanical factor tends in the masculine direction. Each one may be more or less counterbalanced by education or some other element. The rank of dentists, physicians, surgeons, and teachers with their superior and specialized training at a point on our scale below the norm for men of college education we attribute chiefly to the social-welfare factor involved in their occupational choices and activities.

IV. Mechanical Occupations Class.—Turning now from the professions to the occupations it will be seen that our Class IV, mechanical occupations group, is a composite made up of five subgroups which rank from most to least masculine as follows: 7 draftsmen, 14 electricians, 9 engineers (noncollege trained), 43 machinists and mechanicians, and 14 chauffeurs and truck drivers. The relative positions of these subgroups throw further light on the strength of the mechanical element which seems to have such a positive correlation with M-F score. The more technically specialized groups among the five are those whose scores rate as most masculine. The educational factor may possibly also account in part for the order. The draftsmen and the electricians score above the average for Class II, while two of the other subgroups score below Class V, clerical and mercantile occupations. The low position of chauffeurs and truck drivers is thought to be perhaps more a matter of educational limitations than of lack in mechanical interest.

The mechanical occupations rate 36.4 points below the engineers and architects, a significant difference attributable to (1) general educational difference, and (2) a difference in specialization of mechanical training. They score at a point just below the average for men of high-school education. As many of the individuals who make up Class IV have completed far less than 12 school grades, the position of the class on a par with the better educated adults once more stresses the masculinity of the mechanically minded. Class IV does not diverge significantly from the nonmechanical but educationally superior, financial, and administrative Class II. It is also practically equal in M-F rating to III, the class of teachers, physicians, surgeons, and dentists. The feminine social-welfare influence and a higher educational status apparently offset the mechanical factor in Class IV. The other occupational classes rank successively less masculine than IV in the following order and to the extent indicated: V, clerical and mercantile occupations, 1.5 points (difference less than its S.D.); VII, farming occupations, 10.4 points (1.33 S.D.$_{\text{diff.}}$); VIII, public-safety occupations, 15.4 points (1.48 S.D.$_{\text{diff.}}$); and IX, vocational group, 30.3 points (4.76 S.D.$_{\text{diff.}}$). From this enumeration it appears that IX is the only group that is definitely more feminine. However, the placement of the mechanical occupations as the most masculine among the noncollege-trained male groups when considered with other pertinent findings is corroborative of the trends which have been pointed out.

V. Clerical and Mercantile Occupations.—A naturally numerous but well-defined group is the composite V, under clerical and mercantile occupations. This is made up of two subclasses, (1) clerks, bookkeepers, office managers, secretaries, and accountants, 58 cases; and (2) merchants, druggists, and pharmacists, 37 cases. From most to least masculine the clerical constituents fall in the following order: (1) 14 accountants, 50.5; (2) 34 clerks, 49.3; (3) 4 bookkeepers, 30.5; and (4) 6 office managers and secretaries, 3.8. Ranked from more to less masculine the mercantile constituents are as follows: (1) 14 druggists and pharmacists, 46.1; (2) 23 merchants, 37.6. Mechanical interest may be an element in the placement of the accountants, and the social interest a factor in the placement of the office managers and secretaries. The subgroups are too small for more than passing comment. Financial interest is possibly a potent element in the placement of the merchants. Our Class V rates just below the mean for the total population. Its position above the general population which is made up of persons of grade-school and high-school education may be due in part to a somewhat better education, in part to financial and administrative interest, and in part to a slightly greater element of mechanical interest than is present in the three more feminine occupational classes, VI, VII, and VIII. However, the differences are too slight to bear the weight of much generalization.

Class V is less masculine than the engineers and architects (a significant difference), than professional businessmen (a possibly significant difference), than physical-social welfare workers (difference not significant), and than mechanical occupations (difference not significant). On the other hand, the place of Class V on our scale shows that it is more masculine than VI, building occupations, by 7.0 points (difference less than its S.D.); than VII, farming occupations, by 10.4 points (1.33 S.D.$_{\text{diff.}}$). The vocational group comprised of editors, journalists, clergymen, ministers, and artists is clearly and significantly more feminine than V.

In general the placement of Class V may be ascribed in part to its level of education, which is just above that of the general population, and in part to a balance between financial, administrative, and possibly mechanical interest on the one hand against the factor of social interest on the other.

VI. Building Occupations.—Three subgroups have been combined under VI, building occupations. These rank from most masculine to least with scores as follows: 14 contractors and builders, 51.9; 23 builders, carpenters, etc., 32.2; and 8 painters, 20.5. Several factors appear to be exemplified in the relative ranks of these three subgroups: first, the educational, which doubtless in part accounts for the higher placement of the employers and contractors; second, the financial and mechanical, each of which may well contribute to the differences found; and third, the artistic which probably affects the M-F rating of the painters. The score differences between the subgroups appear rather large but are not significant because of the small size of the groups. The trends are similar to those noted among other subgroups and add evidence cumulatively to our analysis.

Class VI rates on the scale approximately at the same position as the general population. This is probably a fair placement from the educational standpoint, as the individuals making up VI are drawn from about the same groupings as our representative general population. Within the group itself the masculine financial and mechanical factors appear to be balanced by the feminine artistic interest represented in the painters. The average score for VI is significantly less masculine than that of the engineers and architects and probably also than that of the professional businessmen. The rating of this group is more feminine (but not significantly so) than the averages for the following groups: VII, farming occupation, 3.4 points (less than 1 S.D.$_{diff.}$); VIII, public-safety occupations, 8.4 points (less than 1 S.D.$_{diff.}$); IX, vocational group, 23.3 points (3.22 S.D.$_{diff.}$). The representatives of the building occupations are thus significantly more masculine than one group only, the vocational.

VII. Farming Occupations.—The group of 58 farmers is probably comprised of individuals of quite varying activities, although no subgroups could be formed. The individuals here grouped are for the most part persons of less than average education. Their occupation, if successfully pursued, of course requires a moderate facility with tools and some understanding of mechanical problems. The chauffeurs and truck drivers rank next above them and the carpenters next below. All three probably benefit in score about equally from mechanical interest. It is likely that this element has pushed all up a little from that position natural for men of their average grade of education. Elements which may weigh against the mechanical masculinity factor are animal husbandry, dairying, and other semi-domestic activities.

The farmers are significantly less masculine than the engineers and architects and than the professional business group. They are less masculine, but not significantly so, than the physical-social welfare group, 12.2 points (1.85 S.D.$_{diff.}$); than the mechanical occupations, 11.8 points (1.44 S.D.$_{diff.}$); and than the building occupations, 3.4 points (less than 1 S.D.$_{diff.}$). Class VII rates more masculine than the following: VIII, public-safety occupations, 5.0 points (less than 1 S.D.$_{diff.}$), and IX, vocational group, 19.9 points (2.93 S.D.$_{diff.}$). Again we find that the occupations are not differentiated significantly among one another as far as M-F ratings are concerned, but the farmers like the other occupational representatives are clearly divergent from the vocational group upon which they have traditionally relied for advice and direction.

VIII. Public-safety Occupations.—The two subgroups that comprise our occupational Class VIII are (1) 10 firemen, average score 28.5, and (2) 13 policemen, average score 27.4. The policemen and firemen rate at the feminine limit of the occupational classes. They are probably not less well educated than the members of many other occupational groups, and we are inclined to interpret the low score as evidence of the social-welfare influence which, as already noted, tends to operate in the feminine direction.[1]   As compared with the educational group to which these men belong, their M-F rating is more feminine, but the difference is not statistically significant.   The average score of the group is more feminine than the mean of either of the two very masculine professional groups.   It is also less masculine, although not significantly so, than the mean for physicians, surgeons, dentists, teachers and those of the four other occupational classes. It is more masculine than the vocational group, but the difference, 14.9 points, is only 1.54 its standard error.   In this fact lies an important bit of evidence in favor of our hypothesis regarding the effect of the cultural element.   It is surely significant that in the policemen and firemen the influences (1) of educational limitation, (2) of social-welfare interest, and (3) of the absence of marked mechanical interest and financial objectives operate to produce a score placement which approximates that of the highly cultured vocational group.   In fact, these civic guardians rate practically at the same point as the editors and journalists. They rate about halfway between those two superior groups, the *Who's Who* men and the husbands of *Who's Who* women.   It thus appears that the positive feminizing influence of culture is

---

[1] Are policemen really as feminine mentally as this rating indicates, or have we through unfortunate chance secured scores from an unusual sampling?   In order to check the result 15 more policemen, members of the force in a large California city, were given the M-F test.   Six men failed to complete the test; the 9 who finished rated an average score of +23.00.   The 6 men who completed only part of the test showed on the work done approximately the same degree of masculinity in score as the 9 who finished.   The average scores for the public-safety group with these 9 men added are as follows:

Occupational group	No. of cases	Mean score
VIII. Policemen and Firemen:	32	+26.5
1. Firemen	10	+28.5
2. Policemen	22	+25.6

almost equaled as far as the M-F trait is concerned by a composite made up of (1) educational limitation, (2) absence of specific mechanical and financial interest, (3) positive social-welfare concern, and (4) selective effect of civil-service positions carrying low salaries but secure tenure.   It would be especially interesting to know whether the last-named factor does tend to exclude from the ranks of civil-service employees the more ambitious, active, masculine type of man.

IX. Vocational Group.—The vocational class is composed of three subgroups with number of individuals and average scores as follows: (1) 12 editors and journalists, 27.2; (2) 63 clergymen, 12.7; and (3) 38 artists, 8.4.   The interests represented by these three classes are most diverse.   Placing them in a single vocational group is, we believe, justified (1) by their score placement as most feminine among the occupational classes, (2) by the evidence which this placement gives and which is supported also by the position of the *Who's Who* groups that some other factor besides education, age, and intelligence almost entirely determines their M-F scores. We have called this factor "culture."   We see it exemplified in the two *Who's Who* groups, men of undoubted superiority and ability, of excellent educational training and experience, who, however, rate on the scale at a point significantly below the norm for persons of college education.   It may well be that not only the positive factor of culture but certain negative factors, generally its correlates, are also operative in the placement of these most feminine of our normal groups.   Lack of mechanical, administrative, and financial interests are perhaps to be considered here.   The social-welfare element may be included in the cultural influence or it may be an additional factor.

The vocational group rates at a point near the average score for the total population in the sixties.   Culture has therefore had for this group an effect similar to that of advanced age. Class IX is less masculine than any of the eight other professional and occupational classes.   The differences are as follows: compared with I, engineers and architects, 68.2 points; II, professional businessmen, 44.3 points; III, physical-social welfare group, 32.1 points; IV, mechanical occupations, 31.8 points; V, clerical and mercantile, 30.3 points; VI, building occupations, 23.3 points; VII, farming occupations, 19.9 points; and VIII, policemen and firemen, 14.9 points. The difference is significant in every comparison except that with the policemen and firemen. Compared with high-school and college levels, which best approximate to them in average of educational training, they are significantly less masculine. They also differ significantly from the general- and from the total-population groups. All these comparisons indicate the unique position of the vocations on the M-F scale. Whether by reason of nature or nurture or by influence of both, the members of Class IX have formed mental habits that register on the M-F test in responses widely divergent from those of the common run of males. They test mentally more feminine than any other male professional or occupational group.[1] They are generally recognized as the least interested in mechanics, in business, in financial aims, and the most concerned with social welfare, religion, and the arts. In a word, they represent the "cultured" interests.

Analysis of the position of the vocational group on the M-F scale is not complete without reference to the difference between this least masculine of the occupational classes and the M-F averages of women's populations. The difference between IX and the total population of women of college education is 87.7 M-F points. The difference between it and the total population of all adult women in our group is 98.1 points. As compared to a group of women which rates among the most masculine of all on the M-F scale, that is, the 25 women listed in *Who's Who*, the difference is 58.5 points. These figures indicate that the contrast between men and women is persistently preserved and that not even the strong influence of the culture element which so modifies the scores of men in the feminine direction can bring them even approximately to the average M-F score of any representative group of women.

[1] The single male group which tested.more feminine was composed of 82 homosexuals of the passive type (see Chapter XI). These are not included in the occupational classifications.

Score Trends of Female Occupational Groups

The M-F tests of women between the ages of twenty-five and sixty-five make up the groups used for occupational classification. These have been separated into housewives and some 15 groups of other occupations containing 10 or more persons engaged in a particular activity. After a preliminary examination of the data each occupational group other than the housewives was subdivided into three sections: single women, married women who state that they are actually engaged in the occupation or profession in question, and married women who state that they are now housewives but that they were formerly engaged in this particular occupation. The three sections in the subgroups were respectively recombined into three large groups for comparison with the occupational, educational, and age classes of adult women. For purposes of interoccupational comparison the original groups have been used, including the persons who state that they are now housewives but were formerly engaged in the activity in question. Means and measures of dispersion have been calculated for the 19 occupational groups and for various combinations of these. The group of housewives has been subdivided, to add to the separate occupational groups in the manner described above. Its menbers have also been recombined on the basis of education, into four groups: grade school, high school, college for one to three years, and college graduates (Table 37).

Combinations of smaller occupational groups into larger were made (1) where the averages were near one another and the dispersions similar, and (2) where homogeneity of activity appeared to be present. The combinations on this basis were more difficult to make for the women than for the men, as homogeneity of score grouping was often not associated with homogeneity of activity. For example, hairdressers and dressmakers might seem to be concerned with equally feminine operations, yet hairdressers are among the most masculine, dressmakers among the most feminine in M-F rating. Again, one might suppose either that women who marry are more feminine than those who do not or else that

TABLE 37.—MEAN M-F SCORES OF WOMEN'S OCCUPATIONAL GROUPS AND SUBGROUPS

Professions and occupations	No. of cases	Mean M-F score	S.D.$_M$	Standard score
I. Professions......................	392	− 74.7	2.22	+.25
1. High-school and college teachers	14	− 48.1	9.36	+.85
2. Nurses......................	64	− 64.2	5.27	+.45
3. Librarians....................	20	− 68.5	8.88	+.35
4. Teachers (not high school or college)........................	149	− 72.1	3.51	+.30
II. Business occupations	303	− 80.9	2.40	+.05
1. Hairdressers..................	10	− 69.5	13.57	+.35
2. Secretaries...................	43	− 74.6	5.74	+.20
3. Secretaries, business administrators.........................	70	− 75.2	4.08	+.20
4. Office managers...............	27	− 76.2	5.34	+.20
5. Clerks, secretaries.............	105	− 77.3	3.84	+.15
6. Bookkeepers, accountants.......	46	− 77.8	6.49	+.15
7. Bookkeepers, clerks............	108	− 78.6	4.04	+.15
8. Clerks, typists................	62	− 79.1	5.14	+.10
9. Saleswomen..................	22	− 85.9	10.60	0
10. Stenographers................	70	− 92.1	5.44	−.15
III. Housewives......................	379	− 81.6	1.11	+.05
1. Married women, employed......	179	− 73.8	3.30	+.25
2. Housewives, college graduates...	108	− 75.1	3.57	+.20
3. Housewives, college education, 1–3 yrs......................	71	− 80.1	4.19	+.10
4. Housewives, grade-school education.........................	105	− 82.1	4.54	+.05
5. Married, formerly employed.....	375	− 83.9	2.14	0
6. Housewives, high-school education.........................	155	− 85.5	3.29	0
7. Housewives, formerly teachers; college education (not graduates)	61	− 91.1	5.41	−.10
8. Housewives, formerly elementary teachers......................	27	−102.8	7.11	−.40
9. Housewives, formerly domestic servants.....................	12	−107.8	10.40	−.50
Single women, employed.............	278	− 74.8	2.57	+.20
IV. Artistic occupations................	55	− 83.3	4.71	0
1. Artists, decorators, photographers	14	− 76.8	10.02	+.15
2. Musicians, music teachers.......	41	− 85.6	5.27	0
V. Domestic occupations...............	38	−100.6	7.05	−.35
1. Dressmakers, hairdressers.......	31	− 90.1	7.03	−.10
2. Dressmakers..................	21	−100.0	7.21	−.35
3. Domestic servants..............	17	−101.3	13.00	−.35

marriage has a feminizing effect. But the data show that married dressmakers differ from single dressmakers by 10 M-F points in the masculine direction, married hairdressers by 100 M-F points in the same direction, while married office managers and business administrators vary in the opposite (feminine) direction from single women in the same activities, as do also married teachers when compared with single teachers. Several trial groupings were made and the resultant means and S.D.'s arranged in scale order within the major classifications. These comparisons showed new trends quite different from any that had been anticipated, yet actually in line with the demonstrated influences of age, education, and intelligence.

TABLE 37a.—MEAN M-F SCORES OF ADULTS (WOMEN) BY EDUCATIONAL CLASSIFICATION

Educational group	No. of cases	Mean M-F score	S.D.$_M$	Standard score
A. College	760	−74.7	1.60	+.20
B. High school	820	−84.7	1.47	0
C. Grade school	287	−86.2	2.53	0
General population: grade school and high school combined	1107	−85.1	1.27	0
Total population	1867	−80.9	1.00	+.05

The occupations exhibit the following trends:

1. The educational-intelligence influence is followed more closely by the women's than by the men's groups. The women's occupations requiring most training and probably presupposing higher intelligence rate most masculine. Conversely, those requiring least training and probably including persons of least intelligence rate lowest. The two occupational extremes of groups of 10 or more persons are held by 14 high-school and college teachers, −48.1, and 17 domestic servants, −101.3. The difference between these extremes is 53.2 points and in spite of the small number of cases in each group it is statistically significant (3.32 S.D.$_{diff}$.). The educational-intelligence trend is shown

by the housewives of college education as compared to the grade-
and high-school housewives.   The latter two with marriage have
exchanged places on the scale.

2. Leadership, the direction of other people, putting over a
program, is apparently also a factor in addition to the educational-
intelligence element.   This tendency is seen first in the position

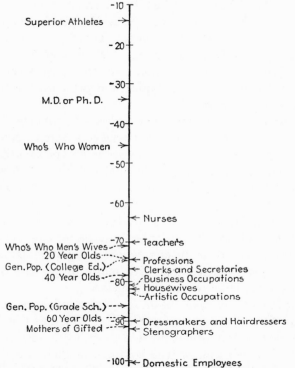

FIG. 10.—Mean M-F scores of occupational and other groups (female).

at the top of the women's range of those whose professions and
occupations involve active dominance of this sort: nurses, librarians, and teachers in the order named.   Similarly the business
administrators and office managers rate highest among the business and clerical groups, while the position of the stenographers
is notably low.   We are inclined to account mainly on this basis
for the position of the artists, photographers, and decorators,

11 M-F points above the musicians and music teachers. The work of the former, if successful, involves essentially more administrative activity than that of the latter. The educational-intelligence factor may, of course, also be present here. A special tendency probably containing many elements related to leadership is that which we may call the influence of interest in athletic sports. This is best typified by a small group of physical education teachers who rate at -36.2, which is above the position of high-school and college teachers. The element of dominance may be the most important here. But since athletic women in general, whether captains or not, show the trend we are inclined to see in this a trait of the typical independent, self-contained, unsentimental woman athlete.

3. Working outside the home appears to influence the M-F score in the masculine direction.[1] Every comparison of large groups of housewives with the women in occupations outside the home yields a statistically significant difference. Women who are not housewives but whose occupation is carried on in their own or other people's homes show the same feminine trend. For example, the dressmakers and the domestic servants, whose horizon is typically circumscribed, are more feminine than the hairdressers and cosmeticians, whose occupation is carried on away from home in contact with many people and under the stimulus of the larger world of business.

4. In general, marriage has a feminizing influence, or else the women who marry are more feminine. That this trend may be counterbalanced by others already described is seen in the fact that the married women who continue in their previous occupations score 10 M-F points more masculine than those who give up outside activities after marriage. Perhaps, however, it is the more able, better trained, and more forceful personalities who continue in occupations and professions after assuming home duties. It may even be that age alone accounts for this contrast. Comparison of the total population norm with that for all housewives and of each educational norm for women adults

---

[1] But see the discussion on pp. 230*ff*.

with the corresponding mean for housewives shows, except in the case of the grade-school comparison, the housewifely group always slightly more feminine.[1]

A corollary to the influence of marriage is a trend exemplified primarily by the 78 mothers of gifted children. The members of this select group are certainly above the general average in ability and training, yet they score more feminine than any of the educational or other adult norm groups.   It appears that this position is due to performance in a single part of the test, word association.   The responses indicate an idealistic, romantic attitude, especially toward the activities of the home and family.   The attitude is doubtless a factor in other married groups.   It may be that it is more pronounced in the better educated and that this, in part, accounts for their greater feminization after marriage.

Summarizing, the trends shown by the female occupational groups are these, arranged as nearly as possible in the order of their importance: (1) The educational-intelligence influence, apparently quite generally operative.   (2) The leadership influence.   Although related to the first trend this appears to have additional constituents, thus justifying its naming as a separate element.   A special form of it is perhaps seen in the athletic-response type.   (3) The influence of the world of business, and interests outside the home. This "broad interest trend" is operative in both married and unmarried women who carry on activities in business or in the world of ideas.   (4) Marital influence.   This usually operates opposite to the three influences enumerated above.   It is exemplified in greater degree by women of better education than by those of little schooling.   A

[1] The exception is perhaps worthy of comment, as it seems to present an interesting compensatory trend.   In so far as M-F score changes after marriage the change can hardly be attributed to the influence of early education or intelligence.   It may be in part associated with age, it is probably to a considerable extent connected with interest and occupation.   Many of the housewives of average or superior education first become interested in household activities when they begin to carry them on in their own homes.   It is possible that their other interests become more circumscribed after marriage.   On the other hand, the women of grade-school training many of whom have had no occupation outside their homes before marriage probably tend to attain a wider mental outlook by association and experience in married life.   (See also pp. 230*ff.*)

special intensification of it is seen in the response type representing an idealization of woman's specific career as wife and mother.

It is obvious from the above discussion that the trends operative in the women's occupational groups are for the most part
quite unlike those discovered in a study of the men's activities.
For the men, type of occupational or professional content was
apparently registered to a considerable degree in M-F score.
This appears to be less conspicuous in the case of the women,
whereas intelligence and, broadly speaking, ability are important
in determining women's scores. A certain analogy may be
drawn: if mechanical interest is the outstandingly masculine
trait, domestic activity is the typically feminine one. With the
men culture operates in a direction opposite to the masculine
mechanical interest, and with women intelligence, education, and
breadth of outlook act in the opposite direction to domestic
interest. Just as the unique position of the engineers implies not
only a presence of a special interest but also the absence of
certain cultural interests, so also the position of the most feminine
of the women's occupational groups implies a limitation in general
interest and culture as well as a specifically domestic mental
preoccupation. The similarity between the trends for the sexes
ends here. For men the influence of intelligence is almost
negligible, that of education is in the same direction as the typical
interest (mechanics), while age acts in the reverse direction. For
the women intelligence is probably an important factor operating
in the reverse direction from the typical interest (the domestic),
education is similarly directed, while age tends toward the
feminine limit.

Women's professions and occupations may be generally grouped
under five heads, from least to most feminine in the order named:
(1) professional, (2) business, (3) housewifely, (4) artistic, and (5)
gainful domestic. Each of the five groups includes, as stated
above, women actively engaged in the work, whether single or
married, and women now housewives who formerly followed the
occupation. This combining seemed desirable by reason of
the small size of nearly all the groups. Where groups or com-
posites were large enough, single and married were originally

isolated for comparison.   In Table 37 the means for the principal subgroups are given.   The five composite groups will be considered in the order of their rank on the M-F scale from the highest to the lowest, with analysis of the subgroup constituents of each in turn.[1]

I. The Professions.—In the professional group are included 64 nurses, 20 librarians, and 163 teachers, who rate on the M-F scale in the order given.   The respective differences between the means of these subgroups are all statistically insignificant.   The subgroups of the three constituents do not follow the same order: married nurses, married librarians, and single teachers are most masculine; single nurses, housewives formerly librarians, and housewives formerly teachers rate most feminine.   But as married and single women occupationally active outside their homes score normally at about the same point, and more masculine than housewives formerly so engaged, the only divergence from the norm is in the position of the unmarried nurses.   However, the small size of the subgroups in question does not permit of any final conclusion being drawn as to the presence or absence of real difference trends.

The nurses' and librarians' groups have not been further analyzed.   The teacher group has been subdivided wherever a sufficient number of cases were available on the basis of (1) level of professional activity, (2) education, (3) type of professional activity.

Regarding the first, level of professional activity, the evidence is of interest.   Among the active teachers a group of 5 single high-school and college teachers rates most masculine; next comes a group of 9 married high-school teachers, principals, and superintendents.   These two high-grade groups combined approach quite near to the rating of the *Who's Who* women; the scale difference is less than 3 M-F points.   Compared with the average for all teachers they are definitely more masculine (difference 29.2 M-F points, 3.02 S.D.$_{\text{diff.}}$).   A group of 5 elementary teachers rates somewhat lower, at −65.5, but this number probably includes only a small fraction of the active

[1] Some of the smaller groups not listed in the table are included in the discussion.

teachers of this rank who are included in the general "teacher" group. A comparison has been made with the teacher group of married women formerly teachers as follows: 13 housewives formerly high-school teachers rate at -80.3, 27 house wives formerly elementary teachers rate at -102.8; the difference is 22.5 M-F points (1.78 S.D.$_{diff.}$). A combined group of 115 housewives formerly teachers above the elementary grades rates -85.3, which is 17.5 M-F points more masculine than the housewives formerly elementary teachers; the difference is 2.12 times its S.D. Apparently when the evidence from both the active and the married, formerly active teacher groups is taken into account, there is considerable basis for belief that higher professional status is generally associated with a more masculine score.

With respect to education the situation is generally similar. The occupational classes may be supposed to correspond to successive educational levels. Further data are offered by a comparison of (1) 61 former teachers, college trained but not graduates, M-F score -91.1; (2) 23 former teachers, college graduates, M-F score -86.0; and (3) 10 teachers whose training extended over five years of college or more, M-F score -47.5. While the groups are small the steps seem fairly definitely to indicate association of M-F rating with educational status.

Comparison with reference to type of teaching is available to a very limited extent. It is presented here purely illustratively because of its possible bearing (1) on the special corollary to the leadership hypothesis, the athletic-objective-independent type, and (2) on the artistic and less dominant, more introverted type. A group of 6 physical education teachers rates at the very high masculine point of -36.2, while the general average for teachers is -77.3 and that for 41 music teachers and musicians is -85.6. The type groups are small but they hold similar positions in relation to the general population and to the groups of which they are a part, as do (1) athletic college women and (2) women music students. Hence, it seems that there is a factor which makes women physical education teachers rate on the M-F scale at a point more masculine than is reached by other women of equal training. We have characterized this group as of the athletic-response type. Similarly, for the music teachers there is some element other than education and intelligence which rates persons of musical occupation below the general mean. It does not appear to be a general cultural factor; culture apparently as often tends in the opposite direction, as witness the *Who's Who* group. Subjective analysis of the activities of music teachers and the personality types involved leads us to suggest that these people represent a fairly superior group of artistically gifted persons who tend to lack the dominant and directive, if not the independent, character of the other active professional women. The music teachers are relatively less interested in controlling other people, and relatively more concerned for ideal artistic standards. Such a theory would account for the M-F rating of this group as compared to the other teachers of equal general ability and status.

The position of the professional group with respect to other large groups gives evidence regarding all the points in our hypothesis. Comparison with the groups, (1) married and working, (2) single and working, (3) married, formerly working, and (4) general and total population, shows the professional women more masculine than any of the others. This is doubtless due to combined factors of age, education, intelligence, activity outside the home, and, in a large proportion of the cases, absence of marital occupation and domestic interests. Data specific to four of the separate heads are as follows: (1) In education and intelligence the professional group undoubtedly stands very high. Its mean M-F score is above the four other occupational classes, although the differences are significant only in the comparisons with the housewives $(2.78 \text{ S.D.}_{\text{diff.}})$ and with the domestic-activity group $(3.50 \text{ S.D.}_{\text{diff.}})$. The professional mean is at the same point as the norm for adult women of college education. It is above the means for the other separate and combined educational levels; the difference between the professional mean and that of women of grade- and high-school training combined is statistically significant $(4.06 \text{ S.D.}_{\text{diff.}})$. (2) Leadership and dominance are demonstrated by a comparison of the professionally active part of the group with the average score of persons of approximately equal education, and with the mean for the whole group, including those no longer active professionally. The active professional women rate 7.5 points above the women of college education (2.27 S.D.$_{diff.}$) and 7.5 points above the group as a whole (2.06 S.D.$_{diff.}$). (3) The masculine influence from working outside the home is found in high scores of the active part of the professional group compared with housewives of college education. The difference is 7.9 points (1.72 S.D.$_{diff.}$). If we include the married members no longer active the professional mean is barely above that for college housewives. (4) Perhaps a feminizing home influence is seen in the lower scores of the members who have given up their professions after marriage as compared to the higher scores of the active members.

Our professional group, constituted of elements (1) variously professional, (2) more or less well trained, (3) with relatively higher or lower intelligence, (4) with more or less well-developed qualities of leadership, and (5) more or less influenced by home duties, finds placement for its subgroups all the way from the highest to the lowest positions on the women's range of the M-F scale. As a unit the group scores in the upper fourth of the women's range and, when reduced to its most active professional element, at a point near the top of all female adult groups. It is still far surpassed by the *Who's Who* women, and rates just less masculine than the *Who's Who* men's wives. Whether married or unmarried, the active part of the professional group is made up of women capable of independent activity by reason of high mentality, superior training, and successful leadership. These traits in so far as they register on the M-F scale have been preserved by the married as well as by the single professional women in the same way, although in less degree than they have been preserved after marriage by the select group of *Who's Who* women. Since the active professional group rates at approximately the same point as the wives of *Who's Who* men we may suppose that occupational activity has done for the former, whose average intelligence may be somewhat lower, what association, native ability, and probably a high type of nonprofessional activity have done for the latter.

II. Business Occupations.—The business group includes (1) 7 auditors, (2) 5 stenographers and secretaries, (3) 10 hairdressers and cosmeticians, (4) 3 telephone operators, (5) 4 merchants and proprietors, (6) 43 secretaries, (7) 27 business operators and proprietors, (8) 46 bookkeepers and accountants, (9) 62 clerks and typists, (10) 22 store clerks and saleswomen, (11) 70 stenographers, and (12) 4 bookkeeper-stenographers. These rank from most to least masculine in the order named. The difference from the highest to the lowest mean score is 25 M-F points. The mean for the first five subgroups is above the total mean for the professions, the mean for the last two is below the mean for the artistic occupations, and the difference between these two extremes is probably statistically significant. The groups were recombined for Table 37.

The three subgroups, (*a*) married and working, (*b*) single and working, and (*c*) housewives who formerly worked, rate from most to least masculine in the order named. In contrast to the usual condition the difference between the married and the single business women (7.8 M-F points) is almost as large as that between the married business women and the married formerly in business. This holds in both the lower and the higher testing groups of the composite and seems to be generally representative of the business class.

Nine of the 12 business groups score between −70 and −80 on the M-F scale, the other three between −85 and −95. The 9 groups contain all the proprietors and independent operators, and the more experienced, better paid, and more responsible types of office workers. The M-F range of means within the business group is as great as the distance from the mean of the professional group to the mean of the domestic-service group. The influences of intelligence, education, breadth of interest, and independence of activity on M-F position are obvious. The business women are 6.2 points more feminine than the professional women (1.90 S.D.$_{\text{diff.}}$). They are 4.1 points more masculine than the artistic group (less than 1 S.D.$_{\text{diff.}}$). They are 6.1 points more feminine than the married working women (1.74 S.D.$_{\text{diff.}}$), and 6.1 points more feminine than the single working women (1.73 S.D.$_{\text{diff.}}$).

They rate at exactly the same position as the total test population and 4.2 points above the general population (1.54 S.D.$_{diff.}$). The business women test more feminine than college women (2.15 S.D.$_{diff.}$) but more masculine than high-school (1.35 S.D.$_{diff.}$) and grade-school (1.52 S.D.$_{diff.}$) groups. Education and intelligence thus practically account for the average ratings of these women. What some of them have gained in M-F score through their more independent activity, others have lost through the influence of domestic activity; the result is a score well above that of the general population but nearer to it than to the professional score.

III. The Housewives.—A group of 379 housewives who have never had any other occupation includes 105 of grade-school education, 155 of high-school education, 11 of high-school and normal-school education, and 108 of college education. The means for the 4 subgroups rate from most to least masculine in the order (a) college, (b) grade school, (c) high school and normal, (d) high school. The difference between the first two combined and the second two combined is more than 2 S.D.$_{diff.}$. The general tendency found elsewhere for education to correlate with M-F score is not eliminated by the element of common domestic experience. Comparison with the total population at successive educational levels shows that housewives of average and above average education are more masculine than the corresponding general groups, whereas housewives of grade-school education are more feminine. The scale positions of the subgroups of college housewives are in the order (1) college education, five years or more, (2) college graduates (four-year course), (3) college one to three years, with a difference of 18.5 points between the extremes.

Compared with the two groups (a) single and working and (b) married and working, the housewives and the housewives who formerly worked are significantly more feminine. This means one of two things: either women whose first and only occupation is that of housewife, and women who give up some other occupation when they become housewives, are intrinsically more feminine than single or married working women, or else they become more feminine as a result of age plus domesticity. The reader may be tempted to say that the mentally feminine woman has a mind like that of the typical domestic servant, the mentally masculine woman like that of women listed in *Who's Who*. This is true so far as total score on the present M-F test is concerned. It would be equally true to say that to be mentally feminine means to have a mind like that of typical mothers of intellectually gifted children (such mothers averaging high in education and intelligence), and to be mentally masculine means to have a mind like that of women athletes and women directors of physical education. Both statements are true, in terms of the M-F test, but either taken alone is misleading. It would be equally true to say, in the comparison of male groups, that to be mentally feminine means to have a mind like that of the typical male homosexual prostitute. We found that so far as total score on the M-F test is concerned, the highly feminine score of the latter group is closely approximated by Protestant ministers, Protestant theological students, and Catholic students training for the priesthood. To say that these groups "have minds like" those of male homosexual prostitutes would be sufficiently absurd to show the danger of generalized characterizations which go beyond the specific items of this particular test.

Only with this emphatic warning do we deem it safe to call the reader's attention, as we have in Table 38, to the percentages in the housewife and other principal groups who reach the two extremes, represented by *Who's Who* women and domestic servants. All the principal trends are exemplified in this table. Superior groups have in general the larger percentages of more masculine women. The exceptions are the artistic women and the mothers of gifted children. The position of the mothers of gifted children may reflect the feminizing influence of their idealistic attitude toward their privileges as mothers.

The housewives' average score on the M-F scale is about midway within the women's range. The education and probably the intelligence of this group is above the general average. But domestic occupation plus age counterbalance the masculine trend of these factors. Various special populations of housewives

TABLE 38.—PER CENT OF WOMEN IN DIFFERENT SUBGROUPS WHO TESTED AT THE LEVEL OF *Who's Who* WOMEN OR OF DOMESTIC SERVANTS

Subgroups	No. of cases	Per cent more masculine than the average Who's Who women (av. −45)	Per cent more feminine than the average domestic servant (av. −101)
Who's Who women..................	25	44	12
Wives of *Who's Who* men..............	24	24	25
I. Professional group:	392	26	38
Married and working...........	179	24	26
Single and working............	278	26	27
II. Business.......................	303	20	31
III. Housewives.....................	379	16	30
Housewives who formerly worked	375	18	34
IV. Artistic occupations:	55	14	29
Mothers of gifted children............	78	8	41
V. Domestic activities	17	0	55

illustrate the relative influences of the several masculine and the feminine trends in our hypothesis.[1]

IV. Artistic Occupations.—The subgroups which form the artistic occupation class and rate on the M-F scale from most to least masculine, in the order named, are 14 artists, photographers, decorators, and 41 musicians and music teachers. The difference between the means of the two main subgroups is statistically significant.

The musicians and music teachers, whether single or married, or housewives who were formerly engaged in this activity, all rate approximately at the same point. The artists, photographers, and decorators, on the other hand, show a fairly wide range from their most masculine constituent, the married members, to their most feminine, the unmarried group. However, all these subgroups are very small and perhaps not truly representative. The average of the group as a whole falls below the mean for the housewives and between the mean for housewives of grade-school training and those of high-school training. The group registers

[1] It should be remembered that the age factor is not constant in the comparisons in Table 38.

at a point intermediate between the total population and the general population. It is 8.6 points more feminine than the professional average (1.65 S.D.$_{diff.}$) and 4.1 points more feminine than the business group (less than 1 S.D.$_{diff.}$). It is 17.3 points more masculine than the domestic-activity group (2.04 S.D.$_{diff.}$). The deviation from the mean of women of college education is the only considerable one in a comparison in terms of education, but this is less than 2 S.D.$_{diff.}$. Similar are the differences between the artistic group and (1) the women married and working and (2) those single and working. We may reasonably assume that these women are above the median for intelligence and training. Their position below the average on the M-F scale may be attributed in part to less than average ability in those traits which exhibit themselves in dominating and directing other people. Because of the high masculine position of the *Who's Who* women, the factor of culture cannot be thought of as explaining the M-F score of the artistic occupations.

V. Gainful Domestic Activities.—This group is composed of 21 dressmakers and 17 domestic servants whose M-F scores rank in the order given. Again, as in the case of the artistic occupations, the married members of the group rate most masculine, the housewives who were formerly engaged in the occupation next, and the single women most feminine. These differences are fairly large in the case of the dressmakers but the numbers are too small to make the contrast definitely significant.

The domestic group is more feminine than any of the large populations, professional, occupational, educational, and housewifely. The differences are from two to four times their respective standard deviations. The very low position of the group seems to indicate the nature of the extreme feminine mental type. In this instance it signifies less than average intelligence and education, and more than average dependence and submission. The group stands in direct contrast to the Ph.D.'s and M.D.'s, the *Who's Who* women, women interested in athletic sports, and women who are active homosexuals.

Summarizing: (1) The women's occupations have an M-F range about half as great as the men's. (2) The more masculine groups tend to be the better educated and the more intelligent. (3) Counter to this tendency operate home interest and housewifely activity. (4) The influence of occupation tends to be stronger than the influence of home duties after marriage. Women are more apt to score with their occupational group than with the housewifely group. (5) Apparently the trend of married experience is toward the mean for the total population of women: the women belonging to the most masculine occupational and educational classes tend to score more feminine if married, those who belong to the more feminine occupations tend to score more masculine if married. Perhaps this is accounted for by the fact that the more masculine scores of the upper group before marriage are in part due to the absence of household occupation and interest, while the more feminine scores of the lower group are due to limitations in general outlook. For the higher testing women marriage brings contact with specifically womanly activities in the home, in the other case it brings opportunity for wider association with less limited ideas.

CHAPTER IX

EFFECT OF INTERESTS ON THE M-F SCORE

Self-rated Interests

Occupation gives a fairly objective expression of interest and we have seen that its influence on the M-F score is marked. We are now to consider the influence of interests based upon self-ratings of "likes" and "dislikes." It is no condemnation of such ratings that they are subjective, for they reflect in an important way certain temperamental and motivational aspects of the personality. When an adult makes such statements as: "I like music very much," "I care little or not at all for travel," or "I suppose I am less interested in politics than the average," these must be taken as significant data; they are probably almost as trustworthy as when in response to ordinary questioning an adult answers, "I am a carpenter," or "I am a trained nurse." Expressions of interest no doubt sometimes have a large element of wish or fancy and may be quite inaccurate registries of the totality of attitudes. But these features by no means brand them as non-significant. For example, musicians rate their interest in music at the highest point, but so do many persons who are not musicians. Thus a high rating of interest in music does not necessarily connote a musician, but rather an individual who values this type of experience; and similarly for other interests. Again temperamental differences may cause some individuals to rate many interests at a high point, others to rate few above average, and such deviations have significance for personality. "Likes" and "dislikes" represent partial cross-sections of the individual at a given time and might well be expected to correlate to some extent with the M-F rating, which is also in a sense a cross-section measure.

Several hundred adult subjects rated their interest in each of twelve type activities on a five-point scale from the highest point,

"having much interest," to the lowest, "having little or none."[1]
The cross-on-a-line method was employed. The twelve activities,
in the order in which they appeared on the blank, are as follows:
travel, sports, religion, mechanics, social life, literature, music,
art, science, politics, domestic arts, and pets. In selecting these
twelve it was our intent to include some that were typically
masculine, others typically feminine.

Correlations were computed between M-F score and interest
ratings on the five-point scale for several age and educational
groups of both sexes. These showed for both males and females a
negative correlation averaging about —.40 between masculinity
and interest in religion. Otherwise the correlations were irregular, contradictory, and usually quite low. The excessive use
of the "average" category in part accounts for this condition.
An attempt was therefore made to derive more usable results
by the computation of mean M-F score for subjects rating themselves as having "very much interest" or "little or no interest."
The discussion that follows is based on the consideration of these
means. Various comparisons of the means with each other and
with the averages of unselected high-school and college adult
populations have been made. The interests found to be characteristic of relatively higher or lower M-F scores have been
combined into typical groupings and the relation of these interest
constellations to the M-F score has been examined. The tendency to rate many interests as either very strong or very weak
has been considered with reference to the M-F scores of the
individuals in the various "enthusiasm" or "indifference"
groupings.

The Masculinity-femininity of Male Interests

Two hundred and twelve men[2] of high-school education
between the ages of twenty-five and sixty-five grouped on the
basis of their expression of "very much interest" earn the mean
M-F scores shown in Tables 40a and 40b. These are arranged in

---

[1] The "interests" appeared only on the final edition of the M-F test. Ratings
are therefore available for only part of our total population.

[2] All of the adult males of high-school education between twenty-five and
sixty-five who had filled out this particular edition of M-F test blanks.

order from the most masculine to the most feminine. Comparison of this and succeeding rank orders of the interests with the original order of presentation for rating (above) on the M-F blank shows no evidence that the presentation order influenced the ratings.

TABLE 40a.—AVERAGE M-F SCORES OF ADULT MALES OF HIGH-SCHOOL EDUCATION EXPRESSING "VERY MUCH INTEREST" IN CERTAIN PURSUITS

Expressing very much interest in	Mean M-F score	No. of cases	Per cent of 212 cases	Standard score[1]
1. Science	+59.6	44	21	+.40
2. Mechanics	+54.8	65	31	+.30
3. Sports	+52.7	73	34	+.30
4. Travel	+51.1	93	44	+.25
5. Social life	+46.8	16	7.5	+.15
6. Pets	+46.6	41	19	+.15
7. Politics	+46.2	28	13	+.15
8. Literature	+42.9	42	20	+.10
9. Music	+38.0	56	26	.00
10. Religion	+31.8	31	15	−.10
11. Domestic arts	+28.8	3	1.5	−.10
12. Art	+16.2	21	10	−.35

[1] The standard score for the population from which these cases are drawn is +.15.

TABLE 40b.—AVERAGE M-F SCORES OF ADULT MALES OF HIGH-SCHOOL EDUCATION EXPRESSING "LITTLE OR NO INTEREST" IN CERTAIN PURSUITS

Expressing little or no interest in	Mean M-F score	No. of cases	Per cent of 212 cases	Standard score[1]
1. Religion	+71.6	57	27	+.65
2. Domestic arts	+60.2	126	59	+.45
3. Art	+59.2	112	53	+.40
4. Music	+57.4	55	26	+.35
5. Pets	+54.9	77	36	+.30
6. Literature	+54.8	46	22	+.30
7. Social life	+53.4	49	23	+.30
8. Politics	+49.2	63	30	+.20
9. Science	+47.6	75	35	+.20
10. Mechanics	+40.7	59	28	+.05
11. Sports	+37.4	26	12	.00
12. Travel	+19.1	7	3	−.30

[1] The standard score for the population from which these cases are drawn is +.15.

The individuals in the same population who express "little or no interest" in a given one of the 12 activities rate from most to least masculine as presented in Table 40*b*. The order in the second list may be seen at a glance to be almost the reverse of the first. The two rank orders together show (1) the masculine-feminine contrast between mechanical or scientific trends on the one hand and cultural interests on the other. This result seems to reflect the trend already noted in connection with the occupations. (2) The tendency for negative interest to rate at a more masculine level than positive interest. Item for item the "little or no interest" rates regularly higher than the corresponding "much interest"; the average difference is 7 M-F points. This tendency to express little or no interest is also more popular (is shown by more individuals) than positive enthusiasms in this group of men. (3) The range from the highest to the lowest average is for the positive interests 44 M-F points (.80 standard score), for the negative interests 52 M-F points (.95 standard score). The smaller of these ranges is more than twice, the larger is more than three times, the range from the most to the least masculine of the three large occupational groups.

With respect to the contrast between the scientific-mechanical interests and the cultural interests the evidence is nonconflicting. The lists agree in denoting as masculine traits (*a*) much interest in science, mechanics, sports, and travel; and correlatively (*b*) little or no interest in religion, domestic arts, art, music, and literature. Relatively feminine traits are similarly found to be (*a*) much interest in art, domestic arts, religion, music, and literature, and (*b*) little or no interest in travel, sports, and mechanics. In general this conforms with the popular view. The difference between the average M-F score of men who profess very much interest in a particular activity and the average of those who say they care little or not at all for it is greatest in the case of art; then follow in the order named religion, domestic arts, travel, music, literature, sports, mechanics, science, pets, social life, and politics. For domestic arts the difference is 2.4 S.D.$_{diff.}$; for religion, art, and travel it is more than 3.6 S.D.$_{diff.}$. The other differences are less than twice their standard deviations.

In both interest lists the contrasted trends are definitely expressed and in three cases the divergences from the general mean for men of comparable educational opportunity are fairly demonstrable statistically.   These three instances show that men who have (1) much interest in art, (2) little interest in religion, and (3) little interest in domestic arts are probably definitely divergent from the generality; the first in the feminine, the second and third in the masculine direction.

Of the negative interests all except mechanics, sports, and travel belong to individuals of more than average masculinity. It is worthy of note that our results indicate that positive interests are not so closely associated with masculinity as the negative ones.   Positive interest in science is the only item in the first list that has a score larger than the lowest of the first six items in the second list.   This seems to indicate a tendency to opposition or outright repudiation of certain interests as a definitely masculine trait.   In this population it is more masculine not to be interested than to be interested, especially along cultural lines, but it should be noted that the extreme type of negative interest represented by the repudiation of religion and domestic arts, and extreme positive interest in art, both connote a demonstrable divergence from the generality.

A further point in this connection is the stronger tendency not to be interested than to be interested.   Positive are more numerous that negative ratings only for mechanics, sports, and travel.   Approximately equal numbers are (a) interested, and (b) not interested, in literature and music.   Negative ratings are considerably more numerous for science, social life, pets, politics, religion, domestic arts, and art.   In the case of the last two activities the differences are very great (58 and 43 per cent respectively).   The average number of men who have much interest in one or another of the 12 lines is 20 per cent, the average number who have little or no interest is 30 per cent.

Another evidence of the negative relationship between the breadth of interest of adult males and their M-F scores is found in a comparison of the averages classed by number of interests, positive versus negative, without regard to what these interests are. From Table 41 it is clear, in spite of the fact that the differences are not definitely significant statistically, that the more numerous the interests the more feminine the score, while the repudiation of interests has the opposite effect. The 35 individuals who avow no enthusiasms whatever score at $+.05$ standard score; those who avow no indifferences score at $-.25$ standard score.

TABLE 41.—M-F SCORES OF MEN OF HIGH-SCHOOL EDUCATION COMPARED ON THE BASIS OF THE NUMBER OF THEIR POSITIVE AND NEGATIVE INTERESTS

Interest direction		In 0 interests	In 1 or more	In 2 or more	In 3 or more	In 4 or more	In 5 or more	In 6 or more	In 7 or more
Positive interests (having "very much interest")	N	35	177	143	97	59	29	12	6
	Mean	$+40.2$	$+51.6$	$+51.1$	$+44.9$	$+38.6$	$+30.5$	$+32.2$	..
	S.D.$_M$	9.94	3.89	4.54	5.75	7.70	10.00	14.62	..
Negative interests (having "little or no interest")	N	19	195	164	146	107	76	45	16
	Mean	$+21.0$	$+52.9$	$+56.6$	$+57.4$	$+53.9$	$+56.0$	$+50.9$	$+63.0$
	S.D.$_M$	13.10	2.71	2.96	4.26	4.87	5.78	7.42	14.35

The positive-interest averages cover the M-F scale range from the vocational mean below to the professional business mean above. The negative-interest means extend from about the same lower limit to cover more than half of the distance between the professional businessmen and the engineers and architects. Having little or no interest in religion apparently tends to place men of high-school education at the same point on the M-F scale as an engineering course places college men. Positive interest in art has almost as profound an effect but in the feminine direction.

The differences between the M-F means of those expressing positive and negative interest in each of the twelve pursuits are shown in Table 42. The arrangement is by amount of difference from the largest positive to the largest negative divergence. In the adult male population of high-school graduates those who are much interested in travel are definitely more masculine than those who have little or no interest in travel. Those who are much interested in sports, mechanics, and science are possibly also more masculine than the men who do not care for these pursuits. Politics, social life, and pets are not diagnostic of masculinity or femininity in this group. The supporters of these interests rate a shade less masculine than the men who repudiate them, but the difference is less than its S.D. Interest in literature, music, and domestic arts indicates a more feminine trend than lack of interest in these matters, while interest in religion or in art is a mark of definitely greater femininity than the avowed lack of these interests. The largest differences in score are not always the most significant, because of the differences in the sizes of the groups.

TABLE 42.—DIFFERENCES BETWEEN AVERAGE M-F SCORES OF ADULT MALES OF HIGH-SCHOOL EDUCATION WHO EXPRESS "VERY MUCH INTEREST" IN VARIOUS PURSUITS AND THE AVERAGE OF THOSE WHO EXPRESS "LITTLE OR NO INTEREST"

Interests	M-F score diff.	Diff. $\overline{\text{S.D.}_{\text{diff.}}}$
1. Travel	+32.1	3.73
2. Sports	+15.3	1.44
3. Mechanics	+14.1	1.53
4. Science	+12.0	1.22
5. Politics	− 3.0	<1
6. Social life	− 6.6	<1
7. Pets	− 8.3	<1
8. Literature	−12.0	1.10
9. Music	−19.4	1.84
10. Domestic arts	−36.4	2.40
11. Religion	−39.8	3.98
12. Art	−43.0	3.64

Thus far we have considered only males of high-school education. Do the same or different tendencies appear in other populations of adult males? In order to answer this question data on interests were collected from a group of men of college education by the same method described for the high-school adult group. The means for the positive and negative interests of this group have been computed and are presented for comparison in Tables 43a and 43b. It should be kept in mind that the general college mean has a standard score index of +.25,

TABLE 43*a*.—MEAN M-F SCORES OF ADULT MALES OF COLLEGE EDUCATION WHOSE SELF-RATINGS INDICATED "VERY MUCH INTEREST" IN CERTAIN PURSUITS

Expressing very much interest in	Average M-F score	No. of cases	Standard score[1]
1. Sports	68.2	101	+.55
2. Social life	66.1	16	+.55
3. Mechanics	65.1	92	+.50
4. Science	64.9	67	+.50
5. Literature	61.8	35	+.45
6. Travel	61.2	112	+.45
7. Pets	56.8	52	+.35
8. Politics	51.7	34	+.25
9. Music	42.1	68	+.10
10. Art	41.8	19	+.05
11. Religion	35.2	30	0
12. Domestic arts	33.8	6	−.05

[1] The standard score of the group from which these cases are drawn is +.25.

TABLE 43*b*.—MEAN M-F SCORES OF ADULT MALES OF COLLEGE EDUCATION WHOSE SELF-RATINGS INDICATED "LITTLE OR NO INTEREST" IN CERTAIN PURSUITS

Expressing little or no interest in	Average M-F score	No. of cases	Standard score[1]
1. Religion	76.6	84	+.70
2. Art	65.2	132	+.50
3. Music	63.5	60	+.50
4. Domestic arts	61.8	154	+.45
5. Social life	61.6	57	+.45
6. Politics	60.6	65	+.40
7. Pets	55.8	88	+.35
8. Literature	54.4	54	+.30
9. Science	47.7	85	+.20
10. Mechanics	45.9	74	+.15
11. Sports	37.8	35	0
12. Travel	28.3	18	−.15

[1] The standard score of the group from which these cases are drawn is +.25.

whereas the general high-school mean index was +.15. An upward trend of all the interest means is therefore to be anticipated for the college group as compared with the figures for the high-school men. In the high-school group the combined positive-interest means averaged +.10 s.s., which is .15 s.s. below the group norm; the combined negative-interest means averaged +.24 s.s., which is .09 s.s. above the group norm. In the college group the combined positive interests show an s.s. index of +.31, or .06 above the group norm; the negative interests of +.33, or .08 above the group norm. Positive interests in college men are therefore associated with greater masculinity than in high-school men, both relatively and absolutely; negative interests on the other hand are absolutely but not relatively more masculine in college men. Putting it in another way we may say that positive interests in college men tend to make them more rather than less masculine than the generality of their group and that this is in contrast to the effect in the high-school group. In one interest, domestic arts, the opposite effect occurs; in religion, music, politics, and science about the expected amount of gain occurs. In travel, mechanics, sports, and art the displacement is larger than was to be expected; in literature and social life much larger. We may say then that almost certainly literature and social life have a stronger masculine influence on college than on high-school men and that to some extent travel, mechanics, sports, and art are associated with greater masculinity in the more highly educated group. We may say further that positive interests are frequently associated with more than average masculinity in men of college training, whereas this is less frequently the case with men of high-school education.

As in the population of high-school education so here too the active mechanical pursuits hold a masculine position, the cultural pursuits a feminine one. Sports, mechanics, and science are three of the four most masculine pursuits and repudiation of them is a negative trend. Dislike of travel connotes in both populations a feminine quality, although great interest in travel is for the college men not so masculine a trait, relatively, as it was for high-school men. Perhaps the term differs in significance for the two groups. In the mind of the man of less education "travel" may mean simply going from one place to another, an independent exploratory and boyishly active pursuit which might perhaps even include hunting and fishing. For the college man it may well have a more intellectual coloring and it is doubtless for him as apt to represent pursuit of culture as it is activity on its own account.   Interest in social life also changes its position in the college ratings.   It has become one of the two most masculine traits.   It is perhaps to be expected that a college experience will cultivate certain interests and discourage others, and that these tendencies would persist in later life.

It is noteworthy that negative interests as a whole do not contrast with positive ones in college men as they did in the men of high-school education.   The average standard score of high-school men with expressed enthusiasms was +.10 s.s., or .05 below the group norm.   The corresponding score for the bar-barians of high-school education, the men who had little or no interest in the pursuits in question, was +.24 s.s., or .09 above the norm.   In the college group the enthusiasms rate at +.31 s.s., the indifferences at +.33 s.s., both being slightly above the norm (+.25) for their group as a whole.   We are inclined to see here a characteristic difference between men at the two educational levels.   In the less educated, positive interest tends to be feminine, indifference a typical masculine attitude; in the more highly educated an attitude of indifference still tends to be masculine, but an attitude of positive interest is almost equally so.   Most masculine of all are still the men who have little or no interest in religion, but it is more masculine to have much interest in sports, social life, and mechanics than to have little or none in any of the other interests.

Table 44 shows for the college adult group the differences between the average scores of the much and the little or not-at-all interested for each of the 12 pursuits.   The rank order and the values are quite similar to those (in Table 42) for the high-school adult group.

The positive-interest means of the college group cover a range excluding the vocations but including all the principal professions except engineering (Fig. 11).   Even the high masculine negative-interest means do not reach to the unusual rating of the professional engineers.   None of the positive or negative interests rates nearly so feminine as the vocations of art and the ministry,

TABLE 44.—DIFFERENCES BETWEEN AVERAGE M-F SCORES OF ADULT MALES OF COLLEGE EDUCATION WHO EXPRESS "VERY MUCH INTEREST" IN VARIOUS PURSUITS AND THE AVERAGE OF THOSE WHO EXPRESS "LITTLE OR NO INTEREST"

Interests	M-F score diff.	$\dfrac{\text{Diff.}}{\text{S.D.}_{\text{diff.}}}$
1. Travel	+32.9	2.69
2. Sports	+30.4	4.06
3. Mechanics	+19.2	2.54
4. Science	+17.2	2.42
5. Literature	+ 7.4	<1
6. Social life	+ 4.5	<1
7. Pets	+ 1.0	<1
8. Politics	− 8.9	<1
9. Domestic arts	−28.0	1.95
10. Art	−23.4	1.84
11. Music	−21.4	2.73
12. Religion	−41.4	5.28

although many individuals in the vocational group, especially among the clergy, are college men. A point of difference between high-school and college men appears in the occupational comparison. Interest, whether positive or negative, is more important than occupation in its relation to the extreme M-F scores of men of high-school education. In college men the extreme positions, both masculine and feminine, are held by professional and not by interest groups. Personal interests are wider than the attitudes developed through occupation, but the complex mental behavior created through the professions and the vocations may develop more conspicuous masculinity or feminity than simple individual interests.

The interests of individuals in such professions as engineering, the ministry, or art might, if measured adequately as constellations instead of separately and incompletely, show a close relationship to the M-F score. Since the average scores of individuals rated on the basis of single interests show definite masculine or feminine trends, the scores of persons who combine two or more of the extreme interests might be expected to show the same trends intensified. Positive interest in science,

mechanics, sports, or travel is associated with masculinity.   Will
not then great interest in two or more of these indicate still greater
masculinity?

Four interest constellations built from the extreme scores in the
positive- and negative-interest series are analyzed in Table 45.

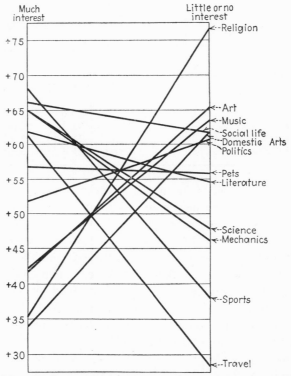

Fig. 11.—Mean M-F scores of adult males with much interest or little or no
interest in various fields.

Men of high-school education who have (1) positive scientific,
mechanical, active interests are compared with an intellectually
related group, namely (2) those who have little or no interest in
music, religion, domestic arts, and art.   (3) Those who have very
much interest in music, religion, domestic arts, and art are then
compared with their theoretical correlates, (4) those who have

little or no interest in science, mechanics, sports, or travel. The tabular values show that where two interests are combined in each of the four groups the negative masculine constellation rates highest, the negative feminine constellation second, and the two positive groups in their expected order in the last two places. The same order is preserved where three interests are combined in each constellation, but here the extremes show an intensified trend. In the last column the intensification of the extremes persists, but here both the positive and the negative masculine trends have become increasingly masculine. In the population analyzed there is evidence of more or less cumulative effect in each of the groupings. It is most pronounced in the negative masculine group and in the positive feminine one. The difference between the average score of 9 men who profess little or no interest in music, religion, domestic arts, and art and the average score of 11 who profess much interest in three of these interests is 93 M-F points. The distance is greater than the range from the mean of the most masculine to that of the most feminine occupational, professional, or vocational groups or subgroups.

TABLE 45.—M-F Scores of Cumulative Interests in Four Typical Constellations (Men of High-school Education)

Interest constellations			Combination of 2 interests	Combination of 3 interests	Combination of 4 interests
Positive masculine	Very much interest in science, mechanics, sports, travel	N	59	20	10
		Mean	+45.4	+44.5	+ 68.5
		S.D.$_M$	6.92	10.21	23.23
Negative masculine	Little or no interest in music, religion, domestic arts, art	N	74	43	9
		Mean	+60.0	+57.9	+106.1
		S.D.$_M$	6.08	6.96	
Positive feminine	Very much interest in music, religion, domestic arts, art	N	26	11	1
		Mean	+34.4	+12.3	− 9.5
		S.D.$_M$	8.55	16.35	..
Negative feminine	Little or no interest in science, mechanics, sports, travel	N	57	20	9
		Mean	+48.4	+48.5	+ 63.8
		S.D.$_M$	6.90	10.67	..

Summarizing the results for the adult males, we may say that interests as rated by the individuals themselves show a relationship with the M-F score that agrees with the occupational findings. Men with objective and mechanical interests tend to rate more masculine than the average, men with cultural interests including those typical of the vocational group rate more feminine than the average. Furthermore, the masculine interests tend to be typically active, the feminine interests to be typically sedentary. The men of college education show the same general trend as the adult population with high-school training. The various interests hold for them about the same relative placements, but the entire series is at a more masculine level in line with the expected influence of education on the M-F score.

In the adult high-school population breadth of interest tends to feminize, whereas barbarianism, *i.e.*, "having little or no interest," even in masculine pursuits, is a masculine trait. The men who are much interested in art are probably significantly more feminine than the population to which they belong, while those who have little or no interest in religion or domestic art are also a group apart but in the excessively masculine direction.

A very *masculine* man in the adult population at the high-school level of education is rather inclined not to admit positive enthusiasms. He may have much interest in science, mechanics, sports, and perhaps travel, usually has no great interest in social life, literature, or pets, and only average interest in politics. He has typically little or no interest in religion, domestic arts, art, or music. An *average* man of the same population may have much or little interest in politics, he has usually average interest in science, mechanics, sports, and travel, and also in religion, domestic arts, art, and music. He is prone to like rather than dislike social life, literature, and pets. A *feminine* man of moderate education is one who is much interested in cultural pursuits, art, religion, music, and literature, and who cares little or not at all for the active or mechanical interests: travel, sports, mechanics, science. He has probably average interest in politics, social life, and pets. He does not dislike domestic arts. He has more positive than negative interests.

The *masculine* individual of college education likes sports, mechanics, and science. He may dislike social life but he is more apt to care for it. He is not likely to be interested in domestic arts and he dislikes or is indifferent to religion, art, and music. Average interests are for him literature, travel, pets, and politics. The well-educated man of *average* masculinity is not extreme in his attitude toward sports, social life, mechanics, science, religion, art, music, and domestic arts. He may care much or little for literature, pets, and politics. He is more apt than not to be a devotee of travel. The *feminine* college man is a man of culture and quiet pursuits. He is not especially attracted to science, mechanics, or sports, and may have little interest in travel. He neither likes nor dislikes social life, politics, and pets.

THE MASCULINITY-FEMININITY OF FEMALE INTERESTS

Self-ratings on interests were available from 533 women of high-school education ranging in age from 25 to 65. The data were obtained in the way described for the men. Averages of the M-F scores for the women expressing "very much interest" or

TABLE 46*a*.—AVERAGE M-F SCORES OF ADULT FEMALES OF HIGH-SCHOOL EDUCATION EXPRESSING "VERY MUCH INTEREST" IN CERTAIN PURSUITS

Expressing very much interest in	Mean M-F score	No. of cases	Per cent of 533 cases	Standard score
1. Mechanics	−66.3	19	3.6	+.40
2. Sports	−70.4	104	19.1	+.30
3. Politics	−71.0	26	4.9	+.30
4. Pets	−77.5	128	24.0	+.15
5. Literature	−79.8	160	30.0	+.10
6. Science	−82.8	33	6.2	+.05
7. Travel	−85.2	235	44.1	0
8. Social life	−86.1	65	12.2	0
9. Music	−86.8	205	38.4	0
10. Domestic arts	−89.3	192	35.9	−.05
11. Art	−90.4	108	20.2	−.10
12. Religion	−93.1	139	26.1	−.15

"little or no interest" for each of the 12 type pursuits in the list appear in Tables 46*a* and 46*b*. As for the men, so too for the women, the positive-interest series if reversed would read almost like the negative series.

TABLE 46b.—AVERAGE M-F SCORES OF ADULT FEMALES OF HIGH-SCHOOL EDUCATION EXPRESSING "LITTLE OR NO INTEREST" IN CERTAIN PURSUITS

Expressing little or no interest in	Mean M-F score	No. of cases	Per cent of 533 cases	Standard score
1. Religion..................	−60.9	67	12.5	+.55
2. Social life................	−74.2	72	13.5	+.25
3. Music....................	−84.2	83	15.5	0
4. Politics..................	−84.7	274	51.4	0
5. Mechanics...............	−85.3	376	70.5	0
6. Art......................	−85.8	171	32.0	0
7. Domestic art.............	−87.7	54	10.1	−.05
8. Science..................	−88.7	287	53.8	−.05
9. Pets.....................	−91.0	178	28.4	−.10
10. Travel...................	−91.0	50	9.4	−.10
11. Sports...................	−92.2	161	30.2	−.15
12. Literature...............	−95.9	44	8.3	−.25

Analysis of the two series reveals certain features. (1) The masculine-feminine contrast for the women seems to be one between active extradomestic interests and the ladylike pursuits of home. (2) Positive interests tend on the average to be slightly more masculine than negative interests. The difference amounts to about 5 M-F points. The negative interests show a wider range at both extremes, but their average is at the norm for the population to which these women belong. (3) The positive-interest range of .55 s.s. extends above the professional women's mean, but does not reach the very feminine position of the gainful domestic activities. The negative interest range of .80 s.s. extends from above the most masculine profession (nursing) to the level of the most feminine occupational average.

The active nondomestic, nonfeminine interests, mechanics, sports, and politics connote masculinity in women of moderate education. There is no interest whose adherents in this population rate as feminine as the enthusiasts for these male pursuits rate in the masculine direction. The three interests that exert a feminine pull are religion, art, and domestic arts. Comparing the two lists extended to include even the small differences from the general mean, we find the contrasting factors to be wide and varied intellectual and scientific interest on the one hand, religious, artistic, and domestic pursuits on the other. The position of literature definitely apart from religion, art, and music is in contrast to the cultural grouping of the feminine interests of the men. The negative interests substantiate the interpretation. Indifference to religion and social life are definitely masculine attitudes. Feminine on the other hand is lack of interest in literature, sports, travel, and pets.

In the women positive interests as such tend to signify masculinity, negative interests tend to be feminine. There are more women in the high-school adult population who express the feminine-(negative-) interest trend (28 per cent versus 24). There are more who are indifferent to mechanics, sports, politics, science, and art than there are adherents of these interests; the numbers for pets and social life are about equal; religion, domestic arts, music, travel, and literature attract more than they repel. The differences are statistically significant (1) between the average scores of the high-school adults and the scores of women who express much interest in sports; (2) between the average scores of the high-school adults and the scores of women who have little or no interest in religion. It seems probable that the high masculine position of the group interested in mechanics is not due to chance and that a larger group would provide a statistically significant difference between this average and the general norm.

There is a certain similarity in the masculinity-femininity of specific interests in the two sexes, but whereas in men of moderate education positive interest was feminine and negative interest masculine, in women of this educational level positive interest is masculine, negative interest neutral. Comparison of the effect of increasing numbers of positive versus negative interests indicates no appreciable differences. Having many or few profound interests is clearly a mark of neither a more nor a less feminine mental quality in the women of this group. The question may be raised, however, whether the neutral values obtained may not be

due to confusion between actual breadth of interest and superficial enthusiasms.

TABLE 47.—M-F SCORES OF WOMEN OF HIGH-SCHOOL EDUCATION COMPARED
ON THE BASIS OF THE NUMBER OF THEIR POSITIVE AND NEGATIVE
INTERESTS

Interest direction		In 0 inter- ests	In 1 or more	In 2 or more	In 3 or more	In 4 or more	In 5 or more	In 6 or more	In 7 or more
Positive inter- ests (having "very much interest")	N	84	451	355	257	172	98	51	27
	Mean	−85.4	−85.3	−84.7	−84.0	−83.9	−85.0	−88.7	−91.0
	S.D.$_M$	4.70	1.96	2.24	2.69	3.28	4.61	5.68	9.48
Negative in- terests (hav- ing "little or no inter- est")	N	31	504	437	349	225	143	83	42
	Mean	−83.7	−85.2	−85.2	−84.9	−88.0	−88.4	−86.4	−85.2
	S.D.$_M$	8.32	1.87	2.05	2.34	2.78	3.67	4.79	6.44

Both the positive- and the negative-interest series cover a
wider range than the means of the five principal occupational
groups (Fig. 12). The positive interests extend upward to a point
usually reached by highly educated and specially trained occupational subgroups only. The women of high-school training who
have much interest in mechanics, sports, or politics are mentally
considerably more masculine than the professional women as
a whole. They are far above the mean of business women and
rate near the office managers, business administrators, and
secretaries. Only a few small scattered occupational groups are
more masculine than this, while among the housewives the college
graduates alone rate higher. The lower end of the range with the
means of the women much interested in art and religion extends
to the very feminine score of the stenographers. There is no
active professional woman's group that rates as far down as this,
although there are some housewives formerly teachers or
librarians who score lower. Similarly in the trained occupational
group it is chiefly the women who because of marriage are no
longer active occupationally that rate below this point. The
gainful domestic activities are more feminine, as are also most of

their subgroups, but none of the groups of housewives whose activity has never been other than this rates so low.

The range of the negative interests is even wider. At the masculine limit the women who have little or no interest in religion score above all the professional subgroups; only a few of the subdivisions of these and some small scattering groups are above this

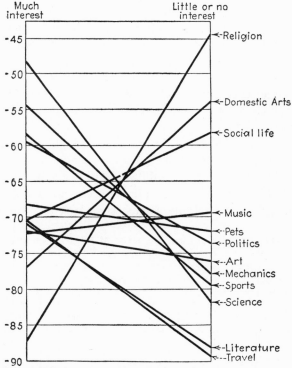

Fig. 12.—Mean M-F scores of adult females with much interest or little or no interest in various fields.

point. Among the trained occupations no more than ten individuals reach this level and among the housewives only women with five years of college training rate so high. No decade level reaches this point. At the opposite limit are the women who care little or not at all for literature and these reach the very feminine rating of the gainful domestic activities. None of the decade norms is as low as this and only a few clerical groups or married women formerly teachers or librarians fall lower. As with the men, the interest ranges of the women are wider than the occupational ranges of the same educational level. Single interests are for both sexes in this population as diagnostic of M-F score as, or perhaps more so than, occupational classification.

The differences in score and their significance between the means of groups attracted or repelled by a given interest appear in Table 48. It is there seen to be definitely more masculine to profess interest in sports than to deny such interest. It is possibly more masculine, but not certainly so, to have much interest in mechanics, literature, politics, or pets. Women who care much for travel or for science are perhaps a shade more masculine than those who do not, but the difference is not statistically significant. Little or no interest in domestic arts indicates practically no less feminine a woman than much interest. But it is true that 36 per cent of the group are among those who have great interest in domesticity, while only 10 per cent repudiate this interest. Interest in music and in art seems to be characteristic of somewhat more feminine women than lack of interest in the

TABLE 48.—DIFFERENCES BETWEEN AVERAGE M-F SCORES OF ADULT FEMALES OF HIGH-SCHOOL EDUCATION WHO EXPRESS "VERY MUCH INTEREST" IN VARIOUS PURSUITS AND THE AVERAGE OF THOSE WHO HAVE "LITTLE OR NO INTEREST"

Interests	M-F score diff.	Diff. $\overline{\text{S.D.}_{\text{diff.}}}$
1. Sports	+21.9	4.18
2. Mechanics	+19.0	1.76
3. Literature	+16.1	2.44
4. Politics	+13.6	1.49
5. Pets	+13.5	2.81
6. Travel	+ 5.8	<1
7. Science	+ 5.8	<1
8. Domestic arts	− 1.6	<1
9. Music	− 2.6	<1
10. Art	− 4.6	<1
11. Social life	−11.9	1.74
12. Religion	−32.3	4.59

same, but the difference in the present group is unreliable. Interest in social life is possibly more indicative of femininity than its opposite, while interest in religion is typically the extreme feminine interest, its opposite being associated with a definitely more masculine average score. Again the small size of the groups makes most of the differences unreliable statistically.

We turn next to the corresponding comparisons for women with one or more years of college training. The means for the two interest series appear in Tables 49a and 49b, where they may be compared with the general college women's group norm represented by the standard score +.25.

TABLE 49a.—AVERAGE M-F SCORES OF ADULT FEMALES OF COLLEGE EDUCATION WHOSE SELF-RATINGS INDICATE "VERY MUCH INTEREST" IN CERTAIN PURSUITS

Expressing very much interest in	Average M-F score	No. of cases	Per cent of 533 cases	Standard score[1]
1. Science....................	−48.3	42	7.9	+.85
2. Mechanics................	−54.5	10	1.9	+.70
3. Sports....................	−58.5	72	13.5	+.60
4. Politics...................	−59.5	30	5.6	+.60
5. Pets......................	−68.3	58	10.9	+.35
6. Travel....................	−70.4	207	38.8	+.30
7. Social life................	−70.5	62	11.6	+.30
8. Literature................	−71.0	169	31.7	+.30
9. Art......................	−72.1	84	15.8	+.30
10. Music....................	−72.3	123	23.1	+.30
11. Domestic arts.............	−77.0	96	18.0	+.15
12. Religion..................	−87.3	87	16.3	−.05

[1] The average M-F score for the college women's population is +.25.

The positive interests show gains over and above those to be expected from the masculine influence of higher education. The entire series averages a standard score of +.38, or .13 higher than the norm, as compared to +.05 for the moderately educated women. Interest in science has advanced to the most masculine position of all. The position of literature has become more feminine. Otherwise the relative standings resemble those of the high-school population. The order still represents the traditional expectation: women with scientific, active, nondomestic

interests are masculine in comparison with the feminine adherents
of the fine arts, literature, and religion.

TABLE 49b.—AVERAGE M-F SCORES OF ADULT FEMALES OF COLLEGE EDUCATION
WHOSE SELF-RATINGS INDICATE "LITTLE OR NO INTEREST" IN CERTAIN
PURSUITS

Expressing little or no interest in	Average M-F score	No. of cases	Per cent of 533 cases	Standard score[1]
1. Religion	−44.3	61	11.4	+.95
2. Domestic arts	−53.9	46	8.6	+.70
3. Social life	−58.3	34	6.6	+.60
4. Music	−69.4	31	5.8	+.35
5. Pets	−72.1	121	22.7	+.30
6. Politics	−73.7	146	27.4	+.25
7. Art	−76.2	59	11.1	+.20
8. Mechanics	−78.1	228	42.8	+.15
9. Sports	−79.6	77	14.4	+.10
10. Science	−81.9	123	23.1	+.05
11. Literature	−88.1	11	2.1	−.05
12. Travel	−89.3	23	4.3	−.05

[1] The average M-F score for the college women's population is +.25.

The negative interests are also if anything masculine rather
than feminine in their influence as a whole.   The range is slightly
greater than that of the positive interests.   Again the masculinity of indifference to social life is evident, while indifference
to travel appears as a feminine indicator.

The ranges of both interest series include all the professional
means, and of the occupational means all except that of the gainful domestic activities (see Fig. 12).   Interests, whether positive
or negative, have little tendency to feminize the minds of these
highly educated women to the degree exemplified by the dressmakers and domestics.   Inasmuch as a large proportion of the
college group is married, this fact seems important.   Most feminine of all at the college level are the women without interest
in four active or intellectual pursuits: travel, literature, science,
and sports.

Masculine college men care for sports, social life, mechanics,
and science; masculine college women for science, mechanics,
sports, and politics.   The difference is in the more intellectual

fourth interest of the women. The masculine negative interests bring out the same contrast. The masculine college man is active and social, the masculine college woman is intellectual and nonsocial. The feminine positive interests are alike for the sexes. The feminine negative interests are found to be, for the men, indifference to mechanics, for the women indifference to literature.

Both positive and negative interests tend to be associated with more than average masculinity in college women. Absence of interest in social life is correlated with masculinity in women at two educational levels, while interests indicative of intellectual breadth are also associated with the masculine trend. The latter tendency is more pronounced in the more highly educated women. The differences between the positive- and the negative-interest means are mainly inconclusive, statistically (Table 50). The trends that they suggest further illustrate the characteristics found in our analysis.

TABLE 50.—DIFFERENCES BETWEEN AVERAGE M-F SCORES OF ADULT FEMALES OF COLLEGE EDUCATION WHO EXPRESS "VERY MUCH INTEREST" IN VARIOUS PURSUITS AND THE AVERAGE OF THOSE WHO HAVE "LITTLE OR NO INTEREST"

Interests	M-F score Diff.	$\dfrac{\text{Diff.}}{\text{S.D.}_{\text{diff.}}}$
1. Science	+33.6	3.83
2. Mechanics	+23.6	2.18
3. Sports	+21.0	2.73
4. Travel	+18.8	2.36
5. Literature	+17.2	<1
6. Politics	+14.2	1.77
7. Art	+ 4.1	<1
8. Pets	+ 3.8	<1
9. Music	− 2.9	<1
10. Social life	−12.2	1.28
11. Domestic arts	−23.2	2.91
12. Religion	−43.0	4.27

There are individual women who score more masculine than the mean for the most masculine profession, higher indeed than the most masculine interest whether positive or negative. There are others who score more feminine than the most feminine occupation, and beyond the most feminine of the interest ratings. M-F scores of the women who combine interest in two or more of the distinctively masculine interests (*a*) positive, and (*b*) negative, and scores of those who combine interest in two or more of the characteristically feminine interests (*c*) positive and (*d*) negative, help to indicate the sorts of persons who score in extreme positions.

TABLE 51.—M-F SCORES OF CUMULATIVE INTERESTS IN FOUR TYPICAL CONSTELLATIONS (WOMEN OF HIGH-SCHOOL EDUCATION)

Interest constellations			Combination of 2 interests	Combination of 3 interests	Combination of 4 interests
Positive masculine	Very much interest in mechanics, sports, politics, pets	N	55	5	0
		Mean	−52.1	−73.5	..
		S.D.$_M$	5.68	..	..
Negative masculine	Little or no interest in religion, social life, music, art	N	75	21	3
		Mean	−78.3	−79.0	− 62.8
		S.D.$_M$	6.04	8.69	..
Positive feminine	Very much interest in religion, art, domestic arts, music	N	124	61	15
		Mean	−88.9	−89.2	−121.5
		S.D.$_M$	3.31	5.07	15.18
Negative feminine	Little or no interest in literature, sports, travel, pets	N	90	18	6
		Mean	−94.2	−88.4	−102.8
		S.D.$_M$	3.86	9.87	..

The masculine constellations show consistently more masculine scores than the feminine groupings. The positive-interest combinations are the most masculine of all. The two feminine combination series persist in the femininity of their scores from the two- to the four-interest groupings. Four contradictions are suggested which the small numbers are insufficient to validate: (1) it is less masculine to have 3 than 2 positive masculine interests and (2) it is less masculine to have 4 than 2 or 3 negative masculine interests; (3) it is more feminine to have 4 positive feminine interests than to have 2 or 3; and (4) it is less feminine to have 4 negative feminine interests than to have 4 positive feminine interests. Although single positive interests are more often masculine than feminine in women of high-school education, there is at least a suggestion that in cumulation they may be feminine in influence. In other words, a combination in one person of several positive interests, each of which may have by itself a positive M-F value, connotes in the combination a feminine trend. Perhaps this occurs because these women are more enthusiastic than interested. The converse is also suggested: women whose single negative interests are associated with a certain score show less increase in the expected direction with combined-interest scorings. The explanation is offered tentatively that while negative interests represent singly a feminine trend, grouped they may incline to the masculine trait of opposition and indifference found to be rather typical of the average man in this population.

The relation between M-F score and women's self-ratings as to interests may be summed up by a few brief characterizations: The mentally *more masculine* woman of *high-school* education tends to care intensely for few rather than many pursuits. She is usually interested in sports or politics, and perhaps also in pets. She also tends to be intense in her dislikes. She is apt to have little or no interest in religion or in social life. As to domestic arts, music, travel, science, and literature, her interests are average. The mentally *most feminine* woman tends to be indifferent to few interests; on the other hand she tends to many enthusiasms. She is interested in religion, but not in literature or sports; her interest in social life is average or above. Otherwise her interests are not specific. The *average* woman of the group expresses moderate interest in art, domestic arts, music, travel, and science. Her interest in religion and in sports is average, while literature, social life, and to a less extent travel and pets are fairly sure to attract her. She is unlikely to be intense in her interests or to limit their number too carefully whether positive or negative. She is apt rather to express a number of varied enthusiasms.

The woman of *college* education whose score is *masculine* tends to positive as often as or oftener than to negative interests. She cares for science, mechanics, sports, politics, or pets; she is indiffer-

ent to religion, domestic arts, and social life.   She does not dislike
travel, literature, or art.   The college woman at the *average* of
masculinity and femininity tends to have some positive and some
negative interests: she may like or dislike music, art, and pets;
she may care much for travel or social life, she is not apt to dislike
either; she may care little for politics, she is not apt to be greatly
attracted by it.   She does not care much for nor is she repelled
by science, mechanics, sports, religion, or domestic arts.   The
feminine college woman is religious and domestic, especially
religious.   She does not usually care for travel, literature,
science, sports, or mechanics.   Her interest in social life is positive rather than negative.   She dislikes rather than likes politics;
she has perhaps average interest in pets.

The high-school and the college level both show that mental
masculinity in women is associated (1) with the profession of
positive interests usually regarded as typically male, (2) with the
assertion of indifference to the acceptedly feminine arts and pursuits.   They show that mental femininity is associated in women
with pursuit of the feminine and domestic interests and denial
of interest in the active and typically masculine pursuits.   In
both groups of women positive interests tend to be more masculine than negative ones.   The difference between the higher and
the lower educational levels consists in the greater intellectuality
associated with the masculine interests of the one, as compared
to the greater activity in the masculine interests of the other.
The meaning of the M-F score is further defined by these
comparisons.

Interests of Men and Women Compared

The interest most popular among men is not the most masculine interest, the least popular is not the most feminine.   The
interest which most often repels men is not the most feminine, nor
is that which least often repels them the most masculine.
Between popularity of interest and M-F score there appears to be
no high correlation for either sex.   The percentages are shown
graphically for the adults of high-school education of both sexes
in Fig. 13.   Travel attracts the largest percentage of both

sexes, yet it is only the fourth most masculine interest for the men and holds the seventh place for the women. Art, the most feminine male interest, attracts 10 per cent of the men, thus rating as more popular than social life (which is most masculine) and more popular than the only less feminine domestic arts. Relative as well as absolute popularity of interests appears to be

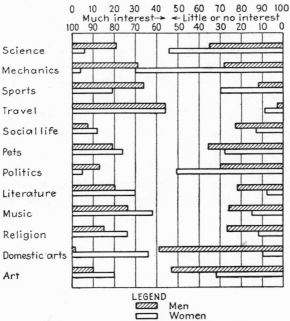

FIG. 13.—Percentages of men and women professing much interest or little or no interest in various fields.

a factor conditioning the masculinity-femininity of the interest. The ratio of the popularity in one sex to that in the other accounts for placements where simple numbers are not sufficient to explain the rank order.

Masculinity in men at either of two educational levels is associated with positive interest in active and mechanical pursuits; it is also associated with indifference to artistic and cultural pursuits. The trends are accentuated in both directions in the less educated population where also the barbarian response,

indifference as such, is strongly masculine.   Femininity in men is
the reverse of masculinity in its relationship to interests.   It is
marked by the presence of positive interests as such, the cultural
emphasis, and usually by the absence of the more active and
mechanical pursuits.

Masculinity in women, whether of high-school or college education, is associated with positive rather than negative interests,
with activity, and, in the more highly educated especially, with
intellectuality.   Femininity in women shows the reverse of the
masculine trends.   It appears associated with less intense positive interests, and these are directed toward the arts of home and
social life.   It may be found also in women who profess a large
number of enthusiasms, for even those interests which singly
are masculine prove to be feminine when clustered.   Mental
femininity is expressed also in indifference to the active, scientific,
and, in the better educated, intellectual interests.   The masculine man has typically masculine interests.   The feminine man
has cultural interests.   The feminine woman has typically
feminine interests.   The masculine woman has intellectual
interests.

CHAPTER X

RELATION OF M-F SCORE TO THE DOMESTIC MILIEU

Youth is masculine, age feminine. Within the area represented by the M-F test, culture tends to make men's minds resemble women's, intelligence and education to make women's minds resemble men's. But every feminine man's score does not come from a cultured greybeard, and masculine men's scores do not necessarily indicate hard-boiled philistinism; nor are all feminine-scoring women dull and uneducated. Some elements of environment and constitution which have been found related positively or negatively with the total M-F score are discussed in this chapter, including the effect of presence or absence of parents in the home; the effect of a large or small number of brothers and sisters, or none; the effect of married life on the scores of spouses; and the effect of children on the scores of their parents.

The Influence of Orphanage and Part-orphanage

There is a popular belief that the sons of widowed mothers tend to become feminized by the resulting relationship, and that daughters brought up chiefly by fathers tend to become masculinized. Table 52 presents the pertinent data on this point for our adult population of males and females. The mean scores of the various groups in the table are given separately for (a) the adult population of high-school education and (b) the total adult population.

In both these populations, strange to say, the males brought up by widowed mothers average more masculine than those brought up by widowed fathers. The difference is approximately twice its standard error. Also, in both populations of males the wholly orphaned rate appreciably less masculine than the total population from which they are derived. Although the N's involved in these comparisons are too small to make the differ-

223

TABLE 52.—M-F Scores of Orphans and Part-orphans

Males, status	Adults of high-school education			Total adult group		
	No. of cases	Mean M-F score	S.D.$_M$	No. of cases	Mean M-F score	S.D.$_M$
Care of mother chiefly or only[1]..	25	+63.3	8.8	85	+52.4	4.82
Care of father chiefly or only[1]...	9	+46.1	14.9	35	+39.1	8.09
Part or whole orphan total......	43	+52.4	7.1	149	+45.8	3.97
Whole orphan total[2]............	9	+28.3	11.5	29	+34.6	10.48
Population from which derived..	344	+45.4	2.9	1083	+43.3	1.57
Females, status						
Care of mother chiefly or only[1]..	72	−74.8	5.8	187	−83.6	3.28
Care of father chiefly or only[1]...	24	−75.3	7.4	63	−86.0	3.25
Part or whole orphan total......	113	−77.1	7.2	303	−83.5	2.44
Whole orphan total[2]............	16	−93.2	11.2	53	−80.1	5.98
Population from which derived..	820	−84.7	1.5	1867	−80.9	1.00

[1] "Only" if other parent died or was absent from before child's sixth birthday; "chiefly" if other parent died or was absent after child's sixth birthday and before twelfth.
[2] Without care of either parent from before sixth birthday.

ences very reliable, our data may at least be interpreted in the negative sense as offering no support to the popular belief stated above. In the case of the females the differences, both in the high-school population and the total populations, are too small to be even suggestive of an influence.

INFLUENCE OF SIBLINGS

The possible influence of brothers and sisters on an individual's masculinity or femininity is a matter of widespread interest. One wishes to know whether masculinity or femininity as measured by this test bears any relation to the number of siblings or to their sex. Does the only child tend to be more or less masculine than the average, and if such a difference obtains, does it hold equally for males and females? Does the lone boy with several sisters tend to become feminized, or the lone girl with several brothers masculinized? Table 53 for the males and

Table 54 for the females present mean M-F scores for groups having various types of sibling relationships. The data are for our adult population of high-school education.

TABLE 53.—INFLUENCE OF SIBLINGS ON THE M-F SCORE OF MEN OF HIGH-SCHOOL EDUCATION

Sibling status	No. of cases	Mean M-F score	S.D.$_M$
Norm of adult population of high-school education with whom these groups are compared...................	212	+50.0	3.3
a. Brothers, with or without sisters:			
Men who have 0 brothers......................	50	+54.9	6.1
Men who have 1, 2, or 3 brothers..............	125	+55.6	4.9
Men who have 4 or more brothers..............	35	+18.5	8.9
b. Sisters, with or without brothers:			
Men who have 0 sisters.......................	59	+52.9	6.3
Men who have 1, 2, or 3 sisters................	130	+51.6	4.7
Men who have 4 or more sisters...............	22	+23.2	13.0
c. Brothers in sibships without sisters:			
Men who have 0 sisters, 0 brothers.............	19	+42.1	4.8
Men who have 0 sisters, 1 or more brothers......	40	+57.0	6.7
Men who have 0 sisters, 2 or more brothers......	21	+61.0	12.7
Men who have 0 sisters, 3 or more brothers......	12	+38.8	15.2
Men who have 0 sisters, 4 or more brothers......	6	+33.8	12.8
d. Sisters in sibships without brothers:			
Men who have 0 brothers, 0 sisters.............	19	+42.1	4.8
Men who have 0 brothers, 1 or more sisters......	31	+62.7	7.7
Men who have 0 brothers, 2 or more sisters......	17	+56.4	9.1
Men who have 0 brothers, 3 or more sisters......	10	+50.5	12.6
Men who have 0 brothers, 4 or more sisters......	5	+42.5	12.0
e. Sibs (of either sex or both):			
Men who have 0 sibs..........................	19	+42.1	..
Men who have 1 sib (either sex)...............	33	+61.4	..
Men who have 2 sibs (either sex or mixed).......	36	+73.8	..
Men who have 2 sibs (mixed)..................	19	+68.4	13.3
Men who have 3 sibs (either sex or mixed).......	27	+42.4	..
Men who have 3 sibs (mixed)..................	18	+42.7	12.8
Men who have 4 sibs or more (mixed)...........	85	+41.1	6.1
Men who have 6 sibs or more (either sex or mixed)	40	+22.0	9.9
Men who have 6 sibs or more (mixed)...........	39	+21.8	9.5

We may examine first section *e* of the above tables. Is there any relationship between M-F score and the size of the family

TABLE 54.—INFLUENCE OF SIBLINGS ON THE M-F SCORE OF WOMEN OF HIGH-SCHOOL EDUCATION

Sibling status	No. of cases	Mean M-F score	S.D.$_M$
Norm of adult population of high-school education with whom these groups are compared............	820	— 84.7	1.5
a. Brothers, with or without sisters:			
Women who have 0 brothers.................	121	— 84.2	3.7
Women who have 1, 2, or 3 brothers...........	332	— 85.0	2.4
Women who have 4 or more brothers...........	82	— 84.9	4.5
b. Sisters, with or without brothers:			
Women who have 0 sisters....................	135	— 81.1	4.1
Women who have 1, 2, or 3 sisters.............	317	— 85.9	2.2
Women who have 4 or more sisters.............	83	— 86.6	5.2
c. Brothers in sibships without sisters:			
Women who have 0 sisters, 0 brothers..........	50	— 82.7	5.4
Women who have 0 sisters, 1 or more brothers...	85	— 80.3	5.6
Women who have 0 sisters, 2 or more brothers...	37	— 89.5	8.8
Women who have 0 sisters, 3 or more brothers...	19	— 90.6	10.4
Women who have 0 sisters, 4 or more brothers...	6	—116.2	17.4
d. Sisters in sibships without brothers:			
Women who have 0 brothers, 0 sisters..........	50	— 82.7	5.4
Women who have 0 brothers, 1 or more sisters...	71	— 85.6	4.8
Women who have 0 brothers, 2 or more sisters...	39	— 85.9	7.1
Women who have 0 brothers, 3 or more sisters...	15	—100.2	10.0
Women who have 0 brothers, 4 or more sisters...	9	— 96.2	12.2
e. Sibs (of either sex or both):			
Women who have 0 sibs......................	51	— 82.4	..
Women who have 1 sib (either sex)............	79	— 77.8	..
Women who have 2 sibs (either sex or mixed)...	83	— 81.8	..
Women who have 2 sibs (mixed)...............	41	— 81.7	6.4
Women who have 3 sibs (either sex or mixed)...	77	— 85.6	..
Women who have 3 sibs (mixed)..............	58	— 85.0	5.1
Women who have 4 sibs or more (mixed).......	229	— 88.0	2.7
Women who have 6 sibs or more (either sex or mixed).................................	118	— 87.0	4.0
Women who have 6 sibs or more (mixed).......	115	— 86.9	4.1

from which an individual comes? The figures show a definite tendency for men from small sibships to score more masculine than the average, and for men of large sibships to score more feminine than the average. The correlation between an individual's M-F score and the size of sibship is in fact —.21 ± .04 for men and $-.35 \pm .03$ for women. One must be cautious, however, in the interpretation of these figures. We have shown in an earlier chapter that M-F score correlated negatively with age, particularly with males, and the question arises whether our subjects from large sibships may not be older than those from small families. It turns out that the correlation between age and size of sibship is $+.29 \pm .04$ for men and $+.13 \pm .06$ for women. It seems, therefore, that age accounts for the negative correlation between M-F score and size of sibship in the case of the males, and to some extent in the case of the females.

The relation of M-F score to number of brothers has been examined without reference to the presence or absence of sisters. In the case of men, those who have four or more brothers score more feminine than those who have three or fewer, a difference which may be due entirely to age. In the case of women the same trend is evident, but in reduced magnitude, and can again be attributed to the age factor. A similar comparison of the relation between M-F score and number of sisters, without regard to presence or absence of brothers, leads to the same general conclusion. The more feminine M-F score of men with four or more sisters, as compared with that of men with fewer sisters, probably represents an age effect. The corresponding data for women suggest that those with a large number of sisters tend to score just more feminine than the average for the entire population, and those with no sisters just more masculine. Again the influence is at least partly one of age.

We may note next the influence of brothers in families in which there are no sisters. The figures for men are inconsistent. Those who have neither brothers nor sisters score just more feminine than the mean for adult men of high-school education. Those who have one or more brothers but no sisters score more masculine than the general mean. Neither difference is statistically significant. Where there are three brothers or more and no sister the relationship is reversed, perhaps because of the negative correlation between age and size of family. In the case of women a more regular trend is observed. Those with one brother and no sister score somewhat more masculine than the general population of which they are a part, and also more masculine than the similar subgroup having neither brothers nor sisters. From this point on there seems to be a definite tendency for each additional brother to have a feminizing influence. The differences all lack statistical significance if considered individually, but their trend is constant. The safest conclusion seems to be the negative one that no evidence is found to support the popular view that girls who have many brothers but no sisters are masculinized, or that the reverse effect is very marked in the case of boys.

Examination of the mixed sibships (Section *e* of Tables 53 and 54) discloses no relationship of importance except the usual negative correlation of M-F score and size of family. This we have attributed to the effect of age. An interesting fact appears, however, when we compare for either sex the scores in Sections *c* and *d* of the tables. Here we find a tendency for men with siblings of one sex only to be more masculine if the siblings are sisters than if they are brothers. This suggests a contrast effect. When a man has both brothers and sisters the contrast effect is not evident. Women with siblings of one sex only tend to be more feminine if the siblings are sisters than if they are brothers. This is the opposite of the contrast effect observed for the men.

RELATION OF THE M-F SCORE TO MARITAL STATUS

Two interesting questions arise in this connection: (1) Is there marital selection on the basis of resemblance or difference in mental masculinity? (2) Does the intimate association of a man and a woman in married life exert a feminizing effect upon the husband and perhaps a masculinizing effect upon the wife, leading to a gradual *rapprochement* with respect to M-F score? A group of 179 married couples was tested in an attempt to answer these questions. The husbands of the group included 83 in the teaching profession (all grades), 9 each in engineering and the ministry, 4 in medicine, 17 in business, 27 in clerical and mercantile occupations, and 21 miscellaneous. They represented all grades of education but half or more were college graduates.

The average age of the husbands was 34.2 years, that of the wives 33.3. The range of ages was from the early twenties to more than sixty. The average number of years married was 9.4.

The mean for the husbands is +44.4, which is just below the mean of the male teaching groups in our general population. The mean for the wives is −76.7, or appreciably more feminine than the female teaching group in the general population. Husbands' scores correlated −.25 ± .046 with number of years married, and wives' scores −.19 ± .048 with number of years married. Taken at their face value these correlations would suggest a feminizing influence of marriage upon both husband and wife, but such an interpretation is unwarranted. The relationship noted reflects chiefly the negative correlation between M-F score and age. When the difference between the score of husband and wife was correlated with length of marriage, no relationship was found ($r = .026 ± .050$).

Correlation of M-F score with number of years married was also computed for a separate group of 161 married men and another of 402 married women, both groups of fairly homogeneous education. For these men M-F scores gave a correlation of −.28 ± .05 with number of years married; for the women −.07 ± .03. But the number of years married correlates with age .89 ± .01 for the men and .86 ± .01 for the women. With age constant the negative correlation between M-F score and length of married life disappears. There is accordingly no evidence that length of married life per se has any appreciable masculinizing or feminizing effect on either husband or wife.

Turning to the question of marital selection, we find in the group of 179 couples a husband-wife correlation of .16 ± .05. It is .16 ± .07 for 89 couples married seven years or less and .20 ± .07 for 90 couples married eight years or more. In the separate exercises of the M-F test the husband-wife correlations are less than twice their probable error for all but two: Exercise 3 (information) and Exercise 4 (emotional attitudes). For these the correlations were, respectively, .26 ± .05 and .31 ± .05. It is probable that the husband-wife correlations of .16 to .20 in total score reflect merely the marital selection that is known to occur with respect to age and amount of education and does not indicate homology based upon mental masculinity or femininity.

EFFECT OF MARRIAGE ON M-F SCORES OF PROFESSIONAL AND OTHER WOMEN GAINFULLY EMPLOYED

It was noted in an earlier chapter that women working outside the home tended to score more masculine than comparable housewives. In the general population group the mean for married women working was -73.8, for single women working -74.8, for housewives with no other occupation -81.6, and for housewives who formerly worked -83.9. These and other data are brought together in Tables 55 and 56.

The contrast in score in the tables is clearly not between married and unmarried primarily, but rather between working and not working. The interpretation might nevertheless be suggested by the figures that it is in general the more feminine women who marry (M-F score -80.7 versus -74.8 for the single women) and that among the married are a less feminine group (M-F score -73.8) who work after marriage. Analysis of the scores of the four categories decade by decade shows that this would be a mistaken interpretation based on figures weighted unevenly at different ages. Equal weighting for the decades changes the order of the categories (least to most feminine) to the following: married and working, housewives, housewives who formerly worked, single and working. Equal decade and category weighting gives an average M-F score of -87.4 (s.s. $-.05$) for the single women and -83.9 (s.s.0) for the married women. In each decade the married women tend, of course, to be the older, hence the difference is not due to age. It seems from this comparison that mental masculinity is not a factor unfavorable to matrimony. However, comparison of the scores of married and single, with age and education made constant, has not been attempted. It seems at present from the figures available unlikely that such analysis would prove more illuminating than the material already available. A final comparison of the means for the married and single groups from age twenty to age sixty with equal decade and category weighting gives prac-

TABLE 55.—M-F Scores of Adult Women in Relation to Marriage and Outside Work

Group categories	Age	No. of cases	M-F score
Single and working...................................	20–29	239	− 72.5
Married and working.................................		92	− 71.5
Married, were formerly working.......................		91	− 84.2
Married, have had no other occupation than that of housewife		74	− 82.5
Single and working...................................	30–39	64	− 80.1
Married and working.................................		96	− 82.2
Married, were formerly working.......................		147	− 86.5
Married, housewives.................................		84	− 92.1
Single and working...................................	40–49	35	− 87.8
Married and working.................................		46	− 84.7
Married, were formerly working.......................		81	− 79.1
Married, housewives.................................		77	− 78.3
Single and working...................................	50–59	18	− 91.7
Married and working.................................		30	− 84.2
Married, were formerly working.......................		60	− 87.8
Married, housewives.................................		55	− 84.8
Single and working...................................	60–69	11	− 93.1
Married and working.................................		13	− 92.6
Married, were formerly working.......................		33	− 97.4
Married, housewives.................................		34	− 79.5
Single and working...................................	70–79	4	− 99.5
Married and working.................................		5	− 65.5
Married, were formerly working.......................		12	− 91.2
Married, housewives.................................		7	− 86.6
Single and working...................................	Total	371	− 74.8
Married and working.................................		282	− 73.8
Married, were formerly working.......................		453	− 83.9
Married, have had no other occupation than that of housewife		332	− 81.6
Equal decade weighting:			
Single and working...................................		371	− 87.4
Married and working.................................		282	− 80.1
Married, were formerly working.......................		453	− 87.7
Married, housewives.................................		332	− 83.9
Equal decade and category weighting:			
Single...		371	− 87.4
Married..		1067	− 83.9
Equal decade and category weighting, ages 20 to 60:			
Single...		371	− 83.0
Married..		1067	− 83.1
Grand total:			
Single...		371	− 74.8
Married..		1067	− 80.7

tically identical scores (M-F score −83). Summarizing all our results so far as they relate to this matter, it appears that with marriage (1) the better educated and widely experienced woman will show a slightly more feminine score as her interests become

TABLE 56.—EFFECT OF EDUCATION ON RELATION OF M-F SCORE TO MARRIAGE AND OUTSIDE WORK
(WOMEN SUBJECTS OF TABLE 55)

	No. of cases	Grade school only	High school		College				Total
Raw scores			1–2 yrs.	3–4 yrs.	1–3 yrs.	4 yrs.	5 yrs.	6–7 yrs.	
Single and working......	371	−106.4 (13)	−86.0 (29)	−82.2 (117)	−80.5 (96)	−64.9 (91)	−62.8 (18)	−46.6 (7)	−74.8
Married and working.....	263	− 84.8 (34)	−87.9 (25)	−72.7 (81)	−87.0 (65)	−68.5 (39)	−64.5 (16)	−16.2 (3)	−73.8
Married, formerly working	453	− 88.0 (68)	−79.7 (48)	−90.4 (131)	−91.4 (114)	−81.9 (76)	−60.4 (11)	−41.5 (5)	−83.9
Housewives.............	332	− 85.0 (93)	−92.7 (37)	−83.5 (94)	−91.2 (59)	−70.4 (42)	−63.8 (7)	..	−81.6
Standard scores									
Single and working......	371	− .50 (13)	0 (29)	+.05 (117)	+.05 (96)	+.45 (91)	+.50 (18)	+.90 (7)	+.20
Married and working.....	263	0 (34)	−.05 (25)	+.25 (81)	0 (65)	+.35 (39)	+.45 (16)	+1.60 (3)	+.20
Married, formerly working	453	− .05 (68)	+.10 (48)	−.10 (131)	−.10 (114)	+.05 (76)	+.55 (11)	+1.00 (5)	0
Housewives.............	332	0 (93)	−.15 (37)	+.05 (94)	−.10 (59)	+.35 (42)	+.50 (7)	..	+.05

more domestic; (2) this tendency will be more or less counter-acted if she continues her extradomestic activities; (3) the less well educated woman of narrow experience will become slightly more masculine in score, as marriage affords her wider experiential contacts. The influence of other factors such as education and intelligence are prepotent and are not overridden by the influence of marriage.

The unmarried male population available for study is practically limited to men under thirty-five years of age. Comparison of the unmarried men (M-F score +60.1) with the married men (M-F score +56.2) from the group of high-school education and of the same age range shows the single men to be the more masculine, but the difference is less than half its standard error. The difference between the same population in its twenties and thirties is larger than this, and the difference between men who care much and men who care little for social life, irrespective of whether they are married, is almost twice as large.

RELATION BETWEEN OFFSPRING AND M-F SCORES OF PARENTS

Data on the relationship between number and sex of offspring and M-F scores of parents are presented in Tables 57 and 58.

Married men and married women without children rate more masculine than the general mean. The unmarried of either sex are just more masculine than the mean of the same sex but less masculine than the married with no children. There is a slight negative correlation between number of children without regard to sex and M-F score for the men; the women show no correlation or a very slight one if one very masculine mother of four boys is omitted. The general trend is in line with the previously demonstrated correlation between age and score, for the number of children is of course correlated with age. The fact that the women show so slight a correlation, if any, between score and number of children seems to indicate that the children have a small but real influence which counterbalances the age effect.

Comparison of the ranges and the trends indicated by the scores of the men who are fathers of girls only, or fathers of boys only, suggests that there may be a small influence of children upon parents which is differential for sex of offspring. The fathers of girls only are increasingly feminine as the number of girls increases. Indeed the four fathers of three or more girls rate as feminine as sixty-year-old men.

TABLE 57.—RELATIONSHIP BETWEEN OFFSPRING AND M-F SCORE OF MOTHER

Group categories	No. of cases	Mean M-F score	S.D.$_M$
Norm for women of high-school education (Series 7)	536	− 84.1	2.3
Unmarried women..............................	124	− 83.5	4.0
Married women, 0 children......................	109	− 79.4	4.4
1· Number of children and M-F score of mother:			
Mothers of 1 child (male)....................	51	− 84.8	5.7
Mothers of 1 child (female)..................	48	− 90.8	5.3
Mothers of 1 child (either male or female)......	99	− 87.7	6.3
Mothers of 2 children (mixed)................	41	− 91.0	4.9
Mothers of 3 children (mixed)................	32	− 86.4	7.1
Mothers of 4 children (mixed)................	30	− 94.8	8.0
Mothers of 5 children (mixed)................	18	− 76.2	11.1
Mothers of 6 or more children (mixed).........	22	− 85.0	7.0
2. Number of boys in families with boys only and M-F score of mother:			
Mothers of 0 girls, 1 boy....................	51	− 84.8	5.7
Mothers of 0 girls, 2 boys..................	18	− 87.3	10.2
Mothers of 0 girls, 3 boys..................	9	− 93.9	..
Mothers of 0 girls, 5 boys..................	1	− 30.0	..
3. Number of girls in families with girls only and M-F score of mother:			
Mothers of 0 boys, 1 girl....................	48	− 90.8	5.3
Mothers of 0 boys, 2 girls..................	26	− 88.0	8.7
Mothers of 0 boys, 3 or 4 girls..............	7	−100.9	16.6

A father who has one boy is more feminine than the unmarried, the married with no children, or the general average. But he is more masculine than the father of one girl, and the addition to his family of successive boys and no girls seems to make him increasingly more masculine. The five fathers of five or more boys and no girls are more masculine than the unmarried and almost reach the high point of the married with no children. Although undoubtedly much older than the average of either of the other two groups mentioned, they exceed even the twenty-

and thirty-year age norms for their own or any other group. It seems strongly suggested therefore that the influence of boys on the father is definitely positive and would be found quite marked were the contraactive factor of age eliminated.

TABLE 58.—RELATIONSHIP BETWEEN OFFSPRING AND M-F SCORES OF
FATHERS

Group categories	No. of cases	Mean M-F score	S.D._M
Norm for men of high-school education (Series 7)...	212	+ 50.0	3.3
Unmarried men....................................	48	+ 60.1	7.6
Married men, 0 children...........................	39	+ 67.4	9.1
1. Number of children and M-F score of father:			
Fathers of 1 child (male)......................	24	+ 41.3	11.8
Fathers of 1 child (female)....................	16	+ 39.2	11.9
Fathers of 1 child (either male or female).......	40	+ 40.5	11.9
Fathers of 2 children (mixed)..................	20	+ 58.5	11.0
Fathers of 3 children (mixed)..................	14	+ 46.2	9.7
Fathers of 4 children (mixed)..................	8	+ 23.0	13.2
Fathers of 5 children (mixed)..................	7	+ 56.2	11.2
Fathers of 6 or more children (mixed)..........	3	+ 33.7	5.4
2. Number of boys in families with boys only and M-F score of father:			
Fathers of 0 girls, 1 boy.....................	24	+ 41.3	11.8
Fathers of 0 girls, 2 boys....................	7	+ 53.4	11.7
Fathers of 0 girls, 3 or 4 boys...............	5	+ 66.5	6.7
Fathers of 0 girls, 5 boys....................	1	+130.0	..
3. Number of girls in families with girls only and M-F score of father:			
Fathers of 0 boys, 1 girl.....................	16	+ 39.2	11.9
Fathers of 0 boys, 2 girls....................	14	+ 26.2	14.0
Fathers of 0 boys, 3 or 4 girls...............	4	+ 20.5	20.6

A difference in the influence exercised by male children as compared to that of female children is also to some extent apparent among the women. The mothers of boys only are more feminine than the general mean, than the unmarried, and than the married with no children. But the differences are very slight and the range from the 51 mothers who have each one boy only to the 27 who have two or more is only .10 s.s. This is certainly not more and may be less than the expected correlation with age. The mothers with girls only are more feminine than the mothers with boys only. The range from the 81 mothers who have one daughter each and no sons to the 7 mothers who have three or more daughters each and no sons is .25 s.s. The 7 mothers with three daughters each and no sons score considerably below any of the decade norms. There is at least a suggestion that the sex of the child may have a real influence upon the M-F score of the mother.

Comparing the two parents, similarity and also difference in the effect of children upon their scores appear. Both fathers and mothers are feminized, though very slightly, by the presence of a single child without regard to its sex. Both are feminized by the presence of daughters in proportion to the number of the daughters. The trend is probably in addition to the feminization expected with age. Both fathers and mothers are masculinized by the presence of sons. The fathers show actually more masculine scores with an increasing number of sons, an effect the more significant since it is the opposite of that expected with increasing age. Mothers show almost complete counteracting of the feminization of age as the number of sons increases. Perhaps we may say that fathers are more diversely affected by sons and daughters, mothers are more similarly affected.

A word may be added regarding the M-F scores of the unmarried and the married with no children. The unmarried of both sexes are slightly more masculine than the general means. This should doubtless be attributed chiefly to the fact of their relatively greater youth. In each sex the married without children are, however, and strangely, more masculine than the unmarried although they are of course older. The difference between the mean for the married men with no children and the general mean is more than three times its standard error. The difference between the mean for the married men with no children and those with one or more daughters is also more than three times its standard error.

Most of the differences discussed in this section are in large part associated with age differences. In so far as age is not the conditioning factor they are to be regarded as suggestive only, since for these small groups the significance of the differences is, except in the few instances mentioned, not established. Where regular trends have appeared and reappeared consistently the possibility of their genuineness should, however, not be denied without the evidence of further data.

FAMILY RESEMBLANCES IN M-F SCORES

Family resemblances in mental masculinity and femininity have not been extensively investigated. In Chapter VI data were presented showing that on a modified M-F test (based upon Strong's vocational-interest test) the correlation between husband and wife is practically zero. In Chapter X the correlation for M-F scores of 179 husbands and wives was found to be slight but perhaps significant. We have found considerable evidence in case history data that the girl who tests extremely masculine is likely to have a father with strong mechanical interests, and that the sons of very religious mothers are likely to test rather feminine, but it remains to be seen whether these indications will be confirmed by statistical evidence.

The only parent-offspring correlations we have are for small populations of gifted children (IQ 140 or higher). These are as follows:

Groups compared	N	r
Sons with mothers....................	46	.138
Sons with fathers.....................	31	.168
Daughters with mothers...............	39	.009
Daughters with fathers................	28	.428
Boys with parental mean..............	26	.413
Girls with parental mean..............	24	.179

As the probable errors range from .10 to .12, only two of the above correlations are statistically significant, and there is a small chance that these also are caused by sampling errors. The problem would repay further investigation. It would be especially desirable to establish parent-child resemblance in M-F score in comparison with the resemblance between foster parents and their foster children adopted in infancy.

SUMMARY

1. Part orphans tend to be contrastingly masculine or feminine in mental traits according as they are brought up by the mother or the father. Whole orphans are if anything more feminine than the average.

2. The brother of one sister tends to be more masculine than the average, and the sister of one brother tends also to be more masculine than other women. Aside from these trends the influence of siblings is not to be distinguished from the influence of age, for the size of sibship is correlated with the age of the individual and the correlation of the latter with the M-F score probably explains the similar correlation of the former.

3. A negative correlation demonstrated between length of married life and M-F score is found to persist only when a wide age range is considered. When the age factor is held constant the correlation disappears. Single and married women rate at the mean when other factors are weighted as nearly equally as possible.

4. Children appear to influence the M-F scores of parents. The fathers of one child are more feminine than the mean and than married men with no children. The latter are more masculine than the unmarried. With increasing size of family both father and mother tend to score more feminine. A single exception is found in the case of fathers of boys only. These fathers are increasingly masculine as the number of boys increases. Mothers show a similar trend in the retardation of feminine emphasis which occurs when the children are all boys.

CHAPTER XI

A STUDY OF MALE HOMOSEXUALS[1]

A study of male sexual inverts was undertaken in the hope that it would contribute information of value in the interpretation of M-F scores and possibly throw some light on the genesis of homosexuality in males. It was entered upon with little first-hand knowledge about the personality traits characteristic of such a group, and with no preconceptions in regard to the causes of sexual inversion. It is believed that the results of the study throw a certain amount of light on both of these questions.

SUBJECTS TESTED

Because homosexual persons in the general population live in constant fear of public exposure and consequent social ostracism, they are not easily accessible for study. Jails, prisons, and reform schools offer the best opportunity for obtaining subjects. A number of such institutions were searched for possible cases with the results shown below. One of the subjects found in the San Francisco County Jail agreed to cooperate in making contacts with additional cases among his associates. By his help and that of others secured through him a fairly large number of noninstitutional subjects have been found. The facts concerning the number of subjects, where found, and the type of homosexuality represented by each group are shown in Table 59.

A few definitions of the terms used in this report should perhaps be given. A *homosexual* is a person who out of preference has sexual relationships with persons of the same rather than of the opposite sex. Since this study deals with male subjects, the term male homosexual refers to a man who has sexual

---

[1] The data of this chapter were collected and treated entirely by Dr. E. Lowell Kelly under the general direction of Terman and Miles. This summary was prepared by Dr. Kelly and Dr. Terman.

TABLE 59.—DATA CONCERNING THE NUMBER OF SUBJECTS, WHERE FOUND, AND TYPE OF HOMOSEXUALITY REPRESENTED BY THE GROUPS STUDIED

Location of Subjects	No.	Classification
State Prison at San Quentin.........................	5	Passive
State Prison at San Quentin.........................	6	Doubtful
Berkeley Police Department.........................	2	Passive
San Francisco County Jail, No. 2....................	11	Passive
San Francisco County Jail, No. 2....................	5	Doubtful
General population..................................	59	Passive
U.S. Disciplinary Barracks at Alcatraz, California.......	46	Active
Total in each classification......................	46	Active
	77	Passive
	11	Doubtful
Grand total......................................	134	All types

relationships with men rather than with women. He is said to be an *active* homosexual if he plays the male role in the copulatory act, and a *passive* homosexual if he plays the role of female. These relationships may be further classified according to the particular type of sexual connection practiced. Rosanoff[1] lists six general types:

1. Mutual masturbation
2. Interfemoral coitus
3. Irrumation
4. Mutual irrumation
5. Sodomy
6. Combinations of these

Irrumation, or *fellatio*, refers to copulation of penis with the mouth. *Sodomy*, used synonymously with *pederasty*, refers to copulation involving the penis and anus. These terms are rarely if ever used by the homosexuals as they have an extensive slang vocabulary of their own.

In this study a subject is called passive if he currently plays the female role in either fellatio or sodomy. A total of 77 such cases

[1] ROSANOFF, AARON J., *Manual of psychiatry*, p. 202, Wiley, 1920.

have been given the M-F test. The 46 army prisoners were all serving sentences for sodomy. Captain G. E. Hesner, staff psychiatrist at the time, reported that in practically every case the prisoners in question were supposed to have played the active part, and the group has therefore been classified accordingly. Those classified as doubtful were persons suspected of homosexual acts, but for whom there was no information as to the role played.

ANALYSIS OF M-F SCORES

The M-F test was given to each of the 134 cases. Form A was used for all except the Alcatraz group, who were given Form B.

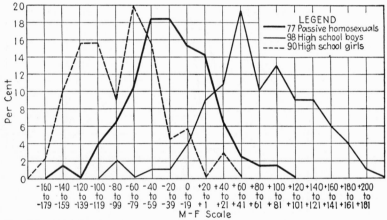

FIG. 14.—Distributions of M-F scores of 77 passive male homosexuals, 98 high-school boys, and 90 high-school girls.

Since the two forms of the test are fairly comparable, the raw scores have been used in all computations.

The distribution of the total scores made by the 77 passive homosexuals, comprising the largest group, hereafter referred to as the P.M.H. group, is shown in Fig. 14, together with the distributions of scores for unselected groups of third-year high-school boys and girls.[1] It may be seen that the curve for the P.M.H. group approximates more closely that for the girls than that for the boys. However, it is distinctly different from that of

[1] The distribution of numerical scores of the P.M.H. group (including three additional cases) is given in Table 10.

either, the difference between the means in each case being statistically significant beyond question.

No other male group thus far studied has tested anything like as feminine as these 77 passive male homosexuals. The male groups nearest to them in mean M-F score are the artists, ministers, Protestant theological students, priests in training, and unselected men in the seventies and eighties. In fact, the mean score of the P.M.H. group (-19.7) is more feminine than that of

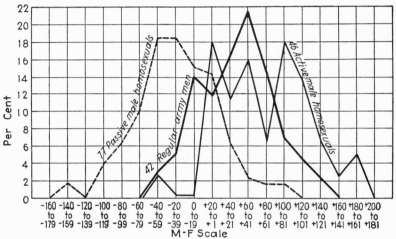

FIG. 15.—Distributions of M-F scores of 77 passive male homosexuals, 46 active male homosexuals, and 42 regular army men.

38 college women athletes (-13.7) and much more feminine than that of a small subgroup of these athletes who rated high in intelligence and low in scholarship (see pp. 115f. and Fig. 6).

Figure 15 gives the score distribution of the 77 passive homosexuals, together with the distribution for the 46 Alcatraz prisoners classified as active, and the distribution for 42 unselected soldiers in the regular army. Although the classification of the entire Alcatraz group as actives involves a certain amount of error, it will be seen that this group not only tests much more masculine than the passive homosexuals, but also significantly more masculine than the army group of roughly comparable ages. If these two groups of homosexuals are fair samples of the active and passive types, it would appear that they in fact present a true dichotomy of personality. It is probable that the small amount of overlap of the two distributions is caused by the errors of classification which must have occurred, particularly in the group classified as active. The distribution of scores for this group is distinctly bimodal, indicating that the group contains two essentially contrasting populations.[1]

Do passive male homosexuals give a preponderance of feminine responses in all the exercises of the M-F test, or only on a part of them? Table 60 gives the mean on each of the seven exercises for the P.M.H. group and for 98 third-year high-school boys, the differences between the means of the two groups, and the ratios of the differences to their standard errors.

TABLE 60.—COMPARISON OF MEAN SCORES OF 77 PASSIVE MALE HOMOSEXUALS AND 98 HIGH-SCHOOL-JUNIOR BOYS ON THE INDIVIDUAL EXERCISES OF THE M-F TEST

Exercise	Homosexuals		H.S. Boys		Diff. Means	S.D.$_{diff.}$	Diff. $\overline{\text{S.D.}_{diff.}}$
	Mean	S.D.$_{dist.}$	Mean	S.D.$_{dist.}$			
1	− 5.72	8.26	− 0.93	8.02	4.79	1.26	3.80
2	− 0.86	1.29	− 0.27	0.56	0.59	.16	3.69
3	− 0.08	8.89	+ 6.68	8.06	6.76	1.30	5.20
4	+21.26	27.26	+15.19	24.16	6.07	3.94	1.54
5	−36.16	30.92	+49.26	31.32	85.42	4.73	18.10
6	− 2.84	5.63	+ 1.72	8.36	4.56	1.06	4.30
7	− 2.70	2.51	− 0.09	1.75	2.61	.34	7.68
Total	−27.97	42.25	+71.52	51.96	99.49	7.08	14.05

Table 60 shows that the P.M.H. group tested feminine on all the exercises of the test except 4 (emotional response), in which it was slightly more masculine than the high-school boys. This reversal of the general trend is probably to be interpreted as a lessening of emotional and moral sensitivity due in part to the

---

[1] A group of 9 homosexual boys was tested at the Preston School of Industry (California). These included one classified by the school officers as active who tested at +56, and eight classified as passive whose scores were: −104, −66, −49, −43, −38, −2, +59, +63. The last two were in all probability active but wrongly classified.

greater age of the P.M.H. subjects, but perhaps more especially to their associations and the type of life they lead. The greatest difference between the two groups is on Exercise 5, dealing with interests, likes, and dislikes. Here the P.M.H. mean (−36.16) is practically identical with that of third-year high-school girls (−36.40).

Can we accept the feminine scores of the P.M.H. group as reflecting the true personalities of the subjects—their actual interests and attitudes—or do they reflect primarily a conscious effort of the subjects to ape the feminine pattern just as they are known to do in physical appearance, carriage, and speech? It has been shown (Chapter IV) that the average man, knowing the intent of the test, can by taking thought score even more feminine than the average woman. These subjects did not know the exact purpose of the test, but many of them knew and others may have guessed that they were being studied because of their homosexuality. Perhaps this knowledge was stimulus enough to make them consciously try to respond as femininely as possible; or if not consciously, perhaps unconsciously, with a result no less misleading than if the score had been purposely faked.

There are several reasons why we do not believe that this theory can account for our findings. When reform school youths or prison groups are tested *en masse* without any of them knowing or even suspecting the purpose of the test, we still find that those known by the officials to be passive homosexuals nearly all score well down in the feminine range, while those known to be active homosexuals usually score well up in the masculine range. We tested a number of individual homosexual subjects who had been completely misled as to the purpose of the test and had no suspicion that they were known by the examiner to be sex inverts, and in these cases too the characteristic type of score is almost invariably found: a feminine score for the passive male homosexual and a masculine score for the active male homosexual.

Even more convincing evidence that the scores of the P.M.H. subjects are not faked, either consciously or unconsciously, is found by comparing their scores in the separate exercises of the test with those of young men who have been instructed to respond to all the items as a very feminine woman would respond. Under these conditions the score becomes more feminine in all the seven exercises, but to an unequal degree. As we go from exercise to exercise, the mean change it is possible for a group to make describes an irregular profile. On Exercises 2, 3, and 6 (ink blots, information, and historical characters) the faked scores are only a little more feminine than the naïve scores; on Exercises 1 and 7 the change is greater but still moderate; and Exercises 4 and 5 (emotional response and interests) are alike in showing changes of far greater magnitude. In other words, males are able to guess better in some fields than others the way in which responses of typical women would differ from their own. They guess best with respect to interests and preferences, and with respect to emotional responses of anger, fear, pity, disgust, and ethical appraisal.

When we examine the divergences of our P.M.H. subjects from normals on the seven exercises we find that they make a profile pattern decidedly unlike that of the intentionally faked scores. For example, Exercise 4, in which it is easy to fake the score of the opposite sex, rates the P.M.H. group even less feminine than the normal group. One may conclude, therefore, that the highly feminine scores of the P.M.H. group on Exercise 5 are genuine. There is no reason why subjects anxiously desiring to appear feminine should respond very femininely in Exercise 5 and more than normally masculine in Exercise 4.

ANALYSIS OF THE P.M.H. GROUP

The average age of the 77 subjects constituting the P.M.H. group is 26.0 years. The distribution of ages has a range from 17 to 44 years and a standard deviation of 6.12 years. It is skewed toward the younger ages, possibly due in part to the selection involved in obtaining the subjects. Since the subject who helped secure cases was only 22 years old, he probably tended to bring acquaintances who were somewhere near his own age. Another possible cause for the skewness may be found in the report that many of the older individuals of this type do not enter into the social life of the group and are therefore not available for study. They have generally better economic status and have more to lose through public exposure.

Nine out of 70, or 12.9 per cent of the group for whom family data are available, were "only" children while 21, or 30 per cent, were firstborn. The average age of the fathers of the group at the time of the subjects' birth was 31.7, of the mothers 26.8, as compared with 33.6 and 29.0 respectively for the parents of 643 gifted children.[1] The average number of brothers is 1.5 and of sisters also 1.5. With respect to the data just given, the P.M.H. group probably differs little from the generality of men of their age and social origin.

Only 4, or 5.7 per cent, of this group were married, as compared with 54.2 per cent of the twenty-six-year-old males in the general population.[2] Six others, or 8.5 per cent, have been married but at the time of this study were divorced or separated from their wives. The entire group of 77 men records a total of only 5 offspring. These figures may be influenced by various selective factors, but they are important in showing the tendency of the members of this particular group in regard to participation in family life.

At the time they were tested, 6 of the 77 were in a state prison and 10 were in jail. Of these 16 institutional cases, 13 regularly practiced prostitution as a means of livelihood previous to incarceration. Of the 54 noninstitutional cases for whom data are available, only 10 were known prostitutes, but it is believed that the actual number engaged in this occupation was at least two or three times as great as the reported number. The current occupations reported and the number engaged in each for the group of 54 noninstitutional cases were as follows: clerks, 7; show workers, 5; waiters, 5; cooks, 5; bookkeepers, 2; hospital orderlies, 2; house-to-house salesmen, 2; nurses, 2; ranch hands, 2; seamen, 2; high-school students, 2; and 1 each for bus boy,

---

[1] TERMAN, L. M., et al., Genetic studies of genius, vol. I, Mental and physical traits of a thousand gifted children, Stanford Univ. Press, 1925, Chapter VI.

[2] Census of the United States, 1920, vol. II, p. 391.

artist, common laborer, cutter and pattern maker for ladies' dresses, porter, truck driver, bellhop, costume designer, house painter, bank cashier, fireman, janitor, ironworker, and schoolteacher.

In order to ascertain whether or not the M-F scores of these 77 subjects bore any relationship to the occupations followed by them, the following correlational study was carried out. Six judges[1] were asked to rate each of the above-mentioned 26 occupations on a scale of 1 to 10 with respect to the masculinity-femininity of the work it involves. Although the masculinity-femininity of an occupation is a rather intangible characteristic, the fact that the intercorrelation of the ratings by the six judges were all between .75 and .92, with a mean of .84, indicates that the judges were fairly well agreed in regard to the thing being rated. Their composite rating may therefore be regarded as a fairly reliable criterion of the masculinity-femininity of the occupations considered.

These composite ratings were then correlated with the M-F scores of the 77 subjects. The correlation between them and the total M-F scores was found to be .24 ± .07, indicating a very small but probably significant relationship. The correlation would certainly have been higher but for the fact that practically all of the occupations listed are those commonly associated with women and so have a restricted range. This fact in itself is significant and agrees with the data presented in Chapter VIII indicating that many occupations exert a selective influence which is reflected in the mean M-F scores of occupational groups.

Approximately nine-tenths of the members of the homosexual group have had at least a grammar-school education, 11 are high-school graduates, and 6 have had one or more years in a college or university. On the whole, the group has a taste for good literature, music, and entertainment, if conversation can be taken as a reliable indication of actual interests and tastes.

[1] The ratings were made by K. M. Cowdery, P. R. Farnsworth, Quinn McNemar, C. C. Miles, E. K. Strong, Jr., and L. M. Terman.

At the time the study was made every subject in the group was accustomed to play the passive role in either fellatio or pederasty, and many engaged in both practices. The majority of them played only the passive role, although a few took the active part if occasion demanded. Practically all of them have lived with men in the relationship of man and wife. These unions are usually brief, although in a few cases they have lasted for as long as two or three years. In such cases, the active member of the pair frequently provided economic support for both. In a few instances the passive masqueraded as a woman and the two were legally married.

FEMININE CHARACTERISTICS OF PASSIVE MALE HOMOSEXUALS

The behavior of these male homosexuals, both as reported by them and as observed during the investigation, is as different from that of a group of average men as one could possibly imagine. It is well known that the average boy or young man makes every effort to keep from appearing effeminate. The passive male homosexual, on the contrary, takes advantage of every opportunity to make his behavior as much as possible like that of women. He not only accentuates any feminine qualities which he may already possess, such as a high-pitched voice, but also attempts to imitate women in his speech, walk, and mannerisms. Practically every subject has adopted a "queen" name by which he is known among his associates. They constantly refer to themselves as "the girls." Their behavior often seems exaggerated and ridiculous, although in some cases the inversion of behavior is remarkably complete.

As was pointed out before, the group tends to follow no occcupation other than prostitution except occupations in which women or very effeminate men commonly find employment. On the whole they are far lazier than any persons of similar age with whom we have come in contact, being inclined to shun any occupation which promises even a small amount of hard work.

Each subject in the P.M.H. group was asked to name his favorite study when in school, his favorite childhood play or game, and his favorite childhood toy or plaything. Replies were received by about 90 per cent of the group, many of the subjects naming more than one preference in one or more of the categories.

The preferences for school studies were as follows, from most to least popular: history, 18; reading, 8; geography, 8; English, 5; spelling, 5; literature, 5; grammar, 5; mathematics, 5; art, 4; arithmetic, 4; foreign language, 4; drawing, 3; music, 3; and 1 each for chemistry, philosophy, typing, and writing. Grouping into larger categories the subjects which are most alike we have: language studies, 33; history, 18; art (or drawing) and music, 10; arithmetic and mathematics, 9; geography, 4; miscellaneous, 4. On the whole the preferences are strikingly feminine; language studies, history, art, and music account for 61 of the 78 named.

The plays and games preferred were as follows: playing house, 17; games played with a ball, 12; marbles, 4; swimming, 3; tag, 3; girls' games (not specified), 3; skating, 2; jumping, 2; and 1 each for blocks, blind man's buff, checkers, chess, croquet, drawing, dressing up, dressing dolls, playing farm, fishing, hunting, hide-and-seek, hopscotch, hobbyhorse, jumping rope, music, ping-pong, post office, puzzles, reading, racing, playing store, theatricals, and tiddlywinks. The list of preferred play activities is even more feminine than the school-subject preferences. Probably no other male group could be found which would rate "house" as its most preferred play. Except for "ball," nearly all of the activities named are more feminine than masculine, and there is such a variety of ball plays that we cannot know how many of the 12 naming this activity had in mind the more masculine types of ball play. Playing house is the third most feminine of 90 kinds of plays, games, and activities according to data collected by the senior author for a large group of unselected schoolchildren in grades 3 to 8.

Applying the masculinity-femininity ratings of these 90 activities[1] to the expressed preferences of the P.M.H. group (omitting the indefinite preference recorded as "ball"), the mean rating of the preferred activities is 10, on a scale in which 13 to 20 is masculine and 12 to 1 is feminine. The mean would have

[1] See Table 1, p. 12.

been still lower but for the fact that the subjects were asked to name their favorite "game." The connotation of the word game is such that it brought no mention of doll play and certain other kinds of feminine activities very popular in this group.

Favorite playthings and toys are in the main such as would be expected from the activity preferences. The order is: dolls, 20; trains, 10; blocks, 5; bicycles, 4; books, 4; balls, 3; wagons, 3; teddy bears, 2; dishes, 2; marbles, 2; skates, 2; and 1 each for cats, dominoes, dresses, drums, engines, girls' toys (unspecified), hobbyhorse, mechanical toys, paints, piano, sailboat, tricycle, and top. It is profoundly significant that the plaything which has a two-to-one lead over its nearest competitor is perhaps the most characteristically feminine of all playthings known to Occidental culture. "Ball" receives only three mentions, which bears out the suspicion that some of those who named ball as a favorite game were not referring to the more masculine types of this activity.

In weighing the significance of the preference reports one must of course bear in mind that they relate to experiences which are for the most part from ten to thirty years in the past (about twenty, on the average), and that the choices given are probably influenced by whatever femininity has been acquired since childhood. That the picture is probably in accord with the facts is, however, strongly suggested by the more detailed information secured in connection with the case-history studies summarized in Chapter XIII. It appears that the large majority of passive male homosexuals are characterized from fairly early childhood by an inversion of interests, attitudes, and activities. The "pansy" type of behavior of adult inverts is not primarily an affectation or the result of "abnormal" or "perverted" sexual practices. The explanation is to be sought either in terms of psychological conditioning or in terms of biochemical factors present from early childhood. If the causes were biochemical it would be reasonable to expect that they would affect physical development, especially the development of secondary sexual characteristics. We turn next to the evidence available for our P.M.H. group on this point.

PHYSICAL TRAITS OF THE P.M.H. GROUP

In order to determine the relation of physique to M-F scores and types of behavior, physical measurements were made on all members of the P.M.H. group whose cooperation could be secured. The data include measures (in centimeters) of total height, sitting height, suprasternal height, pubic crest height, shoulder diameter, hip diameter at the iliac crest and at the greater trochanter, knee width, hip circumference, and head circumference. They include further the approximate net weight in pounds, shoulder slope in degrees, and masculinity-femininity ratings, on a five-point scale, of the hair on the face, chest, legs, and pubic regions. Hair color, skin texture, and condition of genitals were noted. The measurements of height, sitting height, hip diameter, and shoulder diameter were made in the manner described by Dr. W. R. Miles[1] and with the aid of instruments supplied by him. Dr. Miles also gave his personal assistance in planning the techniques for the other measures listed.[2]

The measurements listed were secured for 33 cases, of whom 24 were members of the P.M.H. group. The other 9 cases were obtained at the Preston (California) School of Industry, an institution for older juvenile delinquents. As these were considerably younger than the P.M.H. group their measurements were treated separately. The means and standard deviations of the measures for the group of 24 are given in Table 61 with comparative data when available for 100,000 white army troops, 552 Stanford freshmen, and 100 Smith College women. Table 62 gives the means and standard deviations for the small Preston group.

Table 61 shows that in general the physical measurements of these male homosexuals do not differ markedly from those of army and college men, although there is a slight tendency for

---

[1] MILES, W. R., Human body weight: I, Correlations between body widths and other physical measurements. *Science*, 1928, **68**, 382–386.

[2] Dr. Alvin J. Cox, Jr., Medical Assistant at St. Luke's Hospital, San Francisco, assisted Dr. Kelly in making the measurements.

TABLE 61.—PHYSICAL MEASUREMENTS OF 24 HOMOSEXUAL MEN, 100,000 WHITE ARMY TROOPS, 552 STANFORD FRESHMEN, AND 100 SMITH COLLEGE WOMEN

Item	Homosexual men		Army troops[1]		Stanford men[2]		Smith women[3]	
	Mean	S.D._dist.	Mean	S.D._dist.	Mean	S.D._dist.	Mean	S.D._dist.
Age...............	26.21	5.87	..	..	19.65	..	20.38	1.61
Height.............	170.75	7.67	171.99	6.66	176.0	6.1	163.5	5.21
Weight............	141.45	19.52	144.67	16.92	141.3	16.2	..	..
Sitting height.......	88.9	2.96	90.39	3.51	88.8	3.15	86.29	3.04
Sternal notch height	141.75	3.41	141.18	5.91	..	..	..	..
Pubic height........	86.5	5.87	86.82	5.05	..	..	83.8	4.08
Shoulder diameter..	37.58	2.18	..	..	37.4	2.1	35.1	3.64
Hip diameter, iliac crest.............	28.44	1.50	29.43	2.85	27.9	1.5	27.1	1.93
Hip diameter, trochanter.........	32.29	1.71	..	..	..	..	..	..
Shoulder slope......	111.3°	4.92°	..	..	..	..	..	..
Hip circumference..	90.75	6.22	..	..	..	..	..	..
Head circumference.	56.83	1.89	..	..	..	..	..	..
Knee width........	20.89	1.65	..	..	..	..	..	..
Shoulder-hip ratio[4]..	1.33	.08	..	..	1.34	..	1.30	..

[1] *The Medical Department of the United States Army in the World War*, vol. 15, *Statistics, Part I, Army Anthropology*, p. 234, Government Printing Office, Washington, 1921.

[2] MILES, W. R., *op. cit.*

[3] WILDER, H. H., *A laboratory manual of anthropometry*, Appendix B, pp. 171 ff., Blakiston's, 1920.

[4] Biacromial diameter divided by the hip diameter between the iliac crests.

TABLE 62.—PHYSICAL MEASUREMENTS OF NINE HOMOSEXUAL YOUTHS

Item	Mean	S.D._dist.	Item	Mean	S.D._dist.
Age................	18.7	0.9	Hip diameter, trochanter........	32.28	1.13
Height.............	175.0	6.18	Shoulder slope....	112.33°	3.40°
Weight.............	138.05	15.72	Hip circumference	89.22	4.57
Sitting height.......	88.72	3.50	Head circumference.............	56.83	2.11
Sternal notch height.	141.66	5.33	Knee width.......	21.36	1.05
Pubic height........	90.78	4.56	Shoulder-hip ratio.	1.28	.08
Shoulder diameter...	36.17	2.63			
Hip diameter, iliac crest.............	28.42	2.05			

their means to be somewhat smaller than those of the other male groups. The only statistically significant difference is between the mean height of the homosexuals and that of Stanford freshmen. The latter probably represent a selected group so far as height is concerned; on the other hand, the homosexual group have nearly all reached their adult height while most of the college freshmen have not.

It is commonly believed that men have relatively narrower hips and broader shoulders than women. The shoulder-hip ratios of 1.34 for the college men and 1.30 for the college women support this belief to a slight degree only. The mean ratio for the homosexual group is 1.33, and there is about a fifty-fifty chance that the mean shoulder-hip ratio of another group of 24 homosexuals would be as high as 1.35 or as low as 1.31.

Because of the small number of subjects in the P.M.H. group, the differences between the means for this group and the other male groups are too small to be accepted as evidence that male passive homosexuals are distinguishable from the generality of men with regard to size or body build.

One possibly significant finding is that the group of 24 includes two fairly distinct body types: the small, slender, even delicate, type and the large, fat, voluptuous type. The subjective impression of the investigator that such was the case is confirmed by the following bimodal distributions of the height measurements:

Height, centimeters	Frequency
183 to 185.9	1
180 to 182.9	1
177 to 179.9	5
174 to 176.9	0
171 to 173.9	1
168 to 170.9	2
165 to 167.9	3
162 to 164.9	3
159 to 161.9	3

Again it must be stressed, however, that the data are based on too few cases to justify anything beyond the most tentative of conclusions.

None of the 33 cases for whom a physical examination was possible showed the slightest defect of the genital organs. This is in agreement with the findings of other investigators and with the statements obtained from the subjects to the effect that such defects are practically unknown among their groups.

One other physical characteristic should be noted, namely, the amount and distribution of body hair. Many of the 33 subjects had but a small amount of body and leg hair and as a rule their beards were considerably less heavy than those of the average men.[1] Many of the group reported that it was necessary for them to shave but once every three or four days. A few cases were found with typically feminine distributions of pubic hair, in which the usual male vortex was entirely lacking. Not one of the group was of the extremely hairy type. These facts suggest the possibility of certain endocrine disturbances. It is possible, however, that the small group who were examined physically may not have been a representative sampling of the passive male homosexual population. Further investigation is urgently needed of physique in homosexuals.

THE GROUP OF ACTIVE MALE HOMOSEXUALS

This is the group of army prisoners previously referred to who were serving sentences for sodomy and had been classified by the prison psychiatrist as belonging to the active type.[2] The 56 subjects tested yielded only 46 usable blanks, as several of the subjects were partly illiterate and omitted many items.

The distribution of scores for this group has been shown in Figure 15. The mean of the distribution is +66.2, and the S.D. is 46.3. Both the mean and S.D. are almost identical with those for 130 male college students; the mean is 14 M-F points more masculine than that of 604 adult males in our general-population group. We have also seen that it is more masculine than the

---

[1] It may be noted that depilation, both facial and bodily, is a fairly common practice among homosexual male prostitutes.

[2] The authors are greatly indebted to Commanding Officer Colonel Cralle of Alcatraz for permission to give the M-F test to these groups and for his hearty cooperation throughout the study; also to Captain G. E. Hesner for his assistance in administering the tests and for supplying valuable case-history data for the group.

mean of 42 regular army men of similar education and social status.

The mean age of the group was 26.4 years; S.D. of the distribution 3.5 years; range 17 to 46 years. These figures parallel closely the age data for the P.M.H. group.

The average number of brothers for the members of the active group is 2.2; of sisters, 2.3. Two are "only" children.

Half the subjects were reared in a rural, half in an urban, environment.

Thirty-five were reared by both parents, two by father only, four by mother only, three by grandparents, and two by guardians.

Only six of the group attended high school and only one graduated. A third of the remainder did not go beyond the sixth grade. In education, intelligence, and culture this group is distinctly inferior to the P.M.H. group, which makes their high masculine score all the more significant.

The two favorite childhood games were baseball and football (no other game was mentioned more than once). Neither of these games was mentioned as a favorite by any of the P.M.H. group.

The favorite childhood toys were bicycles and kites. In the P.M.H. group, kites were mentioned once and bicycles not at all.

All of the subjects were unmarried at the time of the investigation; a few may have been married at some time, but information on this point was unfortunately not secured.

Although all had been sentenced for sodomy, only 21 admitted their guilt and 5 of these claimed to have been drunk at the time the offense was committed. The remainder denied guilt and said they were "framed."

The group was classified by the psychiatrist as follows:

1. Inferior type and inadequate personality........... 14
2. Constitutional psychopathic state................. 13
3. Inadequate personality and emotional instability.. 5
4. Mental deficiency............................... 3
5. No mental abnormality........................ 5
6. Miscellaneous.................................... 6

Further studies are urgently needed of the distinguishing characteristics of the active and passive types of male homosexuals, with greater care to secure groups of individuals who belong with certainty to one class or the other. At the same time two other groups should be studied: (a) homosexuals who are equally given to the active and passive roles, and (b) bisexuals who alternate between homo- and hetero-sexuality.

GENESIS OF HOMOSEXUALITY

Certain investigators have stressed the importance of innate constitution in the production of homosexual behavior, while others have insisted just as strongly that it is chiefly the result of environmental conditions. The data collected in this study offer interesting evidence as to the part which environment has played and at the same time fail to disclose any definite constitutional basis for the condition. The fact that the entire group of 77 passive homosexual men studied has produced only five children suggests that group suicide is going on. If this is representative of similar groups, and the homosexual population is dependent on direct inheritance from practicing individuals of this type, it could not survive for many generations.

It is probable that active and passive homosexuality have different causes. With respect to the former we have no data to offer beyond the generally masculine M-F scores of the Alcatraz group. Passive male homosexuals are typically true inverts in the broadest sense of the term; active male homosexuals seem not to be. The latter are masculine in their responses, but the stimulus which provokes their sexual responses is a male instead of a female, though preferably a male of feminine personality. It seems probable that most of them are bisexual, as men have been in certain historic cultures, among the Greeks, for example.

As will be seen later (Chapter XV), the situation seems to be reversed with women. Here it is the active homosexuals who are the true inverts, the passives ordinarily being normally feminine in their attitudes and interests and perhaps usually bisexual. In the making of active male and passive female homosexuals it is probable that chance circumstances often play an important role, also, especially in the case of males, a willingness to experiment in search of new types of sexual gratification. The active male homosexual is rather a pervert, in the primary and nonmoral connotation of the term.

SUMMARY

1. The M-F score mean of a group of 77 passive male homosexuals aged 17 to 44 years is -27.97 with a standard deviation of 42.25. This is by far the most feminine-testing group of males encountered in our investigations, more feminine in fact than our group of outstanding college women athletes.

2. The responses of this group tend to be feminine on all the exercises of the test except No. 4 (emotional response). Exercise 5 (interests) yields by far the most feminine scores of the seven exercises.

3. It is not believed that the test responses of the P.M.H. group were much modified by the deliberate effort of its members to make themselves as feminine as possible. The subjects did not know the specific purpose of the test, and their scores on the separate exercises differ in characteristic ways from those of male subjects who take the test with the instruction to respond as they think women would do.

4. A group of 46 male homosexuals classified as belonging to the active type earned a mean score slightly more masculine than that of unselected soldiers of comparable age and background. The distribution for this group was bimodal, indicating that the population probably contained a number of passive homosexuals.

5. Half or more of the group of 77 passive homosexuals were prostitutes; practically all the 50 other occupations recorded as having been followed at any time were occupations which tend to attract effeminate men.

6. A series of 13 physical measurements applied to 24 members of the P.M.H. group yielded only negative results. Several of the group, however, showed feminine characteristics with respect to quantity and distribution of body hair,[1] and appar-

[1] See note, p. 254.

ently there was some indication of two feminine types (small slender, and large voluptuous).

7. The passive male homosexuals as a group have been markedly feminine in their interests and preferred activities since early childhood. Although exactly comparable data were not secured for the active group, such casual information as was secured presented a strikingly contrasting picture with respect to masculinity-femininity during childhood.

8. Although our data offer no crucial evidence regarding the genesis of homosexuality in males, we believe that they lend considerable support to the theory of psychological conditioning. Additional evidence will be presented in the two chapters which follow.

CHAPTER XII

A TENTATIVE SCALE FOR THE MEASUREMENT OF SEXUAL INVERSION IN MALES[1]

The preceding chapter has shown that passive male homosexuals as a group rate far more feminine on the M-F test than any other group of men comparable in age and education. In fact, their responses are indicative of interests, attitudes, and thought trends that are essentially more feminine than masculine. We have already seen, however, that the P.M.H. group is not equally feminine on all the exercises of the test. Exercise 5 (interests) contributes most heavily to their feminine rating. On this exercise the critical ratio of the group's divergence from our general population groups is 15.3. The critical ratios are also large on Exercise 2 (ink blots) and Exercise 7 (introversion), 6.2 and 5.6, respectively, but these exercises are so lightly weighted as to contribute little to the variance of the total score. On Exercise 6 (personalities and opinions) the invert group is somewhat more feminine than the general-population group (C.R. 2.0), but on Exercise 1 (word association), Exercise 3 (information), and Exercise 4 (emotional and ethical attitudes) their divergences from the general population of males in each case lacks statistical significance. When the P.M.H. means were computed for the four parts of Exercise 4, it was found that in anger and pity responses the group is near average for the general male population, more feminine than the latter in fear responses, rather more masculine in disgust responses, and markedly more masculine in ethical attitudes.

It seemed desirable to investigate still more specific divergences of the invert group from a norm group by the tabulation of

[1] Dr. E. Lowell Kelly, assistant in the M-F investigation, is responsible for bringing together the factual material of this chapter. The summary here presented is the joint work of Dr. Kelly and Dr. Terman.

responses to the individual items of the M-F test. The normal population selected for this purpose was a group of 98 males enrolled in the junior year of high school, whose item responses had already been tabulated for another purpose. The members of this group were younger than the large majority of the invert group and perhaps averaged a little higher in general intelligence. The fact that the two groups were not more evenly matched for age, education, intelligence, and social background detracts in some degree from the value of the resulting comparative data, but probably not to any very great extent; certainly most of the larger differences we have uncovered would be found to hold for groups more carefully matched. The choice of a norm group was dictated by economy, item tabulations for the high-school group being already available.

The comparison of item responses was made with two purposes in view: (1) it would make possible the derivation of a tentative scale for the measurement of sexual inversion in males, and (2) it would afford the basis for a detailed descriptive characterization of the invert group as compared with noninverts of the same sex.

DERIVATION OF "I" SCORE WEIGHTS

The item comparisons could be made only for Form A of the M-F test, as Form B was not administered to the invert group. The techniques used in deriving the "I" scale were essentially the same as those by which response weights were derived in our preliminary experiments with the various parts of the M-F test, except that in this case two contrasting male groups were used instead of a male and a female group. That is, for each item of Form A of the M-F test the percentages of the two groups answering the item in a given way were computed. As each item has from two to four multiple-choice responses, percentages had to be computed for a total of some 1,560 possible responses. The differences between these percentages for the two groups were then translated into "I" score weights, a weight for each of the possible responses.

As in the case of the M-F test, the question arose whether to use unit or weighted scores; in other words, whether to make the weights uniformly +1 or −1, according as a given percentage is significantly higher for one group than for the other, or instead to give larger weights in proportion to the magnitude and reliability of the difference. It will be recalled that in the case of the M-F test weighted scores were finally abandoned in favor of unit scores. The latter reduce the labor of scoring, are about as reliable as weighted scores, and possibly more defensible psychologically in that they avoid overweighting large sex differences that may reflect chiefly the influences of differing environments. The world of men is in reality a very different world from that of women. In the present experiment, however, we are concerned with two male groups, and the psychological objection to the use of weighted scores is less cogent. Weights have therefore been employed. These range from +30 to −30, the plus weights being arbitrarily assigned to responses more frequently checked by the invert group. The weights for all the responses are reproduced in Appendix IV, so that anyone who wishes to use the "I" scale will be able to provide himself with a scoring key. Further investigation is desirable to determine whether a narrower range of weights, say from 1 to 3, would be better than the wide range used.[1]

In order to ascertain whether or not the "I" scores possess a peculiar significance of their own, that is, whether they are measuring something other than that measured by the M-F scores proper, all the test blanks which had been filled out by the invert group were rescored on the basis of the "I" weights. The distribution of the 82 scores[2] resulting is shown in Table 63. As will be noted immediately, the total scores are practically all positive, and, on the whole, quite large. The range is almost two thousand points, which indicates wide individual differences among the members of the group and that the "I" scores are discriminative of these differences.

[1] The "I" score weights were computed by the formula given on p. 54.
[2] In this tabulation five cases were added to the 77 in the original P.M.H. group.

TABLE 63.—FREQUENCY DISTRIBUTION OF THE "I" SCORES MADE BY 82 MEMBERS
OF THE P.M.H. GROUP

"I" Score	Frequency
+1400 to +1499	2
+1300 to +1399	3
+1200 to +1299	6
+1100 to +1199	5
+1000 to +1099	5
+ 900 to + 999	7
+ 800 to + 899	8
+ 700 to + 799	5
+ 600 to + 699	6
+ 500 to + 599	5
+ 400 to + 499	1
+ 300 to + 399	5
+ 200 to + 299	1
+ 100 to + 199	12
0 to + 99	4
− 100 to − 1	4
− 200 to − 101	1
− 300 to − 201	1
− 400 to − 301	1
Mean	+644.0
S.D.	462.2

Perhaps the most interesting feature of the distribution is its distinct bimodality, clearly observable in Fig. 16. By means of the goodness-of-fit technique it was found that such an extremely bimodal distribution would occur only seven times in 1,000 as the result of chance. It appears, therefore, that the invert group is probably made up of two distinct personality types. It will be remembered that every effort was made to include only passive male homosexuals in this group, but in view of the method of obtaining the subjects it would not be surprising if a certain number of the active type were included. It is even possible that a few members of the group were not true homosexuals at all, but were merely posing as such in order to ply the trade of prostitution. Whatever the actual situation may be, the scores indicate a marked heterogeneity within the group.

That the "I" scale is measuring something other than the M-F scale is shown by the fact that the correlation between the two sets of scores was found to be only .09 ± .08. For another group of subjects (46 Catholic priests in training) a correlation of .54 was found. Even here, however, the correlation is low enough to demonstrate that the "I" scores have a special significance of their own. The mean "I" score of this group was −187, as compared with +644 for the P.M.H. group. The range for the priests in training was from −700 to +300. Relative to the mean M-F scores of the two groups (+12 for the student

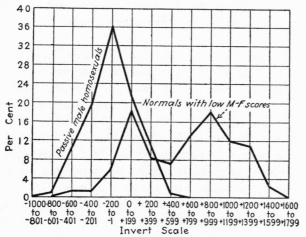

Fig. 16.—Distributions of "I" scores of 82 passive male homosexuals and 46 normal males with low M-F scores.

priests and −19 for the homosexuals), the student priests test much less invert on the "I" scale.[1]

The question may well be raised as to just what a large "I" score signifies in terms of personality and temperament. Without going beyond the empirical findings we can say that a person making such a score possesses a set of interests, attitudes, and thought trends (within the area covered by the test) approximating those of a typical member of the invert group. To the extent that this group is representative of the generality of passive male homosexuals, it might be said that the subject in

[1] Unfortunately the group of 46 male homosexuals classified as actives (Alcatraz group) were given Form B of the M-F test and could therefore not be scored on the "I" scale.

question resembles in personality the typical male sexual invert. There, however, we must stop; a man with a high "I" score may or may not be a practicing homosexual; for all we know he may have made normal heterosexual adjustments. Only extended and careful research can determine the extent to which a man whose personality deviates from the average in the homosexual direction is thereby predisposed to find heterosexual adjustment difficult. One factor which certainly limits the validity of the "I" scale is the fact that the invert group on which it is based is not truly representative of inverts in general but is composed chiefly of invert prostitutes.

There can be little doubt that an "I" scale based upon large and strictly representative groups of homosexual and nonhomosexual subjects would be of value for research and clinical purposes. Subjects at the secondary school level with high "I" scores should be followed up in order to find out what types of sexual adjustment they are likely to make. If it should turn out that young men with such scores are in fact potential homosexuals, preventive measures might be found that would direct their sexual development into normal channels.

The "I" scores may also be found useful in the legal disposition of the cases of homosexuality continually coming before the courts. Although the courts are primarily interested in the criminal act itself, rather than in the factors leading up to the act, it seems reasonable that different types of treatment should be accorded those found guilty of homosexual acts on the basis of whether they are true homosexuals or mere perverts. It will bear repetition, however, that the "I" score cannot be taken as conclusive proof of the presence or absence of homosexuality. It does constitute an entirely new line of evidence, which, interpreted in relation to information provided by the case history, assumes unique significance. In the following chapter, which presents 18 case histories of members of the P.M.H. group, the reader will find it interesting to compare the "I" score of each subject with the obtained behavioral evidence of true sexual inversion.

Analysis of "I" Weights of Individual Responses

By noting the "I" weights assigned to the various responses in the manner described in the last section it is possible to characterize the invert group in terms of the responses which are most or least typical of it. A survey of the items showing significant differences between the two groups will afford a kind of composite picture of the attitudes and interests which go to make up the personality of the male sexual invert.

However, in any use of the response weights for this purpose it is necessary to bear in mind the nature of our invert group. As we have already pointed out, this group is considerably older than the norm group with which it is compared and differs from the latter in experience and social background. There are also differences in education and intelligence, though these are smaller and less important for the present purpose than the differences in age and life experiences. Such differences, having little or nothing to do with sexual inversion *per se*, would doubt-less account for many of the plus and minus weights, especially those of small or moderate magnitudes. There is an additional reason why it is necessary to avoid attaching too much significance to the weight assigned to an individual response. The reliability of a single item weight is so extremely low that even if the groups had been more ideally matched, chance factors alone would have produced many weights of appreciable size. In the total score the chance factors tend to cancel out, as the weights they produce would theoretically fall as often in one direction as the other. Chance factors would very rarely produce a large "I" score, either in the plus or minus direction; such a score could only be obtained by the subject who makes a large number of responses typical (or atypical) of inverts. In item comparisons, however, chance factors must not be overlooked. In the item analysis which follows no account has been taken of weights below $+7$ or -7. Anyone who wishes to extend the analysis to lower weights can do so from the data supplied in Appendix IV. For ourselves we prefer to leave the more detailed comparison until data are available for larger and more representative groups.

Exercise 1: Word Association.—This test, as we have seen, does not effectively differentiate the invert group from normal males. Examination of the separate items shows that only six out of 60 have any of their four multiple responses with weights as large as.+10 or −10. These are as follows:

11. TRAIN   engine(−10)   gown(+12)   travel(+4)   whistle(+2)
16. PASS   car(−3)   mountain(+2)   over(+2)   subject(−10)
37. DEVIL   dare(−2)   evil(−1)   hell(−5)   tempt(+10)
42. CELLAR   basement(−7)   dark(+5)   furnace(+3)   vegetables(+11)
44. DESPISE   coward(−6)   dirt(+10)   dislike(−1)   flirt(+7)
60. MACHINE   engine(−1)   Ford(−5)   ride(+2)   sew(+10)

In No. 11, although the response "engine" has the favored position, "gown," a typically feminine response, was underlined by 18 per cent of the invert group and by not a single one of the norm group. This gives "gown" a weight of +12. "Engine," on the other hand, was underlined by only 40 per cent of the invert group and by 80 per cent of the norm group, which gives a weight of −10 for this response.

In No. 16 the weight of −10 for the response "subject" probably reflects nothing more than the fact that the members of the norm group are still in school and are interested in passing their subjects.

One might explain the weight of +10 for the response "tempt" as indicating a more or less subconscious feeling on the part of the homosexual that he is forever being tempted to engage in a socially disapproved type of sexual behavior.

A plausible reason why in No. 42 the response "vegetables" is given oftener by the invert group and "basement" by the norm group is that "vegetables" represents a more housewifely association. A majority of the invert group have done a great deal of housework and some of them have held positions as cooks.

In No. 44 the fastidious nature of the typical invert asserts itself in a weight of +10 for the response "dirt." It is also interesting to note that the invert group gives a specifically sexual association oftener than the norm group (+7 for "flirt"), and the norm group more often an association reflecting a favorable attitude toward personal courage (−6 for "coward"). Anyone who is acquainted with male sexual inverts knows that physical bravery is not one of their commonly cherished ideals.

In No. 60 the weight of +10 for "sew," as a response to "machine," undoubtedly reflects the preoccupation of the invert group with feminine activities.

We append a list of the items in this exercise which carry one or more weights as high as 7 but less than 10. Weights in this range are of course less reliable than higher ones, but many of them strongly suggest genuine psychological differences between inverts and normal males.

4. SHARP bright(+4) flat(+5) knife(−7) pin(+5)
6. ORDER buy(−2) command(−3) neat(+7) quiet(+3)
8. POST fence(−7) gate(+2) letter(+5) mail(+4)
9. TENDER kind(+1) loving(−1) meat(−4) sore(+9)
14. FLY airplane(−7) bird(+4) nasty(+9) travel(+7)
18. BOOK cover(−5) paper(−7) print(+4) read(+2)
22. DANGER accident(−1) caution(−4) death(+7) escape(+6)
24. FRESH cool(−7) flirt(+6) meat(−1) stale(+2)
29. GARDEN flower(−2) fruit(+7) vegetable(−1) weeds(−4)
30. EMBRACE arms(−6) lover(−1) mother(+3) sin(+7)
31. HOME expenses(+7) happiness(+3) house(−6) sleep(−6)
32. BLUSH red(−8) rose(+7) shame(+4) smile(−1)
34. FELLOW boy(−4) friend(0) good(+7) pal(+1)
35. CHEAT cards(−4) clerk(+7) crook(+1) unfair(−1)
39. DIMPLE baby(+3) cheek(−7) hole(+5) knee(+7)
40. KNIGHT armor(−8) brave(+4) Ivanhoe(+3) man(+1)
41. LETTER love(+4) news(0) paper(−9) stamp(−3)
47. SPOON fork(−2) pet(+8) silver(−1) soup(−2)
48. CHEEK blush(−7) girl(−5) nerve(+8) pink(+1)
51. SACRIFICE cards(+1) kill(−4) money(−6) mother(+7)
56. FAMILY brother(−7) kind(0) quarrel(+5) sister(+1)
57. SIXTEEN age(−8) foolish(+5) number(0) years(+4)

In the above list No. 4 suggests that male inverts are less interested than normal subjects in the knife as a tool ("knife," −7) and more interested in music ("flat," +5) and feminine appliances ("pin," +5). No. 6 again reflects the fastidious habits of the invert ("neat," +7). In No. 8 it is not surprising that "post" more often suggests "letter" to the inverts and "fence" to the normals. One wonders whether the +9 for "sore," in response to "tender," has any connection with the frequent practice of pederasty by the inverts. In No. 14 the plus weight for "nasty" and the minus weight for "airplane" undoubtedly reflect the greater fastidiousness of the invert and the greater mechanical interest of the normal. In No. 22 the weights of +7 and +6 may reflect the invert's timidity in the face of danger. In No. 24 it is hardly surprising that inverts should more often take "fresh" in the sense of "flirt" and normals more often in the sense of "cool." In No. 30 the plus weight for "sin" in response to "embrace" may reflect the invert's bad social conscience over the kind of embrace to which he is accustomed, or it may reflect merely his more intense preoccupation with sex. For the normal youth, "home" (No. 31) is a house or a place to sleep; to the invert it more often suggests expenses. In No. 32 the plus weight for "rose" and the minus weight for "red" in response to "blush" probably reflect the more sentimental and poetic attitude of the inverts. In No. 39 the minus weight for "cheek" and the plus weight for "knee," in response to "dimple," suggest an interesting difference in fetishistic associations. The +8 for "pet" in response to "spoon" (No. 47) is self-explanatory. In No. 48 the −7 for "blush" and the +8 for "nerve," in response to "cheek," may show the tendency to a particular slang usage in the P.M.H. group. The weights of −7 and +5 in No. 56 probably reflect the domestic conflict which so many of the invert group experienced during childhood. We feel less certain of the explanation for the weights in items 18, 29, 34, 35, 40, 41, and 57, though for most of them it would be easy to supply more or less plausible guesses.

Every one of the items in Exercise 1 carries a plus weight for failure to respond, and in the case of 49 of the 60 the weight is +10 or more. The more frequent blocking of associations in the invert group may be a psychoneurotic symptom.

Exercise 2: Ink Blots.—This test is even less discriminative between the two groups than word association. Of the 18 items, only 4 carry a weight as high as 7 and only 2 a weight as high as 10. These are as follows:

6. ax(−11) boat(−4) chopper(+7) moon(−3)
11. Indian(−5) man hanged(−7) scarecrow(−1) tassel(+7)
12. chimney(−4) coil(−7) smoke(+10) thread(+9)
18. a man(−6) bowl(+8) cup(−5) head(−1)

The psychological significance of most of these weights will be obvious. In No. 6 ax is a masculine tool associated with a degree of physical exertion very repugnant to the typical male invert, who is more often interested in such domestic appliances as food choppers. The domestic interest of the invert also probably explains the +8 weight for "bowl" in No. 18. That "cup" was more often checked by the norm group is probably due to the fact that the stimulus looks more like an athletic trophy cup than a household cup. In No. 12 the −7 for "coil" and the +9 for "thread" reflect, respectively, the mechanical interests of the norm group and the feminine interests of inverts. We are uncertain as to the meaning of the +10 weight for "smoke" in this item or the two weights of +7 and −7 in No. 11.

Half of the items in Exercise 2 carry a plus weight of 10 for failure to respond, none bears a negative weight for omission.

Exercise 3: Information.—Although this exercise as a whole does not differentiate the two groups to any very considerable extent, there are 29 items carrying a weight of 10 or more and 10 additional items weighted 7 to 9. Those with the larger weights will illustrate sufficiently the characteristic differences between the groups in this test.

1. Marigold is a kind of fabric(−11) flower(+8) grain(−11) stone(−8)
   Inverts probably have more interest in flowers.
2. Things cooked in grease are boiled(0) broiled(+10) fried(+6) roasted(−6)
   The correct answer is more often given by the inverts, as would be expected, but so is the incorrect response "broiled." Perhaps one could say that the latter is a better error than "roasted," which is more often given by the norm group.
3. The Yale is a kind of hammer(0) lock(−3) screen(0) wrench(−10)
   Lack of interest by inverts in things mechanical.
5. Pongee is a kind of cloth(−1) drink(+6) flower(−10) game(−10)
   It is surprising that all the weights of any appreciable size are carried by incorrect responses, and that the correct answer carries a minus

weight. One would have expected the inverts to have more knowledge of fabrics than this item indicates.

6. The most gold is produced in Alaska(+7) New York(0) Tennessee(−10) Texas(−3)

The inverts' greater knowledge here may be due chiefly to age and experience.

10. Beethoven is known as a composer(+1) painter(0) poet(+4) singer(−10)

More inverts know that Beethoven was not a singer, but the correct response received only a weight of +1. This was a surprise in view of the fact that so many of the inverts seemed to have musical interests.

11. Most of our anthracite coal comes from Alabama(−8) Colorado(−5) Ohio(−11) Pennsylvania(+18)

The greater knowledge of industrial geography on the part of inverts may be due to age and experience.

12. The number of players on a baseball team is: 7(−4) 9(−5) 11(+4) 13(+10)

Inverts are notoriously little interested in games and sports.

14. A loom is used for cooking(+3) embroidering(+3) sewing(−10) weaving(−1)

The one large weight is due to ignorance on the part of the norm group, but it is surprising that the correct answer was not better known to the inverts.

15. Peat is used for fuel(−9) pavement(+9) plaster(+3) road-making(+11)

Peat is a relatively unknown term to the inverts.

17. Tokyo is a city of China(−5) India(+11) Japan(+2) Russia(0)

The one large weight is caused by the relatively greater ignorance of the invert group.

18. The first American naval hero was Hull(−30) John Paul Jones(+30) Lawrence(+11) Winslow(−5)

19. Daffodils are grown from bulbs(0) cuttings(−11) seeds(+8) shoots(+5)

About equal ignorance in the two groups.

20. The baby found in the bulrushes was Jacob(−6) Jesus(−11) Moses(+7) Paul(0)

Inverts appear to have more knowledge of the Bible; a good many of them had a religious upbringing.

21. The boomerang is an animal(−1) plant(+10) tool(+10) weapon(−7)

Greater interest of the norm group in things mechanical.

22. Minnehaha means falling leaves(−10) laughing waters(+2) running brooks(+3) whispering pines(−1)

Nearly equal ignorance in the two groups.

23. A correct expression is I have dove(-6) I dived($+12$) He dove(-11)

The inverts are more fastidious in their language as in other things.

25. The vessel which overcame the Merrimac was the Connecticut($+10$) Monitor(-5) Old Ironsides(0)

The weight of $+10$ for an incorrect response is out of line with the data for No. 18.

28. A shilling is worth about 25 cts.($+6$) 50 cts.(-9) $1.00($-4$) $5.00($-11$)

Superior knowledge of inverts may be due to age and experience.

37. The number of persons on a jury in the U.S. is 8(-9) 12($+8$) 16(-10) 18(0)

Greater knowledge of inverts about legal procedures probably due to age and experience and also to the fact that they live in constant fear of the law.

38. The madonna is a favorite subject for music(-6) paintings($+7$) poetry(-10) stories(-7)

Inverts more often have artistic interests; possibly the madonna motif is accentuated by the mother complex.

46. A buffet is used for books(-11) clothes(-11) dishes($+9$) food($+7$)

Inverts have more housewifely interests.

55. "Mennen's" is the name of cold cream(-8) perfume(-9) collar(-8) talcum($+16$)

Inverts are more given to the use of cosmetics.

58. "Charades" is a running game(-9) game of chance($+3$) guessing game($+6$) kissing game(-11)

Charades is a feminine indoor game that probably holds more interest for inverts than for the norm group.

61. Babies should be weaned at about 3 mos.(-13) 6 mos.(-10) 12 mos.($+7$) 2 yrs.($+13$)

Inverts display more "maternal" or infantile attitudes; are more interested in nursing.

65. A birthright was sold for a mess of pottage by Cain(-6) Esau($+12$) Isaac(-7) Judas(-2)

Inverts have more knowledge of the Bible and probably greater interest in religion.

66. Beam scales illustrate the principle of buoyancy($+1$) elasticity($+10$) leverage(-2) magnetism($+1$)

The only considerable weight is for a wrong response by the inverts to an item concerning mechanics.

69. "Nevermore" was spoken by a general(-11) parrot($+1$) raven($+14$) woman(-4)

Inverts are probably more interested in poetry, or at least in poetry of a certain kind.

70. A famous portrait painter was Rosa Bonheur(-8) Mozart(-2) Reynolds($+10$) Rubens($+1$)
Inverts are more interested in art.

Of the 70 items in this exercise, 11 carry plus weights of 10 or more for omission and two minus weights of this magnitude. The difference could mean either that the invert group has less information than the norm group or that the latter is less timid about guessing. On the other hand it may reflect nothing more than the school youth's greater willingness and readiness to respond to pencil-and-paper tasks.

All in all, the group differences in this exercise seem to us less significant psychologically than those in Exercise 1; the influence of age and experience often seem to outweigh personality factors in producing sizable weights.

Exercise 4: Emotional and Ethical Attitudes.—This is another test which differentiates to only a slight extent between the two groups. The several parts of the exercise will be treated separately for weights of 7 or higher.

a. Anger Responses.

7. Being snubbed by an inferior $VM(+8)$ $M(-2)$ $L(+2)$ $N(-4)$
That inverts more often respond to this situation with "very much" anger probably reflects their sensitiveness and introvertive tendencies.

11. Seeing boys make fun of old people $VM(-7)$ $M(+4)$ $L(+3)$ $N(+10)$
The explanation is not obvious to us.

12. Seeing an honest official thrown out of office by politicians $VM(-4)$ $M(-2)$ $L(+3)$ $N(+7)$
Interpretation uncertain; possibly the inverts are less interested in civic affairs, or possibly they regard the phenomenon as too common to get excited about.

13. Seeing a person laugh at a cripple $VM(-3)$ $M(+3)$ $L(+4)$ $N(-10)$
We see no obvious explanation of the fact that both extremes of response should be more frequent with the norm group.

16. Seeing someone trying to discredit you with your employer $VM(0)$ $M(0)$ $L(-1)$ $N(+7)$
Interpretation of weight for N not clear. Perhaps this represents a common experience for the inverts.

17. Seeing someone laugh when a blind man runs into an obstacle $VM(0)$ $M(0)$ $L(+3)$ $N(-10)$

The N weight here is in line with that in No. 13, but not with the N weight in No. 11. Reason not obvious.

For the 17 items of the test the total of all the plus weights assigned to VM and M is 46; the total of the minus weights is 36. The total of the plus weights assigned to L and N is 65; the total of the minus weights is 54. The difference between the plus and minus totals, though small, is in each case in the direction of a larger plus total. It seems at first a contradiction that the inverts should score higher both for VM and M on the one hand and for L and N on the other. The contradiction disappears when we cast up the totals of VM, M, and L for comparison with the total of N taken alone. These are, for VM, M, and L, $+77$ and -48; for N, $+34$ and -42. The responses accordingly indicate slightly greater proneness of the invert group to say that they would experience at least some degree of anger in situations of the kind presented.

b. Fear Responses.
2. Being lost $VM(-1)$ $M(-7)$ $L(-4)$ $N(+7)$
   Age and experience of inverts may account for the $+7$ weight for N.
4. Becoming deaf or blind $VM(-7)$ $M(-7)$ $L(+6)$ $N(+10)$
   The inverts are probably more careless regarding physical misfortunes.
5. Bulls $VM(+9)$ $M(+2)$ $L(-3)$ $N(-4)$
   Inverts are characterized by greater physical timidity.
11. Garter snakes $VM(+7)$ $M(+1)$ $L(+3)$ $N(-5)$
    The inverts here show a feminine type of timidity.
16. Negroes $VM(+10)$ $M(+6)$ $L(+7)$ $N(-9)$
    We do not know why the inverts stand so much more in fear of negroes than do the norm group, unless it be that negroes take advantage of their feminine timidity to bully them.
18. Punishment in the next world $VM(+1)$ $M(-4)$ $L(+8)$ $N(-5)$
    Explanation of L weight not clear, especially as that for N is in the opposite direction.
20. Windstorms $VM(+10)$ $N(+5)$ $L(-2)$ $N(-1)$
    Physical timidity probably an adequate explanation.

The plus weight total for VM and M is $+107$; the minus weight total, -47. The corresponding totals for L and N are $+58$ and -69. In other words, the invert group inclines more to "much" or "very much" fear, the norm group to "little" or "none." The totals for VM, M, and L are $+142$ and -67; for N taken alone, $+23$ and -49. There can be little doubt that these figures express a genuine difference between the two groups in their attitudes toward situations requiring physical courage.

In this section omission receives only plus or zero weights, for 12 of the 20 items the weight being as high as 10.

c. Disgust Responses.

2. A butcher shop $VM(+4)$ $M(+3)$ $L(+7)$ $N(-8)$
The inverts are a little more fastidious.
12. Seeing a woman smoking $VM(-9)$ $M(-4)$ $L(+2)$ $N(+6)$
Difference probably due to age and experience.
15. Soiled or ragged finger nails $VM(+2)$ $M(+1)$ $L(\pm1)$ $N(-7)$
Again the inverts are slightly more fastidious.

From the small number of items with a weight of 7 or higher one would conclude that no appreciable difference exists between the two groups in disgust response. However, an interesting difference is disclosed when we compare weight totals. For VM and M the plus weights for the 18 items total only $+31$; the minus weights, -63. For L and N the totals are $+64$ and -37. It appears, therefore, that the inverts are decidedly less prone to experience disgust than the norm group, at least in situations of the kind with which we are here concerned. This may possibly be due to the age difference, but we are inclined to think that it reflects a dulling of the invert's sense of disgust by the perverted sexual practices to which he is accustomed. In view of the nature of these practices it is surprising that the inverts are as capable of disgust as the test indicates them to be.

All but one of the weights for omission are zero or plus, nine of them being as high as 10.

d. Pity Responses.

1. A bee that is drowning $VM(-5)$ $M(-7)$ $L(+1)$ $N(+5)$
7. Overworked horses $VM(-3)$ $M(-1)$ $L(+8)$ $N(+4)$
8. Overworked children $VM(-1)$ $M(0)$ $L(+2)$ $N(-10)$
9. A fly caught on sticky fly paper $VM(+9)$ $M(-3)$ $L(+1)$ $N(-3)$
10. An underfed child $VM(0)$ $M(+2)$ $L(-1)$ $N(-10)$
13. A baby bird whose mother is dead $VM(-5)$ $M(-5)$ $L(+8)$ $N(+7)$
14. A wounded soldier who must beg for a living $VM(-8)$ $M(+4)$ $L(+7)$ $N(+9)$

The situations presented in items 1, 7, 13, and 14 arouse less pity in the inverts than in the norm group. The opposite is the case for the situations presented in items 8, 9, and 10. Probably the fact that high-school youths have not often come in contact with overworked or underfed children accounts for the weights in items 8 and 10. Why inverts should feel so much more pity than the norm group for the fly caught on sticky fly paper is puzzling, especially as they feel less pity than the norm group for the drowning bee.

The totals of the *VM* and *M* weights for the 15 items are +25 and −53; for the *L* and *N* weights, +63 and −37. On the whole, therefore, the inverts seem to be less pitying than the norm group, but the difference may possibly be due to age.

Weights for omission are about equally divided between plus and minus; for four items it is −10 and for three +10.

e. Ethical Judgment.—It will be recalled that this test requires subjects to draw a circle around 3, 2, 1, or 0 to indicate whether the act mentioned is "extremely wicked," "decidedly bad," "somewhat bad," or "not really bad." Of the 28 items in the test, 15 received a weight of 7 or more.

M-F test items	3	2	1	0
1. Picking flowers in a public park.............	−10	− 8	+1	+11
2. Stealing a ride on a truck...................	− 9	− 7	−3	+ 9
3. Telling a lie to avoid punishment...........	−15	− 3	+4	+17
6. Making fun of cripples.....................	− 3	+ 1	+3	+10
7. Using slang.............................	0	− 5	−4	+ 7
9. Boys smoking before they are 21...........	− 6	− 7	+5	+ 4
11. Moderate drinking........................	− 5	−11	+1	+10
12. Excessive drinking.......................	− 3	+ 1	+2	+10
14. Swiping fruit out of orchards...............	− 8	− 8	+6	+ 7
15. Laziness................................	− 3	− 5	+1	+10
16. Going to bed without saying your prayers....	− 4	− 4	−3	+ 7
18. Boys fighting............................	0	− 8	0	+ 5
19. Being a slacker in time of war..............	−11	+ 5	+9	+ 8
23. Not standing when "Star Spangled Banner" is played.................................	− 7	− 1	+4	+ 8
27. Having fits of temper.....................	− 4	− 6	+3	+12

There is little to be said about the above items beyond the fact that all of them show the inverts less severe than the norm group in their ethical judgments.   With one exception the groups differ rather uniformly from item to item; telling a lie to avoid punishment is conspicuous for the magnitude of the difference.   Of the entire 28 items in the test there were only two in which 0 received a minus weight, and only two in which 3 received a plus weight. The totals of the plus and minus weights for 3 and 2 were +18 and −229; of the weights for 1 and 0, +243 and −24.   Age doubtless accounts for a considerable part of this tremendous difference, but the low associations of the inverts and their distorted outlook on life are probably the chief factors.   All of them are habitual offenders against the law and many of them have had jail or prison experience.

f. Preferences.—Four of the 7 items in this list have a weight of 7 or higher.   They are as follows, the response "1" indicating preference for the first thing mentioned in each item, "2" preference for the second, and "S" same liking for the two.

M-F test items	1	2	S
1. (1) Make plans (2) Carry out plans................	+ 9	− 8	−1
2. (1) Work involving many details (2) Work involving few details.....................................	− 9	+10	−1
5. (1) Work with men (2) Work with women..........	−11	+11	+3
7. (1) Live in the country (2) Live in the city	− 8	+ 8	−2

The greater preference of the inverts for making plans, as contrasted with carrying out plans, is probably a reflection of their extreme laziness.   This may also explain the greater preference of this group for work involving few details.   That passive male homosexuals usually prefer to work with women rather than with men is well known; we have commented in the preceding chapter on the feminine character of most of the occupations which the members of this group have followed.   The preference of the invert group for city life needs no comment.

Exercise 5: Interests.—This exercise, as we have seen, is the one which differentiates between the two groups more effectively than any other in the M-F test.

a. Occupational Preferences.—"Like" has a plus weight of 7 or more for the following occupations out of the total list of 25: private secretary (+30), singer (+24), nurse (+24), dressmaker (+22), florist (+13), music teacher (+13), chef or cook (+10), social worker (+10), novelist (+9), artist (+8), librarian (+7), and journalist (+7). All these occupations have negative weights for "dislike" ranging from −8 to −25. The occupations with negative weights for "like" are: forest ranger (−12), soldier (−11), building contractor (−9), draftsman (−8), and auto racer (−7). These have for "dislike" positive weights ranging from +5 to +9. All these data are in line with what is known about the occupational preferences of male inverts.

b. Preferences for People.—Of the 12 types of people listed, five have a weight of 7 or more. These are as follows:

M-F test items	Like	Dislike	Neither
8. People who spend freely....................	+19	−14	−7
9. People with gold teeth......................	− 8	− 2	+3
10. Tall women................................	+ 6	− 8	+9
11. Men who take the lead.....................	− 9	+ 6	+6
12. Mannish women............................	+10	− 9	−3

The greater preference of this group of inverts for people who spend freely needs no comment when it is remembered that most of them are prostitutes. That they less often express a liking for people with gold teeth probably means that they are better acquainted than the norm group with dentistry styles, certainly a feminine trait. Their greater liking for tall and mannish women is a common preference of male inverts. They dislike men who take the lead because leadership is a masculine trait.

c. Reading and Movie Preferences.—Six of the 14 items in this list have a weight of 7 or more. The inverts are characterized by greater liking for movie love scenes, poetry, and dramatics, and by greater dislike of adventure stories, mechanics, and science. Comment is hardly necessary.

M-F test items	Like	Dislike	Neither
3. Movie love scenes	+13	−10	− 6
4. Poetry	+ 5	− 7	+ 1
7. Adventure stories	−10	+ 5	+11
9. Radio magazines	−14	+ 9	+ 3
10. Chemistry	− 4	+ 8	− 4
11. Dramatics	+13	−11	− 6

d. Activities and Foods.—Here we find 12 of the 20 items with a weight of 7 or more. Those with plus weights for "like" are: charades (+11), collecting flowers (+8), hopscotch (+7), and cooking (+7), all of which rate high for femininity. The items with a negative weight for "like" are: hunting (−30), horseback riding (−10), repairing a door latch (−8), and strict Sunday laws (−8). Here as elsewhere the inverts tend to repudiate whatever is distinctly masculine.

e. Literary Preferences.—Seven of the 23 items in this list have a weight of 7 or higher. The first 5 listed below illustrate the feminine sentimentality of the male invert; the last 2 his dislike of anything that savors of sternness or adventure.

M-F test items	Like	Dislike	Neither
2. Lorna Doone, by Richard D. Blackmore	+ 7	− 7	−3
3. Through the Looking Glass, by Lewis Carroll	+ 8	−11	−4
5. Daddy Long Legs, by Jean Webster	+10	−4	−3
11. Rebecca of Sunnybrook Farm, by Kate Douglas Wiggin	+10	− 2	−3
12. Christmas Carol, by Charles Dickens	+ 9	− 3	−2
13. The Man without a Country, by Edward Everett Hale	− 8	+11	−1
20. Biography of a Grizzly, by Ernest Seton-Thompson	− 9	+ 4	+5

f. Preferences for Drawing.—Only 2 of the 8 items have a weight as high as 7.

M-F test items	Like	Dislike	Neither
2. Children	+10	−7	−4
6. Flowers	+ 8	−6	−5

g. Preferences for Newspaper Reporting.

M-F test items	Like	Dislike	Neither
2. Sporting news	−23	+12	+ 8
3. Musical events	+ 5	−11	− 1
4. Theatrical news	+12	−12	−10
5. News oddities	+ 7	− 9	− 4

h. Travel Preferences.

M-F test items	Like	Dislike	Neither
2. Hunt lions in Africa	−28	+15	+2
5. Visit many famous battlegrounds	− 8	+ 9	+3
6. Visit many manufacturing plants	− 7	+ 5	+1
11. Learn about various religions	+ 3	− 7	+2

The data in the last three sections can be summarized by saying that the inverts have more interest than the norm group in children, flowers, musical events, theatrical news, news oddities, and religion, less interest in war and manufacturing, and very much less interest in sporting news or such dangerous adventure as lion hunting.

In Exercise 5 there are 19 weights of +10 or more for omission, and 8 of −10 or more.

Exercise 6: Personalities and Opinions.—The first half of this exercise, dealing with preferences for historical and contemporary characters, logically belongs with Exercise 5. Twelve of the 28 characters listed have weights of 7 to 20.

M-F test items	Like	Dislike	Neither
2. P. T. Barnum	+ 9	− 7	− 6
7. Cleopatra	+19	−10	− 8
20. Lenin	+ 7	+ 5	− 1?
22. Aimee McPherson	+13	− 8	0
24. Florence Nightingale	+ 7	− 3	− 4
4. Daniel Boone	−14	+ 6	+11
6. Kit Carson	−17	+ 8	+ 7
13. Congressman Volstead	− 9	+11	− 2
14. Booker T. Washington	− 5	+ 8	0
15. Ulysses S. Grant	−20	+11	+11
17. Herbert Hoover	− 2	+ 8	− 1
26. Billy Sunday	0	+ 9	− 3

Perhaps the only surprises in the above data are the greater preference of the inverts for P. T. Barnum and Lenin. Perhaps the radicalism of the inverts may account for the weight of $+7$ for Lenin, and their theatrical interest for the $+9$ weight for Barnum; certainly neither character could be classed as belonging to the feminine type. Nothing could better characterize the typical male invert than the weights of $+19$ for Cleopatra and -20 for Ulysses S. Grant.

In the second part of Exercise 6, in which the subject is asked to judge the truth or falsity of common opinions, only one of the 14 items has a weight as high as 7. The inverts more often regard as false the statement that Lincoln was greater than Washington, but the weights are not large: true (-5), false $(+7)$. One would rather have expected the preference to fall in the opposite direction. This section of the exercise is interesting in the fact that it shows the inverts do not differ from the normals in the more strictly intellectual attitudes.

In Exercise 6 three items have weights of $+10$ or more for omission, and eight of -10 or more.

Exercise 7: Introvertive Response.—Although this exercise does not differentiate very effectively between the two groups, half the 42 items have a weight as high as 7. They are as shown in the table on page 281.

Three of the items (4, 8, and 34) reflect the fastidiousness of the invert group, the others their introvertive and psycho-neurotic tendencies. Many of them seem to have been more or less maladjusted from childhood, judging from the frequency with which they have had imaginary companions (2) and disciplinary trouble at school (28). Their greater fear of the dark (18) and their night terrors (38) are also suggestive of a neurotic childhood. Other items reveal them as belonging to the shut-in type of personality (1, 15, 40), as nervous and subject to anxiety (12, 17, 41), lacking self-confidence and physical courage (10, 32), weak in self-control (7, 31), indolent and hypo-chondriacal (9, 21, 35). Item 17 (feeling about to "go to pieces") has by far the heaviest weights in the list: $+30$ and -30. Next is item 12 (worry over possible misfortunes) with

M-F test items	Yes	No
1. Do you like most people you know?.................	−10	+11
2 Did you ever have imaginary companions?...........	+10	− 9
4. Do you rather dislike to take your bath?............	− 6	+ 7
7. Do you feel yourself to be lacking in self-control?.....	+ 9	− 8
8. Are you extremely careful about your manner of dress?.	+ 7	− 7
9. Do you work mostly by fits and starts?.............	+10	−10
10. Do you shrink from facing a crisis or difficulty?......	+ 8	− 9
12. Do you worry much over possible misfortunes?.......	+19	−19
15. Have you ever kept a diary?......................	+13	−12
17. Do you ever feel that you are about to "go to pieces"?.	+30	−30
18. Are you often afraid of the dark?..................	+ 7	− 6
21. Do you usually enjoy your meals?..................	− 1	+11
26. Do you ever have the same dream over and over?....	+ 7	− 6
28. Were you ever expelled from school, or nearly expelled?	+ 7	− 5
31. Does it make you angry for people to hurry you?......	+ 7	− 6
32. Can you stand as much pain as others can?..........	− 6	+ 7
34. Would you like to wear expensive clothes?...........	+12	−12
35. Do you feel tired a good deal of the time?...........	+10	−10
38. Are you often frightened in the middle of the night?..	+ 7	− 6
40. Can you do good work while people are looking at you?	− 5	+ 7
41. Do you feel like jumping off when you are on a high place?..	+11	− 9

weights of +19 and −19.   One must remember that the members of the invert group have good reason to feel themselves social outcasts; many of them have suffered legal punishment for their homosexual practices and most of the others live in perpetual fear of the law.   Their psychoneurotic symptoms are no doubt the joint product of their adult experiences and their early conditioning, with perhaps some contribution from heredity in individual cases.

Omitting items 4, 8, 11, 34, and 42 (all of which bear on fastidiousness), we have for the remaining 37 items totaled the plus and minus weights carried by the introvertive, maladjusted, or psychoneurotic responses.   The first total (unfavorable to the inverts) is +252; the second (unfavorable to the norm group) is −9.   Only four introvertive responses carried minus weights and none of these was greater than -3. The four exceptional items are 3, 14, 16, and 39.

Failure to respond is weighted $+10$ or more for ten items, and -10 or more for four items.

SUMMARY

1. On the basis of item tabulations for the passive homosexuals and a norm group of 98 males, "I" (invert) score weights have been derived for all the possible responses in Form A of the M-F test; this permits the computation of a total "I" score for any individual subject.

2. The "I" scores so derived have only a moderate correlation with total M-F scores.

3. The distribution of "I" scores for the invert group covers a wide range and has two modes, indicating that the group probably contains a considerable number of active homosexuals.

4. The 1560 "I" score weights of Form A were examined and the more reliable ones utilized in deriving a composite picture of the invert personality. Some of the leading features of this composite picture are the following:

a. The interests, attitudes, and thought trends of this invert group are more or less typically feminine throughout the test. In general this tendency is evident in all the exercises of the test, though in some more than in others.

b. The feminine personality of the inverts appears in their fastidiousness with respect to dress, cleanliness, and care of person; in their preoccupation with domestic affairs; in their preference for feminine types of occupations and for working with women rather than with men; in their fondness for sentimental movies and romantic literature; in their feminine timidity when faced by physical danger; in their religious interests; and in their liking for literature, art, music, and dramatics.

c. The feminine personality of the inverts is evidenced negatively by their repudiation of everything that is characteristically masculine: aggressive leadership, energetic activity, physical courage, masculine pursuits, and interest in warfare, adventure, outdoor sports, science, and things of a mechanical nature.

d. The inverts show evidence of an excessive amount of sex consciousness, especially consciousness of the forbidden nature of their sex lives.

e. In their anger and pity responses the inverts differ but little from the norm group, but their fear responses are stronger and their disgust responses weaker.

f. One of the most marked differences between the two groups appears in the lax ethical standards of the inverts; whether this difference would be found for a strictly random sampling of the entire invert population cannot be determined without further data.

g. The introvertive and psychoneurotic tendencies of the invert group are reflected in a great variety of responses which indicate social maladjustment, nervousness, lack of self-confidence, a low degree of self-control, and a marked tendency to worry and anxiety.

5. The various parts of the M-F test agree closely with respect to the personality traits which distinguish the inverts from the norm group, each exercise confirms the others, and the resulting picture is surprisingly harmonious. Further, the characterizations of the group based upon analysis of the item responses are reinforced by the case-history data presented in the chapter which follows. The interests and attitudes of inverts as disclosed by the M-F responses can hardly be explained on the theory that they are superficial affectations; we are convinced that on the whole they give an essentially correct picture of the actual type of personality most prevalent in this group.

CHAPTER XIII

CASE STUDIES OF HOMOSEXUAL MALES

This chapter will present the first of three series of case studies of homosexual and other subjects. We recognize that although case studies are of great value to the judicious and cautious reader, they are likely to lure the incautious into unwarranted generalizations. It is therefore desirable to repeat that the behavioral correlates of high and low M-F scores have been little explored and that the reader should constantly be on guard against the temptation to assume that behavior exemplified by a particular case is necessarily typical. With this warning we shall present first the case studies by Dr. E. Lowell Kelly of 18 subjects of the group of passive male homosexuals.

One further warning should be given. In the case of the P.M.H. group it was necessary to depend upon the testimony of the subjects themselves for most of the factual information of the case histories, and in most instances there was no possibility of checking the accuracy of their reports. It is not at all unlikely that homosexual subjects, even when trying to give a truthful account of their early experiences, are prone to exaggerate certain experiences and to forget others. For example, it would not be surprising if they tended to exaggerate with respect to the early age at which their invert tendencies appeared, for practically every member of the P.M.H. group believes that his condition is inborn. He prefers to think of his personality not as something malformed by circumstance, but as a product of nature. It is for him therefore no less "natural" than the personalities of others and one for which he could have no individual responsibility. However, even when we allow for a certain amount of error from this source, the case studies here summarized are, we believe, extremely enlightening. The frequency with which certain factors appear offers impressive evidence with respect to the environmental causes of sexual inversion.

The information for the case histories of this chapter was all obtained by Dr. Kelly in personal interviews with the subjects. Each interview followed a definite routine outlined in the case-history record blank which is reproduced in Appendix IV. As examination of this blank will show, an attempt was made to secure comparable information for all the subjects on physical appearance, personality traits of each parent, treatment of child by each parent and resulting attitude of child, sibling relationships, relationships with other children, favorite toys, games, and other activities, educational history, school subjects liked and disliked, social life after childhood, religious interests, ideals, occupational history, and sex experiences, including autoerotic practices and both homosexual and heterosexual relationships.

We regard such a routinized procedure as essential for securing comparable data, but it has the disadvantage of giving a somewhat stereotyped character to the case histories. In the summaries which follow[1] the effect of stereotypy has been to some extent mitigated by omitting from each history a considerable amount of informational detail that seemed to have no explanatory value.

The 18 P.M.H. cases are presented in order of femininity of score, beginning with the most feminine. Both the M-F scores and the "I" (invert) scores are given for the separate exercises as well as for their total. In reading the "I" scores it should be kept in mind that plus scores are in the direction of inversion. The mean "I" score for 77 male homosexuals classified as passive is $+644$, and the S.D. of the "I" score distribution is 462. The series of this chapter will be designated by the letter H with numerical subscripts to indicate individual subjects.

H-1. "Lady M"[2]

Exercise	1	2	3	4	5	6	7	Total
M-F score	$- 4$	0	$- 29$	-25	-30	$- 15$	$- 2$	-105
"I" score	-50	-6	$+140$	$+27$	$- 9$	$+154$	$+133$	$+389$

[1] The summaries were prepared by Dr. Kelly and the senior author from the original case data.

[2] The names given here are fictitious. However, they are typical of the group discribed.

The M-F total is 3.4 standard scores more feminine than the mean of third-year high-school boys or than the mean of any of our female groups. The "I" score is near the 30th percentile of the P.M.H. group for inversion. The M-F score for Exercise 4 (emotional and ethical response) is feminine, which is unusual for male homosexuals.

H-1, age 26, is in a state prison serving a sentence for fellatio. Son of immigrant parents. Father now about 50 years old, mother 54. Father cold, domineering, ill-tempered and much feared by his children; is a confirmed alcoholic. Mother nervous and emotional.

Subject is below average in height and weight and has never been very strong. Voice soft and gait effeminate.

Was the first of seven children, having two brothers and four sisters. His mother has repeatedly told him that she wanted a girl at the time of his birth. She was very fond of the child, however, and decidedly demonstrative in her affection toward him. This, together with the cold and domineering attitude of the father, resulted in the mother becoming the favorite parent. The relationship between the mother and son has always been very intimate. The feelings toward the parents soon became generalized. As a child the subject was unable to understand men but felt quite at ease in the company of women and girls. In spite of ample opportunity for association with boys he spent most of his time with girls, playing with them almost exclusively. He crocheted, knitted, and took part in their games. He was embarrassed in the presence of other boys and would not go swimming with them because he was ashamed to undress in their presence.

H-1 had very little formal education, not more than three years in all. His favorite studies were reading, history, and geography; arithmetic was much disliked. He is fond of music and plays the violin "by ear."

About the only type of work followed has been in hotels as bellboy, bus boy, or waiter, although on two or three occasions he has gone to work in lumber camps, resolutely determined to become more masculine. At the present time, however, he is still effeminate and constantly refers to himself as "she." He was dressed as a boy throughout childhood, but liked to masquerade as a girl whenever the opportunity presented itself.

When still very young he was greatly thrilled at the sight of strong men, and he practically always falls in love with men of sturdy, athletic build. He has never had a heterosexual experience. Although he is fond of women companions, they have no sexual attraction for him.

He first engaged in sodomy at the age of eighteen with a male lover. At the present time he practices both fellatio and sodomy, always playing the passive role. He prefers fellatio, however, and was arrested and imprisoned charged with this crime.

The subject is convinced that his homosexual tendencies are inborn.

Significant facts: firstborn child; domineering and ill-tempered father; overaffectionate mother; lack of stimulus to play with boys.

H-2. "Louise"

Exercise	1	2	3	4	5	6	7	Total
M-F score	− 6	− 2	+ 2	− 34	− 40	− 8	− 3	− 91
"I" score	−62	+20	+150	−151	+161	+42	+31	+191

The M-F total is more than 3 S.D. below the mean of high-school boys, and more feminine than the mean of all our female groups except domestic employees and mothers of gifted children. Exercise 4 is also feminine, contrary to the rule for this group. The "I" score is one S.D. less invert than the mean of the P.M.H. group.

H-2, age 34, is a female impersonator in dancing and acrobatic stunts for a small eastern circus. He is small and extremely effeminate in both speech and behavior. Seems to be neurasthenic; is nervous, shy, and apparently unstable.

H-2 was the first of 12 children, 8 of whom are still living. The father, now 52, is described as brutal and autocratic in his attitude toward the child. Between the two there was no companionship or intimacy. The mother, now 51, was always the favorite parent. Subject spent nearly all his time with her and the relation between them was unusually close. Mother consistently catered to his every wish and desire. Subject was also the favorite of his maternal grandmother, who lived with the family.

As a child H-2 played more with boys than with girls, although the boys usually regarded him as a sissy. His favorite activities were ball, books, chess, and croquet. His favorite books were romances and he much disliked "Wild West" stories. He graduated from high school but did not attend college because of lack of funds. Most liked subjects, grammar and algebra; most disliked, botany and civics.

Is decidedly social; attends shows, parties, and dances, preferably in the company of men. His friends are usually older than himself and are chosen largely for their beauty. Member of United Brethren Church, but is not very religious now. His ideal (public) character is Woodrow Wilson; the finest person he has ever known is one of his girl cousins.

H-2 has spent the last eight years as a circus performer; had previously worked six years in a paper mill and 18 months as a bus boy. He had also served two years in the U.S. Army in a camp hospital.

Subject claims to have had no conscious sex experiences until the age of 18. At that time he learned to masturbate and thereafter practiced the act regularly. He believes that this made him more effeminate. His first homosexual experience occurred in the same year, when he played the passive role of sodomy with a first cousin. He first practiced fellatio about six months later with an office boy with whom he was in love. Both practices have been continued and both have been commercialized whenever it was necessary to make a little "extra money." The chief sex attraction of men for the subject is said to be an olfactory one.

H-2 asserts that he is attracted to women as well as to men. On one occasion he was engaged to be married, but he broke the engagement because he was afraid he could not give up his male lovers. He receives some gratification from heterosexual experiences and visits prostitutes whenever necessary to keep up appearances with his friends.

Some of the case-history conferences with this subject were held at a time when he was "in love" with a young musician. He was completely infatuated with the lover and thought of him constantly. The least act of indifference on the part of the object of his affections was sufficient to induce grief almost to the extent of despair. His general attitude was typically that of a young girl infatuated with a man who cares little or nothing for her.

Subject worries a great deal over his condition and would like to become normally sexed. However, he feels that the affliction is inborn and incurable.

Significant facts: antagonism toward father; favorite of mother and grandmother; played more with boys than with girls; no tendency to transvestism; is bisexual, but with stronger leaning toward homosexuality; M-F score extraordinarily feminine, even on Exercise 4; low "I" score.

H-3. "Adela"

Exercise	1	2	3	4	5	6	7	Total
M-F score	−1	− 2	− 21	+19	− 68	−7	− 3	− 83
"I" score	+7	+13	+147	+40	+340	+5	−20	+532

The M-F score approximates the median for high-school girls and is 3 S.D. less masculine than the mean of high-school boys. Exercise 4 (interests) is especially feminine. The "I" score is slightly less invert than the mean of the P.M.H. group.

H-3, age 27, was the youngest of three brothers, and the most favored by his parents. The father, who died when the son was about 12 years old, is described as affectionate in his treatment of the boy but somewhat moody. The mother, a trained nurse, died seven years ago. She is described as emotionally unstable and very demonstrative in her affections toward the boy. A close intimacy developed between them and the son worshiped her. Both parents were Catholics.

After the death of his mother H-3 lived with an uncle and aunt in entirely satisfactory relationship. Subject thinks he is less talented than his brothers, one of whom is in training for the priesthood.

H-3 attended only parochial schools and, like his brother, after graduating from high school entered a Catholic seminary and began preparation for the priesthood. After four years this plan of study was discontinued because of the opposition of his aunt, who was a Protestant.

Subject is of large physical build, rather fleshy and voluptuous. He has large hips and breasts but a relatively small head and face. Has never taken part in athletics, in fact made every effort to avoid taking physical training when in school.

Throughout his school life was treated as a sissy and preferred to play with girls "because they did not fight like boys." His favorite toys were dolls; favorite play, house: "I was just like a mother." Most liked school subject was chemistry; most disliked, French and Greek.

After the discontinuance of his preparation for the priesthood the subject obtained, as the result of his interest in chemistry, a laboratory position in a small hospital. He became interested in caring for the sick and took a short course in practical nursing, and has been engaged as a male nurse for the last six years.

At the time of the examination H-3 was a male prostitute in San Francisco. He had come there from Chicago in the company of an aged invalid man. The old man died shortly afterward. Subject claims to have been unable to procure work and that he prostituted himself only to make a living until he could get something else to do.

At the age of 12 he was taught to masturbate by other boys. A short time before that his first homosexual experience occurred. While sleeping with his brother he recalls waking up and finding himself engaged in manustupration and attempting fellatio on him. The brother awoke about the same time and forced him to stop. It is interesting to note, however, that there was considerable rivalry between the subject's two brothers as to which should sleep with him. On a number of occasions one of them even paid for the privilege.

First engaged in homosexual acts regularly while in the seminary, where he reports such practices to be very common.

He prefers fellatio, but will play the passive role in pederasty when it is demanded.

He says he has never had a heterosexual experience, although women do have a slight amount of attraction for him. He enjoys his homosexual practices but feels that he would be much happier if normally sexed. Thinks that he might be able to change over if he could find a suitable girl to marry. Before coming to San Francisco he had been going regularly with a female nurse.

H-3 began having nocturnal emissions at 17 and occasionally has them at the present time. The accompanying dreams are always of men and boys.

Significant facts: favored child; both parents affectionate; loss of father when boy was 12; close intimacy with mother; doll play and preference for girl playmates; segregation in seminary.

H-4. "Lorraine"

Exercise	1	2	3	4	5	6	7	Total
M-F score	−11	0	+ 5	− 30	− 32	− 3	0	− 71
"I" score	−83	−27	+107	−173	+125	−47	−27	−125

The M-F score is about 2.75 S.D. below the mean for high-school boys, and is close to the mean for high-school girls and women teachers. The "I" score is about 1.7 S.D. less invert than the mean of the P.M.H. group.

H-4, age 19, is an attractive Mexican boy, small and plump. He was the third of five children, two of whom died in childhood. Little is known of the father, as he died when the subject was 3 years old. Child was reared by mother and maternal grandfather. The mother, now 40, is very affectionate and sensitive. She and her son are extremely intimate and spend much of their time together. He says, "We are just like two sisters." He has assisted her much in the housework.

There is one brother living and one sister. Although H-4 greatly respects his brother, the relationship between them is much less close than between the subject and his sister, whom he adores.

His favorite childhood toys were dolls; favorite game, playing house with little girls. Here he always insisted on being the "mother." He was always afraid to take part in the rough games of boys, but he was much liked by adults because of his happy disposition.

H-4 attended school as far as the seventh grade. He was considered a sissy by the other children and finally quit school because of ridicule. His favorite subjects were history, geography, and English; he disliked arithmetic. He liked to play volleyball but he "could not get along with the boys."

Subject is a sociable person and spends most of his time in a group. He has no interest in reading. Most of his close friends are women because "they understand me better." He was born a Catholic, but has since become a Protestant. He says he has never had a love affair or even a date with a girl. He thinks that men are far better looking than girls. Ideal character, Ramon Novarro.

H-4 has worked as a bellboy and as a bus boy for periods of one year each. He was also employed in a rubber factory for a year and liked the work.

He obtained his first sex information "from friends" at about 15 years of age. Shortly afterward he learned to masturbate and practiced the act about twice weekly. When 16 he met a "good-looking sailor" in Los Angeles who took him to the home of a male prostitute for the evening. It was there that his first homosexual experience occurred, when he was taught to play the passive role in pederasty. This practice has since been commercialized on numerous occasions. He has engaged in fellatio only a few times; he does not enjoy it and always feels ashamed of himself afterward.

Women are sexually unattractive to him and he has never had a heterosexual experience in spite of many opportunities. Has slept with women without being the least aroused; feels that he would be ashamed if he should force himself to heterosexual intercourse.

Subject says he has had only one nocturnal emission, which occurred about six months ago. The accompanying dream had a young man as the central character.

Significant facts: early death of father, which probably strengthened the bond between mother and son; mother unduly affectionate; fondness for sister; early preference for girls and girls' activities; small size and physical attractiveness: seduced at 16.

H-5. "Dolores"

Exercise	1	2	3	4	5	6	7	Total
M-F score:	−12	− 1	0	+ 9	− 62	− 1	− 3	− 70
"I" score:	+26	+23	+219	+146	+440	+135	+124	+1113

The M-F score is about 2.75 S.D. below the mean for high-school boys and falls close to the mean for women teachers. Exercise 5 is especially feminine. The "I" score is highly invert, being one S.D. above the mean of the P.M.H. group.

H-5, age 21, is an only child. The father is now 62 and the mother 52. The father was a marine engineer and was often away from home for long periods. He is decidedly masculine and quick tempered, though indulgent toward his son whom he has never punished. However, there was little companionship between them, as the father was so much older and so much away from home. The mother is described as well educated, extremely emotional, and the finest person the subject has ever known. Both parents wanted a girl when H-5 was born.

As a child the subject preferred to be alone; he sometimes played with other children but did not enjoy them; was called a sissy by his schoolmates.

Has always preferred girls' clothes and when still a youngster secretly dressed in them. Upon being discovered was made to wear girls' attire as a punishment and gloried in it. Played female roles in several school plays.

H-5 completed high school and attended a western state university for one year. His favorite studies were English, French, and criminology. He disliked mathematics and chemistry.

He dresses neatly and conservatively in dark colors, although he is fond of bright colors in ties, socks, shirts, and underwear. He smokes and drinks and has used morphine. He is a member of the Episcopal Church.

From the age of 6 he greatly enjoyed seeing men's genitals and at 12 indulged in mutual fellatio with a fifty-year-old music teacher who was later sent to prison for his activities with other boys. The practice of fellatio continued for about four years, after which for two years he was inactive because of lack of opportunity and fear of being found out.

At the age of 18 he met a group of "queens" and was fascinated by their life and adventures. They speedily took him into their group and introduced him to a sailor of whom he became enamored and with whom he claims he is still in love.

He practices both pederasty and fellatio and prefers men about 30 who are "not too rough yet not sissified." Women have no attraction for him and he has never had a heterosexual experience.

H-5 is attractive, intelligent, and interested in music. Studied piano for several years.

Significant facts: an only child; father indulgent but much away from home; mother emotional and affectionate; parents wanted a girl; preference for girls and girls' activities; transvestism; seduced at age of 12; scores highly "invert" as well as highly feminine.

H-6. "Leslie"

Exercises	1	2	3	4	5	6	7	Total
M-F score:	− 3	− 2	− 7	+ 2	− 50	− 1	− 2	− 63
"I" score:	−42	+14	+154	+135	+275	+107	+148	+791

The M-F score is about 2.6 S.D. below the mean of high-school boys and close to the mean for female nurses. Exercise 5 (interests) is highly feminine. "I" score is about one-third S.D. more invert than the mean of P.M.H. group.

H-6, age 19, is of very boyish appearance. He was the third of five children. The father, who died when subject was 4 years old, is described as moody, autocratic, cruel, and unstable. He was at various times a house-to-house salesman, a prizefighter, and a politician. The mother, now 43, is energetic and emotionally unstable. After the death of her husband she married her husband's brother, who developed a dislike for the stepchildren. H-6 could not endure being in the same room with his stepfather. Mother the favorite parent; the relationship between her and son very intimate; the mother gave in to the child and spoiled him.

H-6 seems to have had a normal childhood, except that he preferred to be with girls and to take part in their games instead of associating with other boys. He recalls that one of his favorite pastimes was dressing dolls and arranging them for funerals.

Subject attended a Catholic school as far as the first year of high school. Quit because the work became monotonous and his parents had not enough money to send him further. Has read widely in all fields since leaving school and has a good fund of general information. He soon lost all faith in religion, and would often argue for hours on the philosophy of religion with a nun, a friend of his family.

His feminine interests persisted after quitting school. He enjoyed doing housework and taking care of children. About this time, however, he developed a complex against girls and cared nothing more for their company, though he remained fond of his mother.

Most of his friends were older men. He "despised" Boy Scouts and never cared for any kind of club activity. This antisocial attitude has continued; he prefers to live and sleep alone, and likes to take long walks alone. His interest in reading has not diminished.

H-6 worked for short periods as a typist, waiter, office boy, and cashier in a tearoom. He says that he never enjoys any kind of work and will never take another job. He now earns his living solely by prostitution.

He obtained his first sex information from books at about 12 years of age. Masturbation, both alone and with other boys, occurred a short time later. Dreams of boys always accompany his nocturnal emissions.

His first homosexual experience (mutual masturbation and pederasty) occurred at the age of 13, when he was seduced by an older man. No feeling of guilt followed this behavior. He has never practiced fellatio and regards the practice as disgusting.

He has never had a heterosexual experience although a girl with whom he was sleeping when he was 15 years old tried to lure him into coitus. He was disgusted and reports noting a disagreeable odor at the time.

H-6 is timid in the presence of others and talks but little. He finds it almost impossible to urinate in the presence of others. He spends most of his time reading and only goes into a crowd in order to obtain the "business" by which he lives. He reports that the sexual act which follows is never pleasant and is often disgusting. Even so, he prefers it to any kind of work.

Significant facts: early death of father, stepfather who disliked him; mother emotional and excessively affectionate; spoiling; preference for girls; seduced at 13; "I" score decidedly invert.

H-7. "Gypsy Q"

Exercise	1	2	3	4	5	6	7	Total
M-F score:	−5	−1	− 19	−17	− 8	− 2	− 4	− 56
"I" score:	+3	−9	+161	− 1	+130	−36	+66	+314

The M-F score is at the mean for gifted girls and about 2.5 S.D. below the mean of high-school boys. It is feminine for all the exercises. The "I" score is about two-thirds S.D. less invert than the average for the P.M.H. group.

H-7, age 33, is a full-blooded Spaniard of average height and more than average weight. Not especially feminine in appearance. He is decidedly so in behavior, speech, and attitudes. Is extremely talkative and affected in conversation and mannerisms. Looks much younger than his age. Mentioned his "perfect knees" as his most feminine feature.

Subject was the second of seven children, but the first child (a girl) died when only a few weeks old. There are now living four brothers and one sister. The father was a merchant in a small Spanish city and died when the subject was about 14. He seems to have been of a stable disposition and kindly but stern. He was interested in the son but did not show much affection. The mother, on the other hand, was extremely affectionate and soon became the favorite parent. She is well educated and is said to be descended from a prominent Spanish family. Both parents are Catholic; the mother is exceptionally devout and given to mysticism.

H-7 was the mother's favorite child. The father, however, favored the younger sister, who was the only girl in the family. Since the firstborn baby, which died, was a girl, one wonders whether H-7 did not fill the deceased girl's role in the mother's affections. All through his childhood H-7 was treated as a girl both by his parents and by his playmates. He played mostly with girls because boys were too rough to be good playmates. His favorite toys were dolls and doll dresses; the favorite game was playing house.

His mother taught him to read and he attended Catholic schools between the ages of 9 and 20, the last three years of which were spent in a seminary in preparation for the priesthood. He had entered upon this course at the urgent request of his mother, whom he could not bring himself to refuse. He claims to have enjoyed the study of philosophy, history, literature, biography, anthropology, theology, sociology, and psychology; he "hated" mathematics.

At the age of 20, H-7 became attached to a ship officer who agreed to get him a job as mess boy on his ship if he would quit school and go with him. As he did not want to become a priest he gladly accepted the offer. The friendship for this officer gradually developed into love, which finally resulted in the practice of fellatio and pederasty with him, H-7 always playing the passive role. The affair was finally broken up by the transfer of the officer to another ship and the young man found himself alone in Philadelphia. Being unable to speak English fluently and without special training for any occupation, he found it impossible to obtain suitable employment. He was too proud to work as a common laborer. The outcome was that he took advantage of his feminine characteristics and began playing the role of male prostitute, which proved so profitable that he continued to follow it as a means of livelihood. Subject disdains any kind of work; insists that he will not sell his mental faculties or his physical energy for a mere $1.50 a day when it is easy to get $5.00 a day by prostitution.

Obtained his first sex information from schoolmates and engaged in mutual masturbation with them at about 14. Masturbation is still regularly practiced in addition to his other sexual activity; it is carried out with narcissistic admiration of his own naked body.

He has never had a heterosexual experience and women are utterly unattractive to him. During the last ten years he has been the passive member in several semipermanent unions with men. His ideal lover is large, muscular, and athletic, with congenial intellectual interests. Subject is very fond of male statuary.

His first nocturnal emission occurred at 14 and others have occurred intermittently since then. They are accompanied by fantastic and exciting dreams but never include either men or women as a predominant feature.

Considers himself a case of congenital homosexuality and is therefore unashamed; however, he looks upon normal men who patronize "queens" as degenerates.

Significant facts: treated as a girl by excessively affectionate mother, apparently as surrogate for deceased older sister; segregation in a seminary for three years; lack of occupational training and low opinion of work.

H-8. "Iola"

Exercise	1	2	3	4	5	6	7	Total
M-F score:	+ 7	− 1	− 8	+ 47	− 80	0	− 1	− 50
"I" score:	−48	+18	+169	+125	+463	+89	+116	+932

The M-F score is nearly 2.4 S.D. below the mean of high-school boys and close to the average of *Who's Who* women. Exercise 5 (interests) is especially feminine. "I" score is nearly three-fourths S.D. more invert than mean of P.M.H. group.

H-8 is 20 years old, the youngest of nine children (four boys and five girls). Father died five years ago at age 60, mother a year ago at 59, both of heart disease. Parents were of Scotch descent. The father was a candy manufacturer, but was an invalid for several years before his death; the mother had a "good business head." There is no record of crime in the family.

The parents wanted a girl at the time of subject's birth. As a child his favorite toys were dolls and dishes and his favorite game playing house. He played about equally with boys and girls, but was always considered by the boys as "different." His favorite school subjects were English, spelling, and Latin; he disliked mathematics.

H-8 was a constant companion to his father during the latter's illness and so led a rather quiet and secluded life, spending most of his time in reading. The father cared more for him than did the mother.

While still at home, the subject liked to dress up in girls' clothing but was not allowed to do so. After leaving home at the age of 17 he dressed as a woman for three months before being detected. He still attends masquerades in women's clothing at every opportunity. Recently had much newspaper publicity from masquerading as a Russian princess. Usually, however, he dresses as a man in order to evade the police.

He once worked for five weeks as a waitress (*sic.*) and later for two months as a clerk in a mine office.

He is of a Mormon family and is still a nominal member of this church. His favorite amusements are concerts, shows, and books. He drinks to some extent but does not smoke.

H-8 first masturbated at the age of 15, having been taught by an older man. The act was practiced about five times a month until other means of gratification were found. His first heterosexual experience occurred at the age of 16 when he visited a brothel with some school companions. He first committed pederasty at the age of 17 with a boy of the same age, and reports that he did so because he wanted to. This practice has been commercialized and has been practically his sole means of support for the last three years. He first practiced fellatio about six months ago while partially intoxicated.

Significant facts: parents wanted a girl; early preference for girls' activities; companionable with father (unusual in these subjects), perhaps accounted for by the parent's invalidism; transvestism.

H-9. "Rose Marie"

Exercise	1	2	3	4	5	6	7	Total
M-F score:	−15	0	−8	+6	−26	+3	+3	− 37
"I" score:								+964

M-F score is about 2.2 S.D. below the mean for high-school boys, and far more feminine than the mean of women athletes. "I" score total is about three-fourths S.D. more invert than the mean of P.M.H. group.

H-9, age 31, is the only living child in a family of ten children. All the others were born dead or died in early infancy. The parents were remote cousins. The family is reported to be in good circumstances and socially prominent in a middle-western city.

The father, now 68, has been a physician for 25 years. He is said to be very stable, stern, and intelligent, and has a good medical practice. He was autocratic toward the boy but never cruel. The mother, now 62, seems to be extremely emotional and unstable. She was the favorite parent, because—"she would always stick up for me and give me anything I wanted." On one occasion she locked the child in a closet as punishment, but at the end of 15 minutes let him out, gave him $2.00, and in tears begged his forgiveness for her cruelty. The two were together constantly, the mother was demonstrative in her affections, and the boy worshiped her.

Both parents are of French descent, Anglo-Catholic in religion, and well educated. They tried to rear their only child properly but instead spoiled him and perhaps laid the basis for his unhappy and unsuccessful life. They gave him all kinds of toys, books, and games, and tried to make of him a model child. Educated in a private school he was not allowed to play with the other boys of the neighborhood and was always accompanied by a negro servant when he went out of the yard. Was permitted to have girl playmates and he enjoyed playing girls' games. His favorite toys were dolls, although he had expensive mechanical toys for which he did not care. His favorite school subject was history; grammar was disliked.

H-9 is now rather social, but his favorite associates are "queer people and the intelligentsia." He is a member of three fraternal organizations, but he joined them only because his father insisted that it was the thing to do. He was a member of the Episcopal Church but reports that he cared only for the "show"; he acted as an altar boy for a time and liked the part.

Subject obtained his first sex information at the age of 14 from an uncle. Soon he was practicing mutual masturbation and fellatio with a boy friend and attempted sodomy with him. At first these practices were engaged in solely for sexual gratification, but they became quite pleasant and a feeling of love for the other boy developed.

His father tried in vain to get him to work in a drugstore and his mother attempted to persuade him to become a priest. Neither course appealed to him and he ran away to Chicago. There, learning that he could make an easy living by commercializing his sexual practices he entered a "peg house."[1] He stayed there for about two years before deciding to return home to enter college as his parents wanted him to do.

After a French custom, the parents had betrothed him as a child to one of his second cousins. While at home on this visit his father insisted that he get married. The girl he married was reserved and cool, almost frigid. Subject slipped away after the ceremony and did not return for three days. He then decided to settle down, become as masculine as possible, and be a good husband. His first heterosexual experience occurred shortly afterward with his wife, but he found it disgusting. Three months later, on learning that his wife had become pregnant, he ran away from her and went back to the peg house in Chicago. He never returned to his wife but has learned indirectly that he has a son of 11 years. The wife has never remarried.

After a short stay in Chicago H-9 began to roam around all over the country, always making a living by prostitution. Says he has made a large amount of money in this practice and that he was unusually successful on the "Barbary Coast" of San Francisco during the pre-Prohibition period.

He fell in love with a young German bootlegger in Detroit and while posing as a woman was legally married to him. They were happy together until the "husband" was killed in a gun fight with the police. The subject suffered greatly from shock

---

[1] House of prostitution for boys.

and grief, decided to abandon prostitution, and took a course in nurse's training. Since completing this course he has been employed almost solely as a male nurse or hospital orderly.

His homosexual practices have continued, however, and are still resorted to as a means of livelihood when he has no work. When last heard of he was still "on the street."

Significant facts: accentuated case of "only" child; parents overindulgent, especially the emotionally unstable mother; cut off from contact with boys; lack of occupational training; "I" score more invert than average of P.M.H. group.

H-10. "Aimee"

Exercise	1	2	3	4	5	6	7	Total
M-F score:	−16	0	+ 4	+ 4	− 8	−10	− 2	− 28
"I" score:	−62	+1	+124	+23	+184	+61	+41	+373

The M-F score is two S.D. below the mean of high-school boys and more feminine than the mean of women athletes. The "I" score is more than .5 S.D. less invert than the average of the P.M.H. group.

H-10, age 23, is the fourth of a family of six children, four boys and two girls. He is of medium build, somewhat plump, and fairly attractive. He has a soft effeminate voice and tends to be rather quiet.

The father, age 65, is a veterinarian. He seems to possess no outstanding characteristics. There was considerable intimacy between father and son, but also fear on the son's part. The mother is now 53 and a housewife; she worked for a time as a dressmaker. She too is reported as not having any marked peculiarities. The mother was the favorite parent because subject "had been with her more." When pressed for the reason for their constant companionship the subject simply replied that he and his mother "seemed to understand each other." He reports that as a child he worshiped her and helped her a great deal in her work.

The mother wanted a girl at the time of his birth and even prepared for a daughter. The subject was also the favorite of the grandmother who lived with the family and made over him a great deal. An uncle is thought by the subject to be a homosexual.

As a child the subject was considered a sissy by his playmates and treated by them more like a girl than a boy. He preferred to play alone rather than in a group. His favorite toys were trains and dolls; his favorite games, checkers, puzzles, and house. He was most fond of English and mathematics and found manual training very difficult. He graduated from high school, but had no desire for further education.

The only job held by the subject for any length of time was that of clerk in a grocery store. This position he held for two years after leaving high school. Since that time he has earned a living by odd jobs and prostitution.

He is a Catholic but has never been very devout. Contrary to his childhood habits, he is now socially inclined and spends a large amount of time in the company of his friends.

His early sex information was acquired from a middle-aged owner of a pool hall, and it was with him that his first sex experience (mutual masturbation) occurred. Men have always been sexually more attractive to him than women, but he has also been attracted by a few girls. His first strictly homosexual experience occurred at age 15 or 16, when he and a schoolmate with whom he was in love practiced mutual fellatio. He played the passive role in sodomy a short time later with the same boy. Subsequently he engaged regularly in both practices on a commercial basis.

At 18 he was living in a private family and became somewhat interested in one of the girls. It was with her that his first heterosexual experience occurred. The practice was continued regularly during the remainder of his stay with the family (about a month). The subject also has occasional heterosexual experiences at the present time but claims that they are not nearly so satisfying as homosexual experiences.

He had his first nocturnal emission at the age of 14 and usually dreams of men rather than women on such occasions.

He feels that homosexuality is the result of prenatal influences and therefore not subject to change.

Significant facts: mother wanted a girl; mother the favorite parent, but no antagonism to father; early preference for girls; is to some extent bisexual.

H-11. "Myrna H"

Exercise	1	2	3	4	5	6	7	Total
M-F score:	+4	0	− 8	− 5	− 16	+ 1	+ 1	−23
"I" score:	+2	+5	+133	−64	+109	−36	−73	+76

The M-F score is nearly 2 S.D. more feminine than the mean of high-school boys, and appreciably more feminine than the mean of women athletes. The "I" score is relatively low.

H-11 is a diminutive youth of 23 whose whole physical make-up is decidedly feminine. Is one of the best examples of the "queens" in the group. Both parents were English. His father left home before subject's birth and nothing is known concerning him.

H-11 was a premature child, and continued to be sickly until 6 years of age, spending a great deal of this time in hospitals.

He lived alone with his mother, an emotional woman, until he was 18. He was brought up to do housework and all other things commonly done by girls. His favorite toys were dolls, his games were those of girls, and he strongly disliked boyish sports. He liked writing, reading, and history, but disliked arithmetic. He played all the time with girls although there was ample opportunity for association with boys. He has a picture taken at the age of four in which he appears in a dress and long curls.

At various times he has collected stamps, signatures, and girls' pictures. He is very fond of parties and dances, especially when he has an opportunity to play the feminine role.

He has always sought work which would enable him to be with girls. He enjoys their companionship, but is never sexually attracted toward them. He had one female sweetheart who did not like the way he acted toward her—"not like other fellows." He has never had a heterosexual experience nor any desire for one.

When arrested (he is now in prison) he had been working for five months as an instructor in a girls' gymnasium. He has marked religious inclinations, having been a member of a great many denominations at one time or another.

He first masturbated at 14 but had before then felt very pleasurable sensations on looking at men doing manual labor. His first homosexual experience occurred at 18 with a handsome, athletic fellow, an ex-college student. He denies ever having practiced fellatio, which he says is nauseating to him, but admits an extreme liking for sodomy provided he is allowed to play the passive role. He is always the one pursued.

He has masqueraded as a woman whenever possible and says that he would give anything in the world to be able to dream of motherhood. H-11 is passionately fond of babies and consistently calls himself "she." Partly because of the fact that he weighs 100 pounds and is only 5 ft. 2 in. tall, he is very popular as a "queen" among the rest of the convicts. Says he has had 75 love affairs in the 18 months that he has been in prison.

A deep (though soft) voice is his outstanding masculine characteristic.

Significant facts: mother was deserted by husband before child's birth; sickly childhood; treated by mother as a girl; transvestism; feminine physique; "I" score is relatively low.

H-12. "Miss X"

Exercise	1	2	3	4	5	6	7	Total
M-F score:	−18	−1	−7	+17	+12	−1	−2	+00

The M-F score is nearly 1.5 S.D. below the mean of high-school boys. Among high-school and college men about one in ten is as feminine. The score coincides almost exactly with the mean for artists.

H-12, age 24, is slightly below average in height and weight, attractive, and courteous. He is an only child. His father was a stock-and-bond salesman and died when the subject was only 3 years old. His work kept him from home most of the time, and subject has practically no memory of him. The mother died two years ago. She is said to have been gentle, industrious, and much less emotional than the average woman. She worked as a housekeeper after her husband's death.

The death of the father resulted in a very close relationship between mother and son, although there was but little display of affection on the part of either.   The relationship was more like that between an older and younger sister, and involved constant companionship.   The boy helped his mother with the housework and soon became quite efficient.

H-12 developed into a sissy but an unusual one in that he disliked girls.   He associated with whatever boys would tolerate him and tried to play their games.   He did not care for dolls; was very fond of electrical and mechanical toys.   His favorite games were tiddlywinks and ping-pong.   Cared but little for baseball. Liked to be with older people.

Subject quit school at the end of the seventh grade because of his mother's illness.   His favorite studies were history, geography, and reading; arithmetic was thoroughly disliked.   Since leaving school, he has spent a great deal of time in libraries.

When asked how he differed from other children of the same age and sex, subject replied, "I daydreamed a lot, hated vulgar language, liked to argue, and did not believe in religion.   My playmates considered me slightly freaky."

When still a boy he was treated by adults more like a grown person than a child.   He says that he knew everyone in town; preachers, businessmen, and loafers were all his friends.   They were kind to him, kept him in spending money, took him to shows and club meetings, and made him feel that he was one of them. He attributes this generosity to the fact that his father was a thirty-third-degree Mason.

At the present time H-12 is quite social and enjoys being among sympathetic friends.   He belongs to the Y.M.C.A. but to no lodges or clubs.

He worked as a hospital orderly for four years, but quit because he received no advancement.   He has also been employed for varying lengths of time as a bus boy, factory worker, and houseboy, but he does not like to work; thinks he might enjoy being a male nurse, but since he makes plenty of money as a prostitute there is no need to change.

Women are sexually unattractive to him.   He has never had heterosexual experience in spite of the fact that he once worked several weeks for a female prostitute.

Subject obtained his first sex information at the age of 14 from other boys and began to masturbate at that time. Still masturbates at irregular intervals.

Although H-12 claims that he remembers awaking in the act of kissing a friend's penis at the age of six, his first adult homosexual experience occurred at 16, when he played the passive role in fellatio with a middle-aged man who persuaded him to do so. Subject allowed the same man to practice pederasty on him a short time later. Fellatio has remained his favorite practice; pederasty is engaged in only at the request of his patrons.

Nocturnal emissions occur but rarely and they are accompanied by dreams of boys.

Subject says he would rather be a homosexual than change over even if he could. He claims to have monthly backaches and headaches which he fancies are similar to menstrual pains.

Following is a short note written by the subject:

I remember when I was at the age of 13, some friends of mine had as guest a man of 32 years who came for a visit to their house. One day while he was bathing I came into his presence with a towel and would have actually refused to leave if I had been requested to, as I was all a-tremble with passion. I stayed on and offered my assistance. It was laughingly accepted. I helped in rubbing his back and I could hardly keep myself from kissing his buttocks after I was through. Although knowing he had rubbed himself dry in front, I had to do it all over myself for him; I lingered so long over him (and must have actually begun to caress his body with my hands) that he began to have an erection and tried to put it in my face. I refused to accept it, although I wanted to.

Significant facts: absence and early death of father; close association with gentle and kindly mother; a sissy but disliked girls; liked mechanical toys; disliked vulgarity; received favored treatment from adult males; seduced at 16, though homosexual tendencies were evident before this age.

H-13. "Florrie"

Exercise	1	2	3	4	5	6	7	Total
M-F score:	−13	+1	+ 16	+40	− 30	−4	− 3	+ 7
"I" score:	−49	+8	+122	−40	+258	+5	+57	+345

The M-F score is about one and a quarter S.D. more feminine than the mean of high-school or college men, is within the 10 per cent most feminine of men in general, and is close to the mean for the male theological group. The "I" score is about three-fourths S.D. less invert than the mean of the P.M.H. group.

H-13 is a fairly attractive red-headed boy of 23, with effeminate voice and mannerisms. He was the first child of Irish-American parents who are now engaged in the restaurant business. His mother, age 46, is of an emotional type as contrasted with the father, age 52, who is cold and unresponsive. Because of incompatibility the parents separated and were divorced. Both married again but the new partners in each case died and the parents are remarrying.

A sister, age 20, is a waitress in her father's restaurant. She is very sympathetic with H-13 in his failings. A brother, killed by an auto at the age of 11, was much loved by the subject.

Because of her husband's dislike for children the mother did not tell him of her pregnancy for nearly four months. She wanted a girl, while the father hoped that the child would be born dead.

All through childhood the mother was most affectionate with her son. He loved her intensely and feared his father. She made a special point of teaching him to be neat with his clothes, a trait that is still outstanding.

As far back as H-13 can remember he liked to play with girls, wear feminine clothes, and help with housework. He boasts of being an excellent cook and housekeeper. On every possible occasion he would steal his mother's or sister's clothes and dress up as a girl. He says that he did this because he knew that he looked better in girls' clothes. He recalls that he used to dress as a girl and turn somersaults at five cents a "turn" for the laboring men who worked near by. On one occasion he stole a brilliant red dress belonging to his aunt and wore it to the funeral of a neighbor whom he disliked. Apparently his impersonations were successful. He frequently took the feminine role in plays and enjoyed acting.

At school he received good marks, doing especially well in English literature, composition, art, and music. He always contrived to be the teachers' pet and on a number of occasions was taken home overnight with them to be paraded as a model pupil. His grammar and vocabulary are above average. He disliked mathematics and cared little for spelling.

H-13 has a good voice and says he was once known as the best soprano in —— (a large midwest city). On several occasions he has considered joining a vaudeville troupe and posing as a female singer.

Subject has spent most of his time working in a restaurant but was employed as a hospital orderly for several months. He is sympathetic and enjoys caring for others.

His favorite pastimes and hobbies are reading, listening to good music, and seeing good shows. He is also fond of travel, a fact which he attributes to his restless disposition.

Nominally he is a Catholic but his wide reading has rid him of all orthodoxy.

H-13 early noticed that he experienced pleasure at the sight of strong muscular men; would "sit for hours and watch a bricklayer or a blacksmith at work." When at 15 he joined the navy, he found that it was practically impossible to ward off the attentions of his fellow sailors, as they were attracted by his feminine qualities and pursued him constantly. He would move into a new place in order to be alone and immediately two or three men would move in with him. At that time he wanted only to love and kiss his companions, and had no desire for sexual congress. Before long, however, he was forced into playing the passive role in sodomy and was also taught fellatio. For a time these practices were followed by a feeling of shame, but after a time sodomy became a pleasant experience and developed into a habit which has remained his chief type of perversion. He does not practice fellatio, but on request has sometimes played the active role in sodomy.

When he was 17 he became infatuated with a young girl whom he met at a navy dance and had with her his first heterosexual experience. However, he rarely finds a woman for whom he has any desire, and then the satisfaction is only temporary. He says that he has sometimes to imagine his partner a man before he can succeed in the sexual act. He has never been married but has lived with a number of men for two or three months at a time.

H-13 has a very changeable disposition, suggesting a typically unstable personality; he makes friends easily. He has an excessive number of nocturnal emissions, which he considers the result of his extreme emotionality. With these he dreams of both men and women, himself playing the part now of one, now of the other. He has many dreams of motherhood, of labor pains, and of menstruation, with himself as the chief character.

Being above average in intelligence, H-13 is much interested in his case and is not at all reluctant to talk about himself. He feels that homosexuals as a group are misunderstood and mistreated. Regards his feminine tendencies as the product of inborn characteristics and early training by his mother. (About the only subject in the P.M.H. group to suggest any influence of environmental factors.)

Significant facts: cold father, sympathetic mother; mother wanted a girl; neatness of person overemphasized; early and persistent tendency to transvestism; musical; seduced at 15; to some extent bisexual.

H-14. "Jeanette"

Exercise	1	2	3	4	5	6	7	Total
M-F score:	+ 2	+ 1	− 3	+35	− 20	− 8	+ 1	+ 8
"I" score:	+18	−24	+154	−37	+237	+30	−22	+356

Both M-F score and "I" score almost identical with those of H-13.

H-14, age 37, is an interesting case in that he has practiced homosexual acts for more than 20 years. He was the third child of a Dutch contractor and a Scotch-Irish mother. His father is described as very masculine and quick tempered, his mother as above average mentally and not especially affectionate. Both the other children were girls. One of them died at an early age, and H-14 grew up in the company of his remaining (older) sister, who is now a spiritualistic healer. He says that his mother always treated him much better than his father, who was brutal and "did not care what became of us."

The subject's childhood seems to have been normal except that his favorite toys and games were those of girls (dolls and playing house). He also took an interest in boys' games, however, and recalls playing ball and flying kites with much joy. In school he played chiefly with boys and claims to have been considered a roughneck among them. On the other hand, he liked to wear girls' clothes and has attended many masquerade balls dressed as a woman.

H-14 is below average in height, but otherwise of average build. He has a markedly soft, effeminate voice—almost gurgling at times. He dresses conservatively, smokes and drinks, and attends shows, concerts, and baseball games. He is a member of the Spiritualist Church.

Subject has spent 16 years as a cook and waiter, but once worked in a machine shop for two years. At the present time is working as a night clerk in a small-town hotel.

He says that he first masturbated at the age of 10 and continued the practice until about 15 or 16, when his first heterosexual experience occurred. A short time later an older school companion induced him to play the passive role in pederasty, a practice which he has continued throughout his life and which he has often used as a means of livelihood. He says of his first experience, "When we were finished I realized that I had always wanted it, and I have continued to want it." He also practiced fellatio while a youth, but does not care to engage in it now. Prefers a lover who is athletic. Occasionally goes to a prostitute, but only when he is with male companions and accompanies them as a matter of sociability.

Significant facts: brutal father; affectionate mother and older sister; liked both girls' and boys' games; transvestism; seduced at 15 or 16; to some extent bisexual.

H-15. "Bella"

Exercise	1	2	3	4	5	6	7	Total
M-F score:	−11	− 2	+ 6	+ 47	− 18	− 8	− 3	+ 11
"I" score:	+12	+28	+219	+194	+399	−14	+93	+931

In M-F score rates close to H-13 and H-14, but has an "I" score considerably more invert than the mean of P.M.H. group.

H-15 is 33 years of age and the youngest of a family of eight children: four boys and four girls. He was born and educated in Germany, where he finished the *Gymnasium* at the age of 15 years, 6 months, about 1½ years younger than the average. From a very early age he showed feminine characteristics, such as preferring girls' games and toys and playing with girls almost exclusively. Upon receiving a train or other mechanical toy for Christmas he would immediately trade it to his tomboy sister for her doll.

He was taught the practice of fellatio at the age of 12 by a German army officer of high rank. After leaving school he became an apprentice seaman on a German sailing vessel. He found this life distasteful and decided to remain in the United States. As he found himself attractive to men and popular with them, he drifted into the life of a male prostitute. Has held jobs as ship waiter, cook, and bellhop, but his chief source of income has been prostitution; is still an active "hustler."

H-15 has a well-formed body, a pretty face, and a delightfully pleasant voice. He has a quiet disposition, speaks excellent English, and is an engaging conversationalist. Distinctly above average in intelligence.

One brother is also a homosexual.

Significant facts: youngest child; preference for girls' activities; seduction at 12; attractiveness to men; superior intelligence and culture; "I" score above average for the group.

H-16. "Ruby"

Exercise	1	2	3	4	5	6	7	Total
M-F score:	− 4	− 1	+ 9	− 30	+ 40	+ 3	− 3	+14
"I" score:	+72	+17	+28	−157	−145	−27	+117	−95

The M-F score is more than one S.D. below the mean of high-school or college men and close to the mean for male students of music. The minus M-F score on Exercise 4 and the plus score on Exercise 5 are both exceptional for this group. The "I" score is 1.6 S.D. less invert than the mean of the P.M.H. group.

H-16, age 20, is the only son of Welsh parents. His mother was killed in an accident when he was 1 year old; his father was killed in 1917 while a soldier in Shanghai. The father is reported to have been a heavy drinker, quite mean when intoxicated, and sexually promiscuous. An uncle on the father's side is serving a prison sentence for robbery.

The subject was reared by an aunt and uncle, who were kind and affectionate toward their charge. He seems to have been a normal boy, playing the usual boys' games and taking delight in masculine toys such as trains and horses. At school he always played with the boys and took part in all branches of athletics. He completed a high-school course with printing, typing, and mathematics as his favorite subjects, but with a distinct dislike for chemistry and biology.

As might be expected in the light of his other interests, H-16 preferred boys' clothes, and complained that "they made me wear short pants until I was nearly grown." It is interesting to note, however, that on two occasions he attended masquerade balls in female attire.

He has never followed any occupation very long; when arrested (this case was tested in the San Francisco County Jail) was charged with vagrancy. Has worked for brief periods (3 to 17 months) as a seaman (steward's helper), printer, waiter, laborer, and bootlegger.

At the present time, his interests are typically masculine. He smokes a great deal and drinks. Is a member of the Catholic Church but attends rarely.

A chum taught him to masturbate at the age of 10, and his first heterosexual experience occurred at 13 with a girl friend. Subject claims that since that time he has practiced coitus with women at least three times a week. He was married in Seattle in 1927 but was divorced six months later.

He first engaged in pederasty with a German whom he had "quite a bit of love for." This was after he was divorced from his wife, at a time when he says that he was pretty well disgusted with women. Since this first occurrence, he has practiced pederasty (passive role) regularly as a male prostitute.

The subject is somewhat below average in size and very boyish in appearance. As his earlier interests seem to have been entirely heterosexual, it would appear that he is taking advantage of his

feminine physique and simulating homosexual behavior in order
to earn an easy living.   The M-F score of +14, while low, is well
within the normal range.

Significant facts: normal masculinity as child; early and continued heterosexuality; marriage and divorce leading to trial of
homosexual practices; commercial motivation to continuance;
M-F scores on Exercises 4 and 5 contrary to the rule for passive
homosexuals; "I" score indicates no inversion.

H-17. "Vardis"

Exercise	1	2	3	4	5	6	7	Total
M-F score:	+ 2	− 1	0	+38	− 26	+8	− 3	+ 18
"I" score:	−33	+28	+120	+18	+244	−6	+172	+543

M-F score is one S.D. below the mean of high-school boys, close
to the mean for fathers of gifted children, and definitely more
masculine than the mean of artists and theological students.
However, the "I" score is only a little less invert than the mean
of the P.M.H. group, and it is this score, rather than the M-F
score, that is in line with the subject's "queen" characteristics.

H-17, age 22, is the only child of an unknown father, said to be
a Hindu, and a negro-Indian mother.   He is exceptionally neat
in his appearance and has attractive eyes.

Subject was reared chiefly by his grandmother, a very strict
Christian, although his mother visited him from time to time and
helped in directing his training.   Mother, emotional and temperamental, very much wanted a girl at the time of his birth.
He was never allowed to play with the "rough boys" of the
neighborhood, and so took to housework, sewing, and playing
with dolls.   Played almost entirely with girls because "the
boys were too uncouth and diabolical."   He has a good soprano
voice and is an excellent singer.

He has worked as a chef, but his chief occupation has been
that of a female impersonator on the stage; has followed this at
intervals since the age of 13, usually playing the part of a South
Sea Islander or a negro girl.   He has been successful in this type
of work and enjoys it.   He has performed on the stage both
locally and abroad, and has also played in the movies.   He
designs his own costumes, and while in prison (where he was

tested) spends most of his spare time in sewing and doing fancy-work. He has used tobacco and alcohol only occasionally, but was addicted to the drug habit for two years and was arrested in connection with his use of drugs.

H-17 first masturbated at 14, although he remembers practicing manustupration from the time he was 8. His homosexual experience also began about that time, sodomy being his first-learned perversion. He always plays the passive part in this relationship but stressed the point that he practices it only with those he loves. He detests fellatio and has no use for homosexuals who engage in the practice.

He is fond of women as companions and is popular with them, but they have no sexual attraction for him. He says that he has never had a heterosexual experience.

Like most of the others of this group, the subject believes that homosexual tendencies are inborn and for that reason not to be ashamed of. Says he has had no homosexual relations while in prison because he cannot find suitable partners; considers himself superior to others of his kind among the convicts. Although he reports caring most for quiet and refined men, he lived for several years with a prize fighter.

Significant facts: reared by grandmother and mother; mother wanted a girl; was not allowed to play with boys; transvestism; early seduction; actor and singer; possesses exotic attraction to homosexual males.

H-18. M. H.

Exercise	1	2	3	4	5	6	7	Total
M-F score:	−21	+ 1	+ 4	+31	+ 8	−2	−1	+ 20
"I" score:	+ 8	−20	+138	+27	+60	−7	−7	+199

The M-F score is practically the same as that of H-17, though more feminine in Exercise 1 and more masculine in Exercise 5. The "I" score is more than one S.D. less invert than the mean of the P.M.H. group.

H-18 is 44 years old. Although in prison on the charge of rape, he is known to be practicing homosexual acts.

Subject was the younger of two children, but his sister died at the age of 5; he was then 3. His parents were English-American and seem to have had no unusual personality traits.   His mother died when he was 7, and from that time on, although a white child, he was reared by an old negro couple.

He recalls wearing dresses as a small child (does not remember exact age) and that he did not like to play with boys because of their roughness.   He was taught to be neat and to abhor all that was harsh and ugly.   He had practically no toys and played very few games, as he preferred to spend his time alone with books and music.

He began taking piano lessons at the age of 6, was playing a church organ at 11, and began giving piano lessons at about 13. He later established a studio and has spent his entire life in teaching piano, violin, voice, and dancing.   He has also written a few mediocre musical compositions.

He admits having had intercourse with one of his pupils, a girl of 14, but insists that they were planning to be married.   However, several girls testified at his trial that he had attempted the same offense with them.

He first masturbated at about 16, and has visited prostitutes a few times.   He strongly denies homosexual activities although he has been observed in the prison to practice sodomy, fellatio, and manustupration within the course of a few hours.

H-18 has been in prison for about seven years and at the present time is extremely nervous—perhaps as a result of his attempt to conceal his abnormal conduct.   He tries to give the appearance of a goody-goody by feigning to be shocked with the vulgar talk of the other convicts.   He insisted that he knew nothing of the homosexual activities of the other prisoners.   He talks much of his former high social standing and of his many influential and socially prominent friends.

Nominally he is a Protestant with definite leanings toward Christian Science.   Although somewhat matronly in appearance, he has only a few specific feminine characteristics.   His voice is soft and rather deep (he sings baritone).   His speech and carriage are noticeably effeminate, but not so pronouncedly as are those of many true homosexuals.

The following are excerpts from a statement about M. H. written by a fellow convict:

M. H. likes to display himself naked and sleeps naked when possible. Has been reprimanded several times for not keeping dressed. Displays particular fondness for wearing surgical gowns that open in the back, wearing them without other clothing when possible. . . .
When under the influence of sexual desire is excitable, abnormally nervous, shows difficulty in breathing and is apt to be particularly violent toward anyone who distracts his attention from his prospective lover. With "prospect" is very loving; caressing, fondling, and kissing with little caution about being seen. Very passionate, almost insatiable in his erotic desires. Attracted mostly by young fellows of any race or color; Mexicans, negroes, or whites, all are acceptable. . . .

Significant facts: parents not unusual; an only child after age 3; orphan; little contact with either girls or boys; personal neatness overemphasized; precocious in music; bisexual; violent passion and lack of inhibition; "I" score much less invert than the mean of his group.

SUMMARY AND CONCLUSIONS

The regularity with which certain items are repeated in the case histories of this group is very impressive. There are individual differences, but the composite picture is probably less blurred than it would be for almost any other male group one could find.

Thirteen of the 18 were either only children (5), youngest (4), oldest (3), or sickly (1).

Seven of the fathers either died or were away from home when the subject was very young. Eight were described as cold, stern, autocratic, or fear-inspiring; only three as kind or sympathetic. No father was the preferred parent.

Six mothers were described as excessively affectionate and none as antagonistic or unkind; eight as emotional or unstable, one as markedly stable. Only one mother died when the subject was young and one other did not live constantly with the child. In eight cases the relationship between subject and mother is described as very close or intimate, in no case as distant or casual.

Four of the mothers are said to have wanted a girl at the time of subject's birth; five are specifically said to have treated the child like a girl; that the number who did so was probably greater is indicated by the fact that six of the subjects helped a great deal with the housework. Two subjects mention special training in personal neatness.

In four cases a grandmother enters into the picture; in three cases an older sister.

Half the subjects showed marked preference for the companionship of girls, only one for the companionship of boys. Two had no opportunity to associate with boys and three preferred to be alone. Six report that they were regarded by boys as sissies. Normal male companionship has therefore been pretty well out of the picture.

Only two of the subjects (one of these not a true homosexual) preferred boys' playthings; whereas, 11 were fond of dolls and "house" was the favorite play of five.

Six have a history of transvestism, four or five of these being rather extreme cases.

The average school grade completed was the third year of high school, which is significantly above the mean for males of their generation in any part of the United States. It is probable, therefore, that the group is also above the average of the general population in intelligence.

As the most disliked study, mathematics (or arithmetic) was named by eight subjects, one of the sciences by three, and manual training, a foreign language, and grammar by one each. There were two who named mathematics as the preferred study (one of these, H-16, not a true homosexual). The most liked studies are reading, history, and literature.

Five of the group are decidedly musical and three have been actors.

More of the subjects were reared as Catholics than as Protestants, but the group is too small to lend much if any significance to this fact. It is interesting that two of the subjects were trained for the priesthood. One wonders whether they were encouraged to do this because they were seen to lack heterosexual interests, or because the mothers were so attached to them as to want (subconsciously) to make sure that no other woman should have them.

Seven were effeminate in voice and five in manner or gait. Several were of the type that seems especially to attract the active homosexual male (petit, plump, youthful appearing, etc.).

About half the subjects seem to have taken to homosexual practices more or less spontaneously; but there were four or five cases of downright seduction.

Nine of the subjects say that they have never had heterosexual intercourse. Six have copulated with women occasionally but prefer men, and two have maintained regular heterosexual relationships over long periods (one case, no report). The mean M-F and "I" scores of these three groups are as follows:

	Group 1 $N = 9$	Group 2 $N = 6$	Group 3 $N = 2$
Mean M-F score.............	− 50	− 27	+17
Mean "I" score..............	+454	+527	+52

We note here a striking progression toward less feminine score with increased tendency to heterosexuality. The difference in mean "I" score between groups 1 and 2 is not statistically significant, but the "I" scores of both men in group 3 are low for inversion.

Six of the group either deny the practice of fellatio or say that they greatly dislike it, as compared with three who admit that they prefer it to pederasty.

Several of the group give evidence of being neurotic, psychasthenic, or otherwise emotionally unstable, and in several cases there appears to be considerable evidence of instability in one or both parents. Such conditions are probably connected with homosexuality both as cause and effect.

If the case-history data supplied by these individuals can be accepted as anywhere near the truth, the psycho-social formula for developing homosexuality in boys would seem to run somewhat as follows: too demonstrative affection from an excessively emotional mother, especially in the case of a first, last, or only child; a father who is unsympathetic, autocratic, brutal, much away from home, or deceased; treatment of the child as a girl, coupled with lack of encouragement or opportunity to associate with boys and to take part in the rougher masculine activities; overemphasis of neatness, niceness, and spirituality; lack of vigilance against the danger of seduction by older homosexual males. The formula, of course, does not always work. Doubtless many children who grow up in an environment of the kind just described become nevertheless heterosexual; possibly a majority do. In some of these cases the heterosexual adjustment is made only with difficulty; the man may have little interest in sex, he may select a wife much older than himself (a mother surrogate), or if he marries a younger woman she may find it impossible to win first place in his affections.

CHAPTER XIV

CASE STUDIES: MASCULINE AND FEMININE TYPES OF DELINQUENT GIRLS[1]

The M-F test was given to all the inmates of the Ventura (California) Home for Girls, 54 in number. The mean score was −88; S.D. of the distribution, 42. The mean is approximately the same as that of high-school girls (−85.5), and only 10 points less feminine than that of eighth-grade girls. The group as a whole therefore rates as one of the most feminine we have tested. The range, however, is very great: from +103 to −166. The case studies reported in this chapter include two with highly masculine scores, five with scores in the moderately masculine range (−12 to −37), and seven whose scores were very feminine (−166 to −132). Case studies of such widely contrasting groups serve to bring into relief both the value and the limitations of the M-F test as a psychometric tool. The seven most masculine girls of the series will be designated as the M series, the seven most feminine as the F series. The "M" cases follow in order of masculinity of score.

M-1

Exercise	1	2	3	4	5	6	7	Total
M-F score	0	−3	0	+21	+86	−3	+2	+103

M-1 is 17 years old. She is of very superior intelligence, as she was in the ninth grade when she left school at the age of 13. At 16 her IQ on the Stanford-Binet test was 118, and as she passed all but one test in the scale it is probable that her true IQ was not far from 130. Her educational age on the Stanford Achievement Test is slightly better than 18 years, which agrees closely with the intelligence score.

[1] The data for the case studies of this chapter were assembled by Dr. Maud A. Merrill with the cooperation of the officers of the Ventura Home for Girls, Ventura, California (a state institution for delinquents). The summaries here reported were prepared by Dr. Merrill and Dr. Terman.

The father of M-1 is 45 years old. He works in a steel factory, but was formerly a mining engineer. The mother, who is 39, did general housework before marriage. M-1 is the second of nine children, all but one of whom (the fifth) are girls.

M-1 was never in sympathy with either of her parents, though she liked her father better than her mother. She never wanted to do the things the rest of the family did and usually disagreed with their ideas. The father and mother are hard-working people, American born of Slavic peasant stock. Their sole ambition has been to work hard and get ahead. M-1, too, was expected to work hard and to care for nothing else, and her outbreaks against the tyranny of dull routine seem to have been met only with repressive measures. She did not especially care for her sisters. They liked to sew and cook and she did not, and her older sister was "always going to dances."

As a child M-1 played with dolls, but preferred active games and outdoor activities. She played basketball and especially liked to ride horseback until tired out. She also liked to take the children to the basement and "make them do stunts—jumping, etc." She wants and expects to be an aviator. Hates sewing and fancywork and cannot make her own clothes. She likes to use tools; helped her father build a garage and has built chicken houses by herself. Her favorite subjects were algebra and arithmetic; her hardest, reading. Likes the books of Zane Grey, "especially the adventure parts." Preferred magazines are *Saturday Evening Post, Ladies' Home Journal,* and the mining engineering magazine which her father takes. Prefers the sports section of the newspaper. Current news most interesting to her was about Byrd's expedition and Nobile's polar flight. Likes to go out in the rain on stormy nights. Her earliest memory is of "playing in the mine, taking an ax and doing like grown people."

M-1 has no intimates among her fellow inmates and few interests in common with them. At home she belonged to a gang of girls who sometimes dressed up in boys' clothes and went out at night "to stir things up." They are said to have taken automobiles, picked up girls who mistook them for men, and then made the girls walk home. The members of the gang called themselves the "seven devils" and boasted of being able to "lick any boy of their size." Once they held up a dance hall, broke the lights, and robbed the patrons. M-1 displays the staunchest loyalty to her former associates.

The subject is a very attractive girl, frank and jolly. She tells about herself in an objective half-humorous way, but is very positive about her opinions. She is unemotional, self-controlled, of pleasant manner, and respectful in her attitude toward others. Her history shows that she is self-assertive, resistant to suggestion and authority, and not readily guided by advice. Her experiences have been predominantly masculine, and she prefers masculine activities and occupations. Before commitment she was in the habit of drinking to excess. It is not surprising that she claims to have always wanted to be a boy.

M-1 ran away from home, which was in a small town in Ohio, and "hoboed" her way to Los Angeles in 15 days, dressed in boy's clothes. She used a boy's name and succeeded in passing as a boy notwithstanding her distinctly feminine appearance. She is of medium height and has well-developed hips and breasts and a round face. Her expression is merry and she smiles readily when she talks. She says she left home on account of a quarrel with her father over a revolver, but the underlying reason seems to have been her rebellion against routine and her lack of sympathy with her family. Admits that she was "a bit groggy" with liquor when she left and that she hardly knew what she was doing until she got as far as St. Louis. Soon after reaching Los Angeles she was arrested as a vagrant. The medical examination reports her as negative for venereal infection.

Estimates of subject by the officers of the institution differ greatly. According to one, "she is crazy for drink; untrustworthy; would do anything to achieve her ends; is interested only in the things that boys are interested in." According to another she is "very substantial, dependable under supervision." A third says she is "a very worth-while girl; I expect her to come out all right; I don't blame her for wanting to get away from the drudgery of her home or for refusing to return to it." This officer had her detailed to her own home where she (willingly) cooks, waits on the table, and does other housework. In her studies she did well in commercial arithmetic but was so unskillful at typing that she was removed from the class.

The case history of M-1, like the other histories of this series, was prepared by Dr. Merrill without knowledge of the results of the M-F test. However, Dr. Merrill rated this subject as the most masculine of the group and made the notation that unless the test showed her to be the most masculine it would be in error. Her score is in fact at the 73d percentile of high-school boys for masculinity and a full standard deviation more masculine than the mean of the 604 males in our adult population. It is beyond the 100th percentile of high-school girls. The score of +86 on Exercise 5 (interests) is one of the most masculine we have encountered.

M-2

Exercise	1	2	3	4	5	6	7	Total
M-F score	−13	−2	−6	+29	+46	−3	−2	+49

M-2 is 17 years old and in the senior year of high school. At 16 she earned an IQ of 112 on the Stanford-Binet test, which is probably equivalent to a true IQ of 120 for a subject of this age. Her educational age at that time on the Stanford Achievement Test was 16-8. The subject is therefore unquestionably well above the average in general intelligence.

The father of M-2 is a mechanic, 45 years old. The mother died in childbirth when subject was about 13. The father remarried but separated from his second wife when he learned that she had another husband living. M-2 is the second of five children. The first sib is a sister, one year her senior. The next younger is a boy eight years her junior. There is nothing in her family background to account for the masculinity of her score. M-2 never got along pleasantly with either her father or her stepmother; says she never wants to see her father again. The stepmother is said to have had a bad influence on her behavior.

In personality M-2 has a slow, plodding manner. She is moody, visionary, and talkative. Her first conflict with the law came when she was reported for truancy. A home was found for her but she again ran away and was found living with a man as his wife. She had a seven-months miscarriage and accused a second man of being the child's father. Later she lived two weeks with a third man. Has been under treatment for gonorrhea and syphilis.

The subject's behavior is decidedly masculine. She was for a time a reporter, writing sketches and illustrating them with pen pictures. Previous to that she had belonged to a "bicycle gang." After commitment to Ventura she ran away, helped by one of the officers, but was caught and returned. She is quite lacking in the feminine type of emotionality and loves adventure. In many respects she resembles M-1, especially in her spirit of independence and her qualities of leadership. Her sex involvements appear to have been incidental consequences of her insatiable appetite for thrills.

The subject's M-F score is at the 100th percentile for high-school girls and at the 35th percentile for high-school boys. It is most masculine on Exercise 4 (emotional and ethical attitudes) and Exercise 5 (interests).

M-3

Exercise	1	2	3	4	5	6	7	Total
M-F score	−11	−2	−10	+4	+14	−6	−1	−13

M-3 is 17 years old and in the tenth grade. No intelligence score is available, but the educational age of 15-6 on the Stanford Achievement Test indicates that her IQ is at least 100 and possibly higher.

The father, a cook, deserted the family when the subject was 6 months old. The mother was remarried, to a farmer. M-3 has only one sibling, an older sister who is married and has one child. She is companionable with the sister and takes her troubles to her rather than to her mother.

The subject's attitude toward her mother is unsympathetic; "she has such high standards for me." However, the mother is very indulgent and has ambitions for her daughters. The stepfather was not good to the mother when the daughters were at home, and refused to give her money because she spent it for them. The mother was therefore compelled to go out to work and this increased the friction between the subject and her stepfather.

As a child M-3 played mostly with boys, climbed trees, and preferred outdoor games. She never played house and cared little for dolls. "I can only remember having one doll, but my sister always had them." She expects to be a stenographer, but would like most of all to be a doctor. Favorite subjects are her commercial courses; the hardest, mathematics. She prefers to read historical books and stories of adventure; has no interest in love stories. Parts of newspapers liked best are the comics and "topics of interest, like murders." She is fond of tennis, baseball, volleyball, and basketball; is captain of the high-school basketball team. Likes to make things with tools.

M-3 has always been a leader among girls. When in the Alameda Training School for Girls, where she was placed before her commitment to Ventura, she is reported to have developed "a sort of sex complex which reached a climax when the girls scratched her initials on their legs with pins." The subject herself says: "Since I have been shut up with girls I have always had favorites." She prefers the athletic type of girl.

M-3 is a rather attractive girl, pleasant and docile to people in authority, but aggressive in dealing with girls of her own age. Seems to be objective and unemotional. Reports that she always wanted to be a boy and still does. "I've always wanted somebody to pal around with, but there is always a feeling of sex between a boy and a girl and I didn't like that. Never liked to go out with boys on that account. As I got older I wanted to be a boy just that much more."

M-3 ran away from home (in the middle west) to find her father, who had deserted the family when she was an infant. Neither her mother nor her stepfather had any control over her and she was already a sex delinquent. Was sent to the Alameda Training School for Girls. Was paroled and placed in a family where she worked for her board and attended business school. Violated parole by going to gin parties and establishing irregular sex relations. Was returned to Alameda. Paroled a second time, left home and went to Fresno without her mother's consent.

Was committed to Ventura as incorrigible. The officers at Ventura consider her "hard-boiled" and untrustworthy.

The history of M-3 reveals a personality which resembles the masculine more than the feminine type in respect to leadership, aggressiveness, objectivity, interest in tools and athletics, and love of adventure. There is no definite history of homosexual practices, but the subject plays distinctly the active role in her relations with the other girls. Her heterosexual experiences have probably been incidental results of her liking for adventure.

Only one high-school girl in 20 tests as masculine as M-3, and about one high-school boy in 15 tests as feminine. The subject is accordingly about halfway between the norms for boys and girls of corresponding age. She is decidedly less masculine in M-F score than M-1 or M-2, and somewhat less so in her behavior.

M-4

Exercise	1	2	3	4	5	6	7	Total
M-F score	−13	−2	+2	+3	−8	−15	−2	−35

M-4 is 18 years old and a high-school senior. Her Stanford-Binet IQ is 104, probably equivalent to a true IQ of 115. The Stanford Achievement Test gives her an educational age of 17-2.

The father is 46 years old. He is a mechanic and has a garage. The mother, who was 15 years older than her husband, died when M-4 was 10 years old. At the time of her death she had been separated from her husband for two years and was a teacher. The father has remarried. M-4 has an older sister who is married and has three children. There are two half-sisters, still of preschool age, by her father's second marriage. The subject was very congenial with her mother: "The two years mother and I had together [after parents' separation] were the happiest in my life."

After her mother's death M-4 went to live with her father, who had by this time remarried. She disliked her stepmother but did not quarrel with her. The father allowed her little freedom, kept her at home, and established incestuous relations with her. When this became known she was committed to the New York Training School for Girls. After parole she ran away to California where an aunt lived, but the latter refused to take her in or have anything to do with her. Soon afterward she was arrested in an apartment with a man and was brought into the juvenile court on the charge of vagrancy. She was found to be infected with gonorrhea and was committed to Ventura.

M-4 has the dignity and poise of a woman of superior social level; gives the impression of being rather inscrutable and complete mistress of herself. She is reticent but when she talks she expresses herself in good English. Told somewhat reluctantly of the incestuous relationship with her father.

The subject's experience has been predominantly feminine. As a child she preferred girls to boys, but played with both. Liked dolls, but was also fond of skating and outdoor games. Was captain of a girls' baseball team. Her favorite school subject was mathematics; her hardest, English. Her favorite books were Campfire Girls, Gene Stratton Porter's novels, and the Elsie books. She reads *American Magazine* and *Good Housekeeping*. Has never used tools. Can sew and do plain cooking, but does not care for fancywork. Expects to study medicine.

On the M-F test, M-4 rates more masculine than six girls out of seven at the high-school age. In Exercise 3 (information) and Exercise 4 (emotional and ethical attitudes) her scores are more masculine than feminine. Her history strongly suggests, however, that the subject has essentially a normal and well integrated personality, and that her delinquencies were the result of unfortunate circumstances. Her activities and interests have certainly been more feminine than the score would lead one to expect.

M-5

Exercise	1	2	3	4	5	6	7	Total
M-F score	-22	-1	-6	$+17$	-20	-2	-2	-36

M-5 is 15 years old and in the ninth grade. No intelligence score is on record, but the educational age of 16-2 on the Stanford Achievement Test would suggest an IQ appreciably above 100.

Subject's father, aged 40, is an airplane machinist. The mother, also 40, did housework outside her home for a year after marriage. There are five children, of whom M-5 is the second.

The first is a girl of 17, the third a boy of 10, the fourth died at the age of 3, and the youngest is only 2.

The home relationships were anything but sympathetic. "Mother understood me better than my father, but she did not see things from my point of view. She would never let us [subject and older sister] go out; said we could not be trusted. So we went to dances without her permission." Regarding relationship to her sibs, "We didn't play, we fought." However, she was fond of the youngest brother and liked to take care of him.

M-5 played with dolls until she was 6 years old. Liked to climb trees, play games, and go flower picking. She wanted to become a Girl Scout, but the mother was unwilling to let her attend the Scout meetings after school. Had no girl chums. "Only one girl lived near us and mother wouldn't let me have anything to do with her. But they let me go out with a man of 20, a friend of father's." Always wanted to be a boy; "if I were I would be an aviator." She likes to use tools and "can make almost anything." Can sew, embroider, and do plain cooking. Asked what she expected to do when grown up, she said: "Marry; nearly everyone does." Favorite subject, arithmetic; hardest, civics. Likes to read adventure stories. Dislikes athletics.

M-5 is a gloomy and unresponsive girl, bitter, and resistant to advice. She justifies herself and blames her family for all her troubles. Appears sullen, hard, and suspicious. Was committed on the charge of having sexual relations with several boys. However, she denies having had normal sexual intercourse. (Record: "Ruptured hymen; probably has had intercourse.") The house mother in charge reports that M-5 is continually doing things that have a sexual significance, such as handling the other girls. Is described by another officer as "very eccentric and queer."

Only one girl out of seven of corresponding age scores so masculine on the M-F test as this subject. Her most masculine score is on Exercise 4 (emotional and ethical attitudes). It would be interesting to know to what extent her rebellious behavior is the cause and to what extent the effect of her masculine attitudes. As the older sister (not tested) was also for a time in a detention home, it is possible that the domestic situation may be largely responsible for provoking the resistant and otherwise masculine type of personality.

M-6

Exercise	1	2	3	4	5	6	7	Total
M-F score	−15	−2	−4	+18	−28	−3	−3	−37

M-6 is 20 years old.   No intelligence-test record is available, but her high Stanford Achievement Test score and the fact that she reached the twelfth grade before she left school at 16 (or 17) indicate that her IQ is probably above 120.

The subject is an only child, her one sib (just older) having died at birth.   This circumstance has probably been a major factor in the subject's life history.   The father is a retired contractor, 58 years old.   The mother, 57, was formerly a singer; sang with the choral symphony of one of the largest middlewestern cities. M-6 is married and most of her troubles have arisen from her mother's inability to give her up.   "Mother would give her life for me, but she won't give me up to my husband."

The fact that the first child had been stillborn, and that the mother was 37 at the birth of M-6, doubtless accentuated the only-child situation.   From infancy the child was pampered and adored by her mother.   The latter has twice deliberately lured her daughter away from her husband; writes her every day the most effusive letters protesting her affection for her "darling child."   Subject is torn between husband and mother: "I can't live with either of them, and I can't live without them." She resents any show of authority by either.   The father seems to play almost no part in this conflict.

As a child M-6 liked sports and games better than the activities more typical of girls.   Her mother provided her with innumerable dolls, but the only one she cared for was an old rag doll.   She liked to play with other children, preferably boys.   She likes art, music, and dramatics; is in fact very musical and has always been a leader in dramatics.   On the whole, she prefers the stage to music.   She also likes business and has held several office positions.   She is good at mechanical drawing; was the only girl in a class of boys in this subject and was outstanding.   She likes to do things that require fine coordinations and meticulous care. Favorite subjects, English and Spanish; hardest, history and geography. Excelled in swimming and hunting, though her mother thought it wasn't ladylike for her to go hunting. The subject differs markedly from her fellow inmates in the superior quality of her interests, training, and background.

M-6 is vivid, beautiful, charming, and merry; the kind who could hold her own in any social group. She is whimsically objective, interested in everything, happy, dominated by her affections, quick to resent authority, loyal and fearless. Never wanted to be a boy; "I could always play with the boys anyway, and they liked to play with me better than with other boys."

M-6 was committed for forgery. The mother, after luring her away from her husband, encouraged her to accept the attentions of an older man. For a time she was infatuated with this man and, although he was not divorced, lived with him as his wife. He taught her to cash forged checks at department stores after banking hours, and in a spirit of lawless adventure and revolt she entered into this new game. She is not popular with the officers of the institution because they cannot break her spirit. She is never insolent, but she is never cowed.

M-6 was 17 when she eloped and married. All went well as long as she and her husband could live with her mother, but when he took a position in another city the trouble began. M-6, much against her mother's wishes, also got a position. Her mother kept trying to get her to come home, which she did one day after a quarrel with her husband. Later reunited with her husband, but returned home to get her household goods and was persuaded by her mother to stay. The mother's next stratagem was to encourage her to accept the attentions of the other man in order to keep her from her husband. When M-6 was arrested for forgery this man behaved in a most cowardly and disloyal way, yet she refused to turn state's evidence.

From the case history it was expected that this subject would score somewhat masculine, but within the feminine range. Such was the case. One might say that she is a man's woman, par excellence.

M-7

Exercise	1	2	3	4	5	6	7	Total
M-F score	−14	−3	−7	+30	−38	−7	+·2	−37

M-7 is 17 years old, has a Stanford-Binet IQ of 90, and rates a little above 13 years educationally on the Stanford Achievement Test. She is at best not above average in mental ability.

The parents were divorced when M-7 was 5 years old and the mother has remarried. Her stepfather is a carpenter and has served a term in prison. Her mother was a telephone operator before marriage. There are two half-sibs, both boys. Subject is congenial with her mother but has never felt free to talk to her about her affairs.

As a child M-7 never played with dolls and was very fond of outdoor activities. She prefers boys to girls as friends. "Always as a little girl I liked to play with boys better than with girls; you can tell them more." However, she did not want to be a boy. At present gives the impression of being poised, self-confident, and unemotional, which is in line with her very masculine score on Exercise 4, emotional and ethical attitudes.

The subject was only 12 years old when she was first brought into the juvenile court. She was then under treatment for gonorrhea. After a short time in a training school for girls she was released and worked as a clerk while living at home. Because the mother objected to her associates she ran away, was apprehended, and tried to commit suicide. It was after this that she was committed to Ventura.

This case presents no very unusual features from the point of view of M-F characteristics. Although only about one girl out of seven at her age tests as masculine, she is well within the normal feminine range. Her life history indicates that her experiences and interests have presented a mixture of masculine and feminine trends. Her favorite school subjects were civics and hygiene; her hardest, arithmetic and English. She likes dancing, romantic reading and movies, cooking and sewing. Has ushered in a movie theater and would like to be an interior decorator. Has played on a basketball team. One wonders whether the unemotional and somewhat "hard-boiled" attitudes reflected in her responses in Exercise 4 are the cause or effect of her delinquent tendencies.

Before proceeding to the F group of female delinquents a few summary observations may be made regarding the M group of the series.

1. All the subjects in the group are above the 85th percentile of high-school girls for masculinity; two are above the 100th percentile.

2. The group as a whole rates high in intelligence. Four have estimated IQ's between 115 and 130, the highest belonging to the most masculine-scoring subject. Two are at or just above 100, and only one is below.

3. Of the fathers of these seven girls, five belong to occupations of the engineering or mechanical type. The father of the most masculine-scoring and most masculine-behaving girl has been a mining engineer (this occupation is the most masculine in our tested populations). Three other fathers are mechanics and one is a building contractor.

4. The group as a whole has shown far more than the usual amount of interest in masculine activities. This is particularly true of the three whose M-F scores were most masculine, and most of all true of the subject who ranked highest in M-F score. The four least masculine showed a distinctly greater mixture of masculine and feminine interests. Five of the seven cared little or not at all for doll play. Athletics or other outdoor activities figure prominently in the interests of six. Two were members of gangs. Three liked to work with tools. Reading preferences of three were chiefly masculine. Not one was particularly fond of cooking, sewing, or fancywork. Three have always wanted to be boys. Their vocational preferences are for the most part masculine.

5. In general the subjects of the M group are of aggressive, independent spirit; they are self-confident, well poised, and lacking in feminine emotionality. One at least (M-4) is more or less psychopathic.

6. Exercises 4 and 5 contribute most heavily to the masculine scores of the M group, indicating unemotionality of response and a marked tendency to masculine interests.

In going through each of the case histories of the F series which follows, the reader should keep in mind so far as possible the composite picture of the M group in order to note both contrasts and resemblances. The F cases are presented as ranked by the M-F score from most to least feminine.

F-1

Exercise	1	2	3	4	5	6	7	Total
M-F score	−23	−2	−22	−56	−46	−15	−2	−166

F-1 is 18 years old. Both her Stanford-Binet and Stanford Achievement scores indicate that she is of about average mental ability. She is the only child of American-born parents of Spanish descent. The subject's illness prevented the taking of a case history, but the following information is available from the institution records.

F-1 was brought to the San Francisco Detention Home for truancy at the age of 15 and was found to have both gonorrhea and syphilis. She admitted sexual relations with sailors. Was sent to Convent of Good Shepherd, but was soon paroled and continued her former associations. Was again sent to the convent and again paroled. Then her mother died and as the father was unable to control her she was committed to Ventura.

F-1 is said by one of the institution officers to be oversexed. She wants to become a stenographer, is fond of music, public dances, tennis, and roller skating.   Is of the quiet type and reads a good deal.   Feminine interests seem to have predominated, but the available information is scanty. In the absence of full personal history data the case is of interest chiefly as an illustration of one of the extremes of the wide M-F range which one finds among delinquent girls of the late teens.   Only one high-school girl in 50 tests as feminine as this subject, her score on Exercise 4 (emotional and ethical attitudes) being especially feminine.

F-2

Exercise	1	2	3	4	5	6	7	Total
M-F score	−27	−1	−2	−42	−78	−1	−2	−153

F-2, aged 17, is considerably above average in mental ability. Her found IQ of 111 at age 15 suggests a true IQ in the neighborhood of 120, and her achievement scores are correspondingly high.

The mother, now 36, married the father, a preacher's son, when she was 19. F-2 accuses her father of cruelty to her mother and of infecting her with syphilis. Mother deserted husband when subject was 14 months old and after teaching school for several years married a fairly well-to-do man whom she did not love and lived with only three years. Subject's only sib, her twin, was stillborn. F-2 is very devoted to her mother and takes a protective attitude toward her.

As a child F-2 loved to play with dolls. "I still do. Anybody can laugh that wants to. I still have a large doll." Was prevented by her mother from associating with other children, so stayed at home, read a great deal, worked in the garden, and rode horseback. "Most of the things I did were solitary." Her favorite subject was English; her hardest, arithmetic. Favorite author is Gene Stratton Porter. Reads *Pictorial Review*, *Delineator, Ladies' Home Journal, Red Book, American Magazine*, "the sensational parts of the newspaper and the woman's page." Is extremely fond of dancing, pets, embroidering, and sewing. "I love to sew; it is an inherited instinct." Expects to be a stenographer, but would like to be a novelist. Writes poetry.

F-2 is a very unstable girl. She is emotional, but her emotions are shallow. Is uncontrolled, self-centered, selfish, and obsessed with sex interests. Scored highly psychoneurotic on the Woodworth-Cady personal inventory (−2.2 S.D.), at the 100th percentile for instability on the Laird B2, and showed emotional disturbance on the Wells association test, especially on the Jung words that tap sexual complexes. Is described by the institution officers as queer and completely solitary; with one accord they say she is unstable and will probably become insane.

F-2 first came into the juvenile court because of her illicit sexual relations with several men, including two university students. She was placed in a training school for girls, but was found so unstable that she was returned to the court as an unfit subject for training. She was then committed to Ventura.

Significant facts in this case history are (1) the strong mother attachment, probably resulting from the mother's unhappy marital experience; (2) the lack of opportunity to associate with other children; and (3) emotional instability with persistence of infantile egoism. In the M-F test her most highly feminine scores were made on Exercise 1 (word association) and Exercise 5 (interests).

F-3

Exercise	1	2	3	4	5	6	7	Total
M-F score	−32	−2	−21	−6	−74	−9	−3	−147

F-3 is 19 years old. Her score on the Stanford Achievement Test suggests an IQ of 100 to 110. Reached the junior year of high school and became a stenographer.

At the age of 14 F-3 lost her mother; two years later her father, who keeps a fruit stand, remarried. She has one younger brother and two younger sisters.

The subject was committed for forgery. The facts are that she was the trusted stenographer of a businessman in a small California city, fell in love with a young man, allowed him to drive her to Los Angeles, and when he was arrested and fined $50.00 for speeding she signed her employer's name to a check in payment of the fine.

Nothing in her childhood history is noted that is not typically feminine. She is very sensitive, fine spirited, sweet, and gentle. She is extremely remorseful and is regarded by the officers of the institution as essentially trustworthy. She paints well, does needlework, and loves to arrange flowers. Has none of the aggressiveness characteristic of so many delinquent girls. Her score is highly feminine on Exercise 1 (word association), Exercise 3 (information), and Exercise 5 (interests).

F-4

Exercise	1	2	3	4	5	6	7	Total
M-F score	−23	−1	−3	−49	−68	−2	−1	−147

F-4 is 18 years old and in the ninth grade. Her IQ, as estimated from her Stanford Achievement score, is about 90. She is the eighth of nine children in a Spanish family. Her father, owner of a store, died when the subject was 5 years old and her mother when she was 13. A brother, next older, was at the time of this study a featherweight fighter of some note.

F-4 is devoted to her family; her eyes shine when she talks of them. The pugilist brother is her hero. She had a strict upbringing, as is customary in Spanish homes, and was not allowed to play much with children outside the family. Loved to play with dolls. Her favorite subject was arithmetic, English her hardest. She is fond of dancing, and likes to sew and do fancywork. Expects to be a seamstress. Likes to read stories of ancient history and romances. Favorite book, *Ramona*. Reads *Pictorial Review*, *Woman's Home Companion*, *Cosmopolitan*, and *True Romances*. Loves movies. Valentino was her favorite actor, later Novarro. Prefers to be with girls rather than with boys.

F-4 is gentle, amiable, and wants to be loved. She is all sweetness, softness, and charm, has the social and manual interests of her sex, is docile and would do anything to please. She was committed on the charge of "leading a lewd and immoral life." Subject says only one man was involved and that "he was all right, only he was married." Shows no resentment or bitterness over her commitment. Is a devout Catholic. After taking down her case history Dr. Merrill appended the note: "This subject should test feminine if anyone ever did." Her score in fact places her at the 5th percentile of high-school-junior girls for masculinity (95th percentile for femininity). The feminine score was earned chiefly on Exercise 1 (word association), Exercise 4 (emotional and ethical attitudes), and Exercise 5 (interests).

F-5

Exercise	1	2	3	4	5	6	7	Total
M-F score	−31	−1	−8	−22	−60	−20	−2	−144

F-5 is 18 years old and in the tenth school grade. Her IQ, estimated from Stanford Achievement Test, is probably in the neighborhood of 110.

Subject's father, a locomotive engineer, died several years ago and the mother remarried. The only sib is a brother, aged 24.

F-5 is sympathetic toward both mother and stepfather. "Could always talk over problems with my mother. She let me have my way too much." Of her stepfather she says, "He always treated me fairly and was rather inclined to be overindulgent."

As a child F-5 played with dolls until about 11 years old and made clothes for them. She played games, too, mostly with girls. Her favorite subject, arithmetic; hardest, composition. Favorite books, Grace Richmond "and that type, Red Pepper Burns, and love stories." Reads little in the newspapers but the society page. Likes fancywork and makes her own clothes; also plays baseball at Ventura. Likes to go out a great deal, preferably with older companions. When only 14 was permitted to work in restaurants and in private homes with little supervision and formed a number of undesirable associations.

F-5 never wanted to be a boy; says she does not envy them even though she recognizes that they have better business opportunities and can "get by" with things girls can't. In personality she is amiable. A little plump, languorous in speech and movement, but mentally alert and willing to respond; somewhat of the Mae West type. Would probably rate high in physical attractiveness to the opposite sex. The officers describe her as a dependable girl, with wholesome interests, poetic, and "probably strongly sexed." Her score is especially feminine on Exercises 1, 5, and 6.

Subject was arrested as an inmate of a "disorderly house" which was raided by the police. She denies having been promiscuous but the records show that she has had a syphilitic infection.

F-6

Exercise	1	2	3	4	5	6	7	Total
M-F score	−25	−2	−4	−20	−62	−16	−5	−134

F-6 is 18 years old. She is still in the eighth grade, has an educational age of only 14-6, and an IQ of 92.

The subject's parents have been divorced and have both remarried. The stepfather is a traveling auditor, 66 years old; the mother is 40. Subject is in effect an only child; there is one half-sib, less than 2 years old. Got along well with her mother and stepfather ("he was as good as gold to me"), and was congenial with the two grown daughters of her stepfather. Records indicate that her mother is immoral and alcoholic. F-6 was for this reason sent to California to live with her father. She was found to be pregnant when she arrived. An uncle became infatuated with her and at her father's request she was made a ward of the juvenile court and placed at the Business Girls' Club in Los Angeles. She did not do well there and was sent to the Detention Home, from which she ran away.

As a child F-6 liked to play with dolls and "had most fun dressing up in long dresses." Does not like to sew or embroider. Has used tools in making doll furniture, has been captain of a baseball team, and likes athletics. "I would rather swim than eat." Likes to dance. Favorite subject, arithmetic; hardest, history. Likes to read; favorite author is Gene Stratton Porter. Used to like girls her own age but gets along better with boys. Likes older boys and enjoys skating, swimming, and dancing with them. Always wanted to be a boy and still does. In personality is rather colorless, quiet, and unobtrusive, with a certain dignity of manner. Is given to crushes on the other girls of the institution and is the object of their crushes.

F-6 presents a combination of masculine and feminine behavior traits that would lead one to expect her to make a less feminine score than she does on the M-F test. The total score is at the 16th percentile of high-school girls for masculinity.

F-7

Exercise	1	2	3	4	5	6	7	Total
M-F score	-21	-3	$+1$	-25	-80	-1	-1	-130

F-7 is 17 years old and in the fifth grade, though her score on the Stanford Achievement Test shows seventh-grade mastery. Has had no intelligence test but the IQ estimated from achievement score is probably below 90.

Subject has a sister three years older and a brother two years younger; is fond of both. The father is a sheet-metal worker, aged 43. The mother, formerly a housemaid, is 39. Her parents were good to her, but she considered them too strict and ran away.

As a child F-7 played with dolls.   Still likes them.   Also liked to play school, but was not with other children very much. Likes cooking and nursing; "would rather be a nurse than anything."   Can sew and do fancywork.   Favorite school subject, arithmetic; hardest, civics.   Favorite books, Zane Grey's.   In the newspapers reads recipes, advice to young girls, and the woman's page.   Never wanted to be a boy.

In personality F-7 is suave, smooth, and colorless.   Always talks for effect.   Is described by officers as "too nice; quiet and inoffensive, but a talebearer; stubborn, conceited, smug."   She was committed for incorrigibility.   She had run away from home a number of times and in one case was not found for a year. With an older woman was consorting with sailors and had contracted gonorrhea and syphilis.

The experience of F-7, apart from her truancy, has been predominantly feminine.   Her M-F score is especially feminine on Exercises 5 and 1, and masculine on Exercise 3.

The F group of this series presents a very different picture from the M group.   Among the outstanding differences are the following:

1. The members of the group range in M-F score from about the 2nd to the 20th percentile of high-school girls for masculinity (M group 85th to above 100th percentile).

2. The average intelligence is lower.   The group contains one subject of about 120 IQ, three between 100 and 110, and three around 90.

3. Of the fathers of the seven only two were in mechanical occupations (M group, five).

4. The interests and activities of the group have been predominantly feminine.   Only F-6 presents a partial exception. Doll play was engaged in by nearly all and still is by two.   Only one showed much interest in tools, athletics, or other vigorous outdoor activities.   None was a member of a gang.   The reading preferences of at least five are markedly feminine, of none markedly masculine.   Nearly all were fond of sewing and cooking.   The occupational ambitions of nearly all are distinctly feminine.

5. The F subjects, judged by their life histories, lack the aggressiveness, rebelliousness, independence, and self-confidence of the M group. They are more gentle, docile, quiet, and colorless in personality. Although three of the group have been truants, as compared with five of the M group, the truancy of the two groups differs greatly in character. The truant F subjects simply left home to associate with men in the same or a neighboring city; the M truant is more likely to rebel against parental authority and to go to distant parts of the country. There was a somewhat greater amount of sexual promiscuity in the F group. Except for the sexual delinquency prevalent in both groups, one could say that the interests and activities of the M and F subjects show a very small amount of overlap. Even sex delinquency has not always the same significance in the two groups; with M subjects it is likely to be an incidental, with F subjects a more central, factor.

6. The exercises of the M-F test on which the F group scored most feminine are 1, 4, 5, and 6. Two of these, 4 and 5, were most often highly masculine in the M group. So far as the test is concerned, the most characteristic contrasts between the two groups are therefore in (*a*) emotional and ethical attitudes, and (*b*) interests.

CHAPTER XV

CASE NOTES: MISCELLANEOUS

The case descriptions we have brought together in this chapter represent a considerable variety. They have been selected with a view to giving the reader an idea of the limitations as well as the positive value of M-F scores in clinical practice. We have therefore included a number of cases which run counter to expectations with respect to correlation between M-F score and overt behavior or interests. A test of the M-F type has, we are convinced, great potential usefulness in the study of personality in its relation to social and sexual adjustment, but it is only one of many methods of approach to the study of these problems and in the present stage of its development it raises many questions which it does not answer.

X-1

X-1 is our most masculine-testing woman. She is a university professor, not far from 40 years of age, and is an able teacher and researcher.

Exercise	1	2	3	4	5	6	7	Total
M-F score:	+9	−2	+5	+69	+46	+4	+1	+132

The total score is at the 85th percentile for college *men*. She rates on the masculine side in every exercise except the unreliable No. 2.

The M-F score of her husband (+89) although at the 60th percentile for college men, is less masculine than her own by more than one S.D. His scores on the separate exercises are as follows:

Exercise	1	2	3	4	5	6	7	Total
M-F score:	+5	+1	+10	+43	+28	+3	−1	+89

It will be noted that the wife is especially more masculine on

342

Exercise 4 (emotional and ethical response) and on Exercise 5 (interests).

In view of the extraordinarily masculine score of this woman, and the fact that she seems to have made a normal heterosexual adjustment, the following communication from her is of surpassing interest:

I might give a brief case-study of myself, inasmuch as I would classify as a woman brought up by men. My mother died soon after my birth and my education was almost wholly in the hands of my father, grandfather, numerous uncles, and brothers. I did not attend school until I was 15; up until that time I was trained at home by either my father, my grandfather, or a tutor, who was also a man. I dressed in boy's clothes until I was 13, except for such few dressed-up occasions as might warrant a more feminine costume. Occasionally, an aunt or other woman visited us and then I had to wear girl's clothes—which probably started me on my decided antagonism toward women. My amusements were exclusively masculine. I do not remember owning dolls or other girls' toys. I played baseball, football, hockey, went swimming in the "old swimmin' hole," climbed every tree, house, and barn in the neighborhood, and so on. My playmates were all boys; the only girls I recall were girls I was afraid of. My chief amusement consisted in seeing how far I could travel from roof to roof and tree to tree without touching the ground—I think my greatest achievement was traversing some ten blocks before too long a distance between trees, houses, or fences caused me to descend. Another amusement consisted in running along beside some friend who had a bicycle, holding on to the springs under the seat; by the time I was 10 I could run the five miles around a near-by lake without stopping and with the greatest enjoyment. At the age of 15 my father suddenly discovered that he had a first-class boy on his hands, and that I was unable to get along with girls, so he sent me to a girls' boarding school for four years and then to a girls' college. The net result seemed to be that I disliked most girls and women worse than ever, fell desperately in love with a few, and was everlastingly being ruled out of games because I was "too rough." One summer I played professional baseball, my position being catching behind the bat; I still play baseball here on our faculty team in intramural ball. I also play field hockey, basketball, and water polo, but have to be most terribly careful not to hurt someone! My friends are still all men, I don't like girl students in my classes, and I haven't the vaguest idea what makes most women react the way they do; in the company of girls and women I remain utterly silent because I have learned that if I talk I will either bore the poor dears or else shock them.

X-2

X-2 is a woman psychologist of brilliant intellect, age between 34 and 40.

Exercise	1	2	3	4	5	6	7	Total
M-F score:	−8	−2	+9	+67	−2	+15	0	+79

The total score is at the 55th percentile for college men. The score on Exercise 4 (emotional and ethical response) is among the most masculine we have ever had from a woman and is at the 95th percentile for college men. The subject is unmarried but is known to have normal interest in men. She is objective and entirely lacking in feminine coyness. She works better with male than with female colleagues. Both this case and the preceding one are impressive illustrations of the fact that a high masculine score in a woman is not incompatible with heterosexual interests and adjustment.

X-3

X-3 is a 23-year-old woman who was arrested for masquerading in men's clothes. She was tested in jail. The jail physician (female) contributed some of the items of information in the following case summary.

Exercise	1	2	3	4	5	6	7	Total
M-F score:	0	0	−24	−36	+74	0	−3	+11

Stenquist mechanical-aptitude score near to mean for high-school girls.

X-3 attended high school for three years and made good marks. Her father has been dead a year. Her mother is inclined to be suspicious and has a disagreeable temper when angered. The subject has five sisters and one brother. The parents of X-3 wanted a boy and have always treated her as one. She is called "Harry" by the rest of the family. When she was 8 years old she began wearing boys' jeans at her mother's wish, and her father taught her boxing. However, she was sent to a girls' private school, where the girls all called her a tomboy. She never cared for dolls and dislikes housework and babies. In school plays she always took boys' parts and her teachers called her "Tommy." She learned to play the saxophone.

Later she found it fun to dress as a boy and go out with chorus girls and to rouse their emotions by kissing them as boys would. She has no feeling for boys but is sexually excited by girls, especially blondes. Says it would be easier to steal than to be a prostitute.

Shoulders 35½ in., hips 34 in.; breasts well developed and distribution of pubic hair is feminine; large amount of hair on her legs; voice contralto; arms and neck rather muscular; stands with feet apart; avoids color in dress.

In view of the early environmental conditioning it is not surprising that X-3 is more masculine in the M-F test than 95 out of 100 women of her age and education. It is interesting to note that her score is more than normally feminine on Exercises 3 and 4, while on Exercise 5 it is one of the most masculine we have encountered among women.

X-4

X-4 is an artist, aged 27. She was the victim of a homicidal attack by a female "lover" who had learned of her marriage to a man. X-4 had played the passive role in this homosexual attachment, which was of long standing.

Exercise	1	2	3	4	5	6	7	Total
M-F score:	−20	−1	−25	+17	−36	−11	+1	−75

This score is if anything more feminine than that of the generality of women of the subject's intellectual and educational class; possibly not unusual for the passive member of female homosexual partnerships. The subject had an earlier marriage which lasted four years. Her self-ratings on interests were normally feminine. Her homosexual mate who assaulted her could not, unfortunately, be persuaded to take the test.

X-5 and X-6

X-5 and X-6 are members of a homosexual pair. Both are college graduates, teachers, and in their thirties. X-5 the active,

X-6 the passive member of the union.   The score of X-6 is near
the median for college women; that of X-5 is near the 75th
percentile for college men.

Exercise	1	2	3	4	5	6	7	Total
X-5	+ 2	−1	+ 5	+36	+31	+6	+2	+81
X-6	−31	−2	−11	+22	−40	−3	−2	−67

X-5 is tall and slender with boyish build.   Her clothes are
rather severe and lack the feminine touch.   She is quiet and
efficient and is well liked by her acquaintances, especially by
men, who admire her for her intelligence and dependability.
She has marked mechanical interests.   Has had no affairs with
men.

X-6 is small and of feminine build.   Her father was brutal, and
she left home at a tender age.   After graduation from college she
married an effeminate man who left her because he disliked
sexual intercourse.   The subject has since lived with X-5, who
looks out for her in the manner of a devoted husband.   Outside
her work, which she does expertly, she exemplifies the helpless
type of femininity.   There is evidence that but for her
unfortunate marriage she would have been entirely heterosexual.

Our data on homosexual women are too limited to warrant
generalizations, but we are inclined to think that the M-F
scores of these two women are probably fairly typical of the
active and passive types.   Thus far we have found no active
homosexual female with a normally feminine score, and no
passive with a score that was highly masculine.[1]

X-7 and X-8

X-7 is a Canadian teacher, 34 years old.   She is described by a
psychologist acquaintance as "a sublimated homosexual given
to intense heroine worship, and the passive rather than the
active member of these attachments."

Exercise	1	2	3	4	5	6	7	Total
M-F score:	−15	−1	−16	+10	−28	−16	−1	−67

[1] See appendix for data on other homosexual women.

X-8 is a teacher of physical training who has greatly annoyed some of her friends by her homosexual advances, which included impassioned love letters and attempted physical caresses.

Exercise	1	2	3	4	5	6	7	Total
M-F score:	−20	0	−4	+7	+90	+4	+1	+78

These two cases present an interesting contrast, one of them scoring on the M-F test near the average of women and the other near the average of men. It can hardly be accidental that their homosexual tendencies are in opposite directions. The score of X-8 on Exercise 5 is above the 95th percentile for men.

X-9

X-9 is a high-school girl of 17. She was given the M-F test as a result of the high-school principal's suspicion that she was a homosexual. She had developed very intense "crushes" on other girls and had carried her attentions to the point of making them decidedly objectionable.

Exercise	1	2	3	4	5	6	7	Total
M-F score:	−18	0	−11	−12	+16	+10	−1	−17

According to the test, only 1 high-school girl in 20 is as masculine as X-9. She is much interested in travel, outdoor sports, science, and pets, and has little or no interest in religion, music, or domestic arts. These interests, except for the positive interest in pets, are typical of the masculine type of girl.

X-10

X-10 is a psychologist in her late twenties.

Exercise	1	2	3	4	5	6	7	Total
M-F score:	−13	−3	−5	+46	−38	+2	−1	−12

This score is near the 92d percentile of college women for masculinity; about 1 college woman in 12 is as masculine. The score on Exercise 4 (emotional and ethical attitudes) is especially masculine, which seems not uncommon among women psychologists. The subject is married and well adjusted.

X-11 and X-12

X-11 is a male, 24 years old, who was arrested for attempted rape on a girl of 5 years. His M-F score of $+116$ is at the 75th percentile for high-school males.

X-12, female, was tested in a university hospital because of suspected nymphomania. The suspicion was based on numerous improper advances to internes and medical students, with extreme disregard for the presence of observers. Her highly feminine M-F score of -123 (25th percentile for masculinity) is only partly accounted for by her low mental age of 13 years.

Nothing is known as to whether highly masculine and highly feminine scores are, respectively, characteristic of males and females given to unrestrained sexuality.

X-13

X-13, a boy, was 13 years old when brought to the university for examination because a school psychologist had pronounced him an invert.

Exercise	1	2	3	4	5	6	7	Total
M-F score:	$+6$	0	-9	-11	$+22$	-15	-1	-8

The mother of X-13, a teacher in an extremely isolated rural district of California, furnished the following history. She was 40 and the father was 46 when the child was born. Subject has two sisters, aged 22 and 19, and a brother of 15. The brothers have nothing in common. Between the age of 1 and 2 years X-13 did not seem to be developing properly and was given thyroid extract. Improved. Entered school at 6; had "hysterics" the first day. Has never become socialized as far as boys are concerned, but was popular with girls to the age of 7. At recess he always stayed inside unless forced to go out.

The subject was only 7 when he came to his mother sobbing: "Mother, I'm different, I'm different." She tried to assure him he was not. Soon afterward he began to play truant from school and was then sent to a private tutor, a woman. He went to her one day wearing his sister's high-heeled white slippers. Later attended public school but played truant again and was whipped by the principal. Next attended for one year a remote rural school of six pupils taught by the mother. There was no serious problem that year. At 12 he attended school in a large city. The children called him "sissy" and "old woman." The principal tried to get him to fight, but could not. At this time X-13 "behaved like a hunted creature." The truant officer finally decided there was something wrong with the boy and permitted his mother to keep him at home. On a camping trip (age 12) he was with some boys who planned to go swimming: "Mother, I just could not undress before them, and they did not like it." Once more attended an isolated rural school taught by his mother. The other two boys in the school will play with him only when the mother supervises them and they can't avoid it. Recurrence of truancy.

The mother is desperate and feels entirely helpless. She recently took the boy to a psychiatrist who is said to be giving him a hormone extract. The mother thinks effort should be made to "persuade the Rockefeller Foundation to establish a home for the treatment of born inverts."

One cannot say that this boy is not a "born invert." Certainly invert tendencies appeared very early and have persisted in their typical course in spite of all efforts of the mother, school principal, truant officer, and psychiatrist to stem the tide. But there are several environmental factors that cannot be dismissed: the subject is the youngest child in the family and was born when his mother was approaching the menopause; the father is said to be an extreme introvert and not affectionate with his children; the mother is too affectionate and very emotional; much of the subject's life has been spent in isolated places where there were no boys except his older brother.

X-14

X-14 is a male high-school teacher, very old-womanish and censorious.

Exercise	1	2	3	4	5	6	7	Total
M-F score:	−4	+1	−2	−32	−42	−1	−3	−83

Only one third of college women test as feminine as this subject. His score is 3 S.D. below the mean of male teachers.

X-14 was one of five children, the youngest except for one sister. He had two years in college before he began to teach. He is married. In Exercise 4 he checks "very much" for 14 of 17 anger items and for 12 of 18 disgust items. In the ethical attitude section he rates every act in the list as either "extremely wicked" or "decidedly bad." Among those which come in for the most extreme censure are swearing, gambling, and talking back to the teacher! In Exercise 5 he expresses dislike for all the occupations listed except those of interior decorator, jeweler, missionary, and teacher. He claims much interest in religion, social life, and domestic arts, little or none in mechanics, science, music, art, politics, or pets. His special hobby is philanthropy.

X-15

This is a 26-year-old druggist and chemist who stands in striking contrast to X-14.

Exercise	1	2	3	4	5	6	7	Total
M-F score:	+16	−3	+6	+60	+116	−1	−1	+193

The score is more than 2.5 S.D. above the mean of males between 20 and 30. The scores on Exercises 4 and 5 are extraordinarily masculine.

X-15 was an only child. He is a college graduate and unmarried. His hobbies are swimming and shooting. He professes much interest in travel, sports, and science, average interest in mechanics, social life, literature, politics, domestic arts, and pets, and little or none in religion, music, and art.

X-16

Although engineers are our most masculine-scoring group, there are exceptions to the rule. The most feminine score we have encountered in this occupation was earned by X-16.

Exercise	1	2	3	4	5	6	7	Total
M-F score:	−6	+1	+1	+35	−40	−12	−1	−22

This score is nearly 100 points less masculine than the mean of graduate engineers and is near the mean of college women athletes and women doctors. However, the score on Exercise 4 is more masculine than that of the average man.

X-16 was an only child. He began to earn his own living at the age of 15 and put himself through school. He was tested at 29, after returning to the university for graduate work in engineering. He had previously worked as a carpenter, boiler maker, and lawyer. He professes much interest in travel, sports, religion, mechanics, literature, music, science, politics, and pets—an unusual combination of masculine and feminine tendencies.

It is especially interesting that a follow-up of this case five years after he took the test disclosed that he never completed his engineering course. He attended intermittently for three years and left without his degree to work as a civil engineer. He is now married.

X-17

X-17 is a radio engineer, aged 28, who has the most masculine score of the engineers we have tested.

Exercise	1	2	3	4	5	6	7	Total
M-F score:	0	+2	+1	+56	+126	+7	−1	+191

This score is near the 100th percentile of college males for masculinity. The score on Exercise 5 is extraordinarily masculine, and that of Exercise 4 decidedly so.

X-17 rates himself as having much interest in mechanics and science, more than average interest in outdoor sports, and little or no interest in religion, literature, music, art, and politics. We have known this subject since his early youth. He has always been socially diffident and interested only in the most masculine of pursuits. He is married.

X-18 and X-19

X-18 and X-19 are engineers whose M-F scores are almost identical, but who differ greatly in interests.

Exercise	1	2	3	4	5	6	7	Total
X-18	+6	+1	+ 4	+54	+68	+ 2	−3	+132
X-19	−3	0	+10	+59	+76	−11	−1	+130

Although there is a markedly negative correlation between M-F score and interest in religion (approximately −.40), X-18 engages in Sunday School work as his chief hobby. He rates himself as equally interested in religion and science. He has little or no interest in music, art, or pets. The score on Exercise 7 suggests a somewhat introverted personality.

X-19 represents an extreme case of the one-track mind which is extremely inventive and gifted in things mechanical. He was an only child whose hobby through childhood was photography. He was 25 years old when he took the test. He owns and runs a small plant in which he designs and manufactures special kinds of apparatus and appliances. He is extremely nonsocial. At one period he suffered a nervous breakdown and spent several months in a mental hospital.

The only one of the 12 subjects in which he professes much interest is science. He has little or no interest in sports, social life, politics, or domestic arts, and less than average interest in the other activities. He illustrates the predominantly masculine trait of having one great interest in life to the exclusion of all others.

X-20 and X-21

X-20 and X-21 are two feminine-scoring ministers.

Exercise	1	2	3	4	5	6	7	Total
X-20	−5	−3	+ 5	−20	−62	−2	−3	−90
X-21	−7	0	+11	−35	−18	+5	−3	−47

X-20 is 47 years old. He was the oldest of six children, five boys and one girl. He has been married 20 years and has three children. He has much interest in travel, religion, and social life, little or none in sports, mechanics, or pets. His score is more feminine than the mean of adult women and about 2 S.D. below the mean of Protestant ministers. There is no evidence that his feminine attitudes have made his marital adjustments difficult.

X-21 is also a Protestant minister, aged 65. Before entering the ministry he was in turn a clerk, factory worker, mechanic, and assistant foreman. He was the oldest of four children and has always been rather frail. He has been married 28 years and has one daughter. His hobby is men's choral work. The score is nearly one S.D. more feminine than the mean of Protestant ministers and approximates that of *Who's who* women.

X-22 and X-23

X-22 and X-23 are very feminine-scoring stenographers, aged 22 and 26.

Exercise	1	2	3	4	5	6	7	Total
X-22	−18	−3	−30	−60	−64	− 9	−4	−188
X-23	− 5	−2	−36	−41	−48	−24	−1	−157

X-22 had two younger brothers and no sister. Her father died when she was still a child, and the children were reared by their mother. The subject had one year in college before going to work. She has much interest in travel, religion, music, and domestic arts, little or none in mechanics, art, or science. Her score is about 2.5 S.D. more feminine than the mean of female officer workers.

X-23 was the only girl in a family of five children, her brothers all being older than herself. Her highly feminine attitudes may be in part the result of what we have called the "contrast effect"; that is, the tendency of parents and brothers to exert a strongly feminizing influence upon the family's one girl, especially when she is the youngest child.

X-24

X-24 seems to be an extreme example of the unemotional, apparently "hard-boiled," type of masculine woman. She is 26 years old and married.

Exercise	1	2	3	4	5	6	7	Total
M-F score:	−2	0	−5	+60	+34	−4	−1	+82

This score is about 4 S.D. above the mean of adult women. The responses in Exercise 4 were especially masculine. Only 4 of the 17 anger items are checked "very much," and not one of the 20 fear items. Only tobacco chewing in the disgust list is checked for "very much," and no other for "much." Not one of the pity items is checked for "very much" and only four for "much." The subject does not consider any of the acts in the censure list as "extremely wicked."

X-24 has one sib, a younger brother. She finished high school, then attended business college and worked as a stenographer until she was married at 20. Her hobby is playing baseball.

X-25 and X-26

These subjects are both women in their thirties whose M-F scores are 218 points apart.

Exercise	1	2	3	4	5	6	7	Total
X-25	− 9	−1	− 3	+24	+14	− 5	−4	+ 16
X-26	−28	−3	−29	−35	−92	−14	−2	−203

X-25, the more masculine subject, was the oldest of three girls who were reared by their father. She graduated from high school, married when she was 22, and has three children. Her hobby is playing baseball. She has much interest in sports, social life, science, and politics, average interest in travel, mechanics, literature, music, art, domestic arts, and pets, and none in religion.

X-26 scores about 3 S.D. below the mean of her decade group. She was the second of seven children, six girls and a boy, the latter younger than herself. She graduated from high school and worked as a stenographer until she was married at the age of 19. She has since taken a course in dressmaking. Her hobby is choir singing. She professes much interest in religion and music, none in mechanics, and average in the other nine fields.

X-27

This case is an example of the ultrafeminine, old-fashioned spinster in her fifties.

Exercise	1	2	3	4	5	6	7	Total
M-F score:	−7	−2	−22	−69	−26	−21	−4	−151

X-27 was the eldest of seven children. She attended business college after graduating from high school, but has never worked outside the home. She describes herself as a "home body."

She has much interest in religion, little or none in sports, science, mechanics, politics, art, or pets.   In exercise 4 she checked "very much" for 14 of the 17 anger items, for 17 of the 20 fear items, and for 13 of the 15 pity items.   In the censure test she checked 19 of the 28 listed acts as "extremely wicked."

X-28 and X-29

These are female octogenarians, differing in M-F score by about 2.5 S.D.   Both are widows.

Exercise	1	2	3	4	5	6	7	Total
X-28	−29	0	−12	+2	−84	−11	−1	−135
X-29	−19	0	− 9	+7	−22	− 5	+2	− 46

X-28, the more feminine, was the sixth of thirteen children. Her father was a high-school teacher who taught his children at home.   Without other formal education the subject taught school, became a social worker, and edited a small paper.   She is the mother of seven children.   Her hobby is religious work and she is also much interested in literature.

X-29, the more masculine, was one of seven children, including three brothers older and three sisters younger than herself.   She attended college two years, taught school, and later managed a farm.   She is the mother of four children and now widowed after 50 years of married life.   Her hobby is raising horses and dogs.   She professes much interest in travel, literature, music, science, politics, and pets, and average interest in all the other fields listed.   In breadth of interests she presents a striking contrast to X-28, a fact which is doubtless connected with the difference in M-F score.

X-30

X-30 is an unmarried man, 27 years old.   He was the youngest of three children and rates his health as below average.

Exercise	1	2	3	4	5	6	7	Total
M-F score:	−9	−2	+7	+15	−22	−7	−2	−20

Although the M-F score of this subject is near the mean of the group of passive male homosexuals, his "invert" score (−184) is well within the normal range. Since completing high school he has worked as a delivery boy, filing clerk, and bookkeeper. His favorite pastimes are dancing and movies. He has much interest in social life, music, art, and pets, little or none in mechanics, science, politics, domestic arts, or religion.

X-31 and X-32

These two subjects, whose scores are separated by 134 points, illustrate the masculine and feminine extremes for elderly males.

Exercise	1	2	3	4	5	6	7	Total
X-31	−16	+1	+ 1	+15	−56	− 7	0	−62
X-32	−10	−1	+11	+59	+30	−14	−3	+72

X-31 is a manufacturer, aged 64. He was the youngest of four boys and went to school only two years. He was married at 30 and has one daughter. His hobbies are music, geology, philosophy, and collecting stamps and wild flowers. He has much interest in travel, music, science, and politics, little or none in sports, social life, or domestic arts.

X-32 is 71 years old. He was one of six children, five boys and a girl, who were reared by their mother. He attended a country school, and later became a carpenter. He was married at 26 and has ten children. His hobby is horseback riding. He has much interest in travel, sports, and mechanics, little or none in music, art, science, or domestic arts.

X-33

X-33 was an upperclassman in a university when he came to the senior author for counsel regarding his homosexuality. Age 23. Intellectually gifted and the author of several published poems of genuine merit. He was given Form A of the M-F test, the Bernreuter personality inventory, and the Strong test of vocational interests.

Exercise	1	2	3	4	5	6	7	Total
Form A	−18	−1	−11	+62	−60	−7	+1	−34

Application of the "I" key to Form A yielded an "invert" score of +689, which is near the median found for 77 passive male homosexuals.

The Bernreuter scores were as follows: "neurotic tendency" and "introversion" both at about the 90th percentile for college men; "self-sufficiency," 39th percentile; "dominance," 17th percentile.

On the vocational-interest test "A" ratings were secured for the occupations of artist, journalist, and advertiser; "B+" for lawyer, and "B" for doctor, psychologist, architect, real-estate salesman, and mathematician. All other ratings were "C."

The subject reports "much" interest in literature, music, art, travel, and pets; "little or none" in outdoor sports, religion, mechanics, science, politics, and domestic arts. He has at various times worked as a clerk, counter-man, actor, tutor, and chauffeur.

X-33 came chiefly for advice as to whether he should leave college. He was in a wrought-up and nervous condition which he attributed to the fear of detection and to the emotional strain from living in a dormitory with attractive males to whom he dared make no advances. He has a rather slight build and an attractive personality. Voice not unusual, highly sophisticated, rather cynical, no ability at all in sports. As a child was plump, liked to keep his hair long, and tried to attract attention to his looks.

He has two brothers, aged 34 and 28, and a sister aged 36. He is therefore the youngest of the children by five years. The father was 34 and the mother 29 when he was born. The father is a contractor, described as stern, distant, and cold. As a child X-33 feared him and still harbors bitterness toward him; says he is the Babbitt type, coarse, untruthful, and despicable. He deserted the mother for another woman when the subject was 9, but the son's aversion to him goes back at least to the age of 5.

The subject's description of his mother disclosed nothing out of the ordinary as to her personality. She is said to have displayed only an average amount of affection toward her son; there was no unusual fondling; subject not bathed or dressed by mother beyond the age of 6. The mother had been told she could have no more children and on finding she was pregnant wanted the child to be a girl.

X-33 says that his brothers are more talented than he and more favored by the parents.   Much friction has existed between the subject and his brothers.

X-33 was treated by his parents rather like a girl, was considered a sissy by children, preferred to be with girls, played with dolls till about 5 years old, and had no boys' playthings.   His sister was sweet and gentle and let him play with her beads and clothes.   He dressed up often in her clothes till age 12 or 13, and at times till 15 or 16.

He is rather social and prefers friends who are older and have cultured, broad interests.   He never joined the Boy Scouts or any kind of lodge.   His ideal character is Leonardo da Vinci.   His first sex information was from books at age 12.   As an adolescent he was bored by women but interested in men.   Was taught to masturbate at 12 or 13 and continued the practice, probably four times weekly, for years.   His first homosexual experience occurred at the age of 15.   A man accosted him in the library, took him out riding, and persuaded him to play the passive role in fellatio.   The experience was enjoyed by the subject and was frequently repeated.   His first experience in pederasty was at the age of 20.   He prefers fellatio or intercrural connection.

Recently X-33 forced himself to carry through intercourse with a girl.   He had tried before but could not get an erection.   With difficulty he succeeded this time and had an orgasm, but was left with a feeling of disgust.   At present he practices fellatio "quite frequently."   He has no feeling of guilt and does not want to be made "normal."   On the other hand, he looks upon heterosexuality as unaesthetic and unclean.   He wants to leave college and return to the stage "where I can find companionship with others of my kind without risking disgrace."

Significant factors: youngest child; stern, cold father; indulgent older sister; desertion of mother by the father; lack of stimulus to play with children; transvestism not discouraged; early seduction.   The case is typical of a large number of male inverts.

We come next to 12 cases of "gifted children" (6 girls and 6 boys) whose M-F scores deviate excessively from their sex norms. All of them are members of the California group of 1,000 superior children who have been followed by the senior author since 1922. They will be designated as G-1, G-2, etc.

G-1

This is a 13-year-old girl whose masculine score is near the 100th percentile for her age. Her IQ at 7 years was 160.

Exercise	1	2	3	4	5	6	7	Total
M-F score:	−22	−1	+8	+18	+62	−2	+2	+65

G-1 is the older of two daughters of superior parents. The father is a structural engineer. Engineering and mechanical pursuits have been the most common occupations among the male relatives on both sides of the family.

G-1 is outstanding because of her mechanical ingenuity and her all-round masculine interests. Her skill with tools was first noted when she was only 3½ years old. At the age of 4½ she constructed an airplane that was placed on exhibit in Berkeley, California. By the age of 7 she was making sailboats, wagons, kites, "scooters," and bows and arrows. At this age she could understand fairly complicated machinery and was able to construct devices from printed plans or diagrams. At 13 her interest in tools had not diminished and she was considering either engineering or aviation as a career.

At 7 G-1 was making collections of sea shells and birds' nests. By 13 she had collected 900 varieties of stamps. Throughout childhood she preferred boys as playmates and read boys' books almost exclusively. At 13, for example, she was reading adventure stories, West Point series, Tom Swift series, *Trade Wind*, *We*, Boy Scout books, *Boys' Life Magazine*, etc. At this time her mother writes: "Her playmates look for her to start something, and the play she starts usually has to do with the army or navy. She wants to see every movie about West Point or Annapolis and in these days of 'peace talk' her interest in war is somewhat distressing, especially in a girl."

All her school work is excellent, but she prefers science, physical education, and orchestra to other subjects. She plays in the school band, is on several athletic teams, and is an honor student. The interest she has developed in music is rather exceptional in one testing so masculine.

Physically, G-1 is rather small for her age. She is somewhat square featured and her legs show the signs of early rickets. Her movements are noticeably short and jerky and her voice is somewhat squawky and gutteral like that of an adolescent boy.

G-2

This is a 17-year-old college girl whose IQ at the age of 11 was 140.

Exercise	1	2	3	4	5	6	7	Total
M-F score:	−25	+1	+3	+28	+60	+5	−3	+69

G-2 is an only child, the daughter of middle-aged parents who have thought more of the pleasure she could give them than of what they could do for her. Her father is a teacher. Although chiefly of French, German, and English descent, the subject is a direct descendant in the sixth generation of the famous Indian chieftain, King Philip.

She has always disliked housework and is very fond of outdoor games, sports, swimming, and horseback riding. She is a member of several athletic teams. She has shown some mechanical interests but has not worked much with tools. By the age of 13 she had developed considerable interest in music, and on entering college selected art as her major subject. However, she has no great interest in any of her studies, preferring social excitement, dancing, and dates with boys. She shows the effects of her home spoiling. Her class marks, which were very superior throughout high school, have become mediocre.

G-2 is feminine looking and pretty, the kind who would hardly be expected to make a masculine score. She reached puberty at the age of 12½.

There are two facts of special interest regarding G-2. (1) Her father is extremely attached to her and insists on "dating" her to movies and other affairs much as if he were a suitor. (2) Her mother confesses her hatred of men in general; says she "never knew one who was really decent."

A large part of the masculine score in Exercise 4 is due to her responses to the censure items; only one of the acts listed (excessive drinking) is rated as "extremely wicked" and only six as "decidedly bad." In Exercise 5 she expresses liking only for the occupations of architect, artist, building contractor, detective, draftsman, and forest ranger.

G-3

G-3 is a girl of 15 whose IQ at 9 years was 144.

Exercise	1	2	3	4	5	6	7	Total
M-F score:	−1	−2	−8	+20	+40	+8	+2	+59

She is the youngest of three children, two girls and a boy. Her father, of Spanish descent, is a truck driver and was formerly a rancher. The mother taught school before her marriage.

G-3 is exceptionally attractive and is much sought after by her girl friends. She is something of a leader, although she prefers to devote most of her spare time to reading and drawing. She reads chiefly adventure books, detective stories, essays, and books of travel. She is planning to become a commercial artist.

She rather enjoys working with tools and dislikes dances, parties, and housework. She likes active sports moderately well, but is not an enthusiastic athlete. She sews well enough to make her own clothes, but does it only from necessity. Aside from reading and drawing, she is rather indifferent to all activities, masculine as well as feminine. Although she scores almost as masculine as G-1 and G-2, her behavior seems to be appreciably less masculine.

The next three cases are gifted girls who test extremely feminine. The reader will note that in a number of respects they stand in marked contrast to the three cases just described.

G-4

Exercise	1	2	3	4	5	6	7	Total
M-F score:	−32	−2	−4	−55	−56	−8	−5	−162

G-4 was 14 years old when given the M-F test. Her IQ at 9 years was 147. Her Stanford Achievement Test score at the latter age was exceptional in the fact that it showed a mastery of reading equal to the ninth-grade level, three full grades above her score in any other school subject.

She is the eighth of nine children, six of whom are girls. Her father is a revivalist and missionary of Scotch and English descent. The mother's family seems to be of good stock but to have had little education. When G-4 was born her father was 53 and her mother 41 and it is possible that her oldish parents may have had a feminizing effect upon her.

G-4 is greatly interested in English and dramatics and plans to become a teacher of English. Most of her leisure is spent writing poetry or short stories and in reading. She has made collections of poems and short stories. Her reading preferences are almost entirely feminine. She has shown little interest in active games and none in working with tools. She is deeply religious. Her only very low marks in high school were in business methods, practical arts, bookkeeping, and stenography. Her health has always been fairly good, but she is described by her teacher as somewhat nervous, fidgety, and self-conscious.

It is interesting that this ultrafeminine girl is a direct descendant of David Crockett.

G-5

Exercise	1	2	3	4	5	6	7	Total
M-F score:	−12	−3	−18	−14	−102	0	−7	−156

G-5 is 17 years old. Her IQ at the age of 11 was 147, at which time she made a markedly feminine score on the Plays, Games, and Amusements Test. At 17 she is a university freshman, majoring in French, but planning to be a kindergarten teacher. Her scores on the Iowa High School Content Examination are at the 95th percentile except in the science and mathematics section, where she stood at the 75th percentile.

Her father is a merchant and manufacturer, her mother a teacher. Among her ancestors are many teachers, ministers, and inventors.

G-5 is described by her teachers as modest, unassuming, sensitive, sympathetic, and lovable. She early learned to sew, knit, and crochet, and has never shown any interest in sports or the use of tools. A record of her reading over a two-months period when she was 11 years old contains only titles of distinctively feminine books.

G-6

Exercise	1	2	3	4	5	6	7	Total
M-F score:	−21	−1	−8	−6	−114	0	−4	−154

G-6 made the above score at the age of 15. Her IQ at age 9 was 152. Both parents are of Swedish descent. The father runs a small lunch-box factory and does church work as a hobby. The mother, who also works in the factory, is interested in music and social work. The relatives are mostly farmers of the religious, conservative type.

G-6 is the oldest of three children, all girls. She is a striking blonde, good looking and of attractive personality, though slightly overweight. She displayed musical talent at 4, began music lessons at 7, and has learned to play the piano well. She prefers to spend her leisure time reading, sewing, playing the piano, and doing housework. Typical of her reading at 15 are *Pride and Prejudice, Jane Eyre, Ramona, Atlantic Monthly,* and *Pictorial Review*. She is much interested in dancing and dramatics, and has had leading parts in several school plays. Since she was in the middle grammar grades she has been the recipient of many honors and offices. She swims well and plays volleyball and basketball, but these have never ranked among her strongest interests.

At 9 her Stanford Achievement Test score rated her especially high in reading ability and knowledge of literature, and rather low in history and civics. At 15 she stood at the 85th percentile of high-school seniors in total score, but only at the 65th percentile in mathematics and at the 75th in science.

The characterizations of G-6 by her teachers read like the traditional descriptions of the old-fashioned, feminine temperament: "One of the dearest and most dependable children I have ever known"—"Always loyal and eager to help"—"When a task is given her we know it will be done"—"No paint, no slang, no anything to suggest the flapper"—"Studious, friendly, amiable"—"Is terribly upset if she gets a mark below A."

G-6 expects to be a teacher; "I have always wanted to be ever since I could remember."

We next present brief descriptions of three very masculine and three very feminine gifted boys.

G-7

Exercise	1	2	3	4	5	6	7	Total
M-F score:	0	+1	+10	+60	+108	+18	0	+197

This is the most masculine score in our group of gifted boys. G-7 was 17 when he took the test. At 11 he made an IQ of 150 on the Stanford-Binet and a masculine score on Plays, Games, and Amusements Test.

He is the only child of elderly parents; the father was 64, the mother 38, when he was born. The father is a Civil War veteran, a retired lumber merchant, and a former mechanic. Both parents have devoted much time to him, his mother in fussing over him, his father in working with him in the shop.

At the age of 3, G-7 began to build things with his blocks; as soon as he could use a knife, to make boats, planes, swords, etc., and later to draw elaborate plans of his constructions. At 10 he built a steam engine and by 11 had attracted considerable attention by his extraordinary fondness for mechanics. He was rather a solitary child, preferring to work with tools in his shop to playing neighborhood games. The other boys considered him queer because he played so little.

As a child his reading was all adventure stories, the Tom Swift series, the Crusades, stories of mutineers, vikings, aviation, etc. At 17 he reads scientific magazines and books on modern art. His vision is rather defective, $1\%5$ in one eye and $1\%0$ in the other.

G-7 has no desire to be popular with his schoolmates, but his workshop is the delight of the neighborhood boys. He has constructed and reconstructed motorcycles, automobiles, radios, speedboats, and steam engines.

Trait ratings by his parents and teacher place him more than 1 S.D. below the mean of gifted boys in health, musical appreciation, and fondness for large groups, and well above the average in mechanical ingenuity.

His school work in the grades and in high school was excellent. The Iowa High School Content Examination places him at age 17 above the 95th percentile in each of the four parts—English, mathematics, science, and history—and at the 99th percentile for total score.

The case is particularly interesting in that the boy's ambition was to become a construction engineer, but his parents' insistence upon making him an artist led him to elect art as his college major. As his work was only mediocre, and he disliked the university, he left at the end of one year and has not returned. It is hardly surprising that the most masculine-testing of the Stanford gifted boys should have failed to fit into the most feminine of the vocations. This case is further interesting in the fact that the parental situation was the kind that would ordinarily have an effeminizing influence.

G-8

Exercise	1	2	3	4	5	6	7	Total
M-F score:	+3	+1	+11	+20	+120	+9	+1	+165

This is a 15-year-old boy whose IQ at 9 was 150. His excessively masculine score is largely accounted for by Exercise 5. His masculinity score on the Plays, Games and Amusements Test, at age 9, was above average but not extreme. On the Stanford Achievement Test at this age he equaled the norm for grade twelve in history, literature, and general information, but only for grades seven to eight in the other school subjects.

G-8 is the son of a window trimmer. He was an extremely nervous child, stammered, and had a facial tic. He has never been popular with his schoolmates, cares little for games, and is sometimes quarrelsome and antagonistic. He prefers to spend his time alone, reading encyclopedias, scientific pamphlets, history, and adventure stories. He early developed an interest in radio and has constructed several excellent sets. Chemistry and mathematics are his best subjects in high school, languages his poorest. However, he scores in the best 5 per cent of high school seniors in all parts of the Iowa High School Content Examination. He would like to become an army engineer.

Perhaps this boy's most outstanding trait is his solitariness and incapacity for social adjustment, which may be in large part the result of his speech defect. His difficulties in social adjustment have probably in turn accentuated his interests in mechanics. *Things*, he can understand; personalities can be so much more baffling, unpredictable, and disagreeable.

G-9

Exercise	1	2	3	4	5	6	7	Total
M-F score:	−6	+1	+11	+58	+94	+6	0	+164

G-9 is 19 years old, a postgraduate in high school. His Stanford-Binet IQ at 13 was 130, but as the test lacks "top" at this level his true IQ was probably near 140. At 18 he scored between the 97th and 99th percentile of high-school seniors on all four parts of the Iowa High School Content Examination.

G-9 is the second of three children, the oldest a boy, the youngest a girl. His parents, both deceased, were divorced when he was young and he lived with his mother until her death, when he was 13. The father was a civil engineer who "invented" during his spare time. The mother was a teacher before marriage. Males on the paternal side of the family have been chiefly engineers and architects, on the maternal side chiefly lawyers and businessmen. The son exhibited unusual manual skill and mechanical ingenuity at an early age. His ability to mend broken apparatus and to invent new contrivances was always far beyond his years.

This subject, like the preceding one, is strongly inclined to solitude but without marked maladjustment. He is shy, seldom enters into school activities, and has made few friends. He likes to study atlases and his reading includes encyclopedias, adventure stories, and the dictionary, which he is said to have read clear through. His high-school work has been mostly indifferent. He repeated two history courses, chemistry, and advanced algebra, but made A's in solid geometry, mechanical drawing, and one course in English. He expects to be an aeronautical engineer.

The next three subjects are at the opposite extreme in M-F rating from the three just described. Their scores are in the neighborhood of 2 S.D. below the high-school norms and not far from the mean of the passive male homosexual group. On the "invert" scale, however, they all score within the normal range.

G-10

Exercise	1	2	3	4	5	6	7	Total
M-F score:	−16	+ 1	+ 5	− 12	−14	+ 8	0	− 28
"I" score:	−87	−34	+89	−153	−54	−60	−136	−435

G-10 is a 15-year-old boy whose IQ at age 9 was 143. He is of Russian-Jewish descent. His father is a businessman whose hobby is dramatics. The mother was a teacher and is interested in painting. His one sibling is a sister three years his junior.

G-10 has always had frail health and much of the time it has been necessary to limit his school attendance to a half-day schedule and to keep him in bed the rest of the day. Even with this handicap he was a high-school senior when tested. His acceleration of three years dates back to the primary grade, which means that it has been impossible for him to compete in plays and games on equal terms with his classmates, especially as he is small for his age. His natural interest in books has doubtless been intensified by these circumstances. Puberty was late, if we may judge by the fact that his voice did not change until he was 16 years old.

When G-10 was 9 and in the sixth grade his Stanford Achievement Test score equaled the norm for the twelfth grade in literary information, the eleventh grade in history, civics, and general information, but only the eighth grade in science. At 15 he scored on the Iowa High School Content Examination at the 95th percentile of high-school seniors in English, mathematics, and history, but only at the 75th percentile in science. He has always been rated low in mechanical ingenuity. His teachers describe him as exceptionally industrious, faithful, and ambitious. Socially he is well adjusted; was president of his class in the eighth grade, and in high school was captain of the debating team and publicity editor of the high-school paper. Five years after taking the M-F test he won highest honors in the graduate school of law of a leading university.

G-11

Exercise	1	2	3	4	5	6	7	Total
M-F score:	−12	− 1	+ 7	+35	−46	+ 2	− 2	− 17
"I" score:	−70	−19	+138	−21	+29	−75	−83	−101

G-11 is a 17-year-old boy whose IQ at age 10 was 160. He is the oldest of three children. The father is a teacher and both parents are college trained. They live on a farm.

G-11 made his highest achievement test scores in history, literature, and general information; his lowest in arithmetic, spelling, and mathematics. In no subject, however, was he below the highest quartile. Special talent in music was evidenced at the age of 4; he plays the piano well and is a member of the high-school orchestra. Both his mother and his teachers rated him very low in mechanical skill. He is characterized by teachers and field psychologists in such terms as "tractable," "quiet," "unassuming," "retiring," and "inclined to procrastinate." Although mathematics has not been his strongest subject, he plans to become a statistician. He devotes much of his leisure to reading philosophical works and composing music. At age 6 his masculinity score on the Plays, Games, and Amusements Test was below average. Like G-10, he was about two years retarded in reaching puberty.

G-12

Exercise	1	2	3	4	5	6	7	Total
M-F score:	−16	0	0	+ 13	+ 2	− 7	− 4	− 12
"I" score:	−72	−17	+31	−135	−108	−90	−91	−482

G-12 was tested at the age of 16. His IQ at age 10 was 148. The "I" score indicates normality. He has a brother and a sister, both younger. The father is a teacher. Both parents are college graduates and are interested in church work. Several ancestors on both sides have been ministers or church workers.

G-12 has shown more than average interest in music since early childhood, but has not had musical instruction. For years he preferred fairy stories to any other kind of reading, but now enjoys books of travel and adventure. He is well adjusted socially and has been elected to numerous class offices. He takes pride in being popular. When he was just a boy his parents often left him in charge of the younger children and taught him to cook. He is said to be unusually dependable. He became interested in girls at the age of 14. Is noticeably small for his age and very fastidious about his clothes.

G-12 intends to be a physician and scored A for that vocation on the Strong Vocational Interest Test. At the age of 16 his scores on the Iowa High School Content Examination were in English and history near the average of high-school seniors, but at the 85th percentile in science and mathematics. His interest in the last-named subjects appears to be greater than is common with boys who score so feminine on the M-F test.

Although the fragmentary case notes presented in this chapter do not afford a safe basis for generalizations, they illustrate concretely a number of relationships statistically established in earlier chapters and suggest others which call for further investigation. For example, it is no accident that masculine-testing subjects of either sex are much more likely than subjects at the feminine extreme to be interested in sports, science, and mechanics, or that the more feminine subjects are more likely to be interested in religion, music, art, and domestic arts. It appears, indeed, that these positive and negative interests are also likely to characterize the subject's near relatives. The highly masculine female seems especially likely to have a father who is an engineer or has otherwise displayed an interest in mechanics. The daughters, perhaps also the sons, of ministers or other religious workers seem more often than others to score highly feminine. A few cases suggest that frail health or low energy level may operate as an effeminizing influence in males. Other cases among those reviewed emphasize the need of investigation along a number of lines: the influence of early and late puberty on M-F status, the personality differences between active and passive female homosexuals, the M-F status of persons given to unrestrained sexuality (rapists and nymphomaniacs), the vocational success of feminine-scoring engineers and of masculine-scoring ministers or artists, et cetera.

CHAPTER XVI

SEX TEMPERAMENTS AS REVEALED BY THE M-F TEST[1]

The greater part of our treatment of the M-F data so far has dealt with inter- and intra-sex differences in total score of the M-F test or in scores of the separate exercises. In other words, our approach has been primarily quantitative and statistical. Men and women have been compared with respect to mean score on the test as a whole, and subgroups within a given sex have been compared with each other in the same manner. It is interesting and important to know that mean M-F scores of the men and women of our adult population differ by about 122 score points, or two and a half times the S.D. of either distribution; that these distributions overlap to the extent of about 10 per cent; that something like ten out of a thousand of each sex reach or exceed the mean of the other sex; that the M-F score is related in complex ways to age, education, intelligence, occupational classification, expressed interests, and the domestic milieu; that the scores have yielded such and such correlations with scores on a variety of other personality tests; or that extreme scores by individual subjects are likely to connote exceptional types of social and sexual adjustment. The value of an approach which is productive of such generalizations is so obvious as to need no defense. The quantitative method has justified itself.

But the psychologically minded reader will want to know more about sex temperaments than quantitative methods of the totalitarian kind just referred to can tell him. He is unwilling to

---

[1] The material reported in this chapter was assembled by Mr. Horace G. Wyatt under the direction of the senior author and is based on the item-by-item responses of the 550 subjects used in the standardization of the two forms of the M-F test. The chapter as it appears was prepared by the latter from a 200-page summary written by Mr. Wyatt. The authors are greatly indebted to Mr. Wyatt for the psychological acumen with which he performed his task.

stop with sex differences expressed in terms of score-points; he would like to know what is behind these points that can be expressed in a psychological rather than a statistical vocabulary. We may think of this reduction of data to psychological categories as constituting the qualitative as contrasted with the quantitative approach. We regard the two methods as presenting a genuine contrast, notwithstanding the fact that qualitative methods also at times utilize quantitative concepts. In the present case, certainly, our task would be very incomplete if we confined our treatment of M-F differences to just those facts that can be expressed in terms of score points. We must reexamine our data with a view to reducing them if possible to categories that are more strictly psychological than the majority of those which we have thus far employed.

The material to be presented in this chapter seeks to elicit from the responses made by several hundred males and females in the various exercises of the M-F test any important sex differences in interest, sentiment, disposition, and temperament that a comparison of the responses of the sexes to the individual items may reveal. Of the seven exercises in the M-F test, the last four inquire directly into the emotions or sentiments awakened, or professedly awakened, by certain actual or assumed situations or objects. The first three exercises proceed indirectly, on the assumption that sex divergences in associative tendencies (Exercises 1 and 2) and in actual knowledge (Exercise 3) are likely to derive from differences in sentiment and interest.

The exercises were administered to subject groups of both sexes, representative of grade, high-school, and college students, and nonacademic adults, the first two groups predominating. As the populations tested were not quite the same throughout, they are specified with each exercise as it is considered. In the case of each exercise item tabulations were made separately for the male and female groups and the item-by-item differences between the sexes have been used as a basis for the delineation of the outstanding features of the sex temperaments.

No claim, it should be premised, is here made that the exercises or much less the items taken separately are suitable for individual diagnosis, *i.e.*, for determining with confidence from an individual's response the "maleness" or the "femaleness" of that subject's mentality. What we are concerned with are general tendencies that actually distinguish the sexes in the large, and may thus be claimed to constitute "femininity" or "masculinity" without any assumption with regard to the relative influence of genetic and environmental factors as causal agents.

EXERCISE 1: QUADRUPLE-CHOICE WORD ASSOCIATION

As the reader will recall, the subject's task in Exercise 1 is to underline that one of the four given associates following a stimulus word which seems "to go best with" the latter. Each form of the M-F test contains 60 stimulus words, making 120 in all.

In this and all the other exercises with the exception of Exercise 3, the present study of sex temperaments is based upon the weighted scores of the individual items which are given in Appendix IV. The weighted scores were used rather than unit scores in order that magnitude as well as direction of the sex differences could be taken into account.

The population groups used in the derivation of weights for Exercise 1 included roughly 125 pupils of each sex in grade seven, 100 of each sex in the junior year of high school, and 50 college students of each sex; in all about 550 subjects. These are the subjects who furnish the data for our sex comparisons on Exercise 1.

For purposes of convenience, and also because they appeared more promising of results, the responses to Exercises 3, 4, and 5 were examined before those to Exercises 1 and 2. When Exercise 1 was taken up a number of hypotheses had already been reached with regard to the nature of some of the more important psychological differences between the sexes. These hypotheses, based upon an examination of the responses of male and female groups to Exercises 3 to 5 were utilized as a basis for forecasting the sex preferences of associations in Exercise 1. It will be interesting to see how adequately the explanatory hypotheses, empirically arrived at from the responses in certain exercises, explain the sex differences in exercises of a very different type.

Predictive Analysis.—Evidence from the analysis of Exercises 3 to 5 justified the forecast that if word preferences correspond to object preferences,[1] males would be found choosing more often than females word associates symbolizing aggression, activity, adventure, extradomestic (scientific, physical, political, business, and economic) affairs, and customary male occupations; while females would be found preferring words for domestic things or happenings, articles of dress or personal adornment, words for colors, and for artistic technicalities or occupations; words indicative of active, especially maternal, sympathy, and of customary female occupations.

An attempt was therefore made to forecast for Exercise 1 which of the quadruple-choice responses would be chosen more often by males and which by females. Comparison later of these forecasts with the tabulated data disclosed the fact that correct predictions were more than twice the number chance alone would have yielded, and that a majority of the responses wrongly classified had either a zero weight or a very small weight in the opposite direction to the forecast. But as even the most carefully selected groups are never completely representative, and the examiner cannot be completely familiar with their circumstances, and as, in any case, each response is conditioned not only by its relation to the stimulus word, but also by the counterattractions of three other response words, it would be strange if he did not frequently fail in the difficult task of calculating the competing factors for the four responses. That twice the chance number of predictions of sex preferences proved correct, and that it was chiefly where sex preferences were less decided that prediction failed, is so much support for the hypotheses as to dominant sex-distinguishing traits upon which the predictions were based.

The above digression from our main task (the examination of empirical data) may or may not have been worth the time it cost. It does show that the psychologist, with definitely formu-

---

[1] This assumption may not always hold; *e.g.*, some words are more affected by one sex than by the other.

lated hypotheses as to how the sexes differ, can predict with considerable success how men and women will differ in their responses to particular test items. It should be pointed out, however, that the same thing can be done with no small degree of success by young college students who are not psychologists and whose ideas about sex differences have never been clearly formulated. We have already seen that it is possible for relatively unsophisticated subjects to fake their scores so as to make them typical of members of the opposite sex. Truly the psychologist has no monopoly of psychological insight into the characteristic differences which distinguish men and women. Let us turn, however, to an examination of the actual data.

Evidence from the Most Sex-contrasting Choices.—If and in so far as our assumed sex differences hold and govern choices in verbal associations, it is where the choices of four presented associates show most sex divergence that we might fairly expect the assumed differences in sex traits to help determine them; and where, of the four words, two appeal to contrasting sex propensities, we might expect to find between them, other things equal, the widest divergences in the weighted scores. Conversely, where the weight spans are widest, we should anticipate fewest, if any, records contradicting our expectations as to sex preferences.

Confining our scrutiny, then, to those cases, rather less than a third of the whole, in which to the same stimulus word the difference between the sex responses is of six or more units (*e.g.,* stimulus word "Pole" with response "north, -4," "telephone, $+3$," a difference of seven units) we may ask which distinctive associations are referable to our assumed sex distinctions; and whether any results contradict or significantly supplement what we might expect.

Out of the total of 120 items the 40 which exhibit these pronounced contrasts are given in Table 64. In interpreting this table it has to be remembered that a sufficiently pronounced preference of one sex for one response may automatically throw another response on to the other sex, since fewer scores of the former sex remain to be shared among the other responses. Our interpretation, therefore, is adequate if one of the responses in a contrasting pair is "explained." The table shows the contrasting responses with the suggested category of reference, or explanatory trait, assigned in every case to which our hypothesis seems most clearly to apply. The "explained"[1] response is underlined. A query in the column for "explanatory characteristic" indicates that the explanation is doubtful.

TABLE 64.—INTERPRETATION OF CONTRASTED ASSOCIATIONS

No.	Stimulus word	Male response[1] (plus)	Female response (minus)	Explanatory characteristic
Form A				
1	POLE	telephone 3	north 4	Scientific
7	CASE	bottles 4	doctor 3	Domestic and sympathetic
8	POST	fence 4	gate 2; letter 2	Outdoor v. domestic
10	JACK	money 3	toy 4	Domestic v. business
13	BRACE	bit 5	support 4	Mechanical (tools)
14	FLY	airplane 3	bird 3	Scientific. Adventure
18	BOOK	paper 2 print 2	read 4	Literature for the female side; mechanical ("things it is made of or with") for the male
20	MOON	light 4	night 4	?
21	FLESH	meat 3[2]	color 3	Art and decoration
22	DANGER	caution 3	accident 3	?
23	MODEST	bashful 5	shy 5	?
24	FRESH	meat 3[2]	cool 4	?
29	GARDEN	weeds 3; vegetables 3[2]	flower 5	Decorations for the female, and outdoor occupation for the male side
30	EMBRACE	lover 3	arms 3	?
33	BABY	cry 3	darling 3	Maternal sympathy; the male records what strikes him most about a baby at a distance!
46	FACE	pretty 3	powder 4	Personal embellishment
27	SPOON	pet 2; soup 2[2]	silver 4	Decoration
52	MARRIAGE	divorce 4	children 2	Maternal
59	VAIN	impossible 3	proud 4	The female takes the more intimate and personal sense of the word
Form B				
2	LIVE	wire 3	breathe 4	Mechanical (tools)
3	MUFFLER	car 3	warm 4	Mechanical v. domestic
4	NEEDLE	compass 4	sew 2; eye 2	Scientific for the male, and domestic for the female
5	NOTE	mark 3	letter 3	Domestic and personal v. business
10	SHIFT	football 4	gear 3	Male addiction to outdoor activities and emulation throws even the mechanical "gear" on to the female side
12	BUM	hobo 3	tramp 3	?
15	LIPS	kiss 3	mouth 5	?

[1] Weights for female responses are minus, for male responses plus.
[2] That males tend to prefer "food" words is evidenced sporadically throughout the seven exercises.

[1] The word "explained" is here used in the loose, popular sense. A type of response is of course not really explained by merely referring it to a behavior category.

TABLE 64.—INTERPRETATION OF CONTRASTED ASSOCIATIONS.—(*Continued*)

No.	Stimulus word	Male response[1] (plus)	Female response (minus)	Explanatory characteristic
Form B				
18	TOMBOY	girl 8	boy 3; rough 6	?
19	SNAKE	reptile 3	grass 3	Scientific term
23	CHILD	boy 3; kid 3	girl 5; cunning 4	?
25	POWDER	gun 3; explosion 5	rouge 2; face 7	Decoration for the female, and adventure for the male
27	SWEETHEART	kiss 4	friend 2; lover 2	?
34	WAIST	belly 4	belt 2	Unaesthetic and so disliked by females
37	NASTY	filthy 3	horrid 3	?
48	ELECTRIC	generator 4	light 3	Scientific
49	ART	gallery 3	artist 3	Art for the female, and mechanical contrivances for the male
51	DARKNESS	kiss 2	afraid 4	?
52	MAKE	money 3	dress 4	Domesticity v. business
54	SLEN	skinny 3	graceful 4	Aesthetic v. unaesthetic
55	CHAR	snake 4	grace 3	The more aesthetic v. the more "exciting" word
56	WORM	fish 3[2]	squirm 3	Outdoor pursuit

[1] Weights for female responses are minus, for male responses plus.
[2] That males tend to prefer "food" words is evidenced sporadically throughout the seven exercises.

Out of 40 most marked contrasts between the sexes, 26, it will be noted, seem readily explicable in the terms of our hypothesis. Of the 12 queried items, excess of caution prevents us from explaining some on a similar basis. There is no instance of a sex preference reversing expectations. Of the records, then, of these sex-contrasting cases, most support and none contradicts our main hypothesis, leaving—as one might expect—a minority of cases in which the distinctive sex motives are not immediately obvious, and in which no fresh sex difference emerges.

Sex Characters of the Same Associates in Different Contexts.— We must of course evade the snare of taking the response *absolutely*, and considering it "unreliable" if a given word happens to obtain a male score in one context and a female score in another. In choosing one of four given "associates" the subject has in mind not only its relation to the stimulus word, but its relevance to the stimulus in comparison with that of three rival associates—each associate has to pass not only a qualifying but a competitive examination, with different competitors in each case. But where, in spite of variety of context, a word adheres to one sex, we may suspect some rooted sex preference for that word or for what it symbolizes, or some rooted aversion to it in the opposite sex.

The number of associate words presented more than once in the present exercise was 26, and of these 2 were presented five times, 2 four times, 8 three times, and 14 twice. In 7 out of these 26 associates, the "preferring" sex differs with the occasion; but on the whole a sex tends to maintain its preference through varying contexts. Among the 12 offered more than twice, 5 are persistently or predominantly male (money, meat, love, soldier, kiss) and 4 (picture, mother, baby, happiness) persistently or predominantly female. Five of 12 items have the same sex trends here as obtained with the class they belong to in the M-F test as a whole (*e.g.*, words of the class economic are generally male, etc.). These 5, with sex preference and response classification, are as follows: money (male, economic), meat (male, foods), soldier (male, activity and adventure), picture (female, aesthetic), and mother (female, same sex preference). The remaining 4 include love and kiss (both male); and baby and happiness (both female). Clearly the female score for baby is explicable occupationally. We forbear a posteriori explanation of the others. The point to note is that most cases of reiterated distinctive sex preference correspond to sex trends elsewhere evidenced and accord with our main hypothesis. None contradicts it.

Analysis According to Classes of Associate Words.—In this case we shall be taking the associates absolutely, that is, without considering along with them their stimulus or associate context; for though the sex score for any particular associate is obviously influenced in each case by that context, yet we may fairly assume that over a sufficient population particular extraneous influences cancel out, exposing for the two sex groups their sex distinctions.

In Table 65 the quadruple-choice associates have been classified into 17 groups suggested by a separate study of free associations for which space is not found in the present volume.[1] The scores are the totals of the weighted scores for words of the class concerned; *e.g.*, for the words for "parts of the body" selected by a

[1] WYATT, H. G., Free word association and sex difference, *Amer. J. Psychol.*, 1932, **44**, 454–472.

higher proportion of males than of females the weighted male preference scores totaled 4 and 12 in Forms A and B respectively, and for those with the female excess the total female preference scores totaled 1 and 18 respectively.

TABLE 65.—TOTAL WEIGHTS OF SEVENTEEN RESPONSE CLASSES

Response class	Male		Female		Total	
	Form A	Form B	Form A	Form B	M	F
1. Body parts.....................	+ 4	+12	− 1	−18	16	19
2. Dress........................	0	0	− 8	−12	0	20
3. Personal adornment..............	+ 2	0	− 4	−10	2	14
4. Aesthetic......................	+ 5	+ 3	0	−17	8	17
5. Colors........................	+ 3	+ 2	−19	0	5	19
6. Domestic......................	+26	+ 2	−13	−18	28	31
7. Outdoor......................	+21	+30	−10	− 9	51	19
8. Activity and adventure...........	+17	+25	−10	− 6	42	16
9. Emotional.....................	+22	+19	−25	−20	41	45[1]
10. Religious......................	+ 7	0	− 7	− 2	7	9
11. Social........................	+ 5	0	0	− 5	5	5
12. Business, economic, and political...	+ 5	+ 5	− 4	− 4	10	8
13. Scientific and mechanical.........	+14	+13	− 2	− 2	27	4
14. Foods........................	+19	+ 9	− 1	− 5	28	6
15. Personal—male..................	+11	+12	− 7	− 8	23	15[1]
16. Personal—female................	+ 2	+ 9	− 3	−10	11	13[1]
17. Personal—neutral...............	+12	+ 6	− 9	−19	18	28[1]

[1] If we exclude emotional words with a markedly sexual significance, the scores for emotional words run $5\frac{1}{2}{}_{1}$ (instead of $2\frac{3}{4}{}_{9}$) and $\frac{7}{8}$ (instead of $2\frac{5}{6}{}_{0}$), giving total M 22, F 39; and for personal male words M 13, F 7; personal female, M 1, F 7; personal neutral, M 14, F 26.

Table 65 shows a female distinctive associative trend toward, or tendency to think of, words for articles of dress and personal adornment and colors, and words of aesthetic appraisal; a male tendency toward words for outdoor phenomena, of activity and adventure, of science and machinery, and for foods.   Under the categories "parts of the body," "domestic," "emotional," "religious," "social," "business-economic-political" and "personal" in general, sex differences appear slight, perhaps negligible.

Thus this analysis of the associates taken absolutely, that is, without considering their stimulus and associate context, agrees with our previous findings as to the female addiction to aesthetic objects, personal embellishment, and dress; and the male to adventure and to extradomestic (outdoor, business, economic, and political) and scientific and mechanical affairs. There is again a rather marked male preference for foods, and there is a marked female preference for colors; in addition, there are certain neutral areas. The "domestic" associates reveal no marked sex distinction. A reference to details showed, however, that all the "food" words in the exercise happen to fall in Form A, and secure a considerable male preference; while the Form B domestic associates (comprising no "food" words) and the "maternal" words in Form A (infant, baby, toy, mother) score predominantly female. In domestic matters exclusive of foods females appear the more interested.

Summary.—Whichever method of analysis has been used, whether (1) prediction based on hypothesis (derived from an analysis of Exercise 3) as to characteristic sex interests, (2) the most sex-contrasting responses, (3) sex constancy in associations, or (4) sex conformity in preferences with those evidenced in separately administered free association exercises, we find females picking more often than males upon terms for domestic things or happenings, for kindly and sympathetic activities, and for articles or tokens of adornment; males more often than females upon words relating to physical science, machinery, outdoor pursuits, and terms suggestive of excitement and adventure, and rather less predominantly, upon political, business, and commercial words.

Exercise 2: Ink-blot Association

In each form of the M-F test 18 ink blots, or drawings, are presented and the subject is asked to underline one of the four words following each ("the word that tells what the drawing makes you think of most").

The populations used in the analysis of responses to Exercise 2 were the same as for Exercise 1. We have tabulated the responses of the subjects in two ways, one the less illuminative, taking the associations absolutely; the other by considering the more sharply contrasted associations in relation to one another and to the stimulus object. The first tabulation, which is self-explanatory, serves the former purpose:

Form A
   Male preferred associations:
      +6: coil.
      +3: pipe; tadpole; hat; ax; man hanged; cannon; kettle.
      +2: brush; target; flagpole; bell; fish; nose; head.
      +1: tombstone; pear; snow shoe; centipede; boat; moon; torch; fence; lovers; baby; saxophone; bat.
   Female preferred associations:
      −4: mail box; ball bat; coal bucket.
      −3: inkwell; chopper; dish; chimney.
      −2: comb; sword; smoke; thread; incense.
      −1: spoon; teeth; ship; cloud; dancers; scarecrow; tassel; Indian club; jug; idol; snake; flower; star; bowl; cup.
   Neutral:
      jar; ham; cradle; cup; fish; mirror; ring; tire; bird house; letter "E"; tree; Indian; babies; bottle; whip; goat; face; a man.
Form B
   Male preferred associations:
      +5: jack; butterfly.
      +3: glasses; skate; buoy.
      +2: columns; bomb; chain; cow; boat; flower; hook; staff; dagger; stickpin; baby; valve.
      +1: footprints; diamond; vase; cone; lady; tree; hook; boat; hat; stump; sword.
   Female preferred associations:
      −6: bow.
      −5: lady.
      −4: basket.
      −3: lady; question mark; sled.
      −2: vase; bow; funnel; exclamation point; door; flower; stove.
      −1: candle; gate; jar; tie; light; rock; ship; horn; couch; deer; horse; coffin; flame; snake; worm; pyramid; shadow.
   Neutral:
      fireplace; flask; pan; snake; trees; ribbon; bush; mushroom; haystack; umbrella; club; stick; string; airplane.

Throwing the associated words into classes we may compare the sex preference scores as follows:

Forms A and B combined:
1. Terms associated with mechanical and scientific interests.
    Male associations: coil; saxophone; valve; jack.

Total male, 4

2. Terms connected with outdoor activities or adventure.
    Male associations: butterfly; glasses (field); skate; buoy; bomb; cow; boat; dagger; tree; boat (again); sword; stump; cannon; man hanged; flagpole; boat (third time); tadpole; torch; tombstone; snow shoe; centipede; fence; bat; pear; target; fish; ax.

Total male, 27

    Female associations: sled; gate; rock; ship; deer; horse; snake; pyramid; worm; ball bat; sword; star; scarecrow; snake (again).

Total female, 14

3. Terms connected with domestic occupations.
    Male associations: pipe; kettle; bell; baby; baby (again); hat.

Total male, 6

    Female associations: coal bucket; chopper (food); dish; comb; thread; spoon; jug; bowl; cup; basket; funnel; door; stove; candle; tie; couch; jar.

Total female, 17

4. Terms connected with aesthetic experience or personal adornment.
    Male associations: flower; diamond; vase; stickpin.

Total male, 4

    Female associations: bow; vase; bow (again); flower; incense; flower (again); dancers; tassel; comb.

Total female, 9

5. Unclassified terms.
    Male associations: column; chain; hook; staff; footprints; cone; lady; brush; lovers; nose; head; moon.

Total male, 12

    Female associations: mail box; inkwell; lady; lady (again); question mark; exclamation point; light; horn; coffin; flame; shadow; chimney; smoke; teeth; cloud; Indian club; idol.

Total female, 17

The results of the above treatment accord with previous generalizations as to the relative interests of the sexes. Further comment is unnecessary.

We present next, in Table 66, the most strongly contrasted associations.

Seemingly in every case, except perhaps for Item 17 of both forms, the distinctive occupations of the sexes determine the con-

TABLE 66.—CONTRASTED SEX ASSOCIATIONS IN INK-BLOT TEST[1]

Item	Male	Female	Comment
Form A			
1	Pipe[2] +3	Mailbox −4	The male smokes a pipe
2	Tadpole +3	Ball bat −4	Outdoor interest v. a specific female game
3	Hat +3	Inkwell −3	Sedentary clerical occupation
6	Ax +3	Chopper −3	Kitchen v. woodpile
12	Coil +6	Chimney −3; Smoke −2; Thread −2	Scientific or mechanical v. domestic
17	Kettle +3; Nose +2	Coal bucket −4	?
Form B			
5	Jack +5	Funnel −2; Horn −1	The male changes tires
7	Boat +2	Basket −4	Domestic v. adventure
10	Butterfly +5; Glasses (field) +3	Bow −6	Female adornment v. outdoor pursuit
17	Skate +3	Sled −3	?
18	Buoy +3; Baby +2; Valve +2	Lady −5	Scientific and outdoor v. sex-to-sex tendency

[1] With sex divergence span of 6 up, *e.g.*, the span for mailbox −4, pipe +3 is 7.
[2] The associate to which the comment applies is underlined.

trasts. The comments suggest the determining factors in each case. In Item 18, Form B, "baby" is thrown on to the male side by the fact that the female, more discriminative in this case through specific experience, would never associate "baby" with the shape depicted.

Summary.—Females pick more often upon response words associated with domestic occupations, aesthetic experiences, and personal adornment; males more often upon words most obviously connected with machinery, physical science, and outdoor pursuits. The most sex-contrasting responses evidence a preference for words connected with common occupations of the responding sex.

EXERCISE 3: INFORMATION TEST

Each form of this exercise consists of 70 sentences (*i.e.*, 140 in all) to be completed by underlining that word out of four supplied that gives the correct information required. It is a quadruple-choice information-completion exercise, success in which calls primarily for knowledge of fact and would seem, therefore, to depend upon the experience and interests of the subject. Responses were analyzed for the same populations as in the case of the two previous exercises.

We shall briefly summarize the results of our scrutiny before considering the detail.

Within the range of the 140 items set and the subjects who responded to them, a comparison of the sex-preference scores indicates that:

1. Females show more knowledge
   a. About domestic occupations.
   b. About matters of personal or household decoration, adornment, and etiquette.
   c. About literature (fiction), music (or rather musical technique), and conventional taste in colors.
   d. Where the topic is one that appeals to one's active sympathy or feelings of tenderness (including in particular the maternal emotions).
2. Males show more knowledge
   a. Of extradomestic facts and events, political, social, economic, and business.
   b. Of physical and scientific facts.
   c. Of exploit, adventure, invention, whether in fact or fiction.
   d. Where the topic is one that appeals to the pugnacious, aggressive, or vigorously active tendencies.

We can now take the evidence in detail.

Analysis of the Most Sex-contrasting Responses.—This analysis is limited to the *correct* responses carrying plus or minus weights of 4 or larger.[1] They are as follows:

---

[1] As will be seen in Appendix IV, M-F weights were assigned to all the responses in this test, the incorrect as well as the correct, and also to omissions. Our analysis, however, takes account of the correct responses only. The assumption behind our present analysis is that on the average a subject tends to answer more

Form A

Greater knowledge by males (weights +4 or higher):

6. The most gold is produced in   Alaska   New York   Tennessee   Texas
21. The boomerang is an   animal   plant   tool   weapon
24. The "Rough Riders" were led by   Funston   Pershing   Roosevelt   Sheridan
25. The vessel which overcame the Merrimac was the   Connecticut   Monitor   Old Ironsides
31. The Erie Canal is in   Canada   Ohio   New York   Pennsylvania
34. The mossy side of a tree is usually on the   east   north   south   west
40. The proportion of the globe covered by water is about   ⅛   ¼   ½   ¾
43. Mica is an   explosive   food   mineral   vegetable
47. Shinny is played with   bats   clubs   nets   racquets
48. When water freezes it   contracts   expands   does neither
62. The altitude record for airplanes is about   10,000 ft.   20,000 ft.   40,000 ft.   60,000 ft.
66. Beam scales illustrate the principle of   buoyancy   elasticity   leverage   magnetism

Greater knowledge by females (weights −4 or larger):

1. Marigold is a kind of   fabric   flower   grain   stone
5. Pongee is a kind of   cloth   drink   flower   game
32. Red goes best with   black   lavender   pink   purple
41. The turquoise is   blue   red   white   yellow
44. Blue clashes worst with   brown   gray   pink   purple
46. A buffet is used for   books   clothes   dishes   food
51. The amethyst is   green   purple   white   yellow

In the "male" list, Items 6, 21, 31, and 43 demand a knowledge of physical or scientific facts; 21, 24, and 62 are directly or closely related to adventurous activities; all the items except perhaps 47 have to do with the world beyond the home; and 21, 25, and 62 are topics of particular appeal to aggressive and enterprising natures.

In the "female" list, five of the seven items carrying a weight as large as −4 for the correct response have to do with personal

---

correctly on matters in which he is more interested or absorbed.   Whether he also tends to prefer a response word signifying what he is most interested in, irrespective of its being "right" or "wrong," is a separate question not here considered.

adornment. The exceptions call for information about the marigold and a buffet, both related to the domestic situation. The corresponding items in Form B are as follows:

Greater knowledge by males (weights +4 or higher):
4. Robert E. Lee surrendered to Grant Lincoln Sheridan Sherman
13. Sun eclipse is caused by the shadow of the earth Jupiter Mars the moon
16. True silk comes from goats plants sheep worms
21. Paul Jones was a general sea-fighter statesman writer
24. The telegraph was invented by Bell Edison Morse Whitney
33. The large prehistoric reptiles were called anthropoids crustaceans diatoms dinosaurs
36. Of these woods the hardest is cedar oak pine walnut
39. The blacksmith of the gods was called Jupiter Mercury Perseus Vulcan
40. Tides are caused by winds rotation of the earth attraction of the moon ocean currents
41. A shipping term is FOB RST SOS TNT
42. "Pi" is equal to .6666 .7853 1.453 3.1416
46. Heating a piece of iron makes it larger lighter smaller stronger
55. The diameter of the earth in miles is about 2,000 5,000 8,000 25,000
58. Light travels per second about 8,000 miles 25,000 miles 186,000 miles 240,000 miles
59. Among the allies of Germany, in the World War, was Belgium Bulgaria Roumania Russia
60. The "Block System" is used in carpentry mining railroading surveying
66. A noted general in the Mexican War was Burnside Hooker Jackson Taylor

Greater knowledge by females (weights −4 or larger):
23. A mixture of red and blue pigments gives brown green purple yellow
32. A baby usually begins to walk alone at about 6 mos. 12 mos. 20 mos. 24 mos.
37. Topsy was Arabian Eskimo Indian Negro White
38. A chiffonier is used for books clothes dishes silverware
50. Heliotrope is the name of a drug flower gem tree

Examination of the Form B lists shows that the items divide according to the same principles which govern their division in

Form A. Of the 17 in the male list, no fewer than 10 or 11 may be classed as scientific. Four are historical, and three of these have to do with war.

Analysis of Less Divergent Responses.—We shall now consider the items in which the sex predominances, though noticeable, were less conspicuous; namely, those with weights of 2 or 3. If actual differences in sex characteristics are revealed by the differences in the character of the correct responses, then where the response differences are most pronounced the sex differences are most clearly revealed, and where the response differences are less pronounced other factors besides sex differences enter in. As the smaller score weights are statistically less reliable than the larger, the analysis of less divergent responses has been limited to Form A.

Form A
Greater knowledge by males (weights +1 to +3):
3. The Yale is a kind of   hammer   lock   screen   wrench
7. The earth moves around the sun in   7 days   30 days   180 days   365 days
11. Most of our anthracite coal comes from   Alabama   Colorado   Ohio   Pennsylvania
12. The number of players on a baseball team is   7   9   11   13
15. Peat is used for   fuel   pavement   plaster   road-making
16. Marco Polo was a famous   king   philosopher   traveler   warrior
17. Tokyo is a city of   China   India   Japan   Russia
28. A shilling is worth about   25 cts.   50 cts. $1.00 $5.00
36. Turpentine comes from   coal   petroleum   trees   whales
37. The number of persons on a jury in the U.S. is   8   12   16   18
39. The chief cause of the tides is the attraction of   the moon   planets   sun   stars
42. A plant "breathes" chiefly through its   bark   leaves   roots   twigs
49. The Roman numeral C equals   50   100   500   1,000
53. The length of a brick is   6 in.   8 in.   10 in.   12 in.
56. Barometers are used to measure   air pressure   heat   humidity   rainfall
57. Lobo was the name of a   bear   crow   fox   wolf
59. The number of ordinary steps in a mile is about   1,000   2,000   5,000   10,000
63. Limestone originated from   granite   marble   sand   shells
64. An animal that suckles its young is the   alligator   shark   snake   whale

65. A birthright was sold for a mess of pottage by   Cain   Esau
    Isaac   Judas
68. A decisive Revolutionary battle was   Gettysburg   New Orleans
    Valley Forge   Yorktown

Greater knowledge by females (weights −1 to −3):

2. Things cooked in grease are   boiled   broiled   fried   roasted
4. We should drink tea from the   cup   saucer   spoon
8. A stately dance of colonial days was the   minuet   polka   two-
   step   waltz
10. Beethoven is known as a   composer   painter   poet   singer
13. Eggs are best for us when   deviled   fried   hard-boiled   soft-
    boiled
14. A loom is used for   cooking   embroidering   sewing   weaving
19. Daffodils are grown from   bulbs   cuttings   seeds   shoots
20. The baby found in the bulrushes was   Jacob   Jesus   Moses
    Paul
22. Minnehaha means   falling leaves   laughing   waters   running
    brooks   whispering pines
23. A correct expression is   I have dove   I dived   He dove
26. About A.D. 1750 men's sleeves had   bands   lace-ruffles   stiff
    cuffs   stripes
27. A food with much the same food substance as rice is   beans   peas
    meat   potatoes
30. "Speak for yourself" was said by   Annabel Lee   Evangeline
    Juliet   Priscilla
33. Baby gets its first tooth at about   6 mos.   12 mos.   15 mos.
    18 mos.
38. The Madonna is a favorite subject for   music   paintings   poetry
    stories
45. A dinner hostess seats the guest of honor at her   left   opposite
    right
50. Some think "moon over the right shoulder" means   death   rain
    sickness   wish fulfillment
52. Ruth and Naomi are known for their   devotion   hatred   pity
    rivalry
55. "Mennen's" is the name of   cold   cream   perfume   collar
    talcum
58. "Charades" is a   running game   game of chance   guessing
    game   kissing game
60. "Peter Pan" was written by   Barrie   Kipling   Mark Twain
    Stevenson
61. Babies should be weaned at about   3 mos.   6 mos.   12 mos.
    2 yrs.

67. A character in "David Copperfield" is Betty Uriah Heep Sindbad Oliver Twist
70. A famous portrait painter was Rosa Bonheur Mozart Reynolds Rubens

In the male list, Items 3, 7, 11, 15, 36, 39, 42, 53, 56, 59, 63, and 64 demand a knowledge of physical or scientific facts; the others relate to war (68), adventure (16 and perhaps 57), geography (17 and 28), civics (37), and baseball (12).

In the female list, Items 2, 13, 14, 27, 33, and 61 are closely connected with domestic occupations or home life; 4, 8, 26, 45, and 55 have to do with personal adornment or etiquette. Of the remaining items, 20, 30, 52, 60, and 67 are from literature, mostly from works of fiction in prose or poetry. Items 10, 19, 38, and 70 have to do with art, music, or flowers, 20 and 52 call for biblical information, and 50 is a romantic superstition.

Summary.—The information test, scored for correct response, gives valuable clues to the diverging interests and preoccupations of the sexes. The masculine key quality brought out by the test is the aggressive, adventurous, enterprising, outwardly directed disposition; the tendency to pugnacity (in the wider sense) and self-assertiveness. Related to this quality is the greater interest in things physical and scientific. The outstandingly feminine traits are the actively sympathetic, the inwardly directed disposition; the maternal impulse and the tender feelings; concern with domestic affairs, personal adornment, art, and literature.

For masculinity there appear to be two crucial questions: Does the individual under consideration show a taste for adventure, rivalry (up to the fighting point) and aggression? And secondly, does he evince an interest in things outside the domestic circle? Of these the former is the more significant of masculinity. After this in order of importance we may come to such questions as: Does the subject show an interest in physical and mechanical phenomena? and perhaps still lower in the scale: Does he show an interest in social, historical, and business affairs?

For femininity on the other side we may venture a corresponding order: Does the individual concerned show a taste for, or an interest in, topics or events that arouse the sympathetic emotions (those that call for active sympathy) or the maternal interest in infant life? Does he (or she) show a pronounced interest in the intimacies of home and personal relationships rather than in the less personal relationships of external affairs? After this in order of importance may come such questions as: Does the subject show an interest in personal adornment? and perhaps still lower in the scale: Does he or she show an interest in art and literature (especially fiction)?

As regards art and literature it should be noted that all our information exercise suggests is that the girl knows better than the boy who were the great artists, what common technical terms in music signify, and about certain color relationships and conventional judgments of color harmony. We cannot safely infer any superiority in artistic emotional appreciation. And as regards literature the evidence rather suggests a greater attention on the part of the girl to works of fiction and to poetry; one can draw no inference about her taste for literature in general.

EXERCISE 4: EMOTIONAL AND ETHICAL RESPONSE

Exercise 4 falls into six sections, of which four concern occasions of anger, fear, disgust, and pity respectively; the fifth considers occasions of moral reprobation; and the last compares preferences for alternative situations or types of occupation. The analysis of Exercise 4 was based upon data from the following populations: 148 boys and 172 girls in the seventh grade, 116 boys and 128 girls in the junior year of high school, and 50 college students of each sex; in all, 664 subjects.

Anger Reactions.—Here the subject is presented with a number of assumed situations calculated to arouse the emotion in some degree, and with four degrees of emotional intensity: very much (VM), much (M), little (L), or none (N); and is invited to record the particular degree of that emotion which the assumed situation provokes, or would provoke, in him or her.

The first method of analysis adopted was to pair VM with M as representing a tendency to considerable emotion, and L with N to indicate defect and to contrast the combined paired records. But it is clear that on the excess side VM and on the defect side

N indicate more and less emotion respectively than M and L; for instance, a "minus 2 VM" with a "minus 2 M" represents a greater tendency to keen emotion than a "minus VM" with a "minus 3 M." No one of course can tell how much more emotion

TABLE 67.—SEX DIFFERENCES IN ANGER RESPONSE

M-F test items	Excess (2 VM + M)	Defect (L + 2N)	Span
Form A, order for female excess over male defect:			
1. Seeing people disfigure library books	−6	+6	12
2. Seeing boys make fun of old people	−7	+3	10
3. Seeing someone laugh when a blind man runs into an obstacle	−6	+4	10
4. Seeing someone cheat in an examination	−4	+5	9
5. Being called lazy	−4	+4	8
6. Hearing your political views ridiculed	−1	+7	8
7. Being snubbed by an inferior	−4	+3	7
8. Being blamed for something you have not done	−2	+2	4
9. Seeing a person laugh at a cripple	−3	+2	5
10. Hearing someone make fun of your clothes	−2	+2	4
11. Being called stupid	−2	+1	3
12. Being unexpectedly slapped on the back as a joke	−2	+1	3
13. Being deceived by a supposed friend	−2	0	2
14. Being called a thief	0	0	0
15. Being disturbed when you want to work	0	−1	− 1
16. Seeing an honest official thrown out by politicians	0	−1	− 1
17. Seeing someone trying to discredit you with your employer	+2	−1	− 3
Average span between female excess and male defect (85 − 5 ÷ 17)			4.7
Form B, order for female excess over male defect:			
1. Seeing a person treated unfairly because of his race	−9	+5	14
2. Being socially slighted	−5	+7	12
3. Seeing an innocent man punished for another's crime	−6	+6	12
4. Hearing your friends unjustly abused	−7	+3	10
5. Seeing a man sitting in a car with old women standing	−7	+3	10
6. Being marked unfairly in an examination	−6	+3	9
7. Hearing your religion ridiculed	−5	+4	9
8. Being honked at by an automobile	−4	+1	5
9. Being deceived by an enemy	−2	+3	5
10. Hearing someone misspell or mispronounce your name	−2	+3	5
11. Being slapped in a quarrel	−2	+2	4
12. Seeing an animal cruelly beaten	−2	+1	3
13. Being unreasonably prevented from doing what you want to do	−1	+1	2
14. Being cheated in a business deal	0	−1	− 1
15. Being called homely	0	0	0
16. Being called a liar	0	0	0
17. Being called by a nickname you don't like	0	0	0
Average span between female excess and male defect (100 − 1 ÷ 17)			5.8

is signified by a *VM* than by an *M* response; and the differences may vary between subjects and in the same subject on different occasions. But for practical purposes we may recognize the existence and the importance of this difference by giving *VM* and *N* double weight. Hence *VM* and *M* were taken together, and *L* and *N* together, the *VM* and *N* scores being doubled before adding them to the *M* and the *L* scores. The sum of the *VM* and *M* weights will be called the "excess" score, the sum of the *L* and *N* weights the "defect" score. Table 67 gives the items in order of decreasing "excess" score of female over male subjects.

We may contrast the items in which the recorded differences are most pronounced with the items in which little difference appears and ask what is common to the former and absent, or present in less degree, in the latter. The items at the extremities of the scale represent the strongest contrasts. In Form A two of these items, the second and third, representing a high degree of female as compared with male annoyance, are instances of very unsympathetic behavior, while no such cases occur at the other end of the series. Item 9, the only other of this type in Form A, is at about the middle of the scale.

In Form B four out of five instances of very unsympathetic treatment where sympathy is demanded come at the top of the scale, namely, items 1, 3, 4, and 5;[1] the exception being twelfth. Except item 12, all these cases in Form A represent human beings receiving some considerable injury when they need humane treatment. Thus six cases of singularly unsympathetic treatment of human beings when sympathy is meet are also cases of great difference between the sexes in the anger expressed, the female expressing the keener emotion. This corroborates the hypothesis of the greater tendency to active sympathy in the female, at least where human beings are the object.

The other two items at the head of the scale, the first and fourth in Form A and the sixth in Form B, suggest that girls are more annoyed by *school* offenses than boys are ("disfiguring library books" and "cheating in an examination," "being unfairly marked in an examination") and proportionately less angered

[1] The numbers here refer to the order of items in Table 67.

than males by extraschool injustices, since two of the only three items in the whole series against which males record more anger than females include "being discredited with one's employer" and "seeing an honest official thrown out of office unfairly." The former evokes the greatest degree of male anger recorded in the section. In Form B the only case near the top of the sex difference scale we have not accounted for is the female excess of anger over "being socially slighted" (item 2). The female sex is the more concerned about social, the male about business, relations.

The responses in this section accordingly support the view that the female is the more actively sympathetic sex, and is more concerned in her nearer relationships than the male, being proportionately more affected by school and home and "social" vexations, and less by business or extradomestic troubles.

A tendency is seen here, as in all the other sections of this exercise, for females to record in general a higher degree of emotion. Of the 34 items relating to anger, in 26 the excess score is on the female side and in only one on the male side. On the other hand, the defect scores are correspondingly male.

Fear Reactions.—This section of the test is like the preceding except that the subject's response indicates degree of fear aroused by the situations specified.

The rank order of the fear items according to decreasing excess of female over male scores is shown in Table 68.

The influence of cultural bias on responses would seem likely to be stronger for fear responses than for anger responses. For the female sex is allowed by society to be timid, and the male is expected to be brave. The young man fears to be afraid, and the habit of refusing fear expression is bound to weaken his responses in this section considerably. But there is no such sex convention for anger. Hence, we should expect the fear scores to yield us wider spans of sex divergence than the anger scores, irrespective of any really wider divergence in emotional intensities between the sexes. A glance at the table confirms this expectation. The widest "anger" spans are 12 and 14 for Forms A and B, while the widest "fear" spans are 23 and 22. The averages of female

TABLE 68.—SEX DIFFERENCES IN FEAR RESPONSE

M-F test items	Excess (2 VM + M)	Defect (L + 2N)	Span
Form A, order for female excess over male defect:			
1. Floods..	− 13	+10	23
2. Garter snakes....................................	− 12	+11	23
3. Burglars...	− 12	+10	22
4. Bulls..	− 12	+ 9	21
5. Being lost.......................................	− 10	+10	20
6. Thunder...	− 9	+11	20
7. Graveyards at night..............................	− 8	+ 6	14
8. Being in a closed room...........................	− 7	+ 6	13
9. Deep water......................................	− 6	+ 7	13
10. Windstorms......................................	− 4	+ 6	10
11. Lightning.......................................	− 4	+ 5	9
12. End of the world................................	− 3	+ 5	8
13. Negroes...	− 5	+ 2	7
14. Heart trouble...................................	− 3	+ 3	6
15. Automobiles.....................................	− 1	+ 3	4
16. Becoming deaf or blind..........................	− 1	+ 3	4
17. Pain..	− 2	+ 1	3
18. Punishment in the next world....................	0	+ 1	1
19. Insects...	0	0	0
20. Contagious diseases.............................	+ 1	− 2	− 3
Average span for Form A (221 − 3 ÷ 20)......			10.9
Form B, order for female excess over male defect:			
1. Being alone at night.............................	− 10	+12	22
2. Fire..	− 10	+11	21
3. Rattlesnakes....................................	− 12	+ 7	19
4. Earthquakes.....................................	− 9	+ 9	18
5. Crazy people....................................	− 10	+ 6	16
6. Darkness..	− 7	+ 7	14
7. Guns..	− 6	+ 7	13
8. Mice..	− 4	+ 7	11
9. Toads...	− 3	+ 6	9
10. Being on a ship.................................	− 4	+ 4	8
11. Becoming insane.................................	− 6	+ 2	8
12. Crossing an open space...........................	− 2	+ 6	8
13. Ghosts..	− 4	+ 3	7
14. Written examinations............................	− 2	+ 4	6
15. Knives..	− 1	+ 4	5
16. Foreigners......................................	− 2	+ 1	3
17. Horses..	− 1	+ 2	3
18. Becoming crippled or totally disabled.............	− 3	− 1	2
19. Poisoning.......................................	+ 1	0	− 1
20. Old age...	+ 3	− 3	− 6
Average span for Form B (193 − 7 ÷ 20)........			9.3

excess over male defect of expressed anger are 4.7 and 5.8 for Forms A and B, for fear, 10.9 and 9.3.

We shall now examine Table 68 in detail. Our method of analysis was to take Form A first, and to scrutinize the first nine as against the last eight items with a view to eliciting suggestive contrasts. Three contrasts suggest themselves. The items in the first group as compared with the second comprise perceptual events or objects that either (1) are more threatening to life and limb; or (2) are more sudden and occasional; or (3) demand a more immediate display of active courage; or have more than one of these attributes. This contrast is the more obvious the nearer we approach the extremes on the scale. "Floods," "garter snakes," "burglars," and "bulls"—in which the female excess of expressed emotion is greatest—conspicuously fulfill all three conditions, and "punishment in the next world," "becoming deaf or blind," "insects," and "contagious diseases"—items at the bottom of the scale—do not. "Negroes," at the top of the lowest eight items, are not particularly threatening to life and limb, nor do they demand an immediate display of courage; "heart trouble" is a *state* demanding careful treatment, not a quick display of courage; "automobiles" are hardly occasional; and "pain" is a felt state and not a perceived object at all.

The reader may carry the comparison throughout the series. In general there is a descending trend according as the situations fulfill the conditions postulated. But since instinctive fear in man or higher animals is for objects or events that are perceived as threatening immediate danger to life and limb, especially events that are sudden and unfamiliar, and since such situations demand the immediate display of active courage, what the record suggests is not that there are objects or events that in themselves are more or less terrifying to one sex than to the other, but that things that are generally fearsome are, or are declared by them to be, more fearsome to females.

A scrutiny of the Form B spans, while confirming, supplements this conclusion. For there are three out of the eight situations claimed as the most excessively fearsome by females, which do not fulfill our three conditions: namely, "being alone at night," "darkness," and "mice." A social reason for the female dread of darkness and solitude suggests itself. Girls are early taught, in some families more than others, not to go about alone, especially in the dark. Where this practice occurs the sex distinction is likely to be accentuated. "Mice" are also a special cultivated female terror.

In summary, then, a scrutiny of the fear sections in detail suggests minor socially determined differences in the occasions of fear to the sexes; and a general tendency in the female sex to express fears more strongly, and that in proportion to the actual fearsomeness of the object.

Disgust Reactions.—The relevant data for our discussion of this section of Exercise 4 are given in Table 69.

It will be seen from Table 69 that all items portraying actual male rather than female practices, and the two instances of behavior specifically mentioned as male, come high in the scale. These are Items 1, 2, 6; and 5 and 7. The female expresses much more disgust at them than the male does. That practices sanctioned among members of one sex and not the other cease to repel the former is a sufficient explanation. Though, since there are no specifically female disgusting habits included in either Form A or B this leaves us the questions whether and why males have the more disgusting habits. But our present exercise is not designed to answer these two questions.

There remain in Form A two "extreme" items, namely, "soiled or ragged fingernails" and "untidy clothes" (Items 3 and 4) not thus explicable. But here again comes in a social factor. American girls meditating matrimony also meditate their clothes and fingernails, on which they lavish far more care, cash, and cosmetics than is customary with males. The sex is therefore the more repelled by an offense against its idols.

The score graduations on Form B are not disposed of so readily. We may select the first seven items for contrast with the last seven items on the scale. Of the five items that refer to clothes in this and the cognate section, four fall in the higher part of the scale; the keener female concern about dress would seem to explain greater disgust at dress disfigurements; this would cover Items 2 and 5. But the exception, the very low Item 13 in Form A, "food stains on clothing," defeats one.

Items 2 in Form A and 1 in Form B indicate a female repugnance against impolite language.[1] Cultural bias provides the

---

[1] The table on Ethical Discrimination Responses in a later section shows that "swearing" is more censured by females than by males.

TABLE 69.—SEX DIFFERENCES IN DISGUST RESPONSE

M-F test items	Excess (2 VM + M)	Defect (L + 2N)	Span
Form A, order for female excess over male defect:			
1. A drunken man............................	−13	+11	24
2. Foul language............................	−12	+11	23
3. Soiled or ragged fingernails..............	−11	+12	23
4. Untidy clothes............................	−12	+ 9	21
5. Sagging socks on a man....................	− 8	+12	20
6. Spitting in public........................	−10	+ 9	19
7. An unshaven man.........................	− 9	+ 9	18
8. Gum chewing............................	− 7	+11	18
9. Pimples..................................	− 6	+ 8	14
10. Seeing a woman smoking.................	− 8	+ 5	13
11. Smell of decaying flesh..................	− 7	+ 6	13
12. Word "gent" used for gentleman........	− 6	+ 6	12
13. Food stains on clothing..................	− 7	+ 4	11
14. Offensive breath.........................	− 6	+ 5	11
15. Sight of slimy water.....................	− 6	+ 4	10
16. Mushy food in your mouth..............	− 4	+ 5	9
17. Crooked teeth...........................	− 3	+ 2	5
18. A butcher shop..........................	0	+ 2	2
Average span (266 ÷ 18).............			14.8
Form B, order for female excess over male defect:			
1. Words like "belly" or "guts"..........	−18	+10	28
2. Soiled table linen......................	−12	+13	25
3. A boy and girl petting..................	−10	+12	22
4. Tobacco chewing.......................	−11	+11	22
5. Sight of dirty clothes...................	−12	+ 8	20
6. Sniffling...............................	− 9	+10	19
7. Odor of perspiration....................	− 9	+ 8	17
8. Sight of pus............................	− 7	+ 5	12
9. Smell of onions........................	− 4	+ 8	12
10. Hearing a person belch.................	− 7	+ 4	11
11. Seeing a bull..........................	− 2	+ 6	8
12. Sight of anyone vomiting...............	− 4	+ 3	7
13. Smell of cooked cabbage................	− 2	+ 5	7
14. Wienerwursts or stuffed sausage........	− 3	+ 4	7
15. Dirty neck or ears.....................	− 9	− 3	6
16. Seeing a man smoking..................	− 3	+ 2	5
17. A banana..............................	− 2	0	2
18. Bad table manners.....................	− 7	− 5	2
Average span (232 ÷ 18).............			12.9

reason: coarse language is accounted more offensive in the girl than in the boy.

Item 4, "tobacco chewing," aligns with Item 8, "gum chewing," as a disgusting practice, the former being more usual with males and also higher in the scale.

There is also a tendency as in the fear section for the items which might be expected to provoke the keener emotion (whichever the sex) to come higher in the scale. Conversely, a reason why the item "seeing a man smoking" is an apparent exception to the generalization that specifically male practices show the greater spans is that the practice is not repugnant enough to call forth much disgust in any case and is also socially sanctioned in men by women when it is not so sanctioned in women.

As one would expect, it is the more intermediate items that most puzzle one. It is hard to say why "sniffling" (Item 6) should be comparatively more disgusting to females than, say, "dirty neck and ears" (Item 15). There remains Item 3, "a boy and girl petting," high in the scale. If active physical sexual desire is stronger in males than in females, this may more effectively counterbalance moral repugnance, and cultural bias may also come in, for female offenses against "virtue" are the more condemned.

In conclusion, it appears that there are many "nasty practices" which the male tends more than the female to condone or not to find disgusting; that the female sex is more particular about coarse or impolite language, about aesthetic accessories of person or dress, and about sexual morality.

Pity Reactions.—Our discussion of this section of the exercise is based upon the data in Table 70.

A corollary of the tendency already mentioned for the female to express her feelings with the greater emphasis is a general tendency for sex-difference scores and actual emotiveness of a situation to correspond, the most alarming or disgusting situations showing the higher sex spans. This complicates interpretation, for the recorded sex difference in any item now appears as the outcome of two independent variables: (1) this general tendency toward female emphasis; and (2) any true sex differences specific to the

TABLE 70.—SEX DIFFERENCES IN PITY RESPONSE

M-F test items	Excess $(2VM + M)$	Defect $(L + 2N)$	Span
Form A, order for female excess over male defect:			
1. An orphan girl..........................	−8	+ 7	15
2. An insane person.......................	−6	+ 6	12
3. A wounded deer........................	−5	+ 5	10
4. An old person with a fatal disease........	−5	+ 4	9
5. An underfed child......................	−5	+ 4	9
6. A bee that is drowning..................	−4	+ 4	8
7. Very old people........................	−4	+ 4	8
8. A baby bird whose mother is dead........	−3	+ 5	8
9. A dog that must be killed for biting people	−4	+ 3	7
10. A man who is cowardly and can't help it	−1	+ 5	6
11. Overworked children...................	−5	+ 1	6
12. A fly caught on sticky fly paper.........	−1	+ 5	6
13. A wounded soldier who must beg for a living....................................	−2	+ 2	4
14. Overworked horses.....................	−2	+ 1	3
15. A young person totally paralyzed........	−1	+ 1	2
Average span (113 ÷ 15).............			7.5
Form B, order for female excess over male defect:			
1. A mouse caught by a hawk.............	−9	+10	19
2. An old maid who has always wanted children.................................	−7	+11	18
3. A bird with a broken wing.............	−8	+ 6	14
4. A fish caught on a hook................	−6	+ 8	14
5. An orphan boy........................	−7	+ 7	14
6. A boy ambitious to go to college but cannot	−4	+ 8	12
7. A wounded lion........................	−5	+ 6	11
8. An underfed horse.....................	−6	+ 4	10
9. A toad being swallowed by a snake......	−3	+ 4	7
10. A dope fiend..........................	−1	+ 4	5
11. A young person with a fatal disease......	−3	+ 2	5
12. A terribly ugly man....................	−1	+ 3	4
13. A man who is physically a weakling......	−2	+ 1	3
14. A person with no will power............	−2	+ 1	3
Average span (139 ÷ 14)..........			10

item. We have, in other words, always to remember that items in which the true specific sex differences may be the same may yet differ widely in their place on the scale of descending spans because of the first variable.

The reinforcement of general emotiveness by a specific factor appears in the sex divergences in this section, when we compare the first five with the last six items in Form A, and again in Form B.   On the ground of mere emotiveness the items "overworked children" (11 in Form A), "a young person totally paralyzed" (15 in Form A), and "a young person with a fatal disease" (12 in Form B) are surely just as distressing as "a mouse caught by a hawk," "a bird with a broken wing," "a wounded deer," or "a fish caught on a hook"[1] (items high in the scale).

But a glance at the last three items adds the specific factor. They all instance some weak or delicate creature perceived *at the moment* as helpless and in *visible distress*.   The first three items represent a distressing *state*, in which the helplessness and the distress and the weakness of the subject are far less immediately perceptible.   The female claims to be more moved by the sight of the weak and helpless in temporary but palpable distress.

We note again certain exceptions: "an orphan girl" and "an old maid who has always wanted children," although representing distressing *states* rather than *instances*, appear as Items 1 and 2 on Forms A and B.   But here the "normal" female excess over the male is accentuated by the additional specific factor of sympathy with their own sex.   "An orphan boy" registers a slightly lower score than "an orphan girl" and falls considerably lower in its scale.

Again, objects that are unsightly tend toward a low position ("a dope fiend," "a toad being swallowed by a snake," "a terribly ugly man"), suggesting that pity is counteracted by repulsion or disgust.   These explanations for what they are worth (and they at least offer corroborative evidence) cover all the most sex-differentiating items except 2 in Form A—"an insane person."   Why this should seem so much more pitiful to females than to males is not clear.   Why should female pity exceed that of males here more than, say, in the case of "a young person with a fatal disease"?

Summarizing, a comparison of the female and male scores suggests or indicates as distinctive sex characteristics: (1) a

[1] "A bee that is drowning" is less maternally appealing—bees sting.

female sympathy (the maternal instinct?) for the weak and helpless visibly distressed; (2) a tendency for the female to express
more pity for female distress; (3) a tendency to more female than
male sympathy with things attractive in appearance as contrasted with the ugly.

TABLE 71.—SEX DIFFERENCES IN DEGREES OF CENSURE

M-F test items	Excess	Defect	Span	3 Ex-tremely wicked	0 Not really bad
Form A* order of female excess over male defect:					
1. Boys fighting.......................	−8	+7	15	−3	+3
2. Swiping fruit out of orchards.........	−6	+8	14	−3	+3
3. Shooting rabbits just for fun..........	−4	+8	12	−2	+3
4. Boys smoking before they are 21......	−4	+7	11	−1	+3
5. Indulging in "petting"..............	−5	+6	11	−2	+3
6. Going to bed without saying your prayers.........................	−5	+5	10	−2	+2
7. Stealing a ride on a truck............	−6	+3	9	−2	+1
8. Moderate drinking..................	−4	+5	9	−2	+2
9. Not brushing your teeth.............	−4	+5	9	−2	+2
10. Having fits of temper................	−2	+7	9	0	+3
11. Boys teasing girls..................	−3	+5	8	−1	+2
12. Putting pins on the teacher's chair....	−4	+3	7	−1	+1
13. Telling a lie to avoid punishment.....	−3	+3	6	−2	+1
14. Using slang.......................	−3	+3	6	−1	+1
15. Picking flowers in a public park.......	−2	+3	5	0	+1
16. Laziness..........................	−2	+3	5	−1	+2
17. Boy running away from home........	−1	+4	5	0	+2
18. Breaking windows..................	−1	+2	3	−1	+1
19. Insulting the defenseless............	−1	+2	3	−1	0
20. Excessive drinking.................	−1	+1	2	−1	0
21. Not standing up when the "Star Spangled Banner" is played........	−3	−1	2	−2	−1
22. Being a slacker in time of war........	0	+1	1	0	0
23. Neglecting to study your lesson.......	−1	0	1	0	0
24. Making fun of cripples..............	0	−1	−1†	−1	−1
25. Being cross to your brother or sister...	+1	0	−1	+1	0
26. Being a Bolshevik..................	+1	0	−1	+1	0
27. Drinking a great deal of coffee and tea.	+1	−2	−3	0	0
28. Whispering in school................	+2	−1	−3	+1	0
	−73 +5	+91 −5	+163 −9	−31 +3	+36 −2

Average excess and defect scores, and average spans:
Excess: Female 2.6   Defect: Female .18   Span
       Male .18   Male 3.2   5.50

* In Items 1 to 23 the span represents the difference between a female excess and a male
defect in condemnation, in 24 to 28 between a male excess and female defect.
† A negative span indicates greater censure by males than by females.

TABLE 71.—SEX DIFFERENCES IN DEGREES OF CENSURE.—(*Continued*)

M-F test items	Excess	Defect	Span	3 Ex-tremely wicked	0 Not really bad
Form B‡ order of female excess over male defect:					
1. Playing marbles for keeps............	−4	+8	12	−1	+4
2. Swearing..........................	−5	+6	11	−3	+2
3. "Talking back" to the teacher........	−5	+6	11	−2	+2
4. Spitting on the sidewalk............	−5	+5	10	−1	+1
5. Disobeying a "keep off the grass" sign	−4	+5	9	−1	+1
6. Beating your way on a freight train...	−3	+6	9	0	+3
7. Stealing candy from the grocery man..	−3	+5	8	−2	+2
8. Being ashamed of your parents.......	−3	+5	8	−2	+2
9. Being "yellow" or cowardly..........	−2	+6	8	−1	+2
10. Playing hooky from school...........	−3	+4	7	−1	+2
11. Accepting wrong change when it is in your favor......................	−1	+6	7	0	+2
12. Not going to Sunday School..........	−3	+4	7	−1	+2
13. Running away from home............	−2	+4	6	0	+2
14. Losing your temper..................	−3	+3	6	−1	+1
15. Deceiving others without actually telling a lie......................	−3	+2	5	−1	0
16. Shooting craps.....................	−3	+2	5	−1	+1
17. Girls fighting.....................	0	+4	4	+1	+2
18. Playing cards for money............	−1	+2	3	−1	0
19. Discourtesy to people about us.......	−2	+1	3	−1	0
20. Stealing a dollar from your mother's purse..........................	0	−2	2	0	−1
21. Disobeying your parents............	−1	+1	2	−1	0
22. Matching pennies for keeps..........	−2	0	2	0	0
23. Cheating in examination............	0	+2	2	0	0
24. Being extravagant..................	0	+2	2	0	+1
25. Picking on somebody weaker than yourself.......................	−1	−1	0	−1	0
26. Not adding to the collection box at church........................	−1	−1	0	−1	0
27. Stealing a dime from your mother's purse..........................	+1	0	− 1	+1	0
28. Being an atheist...................	+3	0	− 3	+2	0
	−60+4	+89−4	149−5	−23+4	+32−1

Average excess and defect scores, and average span:
Excess: Female 2.1   Defect: Female .14   Span
Male   .14   Male   3.2   5.1
Averages for Forms A and B combined:
Excess: Female 2.3   Defect: Female .16   Span
Male   .16   Male   3.2   5.3

‡ In Items 1 to 25 the span represents the difference between a female excess and a male defect in condemnation, in Items 26 to 28 between a male excess and a female defect.

Taken at their face value the scores also indicate a keener sense of pity in the female and a corresponding callousness in the male. But the true interpretation of the general tendency of females to more emphatic expression of feeling requires separate discussion.

Ethical Reactions.—Here the subject is presented with a list of acts of various degrees of "wickedness" and is asked to grade the badness of each on a descending scale of 3, 2, 1, 0. The response weights are to be interpreted in the same manner as in the preceding sections of this exercise. For example, "stealing a ride on a truck" has the response weights -2, -2, $+1$, $+1$ for the 3, 2, 1, 0 degrees of badness respectively, showing that females more often than males check the 3 or 2, and males more often than females the 1 or 0.

The results are summarized in Table 71 in which the "excess" score is arrived at by doubling the weight for "3" (extremely wicked) and adding it to the weight for "2" (decidedly bad), the "defect" score by doubling the weight for "0" (not really bad) and adding it to the score for "1" (rather bad). Table 71 gives separately the weights for "3" and "0" as well as the "excess" and "defect" scores. Table 72 gives the male and female averages for each degree of censure.

TABLE 72.—AVERAGE SCORE WEIGHTS FOR EACH DEGREE OF CENSURE
(Numbers in parentheses refer to the number of items in which a higher proportion of males or females recorded the particular degree of censure in question)

Degrees	Extremely wicked 3	Decidedly bad 2	Rather bad 1	Not really bad 0
Form A				
General averages............	1.2	1	.9	1.4
Male average................	(3) .1	(7) .3	(19) .8	(18)1.3
Female average..............	(19)1.1	(14) .7	(3) .14	(2) .07
Form B				
General averages............	.9	1.2	1	1.2
Male average................	(3) .15	(7) .25	(14) .9	(14)1.1
Female average..............	(18) .8	(16) .7	(2) .07	(1) .04

A glance at Table 71 reveals the greater tendency of females to excessive censure, as most items show a span of female excess over male defect, few the reverse. Table 72 indicates this difference succinctly. The average scores under each degree of wickedness suggest that the items seem to the subjects as a whole fairly representative of all degrees of badness, since the differences in the general average scores under each degree are not very marked, the most lenient judgment ("not really bad") being slightly the commonest. But the division into female and male scores shows that this conclusion is delusive, for the result is reached by a female tendency to severity of judgment being balanced by a male tendency to leniency. To males more of the offenses listed are trivial, and to females serious. Statistically, the female "extremely wicked" judgments average 11 and 5 times more severe than those of the males (for the two forms respectively), and the male extremely lenient judgments ("not really bad") 18 and 27 times more lenient than those of the females. We may not conclude that females are really morally more sensitive or more particular than males, since the same tendency to excess of expression in the female characterizes the responses for the four emotional sections, including the emotion of anger; and who would claim that females are more pugnacious or more irascible than males are? Moreover, had females been really sterner moralists than males to the extent of the difference in the scores this would have forced itself upon general notice long ago.

But perhaps a closer analysis will reveal specific factors as well as this sex difference in general emphasis. Two questions suggest themselves: (1) Does the female severity apply more to the lighter or the graver offenses? (2) Is a given sex more condemnatory of offenses which characterize the opposite sex?

The first question may be answered by comparing the scores for the most, with those for the least, serious offenses. Although there is not, of course, any one true order of seriousness for this or any other list of offenses, we have from each form selected for comparison three which seem to us among the most reprehensible and three among the least so. The "excess" and "defect" scores for these are given in Table 73, which shows a marked tendency for the female sex to be harsher than the male in judging petty offenses, but to be relatively less harsh in the case of more serious offenses.

TABLE 73.—SEX DIFFERENCES IN THE CENSURE OF SERIOUS AND TRIVIAL OFFENSES

M-F test items	Excess	Defect	Span
Form A			
Serious offenses:			
Excessive drinking.....................	−1	+1	− 2
Insulting the defenseless...............	−1	+2	− 3
Making fun of cripples.................	0	−1	1
Average difference between female excess and male defect of severity is 1.3.			
Trivial offenses:			
Not brushing your teeth...............	−4	+5	9
Whispering in school..................	+2	−1	3
Using slang...........................	−3	+3	6
Average difference between female excess and male defect is 4.			
Form B			
Serious offenses:			
Stealing a dime from your mother's purse.	+1	0	2
Picking on somebody weaker than yourself	−1	−1	0
Cheating in examination...............	0	+2	2
Average difference between female excess and male defect is 3.			
Trivial offenses:			
Losing your temper....................	−3	+3	6
Being extravagant.....................	0	+2	2
Spitting on the sidewalk...............	−5	+5	10
Average difference between female excess and male defect is 6.			

We come now to our second question, whether a sex tends to condemn the more the offenses of the opposite sex. We may divide the items into four groups of offenses: distinctively male, distinctively female, common, and ambiguous. By "common" is meant those committed about equally by both sexes, and by "ambiguous" those about which difference of opinion might be expected, but which are not so obviously special to one sex as to justify their inclusion in our first two classes. Table 74 gives the data according to our own classification of the items.

TABLE 74.—CENSURE SCORES OF MALE AND FEMALE OFFENSES

M-F test items	Excess	Defect	Span
Distinctively male offenses:			
1. Boys fighting..................................	− 8	+ 7	15
2. Shooting rabbits just for fun....................	− 4	+ 8	12
3. Stealing a ride on a truck......................	− 6	+ 3	9
4. Boys teasing girls..............................	− 3	+ 5	8
5. Breaking windows...............................	− 1	+ 2	3
6. Excessive drinking..............................	− 1	+ 1	2
7. Spitting on the sidewalk........................	− 5	+ 5	10
8. Beating your way on a freight train.............	− 3	+ 6	9
9. Swearing.......................................	− 5	+ 6	11
10. Picking on somebody weaker than yourself........	− 1	− 1	0
11. Boys smoking before they are 21.................	− 4	+ 7	11
12. Swiping fruit out of orchards...................	− 6	+ 8	14
13. Boy running away from home.....................	− 1	+ 4	5
	−48	+62 − 1	109
Average span of female excess (109 ÷ 13).......			8.4
Distinctively female offenses:			
1. Girls fighting..................................	0	+ 4	4
2. Drinking a great deal of coffee and tea..........	+ 1	− 2	−3
3. Being extravagant..............................	0	+ 2	2
	+ 1	+6 − 2	+6 − 3
Average span of female excess (6 − 3 ÷ 3)......			1.0
Offenses common to both sexes:			
1. Indulging in "petting".........................	− 5	+ 6	11
2. Going to bed without saying your prayers.........	− 5	+ 5	10
3. Not brushing your teeth.........................	− 4	+ 5	9
4. Telling a lie to avoid punishment................	− 3	+ 3	6
5. Picking flowers in a public park.................	− 2	+ 3	5
6. Laziness.......................................	− 2	+ 3	5
7. Neglecting to study your lesson..................	− 1	0	1
8. Being cross to your brother or sister.............	+ 1	0	−1
9. Whispering in school............................	+ 2	− 1	−3
10. Being ashamed of your parents..................	− 3	+ 5	8
11. Accepting wrong change when it is in your favor...	− 1	+ 6	7
12. Losing your temper............................	− 3	+ 3	6
13. Deceiving others without actually telling a lie.....	− 3	+ 2	5
14. Discourtesy to people about us..................	− 2	+ 1	3
15. Stealing a dollar from your mother's purse........	0	− 2	−2
16. Disobeying your parents........................	− 1	+ 1	2
17. Cheating in examination........................	0	+ 2	2
18. Not adding to the collection box at church.......	− 1	− 1	0
19. Stealing a dime from your mother's purse.........	+ 1	0	−1
20. Being an atheist...............................	+ 3	0	−3
21. Playing cards for money........................	− 1	+ 2	3
22. Using slang...................................	− 3	+ 3	6
	−40 + 7	+50 − 4	87 − 10
Average span of female excess (87 − 10 ÷ 22)...			3.5
Ambiguous offenses:			
1. Moderate drinking.............................	− 4	+ 5	9
2. Having fits of temper...........................	− 2	+ 7	9
3. Putting pins on the teacher's chair...............	− 4	+ 3	7
4. Not standing up when the "Star Spangled Banner" is played....................................	− 3	− 1	2
5. Making fun of cripples..........................	0	− 1	−1
6. Being a slacker in time of war...................	0	+ 1	1
7. "Talking back" to the teacher...................	− 5	+ 6	11
8. Disobeying a "keep off the grass" sign...........	− 4	+ 5	9
9. Stealing candy from the grocery man.............	− 3	+ 5	8
10. Being "yellow" or cowardly....................	− 2	+ 6	8
11. Playing hooky from school......................	− 3	+ 4	7
12. Not going to Sunday School....................	− 3	+ 4	7
13. Running away from home.......................	− 2	+ 4	6
14. Matching pennies for keeps.....................	− 2	0	2
15. Playing marbles for keeps......................	− 4	+ 8	12
16. Shooting craps................................	− 3	+ 2	5
17. Being a Bolshevik..............................	+ 1	0	−1
18. Insulting the defenseless.......................	− 1	+ 2	3
	−45 + 1	+62 − 2	106 − 2
Average span of female excess (106 − 2 ÷ 18)...			5.8

Comparing the average spans of female excess over male defect in severity, 8.4 for specifically male as against 3.5 and 5.8 for the common and ambiguous offenses, and 1.00 for the three specifically female offenses, the statistics evidence a female tendency to be more severe than males upon male offenses, and if we may take three items as enough to judge by, to be more lenient toward female offenses than toward offenses common to both sexes.

An interesting instance of the effect upon the scores of the combination of the general female tendency to excessive expression with the tendency of a sex to condemn the other sex's offenses more severely is afforded by the figures for the parallel items "boys fighting" and "girls fighting."

M-F test items	Excess	Defect	Span
Boys fighting..................	−8	+7	15
Girls fighting..................	0	+4	4

The combination of the two female tendencies to severity in general, and to condemn male offenses in particular, makes the span for "boys fighting" the highest among all the 56 items on both lists; while on the other hand this tendency to condemn in general is in the case of the specifically female offense reduced to insignificance in "girls fighting" by the sex's condonation of its own sex's offense.

We may now ask whether or how far it is ethical discrimination that the responses are revealing. To what extent have the specified types of behavior been judged according to moral standards only?

One way of approaching this question is to have the items ranked by independent moral experts (presumably a chosen few) and then to see of which sex the scores most nearly correspond to their ranking. We might conclude that, other things equal, the less consonant sex admits the more emotional bias; its judgment is more an emotional and less a purely ethical judgment. But this would entail an additional research. And in any case the chosen experts might be expert only in the social morality of their

TABLE 75.—CENSURE SCORES OF FOUR GRADES OF OFFENSES

M-F test items	Excess	Defect	Span
Grade A (the most serious offenses):			
1. Insulting the defenseless....................	−1	+2	3
2. Excessive drinking M[1].....................	−1	+1	2
3. Making fun of cripples.....................	0	−1	−1
4. Picking on somebody weaker than yourself......	−1	−1	0
Average.................................	−0.75	+0.25	1
Grade B (serious but not so grave as A):			
1. Lying to avoid punishment..................	−3	+3	6
2. Accepting wrong change when it is in your favor	−1	+6	7
3. Stealing a dollar from your mother's purse......	0	−2	−2
4. Cheating in examination....................	0	+2	2
5. Deceiving others without actually telling a lie	−3	+2	5
6. Swearing M..............................	−5	+6	11
7. Boys teasing girls M.......................	−3	+5	8
8. Girls fighting F[1].........................	0	+4	4
Average.................................	−1.8	+3.2	5.1
Grade C:			
1. "Talking back" to the teacher..............	−5	+6	11
2. Spitting on the sidewalk M.................	−5	+5	10
3. Losing your temper........................	−3	+3	6
4. Being extravagant F.......................	0	+2	2
5. Boys fighting M...........................	−8	+7	15
6. Beating your way on a freight train M.........	−3	+6	9
7. Neglecting to study your lesson..............	−1	0	1
8. Boys smoking before they are 21 M...........	−4	+7	11
9. Breaking windows M.......................	−1	+2	3
10. Whispering in school.......................	+2	−1	−3
11. Disobeying a "keep off the grass" sign.........	−4	+5	9
Average.................................	−2.9	+3.9	6.7
Grade D (the least iniquitous):			
1. Being an atheist...........................	+3	0	−3
2. Not adding to the collection box at church......	−1	−1	0
3. Being a Bolshevik.........................	+1	0	−1
4. Not brushing your teeth....................	−4	+5	9
5. Moderate drinking.........................	−4	+5	9
6. Using slang...............................	−3	+3	6
7. Playing cards for money....................	−1	+2	3
Average.................................	−1.3	+2	3.3

[1] M and F indicate that the item is considered a specifically male or female offense.

time and place, freedom from which in an unsophisticated child (as indeed in an adult also) might evidence a more genuinely ethical judgment.

The only plan immediately practicable is to take the compared sex responses as they stand and, after ranking to one's own satisfaction the various items in a scale of offensiveness, to see how far one sex shows the more severe judgment than the other for the offenses judged by us more serious, and conversely. For reasons given this method is precarious, but we can with the material at hand apply it. The 30 items which seemed easiest to place at one of four levels of badness are ranked in Table 75.

If our ranking represents a more correct moral judgment than those of the subjects themselves, the analysis shows, after allowing for the effect of specific sex bias:

1. A tendency, except for morally colorless practices enumerated in Grade D, for the male judgments to be nearest the female judgments in severity as the offenses increase in gravity.

2. That as compared with males, females are particularly severe on minor offenses which are yet just sufficiently offensive to merit condemnation; but

3. That when the "offense" becomes so inconsiderable as to be very questionably an offense at all, even the females are apt to relax their proportionate severity a little. But again

4. That even in the morally indifferent items (Grade D) there are still some against which the distinctive female severity is marked ("using slang," "not brushing your teeth," and "moderate drinking").

The results support the view that the male has on the whole a more "objective" moral judgment than the female, who tends to exaggerate minor offenses.

To the question then whether it is ethical discrimination (capacity for reasoned objective valuation) that is being measured, apart from the dependence of the answer upon the particular sentiment tapped by the particular item, and apart from our general human incapacity to keep our judgments clear of bias, our analysis suggests the answer that the female judgments tend, on the whole, to be more emotional and less objective than the male.

This view is supported by such curiosities as the markedly distinctive female condemnation of trivial offenses like "not brushing your teeth" and "using slang."

Preference for Alternatives.—The subject is presented with pairs of situations, occupations, or objects, and records against each pair which of the two, if either, he likes the better.

In Table 76 the items are arranged in descending order of male and female preference (for one rather than for the other alternative in each case). An example will explain the symbols used:

TABLE 76.—PREFERENCE ORDER FOR CHOICE OF ALTERNATIVES
Items in descending order of male and female preference
Forms A and B combined

Male preference		Span	Female preference	
1. Work with men v. 1....	+22	35 or 37	1. Work with women....	−13(−15)
2. Give a report verbally v. 2...................	+ 5	10	2. Give a report in writing................	− 5
3. Camping v. 7..........	+ 4	7	3. A poorly cooked meal, but linen spotless...	− 5
4. A well-cooked meal, but soiled table linen v. 3	+ 4	9	4. Persuade others......	− 5
5. Command others v. 4...	+ 4	9	5. Work of a single kind	− 4
6. An auto with scruffy paint but excellent motor v. 8..........	+ 3	6	6. Book work...........	− 4
7. Great variety of work v. 5...................	+ 3	7	7. Living in good hotels..	− 3
8. Laboratory work v. 6..	+ 3	7	8. An auto with fresh paint but only fairly good motor........	− 3
9. Work involving many details v. 12.........	+ 2	4	9. Interesting work with small income.......	− 3
10. Uninteresting work with large income v. 9.....	+ 2	5	10. Work in one location	− 2
11. Make plans v. 14.......	+ 1	2	11. Live in the city.......	− 2
12. Live in the country v. 11	+ 1	3	12. Work involving few details.............	− 2
13. Change from place to place v. 10..........	+ 1	3	13. Work under a respected superior........	− 2
14. Work for yourself v. 13.	+ 1	3	14. Carry out plans......	− 1

in Item 3 on the male preference side of the table, +4 means that a markedly higher proportion of males than of females say they prefer "camping." "V.7" indicates the alternative, given in Item 7 on the female preference side, to which they prefer it, namely, "living in good hotels." The 7 under the heading "Span" represents the span or sex divergence in preference got by summing the male preference score for "camping" and the female preference score for its alternative, "living in good hotels." (One item, "work with women vs. work with men" occurred in both Forms A and B with female preference scores of 13 and 15 respectively, and male scores of 22 for "work with men" in both cases.)

On the basis of conclusions from our previous exercises predictions were ventured, before consulting the scores, as to which sex would score higher for each alternative. The predictions for Items 1, 3, 4, 5, 6, and 8 on the male preference side of the table and their corresponding alternatives, 1, 7, 3, 4, 8, and 6 on the female preference side proved correct: sex traits now familiar explain the sex differences in response. The sex-to-sex tendency (M 1 and F 1),[1] the male out-of-door interest and love of adventure (M 3 and F 7), the female interest in decorativeness and beauty of appearance (M 4 and F 3 and M 6 and F 4), the greater male interest in the mechanical, and perhaps the female interest in some kinds of literature (M 8 with F 6) suffice or help to explain all the more significant contrasts in which prediction was verified.

The contrast "work with men" and "work with women," appearing in both forms, has the singularly high sex divergence span of 37 and 35, the next highest in the section being 10. But in both cases the item "work with men" has a plus index of 22, its counterpart "work with women" having a minus index of 15 and 13. This indicates that though each sex evinces strongly the sex-to-sex tendency, at the same time more females express a preference for male than males for female coworkers.

The items in which predictions failed run as follows:

[1] "M 1" means Item 1 on the male preference side, "F 1" means Item 1 on the female preference side.

M-F test items	Scores	Span
M F 1. Give a report verbally vs. report in writing.............	$+5 - 5 =$	10
M F 2. Great variety of work vs. work of a single kind.........	$+3 - 4 =$	7
M F 3. Work involving many details vs. work involving few details	$+2 - 2 =$	4
M F 4. Uninteresting work with large income vs. interesting work with small income.................................	$+2 - 3 =$	5
M F 5. Change from place to place vs. work in one location.....	$+1 - 2 =$	3

Predictions in these cases were rash and precarious because the sex differences recorded are not really or clearly derivable from the distinctive traits disclosed by previous exercises, but from other characteristics not contained in them and not so far revealed by our inquiry.

Summarizing: (1) most cases of widest sex span support, and none contradicts, conclusions as to sex differences ventured elsewhere; but (2) the form of the exercise admits of so many variant reactions under the same recorded scores as to make generalizations from the narrower spans precarious.

Sex Differences in Emotional Expressiveness.—The tendency of females to more extreme responses than males has already been noticed, specifically in anger responses and moral censure. We may now consider this question more generally. For all four emotions and for ethical judgment we have summarized the evidence of a distinctive female tendency toward excess, and a distinctive male tendency toward defect, of expressed emotion and censure. The table at the top of page 413 gives for Form A and Form B combined, and separately for anger, fear, disgust, pity, and wickedness, the number of cases in which the highest or lowest degrees of feeling were expressed by each of the sexes. That is, there are 151 items showing female excess as compared with 9 showing male excess, but only 13 cases of female defect as compared with 142 of male defect.

SEX TEMPERAMENTS AS REVEALED BY THE M-F TEST 413

Emotion	Highest degree		Lowest degree	
	Male	Female	Male	Female
Anger....................	1	24	19	5
Fear.....................	2	29	33	4
Disgust..................	0	35	32	1
Pity.....................	0	26	23	0
Censure..................	6	37	35	3
Total..................	9	151	142	13

Moreover, the average score weight in the cases of male excess and female defect were much lower than in the items showing male defect and female excess. These are as follows, for Form A and Form B combined:

Emotion	Excess	Defect
Anger:		
Female................	3.9	.3
Male.................	.06	1.8
Fear:		
Female................	4.2	.25
Male.................	.1	5.2
Disgust:		
Female................	7.7	.17
Male.................	.0	5.4
Pity:		
Female................	4.8	.04
Male.................	.0	3.6
Censure:		
Female................	1.9	.11
Male.................	.24	2.5

The above figures can be summarized by saying that the female tends much more than the male to extreme expression in all four emotions and in moral censure, particularly in disgust, rather less in pity, less still in fear, and least in anger and censure; though her excess, if less marked for censure than for pity, fear, and anger, is more ubiquitous.

How are we to interpret these figures? In regard to the four emotions, two questions await answer: "Why is the female generally more expressive than the male?" and "Why is her excess over the male least in the case of anger?" To the second question it is easy to suggest an answer in terms of social expectation, training, and bias, and to a certain extent in terms of innate factors: the girl is socially trained to express fastidiousness, and permitted to express fear more freely than the boy, and in certain directions to express more pity, but not to show more anger. Again, the female may be innately more prone to fear and active sympathy, and both more especially trained and perhaps more prompted by innate sex motives to shun the ugly and unsightly, but not to express more anger.   It is the girl rather than the boy from whom society exacts the sweeter temper and expressions not of anger but of gentleness.   Hence we can ascribe the comparative mildness of the female in the case of anger to innate or to culture factors, or to both.

But it remains to consider the first of the two questions: "Why does the female still show herself more angry than the male?" and also to compare the results for moral censure with those for the emotions.

Three possibilities suggest themselves:

(1) The female may be really the more emotional sex; she "feels things more" than the male does; or

(2) a greater freedom of expression may be socially encouraged or sanctioned in the female; or again,

(3) her training and occupations promote in her a greater tendency to verbal exaggeration; or

(4) two or more of these may combine.

The first hypothesis cannot be directly tested; the only objective test is through expression, but whether expression corresponds with that which it expresses is the very point at issue.   But there are reasons for mistrusting the adequacy of this hypothesis. Though psychologists might agree that the innate impulses of flight, repulsion, active sympathy, are stronger in the female sex, with their accompanying asthenic emotions of fear, disgust, and pity, surely no one maintains the same of pugnacity with the asthenic emotion of anger.   Though an innate factor—a genuinely keener emotion—may therefore account for some of the excess expression in fear, disgust, and pity, a residuum of excess over the male, represented by the excess figures for anger, remains to be accounted for in all the sections; and this cannot acceptably be referred to greater intensity of feeling.   If then this residuum can be adequately covered by one of the other hypotheses we shall not be justified in referring it to the first.

One inclines rather to seek an explanation from the two environmental factors.   On the one hand, in Western society at any rate, the boy is tacitly and openly expected to be more "Spartan" than the girl.   Crying in a girl is condoned on occasions when in a boy it would be voted "sissy."   No boy may be "as timid as a girl."   To be overnice about dress or deportment is considered effeminate.   Control over feeling, or at least over its expression, is considered manly in a man but not womanly in a woman.   Emotional display is socially expected in a woman (the man rather likes it in her), but emotional control is expected in the man (the woman rather admires him for it).

Moreover, as the sexes mature their customary social milieus increasingly differ, the boy taking to business and the girl to domestic and social life.   Business keeps feeling in the background, social gatherings bring it out.   Emotional exuberance befits the one situation, but reticence the other.   Exuberance easily passes into exaggeration, and the girl forms the habit of saying more than she means, while with boys the tendency is the other way.   The conclusion may be ventured that a cultivated masculine reticence and feminine exuberance combine to account for the scores.   On these assumptions it becomes unnecessary to resort to our unverifiable "greater emotionality" hypothesis.

Lastly, it is easier to explain the sex divergence in severity of moral judgment by the environmental hypothesis.   It indicates why ethical judgments share with anger the lowest place on the sex divergence scale.   With fear, disgust, and pity, special reasons have been found for the additional female excessiveness beyond a general residuum.   That general residuum has been attributed to male inhibition on the one side and to female exaggeration on the other.

EXERCISE 5: INTERESTS, LIKES, AND DISLIKES

Exercise 5 is divided into eight series of likes and dislikes, in the first five of which the subject has to declare whether he likes, dislikes, or is indifferent to

A. Vocational occupations;

B. People with certain characteristics;

C and D. Certain forms of pastime, entertainment, occupations, or situations;

E. Certain books.

The last three series ask him which items from a given program he would like, dislike, or neither like nor dislike

F. To draw (if an artist);

G. To report on (if a newspaper reporter);

H. To do or visit (if on a period of travel).

If the information exercise is an indirect, this one is a direct, inquiry into individual interests, and to that extent would appear to obtain its results less from the accidents of experience and more from the emotional dispositions of the subject, and so to reflect more directly his actual temperament and personal habits of mind. By actual we do not necessarily mean innate, for our likes and dislikes are also influenced by environment.

Our discussion is based upon data from 158 subjects in the grade school, 200 in high school, 52 in college, and 80 nonacademic adults; 590 in all. Each group has an equal number of males and females.

Predictive Analysis.—For the first section in Form A (on occupation preferences) and for 72 cases in Form B where a preferential sex like or dislike seemed deducible from the conclusions of our analysis of Exercise 3, predictions were ventured as to which sex would score higher under "L" (like), and "D" (dislike). If tentative inductions as to the emotional dispositions and consequent directions of interest of the two sexes derived from an investigation of a situation where they were only indirectly exhibited, and might be expected to have been obscured by other circumstances, were confirmed by an immediate inquiry into these very interests themselves, this would mean that the traits were so dominant that, even in a situation where environment and experience (in the shape of factual information) were given every chance of determining the responses, these sex differences in emotional tendencies and interests had proved the one set of differences that clearly emerged all through.

Out of the 48 predictions of L and D sex predominances ventured for Section A, Form A, 41 instead of a chance 16 proved correct. But in venturing a prediction one had to remember: (1) that the question at issue was not of the absolute amount of like or dislike for a given occupation, but of which sex liked or disliked it more, a pronounced *sex* preference being perfectly compatible with an absolute dislike on the part of the sex expressing the comparative preference; (2) that even a very small difference in the sex responses would produce a score for one or other sex, though so small as to be relatively unreliable.

For both these reasons several erroneous forecasts might have been anticipated. That 41 instead of the chance 16 proved correct to this extent supported the hypothesis upon which the predictions were based. The 7 incorrect forecasts concerned four occupations for all of which predictions had been diffident, through inability to estimate or balance conflicting factors. These were as follows:

Item	Forecast	Actual scored result	Preferential index
Architect	$L -, D +$	$L +, D -$	3
Chef or cook	$D +$	$D\ 0$	3
Journalist	$L +, D -$	$L -, D +$	6
Draftsman	$L -, D +$	$L +, D -$	10

It might be added that for two of these four the preference index (or degree of sex divergence) is the lowest for the section, making prediction the more precarious. Of the 25 items on the list, in 9 the forecast had been marked as diffident or dubious; 4 proved incorrect and 5 correct. The correlation of confidence with correctness, and diffidence with half correctness, supports the hypotheses which were the bases of the forecasts.

Of the 72 cases in the various sections of Form B for which prediction as to sex preferences was hazarded on the basis of our assumed sex differences, 68 proved correct.

We may now pass to the a posteriori analysis.

Relative Differentiating Power of the Various Sections of the Exercise.—Of the eight sections it seemed that A (on preferred occupations) would most repay study. As it turned out, this section shows the largest sex difference, and B the least. Table 77 gives our statistical data on the relative amount of sex difference brought out by the eight sections. The figures of Table 77 are reached by amalgamating the two forms, A and B, and averaging the score weights for L, D, and N respectively for each section. The sum of the L and D averages yields one, and the average N score weight another, index of the degree to which the responses divide the sexes. A high "affective span" and to a less degree a low "hesitance" (neutral) score indicate marked sex divergence, and vice versa. The order is that of decreasing significance, as determined by the affective span.

An example will make the method clear. Section A contains 50 items in all, 25 in each form. The average score for L, taking female and male scores together, is 5.4, and the average D or dislike score, 4.7, yielding a difference between them, or affective span, of 10.1. The average score for "neither like nor dislike" is 1.4. We call this the "hesitance index." A high affective

TABLE 77.—DISCRIMINATIVE VALUE OF THE SEVERAL PARTS OF EXERCISE 5

Section	No. of items	Average L	Average D	Affective span	Average N	Hesitance index rank
A	50	5.4	4.7	10.1	1.4	(3)
C	27	4.9	2.9	7.8	2.4	(8)
G	12	3.9	3.2	7.1	.9	(1)
H	22	4.2	2.8	7.0	1.5	(4)
D	40	3.8	3	6.8	1.38	(6)
F	16	3.9	2.8	6.7	1.6	(4)
E	46	4.7	1.7	6.4	1.3	(2)
B	24	1.9	2.2	4.1	2	(7)

span and a low hesitance index shows that the items differentiate the sexes markedly; a low span and a high hesitance index shows that the items are relatively nondifferentiating.

Section *A*: Occupations.—In interpreting the data on this section it is well to remember that in default of actual experience with given occupations the subjects' responses are likely to be influenced largely by cultural sex bias; especially the younger and less intelligent subjects will be unable to dissociate their sentiment toward an occupation from its inherent interest to them. Even in occupations fairly equally open to both sexes a bias may appear; for example, the "he-man" may by his very tendency to be self-assertive affect a distaste for an occupation which women are rapidly taking up. In short, the sex differences that this section

TABLE 78.—PREFERENCE INDICES OF OCCUPATIONS BY SEX
Form A

Occupation	Male preference index	N
Forest ranger.................	+15	0
Building contractor............	+11	0
Stock breeder.................	+11	+3
Draftsman....................	+10	−1
Auto racer....................	+ 9	+1
Soldier......................	+ 8	0
Dairyman....................	+ 7	+2
Detective....................	+ 6	+1
Architect....................	+ 3	−1
Average..................	8.8	

Occupation	Female preference index	N
Dressmaker..................	−25	+1
Librarian....................	−22	+3
Nurse.......................	−18	0
Florist......................	−16	+3
Private secretary..............	−16	+4
Singer......................	−14	+2
Music teacher.................	−13	−1
Social worker.................	−12	0
Bookkeeper..................	−10	+2
Novelist.....................	− 8	0
Artist.......................	− 7	+3
Journalist....................	− 6	0
Clerk in a store...............	− 6	0
Preacher....................	− 5	−2
Optician....................	− 5	−1
Chef or cook.................	− 3	+3
Average..................	11.6	

TABLE 78.—PREFERENCE INDICES OF OCCUPATIONS BY SEX.—*(Continued)*
Form B

Occupation	Male preference index	N
Auto mechanic...............	+16	+1
Factory manager..............	+12	+2
Aviator.....................	+ 9	+1
Fisherman...................	+ 8	+2
Plumber.....................	+ 8	+2
Miner......................	+ 6	+2
Explorer....................	+ 5	0
Farmer or rancher............	+ 4	0
Average....................	8.5	

Occupation	Female preference index	N
Interior decorator............	−22	+3
Teacher.....................	−16	+3
Stenographer................	−15	+3
Barber or hairdresser..........	−14	−1
Waiter or waitress............	−13	0
Jeweler.....................	−12	+2
Poet.......................	−10	+2
Sculptor....................	−10	+1
Magazine illustrator..........	− 9	+1
Missionary..................	− 9	0
Office clerk.................	− 9	0
Furniture dealer..............	− 8	−1
Musician....................	− 8	+2
Landscape gardener...........	− 6	0
Orchestra conductor..........	− 5	−1
Cashier.....................	− 4	+3
Research worker..............	− 3	−1
Average....................	10.2	

reveals may be acquired no less than native, and the factor of "essential sexuality" remains obscure.

Table 78 summarizes the item weights of the various items in a form suitable for exhibiting sex contrast; namely, in two statements, one of occupations preferred by a higher proportion of females, the other of those preferred by a higher proportion of males, in orders of decreasing degree of preference. It must be premised, in explanation of the table, that a high sex record under L (like) predisposes to a high opposite sex record under D (dislike), and conversely, since if many of one sex record a positive liking for an occupation, there remain fewer of that sex but more of the other to record a dislike. Not that the equation will be exact, since there is also a third choice, N (for indecision), which may attract unequal numbers from the sex residues. Therefore, in establishing the total preference of one sex over the other in a given case, account must be taken of both the L and the D records by treating the degree of liking expressed by sex A plus the degree of dislike expressed by sex B as an index of A's preference over B's for the occupation in question.

The "preference index" of an item is found by adding the D weight to the L weight and attaching the sign ($-$ or $+$) for L to the total, thus making it an index of liking. For example, Item 12 in Form A:

12. Dressmaker $-13L$ $+12D$ $+1N$

yields a female preference index of -25. The number against N yields an index of hesitance; it registers the relative indecision of sex choice, a plus registering a higher proportion of males, a minus a higher proportion of females as hesitant or undecided. The preference index records the degree, and an *opposite sign* in the hesitance index the decisiveness, of the relative preference of a given sex for the item concerned. For instance, a $+3N$ signifies that far more males than females were undecided in their attitude. An opposite sign to 3 may thus be considered a decisive, and of 4 or 5 a very decisive, preference.

Let us consider first the data for Form A. A comparison of male with female preferential items brings out the following contrasts:

1. The most indoor occupations fall on to the female preference side. Perhaps "draftsman" and "architect" are exceptions.

2. Not one of the female preferences can be considered primarily an outdoor occupation. "Social worker" and "journalist" come nearest to exceptions.

3. All the artistic and decorative occupations are on the female side.

4. The six occupations on the list that involve direct ministration to individual comfort, convenience, or welfare are all on the female side (cook, social worker, nurse, dressmaker, private secretary, and preacher).

5. All the occupations on the male preference list are also occupations pursued exclusively or predominantly by males, more so

with those having the highest preference indices (forest ranger, building contractor, stock breeder), and less so with those having the lowest (detective, architect).

6. On the female side most occupations are occupations pursued by both sexes, none is a male monopoly; one only, or, if we include "nurse," two are female monopolies, and those two have nearly the highest female preferences.

7. The female exceed the male preferences both in number (16 against 9) and in average degree of preference (11.6 against 8.8).

Turning to the data for Form B, we find all seven points are corroborated. As regards the seventh, the female exceeded the male preference both in number (17 against 8) and in average degree of preference (10.2 against 8.5).

There are no items that indicate occupations carried on in the home, except perhaps "cook," "nurse," and "private secretary" (and these are female preferences), so that interest in that category is not ascertainable from this section of the exercise. We may add two more generalizations applicable to this section.

8. All the items associated with adventure and bodily risk, except missionary,[1] fall within the male preferences (auto racer, soldier, detective, miner, explorer, forest ranger, and stock breeder).

9. All the items requiring muscular strength or prolonged bodily exercise fall on to the male side (forest ranger, soldier, building contractor, stock breeder, auto mechanic, fisherman, plumber, explorer, rancher, miner).

Contrasting for both forms the items that are most preferred by males and females respectively (namely, those near the top of the tables), and comparing them again with those that are less strikingly preferred (those nearer the bottom), we find that vocations representing a combination of artistic and indoor occupations (interior decorator and dressmaker) head the female list on both forms, and a more outdoor occupation concerned with machinery heads the male list for Form B; and an active outdoor

---

[1] The term may suggest to a schoolchild religious ministration and sentiment as much as adventure and bodily risk.

occupation the list for Form A. In general, the occupations that are most sedentary tend toward the upper half of the female lists.

Summarizing: the records for Section A suggest that males have a favorable, and females a less favorable, sentiment toward outdoor vigorous occupations and occupations involving bodily risk and adventure; females have a favorable, and males a less favorable, sentiment toward artistic and decorative occupations and occupations involving immediate care of persons. We may name these the "ministrative" occupations to indicate the probable point of emotional appeal. The results of our scrutiny of this section support our main hypothesis: we find the male professedly the more aggressive and adventurous sex, hardier (perhaps also harder) emotionally, with more direct interest in mechanical (as distinct from human) processes; the female professedly gentler, more sympathetic, with more proclivity to artistic and humane (or humanitarian) than to mechanical pursuits.

Social Sex Bias.—Does each sex tend to like more its own sex's occupations? We have classified the occupations into three groups as predominantly male, predominantly female, or neutral and noted the preference index found in Table 78 for those in each group. They are as follows (index of each occupation in parentheses):

Predominantly male occupations:
 Aviator (9), auto mechanic (16), farmer or rancher (4), factory manager (12), fisherman (8), plumber (8), miner (6), explorer (5), auto racer (9), building contractor (11), forest ranger (15), dairyman (7), stock breeder (11), soldier (8), draftsman (10). These all score male.
Predominantly female occupations:
 Stenographer (15), teacher (16), nurse (18), dressmaker (25), music teacher (13). These all score female.
Neutral occupations:
 The remaining 30.

For the predominantly male occupations, the average male preference index is 9.2; for the predominantly female the average female preference is 17.2. Of the neutral two only are preferred by males, "detective" and "architect," the most questionably neutral of the group.   The average male preference of these two scores is 4.5.   The remaining 28 are all female preferences with an average female preference score of 9.7.   Thus, whereas the male tends to confine his preferences to occupations in which he already predominates, the female would enter neutral territory freely, since she expresses an average preference for 28 neutral occupations as great as the average preference of males for even dominantly male occupations.

Further, the expressed female preference for female occupations (17.2) is almost twice that of the males for male occupations (9.2).   That females are particularly enamored of their present jobs need not be concluded.   The female preference score for the female occupations may average higher than the male score for male occupations, not because the women love women's jobs, but because the men disdain them.   Females score high on their own jobs because men record no preference for them; men score lower on theirs because females are not so chary of occupying male preserves.

Summarizing: both the predictive and the a posteriori analyses confirm previous conclusions; females express themselves as more inclined than males to indoor, artistic or decorative, and ministrative occupations; males as more inclined than females to outdoor, adventurous, and muscular occupations.

We find in addition males preferring their own customary occupations, females, not only their own but also many male occupations.

How far this indicates protest or interest, and how far the preferences in general are genuine or merely professed, the statistical contrasts cannot tell us.

Sections B to H: Idiosyncrasies, Books, Pastimes, Etc.—It would be wearisome and unremunerative to discuss the other sections of Exercise 5 with the same detail with which we have discussed the "sexually" most significant section, A; especially as it needs only a cursory examination of the items to show that most of them fall into categories already formulated.   It will be necessary, therefore, merely to classify them sex-wise, and beyond this to consider real or seeming exceptions.

In classifying items in Sections *B* to *H*, both forms, we shall exclude those with a preference index of 3 or less (38 out of 257 items in all).   The preferences being comparative, the appearance of a response as the preference of one sex may mean, not that the sex espouses it, but that it exemplifies some quality opposite to that favored by the other sex; for instance, unaesthetic objects may thus appear as male preferences.   In spite of this complication the sex divergences evidenced from our previous exercises clearly obtain.   Our classes run as follows:

A. Distinctive male preferences:
  1. Objects, situations, etc., themselves "male" in character.
  2. Experiences implying adventure or aggressiveness.
  3. Experiences implying an interest in mechanisms and mechanical contrivances.
  4. Occupations primarily out-of-doors or involving hard or prolonged bodily exercise.
  5. Business, commercial, and political interests.
  6. Experiences the opposite of those favored by females.
B. Female preferences:
  1. Objects, characteristics, etc., themselves exemplified by females.
  2. Experiences which evoke maternal tenderness or active sympathy.
  3. Aesthetic experiences, including literature.
  4. Domestic experiences.
  5. Social interests.
  6. Experiences the opposite of those favored by the other sex.

According to whether items of the first six classes do actually score as distinctively male, and those of the second six as distinctively female, preferences, our hypothesis is supported or rebutted.

Class A 1. *Objects, Situations, etc., Primarily Concerning Males.*
In Form A:
    Section *B*—Men with beards.
    Section *C*—Charlie Chaplin.
    Section *C*—*Robinson Crusoe, Gulliver's Travels, Adventures of Sherlock Holmes, Little Men, Little Lord Fauntleroy, Boy's Life of Theodore Roosevelt.*
    Sections *F*, *G*, and *H*—None.
In Form B:
    Section *B*—Bald-headed men.
    Section *C*—W. S. Hart, Harold Lloyd.

Section *D*—None.
Section *E*—*The Courtship of Miles Standish, Daniel Boone, Adventures of Tom Sawyer, Bob—Son of Battle.*
Sections *F* to *H*—None.

All these except *Little Men, Little Lord Fauntleroy,* and *The Courtship of Miles Standish* score male preferences. Of these exceptions two are elsewhere accounted for. The third, *The Courtship of Miles Standish,* has a low female preference index, and it will probably be admitted that the title, as well as the contents of the poem, have a female equally with a male reference. It is scarcely a crucial exception.

Class A 2.   Experiences Associated with Adventure or Aggressive Activity.

Form A:
  Section *B*—None.
  Section *C*—Detective stories, Adventure stories.
  Section *D*—Hunting, Dare base (?).
  Section *E*—*Robinson Crusoe, Gulliver's Travels, Adventures of Sherlock Holmes, Boy's Life of Theodore Roosevelt, Rip Van Winkle.*
  Section *F*—Tigers, Ships.
  Section *G*—Accidents, Sporting news.
  Section *H*—Hunt lions in Africa, Visit many famous battlefields, See how criminals are treated.
Form B:
  Section *B*—None.
  Section *C*—Sporting pages, Stories of wild animals, W. S. Hart (?), Harold Lloyd (?).
  Section *D*—Fishing, Swimming.
  Section *E*—*The Swiss Family Robinson, Daniel Boone, The Call of the Wild, Twenty Thousand Leagues under the Sea, Wild Animals I Have Known, The Adventures of Tom Sawyer, The Spy, Bob—Son of Battle, Treasure Island, Two Years before the Mast.*
  Section *F*—Battle scenes, Lions, Ruins (?).
  Section *G*—Crimes, Fires.
  Section *H*—Climb many lofty mountain peaks.

All these, except the questionably adventurous Dare base, score male preferences. Dare base has a low female preferential index of 4.

Class A 3. Topics Implying an Interest in Mechanics and Mechanical Contrivances.

Form A:
Section *B*—None.
Section *C*—Radio magazines, Chemistry.
Section *D*—Repairing a door latch.
Sections *E*, *F*, and *G*—None.
Section *H*—Visit many manufacturing plants.
Form B:
Section *B*—None.
Section *C*—Shop work, Popular science books.
Section *D*—Working with tools, Riding bicycle.
Section *E*—None.
Sections *F* and *G*—None.
Section *H*—Seeing a ship-building plant and, possibly, Visiting the Chicago slaughter-house.

All these score male preferences.

Class A 4. Experiences Connected with Outdoor and Vigorous Bodily Activities.

Form A:
Section *B*—None.
Section *C*—Adventure stories (?).
Section *D*—Hunting.
Section *E*—*Robinson Crusoe, Gulliver's Travels.*
Section *F*—Tigers, Ships.
Section *G*—Sporting news.
Section *H*—Hunt lions in Africa.
Form B:
Section *B*—None.
Section *C*—Sporting pages, Stories of wild animals.
Section *D*—Riding bicycle, Fishing, Swimming.
Section *E*—*Swiss Family Robinson, Daniel Boone, The Call of the Wild, Twenty Thousand Leagues under the Sea, Wild Animals I Have Known, The Adventures of Tom Sawyer, Bob—Son of Battle, The Spy* (?), *Treasure Island, Two Years before the Mast.*
Section *F*—Battle scenes, Lions, Dogs (?).
Section *G*—None.
Section *H*—Climb many lofty mountain peaks.

All score male preferences.

Class A 5. *Business, Commercial, Political Interests.*

Form A:

Sections *A* to *F*—None.

Section *G*—Commercial news, News oddities.

Section *H*—Visit many manufacturing plants (business), Visit many battlefields (political).

Form B:

Sections *B* to *F*—None.

Section *G*—Political news.

Section *H*—See a ship-building plant, Visit the Chicago slaughter-house.

All these are male items excepting News oddities, which has a low female preferential index, 4. But the item is questionably a business, commercial, or political topic.

Class A 6. *Experiences the Opposite of Those Favored by Females.*

There are one or two ugly or disgusting objects or experiences which on our hypothesis might be thrown on to the male side by the females' recording their dislike for them, *e.g.*, People who use toothpicks (Form B, Section *B*); Side-show freaks (Form B, Section *B*); Visiting the Chicago slaughter-house (Form B, Section *H*) and possibly Bald-headed men (Form B, Section *B*). These score male preferences.

We shall now consider the classes of subjects which by hypothesis should be predominantly female.

Class B 1. *Objects or Topics with a Marked Female Signification.*

Form A:

Section *B*—Mannish women, Tall women.

Section *E*—*Rebecca of Sunnybrook Farm, Evangeline, Through the Looking Glass*, etc.

Form B:

Section *B*—Thin women, Women cleverer than you.

Sections *C* and *D*—None.

Section *E*—*Little Women, Mrs. Wiggs of the Cabbage Patch, Janice Meredith*, Helen Keller's *Story of My Life, Heidi*.

All these have a female preference index.

Class B 2. *Topics Which Evoke Maternal Tenderness or Active Sympathy.*

Form A:

Section *B*—Babies.

Section *C*—Movie love scenes.

Section *D*—Pet cats (?).
Section *E*—*Little Men, Little Lord Fauntleroy, Evangeline, Peter Pan and
Wendy.*
Section *F*—Children.
Section *G*—None.
Section *H*—See how criminals are treated.
Form B:
Section *B*—School children, Bashful men.
Section *C*—Love stories.
Section *D*—Pet canaries (?).
Section *E*—*Water Babies,* Helen Keller's *Story of My Life, Janice
Meredith, Mrs. Wiggs of the Cabbage Patch, Heidi, The
Courtship of Miles Standish, The Prince and the Pauper.*
Section *F* to *G*—None.
Section *H*—Study methods of training children.

All these except "See how criminals are treated" score female
preferences. But if from schoolchildren the criminal commands,
not sympathy, but reprobation, the item would not fall into this
category. The effect of the motives in this class in detaching
some "ostensibly male" subjects from the male side will be
noticed; *e.g., Little Men, Little Lord Fauntleroy.*

*Class B 3. Aesthetic or Artistic Experiences or Topics Associated with
Them.*

Form A:
Section *B*—None.
Section *C*—Poetry, Dramatics, Ancient languages.
Section *D*—Collecting flowers, Charades (?).
Section *E*—(See below).
Section *F*—Flowers, Clouds.
Section *G*—Musical events, Theatrical news.
Section *H*—Spend a day in Westminster Abbey, See London Bridge.
Form B:
Section *B*—None.
Section *C*—Music, Fairy tales, Penmanship (?), Painting.
Section *D*—Dancing, Gardening (?).
Section *E*—(See below).
Section *F*—Sunsets, Trees, Portraits.
Section *G*—None.
Section *H*—Study national dress, Visit many picture galleries, Visit
many cathedrals.

These all score female preferences.

Section *E* (on book preferences) has been excluded from this class, since all good books make some aesthetic appeal; but on the other hand, to what extent it is content or style which decides the preference it is difficult in any case to say. With most schoolchildren we can perhaps safely say that the matter is more important than the style. It is noticeable, however, that the three topics of a poetic nature, *Evangeline*, *Tales from Shakespeare*, and Riley's *Poems*, are female preferences.

Class B 4. *Domestic Experiences or Topics Associated with Them.*

Form A:
  Section *B*—Babies.
  Section *C*—Stories of home life.
  Section *D*—Parties and socials, Cooking, Charades, Pet cats, Drop the handkerchief (?), Repairing a door latch, Chess (?).
  Section *E*—(See below).
  Section *F*—Flowers, Children, Cats, Fruits (?).
  Section *G*—None.
  Section *H*—See how people prepare their food.
Form B:
  Section *B*—None.
  Section *C*—None (Love stories ?).
  Section *D*—Washing dishes, Pet canaries, Guessing games (?), Ham and eggs (?).
  Section *E*—(See below).
  Section *F* and *G*—None.
  Section *H*—Visit the homes of many writers, Learn about Japanese houses, Study national dress, Study methods of training children.

With the exception of the rather questionably domestic topics, Repairing a door latch and Ham and eggs,[1] these are all female preferences. The "mechanical" appeal of the former clearly counteracts any domestic appeal it may make.

As regards Section *E* (on book preferences) a glance down the male and female preference columns in both forms will show that the females prefer domestic incident, and the males external adventure.

[1] See discussion of Exercise 1, p. 378, also Table 64, p. 376, which show that "meat" is more thought about by males than by females.

Class B 5. Social Experiences and Social Entertainment, Manners, and Practices.

Form A:

Section *C*—Social problem movies.

Section *D*—Parties and socials, Hopscotch, Charades, Drop the handkerchief, Dare base.

Section *E*—None.

Section *F*—None.

Section *G*—News oddities (?).

Form B:

Section *D*—Jump the rope, Cat and mouse, Guessing games, Picnics.

Section *G*—Social news.

Section *H*—Visit the homes of many writers, Learn about Japanese houses, Study national dress, Study methods of training children.

These all score female preferences.

Class B 6. Experiences the Opposite of Those Favored by Males.

There are none in which this factor seems to be crucial.

So far, then, these comparisons confirm conclusions as to sex differences already suggested from an examination of previous exercises. A scrutiny of response scores for 24 items which do not fall obviously into these classes reveals no important sex difference in addition to, or inconsistent with, those already detected.

Numerical Excess of Female Preferences.—One marked sex distinction which seems to pervade this exercise requires comment. The records show a noticeable numerical excess of female over male preferences, and a corresponding excess of male dislikes. In Table 79*a*, which summarizes the data on this point, the term "pronounced like" means that the preference score for *D* and *N* is of the opposite sex to that for *L*; e.g., $-4L$, $+1D$, $+2N$ means a pronounced female like, while $+2L$, $-1D$, $-2N$ means a pronounced male like.

Table 79*a* shows that in the whole exercise females score 133 and males 99 likes, males 135 and females 87 dislikes. Cases of "pronounced" likes total 85 for females and 44 for males. The reason, however, for the female excess of "likes" does not seem to be that there are more things in heaven and earth pleasing to the female sex, nor merely that the female sex expresses emotion more freely; for in that case its dislikes also would be more emphatic—in contradiction of our records. Taking the sections in detail (Table 79b) we get the clue. This table shows that the differences in numbers of preferences are especially pronounced in

TABLE 79a.—NUMERICAL EXCESS OF FEMALE PREFERENCES

Preference	Form A		Form B		Total	
	Male	Female	Male	Female	Male	Female
Likes.....................	48	68	51	65	99	133
Pronounced likes...........	22	40	22	45	44	85
Dislikes..................	71	40	64	47	135	87
Neutral..................	49	36	62	34	111	70

TABLE 79b.—NUMBERS OF SEX PREFERENTIAL INDICES IN EXERCISE 5

Section	Form A		Form B		Total	
	Number of P.I.'s		Number of P.I.'s		Number of P.I.'s	
	Male	Female	Male	Female	Male	Female
A	9	16	8	17	17	33
B	5	7	4	8	9	15
C	6	8	7	6	13	14
D	6	14	9	11	15	25
E	10	13	12	11	22	24
F	3	5	5	3	8	8
G	3	3	3	3	6	6
H	5	6	3	8	8	14
	47	72	51	67	98	129

some sections, namely, in Sections A and D in Form A, and A, B, D, and H in Form B. In the case of Section A (on occupations) social sex bias is at work. A tendency of males to prefer male occupations, and of females to like male as well as female occupations, accounts for the female doubling the male preferences (33 against 17). Section D is largely composed of social pastimes and occupations of a domestic nature. Section B, with only

12 items, we have reason to suppose is in any case sexually the least significant section, and Section H (Form B) happens to comprise more travel objectives of domestic and aesthetic than of business, political, and scientific interest. Had the list included such items as "Visit big oil fields" or "Visit the spots where dinosaur's eggs were dug up" or "Visit the magnetic pole" or "Visit the source of the Nile," we may be fairly certain that much of the discrepancy would have vanished. In part a special social bias, in part an unbalanced selection, accounts for the differences. There remains probably a greater tendency for the male to disdain the feminine, than for the female to disdain the masculine.

Male Excess in Neutral Scores.—Another feature of the exercise as a whole is the excess of male neutral responses as indicated in the following figures for Form A and Form B combined:

Categories compared	Male	Female
Number of neutral scores	111	70
Score (sum of plus figures for the male and of minus figures for the female)	227	138
Average	2.05	1.97

As the neutral response indicates hesitance or indecision, it might appear that the male is more reticent in expressing a definite preference than the female; or that the female is more decided in expressing her likes or dislikes than the male. She is more sure, or she says she is more sure, exactly what her feelings are. But examination will show that this male neutral tendency is limited to certain sections; namely, to Sections A, both forms; B, Form B; D, Form A; E, Form B; and H, both forms. With the exception of E (Form B) these are just the sections which have already been found exhibiting the most distinctive female preference indices; and this has been explained without resort to any general hypothesis. Reasons have been given why the female should score higher like responses in these cases. But an excess of female scores of like response automatically involves a corresponding excess of male scores to be shared among dislikes and neutrals. In short, the excess of male neutral responses may be occasioned, not by any tendency to hesitance or neutrality in general, but by the particular circumstances already considered which favor a high proportion of female likes.

Summary.—Section *A* has already been summarized. Analysis of the multifarious material contained in Sections *B* to *H* corroborates previous conclusions. We find males expressing more taste than females for situations involving males, for adventures, for outdoor occupations, for machinery, for business, commercial, and political matters; females expressing more taste than males for situations involving females, for indoor and social interests, and for experiences evoking active sympathy or maternal tenderness.

A female tendency to express likes more emphatically and frequently than males, and a male tendency to more dislikes and more neutral attitudes than females, largely explicable by unbalanced selection of items and by acquired social bias, is consonant with a distinctive female proneness to express enjoyment more freely.

Exercise 6: Personages and Opinions

This exercise has two sections, one calling for expression of attitude toward selected historical personages, the other for judgment of truth or falsity of certain statements. Responses to both sections were analyzed for the following subjects: 121 boys and 122 girls in the seventh grade, 102 boys and 118 girls in high school, and 50 men and 50 women in Stanford University; a total of 563.

Personages.—Table 80 gives the preference indices of the 55 items contained in the two forms of the test.

The following points emerge:

1. No woman's name has a male index.

2. One woman (Cleopatra) has a neutral score. The sex-to-sex tendency is here, it seems, counterbalanced by the tendency of females—remarked elsewhere—to be more severe than males on "loose" living.

TABLE 80.—PREFERENCE INDICES OF HISTORICAL PERSONAGES

Form A

No.	Character	Male preference index
1	Jack Dempsey	+10
2	Kit Carson	+ 7
3	P. T. Barnum	+ 6
4	Robert G. Ingersoll	+ 5
5	Ulysses S. Grant	+ 4
6	Bismarck	+ 3
7	Daniel Boone	+ 3
8	Oliver Cromwell	+ 2
9	Mussolini	+ 2
10	Billy Sunday	+ 2
11	Judge Ben Lindsay	+ 1
12	Theodore Roosevelt	+ 1
		Female preference index
1	Florence Nightingale	− 7
2	Jane Addams	− 4
3	Hearst, the publisher	− 3
4	Aaron Burr	− 3
5	Woodrow Wilson	− 3
6	Christopher Columbus	− 2
7	Aimee McPherson	− 1
8	Lenin	− 1
9	Thomas Jefferson	− 1
10	Jefferson Davis	− 1
11	Congressman Volstead	− 1
		Neutral index
	Cleopatra	0
	Wellington	0
	Booker T. Washington	0
	Herbert Hoover	0
	Lloyd George	0

Form B

No.	Character	Male preference index
1	"Babe" Ruth	+10
2	John L. Sullivan	+10
3	"Ty" Cobb	+ 8
4	Hannibal	+ 4
5	John Brown	+ 3
6	Caesar	+ 3
7	Marconi	+ 3
8	Tom Paine	+ 3
9	Charles Darwin	+ 2
10	Anthony Comstock	+ 2
11	Napoleon	+ 2
12	Brigham Young	+ 1
		Female preference index
1	Cornwallis	− 6
2	John Alden	− 5
3	Queen Victoria	− 4
4	Galileo	− 3
5	Carrie Chapman Catt	− 2
6	Eugene Debs	− 2
7	Mohammed	− 2
8	Daniel Webster	− 2
9	Kaiser Wilhelm	− 2
10	Mary Baker Eddy	− 1
11	Henry Ford	− 1
12	Robert E. Lee	− 1
13	Abraham Lincoln	− 1
		Neutral index
	President Coolidge	0
	Jesse James	0

3. There are eight generals. Of these only two—and those were generals who suffered defeat—have a female index; namely, Cornwallis and Lee. Cornwallis, perhaps the least successful of the eight, has the highest female preference score. This supports the view that females are more moved by active sympathy with misfortune, while aggression and enterprise appeal more to males.

4. Unfortunates other than generals are also female preferences: Columbus, Wilson, Galileo, Debs, and Kaiser Wilhelm, all of whom suffered either persecution, misunderstanding, or a reversal of fortune. Possibly we should include Aaron Burr in this class. This again suggests a distinctive female sympathy. Hannibal and John Brown are the nearest approach to exceptions on the male index list; but perhaps the military exploits of Hannibal, and the sporting end of John Brown, suffice to win for them distinctive male preference.

5. All the notorious pugilists and sports champions (and one hunter) score very pronounced male preferences: Dempsey, "Babe" Ruth, Kit Carson, and "Ty" Cobb.

6. Of the women characters (none of whom are on the male side) the most well-known philanthropists—Florence Nightingale and Jane Addams—win the highest, and those noted for more questionable qualities—Mary Baker Eddy and Aimee McPherson —win lower, female preference scores. The active sympathizers with human suffering appeal most distinctively to the female sex.

7. Individuals whose characteristic feature is defiance of conventions score male: Tom Paine, Ingersoll, and Judge Lindsay.

These preference differences confirm previous conclusions. Wellington and Mohammed are the only surprises.

An excess of female omissions to respond—in 43 out of 55 cases the proportion was higher for females—may be due to the fact that fewer girls interest themselves in famous male personages. (There are only seven women characters in the list.)

Opinions.—The statements presented in this section to be marked T (true) or F (false), may, with the exception of two or three, be considered matters of opinion rather than of knowledge, and the section becomes a study of sex prejudices. That a sex tends to favor its own interests explains the response scores in the following items:

Form A:
    Girls are naturally more innocent than boys. T, -3; F, $+3$.
    There should be perfect equality between men and women in all things.
    T, -3; F, $+3$. (Female protest against existing sex discrimination.)
Form B:
    Married women ought not to be permitted to teach school. T, $+1$; F, -1.
    Women are purer than men by nature. T, -2; F, $+2$.
    Wealth, honor, and power usually go to those who deserve them. T, $+2$; F, -2.

Other items testify to the gentler and more sympathetic tendencies of the female, or the harder and more aggressive attitudes of the male:

Form A:
    Children should be taught never to fight. T, -3; F, $+3$.
    We should never give to beggars. T, $+3$; F, -4.
Form B:
    An ugly face usually goes with a kind heart. T, -2; F, $+3$. (We do not know how many of the subjects were ugly, but an ugly face is a more serious matter with a woman than with a man, and she sympathizes more with the troubles of its owner.)
    The hanging of murderers is justifiable. T, $+4$; F, -3.
    Hunting and fishing are wrong because cruel. T, -3; F, $+3$.
    The United States should adopt a more aggressive foreign policy. T, $+3$; F, 0.

Of the sex responses in the remaining items, none seems to oppose, some to support, our previous conclusions.

Summary.—(1) Among well-known historical and contemporary personages, females show a distinctive preference for women, unfortunate people, and philanthropists; males for successful generals, sports heroes, and defiers of convention. (2) The section on opinions indicates that females tend to favor opinions which favor them, and that they subscribe to kindly, males to rougher, sentiments.

Exercise 7: Introvertive Response

The exercise contains 42 questions in each form, with "Yes" or "No" answers, on tastes, habits, emotional and imaginative tendencies, facts of experience, and a few other topics, many of the answers demanding self-scrutiny. In general they are of the type commonly used in tests of introversion or neurotic tendency. The subjects were the same as for Exercise 6, except that the number of high-school girls was 102 instead of 118.

We may arrive at an index of preference (for an affirmative answer) by adding the figures under "Yes" and "No" and attaching to the sum the sign under "Yes," since the weights for "Yes" and "No" responses are nearly always the same and never differ by more than 1; *e.g.*:

"Do people ever say you talk too
   much?"   +2 Yes   −1 No   gives a P.I. +3 (male)
"Are you happy most of the time?"   −3 Yes   +3 No   gives a P.I. −6 (female)

Table 81 gives the items of each form arranged in order of preference index. The latter is starred whenever the "Yes" response indicates introvertive or neurotic tendency; if the item is doubtful in this respect the index is followed by a question mark.

1. A male distinctive tendency toward the aggressive, the independent, the adventurous, accounts for male outnumbering female affirmative answers to some 12 questions: Form A, 15, 17, 30, and 35; Form B, 1, 4, 11, 24, 25, 28, 29, and 33.

2. The female distinctive tendency to feel or affect more fear, or at least to admit its influence on behavior, accounts for female outnumbering male affirmative answers to Questions 2 and 13 in Form A, and Questions 2, 6, 12, and 22 in Form B.

3. The distinctive female care for personal appearance explains the female affirmatives in Form A, Questions 1, 3, and 6.

4. A keener female active sympathy occasions the excess of female affirmative answers to Questions 13 and 18 in Form B.

5. The female preponderance in Form A, Question 4, testifies again to the distinctive female penchant for social gatherings.

All these differences accord with principles by this time familiar. A question of interest is whether the remaining

TABLE 81.—PREFERENCE INDICES OF INTROVERTIVE RESPONSES

M-F test items	Preference index	
	Male	Female
Form A		
1. Are you extremely careful about your manner of dress?	..	12*
2. Are you often frightened in middle of night?	..	10*
3. Do you always remember to brush your teeth?	..	8?
4. Do you like to go to parties, dances, or other social affairs?	..	7
5. Is it easy for you to get up as soon as you wake?	8	..
6. Would you like to wear expensive clothes?	..	6*
7. Did you ever have imaginary companions?	..	6*
8. Do people often say you are too noisy?	..	6*
9. Do you rather dislike to take your bath?	6?	..
10. Are you much embarrassed when you make a grammatical mistake?	..	6*
11. Have you ever kept a diary?	..	6*
12. Do you ever feel that you are about to "go to pieces"?	..	6*
13. Are you often afraid of the dark?	..	6*
14. Can you usually sit still without fidgeting?	..	6
15. As a child were you extremely disobedient?	6*	..
16. Do people nearly always treat you right?	..	6
17. Were you ever expelled from school, or nearly expelled?	6*	..
18. Have you often been punished unjustly?	6*	..
19. Do you often get cross over little things?	..	6*
20. Can you stand as much pain as others can?	6	..
21. Have you found school a hard place to get along in?	6*	..
22. Do you nearly always prefer for someone else to take the lead?	..	5*
23. Have you often fainted away?	4*	..
24. Do you usually enjoy your meals?	..	4
25. Have you the habit of biting your finger nails?	..	4*
26. Does it make you angry for people to hurry you?	4*	..
27. Do you feel tired a good deal of the time?	..	4*
28. Do you hear easily when spoken to?	..	4
29. Do people ever say that you talk too much?	3	..
30. Have you been bossed too much for your own good?	2*	..
31. Do you feel yourself to be lacking in self-control?	2*	..
32. Do you shrink from facing a crisis or difficulty?	..	2*
33. Do you worry much over possible misfortunes?	..	2*
34. Are you worried when you have an unfinished job on your hands?	..	2*
35. Do you ever dream of robbers?	2*	..
36. Do you ever have the same dream over and over?	..	2*
37. Do you ever walk in your sleep?	..	2*
38. Can you do good work while people are looking at you?	2	..
39. Do you feel like jumping off when on a high place?	..	2*
40. Do you like most people you know?	1	..
41. Do you work mostly by fits and starts?	..	0*
42. Are you careful of your personal belongings?	..	0*

TABLE 81.—PREFERENCE INDICES OF INTROVERTIVE RESPONSES.—(*Continued*)

M-F test items	Preference index	
	Male	Female
Form B		
1. Can you stand the sight of blood?	12	..
2. Do you have a great fear of fire?	..	12*
3. Are your feelings often very badly hurt?	..	12*
4. Were you ever fond of playing with snakes?	10?	..
5. Do you know anybody who is trying to harm you?	8*	..
6. Does it make you uneasy to cross a wide street or open square?...	..	8*
7. Do you often have a hard time making up your mind about things?	..	8*
8. Do you think you are getting a square deal in life?	..	8
9. Are you happy most of the time?	..	6
10. Do you usually get to do the things that please you most?	..	6
11. Do you say what you consider the truth regardless of how others may take it?	6	..
12. Have you been troubled by a fear of being crushed in a crowd?...	..	6*
13. Does the thought of hurting a person or animal give you great pain?	..	6*
14. Do you prefer to go without breakfast?	..	6?
15. Do you always get on well with others?	..	6
16. Have others of your age usually let you play with them?	..	6
17. Do you think people like you as much as they do others?	..	6
18. Do you like people to tell you their troubles?	..	4?
19. Do you dislike the company of the opposite sex?	4*	..
20. Do people ever say you are a bad loser?	4*	..
21. Have you often been bothered by blushing?	..	4*
22. Do you dread to have your picture taken?	..	4*
23. Do you think a thing over carefully before you do it?	4*	..
24. Did you ever run away from home?	4*	..
25. Do you like to tease people till they cry?	4?	..
26. Do you usually feel well and strong?	..	4
27. Do things ever seem to get misty before your eyes?	..	4*
28. Do people you are with say you quarrel too much?	4*	..
29. Do people find fault with you too much?	4*	..
30. Do you like to be the center of attention in a crowd?	..	2
31. Do you often introspect or analyze your feelings?	2*	..
32. Do you feel bored a large share of the time?	2*	..
33. Do you prefer to work a thing out for yourself rather than ask help?	2*	..
34. Are you often bothered by the feeling that people are reading your thoughts?	..	2*
35. Do you get tired of people easily?	2*	..
36. Would you rather be alone than with someone?	2*	..
37. Do you like to be praised and made much of?	..	2*
38. Do you sometimes wish you had never been born?	..	2*
39. Do you ever imagine stories to yourself so that you forget where you are?	..	2*
40. Do you prefer to be with older people?	2*	..
41. Do you like to tell your troubles to others?	..	0?
42. Do you take life so seriously that it sometimes bothers you?	..	0*

responses which do not fall clearly into any of these pigeon-holes convey evidence of any fresh sex characteristics not yet encountered.

A number of answers seem to fit the view that the male—presumably the schoolboy—finds, or says that he finds, more difficulties in direct association with his fellows than the girl does. Consider the following items:

Have you found school a hard place to get along in? Male index, 6. (Index of male preference for an affirmative answer.)
Do you know anybody who is trying to harm you? Male index, 8.
Do you always get on well with others? Female index, 6.
Do you feel that you are getting a square deal in life? Female index, 8.
Are you happy most of the time? Female index, 6.
Do you usually get to do the things that please you most? Female index, 6.
Have others of your age usually let you play with them? Female index, 6.
Do you think people like you as much as they do others? Female index, 6.
Do people nearly always treat you right? Female index, 6.
Do people you are with say you quarrel too much? Male index, 4.
Would you rather be alone than with someone? Male index, 2.
Do you prefer to be with older people? Male index, 2.

These answers seem to suggest that the young male finds mixing happily with his fellows a more difficult and troublesome affair than the schoolgirl does. Is it another effect of the greater roughness and aggressiveness of boy society, and the gentler and more sympathetic attitude of girls? The only two responses that at first sight may seem exceptions are:

Do you sometimes wish that you had never been born? Female index, 2.
Do people often say you are too noisy? Female index, 6.

But of these the first has a very small female preference score, and the second may merely result from the girl's being expected to be quieter than the boy, and being the more reproved for noisiness.

Of the remaining items, in some 13 the sex preferences are explicable on the assumption that girls find it easier than boys to admit emotional and physical frailties. The following 17 questions concern such weaknesses admitted in only four cases by a higher proportion of males than of females:

M-F test items	Female P.I.	Male P.I.
Form A:		
Are you much embarrassed when you make a grammatical mistake?..	6	..
Do you ever feel that you are about to "go to pieces"?.....	6	..
Do you often get cross over little things?................	6	..
Can you stand as much pain as others can?..............	..	6
Have you often fainted away?..........................	..	4
Does it make you angry for people to hurry you?..	..	4
Do you feel tired a good deal of the time?..............	4	..
Do you feel yourself to be lacking in self-control?.........	..	2
Do you worry much over possible misfortune?............	2	..
Are you worried when you have an unfinished job on your hands?.......................................	2	..
Do you feel like jumping off when you are on a high place?	2	..
Form B:		
Are your feelings often badly hurt?.....................	12	..
Do you often have a hard time making up your mind about things?.......................................	8	..
Have you often been bothered by blushing?..............	4	..
Do you usually feel well and strong?....................	4	..
Do things ever seem to get misty before your eyes?........	4	..
Are you often bothered by the feeling that people are reading your thoughts?......................................	2	..

Again, more instances of abnormal or "queer" behavior are admitted by females: *e.g.*, imaginary companions, dream recurrences, sleep walking, the impulse to jump off high places, and absorption in daydreaming. Now, if these responses were true, we should certainly expect the female sex to prove more introspective than the male, for most of them accord with the introspective temperament. But when we come to the direct question, "Do you often introspect or analyze your feelings?" more males answer in the affirmative. Introspection conveys no stigma of weakness; and there is no reason why the male should not admit it.

In the two forms there are some 57 items for which a "Yes" answer would class as the more introvertive response in the commonly accepted sense of that term. Of these, 35 have a female, 22 a male, preference index. The difference is probably significant and is in accord with the usual finding that females score somewhat more introverted than males on tests like those of Laird, Thurstone, and Bernreuter.

Summary.—To these questions affirmative answers which suggest a spirit of adventure or independence in the subject are predominantly male; admissions of fear and of humanitarian tendencies, of care for personal appearance, or of liking for social gatherings, are predominantly female. Several answers suggest that boys find school life harder than girls do, perhaps because of the greater roughness of boys at school. On the whole, females admit more emotional and slightly more physical frailties than males and more abnormalities of emotion and "mental" experience. They are more given to introvertive response than the males.

Summary and Conclusions

Before concluding this inquiry with a brief discussion of the outcome it is desirable, even at the risk of seeming tiresomely repetitive, to recapitulate its main findings, exercise by exercise; for their strength rests upon cumulative evidence rather than upon any single decisive experiment. Taken serially they run as follows:

Exercise 1: Word Association.

1. If we take the associated words absolutely, females pick more often than males upon terms for domestic things or things suggestive of kindly or sympathetic activities; and much more often upon terms for articles or qualities of adornment, and for colors; males more often upon scientific and business terms and particularly upon terms suggestive of excitement and adventure, and upon words for foods; and each sex "prefers" names of persons of its own sex.

2. If we take the items which show the most sex-contrasted responses, divergences follow the same lines and also indicate a male preference for words signifying machinery, common tools, and outdoor pursuits.

Exercise 2 : Ink-blot Association.

3. Response words most obviously associated with machinery or science and with outdoor activities and adventure are picked upon more often by males; more of those connected with domestic occupations and with aesthetic experience or personal adornment by females.

4. When we consider the items which show the most sex-contrasted responses, the term which the stimulus figure evokes is in almost every case one connected with a common occupation distinctive of the responding sex.

Exercise 3 : Information.

5. Females are more correctly informed about domestic occupations, domestic and individual embellishment, etiquette, fictional literature, certain points of musical technique, color shades and differences, and on topics that appeal to active sympathy and maternal interest. Males are more correctly informed about political, business, economic, scientific, and physical facts; about exploits, adventures, and inventions; and on topics that evoke aggressive and active bodily propensities.

6. This divergence between the sexes is most marked in knowledge of facts or events that interest aggressive or adventurous dispositions on the one hand, and maternally tender or sympathetic dispositions on the other.

Exercise 4: Emotional and Ethical Response.

7. Females express the most distinctive degree of anger on occasions of very unsympathetic or cruel treatment of human beings where help or sympathy is meet.

8. Females tend to show a more distinctive degree of anger over school offenses and "social" vexations than over business and extradomestic troubles.

9. The sexes diverge more in the fear than in the anger responses.

10. Within the set of fear-inspiring objects and situations presented, the more fearsome the object the greater the female distinctive fear.

11. Females express more disgust than males in general, but particularly at "disgusting" male practices (repugnant habits of dress and person), at coarse language, and at sexual immorality.

12. Females express in general more pity than males, but most for the weak, helpless, and visibly distressed, especially where the object is a human being or a creature attractive in appearance, and for cases of female more than of male distress.

13. Females are in general more condemnatory than males, but more noticeably in petty offenses and in offenses more common in males. In negligible offenses on the one hand and very serious offenses on the other the sex distinction is inconsiderable.

14. The severity of male censure increases more than that of female censure with increased gravity of the offense.

15. Of the alternative occupations and objects presented for choice in the last section of the exercise, males distinctively prefer the out-of-door and adventurous, and the useful rather than the decorative; females prefer indoor and urban conditions of living, and things attractive in appearance rather than the useful.

16. Females express more liking for working with men than men for working with women.

17. Females tend to express a higher degree of the four emotions (particularly of disgust) and of moral censure, than males express; but proportionately less in moral censure and anger than in pity, fear, and disgust.

18. In general, males record more defect of emotion and of moral censure than females, particularly of disgust and fear, with pity, moral censure, and anger following in that order.

19. The interval between female excess and male defect averages greatest with disgust, least with anger and moral censure.

Exercise 5: Interests.

20. The occupations for which females express a distinctive preference are the indoor, artistic and decorative, and the directly "ministrative"; distinctively preferred by males are those entailing adventure, bodily risk, and muscular strength or prolonged exertion.

21. Males distinctively prefer occupations undertaken predominantly by males; females like male as well as female occupations.

22. Females record a higher distinctive preference for predominantly female occupations than males for predominantly male occupations; but also, on the whole, as high a preference for mixed occupations as males for male occupations.

23. Throughout Sections B to H of this exercise a sex tends to prefer objects or topics which more particularly engage or concern members of that sex.

24. Among the various types of material presented for response in Sections B to H, males are found to express distinctive preference for experience implying adventure, aggressiveness, or interest in mechanical contrivances; for out-of-door and physically strenuous occupations; and for business, commercial, and political interests. Females express preference for experiences evoking maternal tenderness or active sympathy, and for aesthetic and domestically social experiences.

25. In the aggregate, female likes considerably exceed male likes, and male dislikes exceed female dislikes, but this holds of some sections more than of others. In three sections of one form male exceed female preferences.

26. In the aggregate, male neutral scores (neither like nor dislike) exceed female considerably; but (with one exception) this excess is confined to those sections in which female likes are most distinctive.

Exercise 6 : Personalities and Opinions.

27. Females show a distinctive preference for women, unfortunate people, and philanthropists; males for successful generals, sports heroes, and defiers of convention.

28. Females distinctively believe statements favorable, and disbelieve statements unfavorable, to the female sex; they subscribe to kindly, males to rougher, sentiments.

Exercise 7 : Introvertive Response.

29. Males affirm distinctively tastes and habits that involve adventure or courage; females habits or experiences that imply

timidity, active sympathy, and care for personal appearance; and with one or two exceptions they more readily confess weaknesses in emotional control and (less noticeably) of physique. Females also admit more psychic abnormalities.

30. **Females more often than males give the introvertive type** of response.

We may now consider two questions to which the present findings give rise: (1) Can we extract from them a single prime principle of sex difference at once not too vague to be ambiguous, and not so particular as to be insignificant? (2) What, so far as our evidence goes, appears to be the relation of the differences we have enumerated to nature and nurture, to endowment and environment? We shall take these questions in succession.

1. *Is there one dominant principle?*

It is obvious that from whatever point we have started, whether from the knowledge shown by the sexes or from their associations or their likes and dislikes for people, vocations, pastimes, books, or objects of travel; or whether we have explored directly or deviously their emotions, tastes, opinions, and inner experiences, we have found ourselves arriving at much the same conclusions— all our ways have led to Rome. But the final scene has two aspects—two sides of the same picture—one showing differences in the direction of interest, the other differences in the direction of emotions and impulses.

From whatever angle we have examined them the males included in the standardization groups evinced a distinctive interest in exploit and adventure, in outdoor and physically strenuous occupations, in machinery and tools, in science, physical phenomena, and inventions; and, from rather occasional evidence, in business and commerce. On the other hand, the females of our groups have evinced a distinctive interest in domestic affairs and in aesthetic objects and occupations; they have distinctively preferred more sedentary and indoor occupations, and occupations more directly ministrative, particularly to the young, the helpless, the distressed. Supporting and supplementing these are the more subjective differences—those in emotional disposition and direction. The males directly or indirectly manifest the greater self-assertion and aggressiveness; they express more hardihood and fearlessness, and more roughness of manners, language, and sentiments. The females express themselves as more compassionate and sympathetic, more timid, more fastidious and aesthetically sensitive, more emotional in general (or at least more expressive of the four emotions considered), severer moralists, yet admit in themselves more weaknesses in emotional control and (less noticeably) in physique.

But we must define some of our terms more precisely, for instance, "aggressiveness" and "self-assertion." The evidence is for initiative, enterprise, vigorous activity, outdoor adventure; "aggressiveness" need not imply selfishness or tyranny or unfair attack. The compassion and sympathy of the female, again, appears from the evidence personal rather than abstract, less a principled humanitarianism than an active sympathy for palpable misfortune or distress. In disgust, in aesthetic judgment, and in moral censure, the evidence is rather for the influence of fashion and of feeling than of principle or reason. Our evidence need not imply the possession of a "truer" taste or a more discerning conscience.

But in asking how deep these sex distinctions go we reach our second question: *What appears to be the relation of our main sex difference to nature and nurture, to endowment and environment?*

The question is not, let us remind ourselves, whether this or that trait is innate or acquired, for every human act or thought is both, but whether the actual sex differences we are discovering are ascribable to biological (genetic) factors dividing the sexes or to sex differences in their training and environment. So far as the evidence of our experiment goes, we are not justified in ascribing the manifest differences to one alternative exclusively. Certainly we do not have enough evidence to exclude the gross physiological differences between the sexes from any part in determining the distinctive preference of the male for heavy muscular work and of the female for less active occupations, or in determining her greater sympathy for the young and weak or her greater interest in home life, with the relegation of outside interests to the male. To actual or anticipated childbearing and motherhood—differences physiologically determined—we have found no reason to deny a part in determining differences in overt habits and emotional dispositions. And in the present state of our ignorance it would be even more rash to deny the possible influence upon sex temperaments of the manifold differences between the sexes in their endocrine equipment and functioning.

Whatever our view as to the innateness of the distinctive tendencies, at least as to maternal tenderness in the one sex and comparative aggressiveness in the other, our experimental evidence is inconclusive. However, when we examine the more direct manifestations of these and other contrasting tendencies in our exercises, and consider how any particular manifestation comes about, the power and reach of what we have named cultural sex bias, its many plain and subtle effects on the upbringing and environment of the sexes within the groups we are considering, keep coming to one's mind. In so many ways too familiar to realize, each sex gives and receives such different treatment as largely to explain the divergences in expression or in fact revealed by the material we have studied. Singularly powerful in shaping our development are other people's expectations of us, past and present, as shown by their practice and their precept. Whether the boy is innately more aggressive and fearless, more handy with the electric lighting than with the cooking stove, more interested and informed about public affairs and about science, more active and enterprising physically; and whether the girl is by nature more sympathetic, gentle, timid, fastidious, more attracted to pots and pans than to rods and guns, more punctilious in dress, personal appearance, manners, and language; at any rate society in the shape of parents, teachers, and one's own fellows of whichever sex expects these differences between the sexes, and literature reflects them. Irresistibly each sex plays the role assigned, even in spite of its own protests. The consequence is that throughout these several exercises, however statistically consistent the distinctive sex responses may prove, we cannot tell how deep the difference lies—or how the deeper and shallower factors combine. And here we must be content to leave the problem, for it is clear that the deciding answer can be wrested, not by a more meticulous struggle with this one set of exercises administered to groups comparatively homogeneous, but from: (1) parallel examinations of socially and racially different groups widely different in social tradition and circumstance, and (2) combined psychological and biological case studies of extreme deviants in sex temperaments within a given culture.

CHAPTER XVII

INTERPRETATIONS AND CONCLUSIONS

<small>THE SIGNIFICANCE OF M-F DIFFERENCES FOR PERSONALITY</small>

Masculinity and femininity are important aspects of human personality. They are not to be thought of as lending to it merely a superficial coloring and flavor; rather they are one of a small number of cores around which the structure of personality gradually takes shape. The masculine-feminine contrast is probably as deeply grounded, whether by nature or by nurture, as any other which human temperament presents. Certainly it is more specifically rooted in a structural dichotomy than the cycloid-schizoid or the extrovertive-introvertive contrasts. Whether it is less or more grounded in general physiological and biochemical factors than these remains to be seen. In how far the lines of cleavage it represents are inevitable is unknown, but the possibility of eliminating it from human nature is at least conceivable. The fact remains that the M-F dichotomy, in various patterns, has existed throughout history and is still firmly established in our mores. In a considerable fraction of the population it is the source of many acute difficulties in the individual's social and sexual adjustment and in a greater fraction it affords a most important impetus to creative work and happiness. The indications are that the present situation, together with the problems it raises for education, psychology, and social legislation, will remain with us for a long time to come.

As long as the child is faced by two relatively distinct patterns of personality, each attracting him by its unique features, and is yet required by social pressures to accept the one and reject the other, a healthy integration of personality may often be difficult to achieve. Cross-parent fixations will continue to foster sexual inversion; the less aggressively inclined males will be driven to absurd compensations to mask their femininity; the more aggressive and independent females will be at a disadvantage in the marriage market; competition between the sexes will be rife in industry, in politics, and in the home as it is today.

Even if it could be shown that the malleability of personality is such as to make the adoption of a single ideal pattern of temperament feasible, no one knows whether the consequences would be more desirable than undesirable. So far only one single-standard society has been described for us, that an extremely primitive one consisting of but a few hundred individuals living in the wilds of New Guinea. Mead's description[1] of this society, challenging as it is, offers no very convincing evidence that a system of unipolarity reduces the difficulties of individual adjustment. Conceivably, in a more complex society it might increase them. It is possible that in an enlightened culture, no longer held in leash by traditions and taboos, dual patterns of sexual temperament are an aid in the development of heterosexuality.

But it is not our purpose to defend the prevailing ideals with respect to sex temperaments. The irrelevance and absurdity of many of their features are evident enough. That in most cultures they have been shaped to the advantage of the physically stronger sex is obvious. It does not necessarily follow that a dichotomy of temperaments is per se an evil to be got rid of. In any case it is not the business of the scientist either to condemn or to praise any given type of human behavior. His task is to understand it. The application of his findings to social betterment he is willing to leave to the social reformer, but with respect to the personality problems with which we are here concerned, he knows that intelligent reform will have to await the establishment of a substantial body of knowledge which does not now exist.

THE NEED FOR MORE ADEQUATE DESCRIPTION OF SEX TEMPERAMENTS

The first step in the investigation of the sex temperaments is to make possible their more adequate description and more exact identification. We have shown that descriptions based upon

[1] MEAD, MARGARET, *Sex and temperament in three primitive societies*, 335 pp., Morrow, 1935.

common observation are often contradictory and that even a subject's intimate friends register little agreement in rating him for degree of masculinity and femininity. This state of affairs betokens the vagueness of current ideas with respect to what constitutes the masculine or feminine temperament and the chaos of opinion with regard to what is valid evidence of its existence. Three sources of confusion may be briefly mentioned.

1. Erroneous ratings may result from the too ready acceptance of overt behavior as the criterion. In this respect the investigator of personality or character is at a disadvantage in comparison with the investigator of intelligence or other abilities. Subjects do not often try to hide their intelligence and they are unable to hide very effectively their stupidities, but character and personality can be rather successfully simulated. Within limits the dishonest can simulate honesty, hatred can be hidden under honeyed words, anger can be disguised, the introvert can force himself to behave as an extrovert, the homosexual may deport himself so normally as to remain undetected in our midst.

2. Errors may be due to lack of a sufficiently large sampling of observational data. The teacher's contacts with her pupils are limited to certain types of situations. The same is true of our contacts with most of the people we know.

3. Among the hardest errors to eliminate are those that arise from traditional biases, such as the notion that the masculine temperament nearly always goes with a particular type of voice, physique, carriage, manner of dress, or occupation. There are doubtless other biases more or less peculiar to the individual or to the class to which he belongs, varying according to whether he is male or female, masculine or feminine, young or old, strongly or weakly sexed, etc.

It is evident that no clear delineation of sexual temperaments is possible on the basis of uncontrolled observation. The M-F test is an attempt to remedy this situation. Its scientific intent is to free the concepts of masculinity and femininity from the irrelevancies and confusions which have become attached to them as the result of superficial consideration of everyday behavior. It is necessary to go back of behavior to the individual's attitudes, interests, information, and thought trends, which constitute the real personality behind the front presented to his fellows.

That the purpose of the test has been accomplished only in part hardly needs to be said.   Our sampling of the universe of mental attitudes and interests which differentiate the sexes is far from adequate.   The sampling used has not been validated by item counts for sufficiently large populations.   Numerous questions remain unanswered with respect to the selection of test items, the best method of weighting responses, and the most meaningful kinds of scores to employ.   The defects of our technique will be remedied by experiment, the technique itself seems to us inescapable however much it may require supplementation by direct experimental procedures.

M-F Ratings of Population Groups by Psychologists

The difficulties encountered by one who is called upon to rate persons for masculinity and femininity are well illustrated by an experiment we have made in which psychologists were asked to rank certain populations in regard to this aspect of personality. The rankings were made by 21 male and 21 female psychologists, selected on the basis of their researches in the field of personality.[1] To each were sent four lists of populations with the request that the populations of each list be ranked in order according to estimated mean with respect to "mental masculinity," the most masculine population to be rated 1.   We purposely refrained from defining the term "mental masculinity" beyond saying that we had in mind primarily "masculinity in interests, attitudes, and thought trends."   (See Table 82 for populations rated.)

Let us examine first the reliability of the ratings.   The averages of the intercorrelations of the individual raters are as shown at the top of page 455.   The highest agreement is among the male judges of male occupational groups; the next highest is for female judges of both male and female occupational groups.

[1] We wish to thank the psychologists for their willingness to devote the necessary hour or more to the painstaking task of supplying the ratings called for.   We are also indebted to Dr. Paul Buttenwieser for assistance in preparing this summary.

Ranks correlated	For male judges	For female judges
For male occupational groups...........	.759	.674
For female occupational groups..........	.428	.663
For special male groups.................	.504	.496
For special female groups...............	.530	.508

These three correlations range from .66 to .76, the other five from .43 to .53. The average rankings by the 21 male judges correlate as follows with the averages of the 21 female judges:

For male occupational groups...........................	.984
For female occupational groups.........................	.991
For special male groups................................	.966
For special female groups..............................	.978

We can say, therefore, that neither the sex of the raters nor the sex of the groups being rated affects very greatly the reliability of the ratings. The one marked exception is in the case of the female occupational groups; here the average agreement among female judges is .66 and among the male judges .43. In general one can say that the agreement among judges of either sex is much greater than we have found for less expert judges who rated individuals rather than groups. Even so, the agreement represented by an average intercorrelation around .50 is in reality very low measured in terms of the coefficient of alienation. The data suggest that even for psychologists the terms "masculinity" and "femininity" do not have very clear connotations.

Our present interest, however, is in the agreement between the M-F scores and the average rankings of the 21 male and 21 female judges.[1] This is as follows for the four groups:

Ranks correlated	Male judges	Female judges
For male occupational groups...........	.349	.347
For female occupational groups..........	.382	.443
For special male groups.................	.656	.720
For special female groups...............	.582	.659

[1] See p. 247 for correlation between M-F scores and scale ratings of 26 occupations of homosexual males.

It is evident from these correlations that the female judges succeed slightly better than do the male judges in approximating the rankings yielded by the test scores.   On the surface, it would seem that the rankings of both male and female judges agree less closely with the test-score rankings in the case of the occupational groups than in the case of the special groups.   This difference, however, is more apparent than real, and may most plausibly be attributed to the fact that the greater spread of masculinity within the special groups has facilitated the task of discriminating between these populations.[1]   When we correct for this factor by adjusting the coefficients to the values that would be expected if the range in M-F test scores were equal for all groups, the ability of the judges to approximate the "correct" order becomes roughly the same for all four classes of populations.

Table 82 shows for each of the four lists of populations the amount of agreement in the rank orders by mean M-F score and composite ratings of the male and female judges.   The reader will find it interesting to examine this table rather carefully for evidence of constant biases.

When we adopt the objective test scores for each group as the standard, and compare these means with the composite rankings of the judges, certain biases are apparent.   Both male and female judges tend to underestimate the masculinity of men engaged in professional and intellectual pursuits, and to overestimate the masculinity of outdoor or manual workers.   Farmers, for example, are ranked 5 in the male occupational list by both groups of judges, but 15 by average M-F score.   Lawyers, bankers, physicians, dentists, teachers (male), and architects are all ranked several grades more feminine by the judges than by the test.   The idea seems to be that the place of a really masculine man is out of doors.   It is unfortunate that we were not able to check this theory further by testing a group of cowboys.

The most pronounced disagreement is the case of city policemen and firemen, who are ranked by both men and women as the most

[1] The range between the highest and lowest mean is as follows in the four groups: Group I, 59 points; Group II, 40 points; Group III, 112 points; Group IV, 79 points.

TABLE 82.—AGREEMENT BETWEEN MEAN M-F SCORES AND PSYCHOLOGISTS'
RANKINGS OF SELECTED POPULATIONS

Selected populations	Rank order M-F test	Composite rank order	
		Male judges	Female judges
I. Male occupational groups:			
Lawyers...	3	7	8
Bankers...	2	9	6
Physicians......................................	8	10	10
Dentists..	7	11	11
Architects......................................	4	14	14
Merchants.......................................	12	6	7
School administrators...........................	10	13	13
Farmers...	15	5	5
Catholic priests in training....................	18	15	15
Professional engineers..........................	1	4	4
High-school and college teachers................	9	16	18
Bookkeepers and office clerks...................	11	18	17
Journalists.....................................	17	12	12
Musicians.......................................	19	19	20
General salesmen................................	5	8	9
Machinists and mechanicians.....................	13	3	2
Contractors and builders........................	6	2	3
Artists (painters)..............................	14	20	19
Protestant ministers............................	20	17	16
City policemen and firemen......................	16	1	1
II. Female occupational groups:			
Graduate practicing nurses......................	1	3	3
Teachers in elementary and high schools.........	4	4	4
Office managers and business administrators.....	5	1	1
Bookkeepers and business clerks.................	7	2	2
Stenographers...................................	2.5	7	6
Domestic servants...............................	11	8	8
Musicians.......................................	9	6	7
Dressmakers and seamstresses....................	10	10	10
Unselected housewives...........................	8	11	11
Artists and photographers.......................	6	5	5
Hairdressers and cosmeticians...................	2.5	9	9
III. Special male groups:			
Juvenile delinquents (typical reform-school population)..	7	5	6
Men in *Who's who*..............................	9	7	7
Unselected tenth-grade boys.....................	2	6	5
Unselected college students.....................	3	3	4
College football players........................	1	1	1
Intellectually gifted boys (ages 16–20).........	4	10	9
Japanese boys (born in America of Japanese parents).	10	11	11
Male homosexuals (typical male prostitutes of a large city)...	12	12	12
Unselected eighth-grade boys....................	6	8.5	8
Unselected men in their 20's....................	5	2	2
Unselected men in their 40's....................	8	4	3
Unselected men in their 60's....................	11	8.5	10
IV. Special female groups:			
Women in *Who's who*............................	3	2	3
Female prostitutes..............................	6	6	8
Gifted girls (age 16–20)........................	4	5	4
Women athletes and directors of physical education...	1	1	1
Juvenile delinquents (inmates of typical reform-school for girls, age 16–20).........................	11	4	5
Japanese girls (born in America)................	8	11	11
Unselected tenth-grade girls....................	10	12	9
Unselected women college students...............	5	9	6
Unselected eighth-grade girls...................	13	10	7
Women holding M.D. or Ph.D. degree..............	2	3	2
Unselected women in their 20's..................	7	13	13
Unselected women in their 40's..................	9	8	10
Unselected women in their 60's..................	12	7	12

masculine occupational group, whereas they score among the lowest on the M-F test.   In rating the latter group it appears that the judges failed to make allowance for the masculinizing effect of a male uniform and for specific occupational selection in terms of stature.   Also they overlooked two selective factors that have probably entered: (1) the craving of some effeminate men for uniforms as a means of enhancing their feeling of masculinity, and (2) the avoidance of ill-paid and rather routine civil-service jobs by men who have in pronounced degree the masculine qualities of aggressiveness, self-confidence, and independence.

The large overestimation of the masculinity of delinquent girls seems to us a relatively "good" error, as the animal psychologist would say, for it probably rests on the rather plausible (though apparently erroneous) assumption that such girls nearly always come into conflict with the law because of their masculine aggressiveness.   Data presented in Chapter XIV in fact suggest that in some cases their troubles can be blamed to the feminine qualities of submissiveness and docility rather than to masculine independence and aggressiveness on their part.

One of the largest disagreements between the two sets of judges is in the ranks assigned to women aged sixty to seventy (rank 7 by male and 12 by female judges).   There is of course an obvious explanation of the fact that the male not yet past middle age finds it hard to think of old women as feminine.   The female judge also finds it harder than the male judge to think of old men as masculine, though here the difference is much less.   It is safe to predict that the old groups would fare still worse in the ratings of opposite-sex judges of the late teens.

The age-of-judge factor is also probably involved in the underestimates of the masculinity of eighth-grade and tenth-grade boys; to the middle-aged, adolescent boys still seem immature and half sexed.   However, to our mature female judges the eighth-grade and tenth-grade girls seem much more masculine than the test shows them to be; only the male judges are able to appreciate their femininity!

In the foregoing discussion we have perhaps seemed to assume that when test and judges disagree the judges are always in error.

It can only be said that the test is right in so far as it samples M-F differences.   To that extent it *is* right so far as the tested populations are concerned.   The items composing the test may sample the totality of M-F differences more adequately than the tested groups sample the general classes to which they belong.   If larger populations had been tested the rank orders for mean score might not have been quite the same.   We have no wish to discredit the ratings our self-sacrificing friends have so kindly furnished us.   Our little experiment will have served its purpose if it has directed attention to some of the types of bias which enter into M-F ratings and to the need of objective scores which are free from censure, uninfluenced by likes or dislikes, and immune to sex appeal.

Suggestions for Revision of the M-F Test

Revision of the M-F test should accomplish two results.   (1) The least reliable sections should be eliminated and only those parts should be retained which can be made reliable enough to warrant profile treatment of individual scores.   By combining Forms A and B, and by increasing the number of items, the desired reliability could be attained for the following subtests: word association, information, anger response, fear response, disgust response, pity response, ethical censure, and interests. The test of introvertive response is less hopeful.   Possibly "interests" could be divided into (*a*) interests in objective things, occupations, and activities, and (*b*) interests in people and their relationships.   (2) The test should be extended to include samplings of sex differences in other fields.   Possibilities in this line include, among others, an annoyance inventory, a sense-of-humor test, and attitude measurement by means of the Thurstone technique.   A test designed to measure intellectual objectivity and emotional bias of judgment might be worth trying, although it is very doubtful whether a satisfactory number of items could be found which would show the requisite amount of sex difference. More promising, perhaps, would be a memory-inventory of childhood preferences in the field of plays, games, and amusements.

A simpler form of the M-F test should be devised which would be applicable to subjects as young as eight or ten years of age. The crude masculinity test used by one of us in the study of gifted children was applicable thus early and seems to have had considerable prognostic value with respect to later development. Probably a much better test for preadolescent children could now be devised.

Until suitable revision has been accomplished we believe the test as it stands will serve many useful purposes both in clinical practice and in research. It is strongly recommended, however, that when the test is used for the appraisal of individual subjects both forms be administered. For the comparison of groups a single form will be found satisfactory.

Nature and Nurture as Determiners of Sex Temperament

The nature-nurture problem occupies a central position in any theory of sex temperament. The M-F test, as we have pointed out in our opening chapter, rests upon no assumption as to the causes responsible for the individual differences it discloses. The aim has been to devise a test which would measure whatever differences may exist in the hope that this would open the way to an empirical estimation of the relative influence of various determiners. At present no one knows whether the M-F deviant is primarily a problem for the neurologist, biochemist, and endocrinologist or for the parent and educator. The question cannot be answered without thoroughgoing search for the constitutional correlates of M-F deviation. The final answer cannot be obtained until both endocrinology and psychometrics have advanced beyond their present stage, though this is no excuse for delaying the initiation of research on the problem at hand. It should be emphasized, however, that failure to find the sought-for correlates can never be taken as conclusive proof that they do not exist. On the other hand, in so far as any such correlates may be demonstrated the nurture hypothesis is to that extent weakened.

In a recent treatise Mead[1] has presented a mass of descriptive evidence favoring the extreme environmental hypothesis for the causes of sex differences in personality. If her observations and interpretations can be taken at their face value it would not be easy to escape the conclusion that among human beings constitutional factors are distinctly secondary to psychological as determiners of the M and F temperaments. Her book is based upon a study of three primitive tribes in New Guinea. She reports that in one of these, the Arapesh, males and females both exhibit in the main a single temperamental pattern, one that corresponds closely to the feminine pattern of present-day occidental cultures. A similar situation was found with the Mundugumors, except that in this case the single standard is typically masculine. The Tchambuli, on the other hand, present both masculine and feminine patterns, but reversed as between the sexes, males approximating what we should call the feminine in temperament and females approximating the masculine. The author describes in considerable detail the cultural influences which she believes to be responsible for these results.

That Mead's contribution offers impressive evidence of the modifiability of human temperament will be readily conceded, but we are by no means convinced that the case for nurture is as strong as a casual perusal of her book would suggest. Psychologists who have investigated personality by means of observational and rating techniques will inevitably question the accuracy of anyone's estimates of the degree of masculinity or femininity of behavior characterizing either an individual or a group of individuals. It is not to be supposed that the field anthropologist, any more than the psychologist, is immune to error in such estimates; indeed, because the groups under observation by him belong to an alien culture, and because his command of the tribal language is almost invariably limited, the anthropologist who attempts to rate the masculinity or femininity of behavior in a primitive tribal group labors under tremendous disadvantages.

[1] *Op. cit.* See p. 452.

We have shown that when subjects are rated by their teachers or intimate acquaintances either on general masculinity-femininity or on specific aspects of personality related thereto, so little agreement is found that the pooled estimates of several independent judges are necessary to increase the reliability of such ratings to a reasonable figure. Even then we do not rule out the types of constant error that result from a common bias among the raters. When subjective methods are employed, greater or less bias is inevitable, however competent and honest the observer may be; and observers who have had a particular kind of training, whether in anthropology or psychology, are bound to be influenced by the effect of biases common to their group—by the "idols of the den."[1]

Notwithstanding the above criticisms, the book in question is one of the most provocative contributions thus far made to the psychology of sex. Written for the general reader, it naturally does not contain the wealth of specific detail that would be necessary to enable the social scientist to judge the correctness of its conclusions. It does, however, present a number of observations which clearly suggest the operation of a nature as well as a nurture factor. The author admits that the cultural pressures in these tribes have not succeeded in forcing acceptance by all individuals of the personality standards imposed. Concrete examples are given of individuals who have become maladjusted

---

[1] In the specific case at hand, it is no reflection upon Dr. Mead to call attention to the fact, verifiable by examination of her earlier writings, that she entered upon her study of sex and temperament with definite leanings toward the environmental hypothesis in the interpretation of human behavior patterns. If the composite verbal pictures of her three New Guinea tribes had been sketched by an equally competent observer of different bias, there is no way of knowing how they would have differed from the dramatic contrasts presented; we can only be certain that they would have differed. It is regrettable that an investigation of the type in question could not have been carried out by the joint efforts of a number of social scientists of widely varying experiential background, including, say, an anthropologist, a psychologist, a sociologist, and a psychiatrist, all recording their observations and making their interpretations independently. Unfortunately, the rapidly growing contacts of these tribes with European cultures will in a few years render such an investigation meaningless, and the student is left to draw from the ingenious but not infallible work of Dr. Mead whatever conclusions seem to him reasonable.

by inability to conform. The author even admits that individual differences within a given sex are about as great as in our own culture, and that the chief result of the pressures has been to shift the location of the distribution of differences on the M-F axis without appreciably diminishing its range.

The literature of anthropology furnishes an abundance of cogent testimony as to the plasticity of temperament and personality. Of the treatises bearing on this question, the above-mentioned book by Mead and another not less notable by Benedict[1] are outstanding examples. Nevertheless, valuable as the anthropological evidence is, it cannot be accepted as a final answer to the nature-nurture problem. Primitive cultures are rapidly becoming more rare; the interpretation of behavior offers many pitfalls to observers unaccustomed to think in quantitative terms; conclusions reached by the anthropologist's field observations are usually not amenable to laboratory checks. For these and other reasons the psychologist, the physiologist, the psychiatrist, and the biochemist need not fear that their contributions to the theory of personality are likely to be rendered superfluous by other approaches.

EVIDENCE OF NURTURE INFLUENCES UPON THE M-F SCORE

Several convergent lines of evidence have been mentioned in preceding chapters which point to the efficacy of nurture factors as at least partial determiners of an individual's M-F score. The latter is definitely, even though not closely, associated with amount of schooling, with age, with occupation, with interests, and with domestic milieu. Perhaps the closest association of all, though its degree is suggested rather than measured, is that between cross-parent fixation and M-F deviation toward the norm of the opposite sex. The data do not define the reasons for these or other deviations. Old men test more feminine than young men, but the causal factor may be either experiential or physiological and endocrinal. Superior culture, in the case of women, tends to be associated with masculinity; in the case of men, with femininity; but our data do not tell us whether edu-

---

[1] BENEDICT, RUTH, *Patterns of culture*, p. 291, Houghton Mifflin, 1934.

cation causes the change, or whether it merely tends to select the already feminine male and the already masculine female. Similarly for occupational classification, though the selective influence of the occupation is more clearly evidenced than in the case of education. Even in instances of cross-parent fixation it is not easy to rule out all possible selective factors: parents may be more likely to foster such an attachment in that particular opposite-sex child who is already a deviant, or, conversely, the already deviant child may be the only one who is affected by the overcherishing parent. Accordingly, although the evidence in favor of a considerable nurture influence is in our opinion very weighty, it is by no means crucial.

From the point of view of science progress could be made more rapidly if experimental and control groups of infants could be artificially segregated and the effects watched in them of reversing nurture influences. Our method for human study can, however, not parallel the "sacrificial" procedure of the physical sciences. Fortunately advance is not blocked by this condition. Comparison of parent-child resemblance in sex temperament with resemblance between foster parent and foster child can be accomplished, also comparison of resemblance between identical twins on the one hand and between like-sex fraternal twins on the other.

Another approach would be to locate parents who belong to one of two extreme types with respect to the kind of influence they have tried to exert in shaping the sex temperaments of their children: (a) parents who accept the usual dichotomy as desirable and have endeavored to inculcate it in their sons and daughters, and (b) parents who adhere radically to the opposite theory and have done their best to counteract every influence that would develop in their daughters the distinctively feminine, or in their sons the distinctively masculine, personality. If enough parents of the second type could be found to permit reliable determinations, the parental influence would be measured by the M-F score difference separating their sons and daughters as compared to the difference separating the sons and daughters of the other parental group. In such an investigation one would of course need to bear in mind that parental pressures may be largely nullified by subtle pressures of the larger social milieu, including playmates, the school, the newspaper, the theater, literature, industry, government, and innumerable other factors. Even so, we believe that a careful study of parental influences upon the sex temperament of offspring would be worth making.

As to what the outcome of such investigations might be, we prefer not to hazard a guess. On the one hand is a respectable body of evidence pointing to nurture effects; on the other is the spectacular and ever increasing evidence from animal laboratories on the effects of hormone concentration upon patterns of sexual behavior. To assume a partisan position at the present time with respect to the relative influence of nature and nurture upon human personality is hardly warranted.

CLINICAL AND FOLLOW-UP STUDIES OF DEVIANT-SCORING SUBJECTS

It is important that we should find the reason for the low correlation invariably obtained between M-F scores and personal ratings of the subjects by their acquaintances. If the mental attitudes measured by the test really have so little observable effect upon behavior, it would hardly seem worth while to investigate them. It may be, on the other hand, that the fault lies with the observers. That this is in part the explanation is indicated by the small amount of agreement between equally competent judges in rating the same individuals. It is further indicated by our case studies of extreme deviants. Clinical reports upon subjects who test 60 or 80 M-F points above their sex mean present a striking contrast to the composite picture of subjects who test correspondingly low. The pictures are blurred by exceptions to the rule, but the contrast is unmistakable. We can only conclude that the test scores do have behavioral correlates but that ordinary observers lack adeptness in detecting them. Perhaps continued use of the test technique will help to clear up the confused notions which are current with regard to what constitutes masculinity and femininity of personality. The fact seems to be that most of us have not acquired the ability to discriminate very clearly the genuinely masculine from the genuinely feminine. We have not learned the art of discovering what is beneath the roughneck apparel of the swaggering male who would disguise his femininity. We are likely to overestimate the masculinity of the big, raw-boned, homely girl and to over-estimate the femininity of the girl who is petite and pretty. Experience has shown that it is possible to talk much more intelligently and intelligibly about a person's mental abilities in terms of test scores than in vague descriptive terms, but the need for objective terminology in the appraisal of masculinity and femininity is even greater.

The interpretation of M-F scores can only be clarified by intensive clinical and follow-up studies of large numbers of individual subjects. Again the situation is paralleled in the history of intelligence testing. It has not been long since even the wisest psychologist was ignorant of the prognostic significance of, say, a mental-age score of 9 years earned by a six-year-old. It was the common opinion, also the opinion of no less an expert in child psychology than Stanley Hall, that such children are especially likely to recede to or below the average as adult life approaches. Not long ago psychologists as well as teachers encouraged the parents of a backward child to believe that the retardation of development would probably be made good by later acceleration. It was only by the testing and follow-up of thousands of subjects that the truth came out. The same process will have to be gone through before we shall know the significance of M-F scores.

APPLICATIONS OF THE M-F TEST IN THE STUDY
OF HOMOSEXUALITY

Hardly any other phenomenon connected with personality presents a more challenging problem than the individual who finds it difficult or impossible to make heterosexual adjustments. From the almost complete ignorance of a large majority of people on this subject one would suppose that homosexuals were exceedingly rare. Such is far from being the case. Estimates by the best informed students of the subject usually place the proportion of males so afflicted between 3 and 5 per cent. The proportion in one of the largest of American universities is estimated by the university medical staff[1] to be in the neighborhood of 4 per cent. Of course not all who are essentially homosexual engage in overt homosexual practices, but the proportion who do, at least in urban communities, must be very considerable. A typical American city of a million population, including possibly two hundred thousand adult males, may support several hundred male prostitutes who must on any reasonable estimate cater to the wants of several thousand men. It is probably safe to say that in our western cultures an average of one man in 30 is strongly enough inclined to homosexuality to find heterosexual relationships difficult. Much less is known regarding the number of homosexuals among females. Although intrasex "crushes" are more common among females than among males, it is probable that the number of true female inverts is relatively small. The female homosexual, for obvious reasons, finds heterosexual adjustment less impossible.

Of course the incidence of an abnormality has no bearing on its merits as a problem for scientific investigation. It has been alluded to in this connection only to emphasize the importance of homosexuality from a social and practical point of view. Any recognizable physical disease which afflicted so many people and caused so much acute unhappiness would attract hundreds of scientific workers and huge research funds. Homosexuality, on the other hand, is at present hardly mentionable; its victims (if males) are hounded as criminals, and the problem attracts from scientists but a small fraction of the attention it deserves.

We are hopeful that the M-F test will prove a useful tool in this field of investigation. It does not measure homosexuality, as that term is commonly used, but it does measure, roughly, degree of inversion of the sex temperament, and it is probably from inverts in this sense that homosexuals are chiefly recruited. For one thing, the use of the test will help to center attention

[1] In a private communication to one of the authors.

on the developmental aspects of the abnormality, just as intelligence tests have done in the case of mental deficiency. It is well known that the milder grades of mental deficiency can now be detected years earlier than was possible a generation ago. The same will in time be true of the potential homosexual. Early identification of the latter deviant is particularly to be desired, because we have so much reason to believe that defects of personality can be compensated for and to some extent corrected.

Tests of a few thousand subjects, and their follow-up into adult life, will ultimately tell us whether M-F scores one or two standard deviations above or below the sex mean at this early age have prognostic value with respect to later social and sexual adjustment. The question involves much more than merely finding out whether and how commonly feminine-scoring boys and masculine-scoring girls develop into homosexuals. It is probable that many who do not so develop will experience other difficulties of adjustment as a direct result of their deviation. One would like to know whether fewer of them marry, and whether a larger proportion of these marriages are unhappy.

Other uses of the test in the study of sexual inversion will readily suggest themselves. The need for more basic cooperation with biochemistry has already been emphasized. Research should also be devoted to the invert female, who has been little studied except by the psychoanalysts.[1] Improvements should be made in Dr. Kelly's tentative scale for measuring sexual inversion in males, and another "I" scale arranged for use with females. A single "I" scale might be devised which would be applicable to both sexes, though it remains to be seen whether this is feasible. Research is needed to clarify the relationship between "I" scores and M-F scores. Our data indicate that a man may have a very feminine M-F score but at the same time a low "invert" score. The value of both the M-F score and the "I" score should be investigated with a view to finding out what

[1] A recent study from the Laboratory of Dr. Carney Landis should be mentioned: STRAKOSCH, FRANCES M., *Factors in the sex life of seven hundred psychopathic women*, State Hospital Press, Utica, N.Y., 1934.

assistance they can render in the psychological differentiation of active and passive types of homosexuals.

OTHER USES OF THE M-F TECHNIQUE

When more reliable subtests are available the profile studies thus made possible may yield important data for clinical use. From the low average intercorrelations of subtests of the kind we have used it follows that subjects who have earned the same M-F total score may present radically different profiles on the subtests. The significance of such differences remains at present almost wholly unexplored. It is known that certain groups tend to score relatively much more masculine on some of the present M-F "exercises" than do other groups; what the divergences signify has been revealed only in part.

Some of the data presented in Chapters VI to IX suggest that the M-F technique may have a contribution to make to educational, vocational, and avocational guidance. The large differences in mean scores of various occupational groups indicate that such occupations exert a selective influence. Engineers, for example, tend to score highly masculine, artists, theologians, and musicians to score highly feminine. Significant relationships have been found between M-F score and the scholastic grades of college students, and between score and avocational interests of adult populations of both sexes. We have not investigated the correlation, if any, between score and success within a given occupation. It would be interesting to know whether, for example, feminine-scoring engineers or masculine-scoring ministers, artists, and musicians have less than average chance to attain success in their professional work.

In Chapter IV it was shown that scores on a substitute M-F test yielded certain small correlations with indices of marital happiness. For example, happily married women tested more feminine than women who were unhappily married or divorced, divorced men more feminine than men who were unhappily married. The differences were in the neighborhood of three times their standard error. At the same time no relationship was found between husband-wife resemblance in M-F score and the index of their marital happiness. The experiment should be repeated with the use of the present M-F test instead of the substitute formerly employed.

Thus far no use has been made of the M-F test with subjects who were suffering from mental disorders. It would not be surprising if reliable differences were found in the scores of the cyclothymic and schizophrenic types or if other psychoneuroses were found to yield characteristic patterns.

The list of suggestions we have made for further M-F research is far from exhaustive and it is impossible to predict which fields of those that confront us will yield the most fruitful harvests. We shall be satisfied if this pioneer attempt to apply psychometric methods in the study of sex temperaments stimulates others to test the soundness of our approach. We hold no brief for finality in the tentative interpretations and conclusions to which we have been led.

APPENDIX I

NORMS FOR TOTAL SCORE

TABLE 83.—PERCENTILE NORMS BASED ON HIGH-SCHOOL JUNIORS

Form A				Form B			
Males		Females		Males		Females	
Percentile scores	Raw scores	Percentile scores	Raw scores	Percentile scores	Raw scores	Percentile scores	Raw scores
100	+190	100	+ 40	100	+185	100	+110
95	+161	95	− 12	95	+156	95	+ 14
90	+142	90	− 27	90	+144	90	− 1
85	+132	85	− 38	85	+134	85	− 20
80	+124	80	− 45	80	+125	80	− 31
75	+117	75	− 51	75	+116	75	− 40
70	+100	70	− 56	70	+105	70	− 47
65	+ 92	65	− 61	65	+ 95	65	− 53
60	+ 84	60	− 67	60	+ 89	60	− 62
55	+ 77	55	− 75	55	+ 83	55	− 69
50	+ 69	50	− 87	50	+ 79	50	− 75
45	+ 60	45	− 97	45	+ 74	45	− 81
40	+ 53	40	−102	40	+ 70	40	− 87
35	+ 48	35	−107	35	+ 68	35	− 92
30	+ 44	30	−115	30	+ 52	30	− 98
25	+ 37	25	−123	25	+ 43	25	−108
20	+ 29	20	−129	20	+ 34	20	−118
15	+ 20	15	−136	15	+ 27	15	−127
10	+ 11	10	−143	10	+ 20	10	−140
5	− 2	5	−153	5	+ 5	5	−156
0	− 90	0	−184	0	− 84	0	−204

TABLE 84.—PERCENTILE NORMS BASED ON COLLEGE SOPHOMORES, AVERAGE OF FORMS A AND B

Males		Females	
Percentile scores	Raw scores	Percentile scores	Raw scores
100	+200	100	+ 41
97.5	+158	97.5	+ 16
95	+139	95	+ 8
90	+125	90	− 4
85	+114	85	− 13
80	+106	80	− 22
75	+ 99	75	− 31
70	+ 75	70	− 40
65	+ 90	65	− 46
60	+ 86	60	− 53
55	+ 82	55	− 59
50	+ 77	50	− 65
45	+ 72	45	− 71
40	+ 66	40	− 76
35	+ 59	35	− 81
30	+ 51	30	− 85
25	+ 41	25	− 90
20	+ 32	20	− 95
15	+ 21	15	−100
10	+ 7	10	−107
5	− 17	5	−117
2.5	− 37	2.5	−124
·0	− 70	0	−140

TABLE 85.—STANDARD SCORES BASED ON HIGH-SCHOOL JUNIORS

	Males			Females	
Raw scores	Standard scores		Raw scores	Standard scores	
	Form A	Form B		Form A	Form B
+200	+2.45	+2.43	+ 60	+3.20	+2.67
+190	+2.26	+2.32	+ 50	+2.98	+2.48
+180	+2.06	+2.11	+ 40	+2.76	+2.28
+170	+1.87	+1.90	+ 30	+2.54	+2.08
+160	+1.68	+1.69	+ 20	+2.32	+1.88
+150	+1.49	+1.48	+ 10	+2.10	+1.68
+140	+1.29	+1.27	0	+1.87	+1.48
+130	+1.10	+1.06	− 10	+1.65	+1.28
+120	+ .91	+ .84	− 20	+1.43	+1.09
+110	+ .72	+ .63	− 30	+1.21	+ .89
+100	+ .53	+ .42	− 40	+ .99	+ .69
+ 90	+ .33	+ .21	− 50	+ .77	+ .49
+ 80	+ .14	.00	− 60	+ .55	+ .29
+ 70	− .05	− .21	− 70	+ .33	+ .09
+ 60	− .24	− .42	− 80	+ .11	− .09
+ 50	− .44	− .63	− 90	− .11	− .29
+ 40	− .63	− .85	−100	− .34	− .41
+ 30	− .82	−1.06	−110	− .56	− .69
+ 20	−1.01	−1.27	−120	− .78	− .89
+ 10	−1.21	−1.48	−130	−1.00	−1.09
0	−1.40	−1.69	−140	−1.22	−1.28
− 10	−1.59	−1.90	−150	−1.44	−1.48
− 20	−1.78	−2.11	−160	−1.66	−1.68
− 30	−1.97	−2.32	−170	−1.88	−1.88
− 40	−2.17	−2.53	−180	−2.10	−2.08
− 50	−2.36	−2.75	−190	−2.32	−2.28
− 60	−2.55	−2.96	−200	−2.55	−2.48
− 70	−2.74	−3.16			

APPENDIX II

NORMS FOR EXERCISES 1 TO 7

TABLE 86.—PERCENTILE NORMS FOR THE SEPARATE EXERCISES OF FORM A
BASED ON HIGH-SCHOOL JUNIORS

Percentile scores	Exercise 1		Exercise 2		Exercise 3		Exercise 4	
	Males	Females	Males	Females	Males	Females	Males	Females
95	+15	− 1	+2	+1	+18	+ 1	+60	+28
90	+11	− 2	+1	+1	+17	− 2	+53	+22
80	+ 6	− 7	+1	0	+15	− 4	+35	+ 5
70	+ 4	− 9	0	0	+12	− 7	+27	− 6
60	0	−12	0	−1	+ 9	− 9	+21	−11
50	− 1	−13	0	−1	+ 7	−11	+15	−14
40	− 3	−16	−1	−1	+ 5	−13	+11	−21
30	− 5	−18	−1	−2	+ 3	−17	+ 5	−28
20	− 6	−21	−1	−2	+ 1	−20	− 7	−34
10	−10	−22	−2	−3	− 3	−25	−20	−44
5	−14	−24	−2	−3	− 7	−28	−25	−48

Percentile scores	Exercise 5		Exercise 6		Exercise 7	
	Males	Females	Males	Females	Males	Females
95	+99	+18	+14	+ 8	+4	+2
90	+92	− 4	+12	+ 7	+3	+1
80	+79	−10	+10	+ 1	+2	0
70	+70	−22	+ 8	− 1	+1	0
60	+62	−30	+ 6	− 3	+1	−1
50	+54	−38	+ 3	− 5	0	−2
40	+46	−47	0	− 7	0	−2
30	+37	−55	− 3	− 9	−1	−3
20	+19	−61	− 6	−11	−1	−3
10	+ 2	−70	−10	−14	−2	−4
5	− 4	−78	−13	−20	−3	−4

TABLE 87.—PERCENTILE NORMS FOR THE SEPARATE EXERCISES OF FORM B
BASED ON HIGH-SCHOOL JUNIORS

Percentile scores	Exercise 1		Exercise 2		Exercise 3		Exercise 4	
	Males	Females	Males	Females	Males	Females	Males	Females
95	+13	0	+3	+1	+16	+ 4	+54	+32
90	+10	− 4	+2	0	+14	+ 2	+48	+26
80	+ 7	− 8	+1	0	+10	− 2	+35	+14
70	+ 4	−11	+1	−1	+ 8	− 4	+27	+ 1
60	+ 3	−13	+1	−1	+ 6	− 5	+21	− 7
50	+ 1	−15	0	−1	+ 5	− 8	+14	−14
40	0	−16	0	−1	+ 3	−10	+ 8	−17
30	− 3	−18	0	−2	+ 2	−12	0	−24
20	− 6	−20	−1	−2	− 1	−16	− 4	−34
10	− 8	−23	−1	−3	− 7	−21	−15	−44
5	−10	−25	−1	−3	−10	−25	−24	−50

Percentile scores	Exercise 5		Exercise 6		Exercise 7	
	Males	Females	Males	Females	Males	Females
95	+114	+19	+16	+ 7	+4	+1
90	+102	+14	+12	+ 4	+3	0
80	+ 89	− 5	+ 7	+ 2	+1	−1
70	+ 79	−16	+ 5	− 1	0	−1
60	+ 70	−25	+ 3	− 3	0	−2
50	+ 64	−33	+ 2	− 5	−1	−2
40	+ 55	−39	0	− 7	−1	−3
30	+ 44	−46	− 1	−10	−2	−3
20	+ 29	−53	− 4	−13	−2	−4
10	+ 22	−72	−11	−16	−3	−5
5	+ 13	−78	−12	−19	−3	−6

TABLE 88.—PERCENTILE NORMS FOR THE SEPARATE EXERCISES, BASED ON COLLEGE SOPHOMORES. AVERAGE OF FORMS A AND B

Percentile scores	Exercise 1		Exercise 2		Exercise 3		Exercise 4	
	Males	Females	Males	Females	Males	Females	Males	Females
95	+12	+ 1	+2	+1	+18	+ 5	+58	+40
90	+10	− 2	+1	0	+15	+ 2	+49	+33
80	+ 7	− 5	+1	0	+13	− 1	+40	+25
70	+ 4	− 8	+1	−1	+11	− 3	+34	+19
60	+ 2	−11	0	−1	+ 9	− 5	+29	+13
50	0	−14	0	−1	+ 7	− 7	+25	+ 6
40	− 2	−16	0	−1	+ 6	− 8	+20	0
30	− 4	−18	−1	−2	+ 4	−11	+16	− 6
20	− 7	−20	−1	−2	+ 2	−13	+10	−12
10	−10	−22	−1	−3	− 2	−17	+ 1	−20
5	−13	−23	−2	−3	− 5	−20	− 8	−26

Percentile scores	Exercise 5		Exercise 6		Exercise 7	
	Males	Females	Males	Females	Males	Females
95	+87	+ 3	+12	+ 9	+3	+1
90	+76	− 6	+10	+ 7	+2	0
80	+63	−20	+ 7	+ 4	+1	−1
70	+53	−31	+ 6	+ 2	0	−2
60	+43	−40	+ 4	0	−1	−2
50	+35	−47	+ 3	− 1	−1	−3
40	+26	−53	+ 1	− 3	−2	−4
30	+16	−60	− 1	− 5	−3	−4
20	+ 3	−67	− 3	− 7	−3	−5
10	−15	−76	− 5	−10	−4	−6
5	−32	−83	− 7	−13	−6	−6

TABLE 89.— STANDARD SCORES FOR MALES, BASED ON GENERAL ADULT
POPULATION OF 552 CASES[1]

Standard score	Ex. 1	Ex. 2	Ex. 3	Ex. 4	Ex. 5	Ex. 6	Ex. 7	Total
+3.00	+20	+4	+27	+86	+127	+22	+5	+197
+2.75	+18	+3	+25	+80	+118	+20	+5	+184
+2.50	+16	+3	+22	+74	+110	+18	+4	+171
+2.25	+14	+3	+20	+69	+101	+16	+4	+157
+2.00	+12	+2	+18	+63	+ 92	+14	+3	+144
+1.75	+11	+2	+16	+57	+ 84	+12	+3	+130
+1.50	+ 9	+2	+14	+51	+ 75	+10	+2	+117
+1.25	+ 7	+2	+12	+46	+ 67	+ 8	+2	+103
+1.00	+ 5	+1	+10	+40	+ 58	+ 6	+1	+ 90
+ .75	+ 3	+1	+ 7	+34	+ 50	+ 4	+1	+ 77
+ .50	+ 1	+1	+ 5	+28	+ 41	+ 2	0	+ 63
+ .25	− 1	0	+ 3	+23	+ 33	+ 1	0	+ 50
0	− 3	0	+ 1	+17	+ 24	− 1	−1	+ 36
− .25	− 5	0	− 1	+11	+ 16	− 3	−1	+ 23
− .50	− 7	−1	− 3	+ 5	+ 7	− 5	−2	+ 10
− .75	− 9	−1	− 6	0	− 1	− 7	−2	− 4
−1.00	−11	−1	− 8	− 6	− 10	− 9	−2	− 17
−1.25	−13	−1	−10	−12	− 18	−11	−3	− 31
−1.50	−15	−2	−12	−18	− 27	−13	−3	− 44
−1.75	−17	−2	−14	−23	− 36	−15	−4	− 57
−2.00	−19	−2	−16	−29	− 44	−17	−4	− 71
−2.25	−21	−3	−19	−35	− 53	−19	−5	− 84
−2.50	−23	−3	−21	−41	− 61	−21	−5	− 98
−2.75	−25	−3	−23	−46	− 70	−22	−6	−111
−3.00	−27	−4	−25	−52	− 78	−24	−6	−124

[1] See note on p. 479 regarding the computation of the standard scores.

TABLE 90.—STANDARD SCORES FOR FEMALES, BASED ON GENERAL ADULT
POPULATION OF 1,107 CASES[1]

Standard score	Ex. 1	Ex. 2	Ex. 3	Ex. 4	Ex. 5	Ex. 6	Ex. 7	Total
+3.00	+11	+3	+19	+67	+ 39	+17	+4	+ 42
+2.75	+ 9	+2	+17	+61	+ 32	+15	+3	+ 31
+2.50	+ 7	+2	+14	+55	+ 25	+13	+3	+ 27
+2.25	+ 4	+2	+12	+49	+ 18	+11	+2	+ 10
+2.00	+ 2	+1	+ 9	+43	+ 11	+ 9	+2	− 1
+1.75	0	+1	+ 7	+37	+ 4	+ 7	+1	− 11
+1.50	− 2	+1	+ 4	+31	− 3	+ 5	+1	− 22
+1.25	− 4	0	+ 2	+25	− 10	+ 3	0	− 32
+1.00	− 6	0	0	+19	− 17	+ 1	0	− 43
+ .75	− 8	0	− 3	+13	− 24	− 1	−1	− 53
+ .50	−10	0	− 5	+ 7	− 32	− 3	−1	− 64
+ .25	−12	−1	− 8	+ 1	− 39	− 5	−2	− 75
0	−14	−1	−10	− 5	− 46	− 7	−2	− 85
− .25	−16	−1	−13	−11	− 53	− 9	−3	− 96
− .50	−18	−2	−15	−17	− 60	−11	−3	−106
− .75	−20	−2	−18	−23	− 67	−13	−4	−117
−1.00	−22	−2	−20	−29	− 74	−15	−4	−127
−1.25	−24	−3	−23	−35	− 81	−17	−5	−138
−1.50	−26	−3	−25	−41	− 88	−19	−5	−149
−1.75	−29	−3	−27	−47	− 96	−21	−6	−159
−2.00	−31	−3	−30	−53	−103	−23	−6	−170
−2.25	−33	−4	−32	−60	−110	−25	−7	−180
−2.50	−35	−4	−35	−66	−117	−27	−7	−191
−2.75	−37	−4	−37	−72	−124	−29	−8	−201
−3.00	−39	−5	−40	−78	−131	−31	−8	−212

[1] See note on p. 479 regarding the computation of the standard scores.

Standard Scores.—The standard scores (S.S.) in Tables 89 and 90 were computed from the test responses of 552 males and 1,107 females between the ages of 20 and 90, all of them people of grade-school or high-school education. The educational level of the combined populations including both males and females averages at about the ninth school year. In formal education the younger members tend to have advanced somewhat further than the older ones. The average age of the males is 40, of the females 41 years. The per cent contributions of the various age groups, as shown in the following comparison, do not differ greatly from similar groupings of the United States general population census (1930) in which the average age falls in the late thirties with the average in education at the eighth grade. Hence, our general population roughly coincides in age and schooling with the general population of the United States.

Standard scores have been computed for the M-F battery in the usual way, *i.e.*, in decimal fractions of the standard deviation of the score distribution on each exercise scale and on the total scale. The respective male and female means

Decades	20's	30's	40's	50's	60's	70's and 80's
U. S., both sexes............	30	25	20	14	8	3
M-F males.................	25	29	16	15	10	5
M-F females..............	26	24	17	15	11	8

and standard score differentials required for the computations appear below. The standard scores reported on our groups have been read from a table with entries in multiples of .05 S.D., the index used being the one on the mean or zero side nearest to the point of entry. The standard scores are larger for males than for females in the total and in Exercises 2 and 5; for the females they are larger in Exercises 1, 3, 4, 6, and 7.

Exercise	1	2	3	4	5	6	7	Total
Male mean....	− 3.37	− .05	+ .87	+16.83	+24.20	−1.39	− .56	+36.48
S.D..........	7.93	1.21	8.63	22.98	34.14	7.66	1.92	53.61
Female mean.	−14.10	−1.02	−10.28	− 5.13	−45.78	−6.94	−2.13	−85.11
S.D..........	8.25	1.18	9.81	24.17	28.41	7.87	1.96	42.30

APPENDIX III

CONVERSION TABLES

TABLE 91.—EQUIVALENT SCORES, FORM A TO FORM B, BASED ON HIGH-SCHOOL
JUNIORS

$$x_A = 1.057(x_B) - 4.812$$

Form B	Form A	Form B	Form A	Form B	Form A
200	207	65	64	− 70	− 79
195	201	60	59	− 75	− 84
190	196	55	53	− 80	− 89
185	191	50	48	− 85	− 95
180	185	45	43	− 90	−100
175	180	40	37	− 95	−105
170	175	35	32	−100	−111
165	170	30	27	−105	−116
160	164	25	22	−110	−121
155	159	20	16	−115	−126
150	154	15	11	−120	−132
145	148	10	6	−125	−137
140	143	5	0	−130	−142
·135	138	0	− 5	−135	−148
130	133	− 5	−10	−140	−153
125	127	−10	−15	−145	−158
120	122	−15	−21	−150	−163
115	117	−20	−26	−155	−169
110	111	−25	−31	−160	−174
105	106	−30	−37	−165	−179
100	101	−35	−42	−170	−185
95	96	−40	−47	−175	−190
90	90	−45	−52	−180	−195
85	85	−50	−58	−185	−200
80	80	−55	−63	−190	−206
75	74	−60	−68	−195	−211
70	69	−65	−74	−200	−216
				−205	−221

TABLE 92.—MENTAL AGE ESTIMATED FROM CORRECT RESPONSES ON EXERCISE 3, FORM A OR FORM B

Correct responses Exercise 3	Estimated M. A.	
	Yr.	Mo.
5	9	8
10	10	7
15	11	5
20	12	3
25	13	1
30	13	11
35	14	9
40	15	8
45	16	6
50	17	4
55	18	2
60	19	0
65	19	11
70	20	9

$$y = 2.04x + 106.14$$
$$r = .675$$
$$\text{P.E.}_{est} = 12 \text{ months}$$

Based on Terman Group Test scores of 333 students in grades 8 and 10 (both sexes).

APPENDIX IV

ATTITUDE-INTEREST ANALYSIS TEST, FORM A

READ THIS FIRST

You are asked to cooperate seriously and carefully in marking the items in this booklet. This is not an intelligence test. We want to find out something about the attitudes and interests of people in relation to their occupations, their home situations, and their hobbies. The items in this booklet have been selected by actual trial out of several thousand. More than 4,000 persons of different ages, occupations, and schooling have filled out test blanks like this one. We are trying to accumulate sufficient returns to discover what the actual standards of response are. Your answers are needed to help do this. Fill in all of the blanks on this page as indicated below. Please do not omit any of the items. All of the information is important. Do not look at the other pages of the booklet until you have finished filling in the blanks below.

Name.. Age......... Sex................... Race...................

City .... State...................

Underline one: Single, Married, Widowed, Separated, Divorced.

Amount of Schooling.

Mark highest point reached: Yrs.

Grammar grades	High School	College
1 2 3 4 5 6 7 8	1 2 3 4	1 2 3 4 M.A. Ph.D. / 5 6 M.D. 7

Other schooling or courses..

Profession or occupation..

Previous professions or occupations if any:

(Married women list occupation before marriage)..........................

Specific hobbies or special interests such as playing baseball, 1. ....
choir singing, chess, collecting stamps, philanthropy. 2. ....

If ever married state for how many years: ....

If you have children state number of boys: .... girls: ....

How many brothers older than yourself reached 16 years of age? ....

How many brothers younger than yourself reached 16 years of age? ....

How many sisters older than yourself reached 16 years of age? ....

How many sisters younger than yourself reached 16 years of age? ....

Were both your parents responsible for your training up to the age of 16? ....

If not, please specify.......................

Underline the word that indicates your usual state of health: Robust, above-average, average, below-average, frail.

Mark a cross on each of the 12 lines below to indicate the amount of your interest in each subject or activity.

	Much	Average	Slight or none			Much	Average	Slight or none
1. Travel					7. Music			
2. Out-door Sports					8. Art			
3. Religion					9. Science			
4. Mechanics					10. Politics			
5. Social Life					11. Domestic Arts			
6. Literature					12. Pets			

NOW READ THIS

Do not look at other parts of the booklet until you are ready to begin the test. When you are ready, turn at once to Exercise 1. Read the instructions carefully, marking the sample items as you come to them. Then go right on to the exercise itself. Work **as** rapidly as you can. As soon as you have finished Exercise 1 go right on to Exercise 2, then Exercise 3, and so on until you have finished the booklet. In each case read the directions with care, and work the exercise **as rapidly** as you can. It should take about 40 or 50 minutes to finish the booklet.

Time began test . . . .   Time finished test . . . .

Do not write in space below.

1	2	3	4	5	6	7

EXERCISE 1

DIRECTIONS: Look at the word in capital letters, then look at each of the four words which follow it.

For example:

HORSE   cow   hay   race   swim

Draw a line under the word that seems to you to go best or most naturally with HORSE; that is, the word that HORSE tends most to make you **think of.**

Second example:

AUTO   danger   gears   machine   ride

Draw a line under the word that seems to go best or most naturally with AUTO; the word that AUTO tends most to make you **think of.** Look at each of the words in the list below. In each case, draw a line under the word that **goes best** or most naturally with the one in capitals; the word it tends most to make you **think of.** Work rapidly; do not think long over any one.

EXERCISE 1.—Continued

1.[1] POLE   barber 0[2]   cat +   North −   telephone +
2. DATE   appointment −   dance +   fruit +   history +
3. BAR   drink +   prisoner −   sand +   stop −
4. SHARP   bright −   flat −   knife 0   pin +
5. TRUNK   baggage 0   elephant +   travel −   tree 0

6. ORDER   buy −   command +   neat −   quiet −
7. CASE   bottles +   container 0   doctor −   grammar −
8. POST   fence +   gate −   letter −   mail 0
9. TENDER   kind −   loving −   meat +   sore 0
10. JACK   cards −   money +   tool +   toy −

11. TRAIN   engine +   gown −   travel −   whistle −
12. DRAW   blood +   bridge +   pencil −   picture 0
13. BRACE   bit +   pair −   strap −   support −
14. FLY   airplane +   bird −   nasty 0   travel −
15. BOND   love +   paper −   security +   tie −

16. PASS   car 0   mountain +   over −   subject −
17. RAIN   clouds +   umbrella −   weather +   wet 0
18. BOOK   cover 0   paper +   print +   read −
19. PURE   good −   milk −   water −   white 0
20. MOON   light +   month 0   night −   round −

[1] The items in Exercises 1 and 2 were not numbered in the test blank, for fear of disturbing the associations. They are numbered here to facilitate reference to them.

[2] In this reproduction of the M-F test the response weights have been added. Responses followed by the sign "+" count one point toward masculinity, those followed by the sign "−" count one point toward femininity, those followed by "0" are neutral.

EXERCISE 1.—Continued

21. FLESH	blood –	color –	meat +	soft –
22. DANGER	accident –	caution +	death –	escape +
23. MODEST	bashful +	good 0	nice 0	shy –
24. FRESH	cool –	flirt 0	meat +	stale +
25. COLOR	black +	blind +	blue –	shade –
26. PICNIC	fun –	hike 0	sandwich 0	Sunday +
27. WEDDING	bride –	happiness –	marriage +	ring +
28. DUTY	God –	honor 0	soldier +	work –
29. GARDEN	flower –	fruit +	vegetable +	weeds +
30. EMBRACE	arms –	lover +	mother 0	sin +
31. HOME	expenses –	happiness –	house +	sleep +
32. BLUSH	red –	rose –	shame +	smile +
33. BABY	cry +	darling –	infant –	mother 0
34. FELLOW	boy –	friend +	good 0	pal 0
35. CHEAT	cards +	clerk +	crook 0	unfair –
36. ENJOY	food +	happiness –	jolly +	laugh 0
37. DEVIL	dare 0	evil –	hell +	tempt –
38. JEALOUS	angry –	green –	lover +	women +
39. DIMPLE	baby –	cheek 0	hole 0	knee +
40. KNIGHT	armor +	brave –	Ivanhoe –	man +

EXERCISE 1.—Concluded

41. LETTER — love + news — paper + stamp 0
42. CELLAR — basement + dark — furnace 0 vegetables 0
43. TRUE — edge + good — soldiers + story +
44. DESPISE — coward + dirt — dislike — flirt 0
45. TWILIGHT — dark + dusk — morning 0 sunset +

46. FACE — enemy + powder — pretty + wash 0
47. SPOON — fork + pet + silver — soup +
48. CHEEK — blush + girl + nerve + pink —
49. WORSHIP — church + God — hero 0 Sunday 0
50. LONGING — absence — child + home — success 0

51. SACRIFICE — cards + kill + money 0 mother —
52. MARRIAGE — children — divorce + happy — license 0
53. RULE — command — footrule + games + obey —
54. BRAVE — fight + honor — protect + soldier 0
55. FLOWER — fields 0 fragrant — vase + violet —

56. FAMILY — brother + kind — quarrel + sister 0
57. SIXTEEN — age 0 foolish + number — years 0
58. ANGEL — death 0 Gabriel + good — heaven —
59. VAIN — peacock — proud — impossible + useless +
60. MACHINE — engine — Ford + ride — sew —

EXERCISE 2

Directions:—Here are some drawings, a little like ink blots. They are not pictures of anything in particular but might suggest almost anything to you, just as shapes in the clouds sometimes do. Beside each drawing four things are mentioned. **Underline the one word that tells what the drawing makes you think of most.**

Examples:—

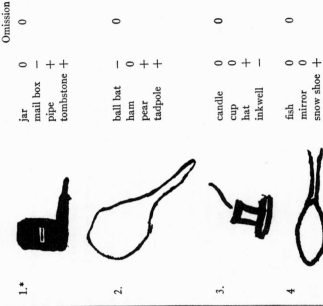

baby
dog
man
squirrel

arm
flame
flower
tail

dog's head
glove
hand
horse's head

			Omission
1.*	jar	0	0
	mail box	—	
	pipe	+	
	tombstone	+	
2.	ball bat	—	0
	ham	0	
	pear	+	
	tadpole	+	
3.	candle	0	0
	cup	0	
	hat	+	
	inkwell	—	
4	fish	0	0
	mirror	0	
	snow shoe	+	
	spoon	—	

* See footnote 1 to Exercise 1.

EXERCISE 2.—Continued

		Omission	
5.		brush + centipede + comb − teeth −	0
6.		ax + boat + chopper − moon +	0
7.		dish − ring 0 target + tire 0	0
8.		bird house 0 flagpole + sword − torch +	+
9.		fence + letter "E" 0 ship − tree 0	+
10.		babies 0 cloud − dancers − lovers +	0
11.		Indian 0 man hanged + scarecrow − tassel −	0
12.		chimney − coil + smoke − thread −	0

EXERCISE 2.—Concluded

		Omission
13.	bottle	0
	cannon	+
	Indian club	−
	jug	−
		0
14.	baby	+
	bell	+
	idol	−
	incense	−
		0
15.	fish	+
	saxophone	+
	snake	−
	whip	0
		0

		Omission
16.	bat	+
	flower	−
	goat	0
	star	−
		0
17.	coal bucket	−
	face	0
	kettle	+
	nose	+
		0
18.	a man	0
	bowl	−
	cup	−
	head	+
		0

EXERCISE 3

In each sentence draw a line under the word that makes the sentence true.
Example: America was discovered by BALBOA COLUMBUS <u>DRAKE</u> WASHINGTON
Work as rapidly as you can. Skip those you do not know.

	Omission
1. Marigold is a kind of **fabric** + flower — grain — stone +	— 1
2. Things cooked in grease are boiled + broiled + fried — roasted +	— 2
3. The Yale is a kind of hammer 0 lock + screen 0 wrench 0	— 3
4. We should drink tea from the cup — saucer + spoon +	0 4
5. Pongee is a kind of cloth — drink 0 flower 0 game +	+ 5
6. The most gold is produced in Alaska + New York 0 Tennessee — Texas —	— 6
7. The earth moves around the sun in **7 days** — **30 days** 0 **180 days** — **365 days** +	+ 7
8. A stately dance of colonial days was the minuet — polka + two-step 0 waltz +	+ 8
9. One must run fast in **fruit basket** — jackstones + tin-tin + wood-tag 0	+ 9
10. Beethoven is known as a composer — painter + poet + singer —	+ 10
11. Most of our anthracite coal comes from Alabama — Colorado — Ohio — Pennsylvania +	— 11
12. The number of players on a baseball team is **7** — **9** + **11** — **13** 0	— 12
13. Eggs are best for us when deviled — fried + hard-boiled + soft-boiled —	0 13
14. A loom is used for cooking + embroidering + sewing + weaving —	+ 14
15. Peat is used for **fuel** + pavement — plaster 0 road-making 0	— 15
16. Marco Polo was a famous king 0 philosopher — traveler + warrior —	0 16
17. Tokyo is a city of China — India — Japan + Russia 0	+ 17
18. The first American naval hero was Hull — **John Paul Jones** + Lawrence + Winslow —	— 18

EXERCISE 3—Continued

	Omission	
19. Daffodils are grown from **bulbs** – **cuttings** 0 **seeds** + **shoots** +..........	+	19
20. The baby found in the bulrushes was **Jacob** + **Jesus** + **Moses** – **Paul** +..........	0	20
21. The boomerang is an **animal** – **plant** 0 **tool** – **weapon** +..........	–	21
22. Minnehaha means **falling leaves** + **laughing waters** – **running brooks** + **whispering pines** 0..	+	22
23. A correct expression is **I have dove** 0 **I dived** – **He dove** – **He dove** +..........	0	23
24. The "Rough Riders" were led by **Funston** – **Pershing** – **Roosevelt** + **Sheridan** –..........	–	24
25. The vessel which overcame the Merrimac was the **Connecticut** – **Monitor** + **Old Ironsides** –....	–	25
26. About A.D. 1750 men's sleeves had **bands** + **lace-ruffles** – **stiff cuffs** + **stripes** +..........	–	26
27. A food with much the same food substance as rice is **beans** + **peas** – **meat** 0 **potatoes** –....	+	27
28. A shilling is worth about **25 cts.** + **50 cts.** 0 **\$1.00** – **\$5.00** 0..........	–	28
29. Punch and Judy are **artists** 0 **dancers** – **musicians** + **puppets** 0..........	–	29
30. "Speak for yourself" was said by **Annabel Lee** + **Evangeline** – **Juliet** + **Priscilla** –..........	0	30
31. The Erie Canal is in **Canada** – **Ohio** 0 **New York** + **Pennsylvania** 0..........	+	31
32. Red goes best with **black** – **lavender** + **pink** + **purple** +..........	–	32
33. Baby gets its first tooth at about **6 mos.** – **12 mos.** + **15 mos.** – **18 mos.** +..........	0	33
34. The mossy side of a tree is usually on the **east** – **north** 0 **south** 0 **west** 0..........	–	34
35. The state whose waters produce the most salmon is **California** 0 **Maine** – **Massachusetts** – **Oregon** +....	0	35
36. Turpentine comes from **coal** + **petroleum** – **trees** + **whales** –..........	–	36
37. The number of persons on a jury in the U.S. is **8** 0 **12** + **16** – **18** 0..........	–	37
38. The Madonna is a favorite subject for **music** + **paintings** – **poetry** 0 **stories** 0..........	+	38
39. The chief cause of the tides is the attraction of **the moon** + **planets** – **sun** 0 **stars** 0..........	–	39
40. The proportion of the globe covered by water is about ⅛ – ¼ – ½ – ¾ +..........	–	40
41. The turquoise is **blue** – **red** + **white** + **yellow** +..........	+	41
42. A plant "breathes" chiefly through its **bark** 0 **leaves** + **roots** – **twigs** 0..........	–	42

EXERCISE 3—Continued

	Omission	
43. Mica is an explosive 0 food + mineral + vegetable 0.........	—	43
44. Blue clashes worst with brown + gray + pink + purple —......	0	44
45. A dinner hostess seats the guest of honor at her left 0 opposite + right —.........	0	45
46. A buffet is used for books 0 clothes + dishes — food —........	+	46
47. Shinny is played with bats + clubs + nets — racquets —........	—	47
48. When water freezes it contracts + expands + does neither —........	—	48
49. The Roman numeral C equals 50 + 100 + 500 0 1000 —........	—	49
50. Some think "moon over the right shoulder" means death 0 rain — sickness + wish fulfillment —......	0	50
51. The amethyst is green + purple — white + yellow +........	+	51
52. Ruth and Naomi are known for their devotion — hatred + pity 0 rivalry +........	—	52
53. The length of a brick is 6 in. — 8 in. + 10 in. + 12 in. —........	—	53
54. The number of Abou Ben Adhem's visions was 1 + 20 40 6 +........	—	54
55. "Mennen's" is the name of cold cream + perfume + collar 0 talcum —........	—	55
56. Barometers are used to measure air pressure + heat — humidity + rainfall —........	—	56
57. Lobo was the name of a bear — crow + fox + wolf +........	—	57
58. "Charades" is a running game 0 game of chance 0 guessing game — kissing game +........	+	58
59. The number of ordinary steps in a mile is about 1,000 0 2,000 + 5,000 — 10,000 0........	—	59
60. "Peter Pan" was written by Barrie — Kipling + Mark Twain + Stevenson +........	—	60
61. Babies should be weaned at about 3 mos. — 6 mos. — 12 mos. — 2 yrs. +........	0	61
62. The altitude record for airplanes is about 10,000 ft. — 20,000 ft. + 40,000 ft. + 60,000 ft. +........	—	62
63. Limestone originated from granite — marble — sand 0 shells —........	—	63
64. An animal that suckles its young is the alligator 0 shark — snake 0 whale +........	—	64
65. A birthright was sold for a mess of pottage by Cain 0 Esau + Isaac — Judas 0........	—	65

EXERCISE 3.—Concluded

		Omission
66. Beam scales illustrate the principle of buoyancy 0 elasticity 0 leverage + magnetism –	–	66
67. A character in "David Copperfield" is Betty + Uriah Heep – Sinbad + Oliver Twist + ...	–	67
68. A decisive Revolutionary battle was Gettysburg – New Orleans + Valley Forge – Yorktown + ...	–	68
69. "Nevermore" was spoken by a general + parrot 0 raven 0 woman –	–	69
70. A famous portrait painter was Rosa Bonheur 0 Mozart – Reynolds – Rubens + ...	+	70

EXERCISE 4

Below is a list of things that sometimes cause anger. After each thing mentioned draw a circle around VM, M, L, or N to show how much anger it causes **you.**

VM means VERY MUCH; M means MUCH; L means A LITTLE; N means NONE.

1. Being blamed for something you have not done..........	VM –	M 0	L +	N 0
2. Being called lazy..........	VM –	M 0	L 0	N +
3. Being called stupid..........	VM –	M 0	L +	N 0
4. Being called a thief..........	VM 0	M 0	L +	N –
5. Being deceived by a supposed friend..........	VM –	M 0	L 0	N 0
6. Being disturbed when you want to work..........	VM 0	M 0	L +	N –
7. Being snubbed by an inferior..........	VM –	M 0	L –	N +
8. Being unexpectedly slapped on the back as a joke..........	VM –	M 0	L –	N +
9. Hearing someone make fun of your clothes..........	VM –	M 0	L 0	N +
10. Hearing your political views ridiculed..........	VM 0	M –	L +	N +
11. Seeing boys make fun of old people..........	VM –	M +	L +	N 0
12. Seeing an honest official thrown out of office by politicians.	VM 0	M 0	L +	N –
13. Seeing a person laugh at a cripple..........	VM –	M +	L 0	N +

EXERCISE 4—Continued

14. Seeing people disfigure library books... VM – M – L + N +
15. Seeing someone cheat in an examination.. VM – M 0 L + N +

16. Seeing someone trying to discredit you with your employer........................ VM + M 0 L + N –
17. Seeing someone laugh when a blind man runs into an obstacle..................... VM – M + L + N +

Below is a list of things that often **cause fear.** After each thing mentioned draw a circle around VM, M, L, or N to indicate how much fear it causes **you.** Be honest and admit all the fears you have. Fears are not disgraceful.

VM means VERY MUCH; M means MUCH; L means A LITTLE; N means NONE.

1. Automobiles.................. VM 0 M – L – N +	11. Garter snakes............. VM – M – L – N +
2. Being lost................... VM – M – L + N +	12. Graveyards at night....... VM – M – L 0 N +
3. Being in a closed room........ VM – M – L 0 N +	13. Heart trouble............. VM – M + L + N +
4. Becoming deaf or blind........ VM – M + L + N –	14. Insects.................. VM 0 M 0 L 0 N 0
5. Bulls....................... VM – M – L + N +	15. Lightning................ VM – M 0 L – N +
6. Burglars.................... VM – M 0 L + N +	16. Negroes................. VM – M – L – N +
7. Contagious diseases.......... VM 0 M + L 0 N –	17. Pain.................... VM – M 0 L – N +
8. Deep water.................. VM – M 0 L – N +	18. Punishment in the next world. VM 0 M 0 L – N +
9. End of the world............. VM – M – L – N +	19. Thunder................. VM – M – L – N +
10. Floods..................... VM – M – L + N +	20. Windstorms.............. VM – M – L – N +

Below is a list of things that sometimes **cause disgust.** After each thing mentioned draw a circle around VM, M, L, or N to indicate how much it disgust it causes **you.**

VM means VERY MUCH; M means MUCH; L means A LITTLE; N means NONE.

EXERCISE 4—Continued

	VM	M	L	N
1. An unshaven man	VM −	M −	L +	N +
2. A butcher shop	VM 0	M 0	L −	N +
3. A drunken man	VM −	M +	L +	N +
4. Crooked teeth	VM −	M −	L +	N 0
5. Food stains on clothing	VM −	M +	L +	N +
6. Foul language	VM −	M +	L +	N +
7. Gum chewing	VM −	M −	L +	N +
8. Mushy food in your mouth	VM −	M 0	L +	N +
9. Offensive breath	VM −	M +	L +	N +
10. Pimples	VM −	M 0	L +	N +

	VM	M	L	N
11. Sagging socks on a man	VM −	M −	L 0	N +
12. Seeing a woman smoking	VM −	M 0	L +	N +
13. Sight of slimy water	VM −	M +	L 0	N +
14. Smell of decaying fish	VM −	M +	L +	N +
15. Soiled or ragged fingernails	VM −	M −	L +	N +
16. Spitting in public	VM −	M +	L +	N +
17. Untidy clothes	VM −	M +	L +	N +
18. Word "gent" used for gentle-man	VM −	M −	L +	N +

Below is a list of things that sometimes **arouse pity.** After each thing mentioned draw a circle around VM, M, L, or N to indicate how much pity it arouses in **you.**

VM means VERY MUCH; M means MUCH; L means A LITTLE; N means NONE.

	VM	M	L	N
1. A bee that is drowning	VM −	M 0	L 0	N +
2. A dog that must be killed for biting people	VM −	M 0	L +	N +
3. A man who is cowardly and can't help it	VM −	M +	L −	N +
4. An insane person	VM −	M +	L +	N +
5. An old person with a fatal disease	VM −	M +	L +	N +
6. An orphan girl	VM −	M +	L +	N +
7. Overworked horses	VM −	M +	L +	N 0
8. Overworked children	VM 0	M +	L +	N 0
9. A fly caught on sticky fly paper	VM 0	M −	L −	N +
10. An underfed child	VM −	M +	L +	N +

EXERCISE 4.—Continued

11. Very old people.................................. VM − M 0 L + N +
12. A wounded deer................................. VM − M + L + N +
13. A baby bird whose mother is dead............. VM − M + L + N +
14. A wounded soldier who must beg for a living.. VM − M + L 0 N +
15. A young person totally paralyzed.............. VM − M + L + N 0

Below is a list of acts of various **degrees of wickedness or badness.** After each thing mentioned draw a circle around 3, 2, 1, or 0 to show how wicked or bad **you** think it is.

3 means "EXTREMELY WICKED"; 2 means "DECIDEDLY BAD"; 1 means "SOMEWHAT BAD"; 0 means "NOT REALLY BAD."

1. Picking flowers in a public park............... 3 0 2 − 1 + 0 +
2. Stealing a ride on a truck..................... 3 − 2 − 1 + 0 +
3. Telling a lie to avoid punishment............. 3 − 2 + 1 + 0 0
4. Whispering in school........................... 3 + 2 0 1 − 0 −
5. Boys teasing girls............................. 3 − 2 − 1 + 0 +

6. Making fun of cripples......................... 3 − 2 + 1 + 0 −
7. Using slang.................................... 3 − 2 − 1 + 0 +
8. Breaking windows.............................. 3 − 2 + 1 0 0 +
9. Boys smoking before they are 21............... 3 − 2 − 1 + 0 +
10. Indulging in "petting"........................ 3 − 2 − 1 0 0 +

11. Moderate drinking............................. 3 − 2 0 1 + 0 +
12. Excessive drinking............................ 3 − 2 + 1 + 0 0
13. Putting pins on the teacher's chair........... 3 − 2 − 1 + 0 +

EXERCISE 4.—Continued

14. Swiping fruit out of orchards.................................... 3 − 2 0 1+ 0+
15. Laziness... 3 − 2 0 1− 0+

16. Going to bed without saying your prayers......................... 3 − 2 − 1+ 0+
17. Not brushing your teeth.. 3 − 2 0 1+ 0+
18. Boys fighting.. 3 − 2 − 1+ 0+
19. Being a slacker in time of war................................... 3 0 2 0 1+ 0 0
20. Boy running away from home....................................... 3 0 2 − 1 0 0+

21. Neglecting to study your lesson.................................. 3 0 2 − 1 0 0 0
22. Being a Bolshevik.. 3 + 2 − 1 0 0 0
23. Not standing up when the "Star Spangled Banner" is played........ 3 − 2 + 1+ 0 −
24. Drinking a great deal of coffee and tea.......................... 3 0 2 + 1 − 0 0
25. Being cross to your brother or sister............................ 3 + 2 − 1 0 0 0

26. Shooting rabbits just for fun.................................... 3 − 2 0 1+ 0+
27. Having fits of temper.. 3 0 2 − 1+ 0+
28. Insulting the defenseless.. 3 − 2 + 1+ 0 0

In each comparison below draw a circle around 1 or 2 or S to show how well you like the things mentioned.
Around 1, if you like the FIRST thing better.
Around 2, if you like the SECOND thing better.
Around S, if you have the SAME LIKING for both.

1. (1) Make plans (2) Carry out plans............................. 1+ 2 − S 0
2. (1) Work involving many details (2) Work involving few details... 1+ 2 − S 0
3. (1) Interesting work with small income (2) Uninteresting work with large income...... 1 − 2 + S +

EXERCISE 4—Concluded

4. (1) Give a report in writing (2) Give a report verbally............ 1 – 2 + S +
5. (1) Work with men (2) Work with women................ 1 + 2 – S –
6. (1) An auto with scruffy paint but excellent motor (2) An auto with fresh paint but only fairly good motor.... 1 + 2 – S –
7. (1) Live in the country (2) Live in the city........ 1 + 2 – S +

EXERCISE 5

For each occupation below, ask yourself; would I like that work or not? If you would like it, draw a circle around L. If you would dislike it, draw a circle around D. If you would **neither like nor dislike** it, draw a circle around N. In deciding on your answer, **think only of the kind of work.** Don't consider the pay. Imagine that you have the ability to do the work, that you are the right age for it, and that it is equally open to men and women.

Don't stop to think long; answer fairly quickly.

1. Architect...........	L + D –	N –
2. Chef or cook........	L – D 0	N +
3. Auto racer.........	L + D –	N +
4. Librarian..........	L – D +	N +
5. Building contractor..	L + D –	N 0
6. Detective.........	L + D –	N +
7. Nurse.............	L – D +	N 0
8. Private secretary..	L – D +	N +
9. Journalist........	L – D +	N 0
10. Forest ranger.....	L + D –	N 0
11. Dairyman..........	L + D –	N +
12. Dressmaker........	L – D +	N +
13. Florist...........	L – D +	N +

14. Stock breeder.....	L + D –	N +
15. Optician..........	L – D +	N –
16. Social worker.....	L – D +	N 0
17. Music teacher.....	L – D +	N –
18. Clerk in a store..	L – D +	N 0
19. Singer............	L – D +	N +
20. Preacher..........	L – D +	N –
21. Novelist..........	L – D +	N 0
22. Soldier...........	L + D –	N 0
23. Draftsman.........	L + D –	N –
24. Artist............	L – D +	N +
25. Bookkeeper........	L – D +	N +

EXERCISE 5—Continued

Do you like or dislike these people?	L	D	N
1. Men with beards	L+	D−	N+
2. Babies	L−	D+	N+
3. Infidels	L+	D+	N−
4. People with loud voices	L+	D−	N+
5. Argumentative people	L+	D−	N0
6. Very forgiving people	L−	D+	N0
7. Very quiet people	L+	D0	N−
8. People who spend freely	L0	D+	N−
9. People with gold teeth	L0	D+	N−
10. Tall women	L−	D+	N+
11. Men who take the lead	L+	D0	N−
12. Mannish women	L−	D+	N−

Do you like or dislike these?	L	D	N
1. Charlie Chaplin	L+	D−	N+
2. Social problem movies	L−	D+	N−
3. Movie love scenes	L−	D+	N0
4. Poetry	L−	D−	N+
5. Detective stories	L+	D−	N−
6. Stories of home life	L−	D+	N+
7. Adventure stories	L+	D−	N−
8. Comic supplements	L+	D−	N−
9. Radio magazines	L+	D−	N−
10. Chemistry	L+	D−	N0

	L	D	N
11. Dramatics	L−	D+	N+
12. Ancient languages	L−	D+	N−
13. Civics	L−	D+	N+
14. Spelling	L−	D+	N+
1. Hunting	L+	D−	N+
2. Skating	L−	D+	N0
3. Horseback riding	L−	D+	N+
4. Hopscotch	L−	D+	N0
5. Dare base	L−	D+	N0
6. Drop the handkerchief	L−	D+	N0
7. Chess	L+	D−	N−
8. Charades	L−	D+	N0
9. Collecting flowers	L−	D+	N+
10. Cooking	L−	D+	N+
11. Studying lessons	L−	D+	N0
12. Repairing a door latch	L+	D−	N0
13. Parties and socials	L−	D+	N0
14. Being with one other	L−	D+	N0
15. Strict Sunday laws	L+	D−	N−
16. Pet cats	L−	D+	N+
17. Near-beer	L+	D−	N0
18. Coca cola	L+	D−	N0
19. Cheese	L0	D+	N−
20. Candies	L−	D+	N0

EXERCISE 5—Continued

After each book you have read, put a circle around L, D, or N to show how well you like it. Skip those you have not read.

	Omission			
1. Robinson Crusoe, by Daniel Defoe	−	L+	D−	N−
2. Lorna Doone, by Richard D. Blackmore	+	L+	D+	N O
3. Through the Looking Glass, by Lewis Carroll	+	L+	D O	N O
4. Westward Ho, by Charles Kingsley	−	L+	D+	N O
5. Daddy Long Legs, by Jean Webster	+	L−	D+	N+
6. Peter Pan and Wendy, by J. M. Barrie	+	L−	D+	N+
7. Huckleberry Finn, by Mark Twain	−	L+	D+	N−
8. Rip Van Winkle, by Washington Irving	O	L+	D−	N−
9. The Wonder Book, by Nathaniel Hawthorne	O	L−	D+	N O
10. Bird's Christmas Carol, by Kate Douglas Wiggin	+	L−	D+	N+
11. Rebecca of Sunnybrook Farm, by Kate Douglas Wiggin	+	L−	D+	N O
12. Christmas Carol, by Charles Dickens	+	L+	D+	N+
13. The Man Without a Country, by Edward Everett Hale	O	L+	D−	N−
14. Little Men, by Louisa Alcott	+	L−	D+	N+
15. The Secret Garden, by Frances Hodgson Burnett	+	L−	D+	N+
16. Captains Courageous, by Rudyard Kipling	−	L+	D−	N−
17. Little Lord Fauntleroy, by Frances Hodgson Burnett	+	L−	D+	N O
18. Boy's Life of Theodore Roosevelt, by Herman Hagedorn	−	L+	D O	N O
19. Gulliver's Travels, by Jonathan Swift	−	L−	D−	N−
20. Biography of a Grizzly, by Ernest Seton-Thompson	−	L+	D O	N O

EXERCISE 5—Concluded

Omission

21. Evangeline, by Henry W. Longfellow.........	+	L—	D+	N+
22. Tales from Shakespeare, by Charles Lamb.........	0	L—	D+	N+
23. Adventures of Sherlock Holmes, by Conan Doyle.........	—	L+	D—	N—

Suppose you were an artist, what would you like to draw?

1. Fruits.........	L—	D+	N+
2. Children.........	L—	D+	N+
3. Horses.........	L+	D—	N0
4. Clouds.........	L—	D+	N+
5. Cats.........	L—	D+	N—
6. Flowers.........	L—	D+	N+
7. Tigers.........	L+	D—	N—
8. Ships.........	L+	D—	N—

Suppose you were a newspaper reporter, what would you like to write about, or report?

1. Accidents.........	L+	D—	N0
2. Sporting news.........	L+	D—	N—
3. Musical events.........	L—	D+	N+
4. Theatrical news.........	L—	D0	N+
5. News oddities.........	L—	D+	N0
6. Commercial news.........	L+	D—	N—

If you had two years to travel, with plenty of money, what would you like to see and do?

1. Visit Holland.........	L—	D+	N+
2. Hunt lions in Africa.........	L+	D—	N0
3. Spend a day in Westminster Abbey.........	L—	D+	N+
4. See London Bridge.........	L—	D+	N+
5. Visit many famous battlegrounds.........	L+	D—	N—
6. Visit many manufacturing plants.........	L+	D—	N—
7. See how people prepare their food.........	L—	D+	N+
8. Spend a year on a sailing boat.........	L+	D0	N—
9. Study social customs.........	L—	D+	N+
10. See how criminals are treated.........	L+	D—	N—
11. Learn about various religions.........	L—	D+	N+

EXERCISE 6

Below is a list of famous characters. After each name draw a circle around L, D, or N to indicate whether you like that character. L means LIKE; D means DISLIKE; N means NEITHER LIKE NOR DISLIKE. Skip those you do not know anything about.

EXERCISE 6—Continued

	Omission						Omission			
1. Jane Addams.............	0	L −	D +	N +		16. Hearst, the publisher.........	−	L −	D +	N −
2. P. T. Barnum.............	−	L +	D −	N −		17. Herbert Hoover.............	0	L +	D −	N 0
3. Bismarck.............	−	L +	D 0	N 0		18. Robert G. Ingersoll.......	−	L +	D −	N −
4. Daniel Boone.............	−	L +	D −	N −		19. Thomas Jefferson........	−	L 0	D +	N 0
5. Aaron Burr.............	−	L 0	D +	N −		20. Lenin.............	−	L +	D +	N +
6. Kit Carson.............	−	L +	D −	N −		21. Judge Ben Lindsay........	−	L +	D +	N 0
7. Cleopatra.............	−	L 0	D 0	N +		22. Aimee McPherson.........	0	L 0	D +	N 0
8. Christopher Columbus.......	−	L −	D +	N +		23. Mussolini.............	−	L +	D 0	N −
9. Oliver Cromwell...........	−	L +	D −	N +		24. Florence Nightingale.......	+	L 0	D +	N +
10. Jefferson Davis............	−	L +	D +	N 0		25. Theodore Roosevelt.......	0	L 0	D −	N −
11. Jack Dempsey............	+	L +	D −	N −		26. Billy Sunday............	−	L +	D −	N +
12. Lloyd George............	−	L +	D +	N 0		27. Wellington.............	−	L +	D +	N 0
13. Congressman Volstead.......	−	L +	D +	N 0		28. Woodrow Wilson........	0	L −	D +	N +
14. Booker T. Washington.........	−	L 0	D 0	N +						
15. Ulysses S. Grant........	−	L +	D −	N −						

Read each statement and consider whether it is **mostly true** or **mostly false**.
If it is mostly TRUE draw a circle around **T**.
If it is mostly FALSE draw a circle around **F**.
Work rapidly. Answer all.

	Omission		
1. The face shows how intelligent a person is............	0	T −	F +
2. The weak deserve more love than the strong............	0	T +	F −

EXERCISE 6—Concluded

	Omission		
3. The world was created in six days of twenty-four hours each.	—	T+	F 0
4. One usually knows when stared at from behind.	0	T—	F+
5. Preachers have better characters than most persons.	0	T+	F—
6. Love "at first sight" is usually the truest love.	0	T+	F—
7. Girls are naturally more innocent than boys.	0	T—	F+
8. Lincoln was greater than Washington.	+	T 0	F 0
9. Opportunity knocks but once for any man.	—	T+	F 0
10. The largest fortunes should be seized by the government and divided among the poor.	—	T—	F+
11. Children should be taught never to fight.	0	T—	F+
12. We should never give to beggars.	0	T+	F—
13. There should be perfect equality between men and women in all things.	—	T—	F+
14. Green-eyed people are not to be trusted.	0	T+	F—

EXERCISE 7

Answer each question as truthfully as you can by drawing a line under YES or NO.

1. Do you like most people you know?	YES+	NO 0
2. Did you ever have imaginary companions?	YES—	NO+
3. Do people often say you are too noisy?	YES—	NO+
4. Do you rather dislike to take your bath?	YES+	NO—
5. Have you been bossed too much for your own good?	YES+	NO—
6. Do you nearly always prefer for someone else to take the lead?	YES—	NO+
7. Do you feel yourself to be lacking in self-control?	YES+	NO—

EXERCISE 7—Continued

8. Are you extremely careful about your manner of dress? .... YES –   NO +
9. Do you work mostly by fits and starts? .... YES 0   NO 0
10. Do you shrink from facing a crisis or difficulty? .... YES -   NO +

11. Are you careful of your personal belongings? .... YES 0   NO 0
12. Do you worry much over possible misfortunes? .... YES –   NO +
13. Are you much embarrassed when you make a grammatical mistake? .... YES –   NO +
14. Are you worried when you have an unfinished job on your hands? .... YES –   NO +
15. Have you ever kept a diary? .... YES –   NO +

16. Do you like to go to parties, dances, or other social affairs? .... YES –   NO +
17. Do you ever feel that you are about to "go to pieces"? .... YES –   NO +
18. Are you often afraid of the dark? .... YES –   NO +
19. Have you often fainted away? .... YES +   NO –
20. Can you usually sit still without fidgeting? .... YES –   NO +

21. Do you usually enjoy your meals? .... YES –   NO +
22. Have you the habit of biting your finger nails? .... YES –   NO +
23. As a child were you extremely disobedient? .... YES +   NO –
24. Do you ever dream of robbers? .... YES +   NO –
25. Do people ever say that you talk too much? .... YES +   NO –

26. Do you ever have the same dream over and over? .... YES –   NO +
27. Do people nearly always treat you right? .... YES –   NO +
28. Were you ever expelled from school, or nearly expelled? .... YES +   NO –
29. Have you often been punished unjustly? .... YES +   NO –
30. Do you often get cross over little things? .... YES –   NO +

EXERCISE 7—Concluded

31. Does it make you angry for people to hurry you? .... YES + NO −
32. Can you stand as much pain as others can? .... YES + NO −
33. Is it easy for you to get up as soon as you wake? .... YES + NO −
34. Would you like to wear expensive clothes? .... YES − NO +
35. Do you feel tired a good deal of the time? .... YES − NO +

36. Do you ever walk in your sleep? .... YES − NO +
37. Do you hear easily when spoken to? .... YES − NO +
38. Are you often frightened in the middle of the night? .... YES − NO +
39. Have you found school a hard place to get along in? .... YES + NO −
40. Can you do good work while people are looking at you? .... YES + NO −

41. Do you feel like jumping off when you are on a high place? .... YES − NO +
42. Do you always remember to brush your teeth? .... YES − NO +

ATTITUDE-INTEREST ANALYSIS TEST, FORM B

READ THIS FIRST

You are asked to cooperate seriously and carefully in marking the items in this booklet. This is not an intelligence test. We want to find out something about the attitudes and interests of people in relation to their occupations, their home situations and their hobbies. The items in this booklet have been selected by actual trial out of several thousand. More than 4,000 persons of different ages, occupations and schooling have filled out test blanks like this one. We are trying to accumulate sufficient returns to discover what the actual standards of response are. Your answers are needed to help do this. Fill in all of the blanks on this page as indicated below. Please do not omit any of the items. All of the information is important. Do not look at the other pages of the booklet until you have finished filling in the blanks below.

Name.. Age...... Sex........................ Race......................

City.................... State......................

Underline one: Single, Married, Widowed, Separated, Divorced.

Amount of Schooling.

	Grammar Grades	High School	College		
	1 2 3 4 5 6 7 8	1 2 3 4	1 2 3 4	M.A. 5 6	Ph.D M.D. 7

Mark highest point reached: Yrs.

Other schooling or courses.................................

Profession or occupation.................................

Previous professions or occupations if any:

(Married women list occupation before marriage)........................

Specific hobbies or special interests such as playing baseball,   1............................

choir singing, chess, collecting stamps, philanthropy.   2............................

If ever married state for how many years: ....

If you have children state number of boys: .... girls: ....

How many brothers older than yourself reached 16 years of age? ....

How many brothers younger than yourself reached 16 years of age? ....

How many sisters older than yourself reached 16 years of age? ....

How many sisters younger than yourself reached 16 years of age? ....

Were both your parents responsible for your training up to the age of 16? ....

If not, please specify............................

Underline the word that indicates your usual state of health: Robust, above-average, average, below-average, frail.

Mark a cross on each of the 12 lines below to indicate the amount of your interest in each subject or activity.

1. Travel
|----------------------|----------------------|
Much   Average   Slight or none

2. Out-door
   Sports
|----------------------|----------------------|
Much   Average   Slight or none

3. Religion
|----------------------|----------------------|
Much   Average   Slight or none

4. Mechanics
|----------------------|----------------------|
Much   Average   Slight or none

5. Social Life   Much |········|········| Average ········| Slight or none

6. Literature   Much |········|········| Average ········| Slight or none

7. Music   Much |········|········| Average ········| Slight or none

8. Art   Much |········|········| Average ········| Slight or none

9. Science   Much |········|········| Average ········| Slight or none

10. Politics   Much |········|········| Average ········| Slight or none

11. Domestic Arts   Much |········|········| Average ········| Slight or none

12. Pets   Much |········|········| Average ········| Slight or none

NOW READ THIS

Do not look at other parts of the booklet until you are ready to begin the test. When you are ready, turn at once to Exercise 1. Read the instructions carefully, marking the sample items as you come to them. Then go right on to the exercise itself. Work as rapidly as you can. As soon as you have finished Exercise 1 go right on to Exercise 2, then Exercise 3, and so on until you have finished the booklet. In each case read the directions with care, and work the exercise **as rapidly** as you can. It should take about 40 or 50 minutes to finish the booklet.

Time began test.................

Time finished test.................

Do not write in space below.

1	2	3	4	5	6	7

EXERCISE 1

DIRECTIONS: Look at the word in capital letters, then look at each of the four words which follow it.

For example:

HORSE   cow   hay   race   swim

Draw a line under the word that seems to you to go best or most naturally with HORSE; that is, the word that HORSE tends most to make you **think of.**

Second example:

AUTO   danger   gears   machine   ride

Draw a line under the word that seems to go best or most naturally with AUTO; the word that AUTO tends most to make you **think of.**

Look at each of the words in the list below. In each case, draw a line under the word that **goes best** or most naturally with the one in capitals; the word it tends most to make you **think of.** Work rapidly; do not think long over any one.

1.* DEAL	business −	great −	hand +	square 0
2. LIVE	breathe −	die +	exist +	wire +
3. MUFFLER	car +	silence +	silk −	warm −
4. NEEDLE	compass +	eye −	pine 0	sew −
5. NOTE	letter −	mark +	money +	pay +
6. BOX	candy −	car +	oranges +	theater 0
7. LIGHT	fire −	gay −	heavy +	smoke +
8. CAN	glass 0	peach −	prison +	tin 0
9. DECAY	apple −	corpse +	rot +	tooth −
10. SHIFT	eye −	football +	gear −	work −

EXERCISE 1—Continued

11. FUSE — cap + dynamite + electric − melt 0
12. BUM — hobo + poor 0 rotten − tramp −
13. FORM — athletic + fit − model − shape −
14. AFRAID — cat + dark − fear + run 0
15. LIPS — kiss − mouth − red 0 whisper +

16. BOSS — employer − foreman + man 0 politics 0
17. GIVE — devotion 0 money + present − take −
18. TOMBOY — boy − girl + rough − tom-cat +
19. SNAKE — afraid − gopher + grass − reptile +
20. AUTOMOBILE — accident − Buick − pet + ride −

21. GENTLE — horse + lamb − meek 0 mother −
22. THIRTEEN — child − number 0 unlucky + years −
23. CHILD — cunning − boy + girl − kid +
24. FAITHFUL — dog + religion − reward 0 true −
25. POWDER — explosion + face − gun + rouge −

26. RADIO — dial + music − speeches − wireless +
27. SWEETHEART — friend − kiss + lover − wife 0
28. SAFETY — first + police − precaution 0 zone 0
29. HANDKERCHIEF — dirty + linen − silk 0 sneeze −
30. RING — bell − diamond − ruby − wedding 0

31. PHYSICAL — body 0 education 0 health − muscle +
32. WISH — bone + good 0 hope − want 0
33. MOUSE — animal + gnaw − scream − trap 0
34. WAIST — belt − belly + clothes − hips +
35. SHOP — barber + bargain − stove + work −

EXERCISE 1—Concluded

36. DARLING	baby –	dearest +	honey +	mamma –
37. NASTY	filthy +	horrid –	words 0	worm +
38. MATE	birds –	pal –	ship +	wed –
39. STAGE	coach +	play 0	scenes –	vaudeville –
40. BIRTH	baby –	children +	death +	suffer 0
41. HUNT	find 0	guns +	search –	shop 0
42. MOTHER	children –	cook 0	mamma 0	father +
43. PLAY	ball +	fun –	games –	school 0
44. THIN	air +	lady –	paper 0	skin 0
45. KILL	murder –	poison +	shoot +	wicked –
46. PAINT	house +	picture –	red +	sticky –
47. DESIRE	beauty –	passion +	praise +	wish –
48. ELECTRIC	bill –	coil 0	generator +	light –
49. ART	artist –	gallery +	picture 0	teacher +
50. YOUTH	age +	beauty –	brave 0	strong +
51. DARKNESS	afraid –	ghosts +	kiss +	stars +
52. MAKE	create 0	dress –	maker –	money +
53. KISS	baby –	lips –	love +	steal +
54. SLENDER	graceful –	long +	skinny +	ugly 0
55. CHARM	grace –	person –	snake +	witch +
56. WORM	fish +	hook +	soft –	squirm –
57. ENGAGEMENT	appointment 0	marriage +	promise –	tardy +
58. ARM	army +	hug –	leg +	strong +
59. MOUTH	chew –	laugh –	teeth 0	whistle +
60. SUCCESS	business +	fame –	fortune +	marry –

EXERCISE 2

Directions:—Here are some drawings, a little like ink blots. They are not pictures of anything in particular but might suggest almost anything to you, just as shapes in the clouds sometimes do. Beside each drawing four things are mentioned. **Underline the one word that tells what the drawing makes you think of most.**

Examples:—

baby
dog
man
squirrel

arm
flame
flower
tail

dog's head
glove
hand
horse's head

			Omission
1.*	candle	—	0
	columns	+	
	fireplace	0	
	gate	—	
2.	bomb	+	0
	flask	0	
	jar	—	
	vase	—	
3.	bow	—	0
	chain	+	
	footprints	+	
	tie	—	
4.	diamond	+	—
	light	—	
	rock	—	
	ship	—	

*See footnote to Exercise 1.

EXERCISE 2—Continued

				Omission
9.	cone	+		−
	pyramid	−		
	sails	0		
	trees	0		
10.	bow	−		0
	butterfly	+		
	glasses	+		
	ribbon	0		
11.	bush	0		0
	lady	+		
	mushroom	0		
	shadow	−		
12.	haystack	0		0
	hook	+		
	lady	−		
	tree	+		

				Omission
5.	funnel	−		−
	horn	−		
	jack	+		
	vase	+		
6.	couch	−		+
	cow	+		
	deer	−		
	horse	−		
7.	basket	−		0
	boat	+		
	coffin	+		
	pan	0		
8.	flame	−		0
	flower	+		
	snake	−		
	worm	−		

EXERCISE 2—Concluded

			Omission
13.		hook	+	0
		question mark	−	
		staff	+	
		umbrella	0	
14.		club	0	0
		dagger	+	
		exclamation point	−	
		stick	0	
15.		boat	+	0
		door	−	
		hat	+	
		stump	+	

			Omission
16.		flower	−	0
		stickpin	+	
		string	0	
		sword	+	
17.		airplane	0	0
		skate	+	
		sled	−	
		stove	−	
18.		baby	+	0
		buoy	+	
		lady	−	
		valve	+	

EXERCISE 3

In each sentence draw a line under the word that makes the sentence true.

Example: America was discovered by BALBOA <u>COLUMBUS</u> DRAKE WASHINGTON

Work as rapidly as you can. Skip those you do not know.

	Omission	
1. The "Glass Slipper" reminds us of Ali Baba + Cinderella − Goldilocks + Queen Mab −	+	1
2. Electric lights were invented by Ampère − Edison + Marconi − Volta 0	−	2
3. Mayonnaise dressing is used with cakes 0 pies + puddings 0 salads −	+	3
4. Robert E. Lee surrendered to Grant + Lincoln − Sheridan − Sherman −	−	4
5. A 3-year-old child likes best to play with blocks − guns + rattles + skates +	+	5
6. Eggs are most easily digested when deviled + fried + scrambled + soft-boiled −	0	6
7. Easter comes in the autumn + spring − summer 0 winter +	0	7
8. The smallest state in the Union is Connecticut − Delaware + New Jersey − Rhode Island 0	0	8
9. The trousers worn in colonial days were baggy + checkered 0 knee-length − long 0	0	9
10. A singing game is poison + blackman + follow-the-leader 0 London-bridge −	+	10
11. Bricks are made of clay + gravel − limestone −	0	11
12. Babies should be bathed daily − every other day + twice a day + twice a week +	0	12
13. Sun eclipse is caused by the shadow of the earth − Jupiter 0 Mars − the moon +	−	13
14. William Tell was an archer + king − orator − prince 0	−	14
15. An important meat-packing city is Chicago + New Orleans − New York + Seattle −	−	15
16. True silk comes from goats 0 plants 0 sheep − worms +	+	16
17. Troubles flew out of the mythical box of Cupid 0 Daphne + Pandora − Venus 0	−	17
18. The bridegroom is the "best man" + the bride's father + the bride's husband −	+	18

EXERCISE 3—Continued

	Omission	
19. Goliath was killed by Cain — David + Moses 0 Samson —	0	19
20. A reel is used in athletics — fishing + hunting — rowing —	—	20
21. John Paul Jones was a general — sea-fighter + statesman + writer —	—	21
22. Hiawatha's bride was Minnehaha — Nokomis + Tallahassee + Wenonah —	+	22
23. A mixture of red and blue pigments gives brown + green + purple — yellow 0	+	23
24. The telegraph was invented by Bell — Edison — Morse + Whitney 0	+	24
25. Little John was Indian 0 negro 0 outlaw + soldier —	—	25
26. The orchid is a flower — fruit + germ + shell + ...	+	26
27. In music the note ♪ is known as eighth 0 half 0 quarter — sixteenth + ...	0	27
28. The length of this page is about 8 in. — 9 in. — 10 in. 0 11 in. + ...	—	28
29. The "Call of the Wild" is the story of a bear 0 buffalo — dog + horse —	—	29
30. The number of U.S. senators from each state is 2 + 30 40 60	—	30
31. The earth turns once on its axis in about 12 hours — 24 hours + 30 days — 365 days 0	0	31
32. A baby usually begins to walk alone at about 6 mos. + 12 mos. — 20 mos. + 24 mos. + ...	0	32
33. The large prehistoric reptiles were called anthropoids 0 crustaceans — diatoms — dinosaurs + ...	+	33
34. Fat people should not eat much of carrots 0 peas — potatoes — spinach + ...	+	34
35. A correct expression is It is they — It is her + It is them + ...	+	35
36. Of these woods the hardest is cedar — oak + pine — walnut —	—	36
37. Topsy was Arabian 0 Eskimo + Indian + Negro — White + ...	+	37
38. A chiffonier is used for books + clothes — dishes + silverware + ...	0	38
39. The blacksmith of the gods was called Jupiter — Mercury — Perseus — Vulcan + ...	—	39
40. Tides are caused by winds 0 rotation of the earth 0 attraction of the moon + ocean currents —	—	40

EXERCISE 3—Continued

	Omission	
41. A shipping term is **FOB** + **RST** − **SOS** − **TNT** −..........	−	41
42. "Pi" is equal to **.6666** − **.7853** 0 **1.463** − **3.1416** + ...	−	42
43. The kidneys excrete **bile** 0 **gastric juice** 0 **lymph** + **urine** −..........	0	43
44. One should eat peas with a **fork** − **knife** + **spoon** +..........	0	44
45. The founder of the Democratic party was **Adams** 0 **Hamilton** + **Jefferson** + **Monroe** +..........	−	45
46. Heating a piece of iron makes it **larger** + **lighter** − **smaller** − **stronger** −..........	−	46
47. Nose-itch is considered a sign of **bad luck** − **company** − **good luck** 0 **sickness** +..........	−	47
48. Low tide comes every **6 hours** 0 **12 hours** + **24 hours** − **48 hours** +..........	0	48
49. The number of chambers in the heart is **1** − **2** + **4** − **6** +..........	0	49
50. Heliotrope is the name of a **drug** + **flower** − **gem** + **tree** +..........	0	50
51. Tetrazzini is known as **actress** + **dancer** + **painter** 0 **singer** −..........	−	51
52. The score in tennis is tied at **deuce** + **love-30** + **vantage-in** 0..........	−	52
53. Mona Lisa is a **novel** 0 **painting** − **poem** + **statute** 0..........	0	53
54. An example of an allegory is **Enoch Arden** + **Marmion** 0 **Pilgrim's Progress** − **Rip Van Winkle** +..........	0	54
55. The diameter of the earth in miles is about **2,000** − **5,000** 0 **8,000** + **25,000** 0..........	−	55
56. A man who argued for the theory of evolution was **John Adams** − **Darwin** + **Galileo** + **Webster** 0..........	−	56
57. "RSVP" means **danger** + **full dress** 0 **please reply** 0 **telegraph** +..........	−	57
58. Light travels per second about **8,000 miles** − **25,000 miles** − **186,000 miles** + **240,000 miles** +..........	−	58
59. Among the allies of Germany, in the World War, was **Belgium** − **Bulgaria** + **Roumania** + **Russia** 0..........	−	59
60. The "Block System" is used in **carpentry** − **mining** + **railroading** + **surveying** 0..........	−	60
61. One of the greatest prophets of the Bible is **David** + **Elijah** − **Samson** 0 **St. Peter** +..........	−	61
62. Sponges are **animal** + **mineral** − **plant** 0..........	−	62

EXERCISE 3—Concluded

Omission

63. A month-old-baby sleeps daily about **12 hours** 0 **15 hours** + **20 hours** − **23 hours** −.............. − 63
64. The Franco-Prussian War was begun in **1648** − **1813** − **1848** 0 **1871** +.............. − 64
65. The air can hold most moisture when **cold** 0 **cool** 0 **hot** + **warm** 0.............. − 65

66. A noted general in the Mexican War was **Burnside** 0 **Hooker** − **Jackson** − **Taylor** +.............. − 66
67. A woman who was an outcast was **Martha** + **Mary Magdalene** − **Naomi** + **Sarah** 0.............. 0 67
68. "The Little Cripple Boy" was written by **Burns** 0 **Holmes** + **Poe** + **Riley** 0.............. − 68
69. Lorna Doone was the daughter of a **fisherman** − **nobleman** − **outlaw** 0 **pirate** 0.............. − 69
70. Mauve is a shade of **brown** 0 **green** + **lavender** − **rose** 0.............. + 70

EXERCISE 4

Below is a list of things that sometimes **cause anger.** After each thing mentioned draw a circle around VM, M, L, or N to show how much anger it causes **you.**

VM means VERY MUCH; M means MUCH; L means A LITTLE; N means NONE.

1. Being called homely.............. VM 0   M 0   L 0   N 0
2. Being called a liar.............. VM −   M +   L 0   N 0
3. Being called by a nick-name you don't like.............. VM 0   M 0   L 0   N 0
4. Being cheated in a business deal.............. VM 0   M 0   L +   N −
5. Being deceived by an enemy.............. VM 0   M −   L +   N +

6. Being honked at by an automobile.............. VM −   M 0   L +   N 0
7. Being marked unfairly in an examination.............. VM −   M 0   L +   N +
8. Being slapped in a quarrel.............. VM 0   M −   L 0   N +
9. Being socially slighted.............. VM −   M −   L +   N +
10. Being unreasonably prevented from doing what you want to do.............. VM −   M +   L +   N 0

EXERCISE 4—Continued

11. Hearing someone misspell or mispronounce your name............ VM – M 0 L – N +
12. Hearing your friends unjustly abused............ VM – M + L + N +
13. Hearing your religion ridiculed............ VM – M + L 0 N +
14. Seeing an animal cruelly beaten............ VM – M + L + N 0
15. Seeing an innocent man punished for the crime of another............ VM – M 0 L + N +

16. Seeing a man sitting in a street car while old women are standing............ VM – M + L + N +
17. Seeing a person treated unfairly because of his race............ VM – M + L + N +

Below is a list of things that often **cause fear.** After each thing mentioned draw a circle around VM, M, L, or N to indicate how much fear it causes **you.** Be honest and admit all the fears you have. Fears are not disgraceful. VM means VERY MUCH; M means MUCH; L means A LITTLE; N means NONE.

1. Being alone at night......... VM – M – L – N +
2. Being on a ship......... VM – M – L 0 N +
3. Becoming crippled or totally disabled......... VM – M + L + N –
4. Becoming insane......... VM – M + L + N 0
5. Crazy people......... VM – M 0 L + N +

6. Crossing an open space......... VM 0 M – L – N +
7. Darkness......... VM – M – L – N +
8. Earthquakes......... VM – M – L + N +
9. Fire......... VM – M – L + N +
10. Foreigners......... VM – M 0 L – N +

11. Ghosts......... VM – M 0 L – N +
12. Guns......... VM – M – L – N +
13. Horses......... VM 0 M – L 0 N +
14. Knives......... VM 0 M – L 0 N +
15. Mice......... VM – M – L – N +

16. Old age......... VM + M + L + N –
17. Poisoning......... VM + M – L 0 N 0
18. Rattlesnakes......... VM – M 0 L + N +
19. Toads......... VM 0 M – L – N +
20. Written examinations......... VM 0 M – L 0 N +

EXERCISE 4—Continued

Below is a list of things that sometimes **cause disgust.** After each thing mentioned draw a circle around VM, M, L, or N to indicate how much disgust it causes **you.**

VM means VERY MUCH; M means MUCH; L means A LITTLE; N means NONE.

1. A banana................	VM –	M +	L 0	N 0	11. Sight of dirty clothes...........	VM –	M 0	L +	N +
2. Bad table manners...........	VM –	M +	L +	N –	12. Smell of onions...........	VM –	M –	L 0	N +
3. A boy and girl petting.........	VM –	M –	L 0	N +	13. Smell of cooked cabbage......	VM –	M 0	L –	N +
4. Dirty neck or ears...........	VM –	M +	L –	N 0	14. Sniffling...........	VM –	M +	L +	N +
5. Hearing a person belch........	VM –	M +	L +	N +	15. Soiled table linen...........	VM –	M –	L +	N +
6. Odor of perspiration...........	VM –	M +	L +	N +	16. Tobacco chewing...........	VM –	M +	L +	N +
7. Seeing a man smoking..........	VM –	M –	L –	N +	17. Wienerwursts or stuffed sausage	VM –	M –	L 0	N +
8. Seeing a bull..............	VM –	M 0	L –	N +	18. Words like "belly" or "guts"	VM –	M +	L +	N +
9. Sight of pus..............	VM –	M +	L +	N +					
10. Sight of anyone vomiting......	VM –	M 0	L +	N +					

Below is a list of things that sometimes **arouse pity.** After each thing mentioned draw a circle around VM, M, L, or N to indicate how much pity it arouses in **you.**

VM means VERY MUCH; M means MUCH; L means A LITTLE; N means NONE.

1. A boy ambitious to go to college but cannot.............	VM –	M 0	L +	N +
2. A bird with a broken wing.............	VM –	M +	L +	N +
3. A dope fiend.................	VM 0	M –	L 0	N +
4. A fish caught on a hook.............	VM –	M –	L –	N +
5. A toad being swallowed by a snake..............	VM –	M –	L 0	N +
6. A man who is physically a weakling.............	VM –	M 0	L +	N 0
7. A mouse caught by a hawk.............	VM –	M –	L 0	N +

EXERCISE 4—Continued

8. A person with no will power............... VM— M0 L+ N0
9. An old maid who has always wanted children............... VM— M+ L+ N+
10. An orphan boy............... VM— M+ L+ N+

11. A terribly ugly man............... VM0 M— L+ N+
12. An underfed horse............... VM— M+ L+ N+
13. A wounded lion............... VM— M— L0 N+
14. A young person with a fatal disease............... VM— M+ L+ N0

Below is a list of acts of various degrees of wickedness or badness. After each thing mentioned draw a circle around 3, 2, 1, or 0 to show how wicked or bad you think it is.

3 means "EXTREMELY WICKED"; 2 means "DECIDEDLY BAD"; 1 means "SOMEWHAT BAD"; 0 means "NOT REALLY BAD."

1. Stealing a dime from your mother's purse............... 3+ 2— 1 0 0 0
2. Stealing a dollar from your mother's purse............... 3 0 2 0 1+ 0 0—
3. Spitting on the sidewalk............... 3— 2— 1+ 0+ 0+
4. Playing hooky from school............... 3— 2— 1 0 0+ 0+
5. Disobeying your parents............... 3— 2+ 1+ 0 0

6. Picking on somebody weaker than yourself............... 3— 2+ 1— 0 0
7. Not going to Sunday School............... 3— 2— 1 0 0+ 0+
8. Shooting craps............... 3— 2— 1 0 0+ 0+
9. Swearing............... 3— 2+ 1+ 0 0+ 0+
10. Playing cards for money............... 3— 2+ 1+ 0 0 0

11. "Talking back" to the teacher............... 3— 2— 1+ 0+ 0+
12. Playing marbles for keeps............... 3— 2— 1 0 0+ 0+

EXERCISE 4—Continued

13. Disobeying a "keep off the grass" sign	3 −	2 −	1 +	0 +
14. Stealing candy from the grocery man	3 −	2 +	1 +	0 +
15. Matching pennies for keeps	3 0	2 −	1 0	0 0
16. Cheating in examination	3 0	2 0	1 +	0 0
17. Running away from home	3 0	2 −	1 0	0 +
18. Losing your temper	3 −	2 −	1 +	0 +
19. Girls fighting	3 +	2 −	1 0	0 +
20. Beating your way on a freight train	3 0	2 −	1 0	0 +
21. Not adding to the collection box at church	3 −	2 +	1 −	0 0
22. Discourtesy to people about us	3 −	2 0	1 +	0 0
23. Being an atheist	3 +	2 −	1 0	0 0
24. Deceiving others without actually telling a lie	3 −	2 +	1 +	0 0
25. Being ashamed of your parents	3 −	2 +	1 +	0 +
26. Being extravagant	3 0	2 0	1 0	0 +
27. Being "yellow" or cowardly	3 −	2 0	1 +	0 +
28. Accepting wrong change when it is in your favor	3 0	2 −	1 +	0 +

In each comparison below draw a circle around 1 or 2 or S to show how well you like the things mentioned.
Around 1, if you like the FIRST thing better.
Around 2, if you like the SECOND thing better.
Around S, if you have the SAME LIKING for both.

1. (1) Persuade others (2) Command others	1 −	2 +	S +	
2. (1) Change from place to place (2) Work in one location	1 +	2 −	S 0	

EXERCISE 4—Concluded

3. (1) Work with men   (2) Work with women........................ 1+ 2— S —
4. (1) Work for yourself   (2) Work under a respected superior........ 1+ 2— S +
5. (1) Great variety of work   (2) Work of a single kind............. 1+ 2— S 0

6. (1) A well-cooked meal, but soiled table linen   (2) A poorly cooked meal, but linen spotless.................. 1+ 2— S 0
7. (1) Book work   (2) Laboratory work........................... 1— 2+ S 0
8. (1) Camping   (2) Living in good hotels........................ 1+ 2— S 0

EXERCISE 5

For each occupation below, ask yourself; would I like that work or not? If you would like it, draw a circle around L. If you would dislike it, draw a circle around D. If you would **neither like nor dislike** it, draw a circle around N. In deciding on your answer, **think only of the kind of work.** Don't consider the pay. Imagine that you have the ability to do the work, that you are the right age for it, and that it is equally open to men and women.

Don't stop to think long; answer fairly quickly.

1. Aviator..............	L +	D —	N +	11. Furniture dealer......	L —	D +	N —
2. Landscape gardener....	L —	D +	N 0	12. Interior decorator.....	L —	D +	N +
3. Barber or hairdresser..	L —	D +	N —	13. Jeweler............	L —	D +	N +
4. Auto mechanic.......	L +	D —	N +	14. Miner.............	L +	D —	N +
5. Cashier............	L —	D +	N +	15. Musician...........	L —	D +	N +
6. Waiter or waitress....	L —	D +	N 0	16. Research worker......	L —	D +	N —
7. Farmer or rancher....	L +	D —	N 0	17. Office clerk.........	L —	D +	N 0
8. Factory manager.....	L +	D —	N +	18. Missionary.........	L —	D +	N 0
9. Fisherman..........	L +	D —	N +	19. Orchestra conductor...	L —	D +	N —
10. Plumber..........	L +	D —	N +	20. Poet..............	L —	D +	N +

EXERCISE 5—Continued

21. Explorer................................ L+   D-   N0
22. Sculptor................................ L-   D+   N+
23. Magazine illustrator................ L-   D+   N+
24. Stenographer.......................... L-   D+   N+
25. Teacher................................. L-   D-   N+

Do you like or dislike these people?

1. Foreigners.............................. L-   D+   N-
2. School children........................ L-   D+   N+
3. People who talk very low.......... L-   D+   N+
4. Quick-tempered people............. L-   D+   N-
5. Very cautious people................ L+   D-   N-

6. Thin women............................ L-   D+   N-
7. Side-show freaks...................... L+   D-   N+
8. People who use toothpicks........ L+   D-   N+
9. Religious men.......................... L0   D+   N-
10. Bashful men........................... L-   D-   N+

11. Women cleverer than you are.... L-   D+   N+
12. Bald-headed men..................... L+   D-   N+

Do you like or dislike these?

1. Harold Lloyd........................... L+   D-   N-
2. W. S. Hart............................. L+   D-   N-
3. Pathé news movies................... L+   D-   N-
4. Fairy tales.............................. L-   D+   N+
5. Love stories............................ L-   D+   N+

6. Stories of wild animals............. L+   D-   N-
7. Sporting pages......................... L+   D-   N-
8. Popular science books.............. L+   D-   N-
9. Painting................................. L-   D+   N+
10. Music................................... L-   D+   N+

11. Modern languages................... L-   D0   N+
12. Penmanship........................... L-   D+   N+
13. Shop work............................. L+   D-   N-

1. Fishing.................................. L+   D-   N-
2. Swimming.............................. L+   D-   N0
3. Riding bicycle......................... L+   D-   N-
4. Dancing................................. L-   D+   N+
5. Picnics.................................. L-   D+   N+

6. Card games............................ L+   D-   N-
7. Jump the rope......................... L-   D+   N+
8. Cat and mouse........................ L-   D+   N-
9. Guessing games....................... L-   D+   N+
10. Gardening............................. L-   D+   N+

11. Washing dishes....................... L-   D+   N0
12. Being alone........................... L-   D+   N0
13. Working with tools.................. L+   D-   N-
14. Giving advice......................... L+   D-   N-
15. Being the butt of a joke........... L+   D-   N+

EXERCISE 5—Continued

16. Pet canaries..................	L –	D +	N +
17. Sherbets.....................	L –	D +	N +
18. Ginger ale...................	L +	D –	N 0
19. Ham and eggs.................	L +	D –	N –
20. Pickles......................	L –	D +	N +

After each book you have read, put a circle around L, D, or N to show how well you like it. Skip those you have not read.

	Omission	L	D	N
1. The Swiss Family Robinson, by Johann David Wyss...........	–	L +	D –	N –
2. Mrs. Wiggs of the Cabbage Patch, by Alice Hegan Rice.......	+	L –	D +	N +
3. Janice Meredith, by Paul Leicester Ford..................	+	L +	D +	N +
4. The Call of the Wild, by Jack London....................	–	L +	D –	N –
5. Water Babies, by Charles Kingsley......................	+	L –	D +	N +
6. Riley's Poems, by James Whitcomb Riley.................	+	L –	D +	N +
7. The Spy, by James Fenimore Cooper.....................	–	L +	D –	N +
8. Adventures of Tom Sawyer, by Mark Twain................	–	L +	D –	N –
9. Heidi, by Johanna Spyri...............................	+	L –	D +	N 0
10. Bob, Son of Battle, by Alfred Ollivant..................	–	L +	D 0	N 0
11. The Prince and the Pauper, by Mark Twain..............	0	L –	D +	N +
12. Daniel Boone, by C. H. Forbes Lindsay.................	–	L +	D –	N –
13. Two Years Before the Mast, by Richard Henry Dana......	–	L +	D 0	N 0
14. Treasure Island, by Robert Louis Stevenson.............	+	L +	D 0	N +
15. Little Women, by Louisa M. Alcott.....................	+	L –	D +	N +
16. Jack and Jill, by Louisa M. Alcott....................	+	L –	D +	N +
17. Boy's Life of Abraham Lincoln, by Helen Nicolay........	–	L +	D 0	N 0
18. The Courtship of Miles Standish, by Henry W. Longfellow..	+	L –	D +	N +

EXERCISE 5—Concluded

	Omission			
19. Story of My Life, by Helen Keller	+	L –	D +	N 0
20. Tanglewood Tales, by Nathaniel Hawthorne	+	L –	D +	N 0
21. Wild Animals I Have Known, by Ernest Seton-Thompson	–	L +	D –	N +
22. The Jungle Book, by Rudyard Kipling	–	L +	D 0	N 0
23. Twenty Thousand Leagues Under the Sea, by Jules Verne	+	L +	D –	N 0

Suppose you were an artist, what would you like to draw?

1. Trees	L –	D +	N +
2. Portraits	L –	D +	N +
3. Dogs	L +	D –	N –
4. Battle scenes	L +	D –	N –
5. Ruins	L +	D –	N 0
6. Cows	L +	D –	N +
7. Sunsets	L –	D +	N +
8. Lions	L +	D –	N –

Suppose you were a newspaper reporter, what would you like to write about, or report?

1. Crimes	L +	D –	N 0
2. Fires	L +	D –	N 0
3. New books	L –	D +	N +
4. Foreign news	L 0	D +	N –
5. Social news	L –	D +	N +

6. Political news	L +	D –	N 0

If you had two years to travel, with plenty of money, what would you like to see and do?

1. Visit Paris	L –	D 0	N +
2. Visit the Holy Land	L –	D +	N 0
3. Visit many cathedrals	L –	D +	N +
4. Climb many lofty mountain peaks	L +	D –	N –
5. See a ship-building plant	L +	D –	N –
6. Visit many picture galleries	L –	D +	N +
7. Visit the Chicago slaughter-house	L +	D –	N 0
8. Study national dress	L –	D +	N +
9. Learn about Japanese houses	L –	D +	N +
10. Study methods of training children	L –	D +	N +
11. Visit the homes of many writers	L –	D +	N +

EXERCISE 6

Below is a list of famous characters. After each name draw a circle around L, D, or N to indicate whether you like that character. L means LIKE; D means DISLIKE; N means NEITHER LIKE NOR DISLIKE.
Skip those you do not know anything about.

	Omission				
1. John Alden..............	0	L –	D +	N 0	
2. John Brown.............	–	L +	D 0	N 0	
3. Caesar.................	–	L +	D –	N 0	
4. Carrie Chapman Catt......	–	L 0	D +	N 0	
5. "Ty" Cobb..............	–	L +	D +	N –	
6. Anthony Comstock........	–	L +	D 0	N +	
7. President Coolidge........	–	L 0	D 0	N 0	
8. Cornwallis..............	–	L –	D +	N –	
9. Charles Darwin..........	–	L +	D 0	N 0	
10. Eugene Debs............	–	L –	D +	N +	
11. Mary Baker Eddy........	0	L –	D 0	N +	
12. Henry Ford.............	–	L –	D 0	N +	
13. Galileo................	–	L –	D +	N 0	

	Omission				
14. Queen Victoria..........	–	L –	D +	N 0	
15. Hannibal..............	–	L +	D 0	N –	
16. Jesse James............	–	L +	D +	N –	
17. Robert E. Lee...........	–	L 0	D +	N 0	
18. Abraham Lincoln........	+	L 0	D +	N –	
19. Marconi...............	–	L +	D 0	N –	
20. Mohammed.............	–	L 0	D +	N 0	
21. Napoleon..............	–	L +	D 0	N –	
22. Tom Paine.............	–	L +	D –	N +	
23. "Babe" Ruth............	0	L +	D –	N –	
24. John L. Sullivan.........	–	L +	D –	N –	
25. Daniel Webster.........	0	L –	D 0	N +	
26. Kaiser Wilhelm.........	–	L 0	D +	N –	
27. Brigham Young.........	–	L +	D 0	N –	

EXERCISE 6—Concluded

Read each statement and consider whether it is **mostly true or mostly false.**
If it is mostly TRUE draw a circle around **T.**
If it is mostly FALSE draw a circle around **F.**
Work rapidly. Answer all.

	Omission	T	F
1. Men are created equal in mental capacity	–	T +	F –
2. Inventors deserve more honor than artists	0	T +	F –
3. An ugly face usually goes with a kind heart	0	T –	F +
4. Married women ought not to be permitted to teach school	0	T +	F –
5. Lines in the hand foretell the future	–	T –	F +
6. Women are purer than men by nature	+	T –	F +
7. The hanging of murderers is justifiable	–	T +	F –
8. Hunting and fishing are wrong because cruel	–	T –	F +
9. There is plenty of proof that life continues after death	–	T 0	F +
10. The United States should adopt a more aggressive foreign policy	–	T +	F 0
11. It is more important to be just than to believe in God	–	T +	F –
12. Wealth, power, and honor usually go to those who deserve them	–	T +	F –
13. It is better to tell your troubles to your friends than to keep them to yourself	0	T +	F –
14. Blondes are less trustworthy than brunettes	0	T +	F –

EXERCISE 7

Answer each question as truthfully as you can by drawing a line under YES or NO.

1.	Are you happy most of the time?	YES –	NO +
2.	Do you like to have people tell you their troubles?	YES –	NO +
3.	Do you like to tell your troubles to others?	YES 0	NO 0
4.	Do you like to be the center of attention in a crowd?	YES –	NO +
5.	Do you dislike the company of the opposite sex?	YES +	NO –
6.	Do you take life so seriously that it sometimes bothers you?	YES 0	NO 0
7.	Do people ever say you are a bad loser?	YES +	NO –
8.	Do you usually get to do the things that please you most?	YES –	NO +
9.	Do you say what you consider the truth regardless of how others may take it?	YES +	NO –
10.	Do you often introspect or analyze your feelings?	YES +	NO –
11.	Do you feel bored a large share of the time?	YES +	NO –
12.	Do you prefer to work a thing out for yourself rather than ask help?	YES +	NO –
13.	Have you often been bothered by blushing?	YES –	NO +
14.	Are you often bothered by the feeling that people are reading your thoughts?	YES –	NO +
15.	Have you been troubled by a fear of being crushed in a crowd?	YES –	NO +
16.	Do you dread to have your picture taken?	YES –	NO +
17.	Do you think a thing over carefully before you do it?	YES +	NO –
18.	Do you get tired of people easily?	YES +	NO –
19.	Were you ever fond of playing with snakes?	YES +	NO –
20.	Did you ever run away from home?	YES +	NO –

EXERCISE 7—Concluded

21. Does the thought of hurting a person or animal give you great pain? . . . . YES —   NO +
22. Would you rather be alone than with someone? . . . . YES +   NO —
23. Do you like to tease people till they cry? . . . . YES +   NO —
24. Do you prefer to go without your breakfast? . . . . YES —   NO +
25. Can you stand the sight of blood? . . . . YES +   NO —

26. Do you usually feel well and strong? . . . . YES —   NO +
27. Do you have a great fear of fire? . . . . YES —   NO +
28. Do things ever seem to get misty before your eyes? . . . . YES —   NO +
29. Do you like to be praised and made much of? . . . . YES —   NO +
30. Do you always get on well with others? . . . . YES —   NO +

31. Do you know anybody who is trying to harm you? . . . . YES +   NO —
32. Does it make you uneasy to cross a wide street or open square? . . . . YES —   NO +
33. Do people you are with say you quarrel too much? . . . . YES +   NO —
34. Do people find fault with you too much? . . . . YES +   NO —
35. Have others of your age usually let you play with them? . . . . YES —   NO +

36. Do you often have a hard time making up your mind about things? . . . . YES —   NO +
37. Are your feelings often very badly hurt? . . . . YES —   NO +
38. Do you sometimes wish you had never been born? . . . . YES —   NO +
39. Do you prefer to be with older people? . . . . YES +   NO —
40. Do you ever imagine stories to yourself so that you forget where you are? . . . . YES —   NO +

41. Do you think people like you as much as they do others? . . . . YES —   NO +
42. Do you feel that you are getting a square deal in life? . . . . YES —   NO +

TABLE 93.—M-F WEIGHTED SCORES FOR FORM A
A. Exercise 1

Items	Responses				Items	Responses			
	a	b	c	d		a	b	c	d
(1)	0	+2	−4	+3	(31)	−1	−3	+2	+2
(2)	−1	+1	+1	+1	(32)	−2	−1	+1	+2
(3)	+1	−2	+1	−1	(33)	+3	−3	−1	0
(4)	−2	−1	0	+2	(34)	−3	+2	0	0
(5)	0	+2	−2	0	(35)	+2	+1	0	−2
(6)	−1	+2	−1	−1	(36)	+1	−2	+1	0
(7)	+4	0	−3	−1	(37)	0	−2	+2	−1
(8)	+4	−2	−2	0	(38)	−2	−1	+1	+1
(9)	−1	−1	+3	0	(39)	−1	0	0	+1
(10)	−1	+3	+2	−4	(40)	+2	−2	−1	+1
(11)	+2	−1	−1	−1	(41)	+1	−1	+1	0
(12)	+2	+1	−2	0	(42)	+1	−2	0	0
(13)	+5	−1	−1	−4	(43)	+1	−2	+1	+1
(14)	+3	−3	0	−1	(44)	+2	−1	−1	0
(15)	+2	−1	+1	−1	(45)	+1	−2	0	+1
(16)	0	+2	−1	−1	(46)	+2	−4	+3	0
(17)	+1	−4	+1	0	(47)	+1	+2	−4	+2
(18)	0	+2	+2	−4	(48)	+1	+1	+1	−3
(19)	−1	+2	−1	0	(49)	+1	−2	0	0
(20)	+4	0	−4	−1	(50)	−1	+1	−1	0
(21)	−1	−3	+3	−1	(51)	+1	+3	0	−2
(22)	−3	+3	−1	+1	(52)	−2	+4	−1	0
(23)	+5	0	0	−5	(53)	−2	+2	+2	−2
(24)	−4	0	+3	+1	(54)	+1	−2	+1	0
(25)	+2	+2	−1	−3	(55)	0	−1	+2	−1
(26)	−2	0	0	+2	(56)	+2	−2	+1	0
(27)	−1	−1	+1	+2	(57)	0	+1	−1	0
(28)	−1	0	+3	−1	(58)	0	+1	−1	−2
(29)	−5	+1	+3	+3	(59)	−1	−4	+3	+2
(30)	−3	+3	0	+1	(60)	−2	+3	−1	−2

A. Exercise 2

Items	Responses					Items	Responses				
	a	b	c	d	O[1]		a	b	c	d	O[1]
(1)	0	−4	+3	+1	0	(10)	0	−1	−1	+2	0
(2)	−4	0	+1	+3	0	(11)	0	+3	−1	−1	0
(3)	0	0	+3	−3	0	(12)	−3	+6	−2	−2	0
(4)	0	0	+1	−1	0	(13)	0	+3	−1	−1	0
(5)	+2	+1	−2	−1	0	(14)	+1	+2	−1	−2	0
(6)	+3	+1	−3	+1	0	(15)	+2	+1	−1	0	0
(7)	−3	0	+2	0	0	(16)	+1	−1	0	−1	0
(8)	0	+2	−2	+1	+1	(17)	−4	0	+3	+2	0
(9)	+1	0	−1	0	+1	(18)	0	−1	−1	+2	0

[1] Omission.

TABLE 93.—M-F WEIGHTED SCORES FOR FORM A.—(*Continued*)
A. Exercise 3

Items	Responses					Items	Responses				
	a	b	c	d	O¹		a	b	c	d	O¹
(1)	+ 2	−4	+2	+2	+2	(36)	+1	−1	+3	−3	−3
(2)	+ 1	+1	−1	+2	−1	(37)	0	+2	−1	0	−3
(3)	0	+1	0	0	−2	(38)	+3	−2	0	0	+1
(4)	− 1	+2	+3	+3	0	(39)	+3	−1	0	0	−3
(5)	− 4	0	0	+4	+6	(40)	−2	−1	−2	+8	−4
(6)	+4	0	−1	−3	−3	(41)	−6	+1	+3	+1	+2
(7)	− 1	0	−1	+1	+1	(42)	0	+3	−2	0	−1
(8)	− 2	+2	0	+1	+1	(43)	0	+1	+4	0	−4
(9)	− 2	+1	+1	0	+1	(44)	+4	+1	+1	−7	0
(10)	− 1	+1	+1	−2	+1	(45)	0	+2	−1	−1	0
(11)	− 1	−2	−2	+3	−3	(46)	0	+3	−4	−1	+1
(12)	− 1	+2	−3	0	−1	(47)	+2	+6	−1	−1	−7
(13)	− 2	+2	+2	−2	0	(48)	+2	+6	−4	−3	−3
(14)	+ 1	+2	+2	−2	+1	(49)	+1	+3	0	−1	−2
(15)	+ 2	−1	0	0	−2	(50)	0	−1	+2	−1	0
(16)	0	−1	+3	−1	0	(51)	+1	−6	+3	+1	+2
(17)	− 3	−1	+3	0	+1	(52)	−2	+1	0	+3	−1
(18)	− 1	+2	+1	−2	−3	(53)	−2	+3	+2	−1	−3
(19)	− 4	0	+3	+2	+2	(54)	+1	0	0	+2	−1
(20)	+ 1	+1	−1	+1	0	(55)	+3	+2	0	−2	−1
(21)	− 1	0	−2	+4	−3	(56)	+3	−1	+2	−1	−2
(22)	+1	−1	+2	0	+1	(57)	+1	−1	−1	+2	0
(23)	0	−2	+2	+1	0	(58)	−2	+2	−1	−1	−2
(24)	− 1	−2	+6	−1	−2	(59)	0	+7	−1	0	−5
(25)	− 1	+5	−3	−2	−2	(60)	−3	+3	+1	+1	−1
(26)	+ 1	−1	+1	+1	−1	(61)	+1	−1	−1	+2	0
(27)	+ 1	+2	0	−3	+1	(62)	−1	+1	+6	+1	−8
(28)	+ 3	0	−1	0	−3	(63)	−1	−2	0	+3	−2
(29)	0	−1	+2	0	+1	(64)	0	+1	0	+3	−4
(30)	+ 2	−1	+3	−2	0	(65)	0	+1	−1	0	−2
(31)	− 2	0	+4	0	−3	(66)	0	0	+4	−2	−3
(32)	−10	+3	+4	+4	+3	(67)	+2	−2	+1	+1	−1
(33)	− 3	+1	+1	+2	0	(68)	−2	+2	−1	+3	−3
(34)	− 1	+4	0	0	−3	(69)	+2	0	0	−1	−2
(35)	0	0	+2	0	−3	(70)	0	−1	−2	+1	+1

¹ Omission.

TABLE 93.—M-F WEIGHTED SCORES FOR FORM A.—(*Continued*)

A. Exercise 4

A. Anger

Items	Responses				Items	Responses			
	VM	M	L	N		VM	M	L	N
(1)	−1	0	+2	0	(10)	0	−1	+1	+3
(2)	−2	0	0	+2	(11)	−5	+3	+3	0
(3)	−1	0	+1	0	(12)	0	0	+1	−1
(4)	0	0	+2	−1	(13)	−4	+5	0	+1
(5)	−1	0	0	0	(14)	−2	−2	+2	+2
(6)	0	0	+1	−1	(15)	−2	0	+1	+2
(7)	−2	0	−1	+2	(16)	+1	0	+1	−1
(8)	−1	0	−1	+1	(17)	−4	+2	+2	+1
(9)	−1	0	0	+1					

B. Fear

Items	Responses				Items	Responses			
	VM	M	L	N		VM	M	L	N
(1)	0	−1	−1	+2	(11)	−5	−2	−1	+6
(2)	−4	−2	+4	+3	(12)	−3	−2	0	+3
(3)	−2	−3	0	+3	(13)	−2	+1	+1	+1
(4)	−1	+1	+1	−1	(14)	0	0	0	0
(5)	−5	−2	+3	+3	(15)	−2	0	−1	+3
(6)	−6	0	+2	+4	(16)	−1	−3	−2	+2
(7)	0	+1	0	−1	(17)	−1	0	−1	+1
(8)	−3	0	−1	+4	(18)	0	0	−1	+1
(9)	−1	−1	−1	+3	(19)	−3	−3	−1	+6
(10)	−6	−1	+2	+4	(20)	−1	−2	−2	+4

C. Disgust

Items	Responses				Items	Responses			
	VM	M	L	N		VM	M	L	N
(1)	−3	−3	+1	+4	(10)	−3	0	+2	+3
(2)	0	0	−2	+2	(11)	−3	−2	0	+6
(3)	−7	+1	+3	+4	(12)	−4	0	+1	+2
(4)	−1	−1	+2	0	(13)	−4	+2	0	+2
(5)	−4	+1	+2	+1	(14)	−4	+1	+2	+2
(6)	−7	+2	+3	+4	(15)	−5	−1	+4	+4
(7)	−2	−3	+1	+5	(16)	−7	+4	+3	+3
(8)	−2	0	+1	+2	(17)	−7	+2	+3	+3
(9)	−4	+2	+1	+2	(18)	−2	−2	+2	+2

TABLE 93.—M-F WEIGHTED SCORES FOR FORM A.—(*Continued*)

D. *Pity*

Items	Responses				Items	Responses			
	VM	M	L	N		VM	M	L	N
(1)	−2	0	0	+2	(9)	0	−1	−1	+3
(2)	−2	0	+1	+1	(10)	−4	+3	+2	+1
(3)	−1	+1	−1	+3	(11)	−2	0	+2	+1
(4)	−4	+2	+2	+2	(12)	−3	+1	+1	+2
(5)	−3	+1	+2	+1	(13)	−2	+1	+1	+2
(6)	−5	+2	+3	+2	(14)	−2	+2	0	+1
(7)	−2	+2	+1	0	(15)	−2	+3	+1	0
(8)	−4	+3	+1	0					

E. *Wickedness*

Items	Responses				Items	Responses			
	3	2	1	0		3	2	1	0
(1)	0	−2	+1	+1	(15)	−1	0	−1	+2
(2)	−2	−2	+1	+1	(16)	−2	−1	+1	+2
(3)	−2	+1	+1	+1	(17)	−2	0	+1	+2
(4)	+1	0	−1	0	(18)	−3	−2	+1	+3
(5)	−1	−1	+1	+2	(19)	0	0	+1	0
(6)	−1	+2	+1	−1	(20)	0	−1	0	+2
(7)	−1	−1	+1	+1	(21)	0	−1	0	0
(8)	−1	+1	0	+1	(22)	+1	−1	0	0
(9)	−1	−2	+1	+3	(23)	−2	+1	+1	−1
(10)	−2	−1	0	+3	(24)	0	+1	−2	0
(11)	−2	0	+1	+2	(25)	+1	−1	0	0
(12)	−1	+1	+1	0	(26)	−2	0	+2	+3
(13)	−1	−2	+1	+1	(27)	0	−2	+1	+3
(14)	−3	0	+2	+3	(28)	−1	+1	+2	0

F. *Likes*

Items	Responses			Items	Responses		
	1	2	S		1	2	S
(1)	+1	−1	0	(5)	+22	−15	−4
(2)	+2	−2	0	(6)	+ 3	− 3	−1
(3)	−3	+2	+2	(7)	+ 1	− 2	+1
(4)	−5	+5	+1				

TABLE 93.—M-F WEIGHTED SCORES FOR FORM A.—(*Continued*)

A. Exercise 5

A. Occupations

Items	Responses			Items	Responses		
	L	D	N		L	D	N
(1)	+ 2	− 1	−1	(14)	+4	−7	+3
(2)	− 3	0	+3	(15)	−3	+2	−1
(3)	+ 4	− 5	+1	(16)	−6	+6	0
(4)	−13	+ 9	+3	(17)	−6	+7	−1
(5)	+ 5	− 6	0	(18)	−3	+3	0
(6)	+ 2	− 4	+1	(19)	−8	+6	+2
(7)	− 9	+ 9	0	(20)	−2	+3	−2
(8)	−10	+ 6	+4	(21)	−4	+4	0
(9)	− 3	+ 3	0	(22)	+4	−4	0
(10)	+ 8	− 7	0	(23)	+6	−4	−1
(11)	+ 2	− 5	+2	(24)	−5	+2	+3
(12)	−13	+12	+1	(25)	−6	+4	+2
(13)	−10	+ 6	+3				

B. People

Items	Responses			Items	Responses		
	L	D	N		L	D	N
(1)	+1	−4	+3	(7)	+2	0	−3
(2)	−3	+2	+3	(8)	0	+3	−3
(3)	+1	+2	−2	(9)	0	+2	−2
(4)	+2	−3	+1	(10)	−2	+1	+1
(5)	+2	−1	0	(11)	+1	0	−2
(6)	−1	+2	0	(12)	−1	+3	−1

C. Reading, Movies

Items	Responses			Items	Responses		
	L	D	N		L	D	N
(1)	+5	−4	0	(8)	+3	−1	−2
(2)	−4	+5	+1	(9)	+6	−1	−4
(3)	−5	+6	0	(10)	+3	−1	−2
(4)	−6	+4	+1	(11)	−6	+3	+2
(5)	+4	−2	−2	(12)	−3	+5	−2
(6)	−4	+2	+2	(13)	−2	+1	+1
(7)	+3	−1	−2	(14)	−4	+2	+2

TABLE 93.—M-F WEIGHTED SCORES FOR FORM A.—(*Continued*)

D. *Activities, Foods*

Items	Responses			Items	Responses		
	L	D	N		L	D	N
(1)	+8	−4	+3	(11)	−2	+2	0
(2)	−1	+2	0	(12)	+6	−6	0
(3)	−1	+2	+1	(13)	−5	+5	+1
(4)	−6	+5	+2	(14)	−1	+3	0
(5)	−1	+3	0	(15)	+5	−2	−1
(6)	−4	+4	0	(16)	−4	+2	+2
(7)	+3	−1	−1	(17)	+2	−2	0
(8)	−4	+4	0	(18)	+4	−4	0
(9)	−8	+4	+4	(19)	0	+1	−1
(10)	−6	+3	+2	(20)	−1	+2	0

E. *Books*

Items	Responses				Items	Responses			
	L	D	N	O[1]		L	D	N	O[1]
(1)	+ 5	−3	−2	− 3	(13)	+1	−1	−1	0
(2)	− 1	+1	0	+ 1	(14)	−9	+3	+1	+6
(3)	− 4	0	0	+ 4	(15)	−6	+2	+3	+4
(4)	+ 3	+1	0	− 4	(16)	+2	−1	−1	−1
(5)	− 9	+3	+3	+ 6	(17)	−5	+4	0	+3
(6)	− 3	+1	+2	+ 1	(18)	+6	0	0	−6
(7)	+ 4	+1	−1	− 3	(19)	+5	−1	−2	−3
(8)	+ 2	−1	−3	0	(20)	+3	0	0	−3
(9)	− 1	+2	0	0	(21)	−4	+1	+2	+2
(10)	− 7	+3	+3	+ 4	(22)	−3	+3	+3	0
(11)	−11	+3	0	+10	(23)	+4	−2	−1	−4
(12)	− 5	+3	+2	+ 3					

F. *Drawing*

Items	Responses			Items	Responses		
	L	D	N		L	D	N
(1)	−3	+1	+1	(5)	−2	+3	−1
(2)	−3	+2	+1	(6)	−4	+3	+3
(3)	+2	−1	0	(7)	+7	−6	−1
(4)	−3	+2	+2	(8)	+3	−2	−2

[1] Omission.

TABLE 93.—M-F WEIGHTED SCORES FOR FORM A.—(*Continued*)

G. Reporting

Items	Responses			Items	Responses		
	L	D	N		L	D	N
(1)	+3	−4	0	(4)	−3	0	+2
(2)	+3	−2	−1	(5)	−2	+2	0
(3)	−7	+6	+1	(6)	+3	−2	−1

H. Travel

Items	Responses			Items	Responses		
	L	D	N		L	D	N
(1)	−2	+3	+1	(7)	−3	+1	+2
(2)	+7	−7	0	(8)	+1	0	−1
(3)	−6	+3	+2	(9)	−5	+3	+1
(4)	−2	+2	+2	(10)	+4	−3	−1
(5)	+5	−3	−3	(11)	−2	+2	+1
(6)	+5	−3	−2				

A. Exercise 6
A. Characters

Items	Responses				Items	Responses			
	O^1	L	D	N		O^1	L	D	N
(1)	0	−2	+2	+2	(15)	−3	+3	−1	−1
(2)	−3	+5	−1	−2	(16)	−3	−1	+2	−1
(3)	−4	+3	0	0	(17)	0	−1	−1	0
(4)	−1	+2	−1	−2	(18)	−3	+4	−1	−2
(5)	−3	0	+3	−1	(19)	−2	0	+1	0
(6)	−4	+6	−1	−2	(20)	−3	+1	+2	+2
(7)	−1	0	0	+2	(21)	−2	+2	+1	0
(8)	−2	−1	+1	+2	(22)	0	0	+1	0
(9)	−2	+1	−1	+1	(23)	−1	+2	0	−1
(10)	−3	+1	+2	0	(24)	+1	−5	+2	+3
(11)	+3	+6	−4	−2	(25)	0	0	−1	−1
(12)	−3	+1	+1	0	(26)	−3	+2	0	+1
(13)	−3	+1	+2	0	(27)	−3	+2	+2	0
(14)	−2	0	0	+2	(28)	0	−1	+2	+1

[1] Omission.

TABLE 93.—M-F WEIGHTED SCORES FOR FORM A.—(*Concluded*)

B. *True—False*

Items	Responses			Items	Responses		
	T	F	O[1]		T	F	O[1]
(1)	−2	+2	0	(8)	0	0	+1
(2)	+2	−2	0	(9)	+1	0	−2
(3)	+2	0	−3	(10)	−4	+4	−4
(4)	−4	+4	0	(11)	−3	+3	0
(5)	+4	−3	0	(12)	+3	−4	0
(6)	+2	−2	0	(13)	−3	+3	−1
(7)	−3	+3	0	(14)	+1	−1	0

A. Exercise 7

Items	Responses		Items	Responses	
	Yes	No		Yes	No
(1)	+1	0	(22)	−2	+2
(2)	−3	+3	(23)	+3	−3
(3)	−3	+3	(24)	+1	−1
(4)	+3	−3	(25)	+2	−1
(5)	+1	−1	(26)	−1	+1
(6)	−2	+3	(27)	−3	+3
(7)	+1	−1	(28)	+3	−3
(8)	−6	+6	(29)	+3	−3
(9)	0	0	(30)	−3	+3
(10)	−1	+1	(31)	+2	−2
(11)	0	0	(32)	+3	−3
(12)	−1	+1	(33)	+4	−4
(13)	−3	+3	(34)	−4	+4
(14)	−1	+1	(35)	−2	+2
(15)	−3	+3	(36)	−1	+1
(16)	−4	+3	(37)	−2	+2
(17)	−3	+3	(38)	−5	+5
(18)	−3	+3	(39)	+3	−3
(19)	+2	−2	(40)	+1	−1
(20)	−3	+3	(41)	−1	+1
(21)	−2	+2	(42)	−4	+4

[1] Omission.

TABLE 94.—M-F WEIGHTED SCORES FOR FORM B

B. Exercise 1

Items	Responses				Items	Responses			
	a	b	c	d		a	b	c	d
(1)	-1	-2	+2	0	(31)	0	0	-2	+3
(2)	-4	+1	+1	+3	(32)	+2	0	-1	0
(3)	+3	+1	-1	-4	(33)	+2	-2	-1	0
(4)	+4	-2	0	-2	(34)	-2	+4	-1	+1
(5)	-3	+3	+1	+1	(35)	+3	-2	+1	-1
(6)	-3	+2	+2	0	(36)	-3	+2	+2	-1
(7)	-1	-1	+2	+2	(37)	+3	-3	0	+1
(8)	0	-1	+3	0	(38)	-1	-1	+1	-1
(9)	-1	+1	+2	-2	(39)	+2	0	-1	-1
(10)	-1	+4	-3	-1	(40)	-2.	+1	+1	0
(11)	+3	+1	-2	0	(41)	0	+2	-2	0
(12)	+3	0	-2	-3	(42)	-1	0	0	+1
(13)	+2	-1	-1	-1	(43)	+3	-2	-2	0
(14)	+1	-1	+1	0	(44)	+2	-3	0	0
(15)	+4	-5	0	+2	(45)	-2	+1	+2	-1
(16)	-2	+2	0	0	(46)	+2	-3	+2	-1
(17)	0	+2	-1	-2	(47)	-1	+2	+1	-2
(18)	-3	+8	-6	+1	(48)	-1	0	+4	-3
(19)	-2	+1	-3	+3	(49)	-3	+3	0	+2
(20)	-1	+2	+2	-2	(50)	+1	-2	0	+1
(21)	+2	-1	0	-1	(51)	-4	+1	+2	+1
(22)	-2	0	+2	-2	(52)	0	-4	-1	+3
(23)	-4	+3	-5	+3	(53)	-1	-1	+1	+2
(24)	+2	-1	0	-1	(54)	-4	+1	+3	0
(25)	+5	-7	+3	-2	(55)	-3	-1	+4	+1
(26)	+1	-2	-2	+1	(56)	+3	+1	-1	-3
(27)	-2	+4	-2	0	(57)	0	+1	-1	+1
(28)	+1	-2	0	0	(58)	+1	-3	+1	+2
(29)	+3	-2	0	-1	(59)	+2	-2	0	+2
(30)	+3	-2	-2	0	(60)	+1	-2	+2	-1

B. Exercise 2

Items	Responses					Items	Responses				
	a	b	c	d	O[1]		a	b	c	d	O[1]
(1)	-1	+2	0	-1	0	(10)	-6	+5	+3	0	0
(2)	+2	0	-1	-2	0	(11)	0	+1	0	-1	0
(3)	-2	+2	+1	-1	0	(12)	0	+2	-3	+1	0
(4)	+1	-1	-1	-1	-1	(13)	+1	-3	+2	0	0
(5)	-2	-1	+5	+1	-1	(14)	0	+2	-2	0	0
(6)	-1	+2	-1	-1	+2	(15)	+1	-2	+1	+1	0
(7)	-4	+2	+1	0	0	(16)	-2	+1	0	+1	0
(8)	-1	+2	-1	-1	0	(17)	0	+3	-3	-2	0
(9)	+1	-1	0	0	-1	(18)	+2	+3	-5	+2	0

[1] Omission.

TABLE 94.—M-F WEIGHTED SCORES FOR FORM B.—(*Continued*)
B. Exercise 3

Items	Responses					Items	Responses				
	a	b	c	d	O[1]		a	b	c	d	O[1]
(1)	+1	−2	+1	−2	+2	(36)	−2	+5	−5	−1	−1
(2)	−1	+3	−2	0	−2	(37)	0	+2	+2	−5	+3
(3)	0	+2	0	−1	+1	(38)	+1	−4	+1	+4	0
(4)	+4	−3	−1	−2	−2	(39)	−2	−1	−1	+4	−1
(5)	−2	+3	+1	+1	+1	(40)	0	0	+5	−3	−2
(6)	+1	+2	+2	−2	0	(41)	+6	−3	−1	−2	−5
(7)	+2	−1	0	+1	0	(42)	−1	0	+1	+4	−3
(8)	−1	+1	−1	0	0	(43)	0	0	+1	−2	0
(9)	+2	0	−2	0	0	(44)	−2	+1	+2	0	0
(10)	+1	+1	0	−1	+1	(45)	0	+1	+1	+1	−1
(11)	+3	−2	−1	0	0	(46)	+4	−1	−2	−2	−2
(12)	−2	+2	+2	+1	0	(47)	−1	−1	0	+3	−1
(13)	−2	0	−2	+4	−2	(48)	0	+3	−1	+1	−1
(14)	+2	−1	−1	0	−1	(49)	−1	+2	−2	+2	0
(15)	+2	−2	+1	−1	−1	(50)	+4	−6	0	+2	0
(16)	0	0	−6	+6	+1	(51)	+2	+2	0	−2	−1
(17)	0	+2	−2	0	−1	(52)	+3	+1	0	0	−4
(18)	+2	+1	−1	0	+1	(53)	0	−1	+2	0	0
(19)	−3	+2	0	−1	0	(54)	+2	0	−2	+1	0
(20)	−2	+2	−1	−1	−2	(55)	−1	0	+4	0	−5
(21)	−4	+4	+1	−1	−2	(56)	−2	+2	+1	0	−1
(22)	−1	+2	+1	−1	+1	(57)	+1	0	0	+3	−1
(23)	+1	+3	−4	0	+1	(58)	−1	−4	+5	+4	−4
(24)	−2	−3	+4	0	+1	(59)	−1	+4	+1	0	−3
(25)	0	0	+3	−2	−1	(60)	−2	+1	+7	0	−5
(26)	−2	+1	+2	+2	+1	(61)	+1	−1	0	+1	−2
(27)	0	0	−2	+3	0	(62)	+1	−1	0	0	−2
(28)	−1	−1	0	+1	−1	(63)	0	+2	−1	−2	−1
(29)	0	−1	+3	−2	−1	(64)	−2	−1	0	+3	−2
(30)	+1	0	0	0	−2	(65)	0	0	+1	0	−1
(31)	−1	+3	−2	0	−2	(66)	0	−1	−2	+5	−3
(32)	+2	−5	+3	+4	0	(67)	+1	−2	+2	0	0
(33)	0	−1	−1	+4	−2	(68)	0	+1	+1	0	−2
(34)	0	−4	−1	+3	+2	(69)	+2	−2	0	0	−1
(35)	−4	+1	+3	0	+1	(70)	0	+1	−2	0	+2

[1] Omission.

TABLE 94.—M-F WEIGHTED SCORES FOR FORM B.—(*Continued*)

B. Exercise 4

A. *Anger*

Items	Responses				Items	Responses			
	VM	M	L	N		VM	M	L	N
(1)	0	0	0	0	(10)	−1	+1	+1	0
(2)	−1	+2	0	0	(11)	−1	0	−1	+2
(3)	0	0	0	0	(12)	−5	+3	+1	+1
(4)	0	0	+1	−1	(13)	−3	+1	0	+2
(5)	0	−2	+1	+1	(14)	−2	+2	+1	0
(6)	−2	0	+1	0	(15)	−3	0	+2	+2
(7)	−3	0	+1	+1	(16)	−5	+3	+1	+1
(8)	0	−2	0	+1	(17)	−6	+3	+3	+1
(9)	−2	−1	+1	+3					

B. *Fear*

Items	Responses				Items	Responses			
	VM	M	L	N		VM	M	L	N
(1)	−4	−2	−2	+7	(11)	−2	0	−1	+2
(2)	−1	−2	0	+2	(12)	−2	−2	−1	+4
(3)	−2	+1	+1	−1	(13)	0	−1	0	+1
(4)	−4	+2	+2	0	(14)	0	−1	0	+2
(5)	−5	0	+2	+2	(15)	−1	−2	−5	+6
(6)	0	−2	−2	+4	(16)	+1	+1	+1	−2
(7)	−2	−3	−1	+4	(17)	+1	−1	0	0
(8)	−4	−1	+1	+4	(18)	−6	0	+3	+2
(9)	−4	−2	+3	+4	(19)	0	−3	−2	+4
(10)	−1	0	−1	+1	(20)	0	−2	0	+2

C. *Disgust*

Items	Responses				Items	Responses			
	VM	M	L	N		VM	M	L	N
(1)	−2	+2	0	0	(10)	− 2	0	+1	+1
(2)	−4	+1	+1	−3	(11)	− 6	0	+2	+3
(3)	−4	−2	0	+6	(12)	− 1	−2	0	+4
(4)	−7	+5	−3	0	(13)	− 1	0	−1	+3
(5)	−4	+1	+2	+1	(14)	− 5	+1	+2	+4
(6)	−6	+3	+2	+3	(15)	− 5	−2	+3	+5
(7)	−1	−1	−2	+2	(16)	− 6	+1	+3	+4
(8)	−1	0	−2	+4	(17)	− 1	−1	0	+2
(9)	−4	+1	+1	+2	(18)	−10	+2	+4	+3

TABLE 94.—M-F WEIGHTED SCORES FOR FORM B.—(*Continued*)
D. *Pity*

Items	Responses				Items	Responses			
	VM	M	L	N		VM	M	L	N
(1)	−2	0	+2	+3	(8)	−1	0	+1	0
(2)	−5	+2	+2	+2	(9)	−4	+1	+1	+5
(3)	0	−1	0	+2	(10)	−4	+1	+3	+2
(4)	−2	−2	−2	+5	(11)	0	−1	+1	+1
(5)	−1	−1	0	+2	(12)	−4	+2	+2	+1
(6)	−1	0	+1	0	(13)	−2	−1	0	+3
(7)	−4	−1	0	+5	(14)	−2	+1	+2	0

E. *Wickedness*

Items	Responses				Items	Responses			
	3	2	1	0		3	2	1	0
(1)	+1	−1	0	0	(15)	0	−2	0	0
(2)	0	0	0	−1	(16)	0	0	+2	0
(3)	−1	−3	+3	+1	(17)	0	−2	0	+2
(4)	−1	−1	0	+2	(18)	−1	−1	+1	+1
(5)	−1	+1	+1	0	(19)	+1	−2	0	+2
(6)	−1	+1	−1	0	(20)	0	−3	0	+3
(7)	−1	−1	0	+2	(21)	−1	+1	−1	0
(8)	−1	−1	0	+1	(22)	−1	0	+1	0
(9)	−3	+1	+2	+2	(23)	+2	−1	0	0
(10)	−1	+1	+2	0	(24)	−1	−1	+2	0
(11)	−2	−1	+2	+2	(25)	−2	+1	+1	+2
(12)	−1	−2	0	+4	(26)	0	0	0	+1
(13)	−1	−2	+2	+1	(27)	−1	0	+2	+2
(14)	−2	+1	+1	+2	(28)	0	−1	+2	+2

F. *Likes*

Items	Responses			Items	Responses		
	1	2	S		1	2	S
(1)	− 5	+ 4	+1	(5)	+3	−4	0
(2)	+ 1	− 2	0	(6)	+4	−5	0
(3)	+22	−15	−4	(7)	−4	+3	0
(4)	+ 1	− 2	+1	(8)	+4	−3	0

TABLE 94.—M-F WEIGHTED SCORES FOR FORM B.—(*Continued*)

B. Exercise 5

A. Occupations

Items	Responses			Items	Responses		
	L	D	N		L	D	N
(1)	+ 5	−4	+1	(14)	+ 2	−4	+2
(2)	− 3	+3	0	(15)	− 5	+3	+2
(3)	− 7	+7	−1	(16)	− 1	+2	−1
(4)	+ 7	−9	+1	(17)	− 5	+4	0
(5)	− 3	+1	+3	(18)	− 5	+4	0
(6)	− 8	+5	0	(19)	− 2	+3	−1
(7)	+ 2	−2	0	(20)	− 6	+4	+2
(8)	+ 5	−7	+2	(21)	+ 3	−2	0
(9)	+ 3	−5	+2	(22)	− 6	+4	+1
(10)	+ 4	−4	+2	(23)	− 5	+4	+1
(11)	− 4	+4	−1	(24)	− 9	+6	+3
(12)	−13	+9	+3	(25)	−10	+6	+3
(13)	− 7	+5	+2				

B. People

Items	Responses			Items	Responses		
	L	D	N		L	D	N
(1)	−1	+2	−2	(7)	+2	−3	+1
(2)	−4	+2	+3	(8)	+3	−6	+4
(3)	−2	+1	+1	(9)	0	+1	−2
(4)	−2	+4	−3	(10)	−1	−1	+2
(5)	+3	−1	−2	(11)	−6	+1	+4
(6)	−3	+4	−1	(12)	+2	−3	+1

C. Reading, Movies

Items	Responses			Items	Responses		
	L	D	N		L	D	N
(1)	+2	−3	−3	(8)	+8	−4	−5
(2)	+6	−3	−4	(9)	−4	+1	+3
(3)	+3	−1	−2	(10)	−6	+5	+2
(4)	−6	+4	+2	(11)	−4	0	+4
(5)	−6	+4	+2	(12)	−5	+4	+1
(6)	+6	−3	−5	(13)	+9	−4	−4
(7)	+7	−3	−5				

TABLE 94.—M-F WEIGHTED SCORES FOR FORM B.—(*Continued*)
D. *Activities, Foods*

Items	Responses			Items	Responses		
	L	D	N		L	D	N
(1)	+5	−3	−4	(11)	−4	+4	−1
(2)	+3	−3	0	(12)	−3	+3	0
(3)	+6	−5	−3	(13)	+9	−4	−5
(4)	−6	+4	+4	(14)	+3	−1	−2
(5)	−3	+2	+3	(15)	+2	−3	+2
(6)	+2	−1	−1	(16)	−4	+3	+2
(7)	−7	+6	+1	(17)	−5	+2	+3
(8)	−3	+4	−2	(18)	+3	−4	0
(9)	−3	+2	+1	(19)	+3	−2	−3
(10)	−3	+1	+1	(20)	−3	+3	+1

E. *Books*

Items	Responses				Items	Responses			
	L	D	N	O[1]		L	D	N	O[1]
(1)	+6	−2	−1	−3	(13)	+ 4	0	0	− 4
(2)	−7	+2	+3	+4	(14)	+ 4	0	+1	− 4
(3)	−6	+3	+1	+4	(15)	−16	+2	+3	+10
(4)	+5	−2	−2	−4	(16)	− 6	+3	+2	+ 2
(5)	−4	+1	+2	+2	(17)	+ 2	0	0	− 3
(6)	−4	+3	+2	+2	(18)	− 3	+1	+1	+ 1
(7)	+3	−2	+1	−3	(19)	− 6	+2	0	+ 4
(8)	+4	−2	−3	−3	(20)	− 2	+1	0	+ 2
(9)	−4	+3	+3	+2	(21)	+ 4	−2	+3	− 5
(10)	+5	0	0	−4	(22)	+ 3	0	0	− 3
(11)	−3	+3	+2	0	(23)	+ 6	−1	0	+ 5
(12)	+6	−2	−1	−5					

F. *Drawing*

Items	Responses			Items	Responses		
	L	D	N		L	D	N
(1)	− 4	+ 1	+3	(5)	+3	−3	0
(2)	− 1	+ 1	+1	(6)	+1	−2	+1
(3)	+ 4	− 3	−1	(7)	−3	+2	+5
(4)	+13	−10	−1	(8)	+6	−3	−2

[1] Omission.

TABLE 94.—M-F WEIGHTED SCORES FOR FORM B.—(*Continued*)
G. Reporting

Items	Responses			Items	Responses		
	L	D	N		L	D	N
(1)	+5	−6	0	(4)	0	+2	−1
(2)	+5	−5	0	(5)	−7	+4	+2
(3)	−7	+3	+3	(6)	+2	−2	0

H. Travel

Items	Responses			Items	Responses		
	L	D	N		L	D	N
(1)	−1	0	+2	(7)	+5	−5	0
(2)	−2	+2	0	(8)	−6	+4	+1
(3)	−5	+2	+2	(9)	−6	+4	+3
(4)	+3	−2	−1	(10)	−4	+3	+1
(5)	+6	−1	−4	(11)	−7	+4	+2
(6)	−4	+4	+1				

B. Exercise 6
A. Characters

Items	Responses				Items	Responses			
	O^1	L	D	N		O^1	L	D	N
(1)	0	−2	+3	0	(15)	−2	+4	0	−2
(2)	−2	+3	0	0	(16)	−4	+2	+2	−1
(3)	−3	+2	−1	0	(17)	−1	0	+1	0
(4)	−2	0	+2	0	(18)	+1	0	+1	−1
(5)	−7	+9	+1	−4	(19)	−2	+3	0	−2
(6)	−3	+2	0	+1	(20)	−2	0	+2	0
(7)	−1	0	0	0	(21)	−1	+2	0	−1
(8)	−1	−2	+4	−1	(22)	−3	+2	−1	+2
(9)	−1	+2	0	0	(23)	0	+6	−4	−4
(10)	−3	−1	+1	+2	(24)	−6	+9	−1	−2
(11)	0	−1	0	+2	(25)	0	−2	0	+1
(12)	−1	−1	0	+1	(26)	−2	0	+2	−1
(13)	−2	−1	+2	0	(27)	−2	+1	0	−1
(14)	−1	−1	+3	0					

[1] Omission.

TABLE 94.—M-F Weighted Scores for Form B.—(*Concluded*)
B. True-False

Items	Responses			Items	Responses		
	T	F	O[1]		T	F	O[1]
(1)	+2	−1	−2	(8)	−3	+3	−2
(2)	+4	−3	−1	(9)	0	+2	−2
(3)	−2	+3	0	(10)	+3	0	−2
(4)	+1	−1	0	(11)	+3	−3	−1
(5)	−1	+2	−2	(12)	+2	−2	−1
(6)	−2	+2	−1	(13)	+2	−2	0
(7)	+4	−3	+1	(14)	+3	−4	0

B. Exercise 7

Items	Responses		Items	Responses	
	Yes	No		Yes	No
(1)	−3	+3	(22)	+1	−1
(2)	−2	+2	(23)	+2	−2
(3)	0	0	(24)	−3	+3
(4)	−1	+1	(25)	+6	−6
(5)	+2	−2	(26)	−2	+2
(6)	0	0	(27)	−6	+6
(7)	+2	−2	(28)	−2	+2
(8)	−3	+3	(29)	−1	+1
(9)	+3	−3	(30)	−3	+3
(10)	+1	−1	(31)	+4	−4
(11)	+1	−1	(32)	−4	+4
(12)	+1	−1	(33)	+2	−2
(13)	−2	+2	(34)	+2	−2
(14)	−1	+1	(35)	−3	+3
(15)	−3	+3	(36)	−4	+4
(16)	−2	+2	(37)	−6	+6
(17)	+2	−2	(38)	−1	+1
(18)	+1	−1	(39)	+1	−1
(19)	+5	−5	(40)	−1	+1
(20)	+2	−2	(41)	−3	+3
(21)	−3	+3	(42)	−4	+4

[1] Omission.

TABLE 95.—"INVERT" WEIGHTED SCORES FOR FORM A
"I." Exercise 1

Items	Responses a	b	c	d	O¹	Items	Responses a	b	c	d	O¹
(1)	+ 2	+ 1	−1	− 2	+10	(31)	+7	+ 3	−6	− 6	+ 7
(2)	− 2	− 4	+4	+ 3	+10	(32)	−8	+ 7	+4	− 1	+10
(3)	+ 1	− 1	−2	+ 1	+ 3	(33)	−3	+ 4	0	+ 3	+10
(4)	+ 4	+ 5	−7	+ 5	+11	(34)	−4	0	+7	+ 1	+ 6
(5)	− 4	+ 2	+6	− 2	+10	(35)	−4	+ 7	+1	− 1	+11
(6)	− 2	− 3	+7	+ 3	+10	(36)	0	− 1	+1	− 1	+10
(7)	− 2	− 1	+1	+ 3	+10	(37)	−2	− 1	−5	+10	+11
(8)	− 7	+ 2	+5	+ 4	+11	(38)	−4	0	+6	− 2	+10
(9)	+ 1	− 1	−4	+ 9	+11	(39)	+3	− 7	+5	+ 7	+10
(10)	+ 1	+ 1	−2	0	+ 3	(40)	−8	+ 4	+3	+ 1	+10
(11)	−10	+12	+4	+ 2	+11	(41)	+4	0	−9	− 3	+10
(12)	0	+ 1	+1	− 2	+11	(42)	−7	+ 5	+3	+11	+10
(13)	− 4	+ 3	−1	+ 1	+11	(43)	+5	− 3	−2	+ 1	+11
(14)	− 7	+ 4	+9	+ 7	+ 7	(44)	−6	+10	−1	+ 7	+11
(15)	+ 2	− 5	−2	+ 5	+11	(45)	+4	− 3	−3	+ 2	+ 7
(16)	− 3	+ 2	+2	−10	+10	(46)	−1	+ 2	−1	− 2	+11
(17)	− 6	+ 3	+3	0	+11	(47)	−2	+ 8	−1	− 2	+10
(18)	− 5	− 7	+4	+ 2	+11	(48)	−7	− 5	+8	+ 1	+11
(19)	0	+ 4	−5	− 3	+ 7	(49)	−1	− 2	+3	− 4	+10
(20)	− 3	+ 3	+1	0	+11	(50)	0	− 3	−1	+ 1	+ 7
(21)	+ 1	+ 4	−3	− 4	+10	(51)	+1	− 4	−6	+ 7	+ 4
(22)	− 1	− 4	+7	+ 6	+11	(52)	+3	+ 1	−4	+ 1	+ 5
(23)	− 3	− 3	−1	+ 3	+11	(53)	+1	− 5	−6	+ 2	+11
(24)	− 7	+ 6	−1	+ 2	+11	(54)	−3	+ 3	−1	− 3	+11
(25)	0	+ 1	+1	− 2	+11	(55)	−4	0	−2	+ 3	+10
(26)	− 2	+ 1	−1	+ 1	+10	(56)	−7	0	+5	+ 1	+11
(27)	+ 2	+ 1	−3	+ 2	+11	(57)	−8	+ 5	0	+ 4	+10
(28)	− 1	− 2	+4	− 3	+11	(58)	+3	0	+3	− 4	+10
(29)	− 2	+ 7	−1	− 4	+11	(59)	+2	+ 2	−6	− 3	+10
(30)	− 6	− 1	+3	+ 7	+10	(60)	−1	− 5	+2	+10	+10

"I." Exercise 2

Items	Responses a	b	c	d	O¹	Items	Responses a	b	c	d	O¹
(1)	+ 4	−1	+1	−2	0	(10)	−4	+1	− 1	+1	+10
(2)	+ 1	+1	+3	−3	+10	(11)	−5	−7	− 1	+7	+10
(3)	+ 3	+3	−6	+1	0	(12)	−4	−7	+10	+9	0
(4)	0	+1	−4	+2	0	(13)	0	−2	0	+1	0
(5)	− 2	0	0	+3	+10	(14)	+4	−2	− 1	+5	+10
(6)	−11	−4	+7	−3	0	(15)	+3	−4	0	+6	+10
(7)	+ 1	−1	+1	−1	0	(16)	−4	−1	+ 5	0	+ 4
(8)	0	−2	+4	−2	+ 3	(17)	0	−2	+ 1	−6	+10
(9)	− 2	0	0	+6	+10	(18)	−6	+8	− 5	−1	+10

¹ Omission.

TABLE 95.—"INVERT" WEIGHTED SCORES FOR FORM A.—(*Continued*)
"I." Exercise 3

Items	Responses					Items	Responses				
	a	b	c	d	O¹		a	b	c	d	O¹
(1)	−11	+ 8	−11	− 8	− 2	(36)	0	− 6	+ 4	+ 6	− 2
(2)	0	+10	+ 6	− 6	+10	(37)	− 9	+ 8	−10	0	− 5
(3)	0	− 3	0	−10	+10	(38)	− 6	+ 7	−10	− 7	− 2
(4)	+ 1	+ 7	− 9	−8	−10	(39)	0	+ 1	− 4	− 3	+ 3
(5)	− 1	+ 6	−10	−10	+10	(40)	− 3	− 4	+ 8	− 4	+ 2
(6)	+ 7	0	−10	− 3	+10	(41)	+ 9	− 9	− 9	− 9	− 1
(7)	− 6	− 5	0	0	+ 2	(42)	+ 3	− 4	+ 3	+ 3	+ 2
(8)	− 4	+ 7	+ 4	+ 3	− 4	(43)	+ 4	− 8	− 3	− 2	+ 8
(9)	− 2	+ 3	+ 4	− 1	+ 1	(44)	+ 1	− 1	− 4	− 5	+11
(10)	+ 1	0	+ 4	−10	− 4	(45)	− 1	− 5	+ 4		− 1
(11)	− 8	− 5	−11	+18	− 2	(46)	−11	−11	+ 9	+ 7	− 4
(12)	− 4	− 5	+ 4	+10	+ 8	(47)	+ 8	− 2	− 4	− 4	0
(13)	+ 4	0	− 6	+ 1	0	(48)	0	0	− 3	0	+11
(14)	+ 3	+ 3	−10	− 1	− 5	(49)	− 4	+ 5	− 1	− 4	− 2
(15)	− 9	+ 9	+ 3	+11	+ 3	(50)	− 2	− 4	+ 5	+ 2	− 1
(16)	+ 3	0	− 3	+ 5	0	(51)	− 4	+ 8	− 7	− 4	− 5
(17)	− 5	+11	+ 2	0	0	(52)	+ 1	− 1	0	− 1	− 1
(18)	−30	+30	+11	− 5	+11	(53)	− 5	0	+ 1	+ 3	+ 6
(19)	0	−11	+ 8	+ 5	+11	(54)	− 1	− 9	+ 9	+ 5	+10
(20)	− 6	−11	+ 7	0	+10	(55)	− 8	− 9	− 8	+16	− 8
(21)	− 1	+10	+10	− 7	+10	(56)	+ 5	+ 4	− 6	− 3	− 2
(22)	−10	+ 2	+ 3	− 1	− 4	(57)	− 6	+ 6	− 5	− 2	+ 6
(23)	− 6	+12	−11	0	+ 7	(58)	− 9	+ 3	+ 6	−11	− 3
(24)	− 4	+ 4	− 1	− 4	+ 7	(59)	− 4	+ 2	− 1	− 2	0
(25)	+10	− 5	0	0	+ 2	(60)	+ 8	− 6	− 4	− 7	− 6
(26)	− 5	+ 2	− 2	− 2	+ 5	(61)	−13	−10	+ 7	+13	+ 2
(27)	+ 3	+ 2	− 3	− 5	+ 4	(62)	− 7	0	+ 2	− 2	+ 5
(28)	+ 6	− 9	− 4	−11	− 1	(63)	0	+ 6	− 3	− 4	+ 4
(29)	− 4	+ 5	− 5	− 1	0	(64)	− 3	+ 1	− 5	+ 4	+ 1
(30)	− 4	− 2	− 4	+ 3	+ 2	(65)	− 6	+12	− 7	− 2	− 4
(31)	− 7	+ 2	+ 1	+ 4	− 1	(66)	+ 1	+10	− 2	+ 1	− 2
(32)	+ 9	− 5	− 6	− 7	− 4	(67)	− 6	+ 4	− 3	0	+ 3
(33)	0	+ 1	− 2	− 6	+ 1	(68)	− 3	− 4	+ 6	− 4	+11
(34)	− 2	− 1	+ 3	− 6	+ 2	(69)	−11	+ 1	+14	− 4	− 1
(35)	− 3	− 5	− 4	+ 5	− 1	(70)	− 8	− 2	+10	+ 1	− 2

¹ Omission.

TABLE 95.—"INVERT" WEIGHTED SCORES FOR FORM A.—(*Continued*)
"I." Exercise 4
A. Anger

Items	Responses					Items	Responses				
	VM	M	L	N	O¹		VM	M	L	N	O¹
(1)	-3	+4	-1	-5	0	(10)	+4	+1	-4	+ 2	0
(2)	-2	+2	-2	0	0	(11)	-7	+4	+3	+10	0
(3)	0	+4	-4	-2	0	(12)	-4	-2	+3	+ 7	0
(4)	-3	+4	+1	+2	0	(13)	-3	+3	+4	-10	0
(5)	-3	0	+5	0	0	(14)	+1	0	0	- 4	0
(6)	-1	-1	+1	+4	0	(15)	-3	-2	+5	+ 2	0
(7)	+8	-2	+2	-4	0	(16)	0	0	-1	+ 7	0
(8)	+3	+5	+3	-6	0	(17)	0	0	+3	-10	0
(9)	0	+3	+1	-1	0						

B. Fear

Items	Responses					Items	Responses				
	VM	M	L	N	O¹		VM	M	L	N	O¹
(1)	+5	+4	+2	- 5	+10	(11)	+ 7	+1	+3	-5	+10
(2)	-1	-7	-4	+ 7	0	(12)	+ 3	+1	+1	-2	+ 4
(3)	+4	+3	-6	+ 2	+10	(13)	- 1	-3	-1	+2	+ 2
(4)	-7	-7	+6	+10	+10	(14)	+ 4	0	-2	0	+ 3
(5)	+9	+2	-3	- 4	0	(15)	+ 4	+3	-1	-4	+10
(6)	-1	-2	+1	+ 1	0	(16)	+10	+6	+7	-9	+10
(7)	-3	0	+1	+ 1	+10	(17)	+ 5	-1	+2	-4	+10
(8)	+5	+1	+1	- 4	+ 6	(18)	+ 1	-4	+8	-5	+11
(9)	+3	-6	-1	- 1	+ 6	(19)	0	+6	+2	-5	+10
(10)	+1	-4	+1	0	+10	(20)	+10	+5	-2	-1	+10

C. Disgust

Items	Responses					Items	Responses				
	VM	M	L	N	O¹		VM	M	L	N	O¹
(1)	+4	-1	0	-1	-10	(10)	0	-1	+2	-2	+10
(2)	+4	+3	+7	-8	+ 7	(11)	+4	-2	+3	-4	0
(3)	-4	+1	+3	-1	+10	(12)	-9	-4	+2	+6	0
(4)	+1	0	+1	-3	+10	(13)	-6	-4	+3	+2	+11
(5)	0	-1	+1	+2	0	(14)	0	+2	-2	-4	0
(6)	-5	-1	+4	+3	0	(15)	+2	+1	+1	-7	+10
(7)	-1	0	-2	+2	+10	(16)	-5	-2	+6	+4	0
(8)	-3	-5	+1	+4	+ 4	(17)	+4	-3	+1	+4	0
(9)	-2	+1	+1	-3	+10	(18)	+4	-4	0	+1	+10

¹ Omission.

TABLE 95.—"INVERT" WEIGHTED SCORES FOR FORM A.—(*Continued*)

D. Pity

Items	Responses					Items	Responses				
	VM	M	L	N	O[1]		VM	M	L	N	O[1]
(1)	−5	−7	+1	+ 5	+10	(9)	+9	−3	+1	− 3	+10
(2)	0	−1	−1	+ 2	0	(10)	0	+2	−1	−10	−10
(3)	−1	+1	0	− 1	0	(11)	−2	+2	−1	0	+ 7
(4)	+2	−2	−1	− 1	0	(12)	−3	−2	+4	+ 3	−10
(5)	+4	−2	−1	− 2	−10	(13)	−5	−5	+8	+ 7	+10
(6)	−2	+1	+2	0	0	(14)	−8	+4	+7	+ 9	−10
(7)	−3	−1	+8	+ 4	−10	(15)	0	0	0	− 5	0
(8)	−1	0	+2	−10	−10						

E. Wickedness

Items	Responses				Items	Responses			
	3	2	1	0		3	2	1	0
(1)	−10	− 8	+1	+11	(15)	− 3	−5	+1	+10
(2)	− 9	− 7	−3	+ 9	(16)	− 4	−4	−3	+ 7
(3)	−15	− 3	+4	+17	(17)	− 2	−4	+2	+ 4
(4)	− 4	− 4	−4	+ 5	(18)	0	−8	0	+ 5
(5)	+ 5	− 5	−1	+ 3	(19)	−11	+5	+9	+ 8
(6)	− 3	+ 1	+3	+10	(20)	− 3	0	+1	+ 4
(7)	0	− 5	−4	+ 7	(21)	− 1	−6	+1	+ 4
(8)	− 3	− 1	+4	− 6	(22)	− 4	+2	+2	+ 1
(9)	− 6	− 7	+5	+ 4	(23)	− 7	−1	+4	+ 8
(10)	0	− 4	+1	+ 5	(24)	+ 4	−5	−1	+ 2
(11)	− 5	−11	+1	+10	(25)	− 6	−4	+3	+ 6
(12)	− 3	+ 1	+2	+10	(26)	− 3	0	+3	+ 4
(13)	− 5	− 2	+8	− 2	(27)	− 4	−6	+3	+12
(14)	− 8	− 8	+6	+ 7	(28)	0	−2	+3	+ 3

F. Likes

Items	Responses				Items	Responses			
	1	2	S	O[1]		1	2	S	O[1]
(1)	+9	− 8	−1	+ 3	(5)	−11	+11	+3	+ 5
(2)	−9	+10	−1	− 3	(6)	− 5	+ 5	+1	+ 6
(3)	−4	+ 4	−1	+ 3	(7)	− 8	+ 8	−2	+10
(4)	0	+ 1	−2	+10					

[1] Omission.

TABLE 95.—"INVERT" WEIGHTED SCORES FOR FORM A.—(*Continued*)
"I." Exercise 5
A. Occupations

Items	Responses				Items	Responses			
	L	D	N	O[1]		L	D	N	O[1]
(1)	− 1	− 3	+3	−10	(14)	− 6	+ 5	−2	+10
(2)	+10	−11	+2	0	(15)	+ 3	− 4	+3	+ 3
(3)	− 7	+ 6	0	+ 4	(16)	+10	−12	+1	+ 3
(4)	+ 7	− 8	+1	+ 6	(17)	+13	−16	+1	+10
(5)	− 9	+ 6	+1	+ 3	(18)	+ 5	− 7	+1	+ 6
(6)	− 6	+ 9	0	+10	(19)	+24	−19	−7	+ 6
(7)	+24	−25	+1	+10	(20)	+ 5	− 6	+5	−10
(8)	+30	−13	−3	0	(21)	+ 9	−12	0	0
(9)	+ 7	−12	+2	+ 3	(22)	−11	+ 7	0	0
(10)	−12	+ 9	+7	−10	(23)	− 8	+ 5	+1	+10
(11)	− 6	+ 3	0	+11	(24)	+ 8	−13	0	+10
(12)	+22	−18	0	+10	(25)	+ 4	− 8	+4	+ 3
(13)	+13	−17	0	+ 3					

B. People

Items	Responses				Items	Responses			
	L	D	N	O[1]		L	D	N	O[1]
(1)	−6	+1	0	0	(7)	+ 5	− 2	−4	−10
(2)	0	+5	−3	− 3	(8)	+19	−14	−7	+10
(3)	+3	−3	+2	0	(9)	− 8	− 2	+3	+ 4
(4)	−2	+1	−1	0	(10)	+ 6	− 8	+9	+10
(5)	−5	+4	−2	0	(11)	− 9	+ 6	+6	+10
(6)	0	−1	0	−11	(12)	+10	− 9	−3	− 3

C. Reading, Movies

Items	Responses				Items	Responses			
	L	D	N	O[1]		L	D	N	O[1]
(1)	− 6	+ 6	+ 4	+ 3	(8)	− 3	− 2	+5	+3
(2)	+ 2	− 4	+ 1	0	(9)	−14	+ 9	+3	−5
(3)	+13	−10	− 6	−10	(10)	− 4	+ 8	−4	−6
(4)	+ 5	− 7	+ 1	0	(11)	+13	−11	−6	−6
(5)	− 3	+ 1	+ 3	+10	(12)	+ 2	− 2	+1	0
(6)	+ 3	− 4	0	− 3	(13)	− 3	0	+5	+4
(7)	−10	+ 5	+11	− 3	(14)	+ 1	− 1	+1	−5

[1] Omission.

TABLE 95.—"INVERT" WEIGHTED SCORES FOR FORM A.—(*Continued*)
D. Activities, Foods

Items	Responses				Items	Responses			
	L	D	N	O[1]		L	D	N	O[1]
(1)	− 30	+19	+10	−10	(11)	+3	−7	+3	0
(2)	− 5	+ 7	+ 3	0	(12)	−8	+6	+2	0
(3)	−10	+ 7	+ 9	− 3	(13)	+5	−5	−8	+10
(4)	+ 7	−10	+ 5	+ 3	(14)	+2	−6	−1	+ 4
(5)	+ 1	− 5	+ 2	+ 7	(15)	−8	+6	−5	+ 3
(6)	0	− 9	+ 8	0	(16)	+5	−4	−3	−10
(7)	− 1	0	+ 1	− 3	(17)	−2	−2	+4	+ 3
(8)	+11	− 9	− 2	+ 5	(18)	0	−4	+6	0
(9)	+ 8	−11	+ 1	− 4	(19)	−1	+1	0	0
(10)	+ 7	−10	0	0	(20)	+2	−7	−2	+10

E. Books

Items	Responses				Items	Responses			
	L	D	N	O[1]		L	D	N	O[1]
(1)	+ 5	−11	− 1	−5	(13)	−8	+11	−1	+2
(2)	+ 7	− 7	− 3	−4	(14)	0	− 1	−1	+1
(3)	+ 8	−11	− 4	−3	(15)	+4	+ 2	−4	−2
(4)	− 3	− 1	+ 2	+1	(16)	0	+ 6	+3	−1
(5)	+10	− 4	− 3	−6	(17)	+4	− 1	−2	−3
(6)	+ 5	+ 4	− 3	−4	(18)	−4	+ 5	+4	+1
(7)	+ 6	− 3	−11	−5	(19)	+1	− 1	+5	−4
(8)	− 1	− 1	+ 2	+1	(20)	−9	+ 4	+5	+3
(9)	+ 3	− 1	0	−1	(21)	+1	− 2	−1	0
(10)	+ 5	− 3	− 3	−1	(22)	+1	+ 1	−1	0
(11)	+10	− 2	− 3	−8	(23)	+2	0	+4	−5
(12)	+ 9	− 3	− 2	−6					

F. Drawing

Items	Responses				Items	Responses			
	L	D	N	O[1]		L	D	N	O[1]
(1)	− 3	+1	+1	+4	(5)	+6	−6	−1	+2
(2)	+10	−7	−4	−1	(6)	+8	−6	−5	−1
(3)	− 1	+1	+2	−2	(7)	−5	+4	+2	0
(4)	+ 1	−4	+1	+3	(8)	+2	−5	0	−1

[1] Omission.

TABLE 95.—"INVERT" WEIGHTED SCORES FOR FORM A.—(*Continued*)

G. Reporting

Items	Responses				Items	Responses			
	L	D	N	O[1]		L	D	N	O[1]
(1)	− 4	+ 1	+1	+11	(4)	+12	−12	−10	+ 3
(2)	−23	+12	+8	+10	(5)	+ 7	− 9	− 4	+ 7
(3)	+ 5	−11	−1	+ 7	(6)	− 6	+ 4	0	+10

H. Travel

Items	Responses				Items	Responses			
	L	D	N	O[1]		L	D	N	O[1]
(1)	− 2	− 2	+3	+ 9	(7)	+4	−5	−2	+4
(2)	−28	+15	+2	+10	(8)	−4	0	+3	+9
(3)	+ 4	− 3	−4	+ 9	(9)	+3	−5	−1	+8
(4)	− 1	− 1	0	+ 9	(10)	+4	−6	−1	+7
(5)	− 8	+ 9	+3	+ 3	(11)	+3	−7	+2	+7
(6)	− 7	+ 5	+1	+11					

"I." Exercise 6
A. Characters

Items	Responses				Items	Responses			
	L	D	N	O[1]		L	D	N	O[1]
(1)	+ 4	− 1	− 4	− 1	(15)	−20	+11	+11	+11
(2)	+ 9	− 7	− 6	− 5	(16)	+ 5	− 1	− 2	−11
(3)	+ 1	0	− 1	+ 1	(17)	− 2	+ 8	− 1	−11
(4)	−14	+ 6	+11	+ 9	(18)	− 5	+ 3	+ 3	+ 1
(5)	− 5	+ 1	0	+ 2	(19)	− 4	− 2	+ 4	+ 6
(6)	−17	+ 8	+ 7	+ 8	(20)	+ 7	+ 5	− 1	− 8
(7)	+19	−10	− 8	−10	(21)	+ 4	+ 4	0	−10
(8)	0	+ 2	0	− 2	(22)	+13	− 8	0	− 4
(9)	− 3	+ 4	− 2	+ 2	(23)	− 2	+ 4	− 4	0
(10)	− 4	+ 3	0	+ 3	(24)	+ 7	− 3	− 4	− 4
(11)	0	+ 2	− 2	−10	(25)	− 5	+ 5	+ 7	−10
(12)	0	− 6	0	+ 1	(26)	0	+ 9	− 3	− 8
(13)	− 9	+11	− 2	− 5	(27)	− 3	− 1	0	+ 2
(14)	− 5	+ 8	0	+ 2	(28)	− 3	+ 1	+ 7	− 8

[1] Omission.

TABLE 95.—"INVERT" WEIGHTED SCORES FOR FORM A.—(*Concluded*)
B. *True—False*

Items	Responses			Items	Responses		
	T	F	O[1]		T	F	O[1]
(1)	+3	−3	0	(8)	−5	+7	−11
(2)	−1	0	+10	(9)	−4	+4	0
(3)	−3	+3	− 1	(10)	0	−1	+10
(4)	+1	−1	+ 4	(11)	+1	−1	0
(5)	−3	+3	+10	(12)	−5	+6	− 6
(6)	−1	+2	− 4	(13)	−1	+2	−11
(7)	0	0	0	(14)	+6	−4	− 2

"I." Exercise 7

Items	Responses			Items	Responses		
	Yes	No	O[1]		Yes	No	O[1]
(1)	−10	+11	0	(22)	+ 5	− 5	0
(2)	+10	− 9	0	(23)	+ 3	− 2	− 4
(3)	− 2	+ 2	+10	(24)	+ 3	− 3	0
(4)	− 6	+ 7	+10	(25)	0	+ 1	− 3
(5)	+ 3	− 3	+10	(26)	+ 7	− 6	−10
(6)	+ 2	− 2	0	(27)	− 4	+ 5	0
(7)	+ 9	− 8	+10	(28)	+ 7	− 5	− 6
(8)	+ 7	− 7	+10	(29)	+ 2	− 1	−10
(9)	+10	−10	+10	(30)	+ 5	− 4	− 3
(10)	+ 8	− 9	+10	(31)	+ 7	− 6	− 5
(11)	0	+ 1	0	(32)	− 6	+ 7	+ 2
(12)	+19	−19	+10	(33)	− 3	+ 5	−11
(13)	+ 4	− 4	0	(34)	+12	−12	− 2
(14)	− 3	+ 3	+10	(35)	+10	−10	0
(15)	+13	−12	0	(36)	+ 2	− 2	− 8
(16)	+ 3	− 3	+10	(37)	− 2	+ 3	0
(17)	+30	−30	0	(38)	+ 7	− 6	− 3
(18)	+ 7	− 6	+ 4	(39)	− 1	+ 3	− 8
(19)	+ 3	− 2	+ 4	(40)	− 5	+ 7	− 6
(20)	− 5	+ 6	− 4	(41)	+11	− 9	− 4
(21)	− 1	+11	−10	(42)	+ 3	− 2	− 5

[1] Omission.

APPENDIX V

TRAIT RATINGS

Name..

DIRECTIONS: (1) In each trait, compare this person with the **average person of the same age.** Then make a small cross somewhere on the line for each trait, to show how much of that trait this person possesses. Note that in each case, one end of the line represents one extreme for the trait in question, and the other end of the line the other extreme. The middle of the line represents an average amount of the trait. Before making the cross, read very carefully the characterizations below the line.

(2) Try to make real distinctions. Do not rate a person high on all traits simply because he (or she) is exceptional in some. Both children and adults are often very high in some traits and very low in others.

(3) Locate your cross **at any point on the line** where you think it belongs. It is **not** necessary to locate it at any of the little vertical marks.

(4) Do not study too long over any one trait. Give for each the best judgment you can, and go on to the next. Please omit none. The ratings will be held absolutely confidential.

Trait 1. LEADERSHIP. By this is meant the degree of this person's talent as a leader; his (or her) leadership among associates of the same age; extent to which he (or she) takes the initiative and is followed naturally by others.

| Extraordinary gifts of leadership. His (or her) suggestion and example always followed | A leader in certain groups | Average in leadership. Apt to join with others but leadership not pronounced | Tends to be a follower when he (or she) joins with others | Never a leader. Always tags on, or does not join with others at all |

Trait 2. PERSONALITY. By this is meant degree to which his (or her) personality is strong and outstanding, making itself felt in any group. Degree of clear and vivid impression, whether favorable or unfavorable, created by this person's presence compared to that of others of his (or her) age.

| Extraordinarily strong personality, conspicuous in any group | Rather strong personality | Average personality | Rather weak personality | No personality, absolutely colorless |

Trait 3. ATTRACTIVENESS TO PERSONS OF THE OPPOSITE SEX. By this is meant extent to which this person is sought out, admired, included in mixed groups, selected as partner or companion by persons of the opposite sex.

| Extraordinarily and conspicuously attractive. Has very admiring associates of the other sex | More than average in attractiveness | Average in attractiveness | Less than average in attractiveness | Utterly lacking in attractiveness to persons of the opposite sex |

Trait 4. ATTRACTIVENESS TO PERSONS OF THE SAME SEX. By this is meant extent to which this person is sought out, admired, included in groups of the same sex, selected as companion by persons of the same sex.

Extraordinarily and conspicuously attractive. Has very admiring associates of the same sex	More than average in attractiveness	Average in attractiveness	Less than average in attractiveness	Utterly lacking in attractiveness to others of the same sex

Trait 5. SEEKS SOCIETY OF THE OTHER SEX. By this is meant the extent to which this person obviously seeks the society of persons of the opposite sex, attempts to win the notice or attention of the opposite sex whether wanted or unwanted.

Always aggressively seeking society of persons of the other sex or encouraging their advances	Definitely more than average interest in seeking society of the other sex	Average in attitude toward the other sex	Less than average interest in persons of the other sex	Never shows any interest whatever in persons of the other sex

Trait 6. SEEKS SOCIETY OF THE SAME SEX. By this is meant the extent to which this person obviously seeks the society of persons of the same sex, or attempts to win their notice or attention whether wanted or unwanted.

Always aggressively seeking society of persons of the same sex	Definitely more than average tendency to seek society of same sex	Average in attitude toward same sex	Less than average interest in persons of the same sex	Shows no interest whatever in persons of the same sex

Trait 7. TYPICAL INTELLECTUAL INTERESTS OF OWN SEX. By this is meant degree of interest in the typical intellectual activities of his (or her) own sex, amount of time and attention devoted to these, and satisfaction or pleasure derived from them.

Has very conspicuously the typical intellectual interests of his (or her) own sex	More than average interest	Average interest	Less than average interest	Has not at all the typical intellectual interests of his (or her) own sex

Trait 8. TYPICAL INTELLECTUAL INTERESTS OF OPPOSITE SEX. By this is meant degree of interest in the typical intellectual activities of the opposite sex, amount of time and attention devoted to these, and satisfaction or pleasure derived from them.

Has very conspicuously the typical intellectual interests of the opposite sex	More than average interest	Average interest	Less than average interest	Has not at all the typical intellectual interests of the opposite sex

Trait 9. TYPICAL SOCIAL INTERESTS OF THE SAME SEX. By this is meant degree of interest in the typical social activities of his (or her) own sex, amount of time and attention devoted to these, and satisfaction or pleasure derived from them.

Has very conspicuously the typical social interests of his (or her) own sex	More than average interest	Average interest	Less than average interest	Not at all interested in the typical social activities of his (or her) sex

Trait 10. TYPICAL SOCIAL INTERESTS OF OPPOSITE SEX. By this is meant degree of interest in the typical social activities of the opposite sex, amount of time and attention devoted to these, and satisfaction or pleasure derived from them.

Has very conspicuously the typical social interests of opposite sex	More than average interest	Average interest	Less than average interest	Not at all interested in the typical social activities of the opposite sex

Trait 11. TYPICAL MANUAL INTERESTS OF SAME SEX. By this is meant the extent to which this person is interested in the typical manual activities of his (or her) own sex, amount of time and attention devoted to these interests, and satisfaction or pleasure derived from them.

Has very conspicuously the manual interests of same sex	More than average interest	Average interest	Less than average interest	Has no interest whatever in the typical manual activities of his (or her) own sex

Trait 12. TYPICAL MANUAL INTERESTS OF OPPOSITE SEX. By this is meant the extent to which this person is interested in the typical manual activities of the opposite sex, amount of time and attention devoted to these interests, and satisfaction or pleasure derived from them.

Has very conspicuously the manual interests of the opposite sex	More than average interest	Average interest	Less than average interest	Has no interest whatever in the typical manual activities of the opposite sex

Trait 13a. TOMBOYISHNESS. (Rate for girls only.) Extent to which this girl likes boys' pursuits and activities, engages in them with boys without regarding sex differences, and wants to follows boys' rather than girls' standards and ideals in performance. Frank and free, rough and ready.

Interested only in pursuits and activities of boys. Wants to be a boy or tries to be like a boy	Definitely more than average interest	Average interest in boys' pursuits and activities	Definitely less than average interest	No interest whatever in boys' pursuits and activities

Trait 13b. SISSINESS. (Rate for boys only.) By this is meant extent to which this boy shuns boys' pursuits and activities, avoids engaging in them, and wants to follow gentler habits and customs. Degree to which he avoids rough play and seeks quiet employment often with women or girls.

Interested only in quiet, non-aggressive activities especially with women and girls. Thinks boys rough. Has attitude and behavior of a girl. A sissy in all his behavior	Definitely more of a sissy than the average; sweeter, gentler, and more like a girl than the average boy	Average	Less of a sissy than the average boy	Has absolutely none of the gentler traits

Trait 14. HAS CRUSHES ON PERSONS OF THE SAME SEX. Extent to which this person attaches himself (or herself) definitely to one or two persons of the same sex, lavishes devotion and attention upon them, is absorbed in their interests, shows lover-like behavior toward them.

| Always having a crush on some person of the same sex. Passionate in such devotion. Lover-like | Tends to have crushes. Shows more than average devotion to friends of same sex | Average interest in others of same sex | Shows less than average devotion to individual friends of same sex | No individual friends of same sex. Either flocks with a group or keeps to himself (or herself) |

Trait 15. AGGRESSIVENESS. By this is meant the extent to which this person puts himself (or herself) forward, attains his (or her) desires without reference to others, achieves his (or her) wishes no matter how much obstruction is offered.

| Extraordinarily aggressive. Always puts himself (or herself) forward. Goes after what he (or she) wants and forces it through | Definitely more than average in aggressiveness | Average in aggressiveness | Definitely less than average in aggressiveness | Entirely lacking in aggressiveness. Always guided by others. Always gives in to others |

Trait 16. OBJECTIVE-MINDEDNESS. By this is meant the extent to which this person's behavior is the result of calm, thoughtful consideration of the merits of any given case. Degree of his (or her) logical, matter-of-fact consideration in every situation. Extent to which this person's action is based on reason, and never influenced by personal considerations.

| Extraordinarily calm in judgment. Never acts without reason. Always logical and matter-of-fact | Definitely more than average in extent of logical and reasoned behavior | Average in thoughtful, logical consideration and action | Definitely less than average in thoughtful, logical consideration and behavior | Absolutely lacking in any thoughtful decision whatever. Behavior never based on reason |

Trait 17. SUBJECTIVE-MINDEDNESS. By this is meant the extent to which this person's behavior is the result of emotion or feeling. Excitable, unpredictable, reaction type, in which action is based on personal attitudes and considerations and never on logical reasoning.

Extraordinarily emotional and excitable. Behavior governed entirely by feeling	Definitely more than average in emotional expression and behavior	Average in emotional expression and behavior	Definitely less than average	Absolutely lacking in emotional reactions. Never excited or moved. Never responds on basis of emotion or personal feeling

Trait 18. EFFECTIVENESS. By this is meant ability to concentrate efficiently toward a given end. Steadiness, sense of responsibility, and dependability. Ability to integrate personal traits in a balanced way.

Extraordinarily effective. Perfectly integrated in behavior. Responsible, dependable	Definitely more than average in effectiveness	Average in effectiveness	Definitely less than average in effectiveness	Absolutely lacking in effectiveness. Never can be counted on. Unreliable. No sense of responsibility whatever

Trait 19. ORIGINALITY. By this is meant independence in thinking, degree of imagination, extent to which this person invents, discovers, or works out new processes or devices.

Extraordinarily original. Always thinking of new methods, devices, or processes. Constantly altering and improving procedure	Definitely more than average in originality	Average in originality	Definitely less than average in originality	Has no originality whatever. Always follows prescribed or traditional procedures. Never alters or improves methods

APPENDIX VI

CASE HISTORY RECORD FOR MALE HOMOSEXUALS

Case No. _____ Name _____ Age _____

I. General Description

    Height _____

    Weight _____

	robust				delicate
Physical fitness:	1	2	3	4	5
General impression:	mas.				fem.
Personal beauty:	handsome				ugly
Attractiveness:	charming				repulsive
Voice	mas.				fem.
Voice	rough				sweet
Voice	low				high
Ability in sports:	excels				incapable

    Which sports

    _____

Shoulders:	broad	narrow
Hips:	narrow	wide
	reserved	responsive
	naïve	sophisticated
	quiet	talkative
	serious	flippant
	petit	voluptuous
	dependent	independent

Physical disadvantages: crippled, lame, cross-eyed, pimples, scars, bad hearing, ugly features, overweight, underweight, glasses, left-handed, excessively youthful appearance, premature birth, sissy voice, _____ _____, _____, _____

Physical features mentioned by subject as most feminine:

    _____

    _____

    _____

II. Family Data

    No. of children _____ Birth order of subject _____

    No. of brothers _____, Ages _____, _____, _____, _____.

564

No. of sisters _____, Ages _____, _____, _____, _____.
Favorite parent _____ Reason_____

Father

Age: now _____, at birth of subject _____, deceased _____
Occupations: now _____, past _____, _____, _____

Emotional stability:	stable				moody
	1	2	3	4	5
Opportunity for contact:	much				none
Interest in subject:	much				ignores
Affection displayed:	very demonstrative				none
Tendency to dominate:	autocratic				complacent
Type of punishment:	brutal				gentle
Companionship:	constant				none
Intimacy with subject:	close				distant
Idealization by subject:	worship				scorn
Feared by subject:	greatly				not at all
Amount of occupational instruction given subject:	much				none
Amount of assistance given by subject in father's work:	much				none

Remarks:

Mother

Age: now _____, at birth of subject _____, deceased _____
Occupations: now _____, past _____, _____, _____

Emotional stability:	stable				moody
	1	2	3	4	5
Opportunity for contact:	much				none
Interest in subject:	much				ignores
Affection displayed:	very demonstrative				none
Tendency to dominate:	autocratic				complacent
Type of punishment:	brutal				gentle
Companionship:	constant				none
Intimacy with subject:	close				distant
Idealization by subject:	worship				scorn
Feared by subject:	greatly				not at all
Amount of occupational instruction given subject:	much				none

Amount of assistance given by
  subject in mother's work: much   none
Remarks:

Siblings
  Comparison of talents: sibs more   subject more

  | | 1 | 2 | 3 | 4 | 5 |
  Popularity in family: sibs more   subject more
  Companionship: much   none
  Competition and jealousy: much   none
  Favoritism of parents   much   none
    Shown to: subject
              sibs
  Amount of friction between sibs: much   none
  Foreknowledge of birth of younger expected and   came as
    sibs: understood   a shock
  In general resemblance to sib-
    lings: very much alike   very different
  Occupations of siblings: _____

Other members of the family group:
  General relation between subject and such persons:
Remarks:

III. Childhood
     Treated
        By parents mostly as: boy   girl

        | | 1 | 2 | 3 | 4 | 5 |
        By children mostly as: boy   girl
        Considered a: roughneck   sissy
        Played most with: boys   girls
        Reason_____

        Played most: in a group   alone

Reason_____

_____

Childhood love affairs

    With girls: many   none

                               1   2   3   4   5

    With boys: many   none

Favorite:

    toys _____ Reason_____

    games _____ Reason_____

    books_____ Reason_____

Amount of education: 1 2 3 4 5 6 7 8 I II III IV 1 2 3 4

Favorite subjects: _____ Reason_____

Disliked subjects: _____ Reason_____

Reason for quitting school: _____

Other details of school life:

How different from other children of the same age and sex:

How considered by playmates:

Remarks:

IV. Social Life

    Attitude in general: social   antisocial

                               1   2   3   4   5

    Attendance at dances: many   none

      Type _____

    Attendance at parties: many   none

      Type _____

    "Dates" with girls: many   none

         with men:

    Type of girl liked for

      1. A date:

      2. A friend:

    Type of boy or man liked for

      1. A date:

      2. A friend:

    Age of friends male: much older   much younger

             female:

    Club activities: lodges, Boy Scouts, etc.

    Religious life:

      Church _____

    Finest person ever known _____

      Reason:

    Ideal characters: _____

Reason:
Other social interests and activities:
Remarks:

V. Occupational Life

Occupation	Duration	Reason for quitting
1.		
2.		
3.		
4.		
5.		

Remarks:

VI. Sexual Life

Method of obtaining sex information:
    Age _____
Early attitude toward men:
Early attitude toward women:
Details of first conscious sex experience of any kind:
    Later reaction to same:
Masturbation
    How learned:
    Frequency:
    Effect on health:
Homosexual Experiences
    Details of first experience:
        Seduced _____
        Forced _____
        In love _____
    Later reaction to this experience:
    Types of practices:
        1. Pederasty _____, age of first occurrence _____
            Occasion _____, present frequency _____
        2. Fellatio _____, age of first occurrence _____
            Occasion _____, present frequency _____
        Remarks:

Chief reason for present practices:
Ever a feeling of guilt:
Ever want to change over: **Why:**
General reaction to homosexuality:
Description of ideal lover:
Heterosexual Experiences
  Details of first experience:
    Sociability _____
    Curiosity _____
    Drive _____
    In love _____
  Later reaction to this experience:
  If subject has had no such experience, why:
  Feeling toward illicit sexual intercourse when a child:
  Remarks:

Miscellaneous
  Nocturnal emissions:
  Presence of anything resembling menstrual pains:
  Genital abnormality:
  Remarks:

VII. M-F Test Results
VIII. Conclusions

APPENDIX VII

GROUP PROFILE COMPARISONS

A few profiles are included to illustrate some of the possible differences in exercise scores that may be present with equal total M-F scores. The profiles are given in terms of the standard scores (Tables 89 and 90) for the five principal exercises and the total M-F score.

A. MALE GROUPS

1. High-school boys vs. engineers.

Exercise	1	3	4	5	6	Total
308 high-school boys	+.30	+.50	−.10	+.95	+.25	+.75
44 engineers	+.15	+.30	+.70	+.35	+.45	+.75
$\dfrac{\text{Diff.}}{\text{S.D.}_{\text{diff.}}}$	<1	1.8	6.3	3.6	1.3	<1

These two very masculine groups differ especially with respect to their emotional and ethical response trends (4) and their activity interests. In the former the adolescents have the slightly feminine rating of immaturity, whereas the engineers give the responses characteristic of mature objectivity. In Exercise 5 both groups are masculine, but the masculinity of superior training and scientific tastes in the adult engineer is far outstripped by that of youthful extroversion and the will to adventure in the teen-age boys. The smaller and less significant differences in the other exercises are in line with expected trends.

2. Gifted boys vs. college men.

Exercise	1	3	4	5	6	Total
75 gifted boys	−.30	+.85	+.20	+.25	+.90	+.55
278 college students	+.50	+.60	+.30	+.30	+.50	+.60
$\dfrac{\text{Diff.}}{\text{S.D.}_{\text{diff.}}}$	6.9	2.7	<1	<1	2.7	<1

570

In profile as well as in total M-F score gifted boys resemble college students of their sex more than they do the adolescent school groups of their life age. From the college men they differ in being more masculine on two exercises (3 and 6) where intelligence tends to masculinize, and in being more feminine on 1 where culture, literary taste, or domestic sentiment may account for femininity.

3. *Who's Who* men vs. general male population.

Exercise	1	3	4	5	6	Total
31 *Who's Who* men	−.55	+.25	+.35	−.50	+.65	−.10
552 general population	0	0	0	0	0	0
$\frac{\text{Diff.}}{\text{S.D.}_{\text{diff.}}}$	3.7	2.4	2.8	3.2	4.5	<1

The average scores for our 31 *Who's Who* men give the profile of a distinguished group in middle maturity whose tastes are chiefly academic or literary. The total score for this group is near that of journalists. The response pattern differs significantly from that of the general population and of college-educated adults in femininity of word-association type, and of occupational choices. We have found that these are the two parts of the test where culture may show a strong feminine influence. In the three subtests where intelligence, education, and breadth of interest may register, the *Who's Who* men are, probably significantly, more masculine than the general population in spite of the apparently feminizing influences of age, domestication, or special pursuits.

4. *Who's Who* women's husbands vs. general male population.

Exercise	1	3	4	5	6	Total
23 *Who's Who* women's husbands	−.75	+.75	+.15	−.70	+.80	−.20
552 general population	0	0	0	0	0	0
$\frac{\text{Diff.}}{\text{S.D.}_{\text{diff.}}}$	4.0	6.0	<1	4.2	6.8	1.4

The profile for the husbands of the *Who's Who* women shows essentially the same trends in divergence from the general-population norms as that for the *Who's Who* men. The only significant difference between the two *Who's Who* groups is in the ratio of masculine to feminine information where the *Who's Who* men show a somewhat greater familiarity with the domestic items (especially those concerning babies) than do the husbands of the *Who's Who* women.

5. Clergymen vs. male adults in later maturity.

Exercise	1	3	4	5	6	Total
63 clergymen	$-.25$	$+.20$	$-.15$	-1.05	$+.10$	$-.50$
119 adults, 60's, 70's, and 80's	$-.05$	$+.05$	$-.25$	$-.55$	$-.10$	$-.50$
$\dfrac{\text{Diff.}}{\text{S.D.}_{\text{diff.}}}$	1.5	1.2	<1	3.8	1.6	<1

In maturity of interests and attitudes clergymen are known to rate high. On the M-F test their score mean is near the same point as that of men in the later decades of life. On Exercise 4 there is no significant difference between the two groups; in general information, in knowledge about personages, and in popular beliefs clergymen show the masculine trend of the younger and the more intelligent groups, but the differences are somewhat dubious. In word associations the clergymen show the more cultivated, more subjective response type. In Exercise 5 their sedentary, helpful, sympathetic, and cultured interests tend to place them at the extreme of femininity among the normally adjusted groups. Protestant theological students score like the mature clergymen on this part of the test. Both of the religious groups, although rating so extremely feminine on Exercise 5, are exceeded in mean score to an extent that is statistically significant by the even more feminine average of the male homosexuals.

6. Male artists vs. passive male homosexuals.

Exercise	1	3	4	5	6	Total
41 artists	$-.75$	$-.05$	0	$-.80$	0	$-.65$
77 passive homosexuals	$-.15$	$-.05$	$+.25$	-1.70	$-.05$	-1.05
$\dfrac{\text{Diff.}}{\text{S.D.}_{\text{diff.}}}$	3.8	<1	1.4	5.9	<1	2.5

These two extremely feminine groups of men resemble one another very little in profile as in I score. In word associations where subjectivity and aesthetic emphasis may be registered the artists are significantly the more feminine. The ratios of feminine to masculine information are approximately equal (Exercise 3) but the artists have answered correctly more of both sets of items. The scores on

Exercise 5 show the contrast between the femininity of culture and the femininity of homosexuality, with a score difference that is nearly six times its S.D.

7. Delinquent boys vs. high-school boys.

Exercise	1	3	4	5	6	Total
153 delinquent boys	+.20	+.20	−.30	+.50	0	+.30
308 high-school boys	+.30	+.50	−.10	+.95	+.25	+.75
$\frac{\text{Diff.}}{\text{S.D.}_{\text{diff.}}}$	<1	2.4	3.3	4.6	3.0	4.9

The older delinquent boys average in age in the middle teens. Their profile and that of high-school boys show generally similar divergences from the general-population norms. But the delinquent boys are less masculine in information, in expressed emotionality and degree of censure, in occupational and activity choices, and in knowledge about personages and attitudes regarding common beliefs. The older delinquents score on Exercises 3, 5, and 6 more like grade-school boys and diverge significantly from the younger boys only on Exercise 4, where the latter show a characteristic childish excess of femininity.

8. Active male homosexuals vs. general adult male population.

Exercise	1	3	4	5	6	Total
44 active homosexuals	+.30	0	+.15	+.50	+.20	+.55
552 adults, general population	0	0	0	0	0	0
$\frac{\text{Diff.}}{\text{S.D.}_{\text{diff.}}}$	2.2	<1	1.2	3.3	1.3	4.1

The profile of 44 army men convicted of sodomy shows especially marked masculinity with respect to activity and occupational choices. This is the part of the test where female homosexuals, especially those who play an active role, show an excessive deviation from general group scores. In word associations the active homosexual males are perhaps significantly more masculine than the general population and they tend in the masculine direction also on Exercises 4 and 6. Their total score is almost as masculine as that of the high-school boys and the engineers, but comparison reveals that the profile is unlike either of these.

B. Female Groups

1. Delinquent girls vs. women's general-population norm.

Exercise	1	3	4	5	6	Total
54 delinquent girls	0	0	−.50	+.40	0	−.05
1,107 adults, general population	0	0	0	0	0	0

$\dfrac{\text{Diff.}}{\text{S.D.}_{\text{diff.}}}$	<1	<1	4.1	3.1	<1	<1

The total M-F scores of the delinquent girls average near the same point as those of a thousand and more adults from the general population of women, but in Exercises 4 and 5 the delinquents show significant divergence from the adult norm. We have found that the two compensating deviations in subtest scores shown by the delinquents are apt to be associated with preadolescent or adolescent immaturity. In these deviations their scores are more remote from high-school girls of their own age and nearer to the younger grade-school girls.

2. Negro college sophomores vs. grade-school girls.

Exercise	1	3	4	5	6	Total
25 Negro college sophomores	−.20	−.10	−.10	−.25	+.60	−.20
256 grade-school girls	+.20	−.25	−.90	+.50	−.30	−.20

$\dfrac{\text{Diff.}}{\text{S.D.}_{\text{diff.}}}$	2.2	<1	4.3	5.7	5.0	<1

The profile patterns of these two groups of equal M-F score are quite dissimilar. Both groups are more feminine in total score than the general population but in information and in emotional attitudes where immaturity is feminine the college group approaches the adult norm, in attitudes toward public characters and in prejudices where breadth of experience tends toward masculinity in women the college girls have a masculine score. The grade-school girls are masculine in word association and in vocational and activity choice, a characteristic trend of preadolescence. Relatively greater femininity in information, in choice of favorite characters, in attitudes toward popular beliefs, and especially a marked excess in emotional reactions and severity in moral censure conceals in the total score the two masculine subtest trends.

3. Gifted girls vs. women college students.

Exercise	1	3	4	5	6	Total
72 gifted girls	−.20	+.50	+.60	+.20	+.60	+.65
295 college women	+.20	+.30	+.65	+.15	+.70	+.70
$\frac{\text{Diff.}}{\text{S.D.}_{\text{diff.}}}$	2.7	2.5	<1	<1	1.0	<1

In total score the gifted girls rate approximately as high as college women. Both groups are significantly more masculine than grade-school or high-school girls, the general adult population or adults of college education. They resemble one another closely in score on emotional attitudes and moral judgments and also in activity and occupational choices. They diverge from one another slightly in score on Exercise 6. Probably statistically significant is the more masculine word-association type of the college women, and the relatively more masculine fund of information of the gifted girls. Both profiles show somewhat less divergence from the general-population norm on Exercises 1 and 5 where intelligence is little correlated with score, relatively more on Exercises 3, 4, and 6 where intelligence may have considerable influence.

4. Women in artistic occupations vs. women adults of the general population.

Exercise	1	3	4	5	6	Total
62 women in artistic occupations	−.20	+.30	+.15	−.35	+.30	0
1,107 adult women of the general population	0	0	0	0	0	0
$\frac{\text{Diff.}}{\text{S.D.}_{\text{diff.}}}$	1.8	2.9	1.6	3.1	3.1	<1

It is not surprising, in view of the femininity of artistic and subjective word associations and of cultural occupational choices, that women in artistic occupations are inclined to femininity in score on Exercises 1 and 5. In information the masculinity of the artistic group was a surprise, but perhaps this was because we had failed to take into account the technical knowledge essential to this group. In Exercise 6 the artistic women resemble the better educated adults rather than the general population. In Exercise 4 they are also more masculine than women of the general population but the trend is less marked. The total score of the women in the artistic occupations shows a balance between femininity in word association and activity interests on the one hand and, on the other, masculinity in the three subtests where intelligence, education, and breadth of experience incline women's scores toward men's.

5. Dressmakers and domestics vs. general female population.

Exercise	1	3	4	5	6	Total
57 dressmakers and domestics	+.20	−.30	−.45	−.05	−.45	−.40
1,107 general population	0	0	0	0	0	0
$\frac{\text{Diff.}}{\text{S.D.}_{\text{diff.}}}$	1.4	2.1	4.2	<1	3.2	3.6

Our most feminine-scoring group has feminine subtest scores where the more intelligent women's groups tend to be masculine (3, 4, and 6), it does not deviate appreciably on Exercise 5 (occupations and activities), and it is slightly masculine in word association. On Exercises 1, 3, and 6 the domestic group more nearly resembles grade-school girls.

6. *Who's Who* women vs. adults of college education.

Exercise	1	3	4	5	6	Total
25 *Who's Who* women	0	+.70	+.70	+.30	+.85	+.90
760 adults, college educated	0	+.30	+.40	−.15	+.35	+.20
$\frac{\text{Diff.}}{\text{S.D.}_{\text{diff.}}}$	<1	3.0	1.9	2.5	3.6	3.4

Twenty-five women listed in *Who's Who* rate in total M-F score among the very masculine groups. In word-association type they differ practically not at all from college-educated adults generally. On the other major exercises they show in excess the masculine trend characteristic of the more intelligent girls' and women's groups.

The wives of *Who's Who* men, except on Exercise 5, where they are contrastingly feminine, register a similar but less extreme masculine pattern.

7. College women athletes vs. college women.

Exercise	1	3	4	5	6	Total
37 superior college athletes	+.40	+.65	+1.30	+.70	+.95	+1.65
295 college women students	+.20	+.30	+ .65	+.15	+.70	+ .70
$\frac{\text{Diff.}}{\text{S.D.}_{\text{diff.}}}$	<1	2.4	4.0	3.4	1.5	9.2

The superior college women athletes (distinguished in intelligence and in sports achievement) rate considerably more masculine on the M-F scale than any other group of 25 or more members. Also their total M-F scores are more homogeneous than those of any other group of this size or larger. Compared with 295 women college students the superior athletes are the more masculine at every point in the profile. But the slightly more masculine scores on Exercises 1 and 6 are not significantly divergent from the similar, if less extreme, scores of the college group as a whole. In information the athletes know fewer of the feminine and more of the masculine items than do the college women. The activity and occupational-choice score of the athletes is more masculine than that of any other college or adult group of women except the homosexuals and the prostitutes. Only a few small adolescent subgroups rate as high or higher. The largest and most significant divergence from the college group is in emotional attitudes and moral censure. Here it proves to be the absence of proneness to anger, to disgust, and especially to fear that gives our sportswomen a masculine, unemotional rating. In attitudes toward misbehavior the athletes are significantly more masculine than the larger group of college women, a divergence characteristic of more intelligent as well as of more athletic groups. In pity we find that the athletes have a truly feminine score that is not significantly divergent from the college women's norm.

8. Homosexual women vs. women of high-school and college education.

Exercise	1	3	4	5	6	Total
18 women inverts[1]	$-.50$	$+.25$	$+.65$	$+.95$	$+.70$	$+1.15$
988 adults, 20's and 30's	$+. 0$	$+.15$	$+.35$	$-.10$	$+.20$	$+ .15$
$\dfrac{\text{Diff.}}{\text{S.D.}_{\text{diff.}}}$	1.5	<1	1.5	6.4	3.0	4.2

The M-F scores of 18 homosexual women when compared with those of women of similar age and schooling (high school and college) show a mean difference which equals more than 4.2 times its S.D. If the total M-F score for these inverts is compared with that of an equal number of professional and business women matched individually with respect to occupation we find a difference of 38 M-F points (.90 S.S.) between the two groups. The standard score for the homosexual women is $+1.15$. Among our many

[1] We are indebted to Miss Jan Gay for securing the cooperation of these 18 women.

female M-F groups it is equaled in masculinity by only one adult group, composed of Ph.D.'s and M.D.'s, and is exceeded by only one, the athletic group. From both of these the homosexuals differ considerably in profile. These 18 women are unique among our female groups in their contrast between a high degree of femininity in word association and an even higher masculinity in activity and occupational choice. It is striking that in word response they are excessive in femininity of score, although in information and in their expression of emotional attitudes and in censure their M-F scores do not differ from the norms for their age and education. In attitudes toward public personages and toward popular beliefs the inverts are distinctly unfeminine and in activity choices (5) they reach the masculine score peak otherwise characteristic of adolescents.

We do not know the psycho-social or constitutional factors that may have been contributory to the homosexual behavior of these women. Certain descriptive information concerning the individuals may, however, be of interest in view of our general lack of knowledge about women who make this kind of life adjustment. The present homosexual relationships are reported as having lasted from 1 to 9 years, with an average of 3 years. The question as to how long they have "been this way" brings a range of years from one to "always," average 10 years. Twelve have wished to be otherwise, six say they have never entertained this wish. Five have been promiscuous in their love affairs, 11 have been constant. Ten claim to be strong in specific sex feeling, 8 say they are relatively weak in this respect. Sex activity with the homosexual partner is generally indulged in several times each week. Adjustment to their way of living is said to be "fair" in one case, "good" in all the rest. The state of personal satisfaction is reported as poor in 3 cases, moderate in 3, fair in 2, good in 8, excellent in 2. Of general interests, travel holds first place with 13 adherents, literature is enjoyed much by 9, pets by 8, art and music each by 6. Social life, science, politics and domestic arts are each liked much by one, religion and mechanics by none. It is perhaps significant that domestic arts are disliked by 12 of the group.

The age range is from 23 to 43 years with the mean at 30. Three have had 3 years of high school, seven are high-school graduates, four have had 2 or 3 years of college. Four are college graduates, one having an M.A. degree. The occupations are those of artist 3, dancer 3, interior decorator 1, office worker 3, advertising and selling 3, housewife 2, nurse 1, writer 1, no occupation 1. Six have been married, of whom four are now separated or divorced. The two married women have children, two and four respectively; one of the divorced women has one child. There are no other children. Health is reported average; height averages 5 ft. 4 in., weight 133.2 lb. Twelve report having been brought up by both parents, six were orphans, or half-orphans. Eight were only children. The voices of 6 are low, 10 medium, 1 is high, and 1 is high and shrill. The last two, and two others, dress in a feminine way. Of the remaining 14, three dress plainly, 8 in sport clothes, and 3 in a masculine style. The style of hair dress is usually short, but may be either severe or curly. Seven of the 18 are said to play a passive homosexual role; 11 participate "mutually" or are the active members in a pair. The M-F profiles of the two groups, (1) passive and (2) mutual or active, perhaps reflect a psychological difference between two types.

	1	3	4	5	6	Total
7 passive	0	+.20	+.20	+ .70	+.30	+ .70
11 active or mutual	−.80	+.30	+.95	+1.10	+.90	+1.60

The group as a whole presents a profile unique among our groups and its characteristics are shown in enlargement when the 11 active or mutual members are viewed apart from those of passive adjustment.

TABLE 96.—M-F SCORES OF MALE GROUPS. MEANS AND S.D.$_M$'s FOR SCHOOL, COLLEGE, ADULT, AND SPECIAL GROUPS ARRANGED IN ORDER OF MASCULINITY OF STANDARD SCORE

Group	No.	Exercises							Total	
		1	2	3	4	5	6	7	M-F Score	S.S.
College athletes.............	46	− 4.4 1.18	− .1 .14	+ 8.7 .88	+30.7 2.57	+51.7 4.20	+ 5.1 .84	− .8 .31	+ 92.54 4.92	+1.00
Engineers.................	44	− 1.9 1.23	+ .4 .18	+ 3.5 .84	+33.7 2.73	+36.6 5.18	+ 2.2 1.00	− .6 .25	+ 77.3 7.33	+ .75
High-school boys.........	308	− .8 .44	+ .0 .06	+ 5.2 .46	+14.4 1.29	+56.7 1.80	+ .8 .46	− .7 .11	+ 77.1 2.98	+ .75
College students (four colleges)......	278	+ .7 .46	.0 .00	+ 6.4 .40	+24.4 1.13	+35.1 2.02	+ 2.5 .36	−1.3 .13	+ 69.3 3.44	+ .60
Gifted boys..........	75	− 6.1 .89	− .1 .06	+ 8.4 .63	+22.2 2.18	+34.2 4.16	+ 5.6 1.12	+ .3 .18	+ 66.2 5.28	+ .55
Army prisoners (active homosexuals)......	44	− .8 1.10	− .1 .17	+ 1.2 1.28	+20.6 3.12	+42.2 5.22	+ .4 1.28	+ .1 .31	+ 66.2 6.97	+ .55
College students (small stature)......	43	− 8.2 1.36	.0 .18	+ 8.5 1.17	+27.8 3.27	+29.6 5.13	+ 4.3 .96	−1.3 .29	+ 61.7 6.72	+ .45

Adults, 20's..........	342	− 2.2 .43	+ .03 .06	+ 3.6 .39	+26.7 1.14	+30.0 1.89	− .5 .37	− 1.2 .11	+ 57.9 2.76	+ .35
Delinquent boys (older group)...........	153	− 1.4 .63	+ .3 .11	+ 3.0 .82	+ 9.3 1.92	+42.2 2.58	− 1.7 .68	+ .2 .23	+ 52.6 4.01	+ .30
Adults, college education........	531	− 2.3 .36	+ .1 .05	+ 3.3 .29	+26.4 .87	+21.9 1.46	+ 1.4 .28	− 1.0 .09	+ 50.4 2.05	+ .25
Adults, 30's..........	330	− 2.7 .45	+ .1 .06	+ 1.8 .44	+23.3 1.18	+26.3 1.87	− .4 .40	+ .6 .11	+ 49.5 3.05	+ .20
Adults, high-school education..........	344	− 3.2 .43	.0 .06	+ 1.93 .46	+20.1 1.24	+27.7 1.84	− .5 .38	− .6 .10	+ 45.4 2.92	+ .15
Delinquent boys (younger group).......	129	− .0 .62	+ .1 .12	+ 5.4 .73	− 7.1 1.93	+46.9 2.71	− 3.1 1.10	+ .1 .28	+ 43.7 4.10	+ .10
Total adult population............	1,083	− 2.8 .25	.0 .04	+ 2.2 .24	+21.5 .67	+23.0 1.03	− .0 .22	− .8 .06	+ 43.3 1.57	+ .10
Grade-school boys.........	260	− .4 .54	+ .3 .08	+ 3.4 .50	− 5.9 1.52	+45.4 2.28	− 1.2 .56	− .8 .13	+ 40.7 3.09	+ .05
Adults, 40's..........	178	− 2.7 .62	+ .1 .08	+ 1.3 .55	+19.5 1.73	+22.3 2.57	− 1.2 .52	− .8 .13	+ 39.7 3.64	+ .05
Army recruits.........	42	− 4.4 .91	.0 .17	+ 4.4 1.35	+ 1.2 3.77	+37.4 3.57	− 1.1 1.16	+ .1 .17	+ 38.8 6.10	0

TABLE 96.—M-F SCORES OF MALE GROUPS. MEANS AND S.D.M.'S FOR SCHOOL, COLLEGE, ADULT, AND SPECIAL GROUPS ARRANGED IN ORDER OF MASCULINITY OF STANDARD SCORE.—(*Continued*)

Group	No.	Exercises							Total	
		1	2	3	4	5	6	7	M-F Score	S.S.
Adults, general population..........	552	− 3.4 .34	.0 .05	+ .9 .37	+16.8 .98	+24.2 1.45	− 1.4 .33	− .6 .08	+ 36.5 2.28	0
Who's Who men................	31	− 8.1 1.2	− .1 .2	+ 3.3 .9	+25.8 3.1	+ 5.5 5.7	+ 3.8 1.1	− .3 .3	+ 31.2 7.6	− .10
English boys....................	59	− 8.3 .92	− .4 .14	− .4 .95	+ 2.3 2.23	+43.3 3.33	− 5.2 .73	− 1.4 .26	+ 28.5 4.62	− .15
Deaf men......................	26	− .9 1.23	+ .2 .19	+ 1.4 1.63	+10.1 3.89	+19.4 5.36	− 2.4 1.57	+ .8 .30	+ 28.2 8.52	− .15
Adults, 50's....................	108	− 4.2 .80	+ .2 .11	+ 1.9 .71	+16.8 1.99	+12.4 2.86	− .1 .72	− .5 .18	+ 26.6 4.46	− .15
Japanese boys (in U.S. schools).....	32	− 6.5 1.07	− .1 .24	+ 5.9 .91	−10.8 3.42	+42.4 5.22	− .0 1.31	− 1.7 .39	+ 25.5 7.60	− .20
Who's Who women's husbands......	23	− 9.7 1.53	− .6 .24	+ 7.4 1.02	+20.7 4.07	+ .3 5.39	+ 4.8 .85	− .9 .41	+ 24.4 7.55	− .20
Adults, grade-school education......	208	− 3.6 .54	+ .1 .09	− .9 .60	+11.4 1.52	+18.3 2.32	− 2.9 .58	− .4 .13	+ 21.8 3.40	− .25

	N									
Fathers of gifted	56	− 8.0 (1.06)	.0 (.14)	+ 3.2 (1.15)	+13.1 (3.55)	+ 6.7 (4.48)	+ 2.8 (.90)	.2 (.27)	+ 19.4 (6.57)	− .30
Student priests	46	−11.8 (1.13)	.2 (.17)	+ 6.5 (.96)	+14.1 (2.91)	+ 7.7 (3.64)	+ 2.4 (.87)	−1.2 (.31)	+ 18.9 (5.14)	− .30
College of music students	50	− 8.9 (1.32)	.0 (.15)	+ 3.0 (1.21)	+26.1 (3.34)	− 4.3 (4.55)	.1 (1.04)	.8 (3.60)	+ 15.7 (6.87)	− .35
Negro college students	51	− 6.2 (.87)	.1 (.14)	+ 3.4 (1.15)	+ 8.1 (2.50)	+ 6.6 (3.95)	+ 2.3 (.57)	.9 (.22)	+ 14.5 (6.15)	− .40
Adults, 60's	75	− 3.6 (.71)	.0 (.14)	+ 1.6 (.88)	+10.0 (2.47)	+ 7.8 (3.15)	− 1.9 (.93)	.5 (.21)	+ 10.8 (4.99)	− .45
Theological students (protestant)	53	− 5.8 (1.08)	.2 (.18)	+ 2.7 (.95)	+29.8 (2.39)	−14.3 (4.01)	− 1.6 (.90)	−2.1 (.25)	+ 9.0 (5.23)	− .50
Clergymen	63	− 5.6 (1.01)	.0 (.17)	+ 2.6 (.64)	+12.8 (2.69)	−11.8 (3.49)	− .6 (.66)	−1.5 (.28)	+ 8.0 (4.52)	− .50
Vocations	118	− 6.7 (.73)	.1 (.12)	+ 1.9 (.55)	+14.6 (2.04)	− 6.7 (2.53)	− .7 (.59)	−1.3 (.21)	+ 7.6 (3.80)	− .50
Adults, 70's and 80's	44	− 4.1 (1.13)	.2 (.22)	+ 1.3 (1.16)	+11.2 (3.57)	− .8 (4.16)	− 2.8 (1.33)	.1 (.31)	+ 3.2 (7.04)	− .60
Artists	41	− 9.6 (1.14)	.5 (.15)	+ .1 (1.10)	+16.2 (3.35)	− 4.3 (3.44)	− 1.2 (1.15)	−1.0 (.28)	+ .3 (6.10)	− .65
Inverts (passive homosexual prostitutes)	77	− 5.7 (.94)	.9 (.15)	− .1 (1.01)	+21.3 (3.11)	−36.2 (3.52)	− 2.8 (.64)	−2.7 (.29)	− 28.0 (4.81)	−1.05

TABLE 97.—M-F Scores of Female Groups. Means and S.D.M.'s for School, College, Adult, and Special Groups Arranged in Order of Masculinity of Standard Score.

Group	No.	Exercises							Total	
		1	2	3	4	5	6	7	M-F Score	S.S.
College athletes (high intelligence)	37	-10.7 / 1.22	-1.0 / .18	-3.8 / 1.28	+26.6 / 3.60	-25.3 / 4.41	+.6 / 1.08	-1.6 / .30	-13.7 / 3.61	+1.65
Ph.D's and M.D.'s	20	-11.7 / 2.27	-1.3 / .28	-2.8 / 1.37	+24.0 / 4.60	-43.5 / 5.38	-1.1 / 1.41	-.9 / .52	-34.5 / 10.85	+1.15
College students (high intelligence)	92	-10.9 / .88	-.6 / .13	-6.2 / .91	+20.2 / 1.79	-36.7 / 3.02	+.3 / .61	-2.9 / .18	-36.2 / 4.38	+1.15
Inverts (active and passive)	18	-18.2 / 2.57	+.3 / .28	-7.5 / 1.74	+11.5 / 5.32	-18.0 / 4.87	-1.6 / 1.24	-1.6 / .49	-36.4 / 9.73	+1.15
Who's Who women	25	-14.5 / 2.08	-1.4 / .24	-3.2 / 1.19	+12.3 / 3.91	-36.5 / 5.80	-.1 / 1.06	-1.49 / .37	-45.5 / 8.47	+ .90
Deaf women	19	-6.6 / 1.78	-.7 / .21	-12.0 / 1.14	+2.3 / 4.43	-20.8 / 7.63	-5.1 / 1.65	-1.2 / .37	-46.3 / 10.97	+ .90
College students (4 colleges)	295	-12.1 / .46	-.9 / .07	-7.0 / .46	+11.3 / 1.25	-41.1 / 1.62	-1.2 / .41	-2.9 / 1.15	-54.1 / 2.47	+ .70

Group	N									
Gifted girls	72	−15.8 / .91	−1.1 / .13	−4.9 / .72	+9.9 / 2.00	−40.1 / 3.69	−2.1 / .77	−2.1 / .24	−57.3 / 5.10	+.65
Adults, college education, M.A.	74	−12.3 / .81	−.7 / .12	−3.5 / .80	+8.9 / 2.61	−46.0 / 3.14	−2.5 / .51	−2.6 / .25	−58.4 / 4.97	+.60
Student nurses	78	−16.7 / .80	−1.2 / .14	−8.7 / .97	+2.6 / 2.12	−29.9 / 3.04	−2.9 / .64	−2.8 / .23	−63.4 / 4.47	+.50
Private-school girls	28	−19.5 / 1.38	−1.4 / .24	−15.4 / 1.78	−2.4 / 4.61	−17.0 / 9.18	−7.6 / 1.20	−2.7 / .46	−65.9 / 11.52	+.45
Prostitutes	12	−11.9 / 2.13	−1.6 / 1.16	−20.7 / 3.19	−7.0 / 4.85	−15.2 / 10.50	−11.0 / 2.34	.9 / .58	−68.2 / 12.80	+.40
Nurses	78	−14.7 / .84	−1.2 / .10	−10.9 / 1.21	+1.6 / 2.66	−39.9 / 3.16	−5.3 / .91	−1.6 / .21	−69.0 / 5.01	+.35
English girls	60	−16.2 / .78	−1.4 / .13	−9.4 / .95	−18.6 / 2.39	−11.8 / 3.65	−11.2 / .59	−2.9 / .22	−70.5 / 4.33	+.30
College of music students	50	−18.8 / 1.04	−.7 / .16	−7.7 / 1.13	+12.1 / 3.13	−51.7 / 3.42	−2.7 / .91	−2.7 / .25	−71.1 / 5.60	+.30
Who's Who men's wives	24	−13.2 / 1.18	−1.5 / .20	−4.5 / 1.21	+8.8 / 5.36	−57.0 / 4.54	−.2 / .96	−2.3 / .33	−71.2 / 8.07	+.30
Adults, 20's	604	−14.2 / .31	−1.0 / .04	−8.5 / .38	+4.1 / .92	−45.5 / .77	−5.6 / .30	−2.7 / .08	−74.2 / 1.82	+.25
Adults, college education	760	−14.4 / .27	−.9 / .04	−6.9 / .29	+4.6 / .81	−51.3 / 1.02	−4.1 / .24	−2.5 / .07	−74.7 / 1.60	+.20

TABLE 97.—M-F SCORES OF FEMALE GROUPS. MEANS AND S.D.M.'S FOR SCHOOL, COLLEGE, ADULT, AND SPECIAL GROUPS ARRANGED IN ORDER OF MASCULINITY OF STANDARD SCORE.—(Continued)

Group	No.	Exercises							Total	
		1	2	3	4	5	6	7	M-F Score	S.S.
Japanese girls (in U.S. schools)	41	-14.1	-1.2	-2.8	-19.1	-31.0	-6.3	-3.4	-74.9	+.20
		1.08	.17	1.17	3.29	3.41	1.30	.31	6.13	
Chinese girls	51	-14.2	-1.3	-6.9	-16.3	-37.7	-8.0	-3.4	-75.0	+.20
		.92	.13	1.35	2.89	3.97	1.15	.33	6.99	
Adults, 40's	297	-13.1	-1.1	-8.2	-1.0	-47.5	-5.8	-2.2	-78.4	+.15
		.45	.06	.49	1.30	2.20	.41	.11	2.54	
Part-time school girls	33	-4.8	-1.2	-12.3	-28.4	-20.9	-9.4	-2.2	-78.6	+.15
		.77	.21	1.47	4.06	3.85	1.67	.45	7.53	
High-school girls	245	-14.3	-1.1	-10.7	-12.9	-32.2	-6.6	-2.4	-79.3	+.10
		.48	.06	.58	1.55	1.85	.50	.13	3.04	
Total adult population	1,867	-14.2	-1.0	-8.9	-1.3	-48.0	-5.8	-2.3	-80.9	+.10
		.18	.03	.21	.54	.66	.17	.05	1.00	
Adults, 30's	466	-14.2	-1.0	-9.5	-.3	-52.8	-5.7	-2.4	-84.5	0
		.38	.05	.43	1.09	1.27	.33	.09	1.93	
Adults, high-school education	820	-14.6	-1.1	-9.7	-2.8	-48.4	-6.2	-2.2	-84.7	0
		.28	.04	.33	.84	.99	.26	.07	1.46	

Group	N									
Adults, general population	1,107	−14.1 .25	−1.0 .04	−10.3 .29	5.1 .73	−45.8 .85	−7.0 .24	−2.1 .06	85.1 1.27	0
Artistic occupations	62	−15.9 .95	−1.3 .13	−7.2 1.01	.5 2.89	−56.8 3.43	−4.5 .73	−2.4 .22	85.6 4.68	0
Adults, grade-school education	287	−12.8 .51	−.9 .07	−11.9 .61	−11.9 1.33	−38.3 1.60	−9.2 .50	−1.8 .12	86.2 2.53	0
Adults, 50's	234	−14.3 .55	−.9 .08	−9.4 .58	−6.6 1.39	−48.6 1.68	−5.6 .51	−2.0 .12	86.5 2.50	0
Adults, 70's and 80's	119	−14.4 .71	−1.0 .13	−10.7 .82	−11.6 2.09	−43.2 2.18	−6.3 .72	−1.0 .15	87.2 3.37	0
Delinquents	54	−14.2 1.17	−1.5 .14	−10.4 1.37	−18.0 3.04	−34.0 3.68	−6.9 1.08	−1.6 .24	88.0 5.73	.05
Adults, 60's	153	−15.2 .63	−.7 .10	−8.5 .76	−9.0 1.74	−47.6 2.16	−6.6 .62	−1.8 .16	89.1 3.02	.05
Mothers of gifted	78	−19.8 .80	−1.1 .14	−6.4 .99	−5.4 2.60	−59.2 2.66	−1.3 .78	−2.1 .20	91.6 4.26	.15
Negro college students	25	−15.9 1.52	−.9 .23	−11.6 .160	−8.5 4.04	−52.9 3.56	−2.1 1.31	−2.7 .49	94.3 8.3	.20
Grade-school girls	256	−12.4 .47	−1.2 .08	−12.9 .59	−27.0 1.47	−30.2 1.81	−9.4 .62	−2.5 .13	95.4 2.98	.20
Dressmakers and domestics	57	−12.5 1.18	−.7 .18	−13.3 1.40	−17.1 2.74	−47.7 2.94	−10.8 1.18	−2.2 .28	103.9 5.01	.40

INDEX

A

Accountants, 159, 172 *ff.*

Activity interests, 104. *See also* M-F Test, Exercise 5

Administrative occupations, 169, 172; educational, 457

Adolescence, early and late, 124, 132 *f. See also* Grade-school groups; High-school groups

Adolescents, **male**, 134, 143; **female**, 134, 145

Adults, college educated, **male**, 126, 138 *ff.*, 143 *f.*, 147, 160, 581; interests of, 201 *ff.*, 208 *f.*; compared with occupational groups, 161, 169; **female**, 127, 138 *ff.*, 145 *f.*, 147, 181, 577, 585; interests of, 215 *ff.*; compared with occupational groups, 180 *f.*; with advanced degrees: M.A., 585; Ph.D. and M.D., 75, 181, 193, 457; housewives, 179 *ff.*, 190 *ff.*

Adults, general population, **male**, 73, 146 *f.*, 156, 477 *ff.*, 571, 573, 582; **female** 73, 147, 156, 477 *ff.*, 574 *ff.*, 587

Adults, grade-school educated, **male**, 126, 138 *ff.*, 143 *f.*, 147, 160, 582; compared with occupational groups, 161; **female**, 127, 138 *ff.*, 145 *ff.*, 181, 587; compared with occupational groups, 180 *f.*; housewives, 179 *ff.*, 190 *ff.*

Adults, high-school educated, **male**, 126, 138 *ff.*, 143 *f.*, 147, 160, 196 *ff.*, 200 *f.*, 207, 224 *f.*, 581; interests of, 196 *ff.*, compared with occupational groups, 161; **female**, 127, 138 *ff.*, 145 *ff.*, 209 *ff.*, 212, 214, 217 *f.*, 224, 226, 586; interests

of, 209; compared with occupational groups, 180 *f.*; housewives, 179 *ff.*, 190 *ff.*

Adults, high-school educated, **male and female**, married, M-F score and age, 134; single, M-F score and age, 135

Adults, total population, **male**, 581; **female**, 586; young adults, 140

Age, 122 *ff.*, 155 *f.*; age and size of family, 225 *ff.*; age groups, **male**, 116, 128, 130, 137, 140 *ff.*, 160, 457, 479, 572, 581 *ff.*; age and occupation, 161 *f.*; **female**, 128, 130, 137, 141 *ff.*, 457 *f.*, 479, 585 *ff.*; age and marriage, 182 *f.*, 230 *ff.*; age and employment, 230 *ff. See also* M-F Test and age

Alcatraz (government prison), 241 *f.*, 254, 263

Allport A-S Reaction Test, 62, 99, 101 *f.*

Anger, *see* M-F Test, Exercise 4

Architects, 159 *ff.*, 163 *ff.*, 456 *f.*

Army prisoners, 126, 580. *See also* Homosexuals, active

Army recruits, 242, 252, 581

Army troops, physical measurements of, 251 *f.*

Art, interest in, *see* Interests

Artistic occupations, **male**, 173, 179, 181, 192; **female**, 179 *ff.*, 184, 186 *f.*, 192 *ff.*, 575, 587

Artists, 74, 116, 159 *f.*, 164, 176 *ff.*, 192 *ff.*, 457, 572, 583

Association, word, *see* M-F Test, Exercise 1

Athletes, *see* College athletes

Attitude-Interest Analysis Test, *see* M-F Test